SIDEBARS

136 / 1036

SIDEBARS

REFLECTIONS BY A MISSIONARY
JOURNALIST IN NEW YORK

TRACY EARLY

WITH BIOGRAPHY BY
GRADY EARLY

Grady Early

Never Again Publishing
San Marcos, Texas

Printed in the United States of America

ISBN-13: 978-0-9791742-0-9
ISBN-10: 0-9791742-0-1

Early, Tracy
Sidebars: Reflections by a Missionary Journalist in New York

Never Again Publishing, 214 Triple Crown Run, San Marcos, Texas 78666
Design by Wendy Tritt, Trittenhaus Design, 111 West Elm Street, Sycamore, IL 60178

To Our Mother

SIDEBARS

TABLE OF CONTENTS

INTRODUCTION

Since we have to put the blame on somebody, Martin E. Marty might as well take the hit. A Lutheran minister, he teaches church history at the University of Chicago, writes a column and handles book reviews for *Christian Century* magazine, and puts out a newsletter *Context*. And he is rightly regarded as one of the most knowledgeable and balanced interpreters of American Christianity. I had written for *New World Outlook* magazine about Will Campbell, a colorful, offbeat minister originally from Mississippi but living in Tennessee at the time he visited New York and let me follow him around for part of the visit. Mr. Campbell is unusual as a white Southerner who disengaged from the racial attitudes of his people without disengaging from them or taking it as his vocation to scold them. He has made himself into a character, and though there is some put on, he has played a distinctive role in American religious life. Dr. Marty observed that writing an interesting article about Will Campbell was easy because all it required was listening in and quoting what he said. But Professor Marty went on to observe, "Let me say that Tracy Early is a religious reporter who is concrete, who has an eye for the vivid and an ear for what will stick in at least my mind. He should write a book."

That was in 1982, and though my reflexes are not rapid, I do not ignore advice from wise professors. Or as was said to King Agrippa, "I was not disobedient to the heavenly vision" (Acts 26:19). The result may not resemble Dr. Marty's anticipation, but he bears responsibility for encouraging me to try.

As a subsidiary factor, I notice some people do show curiosity when they see a reporter at work. I was struck by this one summer when I went up to Fordham University in the Bronx to do a story on a gathering of Focolare, a Catholic movement that originated with an Italian woman, Chiara Lubich. The U.S. leader of the women's branch was another Italian, Sharry Silvi, and she agreed to sit down with me a few minutes to answer my questions about what was going on at this affair they called a Mariopolis. As we were getting settled, suddenly several other people hurried to take the seats around us, and showed not just a casual interest but some eagerness to see this event: "a reporter is about to interview our leader; let's see what happens."

Whether in journalism or otherwise, people do find interest in watching the work of others. It is said that the practice of cutting holes in the board fences around construction sites in New York began with the curiosity of John D. Rockefeller Jr. While Rockefeller Center was under construction, he came by anonymously and stopped to watch the work underway, but was told to "move along, buddy." Imagining that other people probably felt the same interest he had, he went back to his office and sent down instructions that watching would be not merely tolerated but facilitated with viewing spots.

So for any who might be curious about a reporter's work, and perhaps wanted to watch, here is a book. Unfortunately, the reporter in question is atypical and probably does not give a reliable picture of the normal.

Atypical and a bit in the background. Marc Chagall pictured life as a symphony orchestra. Picturing the New York journalistic community as an orchestra, I am the violinist who plays fourth chair on the last row of Kurt Masur's Philharmonic, hardly in the limelight but gratefully in and able to participate in some interesting occasions. Covering religion also means standing a little bit to the side, but I have found it an interesting vantage point for viewing life in New York.

SIDEBARS

REPORTING

For illustrative purposes, I could start out by giving you a few snapshots of the reporting life.

Imagine the FBI wasting its time on me. It was one of the new style agents, female, and not disposed to sound mean, but just wanting to know. She had been assigned. So she came to my apartment to ask what I had been doing. What I had been doing was going to the Soviet Union's United Nations mission on the East Side to interview a member of the Ukrainian staff, then housed in the same building, for a story about Ukrainian Catholics (CNS, November 29, 1989). Now it appeared the FBI kept the mission under surveillance, and had dispatched an agent to tail me as I walked back to my apartment building on the West Side.

The address and my description were turned in, and the nice young lady agent, Jan Fedor, then did a little snooping in the lobby of my building to see if anybody of that description might show up. To her good fortune, I was coming home while she was there, and by chance she heard someone call my name. A blend of ingenuity, pluck and luck. Much like my reporting might be, if I had more ingenuity.

She was not reprimanding or threatening, but only checking, and when I gave my explanation it appeared to satisfy. She did not ask nosey questions about the substance of my interview or try to get a look at the results. And she left in a seeming state of contentment. She sounded somewhat less content, however, when I called some days later, and told her I was now writing a story about her (May 1990 issue of *The Catholic Journalist*, publication of the Catholic Press Association). You might think agents of the FBI would be pleased to find reporters giving them public recognition, and publicizing examples of how the taxpayer's dollar is spent. But in this case seemingly not.

I must report that it is a little disconcerting, even for someone with a conscience clear as mine, to find the FBI has been following you around. But I try for the positive view. There is a kind of honor among prominent personages of the dissident and "activist" communities in contemplating their FBI files grown large, and a corresponding deflation when it turns out the FBI did not consider them dangerous enough to spend time checking on. I suppose my file may be quite modest in size, but at least I am in. And not just some anonymous allegations sent through the mails either, but an actual report by a bona fide agent.

Now imagine me in a small sitting room of John J. O'Connor's office suite, interviewing him for the Catholic News Service. After we have been going on a while, his secretary, James F. McCarthy, comes in and puts an urgent whisper in his ear. The secretary departs and the cardinal continues as before. A little later, Msgr. McCarthy returns and whispers more insistently. Cardinal O'Connor waves him away: "I'll talk to him when I can talk to him."

Is it the pope who must be kept on hold until I get all my questions answered? Is the secretary general of the United Nations begging for a few minutes to consult on developments in the Middle East? I am left to wonder. But whoever, I can congratulate myself on the demonstration of who ranks in the order of priorities.

But now in actuality, returning toward reality, I do know that talking to me will never appear on any cardinal's list of "The 99 Most Important Things To Do This Morning." But for Cardinal O'Connor, making sure he got his view of an issue rightly and fully presented to the Catholic News Service might rank as a matter of some importance.

A circumstance of this sort can lead to a confusion in the minds of reporters. Because they fulfill an important function and deal with important people, they can slip into imagining that they are important personally. For corrective therapy, they generally need only meditate on the size of their paychecks, but in the exhilaration of seeing their words printed under their bylines, they may fail to set aside sufficient time for meditation.

Is the pope a Catholic? One of the sidebar delights of reporting has been an opportunity to turn that old retort into serious inquiry.

The Catholicism or lack thereof attributable to Pope John Paul II came into question through the movement of Marcel Lefebvre, a French archbishop who watched with alarm as the pope conversed with leaders of non-Christian religions as though they might in some sense stand on his level, and even visited the Rome synagogue. Such offenses took him beyond the bounds, said the archbishop.

It remained unclear how serious the Lefebvre movement was until June 30, 1988, when the archbishop ordained four bishops to continue his initiative beyond the years of his own earthly wanderings. One of those was Richard Williamson, rector of a seminary, St. Thomas Aquinas, operated in the United States by the movement's Society of St. Pius X. On July 10, this new bishop celebrated mass for one of the parishes now under his care, St. Michael the Archangel in Farmingville, Long Island, and I was sent out to get the story (NC, July 11). [Ed. Note: NC is National Catholic News Service which later changed its name to Catholic News Service, CNS.]

After mass, Bishop Williamson talked with the handful of reporters who showed up, and explained why a true Catholic could no longer remain in communion with the powers that now governed at the Vatican. He told us that the key issue was not the Latin mass in its old form, but the conviction that Catholicism was "the one exclusively true religion." He repeated charges of Archbishop Lefebvre that Pope John Paul II departed from Catholicism pure and absolute when he visited the synagogue in Rome, prayed for peace with leaders of other religions at Assisi and in 1982 walked up the aisle of Canterbury Cathedral with Robert Runcie, the Anglican archbishop.

Maybe the pope just did not know any better. "I'm sure he does not intend to destroy the Catholic Church, but his confusion is such that this is what he does," Bishop Williamson commented charitably.

How could I resist? "Is the pope a Catholic?" I just had to ask. Bishop Williamson, a native of Britain who had left Anglicanism as a teenager and later found "the one exclusively true religion" in Catholicism, answered by referring to the remark of the Anglican curate who said the egg he had been served was "good in parts."

So now you know. "Pope John Paul II is Catholic in parts," the Lefebvre bishop said.

His group is to be distinguished from others with a nostalgic hankering for the old Latin mass and other aspects of the old pre-Vatican II ways, but who do not separate from the pope. There were enough of these in the New York area to fill St. Patrick's Cathedral May 12, 1996, for a Latin mass in the older form called Tridentine, for the Council of Trent that it came out of (CNS, May 13). Alfons M. Stickler, an Austrian then approaching his 86th birthday and retired from his last post as Vatican librarian and archivist, came from Rome to celebrate the mass, processing up the aisle wearing the old cappa magna (great cape) with train so long it needed train bearers.

Regarding preference for the old mass, there are two issues: the language and the form. In followup to decisions of the Second Vatican Council (*Constitution on the Sacred Liturgy*, 36), mass in the local language became the usual way, though Latin was of course not eliminated. But Catholic authorities also made some changes in the form of the mass, whether in the vernacular or not. In contrast to Archbishop Lefebvre, who insisted on the Tridentine form, Cardinal Stickler told me in an interview before the St. Patrick's mass that he considered the new form valid, and celebrated that way when requested. But he said the old form, which bishops could still authorize if they wished, gave more adequate expression to "the mystery we have in the center of our worship." The new way of putting the priest behind the altar to face the congregation "changes the sense of the mass," he said.

The cardinal said he had celebrated the Tridentine Latin mass in many countries, and I had in fact previously seen him do that in New York. It was at St. Agnes Catholic Church, located near Grand Central Station and famous as the place where Archbishop Fulton J. Sheen used to preach at times, particularly during Holy Week. Cardinal Stickler was celebrating a mass and lecturing to initiate an institute named for Dietrich von Hildebrand, a native of Italy who taught in Germany but left to escape the Nazis, and then taught philosophy at Fordham University.

I had earlier covered Professor von Hildebrand, too. Known in some Catholic circles as progressive for his writings on marriage, he reacted against the new movements of the 1960s and 1970s, and expounded his ultramontane views to a monthly Roman Forum. I still remember him, long white hair giving him the image of the Old World intellectual, closing a session by leading the group in chanting a creed–in Latin (RNS, March 1, 1971).

Despite the fervor in such groups for the old ways, Cardinal Stickler said Cardinal O'Connor was "unique among his brother bishops to place at our disposal his own cathedral in order to give the right expression, in the magnitude and splendor of this church, to the greatness and glory of the Pontifical High Mass in the Roman Rite."

That does not mean Cardinal O'Connor stood heart and soul with the old school. He subsequently pointed out in a column or something I read that the pope celebrated mass according to the new form in his private chapel every morning, and with no shortage of reverence. While not of the age of Cardinal Stickler, the archbishop of New York was old enough to remember the days of yore, when some priests did rattle through the Latin in the old form with excessive speed and little apparent reverence. The lesson we might get: reverence depends more on what is in the mind and heart of the priest than on the particular form of the liturgy.

But Cardinal O'Connor recognized a value in accommodation of varying views. To outsiders, the Catholic hierarchy may seem possessed of such power its members need not accommodate to anything. When I talk with them, however, I find they do not necessarily feel they are privileged to control the world by decree, but need to look for ways of enticing cooperation. In 1986, I

SIDEBARS

interviewed Angel Suquia Goicoechea, the Catholic Archbishop of Madrid, and found him wrestling with a number of challenges he could not meet entirely by command (NC, October 16). Many people might think of Spain as securely or even fanatically Catholic. But Cardinal Suquia told me that he had to deal with anti-clericalism dating to the Franco era, even though the church had lost its favored status as the official state religion a decade before. He was meanwhile trying to get himself through an observance of the 50th anniversary of the beginning of the Spanish Civil War, and avoid anything that might reopen divisions of the past. As a Basque, born near San Sebastian, he was also bothered by tensions over the relation of Basques to Spanish governance. "The situation of the church in the Basque country is very difficult because the situation of Basque society is very conflictive," Cardinal Suquia told me. And he reported that the church was working for peace, but "the religious element" in Basque society had deteriorated.

The cardinal was troubled as well by a recent conference in Madrid that included addresses by two Catholic priests not enjoying the best of relations with church authorities–Hans Kung, whose license to teach as a Catholic theologian had been withdrawn, and a Jesuit who served in the Sandinista government of Nicaragua as Minister of Education, Fernando Cardenal. Attempts to conduct dialogue with Spanish theologians involved in the sponsoring body were hampered because they did not "recognize the magisterium of the church."

How did I come to be talking with people like a Cardinal-Archbishop of Madrid? Maybe the picture will clear as we move along. I had aspired to the free life of the freelance writer for some time before I got into it, and I redoubled my efforts to move in that direction because of some unpleasantness where I did the 9-to-5. I had been employed a few months in the New York office of the World Council of Churches (WCC) as assistant to the communications director. This was a woman who baked cookies for our morning tea and displayed other commendables. But when I made a mistake she not rarely erupted into a fit of temper. So, inasmuch as it has been my custom to make a mistake every once in a while, hanging around where each instance would likely bring me a bashing seemed hardly sensible.

Some of the work also left me with an upset stomach. At my desk, I could adjust to most any tedious assignment that came. But when I had to call up other people and act like an idiot, my comfort level went low. On one morning I remember much too well, my boss went off to a meeting, and left me with one of those chores. A story had just come in from World Council headquarters in Geneva, and to her mind that meant attention must be paid. There had been a meeting or something, and some Catholic had attended or thought about attending or maybe spoke of possibly attending the next one, and in the new ecumenical climate of those days, it appeared there could come another step forward or somewhere. It was the sort of story that in the entire United States maybe around a hundred and fifty people would have some idea what it meant and wish to hear about it. But to my boss it was The Word from Geneva, and must at once go out to the masses. So she gave me a list of key religion reporters that in those pre-fax and pre-email days I was to call and give the story to directly.

The quite different technological style of journalism one can practice today was illustrated when I wrote a story on the funeral of Jacqueline Kennedy Onassis. It was held May 23, 1994, at a prominent Jesuit church on Park Avenue, St. Ignatius Loyola. Mrs. Onassis had attended a smaller church in the area, St. Thomas More, where the memorial mass for John F. Kennedy Jr. and his wife Carolyn was held in 1999, but St. Ignatius Loyola was needed to accommodate the large number invited to the funeral of Mrs. Onassis.

Reporters were not among those invited, but an audio feed was arranged, and was carried by television stations as they showed the outside scene and the people gathered in the street. In this situation, I decided the best thing was to stay in my apartment. So to "cover" the story, I listened to my television set, later got the text of the funeral homily of Father Walter Modrys by fax and interviewed him by telephone. I wrote the story on my computer laptop, and sent it computer-to-computer to editors of the Catholic News Service in Washington. Obviously, it is better to observe bodily on the scene. But that day showed some of the backup alternatives when the best cannot be had. I could be quarantined with leprosy and keep reporting, if my fingers did not fall off.

With fewer resources available for handling the earlier Word from Geneva, I was left with the telephone. I called Elliott Wright at RNS (Religious News Service) first because he would cause no trouble. He was a friend of mine and sophisticated about handling such institutional material. When I called Louis Cassels, religion editor of UPI (United Press International), and started telling him about the blockbuster the WCC was offering, he quickly cut me off with, "Drop it in the mail. It might be something I could use in my column some-time." For The New York Times, I called religion reporters George Dugan and Edward Fiske, and felt relieved when neither answered. I could tell the boss I tried.

My heartburn came at AP (Associated Press). George Cornell, their religion editor, was out, but when I told the man answering the phone that I was calling from the World Council of Churches with a story from Geneva, he decided somebody should take it for George, and turned me over to one his cub reporters. So this nice young fellow took it all by dictation, obscure paragraph following obscure paragraph, to the very end. Then he had a question he did not quite know how to phrase courteously: "Uh, could you, I wonder, is this, how would you, uh, could you tell me, what is the significance of this?" If I had been an honest Christian, I would have told him it did not have any significance so far as I could see. But when you are tied up with an institution, you sometimes find yourself compelled to talk like you have mush in your mouf. So I attempted to tread water a while, and eventually suggested George Cornell would know what (little) it meant.

Then Thomas C. O'Brien, an editor who had given me assignments and encouragement in the past, offered a contract for enough research writing to keep me from starving to death a year or so, and I immediately quit my job, realized my freelance dream and began the process of living happily ever after. More or less. Rejection slips and unfulfilled promises and obtuse editors have brought days of despondency. But even on those days, I have always thought of my glass as more than half full.

The research writing went into a project finally published in 1979–after vicissitudes and a financial rescue by the Sisters of St. Joseph in Philadelphia–as a three-volume *Encyclopedic Dictionary of Religion* (Corpus Publications). I will now hand any potential enemies a sword with which to slay me: they can question me on a great many subjects I researched and wrote about for those volumes, I will reply that I have never heard of such, and they can then point to my name signed to an article on each as though I were an authority. "Pretentious" might well be the precise word to describe that part of my journey.

But overall, the freelance life as I have practiced it has turned out well. I have been fortunate in finding customers who shared my interests, and they have been mostly periodicals and news services operating on a national or international basis. I have the ideal position of not being required to do petty parochialism, because my customers want only articles on topics of some broader interest. And writing for a variety of outlets, I have been able to deal with most any subject that seemed important to me. A reporter on the staff of one particular periodical can be stymied if the chief says no to a story idea. But when one chief told me no, I often found occasion to deal with the topic for another. I have of course gained neither fame nor fortune, but I have survived and, more than that, survived without ever having to write a line about Joey Buttafuoco.

Some religion assignments may take you toward the peculiar, but in my case not really often. I feel comparatively fortunate when I notice stories such as a concert review that critic Jon Pareles wrote for *The New York Times* (January 22, 1996) about one Ozzy Osbourne, apparently something big in rock music: "He dipped his hand in a bucket of water and flung water on the crowd; he sprayed onlookers with a water hose made to look like a gun. He cued fans to shout along, and as the song ended he tore his T-shirt nearly in half." That may be what you wind up writing if you are reduced to covering culture in New York.

Despite the down side of the World Council job, I remain grateful for it, especially because it introduced me to the WCC community and began a continuing connection. I wrote for the WCC magazine, *One World,* until its demise in 1995, and found another market in the news service sponsored by the WCC—called Ecumenical Press Service (EPS) until September 1994, when it transmogrified into Ecumenical News International (ENI) with additional sponsors.

In 1980, John Bluck of the WCC commissioned me to write a small book for the WCC's *Risk* series, a book published that year with the title, *Simply Sharing.* I suggested the series maybe should be renamed *Not Quite So Much Risk,* as he sought to edit out many of my less conventional comments. But he did not follow up on that. Among my learnings from the project were some of the hurdles that must be cleared by any author who wants to protect his pages from editorial mutilation. Mr. Bluck promised to consult me on any proposed changes, and did, but then, alas, he departed for a lengthy holiday in his native New Zealand, and others came in to muck around in the text we had agreed on.

Attempting comic exaggeration, I referred in one passage to "that celebrated creature known to hagiography as Western man." Someone, presumably inspired by the spirit of feminist critique and deaf to the tone of the wording, decided that "man" could not be tolerated. But the rest of the sentence was left, so readers came upon "that celebrated creature known to hagiography as the Western Human" (p. 23). Since nobody had ever heard of any creature with such a designation, the reference to "celebrated" could only move the tone from comic to dumb. Here I got one of my earliest impressions that people operating according to the feminist agenda were often complaining about material they did not really need to feel offended by unless they just wanted to. And that their solution was to make changes in a mechanical fashion that left passages sounding artificial. My goal has been to write English in a way that sounds as natural as possible, and the results of conforming to "inclusive" demands and all that "person" business have never seemed natural to me.

This holds true up to and including God. In *God and the Rhetoric of Sexuality* (Fortress, 1978), Phyllis Trible said she was using masculine pronouns for God in biblical translating, despite disliking reinforcement of the male image, because she did not "know how to resolve the dilemma posed by

SIDEBARS

grammatical gender for deity . . . ." (p. 23). In a commentary on Genesis (John Knox, 1982), Walter Brueggemann also used masculine pronouns for God "because I have not known what else to do" (p. viii). If those two could not solve the problem, surely no one would expect better from me.

But to confess the less fashionable truth, I have never actually felt that calling God "he" caused a problem, or that it oppressed women, or diminished their dignity, or marginalized them or made them invisible, or perpetrated any of the other offenses so often alleged. If Christians have called the church their mother and God their father, that may be simply the fit of the language to the structure of Christian faith, and not a sign of something I keep hearing denounced as "patriarchy."

Now a warning about the freelance life: entering this world means you abandon almost all hope of institutional support. You are out there on your own with nothing to say when you call an eminence of church or state and the secretary insists on knowing not only your name and purpose, but who you are "with." That comes down on you as a daunting demand if you are working on something to offer, but do not yet have a buyer. So for the most part I have waited until I had an editor interested before I started a project, and I could reveal I was "with" some nameable outlet.

After I developed a meaningful relationship with the National Catholic News Service, known from its logo as NC, I got some status from that on occasion. In 1980, several religious groups were sponsoring a conference on the religious broadcasters known collectively as the "electronic church." The program was to put Pat Robertson, Robert Schuller and maybe a couple others of that ilk in a little head butting with their critics. But by the time I learned what was happening and got my assignment to cover it, and called for press credentials, the hour drew nigh. An organizer told me so very sorry but the space was small and the few seats for press were already allotted. When I relayed that response to Richard H. Hirsch, communications officer for the U.S. Catholic Conference, he called the organizers and told them that if NC was not able to do its anticipated coverage, the U.S. Catholic Conference would not be making its anticipated contribution to their budget. Soon I had a call from one of the people making arrangements, who said a recent recount had revealed they did in fact have one vacant seat left, and it had been decided after consideration that this place would be assigned to me.

Quite often, however, the NC connection amounted to less. So I came late to the "seamless garment" story. Joseph L. Bernardin of Chicago worked out a theory he called the "consistent ethic of life" to combine concerns about abortion, euthanasia, capital punishment, war and some other issues under a common rubric, and presented it in 1983 at Fordham, the Jesuit university in New

York. The theory became known as the "seamless garment" approach, and was widely discussed and debated.

You might be surprised: a major thematic address by a cardinal, delivered at a major Catholic university, and the National Catholic News Service was not notified. I later asked the woman handling press relations about my overlookedness, and she said she was not aware the agency had anybody writing for it in New York. I said to myself that if I were press officer for a Catholic institution, I would make a point of finding out how to get news into the Catholic press. She presumably said to herself that if she were the NC reporter, she would make a point of letting Catholic institutions know.

Outsiders might suppose I would have a bigger advantage than I really do covering Catholic stories, since I represent the agency that sends news out to Catholic publications all across the country and to many abroad. Though I sometimes get yardage from that, it is nothing I can count on. For example: St. John's University, which is operated by the Vincentian Fathers and has its primary campus in Queens, became the victim of a sex scandal a while back when several of its white male students got a black female student under their control and took liberties (CNS, May 2, 1990). As a matter of routine, I called first to the office of the president, Donald J. Harrington, to see if he wished to comment. I was told he was busy, and I should talk to the public relations office, which is often the routine when I try to reach CEOs. But then, some weeks later, I was struck by reading Father Harrington's report to the alumni on how he handled the affair. One part of it, he said, was taking time to talk with reporters and explain the university's position.

For Father Harrington, however, it was the New York dailies that were doing the damage among potential students and contributors, and therefore it was the reporters for those dailies that needed the special attention of the president in telling how seriously the university took the issue of sex abuse, and how earnestly it wished to see justice done.

To him, taking this matter seriously meant getting it handled by the criminal justice system as a crime. But it was not clear to me that this was incontrovertibly the best route. The young woman did not immediately report the incident, and then remained hesitant about reliving the trauma in telling the story to the police and filing charges. Officials of St. John's persuaded her finally to do it, and there were trials. But they did not turn out to give great satisfaction. Defense attorneys were able to convince at least some of the jurors that the young woman was acquiescent, or at least to plant doubts about her story, and got acquittals for some of the young men. Meanwhile, St. John's came under attack from some blacks for not immediately expelling the accused, and by friends of the accused for suspending them before they had their day in court.

When I eventually did get to talk with Father Harrington, he still saw the incident as a matter for the criminal justice system (CNS, July 27, 1990). But I raised the question of whether it might have been better handled if it had not been taken to the police. The university could have brought the young men in for a hearing, and if matters stood as they appeared, transmuted them into ex-students in a couple of weeks. Everyone could have quickly seen that the offense against the young woman was taken seriously, without the wait of months for trial, and without putting the victim through the ordeal of testifying in court and subjecting herself to cross-examination in that setting. Handling the case within the university would also have made possible a significant penalty for the perpetrators without burdening their families with huge bills that enriched the defense lawyers. And in the end, the police route did not bring a clear resolution of the case, and the university did expel most of the accused.

One man who has recognized the potential of CNS for getting wider attention for his work is Renato R. Martino, an archbishop from Salerno who has served as the Vatican's ambassador to the United Nations. His formal title actually is "permanent observer" rather than "ambassador," but an Italian ambassador to the UN, Francesco P. Fulci, told us that he found the archbishop doing a great deal more than just observing. When Archbishop Martino has made a statement at the UN, he has usually seen to it that a copy got to me. When he has presented awards on his fund-raising boat cruises, he has made sure to designate a seat for the reporter representing the Catholic press. A pattern of behavior I find admirable in a nuncio.

In my first years as a freelance writer, I did a lot of work for Religious News Service (RNS), now called Religion News Service to indicate the subject is religion but the news is not necessarily handled in a religious way. This agency had been established by coincidence in the year of my birth, 1934, by the National Conference of Christians and Jews (NCCJ) and, during the period when I was writing for it, had space in the NCCJ building on West 57th Street, just a short way over from Tiffany's.

The chief was Lillian Block, a Jewish woman who was apt to order a sandwich with crisply fried bacon when we occasionally went to lunch together, and who apparently spent little time at synagogue. Often I was at RNS offices on a Friday late, and we would pass the evening talking over religious news of the week at some nearby restaurant. "You've been here three hours," an exasperated waitress complained to us one night when we were spending minimal sums and keeping better tippers from getting to use the booth.

But however limited Miss Block's conformity to the traditional rules of her faith, she had a sense of mission. She told me that when the Second World War came along, she was teaching journalism at New York University, but decided she must go work somewhere in a job that would enable her to focus her efforts more directly on building better understanding among peoples. So in 1943 she found her way to the NCCJ and RNS, first as deputy to RNS editor-in-chief Louis Minsky and then as his successor. The level of respect she gained by her handling of that position was shown in 1976, when she became the first non-Catholic, as well as first non-male, to receive the principal annual award of the Catholic Press Association, named for St. Francis de Sales.

She had offered me a full-time job. When I quit the WCC to go into free-lancing, she proposed that I come into her shop at a tempting raise in pay. When I declined, she followed up a couple of days later with an even better offer. But I was set on trying the freelance life, and stayed the course.

I was on her acceptability list because I had already done a few stories for RNS, written in my free time while employed by the World Council, and Miss Block consequently knew my work. My very first RNS story, sent out September 27, 1968, reported the sudden influx of Catholic students into Union Seminary in New York. (There is also a Union Seminary in Richmond, Virginia, run by Presbyterians, but in this book I always mean the one in New York.) "For the second consecutive year, nearly 15 per cent of the total enroll-ment at Union Theological Seminary here is Roman Catholic," I reported. Mae Gautier, secretary to the Union president, John C. Bennett, had brought this to my attention, and it reflected a new interest among Catholics in the post-Vatican II years, opening themselves to Protestant thought.

A year later a Jesuit seminary, Woodstock College, moved to New York and entered into friendly ties with Union. I was told that the first time Union Seminary ever served alcohol at an official affair came when the professors entertained their new Jesuit neighbors and decided that hosting Catholics without offering anything alcoholic might inflict excessive culture shock.

Later developments gave Union an even stronger Catholic presence. Raymond E. Brown, a Sulpician priest and leading New Testament scholar, joined the faculty. And after things moved along further, there came a time when I was able to report that Union was appointing its first Catholic nun as a tenured faculty member (CNS, May 8, 1995). Simultaneously, it appointed its second Catholic nun to a tenured faculty position. Which was first and which was second I do not know, but in alphabetical order they were Mary C. Boys in religious education and Janet R. Walton in worship. By coincidence, both were members of the same order, Holy Names of Jesus and Mary, an order with its generalate in Longueuil, Quebec.

Catholic-Protestant relations were changing in many ways as the spirit of Vatican II reinforced the impact of the nation's first Catholic president. Kay

SIDEBARS

Fraleigh, a Catholic who worked for a United Methodist office at the Church Center for the United Nations, told me that many people assumed she was Protestant, and formerly tried to amuse her with anti-Catholic jokes. But by the time I interviewed her in 1970, she was no longer hearing them (RNS, March 5).

Though Miss Block could offer more than my modest WCC job paid, she ran RNS on a pittance, and some of our journalism there made me wince. Filling in occasionally for staff who were sick or vacationing, I found the way of producing an RNS story was often simply to rewrite an item from *The New York Times* or one of the wire services. I felt ill at ease sitting in Manhattan, often too limited in budget even to check out a story with long distance telephone calls, and datelining my rewrites Albuquerque or Cairo or wherever. Thank goodness, we at least had the decency to keep our bylines off that sort of makeshift.

What I most enjoyed at RNS was getting out and doing real reporting, covering events or interviewing people with something interesting to tell. And over the years I wrote a large number of those stories. In the beginning, I was not given a byline, and then came a period when Miss Block or the managing editor would decide something I turned in could be decorated with a "by Tracy Early." But that happened erratically, so I eventually worked into a routine of putting the byline on myself before I turned the story in, and those who had lacked initiative enough for putting it on now lacked initiative enough for marking it out. During those years, I became widely identified with RNS, and even today some people who are vague about my location in the overall distribution of reality and groping for an identity will introduce me as an RNS reporter, or ask me about my RNS work as though it were current.

I have to give RNS credit for much of my education in church affairs. I did not arrive at RNS offices totally ignorant of what was going on in American church life. Not just through my WCC work but also through earlier years in New York while studying at Union Seminary and then various efforts to keep abreast while away four years in Tidewater Virginia, I maintained some awareness. But I had never before gotten the opportunities for direct observation of events and personal interviewing of leaders that came with the RNS assignments.

One of the last RNS stories in my files (October 20, 1975) reported an occasion commemorating the tenth anniversary of an anti-war organization, Clergy and Laity Concerned about Vietnam, which was then dropping the last part of the name and indicating its members were concerned about things in general. "We have learned that Vietnam was not an exception in American foreign policy but an illustration of it," Robert McAfee Brown wrote in a message to the gathering. The group used the occasion to honor the then-deceased Abraham Joshua Heschel, a rabbi who had helped found the organization in the midst of the war. And the program personalities constituted a sort of roster of the protest community—among them, Richard J. Neuhaus, a Lutheran minister later to become a Catholic priest and part of the conservative protest community; Mary Luke Tobin, a Catholic nun who had pioneered as one of the few women admitted as observers at Vatican II; Balfour Brickner, a rabbi who was interreligious affairs director of the Union of American Hebrew Congregations (Reform) and a prominent voice for a liberal Jewish viewpoint; and Don Luce, who had blackened the reputation of the South Vietnamese government by telling of the "tiger cages" where it kept dissidents.

A curious sidebar story I never followed up was the complaint of George W. Webber, chairman of the organization, that the National Council of Churches was keeping the last $150,000 of a legacy that had been financing Clergy and Laity Concerned and that the organization had hoped to use for its transitional period. Mr. Webber said a wealthy stockbroker, Dan Bernstein, had entrusted the money to the National Council for tax reasons, but with the Vietnam War now over, the Council had decided to use the funds remaining for other purposes. Though conservatives on the outside might consider the National Council of Churches a center of radicalism, I discovered now and then that people leaning leftward were not necessarily always so enthused about it either.

In other stories for RNS, I covered (October 28, 1974) the first celebration of communion by Episcopal women who had been defiantly ordained before the church's bishops made women's ordination legal. I reported on a name day dinner of Greek Orthodox Archbishop Iakovos that focused on the plight of Greek Cypriots and the evil, as the Greeks saw it, of a U.S. decision to sell arms to Turkey (October 14, 1975). I reported on Robert F. Drinan, a Jesuit priest who was a Democratic representative from Massachusetts, telling an American Jewish Committee audience about his commitment to the cause of Soviet Jewry (September 23, 1975). On Betty Friedan and other women at a conference sponsored by the Franciscan Atonement friars (November 3, 1970). On Burgess Carr, general secretary of the All Africa Conference of Churches (February 17, 1970). And many, many more events of equivalent interest

I eventually had to quit working for RNS, however, because of its shoestring budget. RNS charged most of its client newspapers and magazines a bargain rate, and Miss Block kept charges modest in part because of her sense of mission. To her, it was the low budget periodical of some small, isolated religious group that most needed the broadening she hoped would come from exposure to news of the wider religious community. So she would not match inflation with increases to the point of losing such clients. RNS was subsidized by the NCCJ, and Miss Block was also trying to manage affairs in a way that kept the needed subsidy at the lowest possible level, aware that, as later did happen, the NCCJ could decide the burden was too burdensome and throw RNS out on the street.

Even the staff got remuneration so near the minimum wage that most everyone of any ability would soon find another job, moving along to what Miss Block seemed to esteem in a professorial way as the distinguished ranks of her alumni. But keeping the budget low required more especially keeping payments to the outside contributors low. Most of the others who sent in stories would not worry about it so much because they were on salary as religion reporters for daily newspapers or something, and took their RNS checks as only a little gravy for the meat and potatoes already on their plates. Stories were paid at two cents a word, a level Miss Block seemed to feel had once been properly set back in the 1950s or sometime, maybe 1934, and should never be altered, no matter how inflation raged.

I, working freelance and submitting stories done on assignment exclusively for RNS, got the same two cents as someone on salary for some newspaper, and sending in a carbon copy of a story that was written for it and required RNS staff time for rewriting. As a vital supplement, I made a little more money the days I filled in for absent staff, and still more when I began writing the weekly radio script that RNS sent out. But the work I was really there to do, the reporting, was not keeping me alive.

After a few years of that, I decided my apprenticeship was complete, and I should now be paid for my work. Miss Block listened to my request for an increase and spit in my eye. So I bided my time and three years later, in January of the Independence Bicentennial year, declared my own independence. I went in to talk money again with Miss Block, this time not to ask but to tell her compensation must become more compensatory if I were to stay in harness. She squirmed and frowned and looked serious and looked down and looked around and scribbled with a pencil and finally, as though taking some revolutionary action, conceded that she could raise me to three cents. So I left what ought to have remained a natural home base for me.

But I was able to do it without breaking personal ties with Miss Block. By coincidence, she was brought to the WCC offices in Geneva in 1980 for a meeting of some advisory group at the same time I was there to work on the Risk book. She had almost never traveled anywhere before. For one thing, there was no place she wanted to be as much as in her own office, where she could follow the incoming news reports. She also turned down junket offers for fear they might put the unbiased character of RNS coverage in question.

But in 1979 she retired, and so could accept the trip to Geneva without fear of compromising RNS virtue. During that time, we both had a free day the same day, and took a train trip along Lake Geneva to Montreux. There, we walked along the lakefront, enjoying the views across the water as well as the flowers and shrubs along the shore. We made our way eventually to the Castle of Chillon, given fame by Lord Byron's "Prisoner of Chillon," and Miss Block doggedly pushed her short, bulky torso up and down all the steps, still driven by the urge to investigate whatever the world placed before her.

On our way back to Geneva, we stopped off at Lausanne to get some impression of the place where an important gathering, the first World Conference on Faith and Order, was held in 1927. By the time we got there, daylight had about gone, and some rain was falling, so we could not look around much. But we had dinner in the station restaurant, and tried the local wine, and Miss Block set in to see what she could learn from the waitress.

Although Miss Block seemed in more or less normal health, it turned out that she was nearing the end of her life. The next February she broke her hip in a fall, and never came out of the hospital. I went over to New Jersey to pay a final visit shortly before her death, March 21, but had to miss her funeral in order to carry out a reporting assignment, a weighing of priorities I could easily persuade myself she would have endorsed.

In the summer of 1993, I was back in Geneva to do some work for the World Council's news outlet, Ecumenical Press Service (EPS), and set aside time to make a Lillian Block memorial journey to Lausanne one afternoon. To see some of what we had missed before, I carried her in my thoughts down the steep slopes to the lakefront, and along the shore a ways, and took the little train back up the hill. After dark, I ate again in the station restaurant, and remembered the Lillian Block lesson that learning need never stop.

It was at RNS that I first met Thomas H. Dorris. He worked on the staff there for a while, and we saw each other occasionally. Then he edited a news service sponsored by the Lutheran Council in the USA, a cooperative agency for Lutheran denominations, and let me write some articles for him. Later, he became editor of EPS, and I wrote for him regularly during that period. After he left EPS, he took a job in Sweden, and his life ended abruptly there in 1994, when he was driving with visiting family members and ran head on into an approaching car, whose driver was also killed. The family members were not killed, but did not see how the accident occurred, so Tom's life ended in a degree of mystery.

I remember him as notable and rare for a lay piety of depth and intelligence. He was seriously committed to the Christian faith in the classical doctrinal and liturgical forms of his Lutheran tradition. A son of the Missouri

Synod, he eventually moved into the broader Lutheran mainstream, but kept Missouri's seriousness about the faith while dropping its hard and disputatious edge. He was among a small and pioneering few who secured ordination as permanent deacons in the Lutheran denomination. I attended the service at Immanuel Lutheran Church in Manhattan when he was ordained, and later saw him serving liturgically as a deacon there. During my 1993 stint in Geneva, I went to a WCC executive committee meeting in Sigtuna, near Uppsala, and found him there at a smorgasbord sumptuously laid on for the committee. I saw him one last time in the spring of 1994 at an event marking the 60th anniversary of the agency where we first met, RNS. And I closed the circle by attending a memorial service for him at the church where he became a deacon.

One of my more interesting reporting activities in the 1980s was Dorris-initiated. When he got into the EPS post, he suggested that I occasionally write a *Letter from New York* for it. I suppose he took the idea from the *New Yorker* magazine, which occasionally carried a *Letter* from London or Paris or some other locale. It was a relaxed sort of format, allowing the writer to ramble from one thing to another, with the aim of helping readers catch up on whatever interesting events had been happening lately. For EPS, it would not work quite as well because not enough space could be allotted there for a satisfying ramble. And eventually Mr. Dorris decided the series had gone on long enough, and brought it to a halt. But while it continued, it gave me an opportunity to bring in a good many matters of interest that might not have been worth full stories in themselves, and to connect a few developments in ways that showed patterns and trends. I doubt that many of those *Letters* ever got printed by the publications that were clients of EPS, but for any individual readers they were a way of getting not only the bare facts but also some of the flavor of American church life.

In my days contributing to RNS, its principal competitor was NC, the National Catholic News Service, which later dropped the "National" in recognition of its international clients and coverage, and changed its logo to CNS (June 8, 1989; in this book, I refer alternatively to NC or CNS according to the date of the story). Shortly after I began contributing to RNS, the National Council of Churches (NCC) commissioned me to write a series of articles on NCC-Catholic relations that were used by NC. But when Miss Block heard about it, she insisted that my byline come off, and that I foreswear any future attempts to work both sides of the street. After leaving RNS, I was free of her restriction, so I one day asked the NC correspondent in New York if I might occasionally lend a hand. That was Jo-ann Price, in her married life Jo-ann

Price Baehr, the Baehr from an editorial writer for the *International Herald Tribune*, Harry Baehr.

She was indeed glad to have some help, and NC payments, though not overwhelming, surpassed those of RNS agreeably. Jo-ann welcomed a backup for weeks when she went on vacation, or when events came along such as a night program in the Bronx and she did not want to make the long trip from Brooklyn, where she and Harry had an apartment. And at times I picked up a story on my other rounds that had interest for the Catholic press. Jo-ann later died of cancer, and as the disease reached its final stages in 1982, I was called on to do more and more of the NC coverage in New York, and in the last months was doing it all.

After her death, which occurred July 15, the editors of NC followed the line of least resistance and let me take her place. On the evening before her funeral, I was invited to a restaurant in the Citicorp building for dinner with NC editor Thomas N. Lorsung and his chief in the administrative structure, Richard Daw. They were kind and generous, and offered me a retainer such as Jo-ann had been getting. I decided to forego that and retain my freelance insecurity absolute. But to show a cooperative spirit, I offered to accept an increase in my per-word rates, which forthcame.

I also raised the question of my non-Catholicness, which they did not, because I thought it could become a political problem. I had caught just a whiff of that in writing for the Lutheran news service, when one official complained about a couple of my stories and insinuated that I, being outside the fold, could not be expected to report at the desired depth. When people are mad, they reach for whatever rock lies nearest at hand to throw at you. But Mr. Lorsung and Mr. Daw said they had already used enough of my work to become confident my church affiliation would present no difficulty. And these years later I remain somewhat astonished that it has not, or at least I have not been made aware of any.

So I entered into the new relationship with what became my best customer. We have never had a written contract, but operated solely on the old-fashioned basis of a gentlemen's agreement. I agreed to look after their interests in New York, and they agreed to send me some money occasionally, and I have and they have.

Getting into the Catholic world has brought the personal benefit of acquaintance with many agreeable people, which value is not diluted by the fact that I may disagree with them on some points. It recently occurred to me that I have never met a Maryknoll sister I did not like, and I have met a great many. Although I may not necessarily endorse their views on the politics of

SIDEBARS

Latin America, I can testify they are splendid people and seriously committed to giving their lives for any fellow inhabitants of the planet who need help.

My church connections and disconnections are not matters I go around announcing, and not unmentionables I hide. If asked, I explain I am a member of the Riverside Church, an interdenominational congregation, and, for those curious to know still more, that my background is Southern Baptist. But when I tell people I am representing the Catholic News Service, many of them doubtless find it natural to assume I am Catholic.

Daniel W. Morrissey, a Dominican priest, came to Riverside Church as theologian-in-residence for the 1982-83 year. He was giving a class at the church, counseling a few people and contributing in miscellaneous other ways. My Catholic editors agreed that he would make an interesting story, so I got an appointment and went up for an interview.

I pressed Father Morrissey a little on the whys and wherefores of entering into such an unCatholic environment, and how he thought it could fit into the proper ministry of a Catholic priest. I wanted to get material to fill out the story, but he assumed that I was a Catholic and he perhaps feared I was one of the squintier kind, and about to accuse him of unnatural acts. So he began a little lecture to instruct me about the commitment of the Catholic Church to ecumenism, and how there was this document on ecumenism from the Second Vatican Council and so on. Until I finally broke in to let him know I was myself a member of the Riverside Church and hardly needed any convincing about the virtues of ecumenism.

Though I belong to the Riverside Church, I have not taken any active role in its program. The kind of work I do keeps me moving around from church to church on Sundays, and leaves me little time for getting into any sort of regular weekday activities. This practical circumstance got psychological reinforcement early on when I was shocked to receive a letter from one of the Riverside ministers reprimanding me for something I had written about the church. It was a *Christian Century* piece (August 26, 1970) about the New York church scene, and referred to the large endowment of Riverside Church. The complaining minister grew alarmed that members might deduce that they had no need to help out with the budget. He had misread my comments, but I figured that even if I made errors at times, I would find it disagreeable to get a slapping around from a minister of my church, so I had best keep a little emotional distance.

One reason I do not announce my church affiliation on every corner is journalistic. If Catholics I am interviewing sit there viewing me as Protestant, they will likely start explaining the subject in a way they think will help a

Protestant understand it. And that is what I want—not. When I am writing for a Catholic readership, I want matters described and explained in the language normally used in talking to Catholics, terms that will seem natural to Catholic readers. While it is of course important for me to understand, the main point is to convey information to readers in a way that lets it most easily fit into their mental universe. The same considerations, of course, apply when I am writing for other outlets such as publications of the United Methodist Church. And I have done enough of that to leave a few people with the idea I am a United Methodist.

In one of my first assignments for NC, I interviewed Bernard Haering, a Catholic priest of the Redemptorist order and a professor who had written notable works in the field of moral theology, or ethics. Actually, my very first assignment, a story carried March 31, 1977, was to go up to Fordham University's Bronx campus and cover the comments of Father Haering and others about women's ordination. Vatican arguments against it do not persuade, he said.

The need for another, quite different story arose because of potential questions about Father Haering's own ethics. Reports came from Italy that he was featured in a pornographic movie running there, and some people would wonder about that. He normally taught in Rome, but at the time was spending a semester at Fordham. So I was sent up again to the university's Rose Hill campus to ask him what in the Sam Hill was going on.

He explained that some years earlier he had discussed various questions related to sexual ethics for an education film on *The Family Yesterday and Today*. But the director later said he had found a different distributor, and in fact seemed to have put the footage in the hands of someone with different purposes. So it happened that in the United States, Father Haering heard he was featured in a porn film. The patron of the porn house would see the priest talking about contraceptives or adultery or some other problem area, and then would come a pornographic segment to let you see in explicit detail just what Father Haering was talking about.

As he was giving me this account, I sensed a note of pleading in his voice, an undertone of begging me to please understand he never had any idea that his words and image would be used in such a fashion. And this pleading began to seem rather unseemly. Why should a distinguished theologian with a reputation built on decades of work need to justify himself to me? Nobody had appointed me Grand Inquisitor. Yet, if he was to maintain his reputation among people in the church at large, and continue seeing his writings and lectures received with the same respect as in the past, he needed to provide some kind of explanation. And in the fortuitousness of events, it turned out I was the line of communication (NC, April 18, 1977).

Reporters do not represent anybody except the general public. But that is a rather special "except." It is not the function of a court or a legislature or a corporate board of directors, and people talking about the power of the press should remain clear that this is a different kind of power, and find different ways to guard against its abuses. But reporting is nonetheless a function essential to the health of society. The general public has a need and desire to know what is going on. So reporters are doing an essential job, even though they carry no official commission, and want none.

What kind of neutrality do I maintain? Often I am going to report on a sermon or some other aspect of a worship service. If I am a Christian at a Christian worship service, should I pretend for an hour that I have no religion? Can I for the nonce become merely an observer? Do I want to? If the congregation joins in the Lord's Prayer, could I stay silent? If I stay silent during the singing of the hymns, that will enhance the worship for others. But I can hardly go to a church service and stand aloof altogether.

You could say I further violate the rules of journalistic neutrality because, in writing for church publications and agencies, I am usually paid with money that comes ultimately from the churches I am reporting on. But one way or another I am involved in so many conflicts of interest, I can maybe think they cancel each other out, and place me in solidarity with the congressman who takes campaign contributions from groups on all sides of an issue and then figures he can make his own decision about which way to go. Anyway, in my case, the financial returns have been so minimal the issue seems hardly worth agonizing over.

If financial remuneration for my version of the reporting life has not been impressive, a bit of compensation has come from getting entrée to many places I might never see on my own recognizance, such as one of the boxes at the Metropolitan Opera. On my own, I would more likely ascend to the top balcony. But I arranged to do a story about Owen Lee, and that got me into the prestige seating (NC, February 4, 1987). Father Lee, a Basilian priest, taught classics at St. Michael's College in Toronto. But he was also an opera buff of an expertish kind, and came to New York from time to time for the intermission panels during Texaco's Saturday afternoon broadcasts.

On the afternoon of January 24, 1987, the opera was Richard Wagner's *Tannhauser,* and Father Lee was there. So the Texaco people let me listen from one of the chairs in a box they had. For the first intermission broadcast, Father Lee sat at a piano in the little side auditorium, giving an interpretive presentation about the opera, and occasionally playing a few illustrative bars. For the second intermission, he sat on the panel challenged to answer questions sent in by listeners. One asked panelists to identify articles of clothing sung about in certain operatic melodies. As soon as Father Lee heard the first few notes of one example, he smiled and put up his hand. It was the shining white outfit extolled in Richard Strauss's *Rosenkavalier*, he said, correctly. "You can usually rely on him," the quizmaster, Edward Downes, told me.

In an interview, Father Lee said *Tannhauser* was special to him because it was the first opera he ever heard. At age 11 in Detroit, he was told by his piano teacher about the Texaco radio broadcasts, and tried one. That day, the opera turned out to be *Tannhauser*, and "it just swept over me like a tidal wave." So much so that the date was fixed in his memory–February 14, 1942. Nonetheless, another Wagner opera, *The Meistersinger*, later became his favorite.

For a priest, Wagner does of course present certain questions of ethics–the pagan themes in his operas, his personal antisemitism and the way he treated women. But Father Lee told me that admirers of Wagner's music could make the necessary discriminations and "dismiss what should be dismissed." People who heard Father Lee on the radio often wrote to share their reactions, he said. "When a priest says it's all right to like Wagner, they're so grateful."

Another perk of sorts for me was getting shanghaied on a thousand dollar boat ride. It was a fundraising cruise in New York harbor, a benefit for agencies helping unmarried pregnant girls so they might not feel driven to abortion. I went aboard to get the story, thinking I could not spare the time to spend the evening with them, but would go ashore before the boat left the dock. While I was talking with Cardinal O'Connor, an admiral in his earlier life as a chaplain, he apparently felt a familiar motion, looked out, and advised me that I had better get ashore promptly if I were going. But I was already too dilatory.

The thousand dollar price of the ride somewhat exceeded my resources that evening, and quite likely exceeded what NC editors would want to see on my expense account. But the sponsors longed for publicity and were happy to have me along for the full trip, ticket or no ticket. And if you are to suffer mishaps at sea, an evening cruise in New York harbor, getting a closeup view of the illuminated Statue of Liberty with her torch, can serve as the suffering of choice. The lights of lower Manhattan and the necklace across the Verrazano Bridge also entrance, but nothing touches you like the Statue of Liberty.

For civilized elegance, one of my more special treats was a Notre Dame affair at the Plaza Hotel. The university gives an annual award called the Laetare Medal, named for the fourth Sunday of Lent, called Laetare Sunday because part of the mass of the day in Latin begins with the word "Laetare," meaning "Rejoice." Giving that name to a Sunday can serve as a useful reminder that Christian people are people with a religious obligation to rejoice. "Lift up your hearts," a minister often says in liturgies. That is an order. Normally, the Laetare Medal is presented at Notre Dame, but the year it was given jointly to playwright Jean Kerr and her husband, Walter, the drama critic, the ceremony was moved to New York.

Theodore M. Hesburgh, the Holy Cross priest who was Notre Dame's president, believed in operating with panache. Talk suave, and you are talking Father Hesburgh. He engaged rooms at the Plaza, and set up a splendidly elegant, elegantly low key affair for a hundred or so of the most favored. I of course did not rank in the most favored hundred, or hundred thousand, but Lillian Block was included in hopes of getting some RNS publicity, and she took me along to do the work.

After the reception, with a mammoth and memorable shrimp bowl, we sat at round tables for the serving of a gourmet meal. Where every participant but me was a personage, there could intrude nothing so vulgar as a head table. After dinner, along came a cart with various of the more esteemed liqueurs. And the medals were then given in a warmly informal manner as we sipped.

Reporters ought to put aside preconceptions, but the director of the Metropolitan Museum of Art turned out to be exactly what anyone might preconceive. Philippe de Montebello had not only a suitably sounding name for an art environment, but coordinating accent and demeanor. When Philippe de Montebello says "not worthy of response" and gives a disdainful brush of the hand, an interviewer must wonder at his own intrepidity if he persists in suggesting perhaps some response could be in order.

I was talking to Mr. Montebello in connection with the Vatican exhibit that was shown at the Metropolitan in early 1983, and then at the Art Institute of Chicago and the Young Memorial Museum of San Francisco. Partly through the encouragement of Terence J. Cooke, Cardinal-Archbishop of New York and a Metropolitan trustee, the Vatican agreed to let 237 of its art works fly to America, the first time any significant number had gone abroad. At the end of the showing in New York, the Metropolitan declared the exhibition a great success. All the 596,000 tickets it offered the public were sold, and the attendance of museum members, guests of sponsoring companies and others put the grand total at 856,000, officials said. The Metropolitan was happy. Vatican representative Walter Persegati was happy. Cardinal Cooke got one of the last happinesses of his life, soon to end.

As so often with such projects, however, a few people chose to grump. Some in the developing anti-nicotine movement objected to Philip Morris, which gave $3 million and got listed as principal sponsor. Some art lovers worried. What if one of the airplanes bringing the irreplaceables should fall from the sky, and the Apollo Belvedere took a dive in the ocean? But the criticism I thought Mr. Montebello might deal with concerned the style and quality of the exhibition itself. Writing in the *New York Review of Books* (June 2), David Wright, a professor of art history at the University of California in Berkeley, called some of the exhibited works "very feeble stuff," and said the National Gallery in Washington had recently shown it knew how to mount a better show.

Mr. Montebello could not deign to answer such "meaningless" comment from such a "biased" source and, anyway, was the *New York Review of Books* really so important? My impression had been that the *New York Review of Books* normally carried rather intelligent writing. You could often read Garry Wills there, always worthwhile. But no doubt any publication could slip up from time to time. Most critics gave favorable reviews, and the public expressed appreciation in a flow of letters "unmatched in the history of the museum," Mr. Montebello declared.

In 1981, the head of the Maronite community, Antoine Pierre Khoraiche, made his first visit as patriarch to the United States. One Sunday in September, he presided at a mass in St. Patrick's Cathedral, and afterward held a press conference (NC, September 16). A good many people from his entourage and the Maronite community of the United States came into the room where the press conference was held. At the front table, the patriarch was joined by a couple of his key aides, and others lined the back and side walls.

Something of an occasion. But the total number of reporters who turned out for this opportunity to get the latest word on Lebanon directly from the patriarchal mouth, the total number including me, was one. As a partial qualification, I will note that there was also a woman of the U.S. Maronite community who did some radio work, and planned to send back a report for a station in Lebanon. But so far as the patriarch getting this Sunday's message sown across the length and breadth of America, his only media channel seemed to be me.

Patriarch Khoraiche mainly wanted to say that the Lebanon problem was caused by the Palestinian problem, and would the United States please do something about that? By questioning, I also ascertained he would be willing to see the Maronites surrender their monopoly on Lebanon's presidency, provided they were guaranteed certain protections. And by still further questioning I ascertained that he was not disposed to talk about the military alliance reportedly forged by Maronites with Israelis.

Through my previous reporting, I had become aware that there were a few ins and outs to the Lebanon situation. In relation to the surrounding Muslim multitudes, Jews of Israel and Maronite Christians might see some

SIDEBARS

commonality of interest, and were said to find ways of acting in concert. It was also sometimes said that Christians in the United States ought to be joining in more wholeheartedly because the Maronites were their fellow Christians and under threat. But J Richard Butler, Middle East secretary for the National Council of Churches (NCC), had pointed out to me that Lebanon's Christian community included not only Maronites, an Eastern Catholic group, but also Orthodox Christians, a few Protestants and some Catholics of non-Maronite connection. And he said Lebanese Christians were "not themselves monolithic in their analysis or recommendations" (*Christian Science Monitor*, December 9, 1975). Giving Maronites the privilege of always getting to see one of their own as president and another as head of the army did not necessarily please other Christians in Lebanon, nor did it accord with the changed population picture that now put Muslims in the majority. A resolution adopted by the NCC board in October of 1975 said the Lebanese conflict was "essentially political, economic and social," despite some "religious connotations" and some "external pressures."

Finding myself the only reporter at some occasion has not been rare in my experience. It is not so frequent that a formal press conference of a major figure draws nobody else, but because of the nature of my work and the kind of stories my editors want, I am often going to meetings or looking up people that no other reporter has been asked to cover. Rules of engagement in such cases are not clear. Speakers sometimes try to bobble on and off the record. If I am the only reporter in the room, it can become a direct one-to-one issue of whether I will play along.

Then a family tie may develop. If it is a religious meeting, and I am reporting for religious publications, in a sense I sit as part of the family, smiled at and sometimes invited to eat at the family table. Does all this mean that if anything embarrassing emerges, I will avoid mention of it? And if that seems to be the expectation, how do I clear the air without giving offense?

A direct command I can handle. When the North American Academy of Ecumenists met in New York in 1981, a Southern Baptist minister, Glenn Igleheart, conducted one of the communion services. Many Southern Baptists would quickly decapitate any of their ministers they caught leading or participating in a communion service outside a Southern Baptist church, and Mr. Igleheart, as fearful as if I had caught him in a motel with a prostitute, commanded me not to report it. So I reported it (NC, September 28). But displaying strength of journalistic character, I did resist overplaying it, as his attitude had much tempted me to do.

For another example: One day in 1978, NC got a letter saying it had an "obligation" to cover a meeting where some former homosexuals would tell how they had changed to become heterosexual through a philosophy called aesthetic realism. Taught by a man named Eli Siegel, this philosophy held that the whole world, like a work of art, formed an aesthetic unity of diverse elements, including, for example, male and female. And once you saw that, everything fell into place.

A campaign was underway against *The New York Times,* which was refusing to let its readers in on the news about this cure for the ills of the world, and aesthetic realists wore buttons saying, "Victim of the Press." But NC editors saw a story, and since the upcoming meeting was to be in New York, the "obligation" descended to me. I got on the phone to an earnest young woman who was the press representative, and made arrangements. But before I could say goodby, she wanted to know, "Could I ask if you have good will?" I passed it off as something of a joke, and told her, no, she could not ask, and I considered the question rather presumptuous, and so long. But when I got to the meeting, I found she still had "good will" on her mind, and she pressed me further at an intermission. I suggested that insisting on such a declaration was useless since anybody might say what she wanted whether it was true or not. She countered that in her experience it had been otherwise, and when anyone had assured her of good will, it turned out that he really did have good will.

At the end of the meeting, the woman came to me again, and spent a while reporting that she had conferred with her committee, and they had reached the conclusion that if I could not tell them I had good will, there was to be no story at all. Until I finally assured her that the burden of that decision would not fall on her shoulders, and went home to write (NC, July 24).

But then there are the matters of lesser moment. A bishop giving an address wants to tell a just ever so maybe slightly a little bit risque joke, and asks me to let him put it off the record: Today's little girl says, "I found a condom on the verandah." Today's little boy asks, "What's a verandah?" I do not like to have speakers trying to weave off and on the record. If there is a closed session, declare it and I can report they did their business behind closed doors. But what is a little joke among friends?

Some requests seem hardly legitimate. I once wrote an article about the academic work of a Catholic priest, and was surprised to have him ask me not to mention that he was a Catholic priest. He was then applying for another job in a setting where he feared such information might become a liability. But he was publicly known to me and to others as a Catholic priest, and anyway I thought full disclosure might well be a worthy part of any job search. So I "exposed" him. But his fears proved unfounded, and he got the longed-for position in due course. If the exposure had caused him to lose out, I would have felt natural regrets, but would not have thought I was wrong to present the full picture.

The fears of bias were not altogether irrational: appointment of a Jesuit priest of stature, Timothy S. Healy, as president of the New York Public Library drew attacks from people such as Gay Talese, claiming to fear the freedom of intellectual inquiry was about to end. Or perhaps they foresaw Father Healy holding a bonfire behind the library in Bryant Park to burn every book containing a critical sentence about the Catholic Church (NC, March 29, 1989).

Now a more serious example: A priest is telling a group about helping a committee of American Catholic bishops draft a statement, and says they came under some pressure from Rome to change one point, but felt so strongly they resisted. When I later approached him for more detail, he said I could not report that incident at all. Since I did not really have enough information to give a full account, and I did not see the point was worth a direct confrontation with the priest and the organizers of the meeting, I left "Rome" out of the story. But since the priest had made his statement in an open gathering, and it was pertinent and interesting, I decided it should go in somehow. So I merely said the bishops had resisted pressure to change their statement, and left it to my thoughtful readers to reflect on who might have a capability for putting pressure on the Catholic bishops of the United States.

Decisions become even harder when stories involve a church leader working abroad under some harsh dictatorship, and I know suffering could ensue if the dictator gets disturbed. So I avoid establishing any rules with the character of "the law of the Medes and Persians, which altereth not" (Daniel 6:8, 12 KJV).

All in all, I cannot complain much about my treatment from the people I have covered. They likely feel more reason to complain about me, or at least sometimes. J. Blaine Fister was formerly a source at the National Council of Churches for stories on religion and public education. After one of my articles, he jokingly complained that I had taken an hour of his time and quoted only one sentence. The smarty answer to him was that it took me an hour to get one sentence worth quoting. But that was not the reality, either. The hour of conversation gave me a depth of understanding that strengthened the entire article, letting me more accurately identify the main points and their relative importance. And it kept me from putting in other statements that would have been mistaken or misleading.

At times, I may abandon a story when conditions impede. An organization called the Interfaith Foundation for Community Organization (IFCO) bounded into notoriety when a 1969 gathering it sponsored in Detroit, the Black Economic Development Conference, was taken over by a radical named James Forman and turned into a vehicle for pushing his demands, which were $500 million in "reparations" from the white churches. He got a little, but never into the millions. Some years later, with all that subsided, I learned that a black United Methodist executive, Negail Riley, was chairing the IFCO board and funneling some United Methodist money into the organization.

I asked Arthur J. Moore Jr., editor of the United Methodist magazine, *New World Outlook,* if he could use an article. He could. But when I talked to Mr. Riley, I found a case of nerves. He would cooperate only if I would write exclusively about the future of IFCO and say nothing about its past, and only if he could censor the article before it was printed. Normally, officials will do just about anything to avoid the word "censor." Their line usually sounds something like, "Certainly I don't want to censor what you write; no, no, no, not at all; I just want to read it before you publish it, and mark out the parts I think could be misinterpreted." But Negail Riley was made of sturdier stuff, and said "censor" without stuttering or stumbling. So I told him I would drop the project, and he said he was offended by that.

But here now I must avoid any suggestion that I am a hard-driving investigative reporter, since that is rather far from the reality. And even if I were, I would have trouble finding a market. For one immediate preclusion, investigative reporting is expensive. It takes time, and you never know whether it will pay off. As in oil exploration, occasionally you may hit a gusher, but then you may go broke drilling dry holes. In reading about the Carl Bernstein-Bob Woodward investigation of Watergate, perhaps the most celebrated example of investigative reporting in recent times, an aspect impressive to me was how much money *The Washington Post* put into it. Only the strongest journalistic organizations could afford to pay the salaries of two staff members to follow one story for months when there was no guarantee of any significant payoff. And when one of the reporters thought it would help to talk to somebody in California, he could buy a plane ticket, rent a car when he got there, pay a motel bill, eat a few meals and take care of expenses for anything else that might contribute to the cause. Meanwhile, back in Washington, office expenses were covered, and taxi bills and unlimited telephoning all over. The people I have written for by and large thought they were going the limit if they agreed to cover a long distance telephone call or two.

The financial limitations of the church press also limit the opportunities for in depth reporting on programs of a positive character. Many aspects of church life deserve more thorough treatment than they ever get. Where I would find it useful and interesting to take several days and interview many people of diverse viewpoints for a story, I usually find no editor prepared to pay for that much time, and so I must make do with sharply circumscribed investigations.

SIDEBARS

Another brake on investigative reporting of malfeasance in the church field is the reality that most editors of church-related publications are themselves committed to the church, and want to see it advance in strength and public regard. Even if they are willing to face scandal without flinching after it appears, they will not usually want to allocate time and money to dig it out. And they may decide printing it would hurt causes they want to promote. One year when Church World Service, the relief arm of the NCC, became the focus of not criminal scandal but noticeably fierce infighting, the editor of a paper published by one of the NCC's member denominations asked me to report the current state of the question. I spent a good deal of time talking with people on all sides so I could explain to readers with some accuracy and breadth what was going on underneath. But the editor then decided not to print any of it, giving the excuse that it would cause readers to stop contributing to the organization's relief work, and he did not want to see that happen.

Whether journalists really help the church when they cover up areas of scandal, internal conflict and incompetent management could be doubted. If you consider the example of pedophilia among Catholic clergy, which bishops were able to keep quiet in the past but have lately been forced to deal with because of losing million-dollar lawsuits, you could ask about the role of church journalists. Many probably remained ignorant themselves about what was happening, but some of them must have known a little. Were they really serving the interests of the church, or perhaps only storing dynamite for a bigger explosion in the future, when they went along with the bishops' desire to keep the matter quiet, sweep it under the rug and hope it would go away?

But though I am not an investigative reporter in any serious sense, I do make a serious effort to clarify issues. Sometimes I ask a question, and the guy I am interviewing then talks for a while but I fail to see how his comments connect to my question. I never assume he is evading, but figure I have failed to make my question clear, and try asking it in other ways. That procedure has on occasion created some annoyance. I was told that one of my interviewees had reported, "He never lets up till he gets what he wants." That is not really true, though it may have seemed so to some. Many a time I have given up before I got the clarifications I was looking for. There are limits to the possible, but I make an effort.

Some people seem to feel they can psyche me out and determine that there is some specific thing I am trying to push them into saying. In reality, I am not doing that consciously, unless I happen to know already a specific bit of fact I want to get on the record. But more often I am just floundering around in an effort to think of any question that might provoke a worthwhile comment. For my purposes, it usually matters little whether the people I interview say yea or say nay, so long as they say something.

A different kind of challenge came with the terminal illness of Cardinal O'Connor. In August of 1999, he developed a persisting illness, and went to Memorial Sloan-Kettering Cancer Center. His spokesman, Joseph Zwilling, said the choice of hospitals should not be taken to mean that the cardinal had cancer, and when he came out of the hospital September 4, he had Mr. Zwilling put out a press release that conspicuously avoided the c word. We were told that doctors had removed a tumor from the surface of Cardinal O'Connor's brain, and that he would have followup radiation. With that sort of release, you need to think about all the things that someone has chosen to leave unsaid. We were not even told the date of the surgery, or who performed the operation. We were not told whether the tumor was malignant, though you could very well assume that if it had been benign the release would have made sure we knew.

Cardinal O'Connor later told a reporter that he did not use the word "cancer" because it had not been used in the conversations of doctors with him at the hospital. That seemed a little hard to credit. If your doctors decided you needed to visit Sloan-Kettering Cancer Center and undergo tests, and the doctors there told you after tests that you needed surgery for removal of a brain tumor, and that you would afterward need radiation, might it not occur to you to ask, "Do I by any chance have cancer?"

Maybe Cardinal O'Connor had no such curiosity. Anyway, from the beginning all the way through till his death the next May 3, he never told the public that he had cancer, or let people on his staff say the word.

Partly, that may have come from a general disposition to play down the importance of his own health problems. On one occasion, I went to his residence for a scheduled interview and found him suffering from flu or something that should have sent him right upstairs to bed, but he insisted on proceeding as though his physical condition really did not matter. I also saw him in bad shape at an event announcing a drive to raise funds for archdiocesan schools.

But the way the cancer was non-acknowledged went beyond any such measures. Perhaps the idea is that a chief has to pretend there is never anything seriously wrong with him, lest somebody wonder whether he is still up to sitting at the head of the table.

Cardinal O'Connor's predecessor also concealed his cancer for a long time. In *Thy Will Be Done: A Spiritual Portrait of Terence Cardinal Cooke* by Benedict J. Groeschel and Terrence L. Weber (Alba House, 1990), we were told that Cardinal Cooke got treatment for cancer in 1964, four years before he became

SIDEBARS

archbishop, and the archbishop at that time, Francis J. Spellman, had a note sent into the operating room during the surgery directing that "no information" concerning it should be discussed with anyone outside (p. 202). In 1975, doctors discovered that Cardinal Cooke had cancer "diffused throughout the body," and began chemotherapy that continued till his death in 1983 (p. 203). His illness was then identified as aleukemic leukemia (p. 206). All this was kept secret. But even Cardinal Cooke finally allowed an announcement of his terminal illness—on August 26, 1983, about six weeks before his death.

Why did he keep it secret? "If I had not done it, and let everybody know what I had, I would have been a lame duck as archbishop" (p. 86).

We have had such in the secular world, as in Franklin D. Roosevelt refusing to let the American people know his condition when he ran for his fourth term in 1944, or John F. Kennedy concealing his health problems. But there is an ethical question. Can we regard officials of church and state merely as private individuals, with a moral right to conceal their personal travails as they wish? If they want to hold onto their power and authority, should they not perhaps recognize a responsibility to give people a true picture of their physical capacities?

Possibly such thoughts as Cardinal Cooke expressed might have occurred to Cardinal O'Connor as well. After his surgery, the word was always that he was still managing the archdiocese, operating from his residence when he was not able to go to his office, always fully in charge. And that message did not change until the very last weeks, when he was unable even to sit presiding at his Sunday mass in St. Patrick's Cathedral.

In contrast, I recalled the open way hospitalization of another cardinal, Agostino Casaroli, was handled (NC, October 29, 1985). He was visiting New York as Vatican Secretary of State when he hurt himself in a fall, and was taken to Mother Cabrini Hospital. Subsequently, his doctors held a press conference, giving us a well-rounded story: this is what the damage was, this is what we have done about it, this is how he is doing today and this is how we expect him to do tomorrow. You could say these doctors, and the cardinal giving permission, could speak so freely because they had good news to tell, were able to prophesy a full recovery. But more recently we had also seen the openness of Cardinal Joseph L. Bernardin of Chicago in telling his people and the world that he had cancer, and was on his way.

The day Cardinal O'Connor came out of Sloan-Kettering, he had a press release issued saying his schedule would be "somewhat lessened for the immediate future," but that "he is looking forward to returning to the full and vigorous schedule which he has followed since becoming the archbishop of New York." This release also reported that Cardinal O'Connor would have several weeks of radiation. So I do not see how we can avoid calling his handling of the matter deceptive. A 79-year-old man who has just had surgery for brain cancer and faces weeks of radiation knows that his schedule is going to be a great deal more than "somewhat" lessened, and that it is a very iffy matter how long he will be able to continue with any kind of schedule. But when Cardinal O'Connor had to return to Sloan-Kettering six weeks later for treatment of dehydration and a blood clot in the leg, and could not preside as usual over the Al Smith Dinner, he sent a cheery note saying he expected to be on "limited duty" for "a good month" (CNS, October 22).

So my reporting on Cardinal O'Connor's terminal illness had to proceed mostly by indirection, telling what was not said, of the lack of any reports from his doctors, direct or indirect, his inability to appear at times or, when he did appear, to walk far. I had a final chance for a brief conversation with him as he was leaving—in a wheelchair—after receiving a tribute at a dinner of the Cathedral Club of Brooklyn (CNS, January 28, 2000). When I asked how he was getting along, he acknowledged that his feet were unsteady, but said "each day they're getting stronger." He also spoke about plans to continue living in New York after his retirement. But the nervous insistence of his handlers on rushing him back to his residence, and not letting the one other reporter there and I tire him with any more questions gave a clear signal the realities of his health did not match the picture he wanted to paint. Then he became unable to make any public appearances, his weekly column ceased to appear and the unwillingness of the priests living with him to say anything about his daily activities said yet more.

Father Groeschel, the co-author of the Cooke biography and a member of the Franciscan Friars of the Renewal, became the first to give anything I could use to let people know directly what the real situation was. Speaking in St. Patrick's Cathedral on Good Friday, he told the congregation that Cardinal O'Connor was prayerfully preparing "to go home" (CNS, April 25, 2000). I do not know whether Father Groeschel realized he was making an announcement to the entire Catholic press served by CNS, but his brief remarks served the purpose.

Despite the lack of any respectable travel budget, I have been able to report on some distant organizations, such as the United Farm Workers originally headed by César Chávez, when they have decided to show the flag in New York. In the fall of 1988, the union launched a grape boycott against use of pesticides they said were damaging the health of vineyard workers. Mr. Chávez's son-in-law, Arturo Rodriguez, came to New York for some promotional activity, and went with others to a Red Apple supermarket on the West Side to hear John Catsimatides, chairman of the Red Apple chain, declare his support.

SIDEBARS

I wondered whether Mr. Chávez was realistic in trying to launch national boycotts time after time. The initial one, which was also focused on grapes, drew sympathy, and brought enough leverage to get the union into the game. But a national boycott dependent on the general public can hardly be turned on and off like a faucet. Mr. Chávez had been to New York not only to call on his sympathizers to repeat the grape boycott, but at other times to promote one against Andy Boy broccoli or bananas or lettuce. Making such a campaign broadly effective requires an immense educational effort centered on some issue clear enough to draw support from large sectors of the population. But the kind of people who energize these movements give their hearts to lots of causes, and will not all pour into the streets for repeat performances at a moment's notice.

What seemed to me particularly worth noting, however, was the presence at the Red Apple event of two of Robert F. Kennedy's daughters, Kerry and Courtney. People of the upper classes who support movements to aid the lower classes sometimes get sneered at as trendy. But here was an example of consistent, persistent effort on behalf of a cause not merely from one decade to another but one generation to another. The girls' father had given his backing to Mr. Chávez, and now twenty years after the senator's assassination his children were soldiering on in the same company.

The reporting life can also range to events in foreign regions and earlier times. In 1976, Eberhard Bethge came to Union Seminary as a visiting professor, and I got to interview him (*Christian Science Monitor*, December 6). He had been associated with Dietrich Bonhoeffer, married his niece, published his *Letters and Papers from Prison* and wrote his biography.

Pastor Bonhoeffer, though he was hung by the Nazis at age 39 for his connection with the plot against the Fuhrer, Adolph Hitler, might be considered worth devoting a career to. Karl Barth, taking up a theme treated in the opening sections of Pastor Bonhoeffer's *Cost of Discipleship* (1937), wrote, "In these the matter is handled with such depth and precision that I am almost tempted simply to reproduce them in an extended quotation. For I cannot hope to say anything better on the subject than what is said here by a man who, having written on discipleship, was ready to achieve it in his own life, and did in his own way achieve it even to the point of death" (*Dogmatics IV/1*, 533-34). Later, dealing with the subject of his dissertation, published in 1930 as *Communion of Saints*, Professor Barth wrote, "I openly confess that I have misgivings whether I can ever maintain the high level reached by Bonhoeffer, saying no less in my own words and context, and saying it no less forcefully, than did this young man so many years ago" (*Dogmatics IV/2*, 641). And writing to Professor Bethge about his biography, Professor Barth said he had learned from it that "Bonhoeffer was the first and almost the only one to face and tackle the Jewish question so centrally and energetically" (*Letters* 1961-68, tr. Geoffrey W. Bromily; Eerdmans, 1981; p. 250).

We must respect a man who will follow the way he feels led even when he knows it may lead to death. Pastor Bonhoeffer became associated with a group plotting an assassination of Hitler, but was caught and punished by hanging at the Flossenburg concentration camp just a few days before the end of the war. We must also admire Pastor Bonhoeffer's achievement in stimulating so much serious thought among many people in many parts of the world. I pointed out in the *Monitor* that he had two constituencies—one more conservative and evangelical, tuned in to his earlier books because of their intensity of commitment, and the other consisting of radicals excited by his questioning of traditional religion in the *Letters and Papers from Prison.* But Professor Bethge said any true interpretation required seeing the two sides in relation to each other.

I had a question about Pastor Bonhoeffer's understanding of the way of discipleship, however. In the biography, Professor Bethge recorded an incident that occurred when they attended a gathering where everyone was called on to give the Nazi salute. They both abhorred the idea, but when Professor Bethge hesitated, his companion urged him along, saying this was not worth endangering their lives for.

In my interview, I suggested to Professor Bethge that the early Christians living under the paganism of the Roman Empire would not have gone along with symbolic gestures, as seen when they refused to burn incense to the emperors, but they would never have plotted to kill an emperor, close as some emperors apparently were to evil absolute. Was not Bonhoeffer's conception of Christian discipleship a reversal of the early Christian way? Professor Bethge could not give me much help with my question, but only smiled kindly and informed me that Nazi Germany was not the Roman Empire.

I also had the secondary thought, from the standpoint of pragmatics, that the world should be grateful the plot to kill Hitler did not succeed. Even as things stand, we see fringe groups today honoring Hitler's memory and turning back to him for inspiration. If he had been assassinated in what could be denounced as another stab in the back by the liberals, much larger numbers and a broader representation would consider him a martyred hero. For the sake of a healthy political life in Europe and elsewhere, the Nazis needed to be defeated, crushed, so decisively and unconditionally beaten that even their very stupidest baggy-britches in the rear ranks would have to see that his Fuhrer had led him nowhere but to a dead end.

Turning to another foreign region: I was beginning my freelance life in the latter stages of the Vietnam War, and got the idea there would be interest in seeing how military chaplains were reacting to the debate over it, particularly the charge that the American role in the war was immoral. The Army chaplains' school was then located in Brooklyn at Fort Hamilton, so on two or three occasions I got appointments with chaplains who were there for courses after a tour of duty in Vietnam, and did stories for RNS. By calculated preference, I got officials of the school to select the individuals to be interviewed, assuming this would produce the most authentic representation of how the chaplains as an official branch of the Army assessed the conflict.

When critics said clergy should not be serving as chaplains and giving the war moral endorsement, defenders sometimes argued that this work was a ministry to individuals and did not necessarily imply any endorsement of government policy. Sometimes they even could be heard making a comparison with the prison chaplains who offered ministries to inmates without approving their behavior. That seemed to me a dubious analogy, and one I suspected would not inspire whichever soldiers chanced to overhear it. But in any case I found the chaplains, as one might naturally expect, did support the war, and defended the actions of the U.S. military in Vietnam.

Donald L. Crowley, a Southern Baptist from Oklahoma, said he told soldiers who raised questions about the killing in Vietnam, "If we value freedom and the American way of life, we have to share in this common task" (RNS, October 8, 1971). He also confirmed reports that prostitutes regularly worked the American barracks in Vietnam, and U.S. soldiers were fathering many illegitimate children. I had thought that conservative clergy such as himself, normally so firm on sexual morality, might raise some questions about the massive and continuing presence in Vietnam when they saw so many Vietnamese women drawn into prostitution, and saw the damage to Vietnamese family life, as well as the effect on the Americans themselves. But these uniformed clergy, while not declaring approval, seemed not as bothered as they did when preaching on fornication and adultery back home.

In writing an article about an NCC program to help Vietnam veterans who were faltering in their attempts at readjustment to civilian society, I also talked with a former Navy chaplain in the program who told me that he had left the chaplaincy because he came to think U.S. involvement in Vietnam was wrong. But not a single other Navy chaplain he knew of agreed with him, he told me. Theoretically, chaplains might have served without approving the war, but from all I could find out they were true believers in their government's policy.

Among my incidental learnings from the reporter's life was a lesson about translation, gained from the Archbishop of El Salvador, Arturo Rivera Damas. I cannot work in any language but English, and so from time to time must rely on interpreters when I interview people who do not speak it, such as Archbishop Rivera during a 1985 visit he made to New York. He knew some English, but did not feel like trying to use it in answering a reporter's questions about difficult and controversial matters. I saw him at his suite in a modest New York hotel near Gramercy Park, and a woman joined us to translate. But in the course of the interview, I found he would sometimes understand a question more quickly than she did. He did not know English as well, but he knew the issues better, and when he heard certain names and terms he could pretty well guess what I was wondering about.

The times were difficult in El Salvador, and the archbishop had a difficult row to hoe. He followed Archbishop Oscar A. Romero-Galdámez, who acquired mythic status in the minds of many after his assassination, and at the end of a lecture Archbishop Rivera gave at Riverside Church, one member of the audience boldly confronted him with the charge that he was not giving the kind of leadership his predecessor provided. The atmosphere in which Archbishop Rivera had to work was also suggested by the presence of two security guards standing at the front of the room and keeping the audience under scrutiny as he spoke. But he was not really one to inspire hostility. The church in El Salvador was divided over how much criticism should be directed at the government, and Archbishop Rivera, a little phlegmatically, kept to the middle.

Through reporting, and the direct contacts it brings about, you get impressions that could not come from reading alone. You know the atmosphere in Kenya when you interview a visiting Anglican bishop from that country, Henry Okullu, and find him afraid of talking about the governmental situation there. Some people had charged that blacks criticized only the white-ruled countries of Africa, so I asked him whether abuse of human rights by black governments should also be subject to critique. Surely, surely, he responded. Well, then, I inquired, what about President Jomo Kenyatta, who is said to be ruling your country rather dictatorially? He did not want to talk about it, even enough to say "no comment," but gestured me on to other topics.

Nor was he by any means unique in his wariness about offending the authorities he would be going back to live under. A Burmese Protestant leader I interviewed when he was passing through New York, U Kyaw Than, was returning to Burma, and insisted that I send him a copy of my article for checking before publication. That was one of the rare occasions when I agreed to such a procedure, seeing in his case real reason for apprehension.

When I interviewed an Anglican bishop from Spain, Ramon Taibo Sienes, during the days of Francisco Franco (RNS, November 4, 1968), I asked for a thumbnail summary of the bishop's biography. His reply moved conventionally from place of birth and education and so on up until about 1936, the time of the Spanish civil war. Then there was a sudden jump to the recent past and his service as a bishop. So what did you do during the war, bishop? Well, it would not be prudent to say anything about that, particularly if you had been on the losing side.

The abuse of human rights by the new black governments of Africa became a major factor in the life of the continent within just a very few years after the colonial powers granted independence. In New York, I saw a touch of that in 1972 when RNS sent me out to Kennedy Airport to cover the arrival of some Ugandan refugees. Of Asian background, they had been expelled by the Ugandan dictator, Idi Amin, and religious groups in the United States were meeting them and helping them get resettled. One I talked with, B. M. Jaffer, was a Muslim who was getting assistance from a Jewish agency, United HIAS (Hebrew Immigrant Aid Society). An agency official, Hyman Brickman, commented, "President Idi Amin had given the Asians until November 8 to get out, and if they stayed they were faced with concentration camps. Who better than Jews knows what that means?" Mr. Jaffer explained that when Uganda became independent he gave up his British passport to take a Ugandan passport. "But earlier this year they just took it away from me" (RNS, November 3). Considering what was happening to a lot of other people back in Uganda, however, he perhaps should have considered himself lucky to win expulsion.

Though Idi Amin may have been the best known of the African brutalizers for a time, many more were to come into operation. Liberia had what seemed like one of the more stable societies, but I got confirmation of news reports that this was no longer near the truth when I interviewed an official of the Society of African Missions, a Catholic order with a branch office in New Jersey, after his return from a visit (CNS, December 22, 1994). The famous sergeant, Samuel K. Doe, had taken over the Liberian government and killed the president and other top leaders in 1980. Ten years later, the wheel turned and the sergeant-president got his. Thereafter, it was more or less chaos. So S. John Murray, head of the American province of the Society of African Missions, had to report in 1994 that things were so bad two of the three Catholic dioceses in Liberia could not function. Their bishops, priests and others associated with them were forced into exile. The one diocese still functioning, centered in the capital, Monrovia, and aided by priests of Father Murray's society, operated in a situation that was "very tense." Amnesty International reported that "all parties to the continuing civil war were responsible for deliberate killings of civilians."

With my prospects for surviving as a freelancer always marginal and sometimes near the grave, I was predisposed to take most any assignment that came my way. But desperate as I sometimes became, I must report that I had to turn down a few offers, and found in them only education into the ways of the world, but not remuneration.

One instance came when the p.r. director of a most respectable religious organization offered me money under the table if I would get an article about his agency into one of the religious magazines, dealing with the editor as though it were my own idea and selling the article as a matter of great interest to readers. And I later came to understand that a certain amount of that kind of thing was going on. Maybe a writer could sell a feature on the making of church pews, and get a side payment from companies he mentioned along the way. Since religious magazines paid poorly, by and large, such offers could prove tempting, but somehow I found strength to resist.

The idea seemed unsavory on its face, and I would not have considered such an arrangement without letting the editor know. But I was unsure of how such arrangements were viewed in the profession. One second level editor I knew told me that such a deal would never have been considered by his former chief, but a new one just might approve. Since the magazine had only limited funds for buying articles, it might by such maneuvers get some material it otherwise could not afford.

In a grosser corner of dishonesty, a doctoral student at Union Seminary once invited me to lunch, and asked about getting me to write his dissertation. He had a part-time job at the seminary that was taking much of his time, and he had accepted a new job elsewhere that would soon begin. And he just had to get that dissertation done in the all-too-short interval. Under such pressure, the mind displays its capacity for rationalization. Actually he was going to provide me with the ideas, and I would just offer the technical service of putting the ideas into words, he explained. To him, it was merely the next step from hiring a typist, which I and many others had done so we could present our dissertations in some decent form. But though he had justified it all in his own mind, he expressed reluctance when I suggested that I should clear the proposal with his supervising professor. He could not be sure the professor would rise to his level of perspicacity in ethics.

The degree seeker never got around to putting numbers beside the dollar sign he held before me. But that no doubt would have killed the project anyway. I cannot imagine he could have offered the size of payment that would be necessary to get me into the grueling, grinding process of writing another doctoral dissertation. Anguishing enough when you are putting your own ideas

SIDEBARS

into words, the pain would be more than I could handle to do it for somebody else's.

A somewhat peripheral curiosity was an offer from a practicing psychologist to write a book developing some of his ideas. That would have been an open collaboration, but I turned it down anyway because I thought the project was goofy and unworkable in itself. The psychologist had a vague concept, which he thought was a clear concept, about how psychology, philosophy and religion could all be coordinated in a sort of unified theory, like Albert Einstein's $E=mc^2$ in physics. He had it in his mind, but with all the hours he spent counseling his patients, he just could not spare the time to write it down. Ghost writing is hardly to be viewed as an art form in any circumstances, but is workable in some areas, like memoirs of an actress or speeches of a president. For anybody trying to plow new ground in thought, however, putting the thought into words and then figuring out how the words should fit into sentences and paragraphs is intrinsic to the project.

Now, regarding the place where most of my adventures were happening, New York, perhaps I could give you a few words.

NEW YORK

CHAPTER TWO

Walking about the West Side of Manhattan on a Friday evening or Saturday, I often see people who by dress and family grouping would appear to be going to or from synagogue. But on a Sunday morning, I do not get a comparable impression of people headed for church. Orthodox Jews are of course less likely to go by car, taxi, bus or subway. And as a qualification, I should note that dress here does not necessarily give the clue it might in some places. Your liberated New Yorker may slop into church, loins girt with ragged jean shorts and feet shod with thong of Taiwan. To qualify further, some New York churches do attract the crowds. In Harlem, congregations are sometimes large, as they may be in some other ethnic neighborhoods. And a church such as St. Patrick's Cathedral has them standing in the aisles on special occasions. Yet as a generalization, it remains the case that New Yorkers are not big on going to church

That acknowledged, we do have lots of churches, and you will probably find as big a sampling of American religious life in New York as you have come across anywhere. In addition to numerous expressions of other religions, virtually every branch of Christendom has a chapter here.

But the easy availability of so many Christian options makes me skeptical about proposals for increasing church attendance. It is often said that churches are losing their hold because they are too conservative or too liberal or too this, that or the other. But in New York we have churches of most any type anyone might prefer, and throngs of people stay away from them all. In the First Baptist Church we have Bible believers staunch enough to make Billy Graham look wobbly. And Judson Church (American Baptist and United Church of Christ) down in Greenwich Village is liberal as all get out. But at neither place will you need to show up early to find a good seat. Anybody trying to gather a congregation in New York encounters a fierce individualism of people hell-bent on achieving their personal goals. Those goals may or may not allow for church. If you took a poll, my guess is you would find a majority of New Yorkers in favor of ordaining women. But that does not mean a majority will show up at church when a woman is put in charge. We have had some well-regarded women serving as pastors in New York, but the multitudes have not rushed to get the benefit of their leadership.

One of these pastors I observed was a black woman, Suzanne Johnson Cooke, who served some years at Chambers Memorial Baptist Church in lower Manhattan and then moved to a church she herself started up near Yankee Stadium, Bronx Christian Fellowship. At Chambers Memorial, she drew a respectably-sized, mostly black congregation, but lacked a lot filling the house, or did the Sunday I went.

The occasion remains in memory. When I visit churches that ask visitors to stand, usually I stay seated and look around pretending that I am just one of the less faithful they have not seen for a while. But at Chambers Memorial I am conspicuous as Jimmy Carter in Port-au-Prince, so there is nothing to do but stand and give my name as requested. But they also want the name of my home church, and when I comply, Pastor Cooke comments graciously about knowing my pastor. I try to sit back down, but am instructed to keep standing until all visitors have been identified and a speech of welcome has been delivered. And still it is not over. All the members must have time to circulate around to shake hands and greet the visitors (and each other) personally. When you have been welcomed at Chambers Memorial, by golly you have been welcomed.

I should add that in attending many black churches over many years I have never received anything but the warmest of welcomes. That testimony seems obligatory because black Christians have sometimes had to endure rather ugly treatment when they tried to visit white churches, which in some cases would not even let them in the door.

Rev. Cooke is a woman of some height and considerable self-confidence who commands and directs the service authoritatively. We start at 10 a.m. and will not hear the benediction until around 1 p.m. These hours will seem impossibly long for a mainstream white Christian, but groups such as the black churches and the Eastern Orthodox who do enjoy their worship do go on a while. Visiting New Canaan Baptist Church in Harlem one Sunday, I heard the pastor, Wyatt T. Walker, offer his take on scheduling: "People ask me, when do y'all let out up there? I tell them, we let out when we get through." The Sunday I visited Chambers Memorial turned out to be a special occasion, Laymen's Sunday, with a visiting preacher, so we did not get a sermon from the pastor. But we heard enough in the three hours to conclude she was fully capable.

In addition to the sermon and hymns and prayers, and special recognition of laymen, the three hours included three offerings–one with plates passed and two with congregation marched to the front for deposit of gifts into containers there. Very participatory.

Another woman in a New York pastorate until recently, when she became professor of preaching at Union Seminary, is Barbara Kay Lundblad. She had a small Lutheran parish, Our Savior, in the northern end of Manhattan, where you could on the same visit go by to see what remains of the first American canonized as a saint, Mother Cabrini, reposing in a glass case under the chapel altar of Mother Cabrini High School.

At Our Savior, I was a bit startled when I went forward for communion. Pastor Lundblad was moving along according to expected procedure until she got to me, when she halted and asked, "What is your name?" I have knelt at a fair number of communion rails in my time, but never before or since have I been confronted with a demand for identification. It turned out, though, that Pastor Lundblad was not checking my qualifications but just fitting me in when she, as a good shepherd, called each of her sheep by name as she fed them.

She seemed to show a quite serious commitment to Christian ministry, and I was slightly surprised later to hear she was one of the women leading the notorious Re-imagining Conference held in Minneapolis in November of 1993. There, she appeared to swing with the revolution where women were taking a feminist look at religion, and no one was doing anything, as she pointed out pointedly, "in the name of the Father and the Son and the Holy Spirit." I wondered whether even she might not at times have wondered whether that was really her crowd. But a little later she left the parish ministry to join the faculty of Union Seminary, where not much could any longer surprise.

I had not heard of the Minneapolis conference in advance, and would have had no expense account to get me there anyway. But some conservative women who did go as reporters precipitated such a storm that the World Council of Churches magazine, *One World,* asked me to do an article on the fallout (May 1994). A quite considerable fallout it was, especially in the Presbyterian Church. Its 1994 General Assembly, I later reported, gave the official judgment that "some of the theological content of conference presentations and worship rituals not only extended beyond the boundaries of the Reformed theological tradition but also beyond that tradition's understanding of what makes faith Christian" (EPS, July 10, 1994). Mary Ann Lundy, one of the Presbyterian executives at the national headquarters in Louisville, had helped get planning for the event underway with a grant from Presbyterian funds, and she had to go overboard before the waves would subside. (She was later coughed up onto the shores of Lake Geneva for a top job with the World Council of Churches.)

The women who led the conference tied it to Old Testament passages that personify the concept of wisdom, "sophia" in Greek, and on that slender basis claimed that they were proceeding biblically, however otherwise it might appear to some. Critics said they were in fact creating and praying to a goddess as they greeted speakers with the chant, "Sophia, dream the dream, speak the vision." And in one session after another, speakers sought to reformulate Christian theology in non-biblical terms of feminist inspiration.

Critics found many points objectionable. My article was for reporting, not critique, but in my own mind the most questionable part of the conference was its foundational concept of "re-imagining." It seemed to carry an underlying idea that the Christian faith was merely something that certain male persons had made up out of their imagination, and now female persons could do over with whatever new imagery they might prefer. Their guidelines appeared to say, "However I happen to feel about things, that is Christianity to me." Under the First Amendment to the United States Constitution, they no doubt have a legal right to produce and devote themselves to any religion that pleases them. But whether it is intellectually honest to call it Christianity could become another question.

Some of the women who have secured ordination or otherwise sought to open new paths seem quite orthodox in theology. But the Re-imagining Conference revealed that the women's movement in the churches overall lacked any strong sense of fidelity to the Christian theological tradition, or loyalty to church authority. One could conclude that the issue of ordaining women and giving women positions of church leadership is not, for the predominant stream of this movement, simply a matter of women now getting to do the jobs men have been doing, but of moving into a position to turn the Christian religion into something different from what it has been. Presumably they will argue that they have the right, and that Christianity will be much improved when they have redone it. But if some other church members resist, I would not think their reaction could be written off as merely a desire to oppress women.

Something like that was the allegation. When I covered a press conference some of the conference participants held later in New York, I found them contending that their critics were creating "a climate of witch-hunting" and "an environment of violence against women." Perhaps a little shrill. "People frightened by fresh theological insights and by challenges to narrow orthodoxy are attempting to discredit and malign women," they said (EPS, March 20, 1994).

But an orthodoxy would not have to be all that narrow to raise questions about some of the fresh insights, or whatever they were, reported out of Minneapolis. For just one example, consider an attack launched by Delores S. Williams of Union Seminary on the doctrine of salvation through the death of Christ: "I don't think we need folks hanging on crosses and blood dripping and weird stuff."

Squeamish as some of us may feel about blood, however, it remains an unavoidable concept in biblical thought, in the Old Testament, where "without the shedding of blood there is no forgiveness of sins," according to Hebrews (9:22), and in the New. It is, in fact, about as broadly and biblically based as any Christian doctrine. The disciples of Jesus found unforgettable meaning in his reference at the Last Supper to "my blood of the covenant" (Mark 14:24). Paul emphasized that "we are now justified by his blood" (Romans 5:9). And the Gospel of John has Jesus saying that "he who eats my flesh and drinks my blood has eternal life" (6:54). When the chant came, "Sophia, dream the dream, speak the vision," the vision differed much from the vision of John on Patmos, who saw Jesus "clad in a robe dipped in blood" (Revelation 19:13). Weird stuff, to be sure, but that is Christianity for you, a religion of "peace by the blood of his cross" (Colossians 1:20). Whether we think we need it or not, the New Testament thinks it is reporting good news when it says God chose us for "sprinkling with his blood" (I Peter 1:2).

If you wanted to provoke a debate about the way Jesus is presented in crucifixion scenes, you could do that with an analysis that stayed inside a Christian framework, perhaps by taking a new look at changes that occurred in the medieval period. There was an earlier tradition of showing Jesus triumphant in, or through, suffering. Then came a move to emphasize more the suffering itself. The Franciscan movement influenced this shift in Western art, I was told when I reported on an exhibit the Metropolitan Museum of Art presented of Franciscan items from Assisi and related art from the Metropolitan itself and other collections (CNS, February 2 and March 16, 1999). The construction of the basilica at Assisi, shortly after the death of Francis, brought together many of the most creative artists and artisans of Europe, and the styles developed there marked the turn from medievalism to the Italian Renaissance. Part of the Renaissance project was shifting emphasis away from the divine toward the human—for the more secular-minded perhaps back to the view of pagan Greeks that man and not God is "the measure of all things," but for Christians acceptable if properly managed because Jesus is to them fully human as well as fully divine. My reporting did not get into the theological issues, but information presented in connection with the exhibit credited—or debited, however you view it—the Franciscans with encouraging what was considered a more realistic and emotionally moving depiction of the suffering Jesus, body twisted in pain and eyes closed as life was ending. It would be worth a seminary professor's time to launch a discussion of how that approach compares and contrasts with a crucifixion portrayal of Jesus with head erect and eyes open, ready to accept whatever the world wants to put on him. Professors, and others, might usefully spend some time contemplating the question of which is truer to the Christian faith. I remember a comment Patrick V. Ahern, Auxiliary Bishop of New York, made about the death of Cardinal Cooke: "He did not die with dignity; he lived with dignity while he was dying."

But all this about Professor Williams is merely one illustration of the contrast an analyst might elaborate between many of the reimaginings and the biblical tradition. Aruna Gnanadason, head of the women's program of the WCC and a participant at Minneapolis, told me that she found among the women there "strong affirmation of what Christ has taught us," but a feeling that women needed to look for values "beyond just what has come down to us in the Bible." I suspect, however, a good many Christians would not want to join the parade until they got a clearer idea of just where beyond the Bible it was going, and perhaps some idea of how far beyond.

In more general regard to "narrow" orthodoxy, I noticed that Beverly Wildung Harrison, also of Union Seminary, had earlier commented, "We feminist theologians now believe that the development of 'orthodoxy' in theology and church order was the result of an active effort to disempower women in early Christianity" (*Making the Connections,* Beacon, 1985). And she went on to identify a pattern: "Those groups within early Christianity that we viewed as deviant, heterodox or 'sectarian' turn out to have been those parts of the Christian community in which women played an extensive and strong role" (p. 141). From her perspective, that was a point against what have been the predominant patterns of Christian life and thought. But for those Christians who believe, as I do on most days, that the orthodox tradition is basically correct, her insistence on a correlation of female leadership with heterodoxy could inspire different reflections.

We should perhaps recall that this sort of historical reinterpretation for polemical purposes is part of a larger trend that goes back for centuries. People doing a critique of one thing or another project a golden age somewhere in the past when such regrettables supposedly did not exist. Then, in this view, a time of degeneration. The fall of Christianity into a depraved condition is not always but often linked to the Emperor Constantine and his role in bringing it toleration and acceptance into the Establishment in 313–traditionally said to have occurred through an Edict of Milan, though the historical truth of that tradition is uncertain. In any case, many inside critics of the church date the features that most worry them to his reign, and consider the deplorable result to have continued at least until Martin Luther nailed his 97 theses and the Reformation began. Such analysts seem to carry in the back of their minds an interpretive framework that understands church history somewhat along the lines:

33 – 100	real good Christianity
100 – 313	pretty good Christianity
313 – 1517	Christianity that was just awful
1517 – present	Christianity tremendously improved in my sphere but otherwise still pretty much the pits

My guess is that most church historians with modern academic training, maybe even Lutherans, would view that outline as an oversimplification. But it seems to carry weight in parts of the popular mind nonetheless.

If there were a correlation of heterodoxy and female leadership, the orthodox could see it not limited to "early Christianity," but continued in more recent times through such figures as Mother Ann Lee, who became "the female principle in Christ" as leader of the eighteenth century Shakers; Ellen G. White, who became the prophetess of the Seventh-day Adventists in the nineteenth century; Mary Baker Eddy, founder of Christian Science, and Aimee Semple McPherson, who founded the International Church of the Foursquare Gospel in Los Angeles. But unorthodox groups have also been established by men–Joseph Smith's Church of Jesus Christ of Latter-day Saints (Mormons) and the Unification Church of Sun Myung Moon, for examples–so the question of Christian orthodoxy seems not totally correlateable with the politics of gender.

There is another question about what all this means for the Christian ecumenical movement. The Re-imagining Conference was organized by an ecumenical committee in St. Paul and Minneapolis as a contribution to the World Council of Churches program, Ecumenical Decade of Churches in Solidarity with Women. The name, I suppose, must have meant something like "decade of church officials expressing solidarity with leaders of the feminist movement." Since women are members of the churches, it would not make much sense to speak literally of "churches" and "women" as two separate groups expressing solidarity.

But the difficulty presented for the Christian ecumenical movement was illustrated by the decision of the Re-imagining planners to include a young Korean woman, Chung Hyun Kyung, as one of the featured speakers. Her outlook had departed rather far from the Korean Protestantism from which she sprang, and perhaps owed more to the climate of New York's Morningside Heights, where she studied at Union Seminary and where she returned as professor in 1996. She acquired international celebrity from a colorful speech and dance presentation she gave at the 1991 World Council of Churches Assembly in Canberra, Australia, where many delegates responded with intense applause and others intense unapplause. The Orthodox in particular were appalled at how far she departed from the traditions of the fathers. Many liberal Protestants were presumably thinking that the further she departed from the traditions of the fathers the better.

Whatever her gifts and personal appeal, which seemed to be considerable, she was quite conspicuously not a voice for Christian unity. But she kept getting invitations to Christian ecumenical meetings, even as she moved further from anything that could be called Christian. At Minneapolis, she spoke of Hindu and Buddhist goddesses that she found inspiring. And she announced that the women had gathered there "to destroy this patriarchal idolatry of Christianity." I do not suppose Barbara Lundblad or the majority of our other female clergy will go that far. But it is not clear what limits they might accept.

In 1980, Ann Patrick Ware, a Catholic nun of the Loretto order, announced that after serving a dozen years on the staff of the Faith and Order Commission of the National Council of Churches, she was resigning. "I have become increasingly disappointed with some of the official positions of my church and find it difficult to be an enthusiastic exponent," she wrote in her resignation letter (January 10). In a later interview, she told me that she was particularly upset by Catholic statements on women's issues. "I find it very embarrassing in commission meetings when questions of ordination and equality in the church come up," she said (NC, January 31). And a speech she gave a little later revealed that her dissent went deeper than Vatican statements on women's ordination. "The Scriptures are unredeemably sexist," she said (NC, March 7, 1980).

To me, her resignation seemed like a commendable act of integrity. She could no longer honestly represent the position of her church, so she turned in an honorable resignation. Some other feminists, however, seem to want to play it two or three ways. They have grown out of sympathy with their churches, perhaps on many points and not just questions of women's ordination, but they try to keep the jobs that now hardly represent their sense of vocation.

But back to New York's churches: If you were expecting me to tell you where to find the great preachers of New York, forget it. Ours is not a time of greatness. Time was when *The New York Times* considered it worthwhile to carry Monday reports on the previous day's sermons by the more notable preachers of the city. A. M. Rosenthal, later an op-ed regular, recalled in one column "when I was an apprentice reporter covering sermons for $3 a Sunday" (October 1, 1999). But the editors stopped giving those assignments on any routine basis a generation ago.

I have no doubt that the editors' decision was correct, but I do not have any clear thoughts about why the sermons today deserve less space, or no space. The reported preachers were mainly Protestants, though Mr. Rosenthal wrote of covering St. Patrick's Cathedral, and the percentage of interested Protestants among *Times* readers may represent a smaller market share today. Perhaps readers now find less of interest in sermons, but why? Perhaps the quality of men going into the ministry declined. Perhaps the clergy have lost a firm hold on the intellectual structure of their belief, and lack a needed sense of confidence in their message. Perhaps they have become more absorbed in weekday programs and no longer devote long hours to sermon preparation. Perhaps they have gotten too wrapped up in their own psyches. We get a great many sermons that might be generically titled "Me and My Very Interesting Experiences that I Am Sure Will Interest You Ever So Much." Sometimes we get this even from the seminary professors who teach preaching to the preachers of tomorrow. Still, I cannot answer the why question with any confidence.

Leaving aside questions of viewpoint, the most gifted of New York's preachers that I have heard in recent times has been William Sloane Coffin, for several years senior minister at the Riverside Church. Just in general terms he is a man of unusual talents. As an organizer of a Washington demonstration against the Vietnam War, he got a good writeup in Norman Mailer's *Armies of the Night* (New American Library, 1968):

". . . his manner hard, quick, deft and assured, his remarks purposeful, even salient—yes, he would be the kind of man who would know how to talk to reporters. He had a voice which sounded close to the savvy self-educated tones of a labor union organizer, but there was the irreducible substance of Ivy League in it as well, the barking quality, not unlike a coxswain—except the speaker was too large for that—the coach of a crew perhaps. Mailer was not unimpressed" (p. 82).

At Riverside Church, I was not unimpressed by the way Mr. Coffin came into the pulpit and took command, lacking the insecurities that keep too many preachers shifting from one foot to the other, looking in all directions but forward. He was lacking also the overcompensation of others determined to look dynamic, whether they possess dynamism or not. Mr. Coffin was in fact "deft and assured, his remarks purposeful." He also maintained a naturalness of whatever kind of voice he had, a real human voice, and preached in a contemporary idiom, with eschewment of odd words and churchy clichés.

Although Mr. Coffin's crusading on behalf of the liberal social causes naturally got the publicity, he also had theological substance. At Riverside in the 1980s, he could hardly finish a sermon without taking a swipe at Ronald Reagan. But he could also at times move into basic theology in ways most newspaper readers would hardly suspect.

Another good trait was lightening the way with a little humor. Karl Barth observed that God "radiates joy," and that preaching "without sparkle or humor" cannot be persuasive (*Dogmatics II/1*, 655). Mr. Coffin could sparkle.

He drew larger crowds than Riverside Church has had subsequently, but did not build a congregation with strength to endure after him, or enlist the families of means that such a church needs in order to continue in its Rockefeller tradition. And down on the bottom line, he did not find sufficient satisfaction in life as pastor of the most prominent liberal congregation in the country to stay with it, but left to head the anti-nuclear SANE/Freeze movement until, in something of a political joke on him, Ronald Reagan made the movement obsolete by working out his agreements with Mikhail Gorbachev.

Some years later, I saw Mr. Coffin in a less active activism at the United Nations. The Non-Proliferation Treaty was under review at a conference there, and he had been persuaded to join a fast for abolition of nuclear weapons. The fast was announced at a press conference inside the UN headquarters, and a moderately-sized group of supporters showed up. When protest campaigns are launched, it often happens that a good many people will appear at the launching to get their pictures taken and their names recorded for whatever publicity will ensue. But not so many choose to continue on with the subsequent dailiness. I had seen the phenomenon during the Vietnam War in connection with a protest that was advertised to continue at Riverside Church until the war's end (RNS, November 17, 1969), but soon dribbled down to nothingness. In the case of the protesters at the UN, it similarly transpired for most. But Mr. Coffin was one of those who did persist. When I came back to check a few days later, he and Robert McAfee Brown and George William Webber, two other more or less retirees, were about the sum total of the action, and looked a little forlorn out there. When Mahatma Gandhi fasted in India, masses of people felt his pain and exerted their soul force to reinforce him. For Mr. Coffin and colleagues, it seemed nobody much noticed. He told me that in a long life of many protests he had never before engaged in fasting. But he was so concerned about the nuclear issue that he was trying now, at age 70, this new tactic. In other circumstances, in other times, that might have been news. At this point, it seemed not so much. I wrote a story for the Catholic News Service (April 25, 1995) and another for Ecumenical News International in Geneva (April 26). But my reportage was for sure small potatoes to a man whose protest actions of times past had commanded space in major secular media and the pages of Norman Mailer.

Sitting there with the fasters at their post near the Isaiah Wall, across from the UN, I had to reflect that Mr. Coffin's talent and energy could have put him in a position to be making policy inside rather than protesting outside, had he chosen to play his cards differently. Would that have been better? Hard to say. Some people seemingly hear a calling to live as protesters, and could find happiness by no other route.

In referring to preachers, I should mention Gardner C. Taylor, retired pastor of the Concord Baptist Church of Christ in Brooklyn. He has been an especially notable example of an older style of black preaching. There seems to flourish a school of thought in some sectors of black Christendom that says a sermon need not be, maybe ought not to be, anything more than an emotional outburst. Rev. Taylor was not of that school. He was rather part of the tradition that approached sermon preparation as a craft. Preachers of his type–among whites, Ernest T. Campbell, former senior minister of the Riverside Church, has been a good example–saw the sermon as a specific type of communication that required and deserved time and effort deployed in accordance with the nature of the medium. They realized the sermon was not an academic lecture, nor a rant, but an occasion to show and tell a congregation, convey to a congregation, the Christian message and its meaning for them. So a preacher trained in his craft would work out exposition, illustration, assurance and appeal in a way that left hearers feeling well fed. Rev. Taylor retained something of the soothing Southern accent he got from Louisiana origins, and lifted his listeners emotionally with messages built on a considerable amount of scholarship and thought.

Out on the Manhattan streets one day, a young man who was apparently a tourist asked me for directions to St. Patrick's Cathedral. I thought, "Boy, by some providence you sure picked the right person to ask about that. I have been there a few times." My work for the Catholic News Service has entailed frequent visits, sometimes for the story of the day, sometimes just to keep in touch.

Pastor Lundblad's policy of calling each person by name as she gave communion would have been rather much to expect of John J. O'Connor, facing the thousands who show up at St. Patrick's. But he knew me, and would have gently pointed out, as the Cardinal-Archbishop of New York, that I was out of order. It is the Catholic position that Christians divided into different churches can properly share communion only after full unity has been achieved. I think Catholics, along with "closed communion" Baptists and others of the same outlook, are wrong about that, and that sharing in communion is a principal means of drawing divided Christians into unity, much needed whether within single denominations or across denominational lines. Communion in fact has this as its purpose. In the church I attended growing up, we concluded the communion service by singing, "Blest be the tie that binds our hearts in Christian love." So I would say: explain clearly what it is all about, and then encourage everybody who has made his commitment to join in. But I do not want to give public offense, so at St. Patrick's I commune only in my heart.

Though I respect the rules on communion, I may not always conform on lesser points there. One of the diligent ushers caught me indulging my desire to observe from various perspectives and taking notes on the cardinal's sermon one Sunday as I stood back against a side wall, amongst a few other standees opposite the pulpit. Much offended, the usher told me that I, as a reporter, was not allowed to be in the cathedral unless I stayed in the spot designated for reporters. And to make sure I knew my place, he marched me around and put me in it. But on subsequent visits I have not always conformed to his ruling, and have found ways to slip less offendingly into diverse locations.

So I can advise that you should go early enough to get a seat in the center toward the front if you aspire to see and hear. You can sometimes spot someone such as former Governor Hugh Carey slipping in at the last minute and taking a side pew. But he has already seen a lot in his career, and may worry less about the view now.

To give an account of Cardinal O'Connor's preaching, the first point is that he liked to take advantage of his opportunity to occupy the cathedral pulpit and get his message out. He rarely invited anyone else to preach at his Sunday morning mass when he could be present. A second point is that he came prepared to deliver a good bit of substance, and in language the ordinary listener might understand. While many preachers seem to assume a college-educated congregation, he adapted his material more to the high school level. Perhaps because of his many years as a military chaplain, he showed an awareness that the average guy may arrive without much knowledge of the Bible or church teachings. And the third point is that he usually gave attention to the Scripture lessons of the day.

Protestant polemic has traditionally charged Catholics with neglecting the Bible, and doubtless with some truth for some periods. But in the years I have been observing in New York, a worshiper might hear more Bible preached at the "papist" cathedral than a few blocks up at a famous outpost of Reformed Christianity, the Fifth Avenue Presbyterian Church.

That was notably the case when the minister at Fifth Avenue Presbyterian was Maurice Boyd, an Irish Methodist who had a big congregation of the

United Church of Canada in Toronto before playing the Big Apple. Mr. Boyd got to New York because he was a man of ability and capable of making a certain kind of impression upon a certain kind of listener. As much as any preacher I have heard, he deserved the accolade, "If you like that sort of thing, you will find that is just the sort of thing you like." What he did he did very well; whether that was Christian preaching seemed to me in some doubt. He spoke with a self-dramatizing flair, and quoted so many famous authors you figured his Saturday nights must be spent going through *The Oxford Dictionary of Quotations*. Biblical authors may have been included on occasion, but he seemed wary of showing any bias in their favor.

Mr. Boyd eventually lost that pulpit, not because of his preaching, which had its champions, but over disputes with lay leaders of the congregation. Then, if anybody wondered whether he was building a personality cult, the answer came promptly as he led his entourage out of Fifth Avenue Presbyterian and started an independent City Church free of all denominational ties, a swarming with the queen bee to a new hive.

The current pastor of Fifth Avenue Presbyterian, Thomas K. Tewell, operates with a different style, but tries to attract the indifferent secularists with cutesy sermon titles. Walking past, the curious New Yorker sees a bulletin board announcing the sermon of this Sunday will enlighten on "Snorkeling, Scuba Diving and Spirituality" (January 10, 1999), and similarities for other Sundays. I have been able to resist these enticements, but perhaps others have not.

But back to St. Patrick's: If you were buying tickets as to the opera, you would find a rather large number stamped "partial view." The Gothic architecture and the row of pillars running down each side may look spiritual and add texture to the organ tones, but they put many worshipers in a position to not see well. And the acoustics are hell on listeners. If you want a clear view of the three focal points—the chair where the archbishop presides, the pulpit and the altar—a regrettable percentage of seats will not allow it. You better get there early enough to sit in the middle. In 1994, the cathedral staff decided to attempt a technological solution, and placed video screens for people in the outer sections. That helps, but it also gives you something of the feel of watching on television even though you are actually right there.

Some obstruction on a lesser scale confronts you if you go up Fifth Avenue a couple of blocks to St. Thomas Episcopal Church, but not quite so much. That is a church I like to visit because of the beauty and order in its celebration of the liturgy, and its extraordinary music. The church is distinctive for sponsoring a choir school for boys, and bringing them in to sing regularly at services. Gerry Hancock, music master, leads a choir of "gentlemen and boys," all male voices, and does a remarkable amount of fine liturgical music, some composed by himself. I need to keep asking myself, however, whether I am really at church to plead for mercy, or to thrill at the way the "gentlemen and boys" make the Kyrie build and soar and sustain and subside and resonate.

James R. Oestreich, writing music criticism for *The New York Times,* quoted Augustine: "When I find the singing itself more moving than the truth which it conveys, I confess that this is grievous sin" (December 6, 1994). Mr. Oestreich decided that a vocal group, the Hillard Ensemble, singing in Latin at a church without giving translations, became "mere instrumentalists tickling the ear, notwithstanding the sacred setting and ritualistic trappings." In a comparable comment I have been told came from John Wesley, Methodists were instructed that in singing hymns they should "see that your heart is not carried away with the sound, but offered to God continually."

Maybe we could justify indulging the esthetic sense more directly at the end of the service when we have an organist playing a postlude. So many people get up and leave at the last "amen" that we might call postludes "music to walk out on." But that is really a shame, especially in New York, where we have some of the best organists of the nation playing some of the best organ music ever written and on some really excellent organs. And since the offering plates have already passed, the postlude comes as a free extra, so you should consider it something like a sin to miss it.

The basic justification of music in the church, however, is its ability to enhance the impact of the words, and carry them into sections of the soul that might otherwise remain closed off. When James F. Hinchey and Dennis M. Carrado were the priests in charge at the Catholic cathedral in Brooklyn, St. James, I often went to evensong there on the Sundays after Easter to cover bishops they brought in from across the country to speak on topics of general interest. At the beginning of their liturgy, a tenor came out with a large candle and chanted, "Jesus Christ is the light of the world," in a voice so true and clear you could not doubt that Jesus Christ definitely was the light of the world.

But music has an imperialistic drive. It will take over and demote the words to serfdom, given half a chance. I have the impression this commonly happens in Gregorian chant, which may entrance people who know nothing of what is chanted. The same can occur with black gospel, though it so often gives exhilaration. I have a recording in which Marion Williams, who died in 1994, elaborates on "Blessed Assurance, Jesus Is Mine" in a way that brings more assurance than I previously realized the song could convey. But she would sometimes also move on up and out over the edge, in a style that inspires listeners to cheer the vocal pyrotechnics and forget whatever it may be that the song is about.

SIDEBARS

I must immediately add that Marion Williams herself, ordained in the (Pentecostal) Church of God in Christ, would not lose interest in the message. When I interviewed her at Carnegie Hall, while she was there one year preparing to participate in an evening of gospel sponsored by the Newport Jazz Festival, she was proudest to tell me about a little church she had started and was leading (Women's News Service, July 9, 1975). Another year under the same auspices, when she was appearing with Dorothy Love Coates, Willie Mae Ford Smith, Jessy Dixon and others, Miss Williams got everybody to stand and sing "Amazing Grace," on that occasion at Radio City. "Somebody here may want to receive Christ," she said, as she might at an evangelistic service (RNS, July 10, 1972).

Some singers of popular religious music, like many of those singing popular secular music, also seem rather too much into adding body language. I would prefer that they took lessons from the concert style of Marilyn Horn. You know she must be working to a fare thee well, but she stands so calmly on stage you are not made aware of any exertion. It appears that she is so full of music, she has only to open her mouth for it to come out and fill every cubic foot of Avery Fisher Hall with beautiful sound.

I got to discuss liturgical chant a little with the Catholic Archbishop of Milwaukee and former superior general of the world's Benedictines, Rembert Weakland, when he took a six-month sabbatical in 1996 and came east to continue work on a doctoral dissertation he had begun forty years before at Columbia University. He was writing on Ambrosian chant, which had once been viewed as a preliminary stage of Gregorian but had come to be seen as only one of several types used until Gregorian displaced all except the style honored by somehow getting attached to the powerful name of Ambrose. When I asked Archbishop Weakland what practical result in church worship his study might bring, he told me that he had no such goal, but undertook his research only in hopes of advancing historical understanding. More than that, he rejected the whole idea of constructing the ordinary worship service from Ambrosian or Gregorian chant. "Chant is beautiful, but it was never intended to be the song of the people," he said. "I am upset when I see people celebrate old liturgies for the sake of antiquarianism" (CNS, March 22).

Some of the medieval chant has been adapted, however, so that it can serve contemporary needs. And it can along the way perhaps stimulate us to reexamine cliché views about the medieval period. For example, "O come, o come, Emanuel, and ransom captive Israel" originated in an era commonly dismissed as the "dark ages." It has been identified as an antiphon (verses chanted responsively) of the ninth century turned into Latin verse perhaps in the twelfth century. But I am not aware that the twentieth century has produced any better

Advent hymn. What is "dark" and what is "enlightened" maybe depends somewhat on whether I have my eyes open.

The strength of evangelical Protestantism comes partly from conveying its message in music that holds immediate appeal for audiences with no background of musical cultivation. Since its hymns often have lyrics that are doggerel, and melodies that are musical doggerel, frequently decorated with a tinkely-tink by a pianist, churches more culturally ambitious shy away from them. But the alternative too often becomes staid old ponderosities that ordinary people can hardly sing and seldom care to sing. The American churches have not yet produced their Woodie Guthrie. Choir presentation in these upper level churches can also sink to mere esthetics. Frequently they are singing classic works with texts in Latin or German or something, and even when the words are English, the complexities of the music may interfere with comprehension of whatever message the singers are trying to convey. They could be up there singing praises to Isis and Osiris for all I can tell.

To give St. Patrick's Cathedral one compliment, I would say it has the choir properly located in a rear balcony, which is in fact rather common practice among liturgical churches. It is a good rule, reversing the old saying about children, that a church choir should be heard and not seen. Choir members should be up there at the back singing their hearts out in support of the service but not themselves becoming the focus of attention. The back placement helps avoid the danger of a worship service turning into a program of religiously-flavored entertainment—in some places with applause yet!

At the Riverside Church, applause seems to have become routine in recent years. Riversiders now clap for the choir and for soloists and for organists, for preachers and for the more resounding sentences delivered by the preachers, for people who are honored and for people who honor them, for reports of good offerings raised and good deeds done, for whatever the children do. Most anything is likely to set off yet another wave of clappity-clap. As part of the Easter liturgy, we have even been called on to clap for the flower committee. Certainly I hold no grudge against the flower committee. If everybody else is to get clapped, I would not be one to deny a turn for them, stalwart and diligent folk as they doubtless are. But it all can make you wonder whether a different understanding of worship has seeped in, a change from the days when it was understood as a separate time, when the congregation offered itself to God and listened to receive from God.

Maybe something has been spread abroad in the contemporary culture. One day, I noticed that a Jewish Center in my part of Manhattan had posted on a bulletin board an advertisement for customers: "Forget everything you know about Friday night Shabbat services. Now, imagine an atmosphere of laughter, conversation and song. That's the Manhattan Jewish Experience. Our services are vibrant and refreshing, focusing on the most important part of Shabbat, a sense of community." As for the part about God, we are left to wonder.

A back loft is the choir location at St. Mary the Virgin, an influential New York parish in the Anglo-Catholic wing of the Episcopal Church. I do not really know whether the Episcopal Church has an Anglo-Catholic wing of any significance anymore, but when there was one, its more or less cathedral church was St. Mary the Virgin. And in addition to offering the liturgy in the most elevated elaboration of high church, this congregation has maintained musical standards.

You will likewise find the same choir location at the Greek Orthodox Cathedral of the Holy Trinity, a good place to visit for the midnight Easter service. The Orthodox Easter usually–though not always–falls later than the Western, so I often get to celebrate a second time. The dean of the Greek cathedral is Robert G. Stephanopoulos, father of President Clinton's aide, George Stephanopoulos, and those paying attention at Easter services in some years have been able to see the son assisting in an acolyte role.

Here, the service continues about three hours, and you are mostly standing and wishing you had worn more comfortable shoes. About an hour along, everyone goes out on the street so the Resurrection can be proclaimed not just to insiders but to the whole wide world. An admirable missionary impulse, but one that costs the clergy half or more of their congregation. Many Greeks decide they have done their duty just by getting there, and would rather depart now to eat their Easter lamb, or maybe get a little of the anise flavor of ouzo, than stay to receive communion. But those of us who return are musically as well as religiously rewarded, for director Dino Anagnost has his choir singing to the end, when the clergy spoon out communion to their members and hand out Easter eggs to all of us.

As a sidebar, I can tell you that George Stephanopoulos has given about as good a picture of the intermixing of heaven and earth as you are likely to find. So you can check his book, *All Too Human: A Political Education* (Little Brown, 1999), not only for inside dope on the Clintons, but also for a thoughtful look behind the screen of icons in his father's church, where "mystery is rooted in the mundane" (p. 11).

Orthodoxy requires stamina. But at least the Greek cathedral has pews and moments of sitting. At the Russian Orthodox cathedrals the pews are not even there–only a few folding chairs at the back for the most infirm. The Orthodox of Russian background maintain three cathedrals in New York–not, alas, out of devotion to the Holy Trinity but out of a failure of sobernost, the Russian principle of community that makes them, in the minds of some Russians, superior to the many-splintered Protestants or legalistic Roman Catholics. The original cathedral is controlled by the Patriarch of Moscow, and a bishop sent from Russia oversees a couple dozen parishes that want to maintain a direct connection with the spirituality of the mother country. The ultra-conservatives, who fled Russia after the communist revolution and condemned the bishops who stayed and tolerated communist control, operate as the Russian Orthodox Church Outside of Russia, with an adapted mansion on East 93rd Street as their cathedral. The main body of Orthodox of Russian background, autonomous now as the Orthodox Church in America (OCA), use a church on the Lower East Side as their cathedral.

While in the general vicinity of the OCA cathedral, you might also want to check out a church of the Catholic Ukrainian rite, St. George's. It is across from McSorley's Old Ale House, where women were not allowed until a court ruling opened it up a few years ago. St. George's also offers an Easter service in the tradition of the Eastern churches, sung by an impressive choir.

On whatever Sundays, the music of the churches tends to be one of their most unifying features. Christians divided on many doctrinal and organizational points often find they can sing the same words to the same tune. When Harry Emerson Fosdick was preaching his modernist message at the Riverside Church, one of his staunchest fundamentalist adversaries was John Roach Stratton at Calvary Baptist Church. Today, Calvary Baptist, on West 57th Street near Carnegie Hall, remains faithfully fundamentalist, but I notice that its hymnal contains Dr. Fosdick's "God of Grace and God of Glory." And the same hymn also appears in a looseleaf selection placed in the pews at St. Patrick's Cathedral. In fact, these other users now hold truer to Dr. Fosdick's words than Riverside Church, which sings a version altered to "inclusive" language. No more "fail not man nor thee."

The senior minister of All Souls Unitarian Universalist Church, Frank Forrester Church IV, son of former Senator Frank F. Church of Idaho, has made a considerable splash in New York, despite drawing some flak when he changed wives in midstream. He was said to emphasize the theme, "Deeds, not creeds," and attracted a considerable following. Then reports came that he liked the wife of one of the laymen in the church better than his own—as some preachers elsewhere have decided from time to time—and switched over. One of his more remarkable deeds, we were then told (*New York* magazine, October 14, 1991), was that during his campaign of luring the woman, he sent her husband a letter offering him marital counseling. Even some of the deeply-dyed liberals of All Souls considered that a bit thick. But the majority said, "Oh, never mind," and Mr. Church continued on, unabashed as Jimmy Swaggart.

A scene you might not expect in the Broadway theater district is the Times Square Church, a nondenominational congregation in the Pentecostal style. It holds services in a former Broadway theater, near the site of the original Lindy's restaurant, no longer operating but still celebrated in television showings of "Guys and Dolls." Minister David Wilkerson packs them in with a service that is big on excitement and exuberant music of choir and orchestra. Here we praise God with multifarious accompaniment. Praise him with the electronic keyboard. Praise him with the trombones and cornet. Praise him with the drum, the snare drum, the bass drum, the Congo drum, the kettle drum. Praise him with a whole row of saxophones. Praise him to the fever-footed syncopated beat. At times you may feel like you have stumbled upon a New York party, which may be defined as an occasion where they cram too many people into a space too small and turn up the music too loud.

An overemphasis on trying to stir up religious feelings is perhaps the basic error of Pentecostalism. In this view, the more you shout and cry and jump around, and speak gibberish, the more Holy Spirit you've got. A background question for worship is whether you will get something nutritious that provides strength for the days to come, or something more like a drug that takes you high for the moment but afterward leaves you weak as before. Feelings are necessarily ephemeral. For an alternative to the Pentecostal or charismatic view, you could conclude from the New Testament account of Pentecost (Acts 2) that the Holy Spirit is on you when you can speak in ways that connect to people of all cultures. To some extent, Pentecostalism constitutes a church parallel to the Romantic movement in literature, which overemphasized the feelings of the individual and led writers like William Wordsworth to talk misleadingly of poetry as "the spontaneous overflow of powerful feelings" (preface to the 1800 second edition of *Lyrical Ballads*). In Christianity, the important matters are convictions and commitments; whether or not you happen to feel religious is more or less secondary. You may feel up and with it one day, down and out of it the next. But with your mind focused on goals outside yourself, you can hold a steady course. And in the end, you will find that such emotions as love, joy and peace, along with self-control, have come as gifts; you do not need to manufacture them yourself (Galatians 5:22-23).

I have been intrigued to find that a French-American Friendship Foundation has recently started sponsoring an annual mass in New York to commemorate the death of Louis XVI. In Geneva, the editors of ENI also became intrigued, and carried a story I wrote (January 21, 1998). But from the perspective of Washington and the Catholic News Service, it did not seem like a development of sufficient interest to bother with.

A curiosity of covering the New York scene has been reporting on masses held for a number of years at St. Patrick's Cathedral in memory of Joseph R. McCarthy, the Wisconsin Republican who won notoriety as a scourge of (alleged) communists and wound up censured by his fellow senators. These masses were not arranged at the initiative of the archbishop or cathedral clergy, I should quickly insert, but by an independent group, the St. Michael Forum, led by a quite amiable layman, Timothy Mitchell.

If you wonder about the spiritual flavor of the event, consider a sample from the 1981 homilist, a Jesuit priest named Vincent Miceli: "Today we honor the memory of a great American patriot, Senator Joseph McCarthy, who in his public office did not hesitate to fight for the protection of his fatherland against traitors who were scheming to reduce 'the land of the free and the home of the brave' into a gulag run by godless tyrants bent on dominating millions of sycophants and slaves" (NC, May 4, 1981).

One year, Walter Brolewicz, an American-born cousin of the Polish leader Lech Walesa, showed up as a supplementary speaker at the lunch always held after the mass, and told us his cousin thought Senator McCarthy had been "the right man for the time" (NC, May 7, 1985). The role of Senator McCarthy's aide, Roy Cohn, seemed even more curious. He was a Jew who did not practice his own faith, and a homosexual who died of AIDS. And he got a hero's welcome from this little band of ultra-conservative Catholics. He was brought in regularly to speak at the luncheons, and denounced whichever liberals were showing their heads in the political world that year.

While Senator McCarthy was acclaimed as a champion in the fight against the godless communists, I tended to agree with Thurston Davis, a Jesuit priest who had been editor of the Jesuit magazine, *America,* and once told me that the senator did more than anyone else to discredit the fight against communism. After Senator McCarthy, anyone who called for firmness in the battle or questioned Americans drifting into the ranks of fellow travelers would get branded and dismissed by much of the nation's cultural leadership as McCarthyite. It seemed to me that Senator McCarthy was only the most prominent of a good many people who played the same role in those years, not really doing anything detrimental to communism but using anti-communist emotion to promote themselves and slander people they did not like. The commotion created by the McCarthy types became the focus of debate, and people could forget that there actually was a communist party operating in the United States, headquartered in New York, that there actually were fellow travelers, serving Kremlin interests perhaps more effectively by staying in mainstream circles, and that there were in actual fact a number of communist spies operating here.

Taking a quick look now at a dimension of commercial life in New York: The unknowing such as myself would initially suppose that if you are opening a new business, you would select an area without anything in that category. Less competition. And this may be true for some lines. But in other cases, those of a type congregate in an area where customers are accustomed to go. If you want to do business, you go where the traffic is.

So in New York we have a block with several bridal shops clustered for the convenience of brides and their mothers who want to do comparison shopping in one trip. And there are concentrations such as the diamond district just off Fifth Avenue on West 47th. Restaurants show up most everywhere, of course, but they do also have their block on West 46th, where they fill nearly every space on both sides of the street.

I got into restaurant row journalistically to find out about Peter Jacobs (NC, July 5, 1983). He was ordained as a priest of the Catholic Archdiocese of Washington, but had been working in New York as a chaplain for two high schools operated by the Irish Christian Brothers—Rice and Power Memorial. Then, one day he was taken to a high mountain and shown the kingdoms of this world and the glory thereof. Philomene Le Douzen, a French woman who had a building where she formerly ran a restaurant, offered to lease it to Father Jacobs, and held out the prospect he could make $100,000 a year. That was in 1983 when such numbers looked bigger than today, huge though they may still appear alongside a priest's normal income.

The building was well situated, on the end of restaurant row nearest the theater district, and obviously had potential. One fly did appear in the ointment: the priest's superior, Cardinal James A. Hickey of Washington, did not want him to go into business. But Father Jacobs was not a priest to hesitate before an impediment of that sort.

As he talked with me about his various adventures, which ranged far beyond the high schools, I began to think this was perhaps an example of the priest who makes his way among prominent Catholics by personal chaplaincy services such as finding creative detours around inconvenient regulations, maybe on marriages or whatever. He was a name dropper and seemed to know a lot of names to drop, among them Grace Kelly and others of the princely house of Monaco. He called his restaurant the Palatine, which he said was the name of a train running, as his menu would, between Paris and Rome. That also seemed to reflect the world of sophistication in which he was or wished to be at home. He spoke of raising funds for good causes among his wealthy friends, of dining with Walter Cronkite and other celebrities, of preparing a grandchild of Henry Ford II for confirmation, of friendship with apostolic delegates, papal private secretaries and whoever. Shortly before opening the restaurant, according to his account, he was having dinner with Prince Rainier and family in Paris, and they came up with the idea of using the name of the train. He also said that after the death of Princess Grace, in 1982, he was asked to say a mass in her chapel, which he then noticed for the first time was called the Palatine, and this confirmed his choice for a restaurant name.

Father Jacobs had arguments he would offer to support his contention that Cardinal Hickey should let him run a restaurant. He could speak of one priest here and another one there who had been allowed to do that or something similar. He talked of the religious orders that made wine and brandy. He discoursed about all the good he could do, giving jobs to needy students and making profits for the support of worthy charities. He explained his special need for building a retirement resource beyond what he could expect as a priest. He could argue canon law and church history.

Plausible as his spiel might sound in some respects, it seemed to me flawed by the one inescapable and most pertinent point that his boss did not agree. But the restaurant was going, and he was featured in some newspapers, and his priestly faculties were suspended, and consequently also his job with the high schools. He was left with the glory of seeing himself publicized–with what accuracy I do not know–as the first Catholic priest ever to get a liquor license in the State of New York.

Father Jacobs may have had many capabilities, but running a New York restaurant turned out to be not amongst them. He wore his clericals, and greeted his clergy and lay friends who came in, but not enough came. Four years later, I interviewed him again for a story about the closing of the restaurant, and found a priest who had learned unexpected lessons about the greenness on the other side (NC, April 20, 1987). He had learned how expensive it was to hire the quality of staff he needed. He had learned about employees who would take a few steaks home with them. He had learned about burglars who came by after closing time. He learned about water pipes that could break in the middle of the night, and threats of an electricity cutoff in the middle of the day. He learned about city inspectors and their various expectations. He learned the unsettling effects of fights among the staff.

Adding it all up for the final exam, he had learned how a restaurant operator could spend four years and not make $100,000 a year, in fact not make anything, but calculate with relief that he might get out even. "It was more difficult than I expected," he told me.

But hold on. You do not finish off a priest like Father Jacobs that easily. In 1999, I noticed an article in the business section of *The New York Times* (June 23) that told of Martin R. Frankel, a native of Toledo, Ohio, who had been charged with fraud by federal prosecutors, but had fled his home in

Greenwich, Connecticut, to nobody knew where. Insurance companies he had dealt with were also bringing a $950 million civil suit for what they said he had manipulated out of them. And there were reports of maybe a billion or two missing from a Saint Francis of Assisi Foundation he had set up.

Naturally it caught my attention that the *Times* article, by Joseph Kahn and Joseph B. Treaster, spoke of the foundation as "Vatican-linked." But the only link mentioned was that Mr. Frankel had worked closely with "the Rev. Peter Jacobs, a retired priest now living in Rome who has broad connections in American political and religious circles." I rather doubt that the pope would rank Father Jacobs as an authentic representative of the Vatican. But people living in Rome sometimes find it easy to convince the gullible of their inside connections. Later articles in *The Times* identified something closer to a link with Mr. Frankel's operations in Emilio Colagiovanni, an Italian monsignor respected enough at the Vatican to be made a judge on the Roman Rota and allowed to edit an approved quarterly dealing with canon law. But, more convenient for Mr. Frankel's purposes, this monsignor also headed a Monitor Ecclesiasticus Foundation, which had an account at the Vatican bank that enabled him to get Mr. Frankel's Saint Francis of Assisi Foundation tied in to the bank, and thus supplied with appearances of legitimacy. [Ed. Note: A 14 October 2004 AP report compiled by Anthony Ramirez said that Jacobs had pleaded guilty in Frankel's insurance schemes and had received five years probation. Jacobs pleaded guilty in federal court to conspiracy to commit wire fraud and to launder money.]

Priests who are attached to dioceses do have some opening to accumulate personal resources, provided they prosper through enterprises their bishops approve. But members of the religious orders, vowed to poverty, are expected to turn whatever they earn over to their communities. Back when Pedro Arrupe was superior general of the Jesuits, I got to talking one evening with a Jesuit teaching at Fordham University. He told me that he had contracted with a publisher to write a curriculum piece for use in Catholic high schools. He would write it during his free time the coming summer, and for this sidebar activity of his would get thirty or forty thousand dollars. "Does Pedro Arrupe know you are making that kind of money?" I asked. And the Jesuit replied, "Yes, he's the one that gets it."

Now, from commerce to the world of nature: Visitors probably do not often come to New York for nature, but we do have some, and some worthy of special note in Central Park. Going to the East Side, I often walk through the park, which is a pleasure trip and sometimes an occasion. I was passing by the lake one day shortly before Christmas, and was struck by the sight of the ducks swimming about. I suddenly reflected that we had just passed the solstice and moved into winter. "Shouldn't you guys have gone south by now?" I asked. But they acted like they never heard a word I said, and just kept paddling around with their customary insouciance to let me know they could not care less about winter or lakes freezing over or snow covering the ground. This happened to be the winter of 1993-94, which brought us an extraordinary number of freezing days, and when I walked by the lake a few weeks later I saw it had ice thick enough a couple of men were standing on it. I asked a park worker if the crew had any way of supplying the ducks with food or water during the winter, but he said they could look after themselves. Sure enough, when spring came, there they were, gliding along as before. "A New York duck finds ways to survive," one of them now took time to tell me.

Let us now take a look back: New York has a pattern in its religious history that I think is commonly overlooked, but well worth mentioning. A good many Americans like to believe their nation was formed to provide a place for people to enjoy religious freedom, a theory based mostly on the settlement of Massachusetts by the Pilgrim Fathers of Plymouth and the Puritans of Boston. Actually, the theory is not valid even there. Those settlers did not come to set up a system that would provide religious freedom and let every individual do as he pleased, but to build a new society in accord with their common convictions. They did seek freedom from the system they disliked in England, but even that was not the case with some other colonies, such as Virginia, which was settled by people who established Anglican parishes as similar to those in England as the new circumstances allowed.

New York is, however, even more compelling proof that the settlers came with goals other than religious freedom. The Dutch who established New Amsterdam followed exactly the same theological line they had known in old Amsterdam, Dutch Calvinism. There was tolerance of individual members of other faiths, even Catholics and Sephardic Jews, but they had to keep their worship out of the public eye. In *Gotham* (Oxford, 1999), a history of New York, Edwin G. Burrows and Mike Wallace reported that the early Dutch allowed no other public expression of religion except the Reformed "as defined by the Synod of Dort" (p. 59). This defining event was a synod, held in the Netherlands town with the fuller name of Dordrect in 1618-19, that firmly nailed down the most contentious points of Calvinist orthodoxy. In fact, there was sometimes less religious freedom in the colonies than in the mother countries. According to *Gotham*, when Peter Stuyvesant was put in charge of New Amsterdam, he and his associates tried to impose "a degree of religious conformity on the colony that was unthinkable as well as impracticable in the Netherlands" (p. 59). The Dutch felt no need or desire to go off looking for religious freedom, since they had organized their religion the way they wanted it at home. When they came to New York, they were, rather, looking for a place where they could make a little money. And most people who have come to America's largest city in the succeeding years have shared that motivation. As do most immigrants coming today. We provide a haven for some religious and political refugees, of course, but that is not the meaning of America. What this country stands for is opportunity, the chance to start over and see if you can make a better life for yourself and your family, less constrained by structures of the old country. There is no reason to attempt a sanctification of America by trying to give it a more religious meaning than other nations, and good reason not to.

Saying that New York is not America, I realize, has become a cliché, often repeated and I suppose widely believed. But to me it seems an obvious false-hood. If you want to insist that you see differences between New York and Hermleigh, Texas, where my grandfather, Willis Worley Early, once ran a general store and sold too many groceries on credit, pumped gas, kept farm supplies in the back, set up a little lunch counter and occasionally found a free piece of candy for a grandchild, I can of course hardly dispute that. But to say that the largest and culturally most influential city in the country is not really part of the country, but some alien land, to join the witty in the remark that Manhattan is an island off the coast of America, goes too far.

The tradition of putting down New York testifies, I suppose, to its centrality in American life, just as people in the military ventilate their frustrations by putting down the Pentagon. In 1774, en route to Philadelphia for the opening of the Continental Congress, John Adams and others of the Massachusetts delegation passed through New York. He found it unlike Quincy, Massachusetts: "With all the opulence and splendor of the city, there is very little good breeding to be found. We have been treated with assiduous respect; but I have not seen one real gentleman, one well-bred man, since I came to town. At their entertainments there is no conversation that is agreeable; there is no modesty, no attention to one another. They talk very loud, very fast and all together. If they ask you a question, before you can utter three words of your answer they will break out upon you again and talk away" (*Works of John Adams*, Little, Brown, 1850-56; Vol. II, p. 353). But he arrived in August, so perhaps all the real gentlemen had left town to escape the heat.

To me, New York seems very much America. To start with, we might mention Wall Street and the financial institutions associated with it. Who can imagine the American economy without Wall Street? At a different spot on the spectrum, Manhattan also has Harlem, which symbolizes black America. New York is of course the most important center of the arts in this country. The

Broadway stage is the American stage; the New York Metropolitan Opera is what any American who thinks of opera will think of first.

We also have the headquarters of the American Bible Society, which reflects a significant aspect of America's evangelical Protestant ethos. And we have Columbia University and its Teachers College, where John Dewey taught and where influences affecting all American education originated. And the headquarters of Jehovah's Witnesses, a child of the American religious consciousness, is Brooklyn-based. The most important American theologian of the twentieth century was Reinhold Niebuhr, who taught in New York at Union Seminary. From the Marble Collegiate Church in New York, Norman Vincent Peale addressed a national audience, as did Harry Emerson Fosdick earlier from the pulpit of Riverside Church.

Do not the television networks based in New York constitute a central part of American life, a deplorable part you may well say but of undeniable centrality? The book and magazine publishers of New York are fundamental to the national culture, and the jazz community has ranked New York as the Big Apple. Who would claim the events of Madison Square Garden are not America? Even those who do the most clever put-downs of New York are commonly New Yorkers.

The Catholic archbishops of New York naturally take a leading role in the life of American Catholicism. The headquarters of the Greek Orthodox Archdiocese, the largest body of Eastern Orthodoxy in America, sit in Manhattan. Do you want to say none of this is America? And New York is of course the preeminent center of American Jewish life.

Knowledgeable readers may notice that when I refer to New York, I seem to be thinking mainly of Manhattan, now only one of New York's five boroughs. Residents of the others, often called the outer boroughs, complain about the arrogance of us Manhattanites, presuming to make ourselves the center, and relegate everyone else to a peripheral, support role. But so it is. Even they of the less celebrated boroughs commonly concede as much implicitly, talking about a trip to Manhattan as going into "the city." Except for the nearer parts of Brooklyn, the other boroughs are part of New York mainly as an administrative arrangement of convenience, consolidated in 1898. From a cultural point of view, they might as well be New Jersey. Brooklyn is a special place of its own, as is Staten Island. And Queens is a collection of communities. We know not what to make of the Bronx. But most of what identifies New York distinctively as New York belongs to Manhattan, the original settlement that is still New York County. So I do not exclude the residents of the "outer" boroughs from a share in the glory of being New Yorkers, any more than they are excluded from the joy of paying city taxes, but I keep the focus on the center.

SIDEBARS

Perhaps people feel an impulse to put New York down just because it is so important, and they can presume to increase their own stature a cubit by dismissing it with their snidery. If New York oversteps and acts as though it were the totality, and everything outside were nothing, then it needs correction. But it is the most important center of American life, and the mainline Protestant churches have made a fundamental error when they have sought to withdraw from it, or let it drift into their backwaters of neglect.

New York's money has not brought it as much impressive church architecture as it should have, I regret I must tell you. Those in charge seemed usually more disposed to imitate Gothic or Byzantine architecture of past centuries in the Old World, rather than build on the tradition in some fresh fashion more suited to a New World in a new age. I do not care for church architecture that breaks all ties with tradition and experiments with the odd and bizarre, but I saw on a visit to the cathedral built in Coventry, England, to replace the one bombed in the Second World War, that thoughtful architects can design something that is recognizable as a church while also recognizable as a structure of our time.

If bigness guarantees virtue, we can brag about having the world's largest cathedral, the Episcopal Cathedral of St. John the Divine, where the dean until the end of 1996 was James Parks Morton. (For some readers, I perhaps need to explain that St. Peter's Basilica in Rome is a larger church but is not a cathedral, a term that means not necessarily a church of splendor and size, but the place where the bishop has his seat, humble as it sometimes can be. The Bishop of Rome has his seat—in Latin, cathedra—at St. John Lateran.) At St. John the Divine, Dean Morton showed imagination and flair for enticing New Yorkers into the cathedral. He paraded an elephant and representatives of all the other levels of created life up the aisle on St. Francis Sunday. He enlisted celebrities. He displayed art. He rearranged the seating every now and then to accommodate medieval dramas or musical programs. He resumed construction on the cathedral and put several more feet of one tower up.

I have a great deal of admiration for Dean Morton. Episcopalians number not so many, and the cathedral could easily have turned into a museum with only a few pious remnants in attendance. But Dean Morton brought in the New York community. Some observers may object that the program was overly theatrical and insufficiently permeated by real religion. But the cathedral has kept the communion service central to each Sunday's activity. So whatever wanderings the diplomat or poet or whoever in the pulpit has taken you on, at the end you are brought back to the Christian focal point.

So many things go on at this cathedral, anybody is bound to like a few. I like the inclusion of the Sh'ma in the Sunday service, with its reminder that we need to listen. So each Sunday you can hear the choir joining in solidarity with ancient Israel to chant, "Sh'ma Yisrael, Adonai Elohaynu Adonai echad," Hebrew for, "Hear, O Israel, the LORD our God is one LORD" (Deuteronomy 6:4). That is the sort of thing that keeps you connected to your actual roots. You could say that "hear" is one of the most important words in religion. "Receive" and "remember" are a couple more, and I notice the three are brought together succinctly in the warning to the church in Sardis that needed to wake up: "Remember then what you received and heard" (Revelation 3:3).

Aside from all the above, the final truth is that I like New York because it provides the necessary opportunities for the work I do. Not only are many of the newsmakers here, but most of the others will sooner or later come by. If you want to interview the Archbishop of Canterbury and cannot afford a plane ticket to Britain, hold on a while and he will pass through New York. Or likewise if it is a Methodist bishop from Argentina that you want. And if someone like Golda Meier might not have time for a private talk, you could get close enough for a direct and lasting impression when she spoke at a dinner here: the warmth of a grandmother in the steel of a tank commander.

Or you could see Dom Helder Camara, short as he was. In 1980, I got to hear his address and talk with him just a little at Riverside Church (NC, December 9). He was archbishop of the Catholic Archdiocese of Olinda and Recife, in Brazil's impoverished northeast, and had gained an international reputation as a champion of the poor. At times, it could seem as though he spent more days in Europe and North America than with those poor people assigned to his care, and there were reports that the Vatican had suggested he stay home a little more, and tend to his duties there. But he brushed those reports aside when I talked with him, and intimated that he had a personal understanding with the pope.

Brazil had a rough and ready government in those days, ready to dispose roughly of troublemakers, but at Riverside Church I got a pretty clear impression of how the archbishop avoided any serious repercussions. He was a master of the allusive, of the words that pointed your mind in a certain direction, but never actually made the subversive statement. His hands came into play, holding up the structures of society in the old style, and then silently coming down as he gave a little smile. So small, just a wisp of hair on a bald head, so warm as he patted your shoulder. And I was able to confirm this impression when he visited us again in 1983, coming from Japan and receipt there of a peace prize from the Niwano Peace Foundation, an agency of the Buddhist renewal movement Rissho Kosei-Kai. He said that he would visit a couple

SIDEBARS

more U.S. cities and then Paris, Brussels and Geneva before finding time to stop in at the Archdiocese of Olinda and Recife (NC, April 19).

In 1979, a group of Chinese religious leaders were allowed to travel abroad for the first time since the Cultural Revolution, and they came to New York before going to an international meeting held at Princeton by the World Conference on Religion and Peace. I could report their statement that religious freedom had been restored since the fall of the Gang of Four, and that plans were underway for opening of churches and other religious activities (*Christian Science Monitor*, August 29). But the main statement was made just by their presence: they had survived, and Chinese authorities would now let them visit the center of world capitalism.

Without ever visiting Eastern Europe, I could get a view of developments there through agencies such as the Appeal of Conscience Foundation. Established on an interreligious basis by the rabbi of an East Side synagogue, Arthur Schneier, this agency has raised a lot of money from businessmen, amassed a certain amount of influence and carried out an extensive program of support for religious liberty, particularly in Eastern Europe.

In 1986, it sponsored a visit to New York by Konstantin Kharchev, a citizen of the Soviet Union who had recently become its minister of religious affairs. I had never seen one of those before, and had only heard of their strict control exercised from somewhere within the inaccessible interiors of the Kremlin. But here was something new. At a dinner for fifty or so religious leaders in New York, Mr. Kharchev was speaking and began, "My friends." Something was afoot. He met with Cardinal O'Connor. He met with Greek Orthodox Archbishop Iakovos. He met with executives of the National Council of Churches (NCC), who I gathered from the furious way he puffed his cigarette afterward must have pushed him harder than anyone else. Everywhere he worked to convey the message that the Soviet leadership, since the previous year headed by Mikhail Gorbachev, was ready to live and let live. Mr. Kharchev was even willing to talk a few minutes with a reporter representing the Catholic press. The "democratization" campaign of Mr. Gorbachev would also apply to the churches, he reported telling the NCC. "Many questions relating to religious legislation are now being reconsidered," he said.

Would the changes go so far as to allow a visit to the Soviet Union by a Polish pope? the reporter from the National Catholic News Service asked him. But even glasnost would not yet allow an answer to that question–possibly, I would think, because reservations of the Russian Orthodox Church remained as much of an obstacle as governmental views. The millennial anniversary of Christianity in Russia lay not far ahead, and some people speculated on whether Pope John Paul II might go for the occasion. It turned out that he did not. But whatever the outcome of those discussions, the new Gorbachev regime "will never say any bad words about the pope," Mr. Kharchev promised (NC, October 29). Three years before the Berlin Wall was brought tumbling down, it had become clear from a few words on a New York street that the Soviet Union was headed toward some different future.

In the midst of such developments, however, you can never be sure what to believe. Mr. Gorbachev "has proven even more ruthless than his immediate predecessors," said Casimir Pugevicius, a priest who headed the Lithuanian Information Center (NC, November 13, 1986). From a location in Brooklyn, the center was playing a significant role in helping sustain the Catholic Church in Lithuania. Under communist control, Lithuanians could not expect to learn much from local media about activities of the church or efforts to secure greater freedom. But a few people collected information and smuggled it to Father Pugevicius, who transmitted it to Rome, where it was broadcast back to Lithuania by Vatican Radio. So Lithuanians got the officially unapproved news about their country by way of Brooklyn.

I was myself skeptical when I took the long subway and bus ride out to the center one day in the spring of 1989, and heard a visiting priest from Lithuania speak confidently of the coming days of full independence. Fat chance, I thought. The Soviet Union will never let Lithuania out from under its heel, I said to myself. But the priest, a young man named Ausvydas Belickas, told me that "there is no doubt the Soviet empire is beginning to crumble." He had studied at an "underground seminary," courses given privately by priests, when the government refused to let him enroll at the one approved seminary of his country. But the government had now relaxed to the point of recognizing him and other graduates of the "underground seminary." Meanwhile, these graduates were finding ways to work in other parts of the Soviet Union, and he had himself served for a time in Armenia, he said. The Soviet Union might decide to allow freedom for the Baltic states and maybe others such as Armenia and Georgia in an effort to save the rest of its "empire," he speculated (NC, April 6). In elections the next year, a group favoring independence won a majority of seats in the Lithuanian Supreme Soviet, which changed its name then to the Supreme Council, which repudiated the 1940 Soviet annexation of Lithuania. A year later, on September 6, 1991, the USSR State Council recognized the independence of Lithuania, Latvia and Estonia.

Covering the world from New York has of course its down side, because I am often getting only one end of a story, with no chance for independent checking. As on efforts to alleviate the Ethiopian famine. When outsiders suddenly awoke, by way of a television report in the fall of 1984, to a massive drought and famine in Ethiopia, I covered it by interviewing officials of

Catholic Relief Services (CRS), an agency now in Baltimore but then in New York. I found the staff of CRS could be valuable sources on life in many countries of the world. Desk officers stayed up to date on their assigned regions, and field staff were often coming back to check with headquarters. So I got many stories from CRS.

But then a few former employees of the agency, with former Burundi director James MacGuire in the lead, and current staff of sympathetic mind apparently supplying documents from inside, fed material to *The New York Times*, and got a story published there (August 7, 1985) raising questions about CRS handling of funds it received for Ethiopian relief, and about some other aspects of its finances. These critics went public, they said, only after months of unsuccessful efforts to persuade the bishops that new policies were needed.

When the famine got into the news, it became a front page event, and therefore a fundraising opportunity. Americans were told that many Ethiopians were starving to death and millions more would die unless aid came immediately. Reporting on famine in Ethiopia and other parts of Africa, a CRS release in December of 1984 said: "An estimated six to ten million people in Ethiopia alone continue to face starvation–2.5 million in immediate life-threatening jeopardy. Half are children."

Such words seemed to imply that unless Americans sent CRS a lot of money in the next few days, millions of Ethiopians would likely starve to death. The same release said Americans had already sent CRS more than $25 million for Ethiopian famine relief, and this would enable it to "distribute food, seeds and tools and provide farm animals during the coming year." But by the end of July it could report spending only $7 million. And it turned out most of the money had just been put in the bank to pay for long term projects.

No one can deny the value of long term development, of course. And I never got any indication that CRS officials were putting the money in their own pockets. But it was something of a shock to learn that many millions of dollars were just sitting in the bank several months after we had been led to suppose innumerable Ethiopians would quickly die of starvation if Americans did not quickly donate money.

When I did a report on the allegations reported by *The Times* (NC, August 7), the CRS Africa secretary, William Schaufele, told me some people were being fed but "just to feed these people is not adequate" and "does nothing about the future." From the way CRS talked, we had come to fear Ethiopians might not have any future, and Mr. Schaufele acknowledged a problem of perception could arise if some donors thought their money would be used immediately for emergency aid. Mr. MacGuire told me CRS had raised $50 million for food aid and ought to use it for that. Mr. Schaufele said $8.1 million had been used, $22.9 million was being held for use in Ethiopia over the coming 18 months and another $20 million was in an Africa fund for projects in Ethiopia and 17 other African countries over the coming decade.

Lawrence Pezzullo, the former U.S. ambassador to Nicaragua who became CRS director, had also disclosed those plans earlier at a press conference I covered (NC, May 10, 1985). Most of the $30 million CRS planned to spend on Ethiopia by the end of the next year would go to longer-term needs, he said, and CRS hoped to raise $20 million for other development projects in Africa. But he also said that money "inundated" CRS after the shocking television coverage of starvation in Ethiopia. So donors presumably were thinking their gifts would put food in starving mouths.

CRS was meanwhile distributing large amounts of food provided by the U.S. Agency for International Development (AID), and the inspector general of AID issued a report saying CRS had improperly handled some funds and violated regulations by refusing food to people who could not pay. CRS disputed the allegations, and said that if some people were refused food, local distributors were acting against CRS policy.

On this kind of story, you need to check multiple angles, but I was reduced to doing whatever I could just from the New York end.

The French agency, Medecins Sans Frontiers (Doctors Without Borders), worked in Ethiopia a while, and got kicked out after accusing the government of using relief funds to force people in rebel areas to resettle elsewhere. The head of this agency, Rony Brauman, published an article in the October 1986 issue of *Reader's Digest* further publicizing charges that the Ethiopian government misused relief funds to carry out a "murderous policy" of resettlement.

"Nonsense," said Francis Carlin, a CRS official who had directed its Ethiopian work during that period. But after interviewing several CRS officials over a period of years, I was left with the impression that they were not telling quite the whole story about their difficulties in dealing with Ethiopia, then under a communist government headed by Mengistu Haile Mariam. One CRS official just hinted that the difficulty in getting the Ethiopian government to allow the saving of the lives of its people was considerable, but that aid agencies avoided any public protest so they could continue giving food to the starving. In the end, I remained unsure what the true story was. Journalism needs to be played as a team sport like basketball, where a player who finds himself blocked can bounce the ball over to a teammate better positioned to move forward.

A rather distinctive New York story began its unfolding on May 21, 1990, when Mother Teresa wrote New York's Mayor David N. Dinkins to tell him that she would not be able to use two buildings the city had given her for a men's shelter in the Bronx. She said her order, the Missionary Sisters of Charity, hoped to add to its several other projects in New York a home for babies with AIDS. And "I don't think it will be possible for us to handle the extra work of an additional men's shelter."

A few days later (June 3), the New York superior, Mary Dolores, sent the letter to the mayor with a cover letter of her own expressing thanks for his help in dealing with an elevator issue. "Please know that the decision we took was not influenced at all by the elevator matter, except that it created a delay which allowed us to examine again the work we are doing in New York City, and whether we should expand it to include more services to our beloved homeless," she said. And Sister Dolores went on to add, "I want you to know that the director of your Office for People with Disabilities, Anne Emerman, has been of great assistance to us . . . ."

Outsiders knew nothing of all this until September 17, when a columnist for *The New York Times,* Sam Roberts, wrote a piece suggesting, contrary to Sister Dolores, that the shelter project was abandoned because Anne Emerman insisted that the nuns had to follow the law requiring installation of elevators. The result, he wrote, represented "not only a bureaucratic conflict, but a cultural clash" between the secular city and the nuns, who were "forbidden by their religious vows from routinely using modern conveniences and were prepared to carry any handicapped people themselves."

Since Mother Teresa herself routinely boarded airplanes to fly all over the world, no one could really imagine that using modern inventions violated some religious principle of her order. But it entered the folklore that a senseless bureaucracy was keeping the good nuns from serving the needy, and the Dinkins administration got a bit of flak from some people in the Archdiocese of New York.

The Dinkins people did not help themselves much in their handling of the publicity, but after repeated efforts I finally reached a press officer, Catie Marshall, who gave me copies of the letters from Mother Teresa and Sister Dolores, which put the matter in a quite different light, unless you want to accuse the good nuns of lying for the sake of their diplomatic relations with the mayor. And after some delays I finally got to talk by phone with Anne Emerman, who told me that an agreement had been worked out for an elevator going up only one floor and costing only about $25,000, for which a donor had been found (CNS, October 3, 1990).

But perhaps the bigger mistake was the failure of the critics to get the point of the campaign for the handicapped. Inspiring as it may sound to some people to hear of the good nuns, smiling as their backs are breaking, taking cripples on shoulders and trudging up stairs, what the handicapped want is the freedom to get themselves up and about, not to be left dependent forever on the goodhearted to carry them. But people were angry with Mayor Dinkins for other reasons, so the charges of frustrating the good nuns of Mother Teresa served as a convenient stick for beating him.

So much for New York. But for journalists, perhaps as important as location are the editors they have to work with, through, under and sometimes around.

EDITORS

CHAPTER THREE

One Sunday morning, I went to Riverside Church and heard Edith Lerrigo, a YWCA executive who chaired a search for a new senior minister, report that her committee was unanimously recommending William Sloane Coffin. She said the recommendation had been conveyed to the deacons, a body of church lay leaders, and they unanimously endorsed it. After the service, I learned by nosing around that the trustees also approved the nomination, and that it likewise brought happiness to the church staff. So I thought: I have a little story here.

I called the editor in charge of a daily page of brief items in the *Christian Science Monitor,* and got his agreement that Mr. Coffin's selection would be suitable for one of those. Mr. Coffin had for some years been chaplain at Yale University, and had become nationally known also for leadership in the civil rights and anti-Vietnam War movements.

With an okay from the *Monitor* editor, however, I confronted a writing challenge. The selection of the new senior minister would not become official and final until the congregation voted some two weeks later. I could not say Riverside Church had called him. At the moment, I could not say Riverside had done anything. Still, this was pretty nearly a done deal. So how could I write the story as strong as it actually was without overstating?

Pondering a few minutes, I arrived at a quite clever solution. I began in the passive voice, writing in the first sentence that William Sloane Coffin had been chosen to serve as senior minister at Riverside, but without saying at what level the choice was made. In the second sentence, I reported that Edith Lerrigo had announced her committee's choice, and in the third I covered myself by giving the explanation that the membership was yet to vote but seemed certain to affirm. Then I went on with background about the role of Harry Emerson Fosdick and John D. Rockefeller Jr. in the church's history.

The editor, looking as editors often do for ways to compress, decided he would dispense with my third, covering sentence if approval was considered a sure thing, and save more space for the background material. Thus edited, the story moved to a headline writer, who did the obvious thing and in the big type announced, "Riverside Church Hires William S. Coffin" (August 2, 1977).

Which went beyond unfortunate. The congregation at Riverside guarded its right to a final say most jealously, and the search committee tiptoed to avoid any display of presumption. So now as they saw my story and its headline, "there were flashes of lightening, voices, peals of thunder, an earthquake and heavy hail" (Revelation 11:19). The church tower began swinging in circles like a radar screen, and the Resurrection Angel on the church roof, poised to blow his trumpet when the time came to announce an end to the perversities of human history, was alerted to stand ready for the signal at any moment. But the *Monitor* sportingly printed a quick apology and correction (August 4), and the earth cooled, and Mr. Coffin did get his approval in due course.

In the 1970s, I did a great deal of writing for the *Monitor*. That did not bring me much money, but nothing I did brought much money, and the *Monitor* was a paper of considerable standing among knowledgeable people, more so than today. A byline there brought satisfaction I would not have gotten from some forms of more lucrative writing.

From a check of my files, it appears my first article for the *Monitor* was based on an interview with Cynthia Clark Wedel, president of the National Council of Churches (January 3, 1972). Looking at the article these years later, I have to report that she spoke too optimistically about the future of the NCC and other ecumenical endeavors. But from the interviewee, who in the older tradition still identified herself on her stationery as Mrs. Theodore E. Wedel, the article brought a letter of characteristic graciousness: "I'll be glad to be interviewed by you anytime." And for my interest in writing for the *Monitor,* it provided a good launch. When I called a *Monitor* editor for a follow-up conversation, he told me a recent retrenchment had left the paper without a staff reporter covering the religion field, so I might be able to make further contributions.

My *Monitor* work started slowly and gradually built to a flowering, but then after a time faded back to nothingness. At first I was galled by an editor who seemed to make a point of changing every lead I wrote just for the sake of changing it. Always in journalism, what you see in print is the composite result of what reporters turn in and what editors do with it. But the proportions in the mix vary widely. I have read the opinion that a good editor is one who helps the writer say more effectively whatever he is trying to say, not replace it with what the editor himself might have written. But my *Monitor* man operated with the latter mindset. And the changes revealed no logic that would enable me to learn the approach he favored and perhaps follow it in my later submissions. However I did a story, he changed it around to go some different way. Brooding on this behavior, my mind, of its own accord and without direction, began recalling something I had read about certain animals marking their territory by spreading the scent of their urine over it.

One of the editing jobs that especially impressed me was perpetrated on a story about a project of the World Council of Churches' Fund for Reconstruction and Reconciliation in Indo-China. After my version was de- and re-constructed, and not reconciled with what I had written, a fairly lengthy story appeared that nowhere told readers that all the sentences were about the Fund for Reconstruction and Reconciliation in Indo-China. I wrote out a page of complaints about errors and misleading phraseology that had been introduced, of which the decision to keep secret what the story was about came last. But then I decided it was pointless to send it to an editor who had repeatedly demonstrated he did not really care all that much about factual accuracy, logic or coherence.

Then there were things minor but annoying. At that time, the United States had two Lutheran denominations with similar names–American Lutheran Church and Lutheran Church in America. They are now merged, but in the years of separate operation, their officials naturally desired that you get the names right. So I was made aware of dismay when I wrote a *Monitor* article that quoted the head of the Lutheran Church in America, and his identification was changed in the slapdash editing to put him in charge of the other body.

If such editors were starting from scratch and writing something of their own, we would all consider it quite forgivable if they failed to realize the names that sounded the same were not. But if they had a contributor with a little specialized knowledge, why would they not choose to let his wording stand, absent some special reason for changing it? Doubtless I would let a few mistakes of that type slip in if I were rewriting somebody else's stories, but I failed to see why the *Monitor* editor felt a need to do all that much rewriting. I have had enough of my articles used more or less as written to be confident the rewriting was less a matter of deficiency in my style than surplus in editorial ego.

A more ridiculous error got written in when I did an article for the news service of the Lutheran Council in the USA about a mission outpost of the Church of Sweden selling air rights over its midtown Manhattan building (June 4, 1982). I wrote, accurately, that the pastor, Evert Olson, was "a short, slender man." But the editor of the news service, who seemed to have even more of an ego problem than my *Monitor* headache, decided he had to set to and rewrite the article according to his own stylistic preferences. Failing, I suppose, to keep in touch with my original, he presumably carried in the back of his mind the recollection of something about height, and so grabbed a cliché from his Swedish file, and made the pastor "six-foot tall." Such days do weary one.

Once upon a time, I got a peek at one of my manuscripts after editors at another place had gone over it, and saw that one of them had written the word "idiosyncratic" (a word linguistically related to "idiot," my dictionary tells me) alongside a paragraph elaborating one of my more unconventional thoughts. I suppose that some editors might feel inclined to use the same word about my entire output. But that bit of realism has not kept me from holding onto my own wayward views about overly-diligent editors.

At the *Monitor*, however, the offender departed after a while, and for a period I had editors I could work with more easily and happily. The one I remember with most appreciation was Jak S. Miner, an assistant American news editor who was my principal conduit for a time. He had the greatest gift: good judgment. I would offer a suggestion, he would consider it a couple of seconds and then I could expect a straightforward yes or no. If it was yes, I did the story and he printed it. If it was no, I forgot about it–at least so far as the *Monitor* was concerned.

But after he went on to something else later in the decade, there came the chilling, with one editor announcing he wanted to do the religion stories himself, though not actually doing many, and another making such demands and moving so erratically I had to conclude the tiny fees no longer justified the hassle.

The *Monitor* had a certain relation to Middle East questions that left Jews admiring the paper less than they might have otherwise. One second level editor who was unhappy with the *Monitor* stance did once use the word "anti-semitism" in talking with me about something or other the *Monitor* was printing or not printing, though I do not assume this would necessarily have been his final, overall judgment. Other people would describe the *Monitor* approach as fairness toward the Arab side. In neutral, an analyst could observe that people who felt much of American journalism was slanting Middle East coverage along a pro-Israeli bias tended to say the *Monitor* did better.

I wrote an occasional story related to the Middle East, but more often I was encountering an unexplained unwillingness of *Monitor* editors to take stories about the Catholic Church. They would accept a story about what was going on in the Presbyterian or United Methodist or Baptist churches. They seemed to indicate a special receptivity to reports about the conservative-moderate conflict in the Lutheran Church-Missouri Synod, perhaps reflecting some views among Christian Scientists about literal Scripture interpretation. But the Catholic Church, which had more members than all those denominations combined, apparently was not considered a worthwhile subject for a *Monitor* article. Editors would allow a Catholic paragraph or two in a roundup, but never a Catholic theme for a whole story. My perceptions on this point got reinforcement when one editor did approve my proposal for reporting on a development in the Catholic Church, and after I had done it told me editors at higher levels turned thumbs down. Maybe bad vibes from Boston struggles of earlier days still reverberated somewhere in the upper management levels. I was told the higher authorities kept their eyes sharply focused on what the editors printed, scanning it line by line. And I later read that the church's founder, Mary Baker Eddy, had a thing about Catholics (not that such would have been so unusual in her time and place).

Some *Monitor* editors seemingly did not want to admit the restrictions their church imposed. I knew Christian Scientists did not speak of people "dying," but preferred to say they passed on to another life or something. But when there was a possible story about some other churches dealing with death as a topic, I asked a *Monitor* editor whether the very word "death" was forbidden. He said no, it did not have to be ruled out in a story such as I was proposing. So I sent the story, and back it came. Sorry, not for us.

What made contributing to the *Monitor* a delight, however, was the opportunity to do serious stories. There was no call for jazzing up and no need for dumbing down, and no tolerance for sensationalizing. And an advantage to me, the editors of the various sections of the paper operated in some independence, so if something I wanted to do failed to interest one, I might try another. At other publications as well I have found that the editor blocking entry might be worked around by selling something to a sub-editor in charge of one page or department. In time, I came to place stories in several sections of the *Monitor,* not only domestic news but also sometimes foreign as I interviewed church leaders from abroad or reported on U.S. church involvement in other parts of the world. Also I wrote stories for the education page, dealing with church contributions to education and sometimes commissioned by the education editor, Cynthia Parsons, to reach into the secular sphere. And when the churches moved aggressively into the corporate responsibility movement, I wrote an article or two about that for the *Monitor*'s business pages. Contributing occasionally to *The Home Forum* page edited by Henrietta Buckmaster, I even got into the art world when I bought a print of an El Greco "St. Jerome," which had struck me when I saw one version (my print is from the Frick's original) in the Metropolitan Museum of Art, and wrote an appreciation she found usable (April 3, 1978). Mrs. Buckmaster also saw reason to print (February 2, 1979) an interpretation I wrote of an Albrecht Dürer drawing, "The Adoration of Kings" (original in Musée Bonnat, Bayonne, France). In view of how little I know about art, and how much she did know, I had to take her decision as a professional encouragement.

But as the 1970s moved toward their close, new editors made relations increasingly difficult. Instead of consulting with the man who could say yes and no, I was finding on the other end of the line a kid who had no idea what he wanted, but was full of recommendations about by-roads I might explore just to see if something worthwhile would come of it, the fantasies of a staffer on salary who never had to worry about whether his explorations would lead to a check. So a few contributions in the early 1980s brought my *Monitor* career to a close. A brief item on an NCC meeting in 1983 (November 15) became the very last, my records indicate. A new editor on the education page asked for a story in 1984, and when I sent it in wrote me that it was just what he wanted. But it appears higher authorities blocked him from ever getting it into print.

At the *Monitor,* even if several days work did finally produce something it would use, my payment was still only fifty dollars or so. I thought about those numbers when I read in later years of the millions the Christian Science Church flushed down the sewer in an ill-considered effort at television operation, and of the resulting financial bind that pushed the church to accept a legacy with quite dubious conditions attached.

When Earl W. Foell, one of the more distinguished editors who had been associated with the *Monitor,* died in 1999, his obituary in *The New York Times* (July 13) included the information that he became editor of a new Christian Science publication, *World Monitor Magazine,* that was started in 1988 but abandoned only five years later. The obituary also mentioned the television boondoggle, which we had heard earlier was launched at the insistence of Harvey W. Wood, the chairman of the church's directors, and John H. Hoagland Jr., manager of its publishing society. And we had heard the church may have lost a hundred million dollars or more on the operation. The magazine was also a big loser, so church leaders were feeling the pinch. Now, the perhaps not totally unrelated item: In 1991, *The New York Times* reported that a book by Bliss Knapp, *Destiny of the Mother Church,* about the church's founder, Mary Baker Eddy, had been ruled unacceptable on its publication in 1947, but Mr. Knapp, his wife and her sister had willed the church their $90 million estate–provided the book was published as an "authorized" text and placed in the church's reading rooms. The church had decided to go along, though there were complicating reports of Stanford University and the Los Angeles Museum of Art getting mentioned in the will and sharing in the estate.

Meanwhile, to finance the short-lived television and magazine projects, resources had been taken away from the *Monitor*, which brought protest resignations from some key staff, including the editor, Katherine W. Fanning. So at the time of the Foell obituary, circulation had fallen from 200,000 to 80,000. Truly sad. The *Monitor* was the best thing the Christian Science Church had going for it, so far as gaining recognition in the outside world was concerned, but instead of building on strength, the church chose to divert the money flow to irrigate mirages.

Reporting for the *Monitor*, I dealt with issues affecting many churches, but not with Christian Science. Later, however, writing for ENI, I had one occasion to touch on the Christian Science view of healing. Douglas and Rita Swan were former members of the church who said they left it to become United Methodists after they followed the advice of Christian Science practitioners that prayer could cure their 16-month-old son of meningitis. After his death, they formed CHILD (Children's Healthcare Is a Legal Duty) to oppose legal recognition of Christian Science as an alternative form of medicine. My ENI story (August 14, 1996) reported a victory they had just won, a ruling by Federal District Judge Richard Kyle of St. Paul, Minnesota, that Medicare and Medicaid payments to Christian Science nursing homes violated the constitutional ban on establishment of religion.

I do not know exactly how Christian Scientists develop their theories of healing, but it seems rather clear they operate with a bedrock misunderstanding of what prayer is, and that they could hardly carry the theories through with consistency. The summary judgment that Christian Science is neither Christian nor scientific has become an aged cliché, but nonetheless seems basically correct. To start with, all Christians know that if your body is left nailed to a cross, you are going to die, however close your communication with God. Life cannot be reduced to the physical realities, but these realities can hardly be ignored. Christian Scientists favor feeding the hungry, I gather, and do not try to cure malnutrition by prayer alone. They are aware that we do have physical bodies and that these bodies do require physical food and water, and of the right quality. It should be equally evident that when you have a tumor interfering with the operation of your colon, the tumor needs to be cut out. Christian Scientists also realize well enough that alcohol and other drugs can have a detrimental influence on the body, and if that is the case, how could they rule out the possibility some drugs might produce beneficial results?

Certain aspects of Christian Science seem only a different way of describing events. Christian Scientists may not use the word "death," but they recognize that their earthly lives come to an end, just like everyone else's. Other aspects seem to involve taking different actions, however, and in this sphere problems can develop, particularly when a Christian Scientist is making decisions for another person, such as a child in need of vaccinations, medicine or surgery. We would have to follow the lives of Christian Scientists closely over a lengthy period to see just how consistently all their theory is lived, but you have to wonder about the practicalities. I once had a dentist who told me that he had accumulated a number of Christian Scientists as patients, and he attributed his success partly to his restraint in talking about what was going on. When he thought medication of gums was called for, he just medicated them, chattering along about something other than medicine. I have never heard how Christian Scientists may theorize on tooth decay, and I have wondered how many of them succeeded in making it vanish solely by the techniques taught in their church. I have also doubted that many Christian Scientists with severe toothaches would stay long away from the aspirin bottle and the dentist. Actually, prayer means getting into the stream of God's action, so you act in accordance with it, not a substitute for action. If you have gums that need medication, you thank God when you can get a dentist to do it. You do not try to put God and the dentist in separate offices, and assume you have to make a choice of going to one or the other.

Editors at the *Monitor* were, of course, not the only ones who acted in puzzling ways. And I might mention that editors everywhere will change stories by deleting as well as by rewriting. To me, it is not so bad to have material cut out. It may be an annoyance, particularly when the editors have requested extra work for extra material they decide not to use. But the result is not normally a misstatement.

Sometimes deletions may mystify. In 1998 I covered a Holy Spirit Conference of charismatics who met in the Hunter College auditorium (CNS, June 9), and who had a program led by Ralph Martin and others from his organization, Renewal Ministries in Ann Arbor, Michigan. Among other gleanings, I gave the news: "Martin conveyed reports from India of 200,000 Hindus converted to Christ and of an evangelist working among tribal people in the northern part of the country who had seen four people raised from the dead." It seemed to me that a report of four people being raised from the dead would have drawn the interest of readers. But the editors somehow decided that this sentence was one they could remove to make the story more succinct.

Some problems of actual difficulty occurred in my earlier days with CNS when editors were operating with the rule that everything I wrote should be

SIDEBARS

attributed to some source. If I introduced a bit of explanatory background on my own, they would often reach for the name of somebody I had quoted on other points, and attach it to something the person may never have even thought about saying. Or the comment might be something with an undiplomatic slant to it that the person would have deliberately chosen to not say, even if the thought had occurred. But after a few awkward passages, and a few bits of counseling, we were able to get that editing tradition modified.

Overall, the worst editing experience I have endured came at *Christianity and Crisis,* a small circulation but high prestige journal of opinion founded by Reinhold Niebuhr, and now regrettably defunct. The editors called on me for a general piece on church involvement in day care that they had decided they wanted (November 1, 1982). So I went around interviewing a lot of people, and put together an article reporting what was going on. But also raising questions. It seemed a good many infants and other young children were left in the hands of strangers for a high percentage of their waking hours, and I thought more time at home might be preferable, quantity time as well as quality. A common line held that mothers had no choice, and I questioned that, too. While many hardship cases no doubt could be found, I suspected in most cases a choice was being made, and in not a few cases a questionable choice.

But raising questions of this kind proved unbearable to the editors of *Christianity and Crisis.* It appeared that I was offending against what would come to be called political correctness, though I do not recall hearing that phrase much if any at the time. I gathered that day care had been certified as one of the causes championed by the women's movement, and only one reaction could therefore be allowed: "How wonderful!" I had previously been asked to write an article on the Nestlé boycott for *Christianity and Crisis* (June 23, 1979), and sailed into it, too, with a questioning style. It seemed clear that infant formula was a godsend for mothers who needed it, but should never be promoted as though it were an advance over the Creator's own arrangement, and most especially should not be promoted in poor regions of the world where mothers were short of money as well as refrigeration and equipment for sterilizing bottles.

From doing that article, I got the impression child care authorities more or less agreed that breast feeding was better both emotionally and physically for both mother and child. So I would think any setup for day care that interfered with this need would be automatically suspect. The government was under great pressure to provide day care. But it seemed to me that if the government was going to pay somebody to take care of a child, the better plan would be to pay the child's mother, as was providentially arranged in the case of Moses (Exodus 2:1-10).

If a mother gave thought, would she not, a little further along, also want to be the one who taught her children their mother tongue, who would accompany them in their moments of discovering the world, and give them words they could use to name the objects outside and the feelings inside? For a mother, is it really more glorious to keep slogging up the career ladder in hopes of one day getting promoted to assistant general manager for widget sales in the eastern district?

In the case of Nestlé, a pointed, questioning analysis served splendidly in the view of *Christianity and Crisis* editors (not Nestlé's), but for day care became a no-no. The editors insisted on writing in material I thought should be left out, and taking out material I thought should be left in. And where they could not absolutely deny some factor I had identified, or could not explain exactly why they felt bothered by it, or felt threatened by possible reactions of those whose lives were intertwined with the day care movement, most especially if it might be their board members, they found ways to bury it inside some subordinate clause of a long and meandering sentence, which had been elaborated to hide the unwanted suggestions in the middle of a lengthy paragraph, with the hope maybe it would not register clearly enough for anybody to notice it, or at least would induce readers to pay it not much attention.

To be sure, I could and should have withdrawn the article. But I had taken hours from a good many people on the claim that I would publish something in this prestige journal, and in a few cases cross-examined them with some intensity. After all that, I did not have the guts to go back and tell them that nothing would come of it all. The final result was not absolutely impossible, and I found ways to rationalize. But the episode remains in my memory as the most painful point where my journalistic integrity was at stake and I chickened out. The lesson is: beware trying to write for a journal of opinion unless you have checked to make sure you have the same opinions as the editors.

If you have some curiosity about *Christianity and Crisis,* and the influence it exercised among many leadership types, particularly liberal Protestants, you might read Mark Hulsether's book, expanded from a dissertation, *Building a Protestant Left: Christianity and Crisis Magazine,* 1941-1993 (University of Tennessee Press, 1999). Some readers might be misled by the reference to the "Left" in the title. By the time Reinhold Niebuhr founded *Christianity and Crisis,* he was far beyond any Marxist leanings, and was operating as a liberal Democrat in the style of people like Hubert H. Humphrey. And among others associated with the magazine, the amount of "leftism" desired or expressed could vary a good bit. Professor Hulsether sympathized with the editorial lines taken in the journal's later years, and in fact seems to find them superior to those of Professor Niebuhr and associates earlier, when writing that came "almost exclusively from a white male Protestant standpoint" was "linked to limitations in its domestic social vision" (p. 49). But Professor Hulsether also had to recognize that in the final period *Christianity and Crisis* "really did dumb down" and try to expand circulation by "simplification and popularization" (p. 253). Actually, worse than the way he expressed it, there came a sort of perversely willed move against intellectual quality in the name of anti-elitism, a see-from-underneath kind of obsession, which was self-destructive for a journal whose only reason for being was to serve as a communications medium of the elite for the elite. Publishing writers on a quota basis just because they are non-white and non-male and non-Protestant does not help circulation much if they are writing nothing of interest to other non-whites and non-males and non-Protestants. As another criticism, some people would say that *Christianity and Crisis* did not show enough interest in religion. "Too much crisis and not enough Christianity" was a jest one might hear. But that depends partly on what you understand Christianity to be.

On a smaller scale than with the day care episode, I found the same political correctness stood in the way of good journalism at *Christianity and Crisis* some years later when I was asked to do an article on the Fund for Theological Education, an agency that gave scholarships to seminarians (April 8, 1991). It had been started in the 1950s at the initiative of Nathan Pusey, president of Harvard University, who decided that seminaries were not getting their share of the better students, and persuaded the Rockefellers to finance a trial year for brighter people who could be encouraged to explore seminary life and see where it led them. *Christianity and Crisis* wanted an article because the fund, while continuing some of the original program, had shifted to concentrate on helping black and Hispanic seminarians. But along with reporting on that development, I also raised the question of what had happened to Dr. Pusey's original goal. I talked with the board chairman of the fund, G. Wayne Glick, retired president of the Bangor (Maine) Seminary, and he said the academic quality of seminarians was "worse now than it was in the fifties."

That comment mainly had the Protestant seminaries in view, but I gather the condition is not limited to the Protestant world. In the Catholic Church, the sharp decline in young men volunteering to study for the priesthood is said to have brought a lowering of admission standards. I have even heard it alleged that a few bishops now seem to prefer candidates who are dumb and docile.

Christianity and Crisis would not allow Dr. Glick's judgment to be printed, however, because there were now more female and minority seminarians than in the 1950s, and they might take offense. I had not presented the statement as necessarily true or final, but only as the judgment of Dr. Glick, and I assumed it was pertinent to quote his opinion since he chaired the board of the agency I was assigned to write about, knew the scene as a former seminary president and kept himself involved with the seminary world in retirement. And his statement, of course, had no reference to the gender or ethnic issues. But when political correctness rules, no other consideration counts for anything. I could back up the chairman's statement with one from the fund's director, J. Oscar McCloud: "It is generally said and felt that seminaries are not getting the best students today." But the editors could not stand to print that either.

I was grateful one year, though, that I had no editor ready to take what I was ready to give. By logical analysis, I came to the conclusion that the next president of the National Council of Churches (NCC) would have to be Robert J. Marshall. He was a man of ability and president then of one of the NCC's largest member bodies, the Lutheran Church in America. There had never been a Lutheran president of the NCC, so the demands of ecumenicity made it seem advisable to give this denomination its turn. And Dr. Marshall was obviously the Lutheran of choice. Fortunately, I did not find any editor willing to put my conclusions into print. When the announcement of the next president came, it was not Dr. Marshall or any other Lutheran. And there still has never been a Lutheran president of the NCC. I got a salutary lesson: after events happen, analysis can perhaps find a rational pattern leading up to them, but that will not work for predicting the future.

A degree of consolation came in finding that Reinhold Niebuhr could also overlook this truth. In 1937, as Pope Pius XI approached the end of his life, Professor Niebuhr wrote an article for *The Nation* (January 30) speculating on who might become the next pope. Some people had suggested Eugenio Pacelli, the Vatican Secretary of State. But Professor Niebuhr undertook an elaborate historical analysis and found "a long tradition against elevating the secretary of state to the highest eminence." So he concluded, "Cardinal Pacelli is not likely to be the new pope."

Reading that, I wondered how many cardinals a Protestant such as Professor Niebuhr could have had contact with in the state of 1930s Protestant-Catholic relations. He had not yet achieved the status that came with his delivery of the Gifford Lectures, *The Nature and Destiny of Man* (Scribner's, Vol. I, 1941; Vol. II, 1943), and his later recognition by popular media. It was the cardinals who were going to choose the next pope, and I could not imagine Reinhold Niebuhr had gotten much opportunity to test their thinking. How many cardinals could he even have known? He quite likely made his prediction without talking to a single one.

Contrary to all the depth of historical analysis, Cardinal Pacelli did in fact get elevated to the highest eminence, and served as Pius XII. But D. B. Roberts still considered the Niebuhrian analysis interesting enough to reprint more than two decades later, when he edited a collection of the theologian's shorter writings under the title, *Applied Christianity* (Meridian, 1959, pp. 201-07).

As it oddly happens, I have had occasion to talk with a good many cardinals. I once interviewed the Cardinal of Manila, Jaime L. Sin, who was a jovial fellow and enjoyed making little jokes, though I do not remember any about "cardinal sins." Cardinal Stephen Sou Hwan Kim of Seoul expressed concern about the state of democracy in his country. I talked with Cardinal Godfried Danneels of Belgium about his roles as international president of the peace group, Pax Christi, and as head of his country's Military Ordinariat, which roles he found not in conflict, not even in tension. And I talked with Cardinal Cahal Brendan Daly of Armagh about peace prospects in Northern Ireland. I have been able to get impressions of some cardinals at press conferences—Carlo Maria Martini of Milan among them. Mario Paredes of the Northeast Hispanic Catholic Center has brought a stream of Hispanic prelates from other countries to New York, and through his facilitation I have interviewed cardinals from places such as Mexico City, Bogota, Santo Domingo, Santiago and Buenos Aires. In 1989, I got to interview the visiting cardinal from Hungary, Laszlo Paskai, and get direct information about moves then just beginning to restore the reputation of his predecessor, Jozsef Mindszenty. I have interviewed Cardinal Franjo Kuharic of Zagreb, who told me the difference for the church made by the end of communism: "There is no fear any more." And I talked at a reception with Cardinal Franciszek Macharski of Krakow, former diocese of John Paul II. I was in on a press luncheon for Cardinal Jean Marie Lustiger of Paris. Some cardinals are not always disposed to converse, however. Cardinal Jean Jerome Hamer, head of the Vatican Congregation for Religious and Secular Institutes, declined my request to talk about a controversy that arose over an October 1984 pro-abortion ad in *The New York Times,* and the demand of his congregation that members of Catholic religious orders who signed it must publicly retract. He first sent word he wanted me to submit written questions, and when I complied with that request, he gave me the semi-compliment of sending word that the questions were too sensitive for him to deal with (NC, August 16, 1985). But I have interviewed other Vatican cardinals—Josef Tomko of the Propagation of the Faith (Evangelization of Peoples), Alfonso Lopez Trujillo of the Council for the Family, former Secretary of State Agostino Casaroli and others. Occasionally, I have met cardinals-to-be in the years when they were able to talk more nearly as their natural selves. I interviewed Fiorenzo Angelini, head of the Vatican unit dealing with health issues, in 1989 on AIDS and in 1991, a few months before he became a cardinal, on drug and alcohol addictions. Cardinal Anthony J. Bevilacqua of Philadelphia even took me into his residence and fixed a lunch for me while he was still a monsignor in Brooklyn and dealing with immigrants, my interest the day I met with him. When I talked with Boston's Cardinal Bernard F. Law at the Brooklyn cathedral, he was not ready to entertain any of my queries until he cleared up one matter puzzling him: "Where are you from?" He had himself started out as a priest of the Diocese of Jackson, Mississippi, and my accent reminded him not a lot but a little of home. It was not Brooklyn for sure. A couple of cardinals, since deceased, early in my reporting days showed what diversity existed within the college. Angelo Rossi, a Brazilian who preceded Cardinal Tomko at Propagation of the Faith, exemplified the formal Latin American style of a past generation. Sergio Pignedoli, head of the Secretariat for Non-Christians, epitomized the informal and vivacious Italian who might take your arm on a first meeting and start a free-flowing conversation on whatever came to mind.

None of them ever hinted at a choice for the next pope. But Cardinal Juan Landazuri-Ricketts of Lima did make a point of telling me emphatically, "I know how to elect a pope." He was among a tiny group who participated in the conclave that chose Paul VI in 1963, lived to help elect John Paul I and John Paul II in 1978 and at the time of our conversation were still young enough to help pick a fourth if the occasion called.

But with all that, I would consider it preposterous to attempt a prediction of who it is the cardinals might choose as the next pope. Very likely, they themselves do not know how their thinking will run when they get into conclave, look around and face the reality that "we're what we've got to choose from."

Now, you are wondering whether all the people I have written about got a glow from the way my stories turned out. Not bloody likely. Actually, that is not my goal. I am trying to serve my readers, and give them material I think might interest them, not please the people I am writing about. Sure, it would be nice if everybody in the world could be happy about everything that happens. But if people I am covering get upset at reading the results, their temperature is not my first concern. And the fevers do rise occasionally. For all the efforts of some editors to avoid controversy, others have let enough go by to generate a few disturbances.

Sometimes it is more the editing that gives the headaches. In journalism you learn that the important thing is not whether you win or lose, or how you play the game, but who gets credit in the write up. When I talked with Janet Carroll, a Maryknoll nun, about a new China Bureau she was directing, many people were giving support, but the Maryknoll Fathers and the California Jesuits seemed most prominent, so I spotlighted them in my story (CNS, November 28, 1989). And down in the latter part, I mentioned some of the actors I considered secondary. I do not suppose anybody joining in such an

SIDEBARS

effort considers himself secondary. But worse than that, the CNS editors decided my story was running unduly long, and cut off several of the latter paragraphs, leaving some creditable people totally uncredited. Sister Carroll indicated that from her political standpoint this was not the most convenient way for things to have turned out.

But the editor who cut the concluding sentences did better than some editors who have wanted shorter. Regarding news articles, traditional journalism has said that a story should begin by succinctly stating the main development to be reported, and then work in supplementary facts in descending order of importance. Then a newspaper editor short of space can easily drop off from the bottom however many lines do not fit, and will not have to take time to rewrite the entire article in some condensed form. And I generally try to write news stories that way. But in not a few cases an editor dealing with one of my articles has decided it was all interesting and pertinent, and he wanted it all, though in a smaller space. So to understand his procedure you could imagine someone who wants to put a cake in a box that is too small, wants to take the whole cake and not just cut off however much will fit, and so decides to squash it together till it will all go in. The cake then may not look so good.

But often the discontent arises from my own writing, and not from the editing. At a forum on racism held at Fordham University's Lincoln Center campus, a black professor, Clement London, got up and rather boldly confronted the president, Joseph A. O'Hare, with the charge that "insensitivity" to black concerns existed right there at Fordham, and specifically in the Education Department, where the professor was employed. Father O'Hare, a Jesuit who previously edited his society's magazine, *America,* had only recently come to his post, and had not very much to say in response, but such as it was I put in my story as answer to the allegation (NC, April 22, 1985). Such as it was was far from enough, and I was derelict in failing to research and report the truth that the allegations were unfounded, Father O'Hare let me know.

For another example: Ronald S. Michels, a Maryknoll priest, was disturbed over my selectivity in reporting on an interview with him (CNS, October 2, 1990). He was the Maryknoll superior for Central America, and I got him to give some assessment of the current status of Miguel F. D'Escoto, the Maryknoller who had upset Pope John Paul II and Cardinal Miguel Obando Bravo of Managua by serving as foreign minister of the Sandinista government of Nicaragua. An electoral defeat of the Sandinistas bringing that job to an end, what next for Father D'Escoto? Well, this was a bit of a headache, Father Michels revealed. It seemed no bishop wanted his diocese graced with the service of this famous priest. I also talked with Father Michels about other matters, but when I came to write the story, the case of Father D'Escoto seemed the most interesting. So that was the lead and headline and a good part, though not all, of the story.

Some people who are interviewed think a fair article about the conversation must be more or less a summary, giving all the main points covered and in some proportion to the time spent on them. Or a preacher will think a proper news report on his sermon is one that is a sort of condensation: "The Reverend Mr. Whoever began by saying how humbly privileged he felt to have this privilege of speaking to this great congregation of God's good people, and in his first point called on everybody to defend our precious faith, and secondly insisted that every true believer must perform the works of mercy, including the extermination of heretics, but in his third point expressed confidence everything would eventually work out and, with tears in his eyes, concluded by reciting some deeply moving lines from Edgar A. Guest."

I doubt that you could find many reporters who think of their task in such fashion. But if one of them should single out that subordinate point about extermination of heretics for the lead, as I can imagine might very well happen, and the preacher should feel some heat from reader reaction, he would consider himself yet again the victim of unbalanced reporting, sensationalizing, media bias, taking out of context and all those other manifestations of media malice.

To this I should add that sensationalizing really is a vice that some reporters do cultivate and some editors do encourage. Cardinal O'Connor for a while was giving a little time after his Sunday morning mass for a standup press conference where reporters would gather round and ask whatever lay upon their minds that week. But he finally decided–correctly, as I saw it–that the practice was counterproductive. Some reporters sent by the tabloids came with little awareness of what the church was doing, and had no apparent purpose but to find something that would make a tabloid headline. On one unfortunate occasion the cardinal fed into this by preaching and commenting at unnecessary length and with superfluous detail on the devil, exorcism and rock music (CNS, March 6, 1990). But however soberly he might subside on other occasions, a reporter told by his editor to find a tabloid headline would discover some way to turn whatever he got into a tabloid headline.

Still, in the best of journalism, if a reporter finds one incidental, off-the-cuff remark the most interesting point in an hour-long address, that remark will likely be featured, while many substantive points prepared with deep drilling and heavy lifting pass unreported. Life with the journalists is unfair as anywhere else. So we can understand that Father Michels wrote a letter voicing his upsettedness when the article about his interview gave primary attention to a rather disagreeable hangnail issue that he considered more or less peripheral to his overall work in Central America.

I never got a chance to interview Father D'Escoto himself, though CNS was of course always ready to report his side of his story. I once was able to speak to him briefly at a public appearance he made in New York and ask about an interview. But I got the reaction not uncommon in dealing with prominent personalities: the notable cordially agrees and says, "Call my office to set a time"; I call an aide, who says, "I'll see what I can do"; I hear nothing; when I call back, I am told, "So sorry, we were not able to work it in."

To give you another glimpse of editing: In 1978, I wrote an article for the North American Newspaper Alliance (NANA) that began with the news, "Adrian Wijemanne, an Anglican layman from Sri Lanka, has been in the United States lately talking to church leaders about a new place to put some of their investment capital" (January 19). And I went on to explain that he had recently been named manager of a new agency, the Ecumenical Development Cooperative Society, set up by the World Council of Churches and the Netherlands Council of Churches to serve as a mini-World Bank, a source of development loans for poor areas. The idea was to get the relatively affluent churches to invest a little of their pension or other reserves through this agency, and thereby help "the poorest of the poor" improve their condition while the investors got some modest return. But at NANA, a bored editor, feeling an impulse to turn out more attention-getting material, rewrote my lead: "U.S. churches don't know what to do with all their money these days, but Adrian Wijemanne, an Anglican layman from Sri Lanka, has some ideas." If some people become wary of the world of journalism, they have a few legitimate reasons. William P. Thompson, chief staff executive of the United Presbyterian Church at the time, wanted to get his denomination interested in putting money into the new agency, and did not find my (edited) article helpful. Informing me courteously in advance, he used it as an example of problem areas when he gave a talk to a journalistic group. I was able to explain to him how the over-jazzy lead came about, but that did not make it any less of a difficulty from his standpoint. In a team sport, when one player is off sides, the whole team gets penalized. But Mr. Thompson also took the trouble to be complimentary when he found something worthy, and on another occasion sent me a note commending my "responsible and accurate reporting" of "controversial issues."

Although I never got any complaints from Cardinal O'Connor about my reporting on him, his vicar general, Joseph T. O'Keefe, later Bishop of Syracuse, did write my editors at the National Catholic News Service once to voice some disapprobation. While the New York Archdiocese was opposing a homosexual rights bill before the City Council, a group of liberal priests and nuns held a press conference to advocate passage, and I wrote a story on their action (NC, March 4, 1986). I identified individual participants as they identified themselves to me. But Bishop O'Keefe had additional information that he thought the story should have included to discredit them, showing that certain ones were not in good standing and others had sundry black marks against their names.

Were there world enough and time, we might employ detective agencies to do background checks on all the people we quote. But journalism is usually done in a hurry. How much material of that kind should go in a story is in any case a matter of debate, assuming you have it. Must every reference to Richard M. Nixon drag behind it a recitation of his Watergate record and other dirty tricks, and where would you stop if you did not care to run all the way back to Helen Gahagan Douglas and H. Jerry Voorhis?

One of the nuns at the press conference was Jeannine Gramick of the School Sisters of Notre Dame, who put out a statement in the name of an unofficial group called the National Coalition of American Nuns: "We are scandalized by the present public stand of John Cardinal O'Connor of the Archdiocese of New York and Bishop Francis Mugavero of the Diocese of Brooklyn, whose opposition to this piece of civil rights legislation erodes the credibility of institutionalized Catholicism, which should be marked by the compassion of Jesus." And this advocate of the compassion of Jesus said the "ignorance" exhibited by these leaders in her church embarrassed "any moderately intelligent Catholic."

According to the line taken publicly at the press conference, upholding the rights of homosexuals did not necessarily imply approval of homosexual activity. But when I talked with Sister Gramick, it seemed clear enough that she did reject the teaching of the Catholic Church on this point.

In something called New Ways Ministry, she was associated with C. Robert Nugent, a priest of the Salvatorian order. He had a lot of trouble with church authorities over his work with homosexuals, implicitly supportive of them, implicitly subversive of church teaching, and in 1987 he was planning to go public with a challenge to one archbishop through church courts. That was to appeal the decision of Theodore E. McCarrick, Archbishop of Newark, not to renew his faculties, which meant he would not be able to continue the masses and other activities that had occasionally been part of his life in the archdiocese. Father Nugent talked with me about all this, and I wrote a story for NC. But before writing, I called his Salvatorian superior in Milwaukee, Barry Griffin, and included in my story his statement that the order was taking no position on the appeal. Presumably, Father Griffin decided on reflection that he would just as soon miss out on the publicity, and before NC could run the story, I got a message on my answering machine from Father Nugent, telling me that after talking with his superior he had come to see wisdom in dropping the appeal.

Despite the opposition on many fronts, however, Sister Gramick and Father Nugent were able to keep their work going for what to me seemed like a surprisingly long time before getting a final crackdown. It was not till 1999, after extensive and prolonged investigations and interrogations, that the Vatican Congregation for the Doctrine of the Faith declared that Sister Gramick and Father Nugent were "permanently prohibited from any pastoral work involving homosexual persons." Concerning the rights of homosexuals, the statement said they had "the right to receive the authentic teaching of the church from those who minister to them."

A different kind of internal dispute among Catholics occurred in regard to a couple of pastorals their American bishops issued. Some of the more conservative types registered alarm in 1983 when the bishops issued a pastoral letter taking a dim view of threats to obliterate civilian masses with nuclear bombs. The following year, when the bishops set out to write a pastoral on economics, fears that American capitalism might next undergo moral critique got the conservatives into gear. In the spirit of American competition, a group of the richer and more conservative lay Catholics organized to write their own pastoral. Though not being pastors, they were not authorized to issue a pastoral, and so called their document a lay letter, and their group the Lay Commission on Catholic Social Teaching and the U.S. Economy.

The bishops' committee drafting the pastoral, headed by Rembert G. Weakland of Milwaukee, held hearings to get the views of all parties, including some who were not Catholic. I covered one hearing when Archbishop Weakland and some of his committee members came to New York to get suggestions from the National Council of Churches and the Jewish community (NC, July 30, 1984). The Lay Committee followed suit and held hearings, too, though I wondered about the seriousness of their imitative process when key people failed to attend the ones I covered (NC, July 12 and 31, 1984). There were two hearings in New York. But President Nixon's Treasury Secretary, William E. Simon, the muscle of the group, and Michael Novak, the talent, both failed to appear.

I found people on the committee and staff associated with them walking on eggshells. As conservatives, part of their act was to come off more loyal to the church than other Catholics, and yet the whole point of their enterprise was to fight the bishops. Could they think organizing laymen to fight the bishops expressed integral Catholicism?

Since I attended the hearings as a representative of the National Catholic News Service, they would likely assume I represented the bishops, though that was not my assumption or the assumption of my editors. So people associated with the Lay Committee could feel reason to be formally polite as the dickens, but much on edge.

Thus it was with the woman serving as chief staff operative when I interviewed her at the tired end of a day of hearings on welfare. She was very nice and very patient in answering my questions. Until I asked why, since such a lot had been said during the day about the problem created by the presence of so many black women on the welfare rolls, no black woman on welfare had been brought in to offer her perspective. Then the staffer lost it.

All that she had told me to that point was now off the record and I was not to use any of it, she said. I replied that, actually, putting material off the record retroactively was not the way we operated. An understanding on such a point should be reached in advance. In that case, I would have to submit whatever I wrote to her for checking before I sent it to my editors, she said. Then I had to inform her that, well, actually, we did not do it that way either.

But in the end, to demonstrate that I was really a good fellow at heart, I agreed to call her at home later that evening and go over my notes from the interview, though without any promises about procedures thereafter. When I called her, she denied making one of her more unguarded remarks. She certainly did not say any such thing, she insisted. And I can well believe she did not believe she had. I suspect we would all be shocked to hear a recording of statements we have made reacting to pressure and emotion, and without a tape could not believe them at all.

I left the woman's unguarded remark out of the story. It was not all that important, and journalistically the more useful contribution is to report the position people are stating and staying with. What we say in the throes of passion or just by inadvertent carelessness no doubt reveals much about us, but probably we could all be hung if everything we said were printed in the newspapers.

During this period, I interviewed a Catholic bishop who was annoyed with the Lay Committee, and who along the way accused them of organizing as a faction outside the church. "Outside the church?" I asked, looking up before writing down. "No, inside the church," said the bishop, grateful for a chance to rephrase and refrain from excommunicating them. "Thank you."

When the bishops put out a preliminary draft of the economics pastoral, I got an interview with Mr. Simon for reaction, and with it came as lagniappe the opportunity to see the tycoon style in operation (NC, November 26, 1984). For Mr. Simon, the Lay Committee was only one of numerous items on a full agenda that included making millions in business every once in a while, and keeping abreast of the political world. His basic message to me was a dismissal of the bishops' document as "a Santa Claus wish list," and he said they were proposing solutions that had already been tried, and failed to work. "Government has a role, but it is not the expanded role the bishops recommend." His response to the bishops of his church, expressed not just to me but elsewhere, was really a bit condescending. In one speech he allowed they were "well-intentioned," but said their pastoral was "merely a bid to recycle the worn-out government programs of the Great Society" and "bears no resemblance to economic reality."

In the midst of giving me his critique, however, he was doing a dozen or so other things—looking at papers, talking with assistants, taking telephone calls. Once, he jumped up and went out of the room, and left me to get his thoughts from one of his aides, Michael Joyce, as he might leave the details of writing a contract to his lawyer. Which may have been all the more logical because Mr. Simon conceded to me later on that he had not yet finished reading what the bishops had written, which was rather extensive and substantive. He cut to the bottom line, saw that the bishops wanted the government to do more, and knew immediately that he did not cotton to it.

I got to observe a similar working style used by a man with a different political outlook when I interviewed John V. Lindsay, mayor of New York, for a *Christian Century* article (March 31, 1971). At the time, some speculators were suggesting he might become a presidential candidate, and later turned out to be correct about that, though he got only as far as nomination candidacy, and not to party nomination. With his opinions maybe becoming matters of national significance, I asked for an interview to get his thoughts on the role of churches in dealing with issues of public policy. I had learned that he was a parishioner at St. James Episcopal Church on Manhattan's East Side, and assumed he would likely have some views.

His press officer arranged for me to sit beside Mr. Lindsay for a rather lengthy car ride from an appearance far out in one of the outer boroughs back to City Hall. It worked well enough, but as we rode along, Mr. Lindsay regularly interspersed his comments on the churches with comments to a staff aide in the front seat about upcoming events, instructions to the driver, calls on the car phone, checking every few minutes on somebody who had to be met at the airport, and study of papers he pulled from his inside coat pocket. I figured I had about sixty per cent of his attention, but he was still able to keep his train of thought, and say what he wanted to tell my readers. And I had him trapped in a spot where he could not jump up and leave me.

What he thought in essence was that the churches ought to address public issues. "They should be totally engaged in an effort to bring about changes in the system. They should be pursuing specific legislation, lobbying for it, talking about it publicly, using the pulpit as a forum for debate on the question, explaining its relation to questions of morality. I'm for all that." When he went to church and heard a sermon on the same type of issues he was dealing with as mayor, did he not feel the clergyman was getting outside his area of competence? "No, I like to hear him discuss it," the mayor said. "I usually learn something."

Reviewing in retrospect, I can see that on occasion my reporting would have drawn even more flak than has been the case, had not cautious editors done a little toning down. In 1981, on August 31, the board of an ecumenical agency called Church Women United (CWU) met by conference call and voted over some opposition that their chief staff executive, Nan Cox, as of that very day was no longer their chief staff executive, or on their staff at all. Such is the sort of alteration that will attract a reporter's interest, but some of the CWU leaders seemed not only to wish such an untoward event might pass unnoticed, but to suggest that reporters had some moral obligation to ignore it. When I published a story anyway (*United Methodist Reporter,* September 25), it drew protesting letters to the editor that among other complaints spoke of "yellow journalism." But my hide would probably have been more ferociously flayed had the editors not deleted my dismissal of the organization's press release as laughable.

In it, the CWU President, Thelma C. Adair, announced that Dorothy C. Wagner had been appointed interim general director. The press release left readers to wonder for a right good while why an interim general director might be needed, and went on for several paragraphs about Miss Wagner's background. And then, in the very last sentence, revealed that Nan Cox "completed her services" on August 31.

Most any journalist would say there was obviously a story to be written, and a story that ought to be told so people would get some information about what was happening. The board, formally called the executive council, was scheduled to meet in October, and a celebration of the organization's 40th anniversary was set for December at the Cathedral of St. John the Divine in New York. What was so urgent as to require an immediate ouster of the CEO by conference call?

I was never able to uncover the motivation. But fortunately one board member, Frances Kennedy, wife of Union Seminary Professor William Kennedy, agreed that the story was legitimate and the general public should get some report. She did not give me any salacious details, but confirmed the basic facts of the dismissal. Some others, however, did not want even the bare external facts reported. "These things are not relevant to the people outside," Miss Wagner told me. President Adair was not in a mood to offer explanations. The attitude of the leadership went something like, "If you want to do a story, why don't you write about the great literacy program we're supporting out in Mozambique?"

Despite the experience of subsequent years, I have never found ways of preventing all reader unhappiness. In 1997, I got a little knocking about because of a story on a controversy over the direction some Catholic nuns had been taking (CNS, October 22). My own first sharp awareness that we were sometimes dealing with a new breed had come very early in my journalistic career, when a nun set up an interview with a priest at her convent. After talking with the priest about whatever cause it was he wished to promote, I got permission to use the restroom, and was surprised to find it was filthy. My image of nuns pictured them as practitioners of the theory that cleanliness is right up there next to godliness, and in my other (quite limited) opportunities to observe, that has seemed to be more or less the case. But the convent that showed me another style was inhabited by some nuns who were too busy bringing about the revolution to waste time on housecleaning. And in a little while, I heard that the nun who set up my interview had moved along with whatever movements she was into, and moved out of her order.

For the most part, however, my reporting assignments did not include the debates over which direction nuns should take as they went about their updating after Vatican II. Then came the announcement of a program where Ann Carey would expound on the criticism of "radical reformers" she had made in a book, *Sisters in Crisis: The Tragic Unraveling of Women's Religious Communities* (Our Sunday Visitor press, 1997). About 100 nuns from various orders, joined by a handful of men, came out to get her thoughts and those of a couple of other speakers, who took a more positive view of the changing styles.

At the question period, it became clear that the listeners by and large rejected the Carey critique, and I pointed that out in the lead to my story. But as I was leaving the event, I happened to ride down in an elevator with a couple of nuns who let me know they found the criticisms true to their experience, descriptive of a situation they had encountered in their own order, a Franciscan group in the Archdiocese of New York. One of them, Lucy Sabatini, said she was part of a minority who thought they should give more emphasis to the distinctively religious roles of their life. So I put that in at the end of my story to show a smattering of diversity.

Which more than a little upset Jean Pruitt, a Maryknoll nun who sent a letter to the New York archdiocesan paper, *Catholic New York* (November 27, 1997), charging that I had given Mrs. Carey's criticism too much space, and "let the minority set the agenda for his reporting." That kind of complaint I can recognize as more or less normal. But I was surprised by another part of her indictment: that "he did most of his reporting by interviewing the nuns wearing traditional habits" when "it was the sisters in contemporary dress who spoke" about the study of Vatican documents "leading them to leave their comfortable chapels, classrooms and offices to seek out the images of God in shelters for battered women, in the streets for homeless families, the soup kitchens, the prisons and slums." I do not know about those "comfortable" chapels that Vatican documents inspired these nuns to leave, or even the offices. But for my part, I can hardly imagine that being put in a classroom with a couple dozen fourth graders would be anybody's idea of comfort. Give me the prisons; there at least you stand some chance of maintaining control over your fate.

But back to my reporting on that program: actually, I did it mostly on the basis of what was said publicly in the meeting, not any interviewing, and only by coincidence talked with the two dissenters, who were wearing updated habits, not traditional. In any case, I would have expected the onward-moving nuns to be the ones who would argue it was of little importance whether a nun wore a habit or not. Pope John Paul II had indicated that he thought wearing a habit, suitably updated, was a good idea, and I had sometimes wondered a little whether maybe a few, maybe quite a few, nuns wanted to demonstrate a defiant attitude by making it clear they would not let themselves be influenced by what some pope said. But I expected the strategy of the non-habited would be to play down the issue, and try to tell people that dress was not of the essence, and did not determine what kind of nun you were. Now, here was this most up-to-date Maryknoller telling the whole wide world—at least, that percentage of it reading the letters columns of *Catholic New York*—that I was wrong. Dress does tell you who are the OK nuns and who are the non-OK, her letter (maybe) disclosed.

Now on another hand: Although I find editors much too often changing my articles to fit their understanding of proper style or correct viewpoint, I do not find them often enough catching real mistakes. I have on occasion ordained people who were lay, and left in the lay estate those who were clergy. I misspell. And other such. Editors sometimes catch my real mistakes, but not as frequently as I would like. In 1997, I was asked to do a story for Ecumenical News International (ENI) on moves in the U.S. Episcopal Church to add Florence Nightingale to the list of model Christians authorized for commemoration in the church calendar, something like a Catholic calendar of saints. The General Convention of the church had approved a step in the process, but somehow I jumped to the conclusion that the process had been concluded.

SIDEBARS

And I stayed with that misapprehension through some reading about the matter. And my wrongheadedness remained invincible as I talked with Ted Karpf, an Episcopal priest who was leading the campaign as director of the National Episcopal AIDS Coalition. He said Miss Nightingale, the founder of modern nursing, was considered a good model for AIDS patients because she suffered from a debilitating illness herself for many years and because "nurses have been the backbone of AIDS care." Astonishingly, all my reading and talking, exploring this aspect and that, never shook my initial misconception. So my story went out saying Florence Nightingale had been added to the calendar, and then it had to be followed forthwith by another saying she might be later (both dated August 4).

To illustrate my vulnerability to the common garden variety error of fact: I was writing an article related to the United Nations, back when I had even less familiarity with it than today, and inexcusably gave UNESCO's full name as the Economic and Social Council, which is ECOSOC, instead of properly writing UN Educational, Scientific and Cultural Organization. The article, for *Response* magazine (October 1985), was based on an interview with Bradford Morse, administrator of the UN Development Program. And he wrote me a letter that gently said it was a matter of nitpicking perhaps, but actually UNESCO was not the Economic and Social Council. Another reader, more exasperated, wrote that she was greatly interested in the UN and gratified to see an article on it, but could not bear to continue reading after she hit my disheartening error.

There is a kind of argument from the small to the great, contending that if you are unreliable on the minor points, you cannot be trusted on the larger. If you do not know enough to tell people what UNESCO stands for, nobody should put any confidence in what you say about the UN and its accomplishments or deficiencies overall.

I do not think that argument is necessarily valid. A writer could make mistakes on several matters of detail, and still get the overall picture right. But the reality is, when we find mistakes on simple matters of fact, our confidence in the author lessens. So writers had better take time for adequate fact checking if they want to have people paying any attention to what they publish. As a further consideration, people who object to the general thrust of an article will often develop a desire to undercut the credibility of the writer, and in pursuit of this goal will search for any little error they can use. Accuracy, even on the smallest points, is always better.

In 1984, I covered the installation of Father O'Hare as president of Fordham University, and his presentation on the same occasion of an honorary Doctor of Laws degree to Cardinal O'Connor, who had arrived in New York earlier that year and was not yet a cardinal (NC, October 1). Less than a month later, I covered another Fordham event where Justice Sandra Day O'Connor spoke, and Father O'Hare gave her an honorary Doctor of Laws degree (NC, October 25). Since Justice O'Connor's husband is John J. O'Connor, I might tell you I had witnessed Father O'Hare giving honorary degrees to Cardinal and Mrs. John J. O'Connor. But journalists get in trouble when they draw connections too quickly. For one thing, a more thorough checking would turn up the detail that Cardinal O'Connor's name is John Joseph and the justice's husband is John Jay III.

A different kind of reporting challenge comes where writing a good story requires making a speaker look better organized than he is. However chaotic a talk may be, editors will insist my story about it must cohere. A speaker may wander from disconnected point to irrelevancy, follow some inner train of consciousness known only to himself, and eventually stop without drawing any discernible conclusions. But if I am assigned to report, I must puzzle through my notes, find something that can be considered more or less the main or most significant point, identify a logic somewhere and try to show how at least a few of his remarks relate. We could call the procedure here one of the deeper forms of deception. If some speakers justly complain that my stories have not shown them in their true splendor, others should give me thanks for helping them sound more together than they really were.

Here I would feel safer if I avoided giving examples. But Joseph M. Sullivan, an auxiliary bishop of Brooklyn, is a genial fellow who probably would not protest too strenuously if it were suggested that in some respects he might tend toward the incompletely coordinated category of which we now discourse. As he points out a social need the church should address, suddenly it occurs to him to talk a while about something the church did in the nineteenth century, and then he is to the West Coast or to Canada, and to a time earlier in his career, but then just the other day he was at a meeting in St. Louis, and somebody there told him of how one institution had proceeded, and if you look at what the bishops had said in some of their statements, considering that passage in the Bible, and the latest government regulations, and we have to think about that bill pending in Congress. His free association is free indeed. It is all presented with good vibes, and carries a certain interest, and the people who hear Bishop Sullivan probably go away feeling they have had a time of uplift. But I have some difficulty figuring how to put together a few paragraphs that will tell readers in Paducah just what was said.

Another form of editorial interaction has occurred as I did anonymous writing on the side for editors commissioning promotional material. Much of this was done for the United Methodist Board of Global Ministries, which is located in New York and publishes a great many information and fundraising pieces. Since my name does not go on these items, I can stay more relaxed about the editorial mutilation process. I recognize that the piece has to present the agency's point of view and serve the agency's purposes. I am there simply to serve a technical function—and make a little money to help pay my bills. So as long as I do not become a party to outright fraud, I can go along with editing, however heavy-handedly it falls.

One thing I learned from this kind of work was that church bureaucrats, in the case of more than just a few, do not slip into using clichés. On the contrary, the cliché is the substance of their life. Their work is organized around certain words and phrases, and their future depends, or is felt to depend, on securing a future for them. So there can be no slippage. The naïve—taking myself as an example—might suppose that church executives fall accidentally into a habit of repeating certain terms so often they become deadeningly trite. And then one might suppose that the offer of a fresh approach with different terminology would be welcome. One ought not so suppose. The officials who turn program language into clichés love those words, hold them to their bosoms and yearn to see them repeatedly present on every piece of literature they control. Partly this comes from battles over budgeting. If certain kinds of work have been identified as funding priorities, every agency executive will want to emphasize the words that suggest alignment with those priorities. If "empowerment" is the name of the budget game, then all literature coming out of your department must drop in the word "empowerment" every couple of lines.

A related difficulty emerged when people in the United Methodist Board of Global Ministries responsible for publishing the annual report articles in *New World Outlook* got the idea it might be interesting to have them written by independent, outside journalists, rather than by in-house staff as previously. This was proposed for reports on 1975, got okayed by the chief of the unit concerned, Beverly Jean Chain, and led to results published in the April issue of 1976. Each division of the board got a separate article, and I was assigned to write on the World Division and the Education and Cultivation Division. But heads of the divisions found it too much of an ordeal. For positioning in budget battles, they needed more control over how their work was presented. So later years heard no talk of bringing in the independent writers.

It occurs to me now that in these recountings of my adventures in the church world, I am probably failing to give the conservative evangelicals as much attention as might seem advisable, given their numbers and sometimes-assertive role in American society. They lack a capacity to assert so much in New York, but in any case they should have their chapter.

CONSERVATIVE EVANGELICALS

CHAPTER FOUR

William F. Brown explained to me that a stadium did not automatically fill up just because somebody announced his boss, William F. Graham Jr., was going to preach there. I found Mr. Brown was the man responsible for nuts and bolts when I covered Billy Graham's 1970 "crusade" at Shea Stadium, and a man willing to talk with some frankness about what that responsibility entailed. Local sponsoring committees too often fell prey to overconfidence, Mr. Brown told me. These people were Graham fans, and imagined the multitudes would appear spontaneously if somebody put an ad in the newspapers. But in reality, behind the arrival of those crowds that you found surrounding you if you attended one of the services, or might later see on television, lay months of planning, preparation and promotion. All the churches in a 50-mile area got letters. And whenever any gave a positive response, arrangements were made for the churches to enlist busloads of people, including, preferably, many prospects for evangelization.

An earlier, lengthier series of meetings Mr. Graham held at the old Madison Square Garden, in the summer of 1957, had become something of a legend of triumph among his followers. But checking back, Mr. Brown found the Garden had not filled up every night, even though groups came not only from throughout the New York region but also from distant states to show support.

This, I think, created a general illusion for Grahamites as well as a practical hurdle for Mr. Brown. The evangelical world longed to think Mr. Graham's message was exerting a transformative influence on New York, and on the New Yorkers who were exerting so much national influence from their base here.

But a presence geographically in New York did not necessarily mean a "crusade" affected New York in that sense, and of course even less with so much of the attendance bused in.

I had covered a briefer series of services Mr. Graham led at the new Madison Square Garden in 1969, and found he was able to draw a full house there for ten nights (*Christian Century,* August 6). No doubt some local churches got a boost, but the effect on New York was not observable. I could not see the wave of regeneration that Graham enthusiasts were always reporting wherever he went.

Mr. Brown also told me that overconfidence became an enemy in raising the necessary budget for the services, as committee members imagined just sending out letters would suffice, and they need not follow through with the tougher task of direct personal asking. And he had problems of other types. He visited Shea Stadium two or three times before signing the contract to rent it, he said. Then, when Mr. Graham came to look it over and hold a press conference there, he was concerned and Mr. Brown was shocked to hear what had not been heard before, airplanes from LaGuardia Airport flying over about one a minute. But Billy Graham being Billy Graham, he had friends at levels high enough to divert flight patterns for the hours he would be preaching.

It has been part of the Graham strategy to cultivate people of high standing in the rankings of this world, up to and always including presidents of the United States. Harry S Truman was put off by the young Mr. Graham's callow self-promotion, but with savvy quickly acquired, he has made all the presidents from Dwight D. Eisenhower on his friends.

When Marshall Frady became the first or one of the first serious biographers to do a book on Mr. Graham (Little, Brown, 1979), I reviewed it for *Worldview,* a monthly published by the Council on Religion and International Affairs (September 1979). At that point, one of the more impressive parts of the Graham record was his success in profiting from a close bonding with Richard M. Nixon when Mr. Nixon was ascendant, and then smoothly disengaging from Mr. Nixon in descent. Drawing on Mr. Frady and others, I collected a series of year-by-year, how-well-I-know-him quotations that showed Mr. Graham reaching a height in Mr. Nixon's 1972 triumphant reelection campaign:

"I know the president as well as anyone outside his immediate family. I have known him since 1950, and I have great confidence in his personal honesty. I voted for him because I know what he's made of" (Frady, pp. 454-55).

Then after Watergate, and the revelation through the tapes of the vulgarity of Mr. Nixon's mind and tongue, it came down to: "I wasn't really one of his confidants, either to have a game of golf or to sit down and have a serious discussion. I didn't really move at the level with Nixon that the press thought I did" (p. 482).

In private, there appears to have been a good deal of what the secular world calls sucking up. One of the Nixon tapes released in 1996 revealed Mr. Graham calling to flatter the president the next day after his dishonest April 30, 1973, televised speech, in which Mr. Nixon said the facts of Watergate were now out, that he knew nothing about what had happened but took responsibility, that there could be no whitewash, that he was accepting the resignations of his key aides, H. R. Haldeman and John D. Ehrlichman, and that he "must now turn my full attention once again to the larger duties of this office." Mr. Graham called up to tell the only president in American history who had to resign and accept a pardon for abusing the powers of his office, "Your sincerity, your humility, your asking for prayer–all that had a tremendous impact." The unindicted co-conspirator: "You really think so, Billy?" The Bible-waving evangelist: "I really mean it" (*New York Times,* November 24).

Though Mr. Graham deftly distanced himself from Mr. Nixon in the immediate aftermath of Watergate, he reestablished his ties as the former president reestablished himself in the succeeding years, and so was in place to represent the religious community at the funeral in 1994.

Mr. Graham had some special affinities with this president, and both got their initial boost up the career ladder about the same time from powerful conservatives in the same part of the country, southern California. But the evangelist-president relationship remained workable through all administrations, largely because the evangelist was determined to make it work. Each party got enhanced by association with the other, and the melding of constituencies. If Mr. Graham succumbed to the temptation to serve foreign gods, they were not the gods of power or Mammon, but of popularity. Where other church leaders might push a president to do more for the needy or to become more assertive for or against abortion or to shift policy on some foreign country, Mr. Graham would give the publicity benefit of his association, and ask for nothing in return except the publicity benefit to himself of association with the president. Or at least nothing related to presidential policy. I suppose there might have been a few personal favors requested from time to time.

I never interviewed Mr. Graham, but I had a form of contact standing in a corridor once at Shea Stadium when he came by on his way to the platform. It is true that I am a little slow, but it is still remarkable that he spotted me, strode over, shook my hand and got halfway to the platform before I realized what was happening. The impression was one of really extraordinary energy. That of course might be presumed of anyone who did as many things and went as many places and kept the attention of as many people as Billy Graham. Still, I was startled by the force of the man.

As for other factors that might help explain his success, I have always thought his truly distinctive gift was a capacity to sense what his audience of the moment would like to hear from him, and then say it in ways that gave the least possible abrasion to people of other views who might overhear. With that went his willingness—within broad limits—to say whatever people wanted to hear. He had early recognized he could never satisfy the very left or very right without losing the majority middle, and fundamentalists such as those associated with Bob Jones University in Greenville, South Carolina, withdrew their approval, decisively in 1957 when he sought and got the support of New York clergy who were conspicuously not fundamentalists. But for the broad spectrum that came to be called Middle America, he was ready and able to reflect and support their feelings in the general terms of evangelical Protestantism.

Another strength that should not be overlooked was Mr. Graham's ability to hold the loyalty of some talented staff over the decades, an inner core for his whole career and others for significant periods. While my observation may not be true of each and every one of them, I would say generally that in style and substance they have appeared to operate nearer the narrow, hard-edged traditional evangelicalism that their leader in some ways outgrew. But they served his purposes well.

To me, one of the most remarkable aspects of Billy Graham's career has been his ability to reign as the world's premier evangelist without himself ever having gone through the particular type of "born again" experience that his kind of evangelism was designed to manufacture. Nor does it appear that his parents, deeply committed and deeply conservative Presbyterians, had gone through that specific sort of religious processing, and he presumably considered them nonetheless "born again."

For his credentials, he would point to an evening in 1934 when, as a teenager, he attended a revival led by the antisemitic tub thumper, Mordecai F. Ham, and went forward in response to the invitation at the close of the service. But as Mr. Graham reported on the event himself, and as the steady course of his life before and after that night confirmed, there was no significant reorientation such as the report of getting saved would reflect. In the revival culture, walking forward at the end of an evangelistic service had become a formality that was the standard and expected path of young people. For a few converts, there might be a visible shift from an irreligious to a religious life. But for the ordinary forward-walker, the act would have a meaning similar to that of a confirmation ceremony for a serious young Catholic or Episcopalian, or a bar mitzvah for a serious young Jew. Beginning to come of age, a youth now publicly becomes a part of the religious community by his own commitment, and not just as a child operating under parental influence.

But for Baptists, such a walk down the aisle and "getting saved" would have led to baptism. But it did not for Billy Graham—not immediately. Born to a Presbyterian family, the infant Billy Graham got a baptism that he broadmindedly seemed always to credit as true and valid. But he was persuaded later, while attending a Bible institute in Florida, that he should be baptized by immersion. And later still, for frankly stated career reasons, he accepted another immersion, when he was preaching to some Southern Baptists and found his standing with them depended on baptism under their auspices. So Mr. Graham would cheerfully report in his autobiography, *Just As I Am* (HarperCollins, 1997, pp. 55-6), that he had been baptized three times. But none of the three baptisms was connected with the occasion when he supposedly was born again. Presumably, he could just as cheerfully have gone for another dozen baptisms if someone had convinced him they would bring him more preaching opportunities. The once-for-all event of Christian life was the walking down the aisle.

Strange that the world's most famous Baptist preacher would be one to trivialize baptism. Baptists justify their existence as a separate denomination in large part by their belief about baptism—that it is valid only for believers, not for infants, and secondarily that its symbolism of death and resurrection should be portrayed through immersion. But growing up in the Southern Baptist Convention, I found many Southern Baptists putting primary emphasis on the secondary point of external form, and on the negative points that baptism was not for infants and not for salvation. Relatively little attention was given to the question of what believers' baptism did mean. And when I have seen Southern Baptist clergy transferring to denominations that baptize infants, as happens with some frequency, I have gotten the impression that they saw their shift of position and practice on baptism as a matter of no great moment. It had never really become embedded in their thinking, but was only a sort of uniform they might wear for a time and discard when they decided to start playing with another team.

In the years of rethinking following the Second Vatican Council, some Catholics were giving baptism more fresh consideration than Baptists were. I reported on just a little of that for the news service of the Southern Baptist Convention, Baptist Press, when I came across John Gallen, a Jesuit priest teaching at the theological school, Woodstock College (April 22, 1974). Changes in the thinking of some Catholics had come about as liturgical scholars studied more texts of the ancient rituals, he told me. "Knowing the liturgical tradition, we know that the Christian initiation liturgy was not originally constructed to deal with infants. It had a different orientation." Father Gallen said he differed from Baptists in thinking baptism of infants was valid, and those who had received baptism in infancy should not be baptized again (the meaning of "Anabaptist," a name given to some Baptists in the early Reformation period). He also saw some significance in the form of baptism, and expressed a preference for the Baptist tradition of immersion, whether for infants or for adults. "Immersion has always been an option in the Roman liturgy, and though rarely practiced, never completely died out," he noted. So he would have made immersion of adults the standard practice, and baptism in infancy and by pouring allowable variations.

Father Gallen did not anticipate such far-reaching change would come to the Catholic Church quickly, but he reported that he found a good many specialists in liturgy taking the view that it should come. The same year as my Baptist Press article, a supplementary Volume 16 to the *New Catholic Encyclopedia* was published (Publishers Guild/McGraw Hill), and for it Gerard Austin, who taught liturgy at the Catholic University of America, wrote an article that asserted, "Both immersion and infusion (pouring) are acceptable, but immersion is preferable since as a symbol it is more apt for signifying participation in the death and resurrection of Christ" (p. 20).

A few years later, I noticed that Peter Steinfels, religion reporter for *The New York Times,* was writing about an adult woman who was preparing to go to a Catholic church for the Easter Vigil liturgy, and would "enter a pool" and "lie down, let the water close over her head and then rise, baptized" (March 25, 1989).

In Southern Baptist minds, however, there had been another drift, the placement of the beginning of the Christian life not at baptism but in that moment at the end of a church service when someone walked down the aisle to the front as a sign of a readiness to put faith in Christ and join the church. People who have not attended churches with this custom can get the idea from the televised services of Mr. Graham, who concludes his sermons by asking people to walk forward. Because those of different denominational backgrounds may interpret the meaning of what they are doing in different ways, the Graham organization puts the statistical report on how many responded under the general heading of "decisions for Christ." This shift of focus away from baptism on the part of Mr. Graham and other sectors of the evangelical community, even the denomination that got its name from its teaching about baptism, could be connected to the theological shift in the American revival milieu from Calvinism, with its emphasis on salvation as something received by grace, to Arminianism, and its tilt toward salvation as something achieved by human decision and action (under divine direction, of course). Methodism

SIDEBARS

was also at work, its Wesleyan style of stirring emotion influencing Baptists in a manner similar to what was called Pietism on the European continent, and in America not only influencing Baptists but moving even more emotionally into the Holiness sects and then into Pentecostalism.

Many evangelicals speak of a "plan" of salvation, with certain steps you or anybody can take one-two-three-four to reserve a place in heaven at any time the impulse arises, as routine as baking a cake. The concept, as with some theories of the sacraments, reminds you of a self-service filling station: God has left a tank full of grace and directions on how to get some for your car. There is still an ultimate dependence on God, but under this plan the customer is allowed more control, and gets what he wants without having to engage in some direct contact with the manager.

Everybody in the world needs to know about this plan evangelicals have worked out, the theory goes, because it provides the only possibility of achieving salvation. It depends on the individual following this plan, not on Christ. Consequently, whether some poor fellow over in Ouagadougou goes to hell or not depends on how much you contribute to the missionary offering.

Liberals who recoil at that scenario tend to say God is so good he will let anybody go to heaven who does the best he can with what he knows. But Christians will not be able to take much comfort in that, aware as they are that nobody does the best he can. A better way of understanding the reality was offered by Pope John Paul II in his book, *Crossing the Threshold of Hope* (tr. Jenny McPhee and Martha McPhee; Knopf, 1994). Christ came into the world for all peoples, the Chinese, the Tibetans, the Australian indigenous, whoever, redeemed them all and "has his own ways of reaching each of them," the pope said (p. 83).

The priority given to human decision in the evangelical planning for salvation differs from what you see in the New Testament story of Paul's conversion. In that case, things happened the other way round: Paul did not make a decision for Christ; all his decisions were against Christ. "I persecuted the church of God," he confessed. But Christ made a decision for Paul. So Paul's ultimate decision was to accept the decision made for him when the Son of God was revealed to him—or, literally, in him (Galatians 1:13-17). Jesus had said the same to his disciples: "You did not choose me, but I chose you" (John 15:16). And the Old Testament gave a similar picture of how things work. According to Exodus, the Hebrew people did not decide to leave the bondage of Egypt. They were afraid to defy Pharaoh (14:10-12), and after they got out of Egypt, they wished they had never left (16:2-3). But God had decided to take them out (3:7-8), so that was that, and they were off to a new land.

In parts of the conservative evangelical community we used to hear even more of this talk about "getting saved" than today. Although that language can sound a bit primitive, and is a bit primitive, its understanding of salvation as something received puts it closer to describing the reality than many alternatives. With similar passive voice, the song "Amazing Grace" presents the truth that "I once was lost and now am found," not that I as a clever self-starter found my own way out of the woods. Those who would like a more sophisticated sound of the passive voice could consider Paul Tillich's references in books such as *The Courage to Be* (Yale University Press, 1952) to "the state of being grasped by the power of being-itself" (pp. 156, 172).

But rambling back, the anything goes view of baptism provides an introduction to Billy Graham's churchmanship, or lack thereof. From baptism, we could go on to communion, also called the Lord's Supper and the Eucharist (giving of thanks). Writing something about Mr. Graham a while back, I wondered what his thought and practice on this subject might be. But looking at one of the better recent biographies, *A Prophet with Honor* by William C. Martin (William Morrow, 1991), I could not find anything, and so called to talk with Mr. Martin. He was a university professor who had spent years researching the Graham story, and had spent a good many hours talking personally with his subject. And he told me that he did know what if anything Mr. Graham thought about communion, or about officiating at a communion service, or what his practice was in communing or not communing with people who were not Baptist, or in what circumstances he might or might not.

That is really remarkable when you reflect on the central role that communion and its interpretation have played in the history of the Christian church, including Baptist history. Efforts to grasp the meaning of the Christian faith have often centered on theological debate about communion–what it is, what it signifies, who participates, who decides.

That has been the case not only with theologians and bishops, but a philosopher such as Georg W. F. Hegel could also see interpretation of the Lord's Supper as a decisive point. In his 1831 *Lectures on the Philosophy of Religion,* he called communion the "midpoint of religion," and said differences on that topic "endow all the other differences in religion with their significance" (University of California Press, 1985, Peter C. Hodgson, ed.; Vol. III, p. 372). To Hegel, a Lutheran, it naturally appeared that the Lutheran interpretation got it best. But Mr. Graham would know it could not help his career to say Baptists got it best. His potential audience was divided on questions about communion, so it would serve his interests to ignore the whole topic, and not worry about what was good, better or best on communion.

Next, consider ordination, another practice central to church life and a focus of debate in regard to its meaning and administration. In *Just As I Am,* Mr. Graham reported that he sought ordination after a friend told him it would give him "standing" with the Baptist denomination and "be of great benefit to you in many ways" (p. 56). If it is pragmatism you want in religion, there it is, full and frank. To Mr. Graham, we might also note, ordination did not mean, as it would to many clergy, accepting accountability to a church for the way he exercised his leadership role. In old age, Mr. Graham still was bragging about how "my patience ran short," and he faced down a member of his ordination council who wanted to know more about his theological beliefs. So Mr. Graham got ordained and "had sanction to perform weddings, conduct funerals and officiate in church activities not open to me before" (p. 57). But still, what a large part of the Christian community would consider most important, authorization to officiate at the communion service, does not make his list.

Another unmentioned benefit of ordination that showed up a little later was keeping Mr. Graham out of the army. At the time of Pearl Harbor, he was a healthy, unmarried young man of 23, and a cadet in the Army training program at Wheaton College. Most of his contemporaries had to put their careers on hold for a few years to go out and defend their country against its enemies. But Mr. Graham did not, and explains only that he lacked sufficient education early in the war to become a chaplain and his desire to volunteer late in the war happened to not work out (pp. 67, 89-90).

Ordained a Southern Baptist, Mr. Graham did not need to consider the authority of a bishop. But during a brief period when he was pastor of a congregation that was unhappy with his frequent absences to preach elsewhere, he also made a point of not deferring to what Baptist tradition has regarded as the authority of the local church. For all we can see, Mr. Graham never in his life as a minister accepted any religious authority except his own personal interpretation of the Bible.

The three rites of baptism, communion and ordination are the ways the Christian faith becomes concrete, and Christians are bound together across all human divisions, across the separations of time and space, into one community. Early Lutheranism developed a concept called adiaphora (not making a difference), meaning topics that could be considered matters of individual opinion and not serious enough to split the church over. It is perhaps worth pondering: Can the three topics of baptism, communion and ordination be set aside as adiaphora, the way evangelicals such as Mr. Graham seem to do?

For evangelicals of this stripe, the only important matter is accepting a message from the Bible, and accepting it by inward belief. As the rationalist philosopher Rene Descartes might have said, the important point is getting hold of the proper "clear and distinct ideas" about religion. Karl Barth has explained that biblicism, the shift of emphasis from the one the Bible is talking about to the text of the Bible itself, is a form of rationalism (*Dogmatics IV/1*, 368). Evidence that the conservative evangelical tradition, in carrying on a church life that centers in revivalism, has become a form of rationalism may be found in Mr. Graham's setting aside all concern with the three community-building rites I have mentioned. And it appears his influence has led his fellow Southern Baptists to a softening in this area. They formerly maintained strict views and practices on these points, but he seems to have convinced them that the success they desired was to be found along other lines.

This has a positive side. What from one perspective could be viewed as fuzzy thinking and a desire to find customers on whatever street they might live, at the same time made Mr. Graham a force for unity in the nation as a whole. And he served to draw others of his denomination, Southern Baptists, out of their narrow denominationalism.

The narrow denominationalism was evident especially in the attitude toward Catholics. In 1964, while I was pastor of a Southern Baptist church in Virginia, I wrote a review article for the state Baptist paper, *The Religious Herald,* about some of the books on the Second Vatican Council, then in progress (October 7, 1965). I was able to point out that many of the developments in Rome took account of criticisms that Protestants and others had made through the years, and some speeches of bishops, such as those emphasizing the importance of the local congregation, could be of special interest to Baptists. In response, I got a letter from one of the denominational officials in Nashville expressing appreciation for my article as a contrast to the executive committee of the Southern Baptist Convention, which not only refused to acknowledge that anything worthwhile could be going on at the Vatican but remained explicitly "condemnatory."

At that point, after President John F. Kennedy and Pope John XXIII had changed the attitudes of many Protestants, Southern Baptists, especially in the leadership, tended to keep looking on Catholics as pagans, with evangelism programs continuing to speak of winning Catholics to Christ. Over the years, such attitudes gradually softened, and Billy Graham made a contribution to the change–though on the underside he helped reinforce the fundamentalist outlook that was divisive otherwise.

The absence of any actual event of getting "born again" in the primitive sense of such raw experience was perhaps part of what set Mr. Graham apart from much of the evangelical world that honored him as its preeminent figure. Many of his more ardent followers seemed a couple of notches below him in sensitivity. One illustrative event occurred during a 1972 visit to Northern Ireland. In *A Prophet with Honor*, Professor Martin reported that Mr. Graham was taken out on the streets of Belfast for some one-on-one soul winning with Arthur Blessit, an overabundant character who at other times publicized himself by carrying around a large cross (pp. 401-2). Mr. Graham expressed his hesitation in humble terms: "You're going to have to teach me and consider me a student of personal evangelism. I don't consider myself to be a man that's gifted of God just to deal with an individual." Though in fact he built his career developing friendships with individual supporters, he had sensitivity enough, as many in his genre did not, to realize that accosting individuals on the street in an attempt to sell Jesus like umbrellas could be offensive to many of those accosted, as well as demeaning to the religion he represented.

Covering the Graham "crusade" in New York was somewhat unusual in my reporting experience. Conservative evangelicals do not manifest a strong presence in New York, and I got only limited opportunities to observe them. But New York does of course have some. Helped in part by Mr. Graham's 1957 preaching at Madison Square Garden, his fellow Southern Baptists got a group going and organized a congregation the following year in Manhattan. By coincidence, I was then attending the Army chaplains' school at Fort Slocum, on a little island off the East coast of Westchester County, just above New York, and attended the service that brought the church officially into existence. Later, I was a member for a time, and since then I have watched it, now in the form of a successor called Metro Baptist Church.

In 1958, Southern Baptists thought they were on a roll, and could roll over any obstacles. But they had not really taken the measure of Manhattan. Failing in these intervening years to achieve numerical success in the expected pattern of the denomination's churches in the South, the efforts here have more or less fallen between two stools. The underlying concept of Southern Baptist expansion was that Baptists of the North, and other Christians in Yankee territory of course even more so, had wandered from the faith, and Southern Baptists should come and offer the people authentic Bible religion again. But the Southern Baptist outpost in Manhattan naturally drew first from transplanted Southern Baptists who had come to New York for schooling and jobs.

Here lay a dilemma. Should the church in New York reproduce the conservative evangelistic, common people pleasing style they had known down home in the South, or out in the Southwest, or should it become something a little more culturally upscale to fit the career upward mobility of many in its New York constituency? Some wanted an improved model, and a few even became so radical the church split, though the more radical group evaporated rather soon. But the moderate element was indeed "moderate" in the political sense of the denomination's wars, and never could do the all-out soul-saving evangelism that might have attracted the old-fashioned element. One of their pastors left to become an Episcopal priest, which revealed a mentality rather far from what the original promoters of this northern invasion had in mind.

Not that the older form of conservative evangelicalism remained immune to cultural influences either. That became evident when many people of this community emerged as zealous supporters of Ronald Reagan. That allegiance puzzled me in relation to Mr. Reagan's personality and ideas, though I recognized his political skill. I got to make my own observations close up when he visited Covenant House in 1989 (CNS, November 15) to talk with some of the young people there. His audience could hardly have been more alien—mostly black and Hispanic homeless youth from the inner city. But Mr. Reagan, still a political animal when he was out of the White House and no longer running for anything, did very well. He perhaps did not persuade these young people in the one talk to go out and register as Republicans, but he reached out to them in pertinent ways. He told them that his father was an alcoholic, and that this created problems for his family, as similar behavior probably had done in many of theirs. But this was something you had to deal with and move on. He told them he was hurt when as a young fellow he failed to get a job he applied for, and badly wanted and needed, and felt he was qualified for. His listeners probably had gone through something like that, he recognized, but you had to keep trying, and later something else came along that worked out even better for him. And they could hope the same would prove true for them.

When a man has gotten himself elected governor of a populous state, and reelected, and has then defeated a sitting president to get himself elected to the highest office in the United States, and after four years reelected by an impressive margin, it may seem superfluous to report that he shows signs of possessing political talent. But I think in this case it is not superfluous, because so many people aghast at Mr. Reagan's ideas seemed to assume his electoral success must have been some kind of trick, or backstage manipulation by other people.

By contrast, James Earl Carter Jr., also known as Jimmy. Admirable in many ways, but strange, you have to say of the Carters. I did not get to talk with President Carter or ever catch anything more than a brief glimpse of him until after he left office. But in 1984, he came to New York to speak at a service marking Archbishop Iakovos's 25th anniversary as chief of the Greek Archdiocese (EPS, May 15). There, the featured personality at a celebratory event, the former president delivered a message about as inappropriate to the occasion as any I have ever heard. He was still devastated by the voter rejection of 1980, and made "frustrations and disappointments" the theme of a long, long, much too long address. He had certainly experienced frustrations and disappointments, we were informed. In fact, we all encountered frustrations and disappointments, did we not? Iakovos, too, reportedly had known frustrations and disappointments. Come to think of it, Jesus had frustrations and disappointments. Hopes often failed of fulfillment, so Jesus wept. And we learn right from the Bible that Christ was a man of sorrows. And so on almost interminably. One listener told me afterward that he initially anticipated a Hegelian dialectic–the difficulties of existence countered by the resources of faith, which would lead then to the final triumph in glory. But for Jimmy Carter, it was frustrations and disappointments all the way to the end of the line. I had admired his work from many standpoints, and his post-presidency contribution to Habitat for Humanity and so forth deserved commendation. Thank God, he did not put the ex-presidency up for sale. But no doubt something was missing.

Maybe there was a wrinkle in the family genes. I saw Mr. Carter's sister, Ruth Carter Stapleton, once while he was president, and had to wonder a little about her, too, fine serious-minded lady as she evidently was. She had some sort of religious ministry, not too clear in its exact dimensions, and got to see her career flourish briefly during her brother's presidency. The charismatic movement was also blooming in those years, and in 1978 she was invited to speak to a charismatic "Jesus Rally"–yes, Jesus Rally; would I kid you about a thing like that?–at Giants Stadium in New Jersey on the Saturday before Pentecost. It was a large, mixed crowd of Catholic and non-Catholic charismatics, and Cardinal Terence Cooke of New York and other eminences came to give official backing (NC, May 15).

It was all rather much. The electronic scoreboard told us the score was "Jesus 78." Speakers were coming on like cheerleaders. "If the Lord grants you the gift of tongues, use it," said one. "Glory!" said the scoreboard. We heard from people such as Jim Bakker, the PTL Club host later shorn of luster by revelations of adultery and sent to prison for financial shenanigans. "Hallelujah!" said the scoreboard, perhaps with foresight into Mr. Bakker's future. Greetings from "messianic" Jews who had been "baptized in the Spirit" were brought by one Michael Evans. And the name draw for all this, featured in the press release, was a sister to the president of the United States, who told us about her friendship with *Hustler* publisher Larry Flynt and other far out adventures with God.

But speaking of Ronald Reagan, as we were, I was puzzled by the attachment of religious conservatives to his political cause. In the conservative circles

I knew growing up, the whole Hollywood scene was rated low by the stricter sort. Then to find in those very same circles a gushing over a Hollywood actor, and one who had further sinned grievously against conservative standards by divorcing his wife and marrying another woman, a politician whose tax returns showed he gave virtually nothing to any church although he was a man of affluence, and who made no apparent effort to rear his children in any church tradition, or even have much to do with them—for such a man to become the hero of the religious right, Protestant and Catholic, the family values crowd, did boggle the mind.

To put the cream on top, White House chief of staff Donald Regan then revealed that the second wife, Nancy Reagan, relied on a practitioner of astrology to advise on good and bad days for presidential travel. It was instructive, by the by, to find this revelation did not hurt Mrs. Reagan in her social circles. If she had been compelled to admit she talked to Jesus about her anxieties, the fashionable world, the world of her fashion designers and the ladies who lunch, would have laughed. But the astrology report was somehow more respectable. It appeared quite a few prominent people were getting their enlightenments the same way, giving some of the more fashionable astrologers social eclat. And now we see psychic programs on cable television.

In New York, we have everything, so no one can be surprised to find fortune tellers in what Harvey Cox extolled as *The Secular City* (Macmillan, 1965). But I have been amazed to see how many can make a living here. You can see their signs all over. Actually, though, their presence does not constitute evidence against the secular character of the city, but further support. I suppose some people see the psychics, astrologers, palm readers, Tarot card interpreters *et al.* as alternative forms of religion. But to me they represent the opposite of religion, human schemes to get supernatural benefits without having to rely on God. Which schemes appear advantageous, because if you turn to God for help, he may want to help you by changing the way you live your life. And not so many of us would like that.

Somewhere along here, I perhaps should note that religion as such is not necessarily something Christians must always applaud. The Bible is replete with criticism of religion, both in the Old Testament and in the New. The biblical word is: "You shall make no covenant with the inhabitants of this land; you shall break down their altars" (Judges 2:2). And to make it rather personal and comprehensive, Jesus warned in the Sermon on the Mount, "Beware of practicing your piety before men" (Matthew 6:1). So you need to be not just critiquing the religions of others, but subjecting your own religion to critical review. (By "your own religion," I do not mean the religion of your parents, which rebellious children always find all too easy to criticize, but what has been

SIDEBARS

receiving your very own most devout attention.) From a biblical perspective, or looking at the Balkans and some other places in recent times, you could easily make the argument that bad religion is worse than no religion, although it may alternatively be that everybody implicitly has some religion and serves some god. Reinhold Niebuhr told of his Detroit parishioner who had come up with the simple rule that religion was good for good people and bad for bad people, suggesting bad people can become even worse when they find ways to use religion to serve themselves rather than God.

A ways back, when I was the newest chaplain at Fort Bliss, Texas, I learned the significance of seniority by getting what was considered a bottom assignment, the post stockade. But I found it an interesting and educational assignment, and never resented it. There was a chapel within the stockade compound, and exploring one day I found that a resourceful prisoner had discovered the altar was open at the back and offered a convenient place to hide. He had brought in a little mattress for comfort, and a candle and a copy of the *Reader's Digest* for times when he felt like reading himself to sleep. I have since taken that as a parable of the way we can use religion to escape and evade. It is said that people wanting to hide from God may even try going to church as a last resort. "He'll never think of looking for me here."

Mr. Reagan's association with the right wing clergy brought him criticism from people of more liberal views on religion. But his record could be seen as another demonstration of political skill. It always seemed to me that he had those clergy serving his purposes more than he served theirs. And the final result was defusing a lot of raucous energy of the Bible swingers by channeling it into the political system. How many people will lie awake tonight worrying about Jerry Falwell and his Moral Majority?

Billy Graham reported in his autobiography that he was present when, in just one conversation, Mr. Reagan changed the Dallas fundamentalist W. A. Criswell from declaring the whole movie industry was "of the Devil" to declaring, "I'm going to start going to some movies, and I'll tell my congregation that it's not a sin to see certain types of movies" (pp. 528-29). As with many conversion stories, some of us might wonder whether it all happened that quickly with immediate expression in just those words. But looking at the overall picture, I do not doubt that Mr. Reagan enjoyed more success converting religious conservatives to his causes than they had enlisting him in theirs.

The religious right justified adoration of Mr. Reagan largely on the grounds that he promised to get a constitutional amendment against abortion. But he did not get one and, so far as I could see, never tried. In a fallback line, he said the amendment was not really needed because abortion could be stopped by correct Supreme Court decisions. But then his very first appointment to the Supreme Court, Sandra Day O'Connor, turned out pro-abortion, part of the majority in the Planned Parenthood *v.* Casey decision of 1992 that allowed state (Pennsylvania) regulation of abortion in some respects but reaffirmed the basic elements of Roe *v.* Wade. Another tribute to Mr. Reagan's political skill, he got the support of the religious right for his presidential ambitions even though he had a solid pro-abortion record in California. As governor, he signed a bill that liberalized what he condemned as the state's "outdated abortion law," and that led to a rapid increase in the number of abortions there.

As for his record in the presidency, in 1980, the year of his election, there were 1,553,890 legal abortions in the United States, according to official statistics; in 1988, his last full year in office, there were 1,590,750. Not as disastrously downhill as his record on another of his major campaign promises, balancing the budget, but still thought-provoking.

When the contest for his successor was underway in 1988, I wrote a report for EPS and recalled the revolutionary enthusiasm he had originally aroused among conservatives with his promises of radical change toward their side. Then I summarized the record: "But his eight years brought no end to abortion; no federal aid to church schools; no ouster of the Nicaraguan government; no halt to foreigners taking Americans hostage; no magic wand eliminating crime, drug addiction, pornography or family breakdown" (October 25).

Still and all, the religious right cheered on for Mr. Reagan, even as it became clearer and clearer he was doing little to deal with their concerns. Assuming their concerns were as purported. If, on the other hand, you think that surely at least a few of the conservative clergy must have been intelligent enough to see that President Reagan was not stopping abortion or insisting that court appointees must be anti-abortion, then you would need to ask whether these clergy were actually more interested in the military and economic goals he did faithfully work for.

Many people of the same type also supported Barry Goldwater when he ran for president in 1964, and recommended him as Mr. Conservative, a man of the old-fashioned true American values and all that. In later times, they expressed dismay at hearing him endorse abortion and homosexuality. But they should not have been surprised, because it was always evident, for anybody willing to see, that Mr. Goldwater was not really a conservative but a radical individualist. During his political career, he focused this individualism on the interests of businessmen, a position that commonly appropriates the term "conservative" for itself. Senator Goldwater supported the desire of the individual businessman to do whatever he considered best for himself, without having to take into account labor unions or government regulations, and with

SIDEBARS

only the most minimal demands from the tax collector. Just the amount needed for the police and the military. When the abortion and homosexual movements came along, Mr. Goldwater simply applied the same radical individualism to his analysis of them. What could be more radically individualistic than breaking society's bond of male and female, or setting the interests of a mother over against those of the child developing in her own womb? I do not know what Russell Kirk thought about Mr. Goldwater personally, but if you look at the mentality described in books such as Mr. Kirk's *Conservative Mind* (Regnery, 7th ed., 1985), the respect for tradition and "the immortal contract that unites the dead, the living and those yet unborn" (pp.68-69), the belief in maintaining "continuity of political development" (p. 19), the regard for a "balancing and compromising of interests in which all important elements of the population concur" (p. 175), you are struck by how little of that could be found in the mind of the politician who got and claimed the title of Mr. Conservative.

In neither politics nor religion, however, would I think dissatisfaction with the dominant sectors of those called conservative obligates us to go the way of the liberals, who are also individualists in their separate way. Liberal religion as it exists in the popular culture seems seriously deficient, marked by a persistent underlying desire to water down. Among liberals, you can sometimes hear a theory that Jesus was a nice man who came with simple sayings like the Golden Rule, and that Paul was a meanie who took over and messed it all up. This theory cannot be maintained by anyone who takes time to look at the New Testament carefully. To mention just one point, Luke, who gives a picture of Jesus that liberals tend to favor, is the same author who wrote Acts, and there presented Paul as a key figure in spreading the word about Jesus. Scholars also commonly tell us the writings of Paul came before the Gospels, and are therefore closer to the source, for whatever weight that carries. But among certain liberals, attention is more exclusively directed to the teachings of Jesus, especially those in what are known as the Synoptic Gospels—Matthew, Mark and Luke. Religion is then reduced to ethics and ethics to a simple rule or two that each individual can follow on his own. Like, do unto others as you would have them do unto you (Matthew 7:12; Luke 6:31). Golden as such a rule may be, nobody lives up to it, so I find it hard to understand why so many people seem to be always putting it forward as though it were some kind of panacea.

Liberal religion really is for the complacent, those who feel they are good enough to make it on their own. They talk of doing lots and lots of good unto others, but fail to consider the prior question raised by Paul, "Who will deliver me?" (Romans 7:24). A full-bodied biblical theology is welcomed by those who need to be forgiven and changed. Justification and sanctification, salvation and atonement, reconciliation, redemption, regeneration and whatever—we need all we can get.

Taking it in the overall, the Protestant churches commonly called "mainline" have been enervated by a pervasive liberalism that initially looks like it should be popular but in the long run fails to satisfy because it cannot build and sustain a satisfying sense of community. Rabbi Isaac Mayer Wise, father of Reform Judaism in the United States, imagined that all Jews would follow his lead sooner or later. They have not, and today Reform Judaism moves toward greater regard for tradition. Thomas Jefferson imagined similarly that American Christians would follow his lead into the shallow waters of Unitarianism. They have not. Throwing off the conservative shackles may exhilarate, but you can hardly make a religion out of it. After you have thrown off, what then? Think whatever seems rational to you personally? Do whatever seems right to you personally? Who needs a religion for that? So I would recommend following the example of the good King Josiah, who "did not turn aside to the right hand or to the left" (II Kings 22:2).

As the 1976 election approached, I reported the notable fact that all three of the most important candidates for the presidency were associated in one way or another with the conservative evangelical tradition—Jimmy Carter on the Democratic side, Gerald Ford and Ronald Reagan battling for the Republican nomination (*Christian Science Monitor,* August 16). "In the nation's bicentennial year, the leading candidates for national leadership all stand closer to the evangelical faith of Jonathan Edwards than to the deism of Jefferson," I pointed out.

Of the three candidates, Mr. Reagan, beloved of the religious right, had the softest focus. "In my own experience there came a time when there developed a new relationship with God, and it grew out of need," he said. "So yes, I have had an experience that could be described as 'born again.'"

Mr. Ford, more explicit, wrote Billy Zeoli, a Michigan evangelist he maintained a close tie with, to say he "trusted Christ to be my savior," and to thank Mr. Zeoli for taking time to help him "learn more about our savior." And Mr. Carter, as everyone became well aware, talked so much about his evangelical faith he made people nervous, even some who were predisposed to like him. I thought Mr. Carter's practice on religious talk might be compared with a man's declarations of love for his wife: expressions suitable for use in personal communication might not be quite the thing for the public street, proper as it would certainly be to show his love there, too, in appropriate ways.

On the other hand, there is a lot on the other hand. A close look at conservative evangelicals shows that they do not hold the keys to the kingdom either. I have been acquainted with them particularly through Southern Baptists, and at least until a fundamentalist takeover of their national machinery brought a period of disruption, people could point to the Southern Baptist Convention and say, "Way to grow!"

Southern Baptists did avoid some of the errors of the liberals. But they experienced a steady erosion of their more educated clergy and lay leaders, and they exerted an influence on American life impressively small relative to their numbers. Aside from the special case of politicians who needed the votes, most any Southern Baptist with the ability to take a leadership role in cultural life either left the denomination or made it marginal to his work.

In my own case, the question of cultural leadership would of course never arise, and I made no formal break with Southern Baptists. But after study in a Southern Baptist seminary and service in a Southern Baptist pastorate, I just decided it was time to move along. I departed with no bitterness, and in fact had a quite congenial place to work as pastor of the Urbanna Baptist Church in Virginia, but did not feel disposed to stay identified directly with the denomination as such.

As I was growing up, I heard and read Southern Baptist leaders constantly making claims to offer the world a purer vision of Christianity, truer to the New Testament than that of other denominations. But over the years I began to wonder about that.

The more usual objection to Southern Baptists has been that they are too narrow-minded in their morality, too fundamentalistic in their doctrine and either too formalistic or not formalistic enough in the way they carry on their church services. That indictment contains much truth. Verily, Southern Baptists do include plenty of fundamentalists who want to twist your arm and make you say you think all those miracle stories in the Bible are literal historical accounts. But I also had a few specific points bothering me, points not unique to Southern Baptists, but characteristics to some extent pervading the conservative evangelical Protestantism of the nation and coming to prominence among Southern Baptists.

One was sabbath observance. How did they come to make such a production of that? It was not a Southern Baptist peculiarity, I knew, but in fact infected much of Christendom one way or another, not only in the United States but also in Europe and other parts of the world. But it eventually struck me as a curious contradiction for a denomination that made such a boast of basing its teaching on the New Testament.

Sunday was given a special character as the day on which certain activities otherwise acceptable or even virtuous, like work, became sinful. There should be no unnecessary labor on Sunday, but recreation was also suspect. Commercial amusements, such as going to the picture show, must be avoided because that involved labor for other people. In recent years, this aspect of conservative religious teaching has been muted, in large part I would guess because of the popularity of professional football. The kind of people who supported fundamentalist preachers such as W. A. Criswell at the First Baptist Church of Dallas also went for the thrills of the Dallas Cowboys. If a preacher is playing to the galleries, which is a big part of what the conservative evangelical movement is about, he can hardly afford to condemn Sunday football, professional though it is.

Sabbath observance perhaps got excessive emphasis because of its inclusion in the Ten Commandments, and the concept of the Ten Commandments tended to get excessive emphasis. The New Testament contains reference to the "Ten Commandments" as such, and even when Jesus (Mark 10:19) and Paul (Romans 13:9) enumerate some of them, they do not mention the one about the sabbath. In fact, even the Old Testament makes explicit reference to them as something like a code only in the two books where they appear–Exodus (20:1-17; 34:28) and, the later variant, Deuteronomy (4:13; 5:1-21; 10:4). So if you are in a church where you hear more about the Ten Commandments than the Beatitudes of Jesus or Paul's listing of the gifts of the Holy Spirit, you have to wonder about the preacher's sense of balance. What Jesus asked of his followers was not that they obey the Ten Commandments, but that they obey his new commandment, which was to "love one another as I have loved you" (John 15:12), and spread the word (Matthew 28:19-20).

I could mention more broadly that interpreting the Bible is not the simpleminded matter some people try to make it, even in ethics. Prohibitions such as we find in the Ten Commandments against murder, theft, adultery and lying are of course useful. But recommending the Bible in its totality as an ethical guide has its dangers, as village atheist types announce from time to time. Suppose you come across the story of Moses growing angry that his followers did not kill enough Midianites? You will find him giving the wipe-up guidelines: "Now therefore, kill every male among the little ones, and kill every woman who has known man by lying with him. But all the young girls who have not known man by lying with him, keep alive for yourselves" (Numbers 31:17-18). The point of studying the Bible is not necessarily to imitate the behavior of the biblical characters, who are really a mixed bag, but to see how God worked out his purposes through and despite the actions of sinful men. After the walls of Jericho came tumbling down, Joshua, who succeeded Moses as leader, instructed that "the city and all that is within it shall be devoted to the Lord for destruction" (Joshua 6:17). So his army "utterly destroyed all in the city, both men and women, young and old, oxen, sheep and asses, with the edge of the sword" (6:21). The lesson is not "go thou and do likewise."

In reading of the treatment of the people the Israelites saw as enemies of

God, we can also recall that the Hebrew Scriptures with remarkable even-handedness reported similar punishment received, and deserved, by the people of Israel. The Hebrew Bible, at some variance from the ordering in the Christian Old Testament, places I and II Chronicles as the last books, and the final chapter of this history records that in reaction to "mocking the messenger of God" and such sins "the wrath of the LORD rose against his people." Expressing this wrath, God "brought up against them the king of the Chaldeans, who slew their young men with the sword in the house of their sanctuary, and had no compassion on young man or virgin, old or aged; he gave them all into his hand" (II Chronicles 36:16-17). What lessons we are to draw from such passages for contemporary guidance will emerge only after a certain amount of reflection.

The collection known as the Ten Commandments is another matter, and is not a bad code as codes go. But it is not the final word for Christians, who "serve not under the old written code but in the new life of the Spirit" (Romans 7:6). In special particular, the sabbbath commandment should not be inter-preted as though it stated a law for the church. Sabbath observance is not real-ly a part of the Christian faith as portrayed in the New Testament, although many church leaders have sought to establish a Christian form of the Jewish sabbath, with the day shifted from Saturday to Sunday. For American evangel-icals of the nineteenth century, this deviation brought its due punishment in the emergence of Seventh-day Adventists and a few Seventh-day Baptists, who logically argued that if they must follow the Old Testament law on sabbath observance, they should follow the Old Testament instruction to observe the seventh day. Actually, I do not know how anyone could determine whether Saturday is the seventh day of the week on God's reckoning, or whether Sunday is counted as the first day of the week in the calendar of heaven. But leaving that aside . . . .

What the early Christians did is not correctly described as changing the sabbath from Saturday to Sunday. What they did was quit observing the sab-bath and start doing something else. Some of them may have continued to observe the sabbath also as part of their religious tradition. Christians of Jewish background might continue to carry out prescribed rituals, as Paul is reported to have done for public relations purposes on a visit to Jerusalem (Acts 21:17-26). Jewish authorities might object, but from the Christian point of view there was no reason why someone could not live as a Jew and a Christian at the same time, provided he did not teach that the Jewish observances were essen-tial for salvation or try to impose them on Gentile converts.

As the day of Christ's Resurrection, Sunday became the day Christians gathered for worship. Their gatherings were in fact a celebration of his continuing life among them, and of the eternal rest, not just one-day-a-week rest, that he gave (Hebrews 4). This was explained by Ignatius, a second century bishop of Antioch: "Those, then, who lived by ancient practices arrived at a new hope. They ceased to keep the sabbath and lived by the Lord's Day, on which our life as well as theirs shone forth" (Letter to the Magnesians 9:1; tr. Cyril C. Richardson; *Early Christian Fathers,* Macmillan, 1970).

Of course, setting aside a day each week for physical rest shows good sense, and giving slaves and servants a day off was a matter of humanitarian responsibility. And when Christians got in a position to make the laws of the state, and wanted a day for worship and rest, they naturally designated Sunday as the day.

A rhythm in which everyone gets a day of rest each week, and turns from obsession with making a living to reflection on making a life, also has obvious moral value. Perhaps even better would be finding a way to ensure that you are making a life all the time you are making a living. But clergy inclined to turn the Christian faith into a religion system have yielded to the temptation to use biblical authority for a day devoted to the system. Certainly they do not themselves rest on Sunday. Nor do I customarily. I could not continue in my present work if I insisted on resting every Sunday, or taking off any set day every week. Getting the work done sometimes has moral value overriding any particular schedule we might set up. So a part of church reform always needs to be liberation from religion systems, and such liberation was one of the points taken up by John Calvin.

In discussing the Old Testament requirement of sabbath observance given as part of the Ten Commandments, "Remember the sabbath day, to keep it holy" (Exodus 20:8), he pointed to the New Testament teaching about its fulfillment: "Let no one pass judgment on you in questions of food and drink or with regard to a festival or a new moon or a sabbath. These are only a shadow of what is to come; but the substance belongs to Christ" (Colossians 2:16-7). Calvin did not advocate giving up the use of Sunday as a day of worship and Christian teaching, but he denied that the sabbath commandment justified what came to be called sabbatarianism: "There is no doubt that by the Lord Christ's coming the ceremonial part of this commandment was abolished. For he himself is the truth, with whose appearance the shadows are left behind . . . . Christians ought therefore to shun completely the superstitious observance of days" (*Christian Institutes II,* VIII, 31; tr. Ford Lewis Battles; Library of Christian Classics, Vol. XX, ed. John T. McNeill; Westminster, 1960).

In England, the Puritans took a different line, alas. To them, reform meant not liberating the church from systems of legalism, but enforcing legalistic requirements more strictly. So while they might forbid any observance of church festivals such as Christmas, superstitious observances or not, because the Bible made no mention of such, the Puritans insisted on sabbatarianism because the sabbath commandment was there.

The Puritans put this viewpoint into the *Westminster Confession* (1643), with a (mistaken) declaration that the Lord's Day did in fact continue the Old Testament sabbath "changed into the first day of the week" (XXI, 8). Although the Restoration of Charles II ended the Puritan attempt to exercise absolute legal control over the religious life of the British people, the *Westminster Confession* and the outlook it encapsulated remained enormously influential, became a standard of the Church of Scotland and deeply affected the religious culture of the United States and other areas reached by British missionaries.

Some of the more thoughtful Southern Baptists recognized sabbatarianism as an error. The "sabbath" article in an *Encyclopedia of Southern Baptists* published by the Southern Baptist agency, Broadman, in 1958 said, "The Christian's Lord's Day is of separate origin," and explained that there was "no connection" between it and the Jewish sabbath. Nonetheless, among Southern Baptists in general, as among many others, sabbatarianism was promoted and helped solidify a religion system in which Sunday observances left many people sensing constraint rather than resting from the labors of self-justification.

As a sidebar here, I might note that Christians through the centuries have also made other attempts to establish a religion system with counterpart elements matching practices of the Old Testament, rather than taking a fresh look at the whole operation from a New Testament perspective. Calvin rejected efforts to justify the existence of Christian priests, who are not part of the Christianity of the New Testament, as a counterpart to Old Testament priests (*Institutes* IV.xix.28-31). In the New Testament, Christ is "the" priest in the ultimate sense (Hebrews 4:14), and all those who believe in Christ form a community of priests (I Peter 2:9), commissioned to do the priest's work of connecting God to the world. But there are no priests as a separate caste within the Christian community. However, like some other theologians, Calvin in another chapter of the *Institutes* tried to interpret baptism as a counterpart to Old Testament circumcision (IV.xvi) in order to justify baptizing babies, which could hardly be done on the basis of the New Testament, or Calvin's own teaching in the preceding chapter that baptism is "our confession before men . . . the mark by which we publicly profess . . . by which we testify . . . by which finally we openly affirm our faith" (IV.xv.13).

Actually, baptism is not a New Testament equivalent of Old Testament circumcision, but something quite different. For one elementary and rather significant difference, circumcision, however you interpret it, is only for males, whereas baptism is for both sexes and has the same meaning for both. Attempting to equate the two practices also overlooks the fact that the first

Christians were themselves Jews, and male Christians did not think they could skip baptism because they had already received something more or less equivalent. Paul emphasized that he was circumcised the eighth day and otherwise had a life conforming to all the Hebraic traditions (Philippians 3:5-7), which from one perspective he could value highly (Romans 3:-2) but in comparison with the new life he had been given meant little. So according to Acts, he got baptized to mark the event that gave him a new outlook (9:18). In the paradigm story of Jesus' baptism, we have another man who had received circumcision in infancy (Luke 2:21) but showed there was something new he wanted to say by going, at age 30, to get baptized (Matthew 3:1-17; Mark l:1-11; Luke 3:1-23; John 1:19-34). Circumcision was a way of saying, "God has chosen you to be part of his people." Those who get baptized say they are ready to be the people they have been chosen to be.

Another point of questioning I had about Southern Baptists concerned tithing. The teaching that Christians should give the church a tenth of their income was heavily stressed in Southern Baptist life. It was no secondary element but a central aspect of preaching and teaching, and an aspect presented with a strong emphasis as a divine law—a kind of flat tax of ten per cent for rich and for poor.

A generous spirit is of course basic to Christian character. And Christians who care about their churches will want to give them adequate support. But the percentage of a family's gross domestic product that should be spent on church personnel, church buildings and church programs is a matter for balanced judgment according to circumstances, not for calculation according to some legal formula. Tithing as such is not a requirement of the Christian life, any more than sabbath observance, or circumcision, or abstaining from pork, or stoning blasphemers, or other practices that in the Old Testament religion gave external form to the inner commitment.

Lest I be suspected of introducing novelties, I should perhaps point out that a little after Ignatius, another of the early church fathers, Irenaeus of Lyons, made this point on tithing while also expressing his own rejection of sabbatarianism. In *Proof of the Apostolic Preaching,* he wrote that the law would not "demand tithes of him who has vowed to God all his possessions." And he continued, "Nor will he be commanded to leave idle one day of rest, who is constantly keeping sabbath, that is, giving homage to God in the temple of God, which is man's body, and at all times doing the works of justice" (chapter 96; Newman Press, n.d., imprimatur 1952; tr. Joseph P. Smith).

Tithing, devotion of ten per cent of one's income to religion, was required in Old Testament law, but its only mention in the New Testament came in a

SIDEBARS

critique Jesus made of the scribes and Pharisees. He pronounced woe on them because "you tithe mint and dill and cummin, and have neglected the weightier matters of the law, justice and mercy and faith; these you ought to have done without neglecting the others" (Matthew 23:23). Even in the Jewish context that elicited this statement, the point is that more emphasis should go to matters of greater moment. But I found Southern Baptist preachers tended to ignore that basic point and stress rather the part about "these you ought to have done," expounded as a way of trying to make church members believe tithing to the church was a command binding on them. But these preachers did not observe that Jesus directed the command only to the scribes and Pharisees. Jesus never said or suggested that his disciples were expected to give a tithe to the new community he was forming, the church, and tithing does not appear in any of the New Testament records as a practice of the early church. For a denomination claiming to preserve New Testament Christianity in its absolute purity, Southern Baptists seemed much out of joint in making a central emphasis of a practice that was not in the New Testament at all. They had to rely here again on the Old Testament, and usually hammered away at one verse they found in Malachi: "Bring ye all the tithes into the store house" (3:10 KJV). And at this point, they forgot all they might say on other occasions about the way Old Testament law related to New Testament gospel.

Jesus had his own version of the flat tax, for rich and for poor, but at a hundred per cent. I cannot recall that he ever asked for a tenth of anything. To the rich young ruler, Jesus said, "Sell all that you have and distribute to the poor" (Luke 18:22). And he commended the poor widow who put her two mites into the temple treasury because she was giving everything she had (Mark 12:41-44). The point here, we might add, is not necessarily that you give to the poor, or that you give to the temple, but that you give with your whole heart, wherever God leads you to give. Just from the general religious standpoint, there is something disconcerting about the thought of a man sitting down before a stack of bills and dividing out his profits: "One for God and nine for me, one for God and nine for me, one for God and . . . ." Jesus had a different concept: a man sacrificing his entire portfolio to obtain one particular pearl that he saw had value beyond all others (Matthew 13:45-46).

A third point of my questioning of the Southern Baptist and general evangelical ethos concerned the insistence on abstaining totally from drinking alcoholic beverages. This was no secondary or incidental teaching either, even long years after repeal of the Prohibition Amendment, but a central emphasis, propounded frequently and fervently, with something like Muslim fervor, a mark to set off the truly spiritual from the worldly sort. In the years when I was growing up after repeal, the continuing campaign for legal prohibition of alcohol county by county was one of the rare points where the conservative evangelical community would organize for political action–this before the era of Jerry Falwell and Pat Robertson. Even at communion, the wine had to be replaced with Welch's grape juice.

The total absence of any support for this position on any page of the New Testament did not inhibit Southern Baptist preachers who boasted that they preached nothing but New Testament Christianity. They did not deign to notice that they were proclaiming Muslim doctrine and not Christian. Actually, the New Testament not only omits any backing for the teetotalers, but presents the drinking of wine as a normal part of life. Jesus' own practice was so far from the ascetic that his critics called him "a glutton and a drunkard." We may suspect perhaps they exaggerated, as commentators on such matters often do, but Jesus himself distinguished his "eating and drinking" from the abstemious mode of John the Baptist (Luke 7:33-34).

That was because the ascetic way of giving up things such as food and drink does not get to the root of what is wrong with us. Aside from any religious considerations, self-discipline on such points can be recommended for greater human effectiveness. We can think of an athlete giving up indulgences in order to become a more effective performer. But if he wants to become a more effective performer in order to bring more glory and money to himself, he still falls short of the life Jesus came to offer. We do not make progress in that direction by giving up things, but by giving up possession of ourselves, and letting someone else into our hearts.

At the Last Supper, Jesus used wine as the material means of conveying the new life given by his sacrifice of himself. He gave his disciples the "fruit of the vine" (Mark 14:23-24) to drink as his blood. Thinking about these matters, I began to find it curiouser and curiouser that preachers would take a stance directly contrary to both the example and the teaching of Jesus, and do it in the name of a supposedly purer form of Christianity.

Sometimes, Southern Baptists and other conservative Protestants of similar outlook concocted theories about the Greek word for wine meaning unfermented grape juice. But that could hardly convince anybody who recalled that people did get drunk when they consumed too much of this commodity (I Corinthians 11:21). And who can imagine Jesus at the wedding feast of Cana (John 2:1-11) turning the water into Welch's grape juice?

Southern Baptists could find a passage or two in the Old Testament to support their anti-alcohol stance. "Wine is a mocker, strong drink is raging; and whosoever is deceived thereby is not wise," says Proverbs 20:1 in the King James Version. And preachers would also quote Proverbs 23:31-32:

Look not upon the wine when it is red,
When it giveth his color in the cup,
When it moveth itself aright,
At the last it biteth like a serpent,
And stingeth like an adder.

A worthwhile caution for any who slide toward going too deeply into their cups. But I never heard a Southern Baptist expound the teaching of Psalm 104 that one of God's blessings was "wine to gladden the heart of man" (v. 15).

In the New Testament, a famous passage has Paul advising Timothy to "use a little wine for the sake of your stomach and your frequent ailments" (I Timothy 5:23). I still remember Professor Cyril C. Richardson at Union Seminary reporting on the observation of one commentator that Paul surely did not mean for Timothy to rub the wine on the outside of his stomach.

In 1980, when the Christian Brothers were observing their 300th anniversary, their San Francisco province marketed a special wine, and I wrote a story for NC (April 3) about their cellarmaster coming to New York on a promotional tour. For a sparkling coincidence, he had the name of Brother Timothy, one he had taken before his appointment to this special job in the order. He told me another brother used to quote Paul's advice to him regularly, and always put heavy stress on "a little" to suggest a need for greater moderation.

A fourth point on which representatives of the Protestant evangelical culture showed they were operating outside the sphere of New Testament thought was a frequent reference to building the kingdom of God, or extending it or promoting it or other such presumptuous words. At the annual convention of Southern Baptists in 1957, the year of my ordination, C. C. Warren of Charlotte, North Carolina, delivered a presidential address that called the church "the greatest medium on earth for establishing the kingdom of God," and with related exuberance spoke of Southern Baptist churches "providing spiritual leadership for the greatest advance in the history of Christianity."

Strange to note, talk about somehow constructing the kingdom of God also came from the mouths of liberals advocating the social gospel. People on the left had a different conception of what building the kingdom meant, of course. For them, it was changing society in the direction of socialism. For Southern Baptists and other conservatives it was enlisting more people for membership in their churches, and expanding church programs. But in both cases, it was something they felt sure they were to bring about.

In the New Testament, the kingdom of God, or in Matthew's terminology, kingdom of heaven, is not something anybody establishes or builds, however he conceives it. It is something that already exists, a reality we need to take account of but not presume we can construct.

The kingdom of God is something we get by inheritance (I Corinthians 6:9-10; 15:50). Jesus spoke of the kingdom coming to us (Matthew 12:28), and of our entering the kingdom, something more difficult for the rich than a camel going through the eye of a needle (Mark 10:25), but which the tax collectors and harlots may do before the chief priests and elders (Matthew 21:31). Does that leave us with nothing to do? Well, we can pray, "Thy kingdom come," in the Lord's prayer (Matthew 6:10), seek the kingdom before anything else (Matthew 6:33), join Joseph of Arimathea in looking for the kingdom (Mark 15:43), hear Jesus proclaim that the kingdom is now "at hand" (Mark 1:15), join the Twelve in receiving his commission to "preach the kingdom of God" (Luke 13:29). That would be doing quite a lot. But what we never ever do, when moving within the realm of New Testament thought, is imagine we could establish or build this kingdom. Rather, we give thanks that God the Father "has delivered us from the dominion of darkness and transferred us to the kingdom of his beloved Son" (Colossians 1:13).

We should acknowledge that the mistake of thinking human effort would produce the kingdom of God is not just the error of certain limited groups, but has prevailed far and wide. Karl Barth in fact found it a dominating view in the history of Christian doctrine, and he cited an example in the reference of Augustine to building up (aedificare) the kingdom through the activity of the church. Barth sympathized with religious socialism, particularly in his earlier years, but found it guilty of "a good deal of misguided if zealous talk of fighting for the kingdom of God" as it hoped for "a better world beyond the sway of capitalism, nationalism, militarism, alcohol and so forth" (*Dogmatics IV/4*, 243-44). However socialist he may have been personally, Barth felt it necessary to separate himself from some theologians who "combined the Christian expectation of the kingdom of God and the socialist expectation of the future" (*Dogmatics II/1*, 634).

The concept of the kingdom of God has often been used by church leaders who wanted to serve that kind of political agenda. In *Russia Under the Bolshevik Regime* (Knopf, 1990), Richard Pipes reported that a group of Russian Orthodox priests calling themselves the Living Church cooperated with the Bolshevik assault on the church, and defended their action with the argument that Lenin's regime was the only one in the world that sought to realize "the ideal of the kingdom of God" (p. 361). Actually, the kingdom is not an ideal to be realized, but a reality to be acknowledged. And it is not all that clear what connection this reality had to the realities of the system imposed on the Russians by Vladimir Ilich Ulyanov (Lenin).

In 1892, while serving as pastor of a German Baptist church in the Hell's Kitchen area of Manhattan's West Side, Walter Rauschenbusch, a socialist, joined with others interested in making Christianity a force to overcome poverty and injustice, and formed a Brotherhood of the Kingdom. In a biography, *Walter Rauschenbusch: American Reformer* (Macmillan, 1988), Paul M. Minus reported, "Rauschenbusch contended that when the church places Jesus' teaching about the kingdom at the center of its faith, it will constitute a historic change comparable to the Reformation of the sixteenth century" (p. 89). But Mr. Minus went on to record that the only time the Brotherhood of the Kingdom took direct action on a social issue came when they asked the New York Park Board to "install sandpiles in city parks for small children," and the board agreed to place one in the East River Park (p. 93). Anybody trying to help children wins our sympathy. But the Rauschenbusch contention about "change comparable to the Reformation" amounted to a recognition that his view differed from what had previously been considered Christian teaching. And the one practical result of this "historic change" illustrated the orientation to the physical environment rather than the inner and inter-personal life.

The church that this socialist pastor built, helped by a good many dollars from a fellow Baptist of non-socialist tendencies, John D. Rockefeller the First, still stands, but in these later times has been converted into a theater. I had occasion to go there when I was assigned to do a story on a play about a nun's friendship with George Bernard Shaw (CNS, April 1, 1993). Called *The Best of Friends*, the play was put together by Hugh Whitemore on the basis of letters the nun, Laurentia McLachlan, and Shaw wrote each other, supplemented by letters of an agnostic who got them connected, Sir Sydney Carlyle Cockerell, a museum curator.

Diana Douglas, mother of actor Michael Douglas and former wife of actor Kirk Douglas, played the nun, and I was invited to have lunch with her at a pleasant restaurant near the theater. She told me that she had little prior experience with nuns, but was fascinated by Dame Laurentia "because of her intellectual curiosity." And she herself had been given lunch at Stanbrook Abbey, near Cardiff, Wales, with the nuns then in the convent where Dame Laurentia had lived. "We kept talking and I didn't leave until 6 o'clock," she told me. So New York is not the only place where business gets done by lunching.

If evangelicals take a relatively minor role in New York, a group you must say the opposite about are the Jews. And I have had numerous opportunities to cover developments in their community, particularly in Jewish-Christian relations.

JEWS

CHAPTER FIVE

Covering a symposium on Christian-Jewish relations held by the Cathedral of St. John the Divine in 1974, I found Yosef H. Yerushalmi, a Harvard professor then, later at Columbia University, the most thought-provoking speaker. If Christian theology is to be blamed for the Holocaust, he asked as a Jew and as a specialist in the Inquisition, why did it not happen in the centuries when the church had the power to inflict genocide? When the penalty for heresy was death, Judaism was not regarded as a heresy. Professor Yerushalmi was not declaring Christianity innocent of all charges against it, of course, but advancing the dialogue by raising questions about a common charge, and attempting to encourage a deeper analysis.

Such delving has not been so frequent in the Christian-Jewish dialogue I have heard. And when I extrapolated on some of Professor Yerushalmi's comments and other questions in reporting on the symposium for *Christianity and Crisis* (October 28), I had to defend myself later (December 23) against a rather furious assault by Gregory Baum, a Canadian Catholic of Jewish background who was a symposium participant.

In the intervening years, I have continued to follow the dialogue in a general way, and have found it troubled on several fronts. For the Christian participants of Jewish background, inner tensions come into play. One man in this category, Gerald S. Strober, who worked for the American Jewish Committee, eventually felt led to disconvert and return to Judaism, and wrote a book casting doubt on the value of efforts to strengthen interfaith relations. In *American Jews: Community in Crisis* (Doubleday, 1974), he advised Jews against "alliances of any sort with the liberal Protestant community" (p. 83), and

REFLECTIONS BY A MISSIONARY JOURNALIST IN NEW YORK   141

warned of "the growing gulf that exists between the Catholic and Jewish communities" (p. 84).

An unease also can be found among some Jews facing other Jews who have converted to Christianity, or Christians with some Jewish ancestry. A while back, the World Jewish Congress made a public protest when it observed that the Jewish relations secretaries of the World Council of Churches (WCC), Hans Ucko, and National Council of Churches (NCC), Jay T. Rock, and the general secretary of the Catholic Near East Welfare Association, Robert L. Stern, were all Jewish or part-Jewish in background.

Some of the Christian participants in the dialogue who do not have Jewish family ties tend to form something of a cult, a group absorbed in the issues but somewhat isolated. "You always see the same people in these meetings," one of them complained to me. And some in this category seem to feel such a sense of guilt for Christian treatment of Jews over the centuries, and such desire to make nice, that they do not really engage in dialogue. It is more a matter of attacking their fellow Christians and Christianity overall, and showing they can support Jewish causes as fervently and uncritically as any Jew might. It can seem that some Christians view the dialogue as just an occasion of wallow and grovel. Then there are those Christians operating out of such a generalized psychological unhappiness with their own community that they look for all possible ways to denigrate it, and find in the history of Jewish relations ammunition they can use.

Listening to some of these Christians, I get an impression they arrive at the dialogue ready to tell their Jewish partners, "If there is anything about Christianity that could bother you, I'll just throw it out." I have gone to a certain number of events such as a 1978 panel at the American Jewish Committee on the centennial of the birth of Jules Isaac, a French assimilated Jew who wrote an influential book, *Jesus and Israel* (1949), challenging the church to remove anti-Jewish elements from its teaching. One panelist, United Methodist minister A. Roy Eckardt, went on way beyond M. Isaac and called for recasting basic Christian doctrines. After the burning of children in the Holocaust, the crucifixion of Jesus had "relative nonsignificance," he said, and the Resurrection should be reinterpreted as a future event (NC, January 13). It had to leave a listener wondering if whatever Mr. Eckardt had left could be called Christianity in any sense that made sense. The Christian faith, Resurrection and all, remains whatever it is, regardless of what any individual Christian may wish to discard. And it cannot be helpful for individuals in dialogue to mislead about what a community as a whole might do.

I would suppose that any Christian who was in any way serious about the Christian faith would join Paul in asserting that "if Christ has not been raised,

SIDEBARS

then our preaching is in vain and your faith is in vain" (I Corinthians 15:14). But detecting a tendency among some Christian theologians to ease away from that, Gerald G. O'Collins, a Jesuit priest teaching at the Pontifical Gregorian University in Rome, got together with a Presbyterian, Stephen T. Davis of Claremont McKenna College in California, to organize an ecumenical and international corrective. At their Resurrection Summit, they even brought in a Jewish scholar, Alan F. Segal of Barnard College in New York, to discuss concepts about resurrection held by Jews in the time of Jesus. Summit participants gathered at the seminary of the New York Archdiocese, St. Joseph's in Yonkers, and held a press conference at the end. In a story for CNS (April 15, 1996), I reported that the Catholics and representatives of several Protestant denominations there could agree that the Resurrection should take a larger place in preaching, ethical reflection and spirituality. But while they also agreed the Resurrection was something that happened to Jesus, and not just something going on in the minds of the disciples, they did not reach a common mind on the type of seeing involved when the disciples saw Jesus after the Resurrection.

To me, that seems like a place theologians and preachers could do more work. The form of the New Testament story in which the Resurrection is presented remains indispensable, and Christians never get beyond needing to hear it. But they only make agonies for themselves when they spend time trying in some literalist, fundamentalist fashion to figure out how laws of the physical sciences could accommodate this kind of event. And even if they got over that hurdle, they would still face the task of explaining how the Ascension fit into an astronomer's view of the universe. If a whole busload of tourists had pulled up just at the moment the Resurrection happened, not one would have caught it on his camcorder. It was not that sort of event. Trying to figure out some way of proving it all by the laws of physics and astronomy can only lead you to despair or, worse, to the false pride of imagining that you did somehow succeed in proving it. The *Catechism of the Catholic Church,* issued by the Vatican in 1994, points out that what happened in the Resurrection of Jesus was "essentially" different from what we get when we read the miracle stories about the raising of people such as Lazarus, who were brought back to continue their earthly lives for a while longer but then would have to die again (paragraph 646).

Regarding Jewish relations, the crunch point for a Christian comes in dealing with the New Testament, and I do not suppose this issue can ever be solved intellectually, since everything depends on how the texts are used. If antisemites wish, they can surely find plenty to work with there, but others can read the texts in other ways. Take the report so often quoted of the Jews crying out at the Crucifixion, "His blood be on us and on our children" (Matthew

27:25). For people who understand this blood to be saving blood, the text can take on a meaning different from what others might hear. Like many characters in the Gospel story, those who cried out were saying more than they realized.

Paul is also a figure of ambiguity in this regard. He described himself as a "Hebrew born of Hebrews, as to the law a Pharisee" (Philippians 3:5), became a believer in Christ and later spoke of "the Jews, who killed both the Lord Jesus and the prophets, and drove us out, and displease God and oppose all men" (I Thessalonians 2:14-15). What is to be made of this depends on the interpreter.

I would not want to provide research services for antisemites, but if they checked the Old Testament, they might find as many quotable verses in it as in the New, or maybe more. In the opinion of God, and of Moses, we have there to deal with a community that is "stiff-necked" (Exodus 33:5; 34:9). The Israelites rebelled against Moses, the one sent to them from God for their deliverance, and made the golden calf to serve as the focus of their devotion. According to the Torah, Yahweh declared that they "have corrupted themselves, they have turned aside quickly out of the way which I commanded them; they have made for themselves a molten calf, and have worshiped it and sacrificed to it, and said, 'These are your gods, O Israel, who brought you up out of the land of Egypt'" (Exodus 32:7-8). Or, as the Old Testament also says, "They exchanged the glory of God for the image of an ox that eats grass" and "forgot God, their Savior" (Psalm 106:20-21). At bottom, the New Testament really adds nothing more damning.

But the point is not to use Scripture, Old Testament or New, Koran or whatever, in the conflicts of one group with another, as justification for hostility, or for self-justification in the human struggles of this world. How much respect for the Bible does it show when you tear out pages and wad them into spitballs to shoot at the kid on the other side of the room? Christian theology can recognize in the story of the rebellion and redemption of the chosen people, Israel, the Jews, the story of every community and the human race. Christians sometimes sing a hymn, by one Johann Heermann of the 1600s, that begins, "Ah, holy Jesus, how hast thou offended, that man to judge thee hast in hate pretended?" And in the second verse they sing, "Who was the guilty? Who brought this upon thee? Alas, my treason, Jesus, hath undone thee. 'Twas I, Lord Jesus, I it was denied thee; I crucified thee." Gentiles who want to use Christian theology against the Jews will repress that insight, but the hymn, and not Mr. Eckardt's revisionism, gives us the Christian truth.

Much of the news on Christian-Jewish relations, however, has emerged at some remove from theology. In considerable part it has been the Jewish community pressing Christians in the mainline churches to take a more pro-Israel stand, and the mainline churches pressing for Israel to take a more conciliatory stance toward Arabs. I have never found the mainline churches questioning the right of Israel to exist, or going along with the (now-repealed) United Nations condemnation of Zionism as racism. But much of their leadership has contended that Israel should concede more to the claims of the Arab side, and particularly to the Palestinians. That commonly produces not dialogue but attacks and charges that Christians are anti-Israel, biased against Israel or, in the darker imputations, revealing yet again their unchanging anti-semitic stripes.

In 1976, I interviewed Leopoldo Niilus, director of the WCC's Commission of the Churches on International Affairs, about the Middle East. He told me that he had helped draft a statement issued by Philip A. Potter, the WCC's general secretary, declaring "unequivocal opposition to the equation of Zionism with racism" (*Christian Science Monitor,* May 12). But he did not consider it smart, as had just been done, for Israel to bring in the prime minister of South Africa, the most conspicuous example of governmental racism in the world, for a visit at the exact moment people were thinking about the UN resolution. Also, four years before the NCC would upset Jews with talk of taking the Palestine Liberation Organization (PLO) as a negotiating partner, this representative of the World Council was stating that Israel should do that, and without pre-conditions. He was also reporting that the World Council already supported the right of Palestinians to establish their own state. Announcing such positions bothered some people, Mr. Niilus acknowledged, but he was plowing ahead nonetheless. "Somebody has to stick his neck out, and I have been doing that for a couple of years," he told me.

Botherment of enlarged dimensions appeared on the U.S. scene in 1980, when the NCC adopted a new policy document on the Middle East, and in it said the Palestine Liberation Organization was "the only organized voice" of the Palestinians, and "the only Palestinian body to negotiate a settlement on their behalf." The United States should "engage in open dialogue" with the PLO, it said. In the same document, the NCC said the PLO "must" amend the call in its charter for destruction of Israel, or by other means "remove any doubt" regarding Palestinian acceptance of Israel and Jewish self-determination. But Jews wanted nobody to have any dealings with the PLO. Even before the 1980 document came along, the Anti-Defamation League and the American Jewish Committee had done studies of the NCC record on Middle East issues, and reported finding an anti-Israel bias. Now came this formal paper, unanimously approved, that prominent sectors of the Jewish community could not tolerate, even for purposes of discussion, and the NCC was made much aware of Jewish resentment (NC, November 20).

While production of the document was in process, just a few days before the NCC was to meet and vote, the Anti-Defamation League called a group of its Catholic and Protestant allies to New York for a preemptive strike (NC, October 28). "We are troubled by Christian leaders who ask the Jewish people to brush aside the most ominous threats of the Palestine Liberation Organization as mere rhetoric, and to negotiate with the PLO before it abandons its commitment to Israel's annihilation," said the group. That, of course, would not be the way the NCC saw what it was doing, but Jews and their Christian allies did not want to see the PLO given any respectability. Later, when the NCC board took up the proposed statement, several of the major Jewish organizations moved into heavy lobbying. And when the document was adopted anyway, the protests sounded. Alexander M. Schindler, a rabbi who was president of the Union of American Hebrew Congregations (Reform), called the NCC document "an unconscionable statement supporting the PLO" (UAHC news release, November 22).

In 1982, Nathan Perlmutter, director of the ADL, attacked the NCC for this statement and others in a book unsubtly titled, *The Real Anti-Semitism in America* (Arbor House). Although the liberal Protestants represented by the NCC were personally more tolerant of Jews than many conservative Protestants were, that was less important to Jews than the "constant, persistent mounting pressure by the National Council's ruling hierarchy against Israel" (p. 161). Mr. Perlmutter, who credited his wife, Ruth Ann Perlmutter, with co-authorship of the book but wrote much of it in the first person singular, reported that early in his career "I found myself preferring the mainline Protestants" to the fundamentalist types (p. 144). But he had subsequently decided "liberal Protestantism's tolerance is not so helpful to us as its political hostility to Israel is damaging to us" (p. 155). Jews had much better friends among the fundamentalists such as Jerry Falwell and Pat Robertson, he now believed. (Rabbi Schindler, contrariwise, said Jewish "flirtation" with right wing Christians, as in the ADL giving a platform to Mr. Robertson, was "madness and suicidal as well.")

A lot of flak went to Bailey Smith, president of the Southern Baptist Convention, when he was taped in 1980 declaring, with perhaps some deficiency in nuance, that "God Almighty does not hear the prayer of a Jew." Mr. Perlmutter indicated that he himself held other views, but still placed Mr. Smith closer to his own heart than the NCC types because the Southern Baptist wrote President Reagan to express support for Israel, and joined Jews in opposing the sale of AWACs to Saudi Arabia (p. 166).

"The security of the state of Israel is far more crucial an issue, in terms of that nation's life and death and in terms of the lives and deaths of its

SIDEBARS

population, than the issues on which many fundamentalists and many Jews differ," according to the ADL director (p. 171). So, in contrast to liberal Protestants of the NCC, the fundamentalists were "friends in deed" because they were "friends in need."

Outsticking of necks by Mr. Niilus and associates led to similar results for the World Council of Churches (WCC). Marc Tanenbaum, who had been director of interreligious relations for the AJC and moved over to become its international relations director, was an invited visitor to the 1983 WCC Assembly in Vancouver. But that did not lead him to speak well of the WCC. Reporting–August 21–in the commentary series he delivered for a New York radio station, he charged that a Middle East statement adopted in Vancouver sought to "isolate Israel as a pariah among the nations," that it "dishonestly" accused Israel of inhibiting Muslim and Christian access to Jerusalem, and that it "demonically" sought to replace Western Christian guilt for the Holocaust with guilt for the plight of the Palestinians. He called William P. Thompson, who chaired the committee drafting the statement, a "self-righteous American Presbyterian," and accused the WCC as a whole of "moral hypocrisy." Mr. Thompson declined to respond. Church leaders have not always practiced the Christian virtue of turning the other cheek, but in recent times it seems to me a good many of them have done so in the face of strong and sometimes personal attacks from leaders of the Jewish community.

Rabbi Tanenbaum did not stand alone. The rabbi coordinating interreligious affairs for the ADL, Howard Singer, said the WCC was "forfeiting any role as a world moral authority" because the Middle East statement "elevates the PLO to the position of negotiator and describes East Jerusalem as occupied territory" (ADL press release, September 8).

During the process of voting on the NCC's Middle East statement, there did come one narrow escape for Zionism, when a proposal to drop "as a Jewish state" from the formula commitment to the right of Israel to exist was defeated by only a very narrow margin. Whether that revealed some seriously-developed alternative, or just a failure to understand what was involved, I could not determine.

If the NCC seemed to stand most continuously in the line of fire, what it got was nonetheless mild compared to the condemnations poured on the head of Pope John Paul II in 1982 when he met with Yasser Arafat and let the world get a picture of the two of them together. In 1995, when Mr. Arafat came to Bethlehem to assume control for the Palestine Authority, he put that picture on a postage stamp to commemorate the meeting and record his continuing awareness of the importance of the gesture of papal recognition. But Bishop Francis J. Mugavero of Brooklyn, moderator of the U.S. Catholic bishops' committee on Jewish relations, told me shortly after the pope-Arafat meeting that he had a pile of letters from unhappy Jews. He expressed no resentment toward the protestors, but only commented that the pope did not do things without reflection, and that people should look for his reasons (NC, September 30, 1982).

The *Jewish Press,* an Orthodox Jewish weekly published in Brooklyn, "the largest independent Anglo-Jewish weekly newspaper," looked at the pope and found not reasons but dark, dark guilt. His meeting with Arafat—on September 15—led to the murder of the Palestinians at the Sabra and Shatila camps in Lebanon September 16-18, in the view of the editors. "The Pope Shares the Blame for the Palestinian Massacre," said the headline. The editorial said the pope "sent a signal to all the Christians that murder for a cause is to be applauded," and that "following his guidance the Christian Phalangists began murdering for their cause" (September 24). Others were suggesting it was Israel that should be identified as an accomplice of the Phalangists. But when the Catholic League for Religious and Civil Rights demanded a retraction from the *Jewish Press,* the editors gave a reiteration (October 8), and asked why the League was not shocked "when the Vatican issued the picture showing the pope greeting the master terrorist, Arafat, with a warm head-of-state hero's welcome."

An illustration of the power of photo journalism, the picture was widely published and inflamed relations more than a written report of a meeting would have by itself. I covered the National Workshop on Christian-Jewish Relations the next spring in Boston, and heard Eugene J. Fisher, Jewish relations secretary for the Catholic bishops, comment on the different captions given the picture. In the Catholic press, he recalled, it would run something like, "Pope reaches out for peace," but in Jewish papers more like, "Pope meets with successor to Hitler" (NC, April 28).

So time moves along. And on September 5, 1996, I looked at *The New York Times* and on the front page saw a picture of Benjamin Netanyahu, the Likud leader elected Israeli prime minister on a pledge to take a harder line against the Palestinians, and he was shaking hands with Yasser Arafat.

But the Middle East has not been the only trouble spot. When Pope John Paul II visited Auschwitz in June of 1979, he noted the plaques in various languages indicating deaths of people from many backgrounds. As he directed attention from one to another, he paused at the one in Hebrew. "It is not permissible for anyone to pass by this inscription with indifference," the pope said with concentrated solemnity. Mr. Perlmutter wrote that in a meeting he told the pope his remarks were "moving and well noted by Jews" (p. 149).

But I was a little astonished when I went to cover a forum on "Jewish and Christian perceptions" of the visit, and heard a largely negative tone (NC, September 2, 1979). Thomas E. Bird, a Catholic layman teaching Slavic and Eastern European languages and literature at Queens College in New York, said the pope's statements were good as far as they went, but went not far enough. They should have included more direct reference to "the Jewish people" as Holocaust victims, he said. And Professor Bird criticized the pope for bringing up Maximilian Kolbe, a Franciscan priest who gave his life to save another prisoner at Auschwitz, and Edith Stein, a Jewish convert to Catholicism who was executed there. The idea that a religious leader might visit the place where such noted members of his community were killed and make no reference to them seemed to me unlikely to sell. Catholics who looked to those individuals as inspiration for their own lives would have felt their Holy Father let them down. But another professor, Gershon Bacon of the Jewish Theological Seminary in New York, also objected to mentioning the two, and said it played down the specifically Jewish aspect of the Holocaust.

I do see that as a valid concern, aside from whether or not the pope's way of speaking at Auschwitz deserved the critique. And it leads to the broader issue of whether Hitler's attempt to destroy the Jewish people should be viewed as a unique event, or just another in a series of tragedies affecting many groups. In 1978, the Cathedral of St. John the Divine followed up on its symposium by placing a work by a Jewish sculptor, Elliot Offner, in one of its side bays as a memorial to the Holocaust. Such memorials had been extremely rare in churches, as I suppose they still are, and I reported on the installation and other Jewish relations activities of the cathedral in articles for the *Christian Science Monitor* (May 30) and the World Council of Churches monthly, *One World* (September). But the significance of the cathedral's action seemed to shrink when officials later placed in the same area memorials to the Armenian massacres and to victims of the Bosnian conflict. Making it a generalized acknowledgment of various who have suffered atrocities seemed to obscure the original point.

Jews are right, as I see it, when they insist on the uniqueness of the Holocaust, or the Shoah, as it is known in Hebrew, and demand attention for the specific challenge it presents. The response of people who say, "Oh well, lots of bad things have happened to other groups in history, and the centuries have been marked with many Holocausts," seem not merely wrong but perhaps badly motivated. It sounds like an effort to evade the horror of "the" Holocaust, and the need to think through how it happened. Attempts at group extermination occurred in ancient times, such as we read about in the Old Testament, and in out-of-the-way corners in later centuries. But the Nazi project is unparalleled as a calculated, cold-blooded attempt by an advanced society, with fullest access to the religious and cultural heritage of thousands of years, to exterminate an entire race of people, and to kill every single one of them simply because of the group they belonged to by ancestry, charging that the group was evil and every member stood corrupted, and not because of anger at any particular actions proved or alleged against the victims.

The Armenian massacres, horrible as they were, did not really have the same character, and I do not suppose Armenians themselves would rank the Turkish society of the Ottomans as an advanced civilization. The Turks apparently felt threatened and erupted in a frenzy. Many of them no doubt went rampaging with a lust to kill every Armenian they saw. But they were not operating on the basis of a developed ideology and program such as that of the Nazis, or using the administrative machinery of a modern state in bureaucratic efficiency. The same could be said about the Pol Pot massacres in Cambodia or the mutual hacking of Hutus and Tutsis in Rwanda and Burundi.

In what is called victimology, groups of various sorts try to get sympathy, political backing and maybe material benefits by talking of how badly they and their group have been abused in times past. I elevate myself to a position of privilege by talking about how much my ancestors suffered. To some other groups with grievances, it appears that Jews get more of all that because of the Holocaust. So the others begin to ask, Can't I get some of that concern for my pain? And ain't I a victim?

I see even some Catholics in New York want to complain about Catholic "bashing" and assert their right to enjoy the victim status in their very own lifetime. But when Catholics are electing mayors, governors, senators and representatives by the car load, it becomes hard to believe the general population holds ingrained prejudice against Catholics *per se*. The pollution has cleared considerably since Alfred E. Smith unsuccessfully and John F. Kennedy successfully ran for president.

Under a new chief, the Catholic League for Religious and Civil Rights has set out in recent years to surpass the ADL in finding grievances to get outraged about. William A. Donohue, who became president in 1993, even stretched down to publish a complaint about one of my stories, apparently short of worthwhile outrages to keep him occupied that day. When I reported that during the League's demonstration against Terence McNally's homosexual play, *Corpus Christi*, People for the American Way held a counter-demonstration, but with "somewhat smaller" numbers (CNS, October 14, 1998), Mr. Donohue grumbled that I did not show the difference starkly enough. He presumably thought I should have written "awfully much smaller" or "humiliatingly smaller" or maybe "ridiculously littler." No doubt, people are sometimes expressing a hostility to Catholicism or some aspects of the Catholic Church. But Mr. Donohue's way of making a career out of looking for a grievance makes us suspect he is yet another of those who enjoy taking the victim role in order to justify their zest for hitting people.

I think what such warriors label anti-Catholicism might in many cases be more accurately called anti-clericalism, something often found in Catholic countries but a phenomenon the United States has largely escaped in the past. Its occasional emergence here in more recent times has derived mostly from the way bishops try to use their influence on issues related to sex, and has come from Catholics as well as non-Catholics.

If you would like to see another step in grievance collecting: when the first Polish pope was about to make his first visit to the United States in 1979, President Eugene Kusielewicz of the Kosciusko Foundation released an open letter to him complaining of the way the U.S. Catholic Church treated its Polish-American members (NC, October 1). In the Kusielewicz view, they were getting no respect. So now which should we say—that he was anti-Catholic or that American Catholics were anti-Polish? If victimology becomes the coin of the realm, everybody will scramble to come up with enough to buy a little public sympathy.

One place I have sensed the anti-clericalism has been in the debates over church-state relations. Champions of the strict separation view have often accused Catholic bishops, and in New York sometimes especially John J. O'Connor, the Catholic Cardinal-Archbishop, of threatening the "wall" of separation, and undermining the First Amendment and our constitutional government and so on. In New York, the black Protestant clergy have been the most explicit and conspicuous in using their churches for political purposes, but the line of these ministers is generally liberal, and white liberals perhaps would not want to criticize their allies, white critique of blacks not being considered good form in any case. Black Protestant clergy use their pulpits to campaign for political office themselves, endorse favored candidates from their pulpits and invite these politicians to campaign from their pulpits. It is not conceivable that Cardinal O'Connor would have done anything like that, or allowed anything like that, from the pulpit of St. Patrick's Cathedral. But if he commented on public issues, in or out of the pulpit, he could get accused of trying to destroy the American form of government—if the separationists disagreed with the position he was taking at the moment.

After the folding of *A.D.,* a monthly magazine published jointly by the United Presbyterian Church and the United Church of Christ, one of the *A.D.* editors, James A. Gittings, started a Presbyterian monthly he called *Seventh Angel,* with reference to the angel of Revelation that pronounced the final judgment on the world of wickedness (16:17). There were not sufficient resources or backers to keep it going, but in the few months it lived Mr. Gittings asked me to do a number of articles. In one (November 1984), I surveyed the church-state scene, and among other items included a report on a sermon delivered by Donald S. Harrington, retired pastor of the Community Unitarian Universalist Church in New York. Speaking at another Unitarian Universalist church on September 30, into the political season, he attacked Catholic bishops and Protestant fundamentalists for their "concerted" effort, with President Ronald Reagan, to "break that wall of separation between church and state which our founding fathers so painfully constructed." And he attacked the tv evangelists for promoting Mr. Reagan on tax-exempt broadcast time.

Curious to me, Mr. Harrington was himself among the most political of ministers. He was, at least in title if perhaps not in substance, the head of a political party, the Liberal Party. But he exempted himself from criticism because, he claimed, he had "meticulously kept my church out of partisan politics." All this came in the midst of a political campaign in which the Liberal Party was supporting Mr. Reagan's Democratic opponent. So I pointed out: "This attack on Reagan and friends by the head of a political party supporting Walter Mondale was, of course, delivered in a church we may presume is tax exempt." In any case, I cannot see how a church can be kept out of party politics, meticulously or unmeticulously, when its chief cleric is a party chief.

In reference to the topic at large, I also observed, as many have, that the Constitution nowhere mentions a "wall" between church and state, and that if Thomas Jefferson spoke of a "wall of separation," this did not prove there actually was one, or ought to be one, or that the American people as a whole agreed with him in wanting one. My guess would be that most Americans prefer to see church and state working together harmoniously, as they have been doing in several areas: chaplaincies in the military, social welfare programs, overseas relief, *etc.*

Growing up as a Southern Baptist, I heard much about the need for church-state separation, but I gradually came to realize that we were getting mostly code language for what was then actual anti-Catholicism. And from the side of liberal Protestantism, John C. Bennett could observe in *Christians and the State* (Scribner's, 1958), "The attitudes of Americans toward church-state relations depends in considerable measure on their attitude toward Roman Catholicism" (p. 252). I suppose in general you could say the "wall" people are usually thinking of specific groups they want to wall off from public influence. Protestants, whether liberal or conservative, never thought their own role in the public sphere should be diminished, and when the Supreme Court began to do that by ruling out prayer and Bible reading in the public schools, a shift in Southern Baptist thinking became discernible. As a New Yorker cartoon had the boss declaring to a subordinate, "When I said, Let the chips fall where they may, you knew very well I did not mean on me."

Southern Baptists, while operating colleges to protect their young people from malign influences of higher education in the secular mode, had supported the public school concept at the elementary and secondary levels against parochial schools because they could feel the ethos of conservative evangelicals pervaded the public schools. If you want to believe in some historic American tradition of building a wall between church and state, you will need to find a way of fitting in my great-grandfather, Thomas Rockhold Early, who moved to a rural community near Mountainburg, Arkansas, in 1883, served as pastor of the Baptist church there and taught the public school in the same building. I doubt that there was any wall through the middle of the building, or the middle of my great-grandfather's mind, to keep one aspect of community life from influencing the other.

Paul Blanshard, who carried on the separationist campaign through his writings and speaking, and through an organization, Protestants and Other Americans United for Separation of Church and State, got much of his support from Southern Baptists. But when I read his writings such as *Catholic Power and American Freedom* (Beacon, 1949), which was sometimes found in the little libraries of Southern Baptist churches, I could see his attack on the Catholic Church came ultimately from a secular outlook, and if thought through would also hit Southern Baptists or most any religious community. And eventually he did reveal that he was a secular humanist.

I do not mean to suggest here that I see no peril in church-state entanglement. Obviously, dangers abound for the church as well as for people outside who may feel put upon if the churches, or one dominating church, find ways to push a controversial agenda with government money and authority. In 1978, I began to wonder a little about the National Council of Churches coming to rely more and more on government money. In a piece that the *Christian Science Monitor* printed in its "opinion and commentary" section (July 3), I noted that the NCC's guidelines said it would "normally" rely on "voluntary contributions rather than government resources." But just one of its units, Church and Society, had received authorization in one board meeting to accept $1,440,000 from the government for one project, $200,000 for another and an unspecified amount for a third. Since this unit already had permission to accept other government grants, and since its 1978 budget anticipated that it would get less than $900,000 from church sources, I wondered about the ultimate import of this drift. For one thing, the churches could not talk much about their religious beliefs when using government money. And I mentioned as a subtler problem the reduced need of NCC staff to stay in rapport with their constituency when they could finance the programs they wanted by going to the government for funding.

So while I would not advocate any rigid "separationist" policy, I could conclude in the *Monitor* analysis, "The dominant American tradition has held that the churches will be strongest–and ultimately most useful to their society–when they are most independent of the government and most reliant on their own resources."

Now, speaking again of victimology, I notice that blacks are sometimes among those who want to hook other causes onto Holocaust language and emotions. So blacks on occasion argue that they, too, have been victims of a Holocaust and genocide, and suffered more deaths than the Jews. Bad as slavery was, however, and whatever number of blacks died in the slave trade, I do not see how you can properly call their American experience genocide. Those who brought slaves to America and those who bought them did not adopt anything like the Nazi view. Owners exploited the labor of black people, and when they felt so inclined, treated them brutally. But they did not want blacks exterminated. Quite the opposite: they felt a need for the presence of blacks in their midst, and they wanted blacks to continue to be, to be in America and to be in America in growing numbers. They wanted blacks to get to America alive, because only so could the profits come, and in America they wanted blacks to live long and healthy lives, because only so could whites enjoy their labor to the fullest. And they wanted blacks to reproduce, and the country through succeeding years to see new generations of the black race. That is treatment far removed from genocide.

The Nazis could not content themselves with confiscating the property of Jews and exploiting their labor. Dominating the Jews and depriving them of all rights was not the final solution. The Nazis did not aspire merely to drive Jews away and force them to live in an alien land. They wanted Jews, all Jews, every Jew, to not be. And for that the Nazis were willing to act against their own immediate interests—renouncing the benefit of Jewish labor and, in the extreme crisis of a desperate war effort, diverting scarce resources to the goal of racial extermination. And the goal was set without regard to any particular acts of individual victims, but solely because they were Jews. It was a depth and darkness of evil beyond what any rational mind could conceive. So we need to contemplate this history in its malign singularity.

For Christians, some special contemplation is in order, uncomfortable though it is, because the Holocaust occurred in an area under Christian influence for long centuries. When people say it happened in the heart of Christian

SIDEBARS

Europe, we can suggest it is perhaps more accurate to say it happened in the heart of pagan Europe, because baptism had become only a cultural tradition for large numbers who retained some formal church relationship. Still, it would be salutary for Christians to remember that the Holocaust was carried out mostly by people in some sense Christian, baptized people, and the Nazi perpetrators were supported by significant numbers of those committed with some seriousness and theological awareness to the Christian religion. How could that happen?

On innumerable occasions, I heard Cardinal O'Connor tell of going to Dachau, putting his hand on an oven and asking, "Could human beings actually do this to human beings?" But I cannot recall him ever going on to ask the more specific questions: How could so many Christians have so enthusiastically joined in doing this? How could so many clergy, Catholic and Protestant, have gone along with this? How could the Catholic bishop for the German armed forces, Franz Josef Rukowski, as recorded in Gordon C. Zahn's *German Catholics and Hitler's War* (Notre Dame Press, 1989), have issued a statement for Adolph Hitler's birthday in 1940, appealing to Catholic soldiers to "let our gift to the Fuhrer be the inner readiness for sacrifice and devotion to the folk"? How could it have emerged as the teaching of a Catholic bishop that Hitler "has discovered the life principle of the German folk and by his acts has made it effective" (p. 160)?

I might add that Christians have an additional obligation to give these matters attention because of the inward relationship with Jews. Christians cannot regard Jews as just adherents of another non-Christian religion. The tie starts with the fact that Jesus was a Jew, and a Jew not just incidentally. His human culture was fully Jewish. The New Testament presents the center of Christian faith as a descendant of King David, born in David's royal city, Bethlehem, a child dedicated in the Jerusalem temple and carried there later in life by his parents for festivals, a child who recapitulated the experience of ancient Israel in the flight into Egypt. The New Testament authors apparently did not think it was of any importance to tell us what he looked like, but only what he did and what he said, who he was. Or as my grandmother would tell you, pretty is as pretty does. But it has been observed that the one thing we do know about the physical appearance of Jesus is that he was circumcised. He began his ministry in the local synagogue, chose twelve apostles to represent the twelve tribes of Israel, developed his teaching out of the Jewish Scriptures and died in Jerusalem. A real Jew.

The other basic tie of Jews and Christians derives from the Hebrew Scriptures. The church has canonized these writings in their entirety, declared them to be the Word of God and placed them with the New Testament writings to form together the Christian Bible. That has not been done for the writings considered sacred by any other religion. So whether or not Jews and Christians like each other, they are bound together, and always will be.

How we will understand the common heritage is another matter. In conventional goodwillism, we hear appeals to the common positions of Jews and Christians as believers in monotheism. And sometimes Islam is brought in so there can be a mutual embrace by adherents of these three monotheistic religions, each looking to Abraham as the original father of believers. No doubt it would be a good thing if believers in these–and other–religions could get along and avoid killing each other. But it is not necessarily a good thing to oversimplify.

Karl Barth has taught that though Christians do of course believe in one God, a monotheism that is trinitarian differs much from one that is not. And Georg W. F. Hegel suggested that we could gain little of value from "mere" monotheism (*Philosophy of Mind,* paragraph 573). For Christians, one could say in elaboration, value comes when, helped by the Holy Spirit, they see the one God in the face of Jesus, hear him speaking the Word of God and feel his hand lifting them up as they are about to sink. If monotheism is understood to require rejection of a belief in Christ as the one and only eternal Son of God, then it represents a different kind of religion and, Professor Barth argued, different from the faith expressed in the Old Testament. To suggest the depth of difference between concepts of the oneness of God, he observed that after the Gospel of John reports the statement of Jesus that "I and the Father are one" (10:30-31), it adds that his hearers then "took up stones to stone him" for blasphemy (p. 456).

Islam raises the question, Professor Barth wrote, of whether the oneness and uniqueness ultimately belong to God or to his prophet Mohammed, or maybe the individual Muslim. "It is, therefore, unthinking to set Islam and Christianity side by side, as if in monotheism at least they have something in common. In reality, nothing separates them so radically as the different ways in which they appear to say the same thing–that there is only one God" (*Dogmatics II/1,* 449).

Just in passing, we could note that Christianity also shows its difference from Islam quite concretely in not requiring anything comparable to the Muslim's visit to Mecca. To be the best kind of Muslim, you must go there at least once in your life. Christians do often make religious pilgrimages to places associated with the life of Jesus, or go just out of historical interest, but they have no obligation to do so. Nor is there anything comparable to the obligation some Jews have asserted for all Jews outside Israel to "return" to Israel, making what is called in Hebrew "aliyah," meaning "to go up."

SIDEBARS

In *Israel for Christians* (Fortress, 1983), A. James Rudin of the American Jewish Committee explained that "making aliyah" had "deep religious meaning, for it is considered the fulfillment of a divine commandment." And he continued, "Jewish religious tradition finds profound significance in residing in the land of Israel" (p. 107). Rabbi Rudin did not go live in Israel himself, an indication the commandment is perhaps not considered always binding on every Jew. But in any case, the religious attachment of Muslims and Jews to particular locations remains unmatched by anything in Christianity.

We are rather often reminded that the one important matter in real estate is location, location in triplicate, but for Christianity real estate itself is not all that important. As children of Abraham, they stand always ready to respond to the call: "Go from your country and your kindred and your father's house to the land that I will show you" (Genesis 12:1). With the focus shifted from location to vocation, the disciples of Jesus were called to leave whatever spot they occupied before he came along, follow him wherever he went and then carry out his commission to go into all the world. "Foxes have holes, and birds of the air have nests; but the Son of man has nowhere to lay his head" (Matthew 8:20). The church uses whatever locations it can, but has no particular need to control any particular part of the earth's surface. So what if you never ever see Bethlehem, Nazareth or Jerusalem, or Rome, Constantinople, Wittenberg, Geneva or Canterbury, or even if you never get to the Interchurch Center in New York? All interesting places to visit, but you can live the Christian life to the fullest without ever seeing any of them.

Sometimes Christianity is grouped with Judaism and Islam under the common category of "religions of the book." I do not know exactly how Jews and Muslims understand that, but for Christianity it is misleading. Christians do, of course, give all due reverence to the holy writings. But Christianity is person-centered, not book-centered. To some religious people that Jesus thought were too much people of the book, he observed that they were trying to find eternal life in the Scriptures, but really the reason for reading those words was that "it is they that bear witness to me" (John 5:39).

German mission agencies interested in converting Jews held a conference in Stuttgart in 1930, and invited Martin Buber to come help them better understand the people they were trying to convert. Considering Buber's belief in I-thou relationships, it is perhaps not surprising that he accepted even such an invitation as theirs. He began, as we might have guessed, by telling his audience that they had the wrong mission, but went on to give a thoughtful address on "The Two Foci of the Jewish Soul," an address I suppose may have been published in various places but which I found translated in a volume edited by Fritz A. Rothschild, *Jewish Perspectives on Christianity* (Crossroad, 1990).

Buber said Jews and Christians had in common "a book and an expectation," but differed in their understanding of both. Regarding the Bible, he said, "To you the book is a forecourt; for us it is the sanctuary" (p. 130). Christians, I might explicate, would say they come into this "forecourt" because it, Old Testament and New, is a witness to the living Word.

You can see another difference between Christian and Muslim views if you look at their opposite positions regarding translation. When I cover the American Bible Society, I am constantly getting updated reports of how many more languages the Bible is in. That is in fact a major goal of the organization–getting the Bible translated and printed in enough languages that every literate person in the world could read it, and maybe putting oral versions on tape for those who are not literate. The earliest Christian communities started the tradition by using Greek translations that Jews had made of the Hebrew Old Testament. Did those translations always represent the Hebrew original in absolutely perfect form? No, not at all. Did that bring on a migraine for the early Christians? No, not at all. If you check your Bible, you will likely find that some of the quotations in the New Testament do not so well correspond word-for-word with the Old Testament sources. But Christians have never considered that such a big worry. Whenever anyone is translating the Bible, or anything else, he should strain every mental muscle to make it as true to the original as possible. But our eternal salvation does not depend on the perfection of translators, or on all of us learning to read the Bible in its original languages.

However, if you go to the HarperCollins *Dictionary of Religion* (1995) to learn something about Islam, you will read, "Muslims have maintained an aversion to translations, maintaining that the inimitable Qur'an is truly itself only in Arabic, the language of God's revelation" (p. 517). Islam has spread to people of many languages, but for religious purposes the Koran (Qur'an) must everywhere be learned and recited in Arabic. And you will be told that, to Muslims, this text has the religious significance that Christians find in Christ.

In theory, Christian fundamentalists try to uphold something like the Muslim view, though they of course do not and cannot carry it all the way. They yearn to find the religious absolute, the ultimate truth, infallible truth, in the human wording of a book they can hold in their hands and quote at their opponents to batter them down. "The Bible alone, and the Bible in its entirety, is the Word of God written and is therefore inerrant in the autographs," says the Evangelical Theological Society. We will have to think a bit about that matter of "autographs." But psychologically, the fundamentalist emphasis on the infallibility of a text, like the Catholic doctrine of finding infallibility in certain statements of popes, is a worldly effort to claim a kind of security in verbal formulations that God has not granted to finite minds.

When Christian fundamentalists wave a Bible at you as they preach, and declare that they are preaching from an infallible book, and you had better not question anything they say, they are engaging in a double dishonesty. This I assert in the sense of objective dishonesty; I of course do not claim to read their subjective thoughts. But dishonesty is the word I feel called to use when they are waving an English version of the Bible or some other translation. If they have thought at all about what they are doing, they would have to acknowledge that the book they are waving is not infallible, even on their theory, because, as Muslims might emphasize, no translation can reproduce the original text perfectly, with all the nuances. And they are acting dishonestly on a second level because they know the versions they might hold of the Hebrew Old Testament and Greek New Testament, whatever versions served as the basis for the English translations, have been affected by copyists through the centuries, introducing at least a few mistakes, we know, because we find one manuscript differing from another at various points.

We do not have the originals of any of the biblical books, those autograph copies, where the more aware fundamentalists postulate infallibility, and in the case of some books, there may not ever have been any one piece of papyrus or parchment that could be called "the" original. Paul seems at least in some instances to have dictated his letters to a scribe, so a theory of infallibility would have to move beyond his oral infallibility, and assert scribal infallibility. Not conceding a single typo, or whatever a fallible scribe would make. But for many of the biblical books, such as the Psalms, we have no clear idea of how they were produced. The material may have been gathered by various people over a period of time, and have existed for a few generations in varied formats. Some of the "autographs" may have been only oral for a while, recoverable only when scientists give us that machine to record all the sound vibrations of past centuries.

Writing in the *Anchor* commentary on John (Doubleday, 1966), with the imprimatur of Terence J. Cooke, later Cardinal-Archbishop of New York, Raymond E. Brown suggested that this Gospel was developed in five stages, in which original material (1) was shaped orally by "more than one man" (2), and produced in a "first edition" (3) with "secondary editing" (4) by the main shaper of this tradition, and "final editing" (5) by someone else (pp. xxxiv-xxxix). If you know where you can lay your hands on some "autograph" manuscript of John with infallibility, scholars would be interested to hear from you.

People studying the history of the Koran suggest there can be similar questions about finding any original version of it to be called infallible. The material had not all been put in written form at the death of Mohammed in 622, it appears, and scholars cannot certify the standard version commissioned by Caliph Uthman (644-56).

For Christians operating on the basis of common sense, such considerations do not wrinkle the brow, because biblical material seems to have been handled carefully enough through the centuries. So if you focus your eyes on what the Bible is telling you about, and do not try to worship the text itself, you suffer no distress. But fundamentalists do not operate on the basis of common sense. They insist on absoluteness. And logically enough, Christians of this outlook react much like Muslims against scholars who engage in historical analysis of the sacred texts.

As for papal infallibility, it seems to me that its real function is symbolic and political, a device for keeping everybody marching together at the cadence of the chief. The overwhelming majority of papal statements do not carry the certification of infallibility, but we read of "trickle down infallibility," a suggestion the infallibility of the few dogmatic statements up at the top serves to give popes a luster that helps reinforce demands for everybody to go along with whatever decisions they are making at ground level. Similarly, the biblical infallibility we hear about from preachers in the Protestant fundamentalist camp seems like a device they are using to make themselves sound more authoritative as they move from point A to point B and eventually to XYZ.

When I wrote an article for the *Christian Century* (July 1, 1970) on the centennial of the First Vatican Council, I pointed out the circumlocutious language used in formulating the doctrine of papal infallibility. The council did not just straightforwardly assert that the pope was infallible, or infallible on specified topics. Instead, the decree, Pastor aeternus, said the pope was "possessed of that infallibility with which the divine Redeemer willed that his church should be endowed." And I pointed out, further, that such phrasing "might be analyzed at length." You could also ask whether the pope is infallible in deciding on which occasions he is speaking infallibly. It may turn out that only those papal statements will continue to be considered infallible which church members by consensus continue to believe express their faith. In the article, I noted the apparent inability of Catholic authorities to give us a list of all the infallible statements that popes had made. It seems agreed that Pius XII's assertion in 1950 of the dogma of Mary's assumption into heaven at her death was the only one since Vatican I, unless maybe you accept Joseph Ratzinger's view that Pope John Paul II was speaking infallibly when he ruled out ordination of women. But infallibility presumably did not wait till 1870 to start existing, but would apply to each and every pope of each and every century. And presumably it would be important for us to know about all the truths we have

SIDEBARS

been told with infallible certainty. Why has there not been a greater effort to collect all these statements and give them to us in convenient form?

To some extent, Christian acceptance of the Jewish Scriptures as the Old Testament gives Christians and Jews a shared ethical tradition, though they have different standpoints from which to interpret this material. Christians interested in social reform have often turned especially to the critiques of society found in the Hebrew prophets, and interpreted the Christian life as an attempt to act in accordance with them. In *Man's Nature and His Communities* (Scribner, 1965), Reinhold Niebuhr quoted Charles D. Williams, Episcopal bishop of Detroit, as saying that there were only two real Christians in the whole city–"and they are both Jews" (p. 18).

There is also a general question about how Christianity as a religion is related overall to Judaism. Sometimes Christians call Jews their elder brothers, but that could carry an unfortunate connotation for those acquainted with the hardhearted elder brother in the parable of the Prodigal Son (Luke 15:11-32), which parable I suppose might actually have the Jewish-Gentile relationship in its ancestry. At other times, Christianity is called a daughter of Judaism. To me, it seems more accurate to say Christianity and Judaism are both daughters of the same mother. In the first century there was a division among Jews about how the faith of Israel was to be carried forward. Two communities rooted themselves in the Old Testament, but neither sought to continue its patterns exactly, and after the Romans moved in could not continue the patterns exactly. Judaism without the temple, without the priesthood and without the sacrifices of the Old Testament, a Judaism oriented to the rabbinic teaching of the Mishnah and the Talmud, is something considerably different. So what is now called rabbinic or Talmudic Judaism is not precisely a reproduction of the Israelite religion of the Old Testament but, like Christianity, a daughter.

It is a historical curiosity that the little region of Galilee holds central importance for both. Judah ha-Nasi (the prince), a key figure credited with leadership in putting basic materials of the early rabbinic tradition together in the Mishnah, was based in Sepphoris, a city near Nazareth.

A common error of Christians, however, has been using the rabbinic tradition in an insufficiently careful way to interpret the New Testament. I picked up this point from a Jewish scholar, Burton L. Visotzky, a professor of rabbinics at the Jewish Theological Seminary in New York. He was a panelist at a conference Union Seminary held in 1987 as part of its 150th anniversary celebration, and that I reported on for a New York publication, *Jewish Week* (April 24). He referred to the frequent attempts to add background interpretation of the New Testament by saying, "Jewish law at the time required" this, that or the other, but called the procedure "hazardous."

Interpreters making such attempts are usually drawing on material in the Mishnah, not compiled until perhaps around 200 A.D., and in the Babylonian and Jerusalem versions of the Talmud, a couple of centuries later. These works may preserve material that dates to the time of Jesus or before, but scholars cannot tell us with much assurance which parts go back that far, or what form they had then, or to what extent people of the time obeyed whichever of the rabbinic laws that may have been taught. So it will be well to question the conventional efforts to interpret incidents in the life of Jesus or the New Testament church by using the rabbinic traditions, and saying this was the way Jewish life was supposed to go in the years before the destruction of Jerusalem.

At the Union conference, a Christian scholar, James A. Sanders, suggested that study of the Mishnah and Talmud remained useful for Christians, nonetheless, because it would help them see a "trajectory" of development from the period before the New Testament to the period after. That approach no doubt has value, but it seems to me that the more basic structure is two trajectories that we can compare for our instruction, two ways the development proceeded.

Some people have tried to minimize the differences between Judaism and Christianity by asserting that it is only a difference between thinking the Messiah came in the past and will come again, or thinking his future coming will be his first. "Have you visited our planet before, or is this your first time here?" they plan to ask him whenever he appears. So the disagreement reduces to a little witticism about timing, the supposedly incidental matter of believing in one coming or two, a question equal in importance to whether you prefer one lump of sugar or two in your tea.

But to me, that approach presents difficulties of both form and substance. Belief in the Messiah is a matter of considerable significance in the religious life of many people, and it seems not good form to make a joke out of it, or slight the importance of understanding it aright. On substance, the complication is that Christians not only believe the Messiah did come, and give his life for all of us, Jew and Gentile alike, and that at the end he will come again to complete all he has begun, but that he is present today, with us right here and right now, really present. So the message of Emmanuel, God with us, speaks with immediacy, and not just as a recollection of great days in the past or expectation of glorious events yet to come.

For Christians, we might add, the connection between what happened then and there, in the ministry of Jesus, and what happens to us, here and now, is found in the doctrine of the Holy Spirit, the same Spirit present to us that was at work in him. I would guess that a lack of concentration on this point is what has led some Christians to feel the biblical world was too remote in time and space, and to decide they might make it more immediately present to American life by producing stories such as the one Mormons got from the gold tablets of Joseph Smith. But if you believe in the Holy Spirit, you already have as much immediacy as you can ever use.

In other Christian-Jewish news, we were to have the conflict over the Auschwitz convent and non-felicitous interventions by the Warsaw archbishop, Jozef Glemp. Some Polish Catholics reacted with outrage to pressures for removal of the convent, and charged that Jews were trying to monopolize Auschwitz and make the world forget that Catholics also suffered and died there. People asking how Christians could have treated Jews so cruelly are challenged also to ask how Christians could have treated fellow Christians so cruelly. So the way of giving special attention to the Holocaust as a distinctively Jewish trauma without ignoring the suffering of others remained a live issue.

I got to see the Glemp controversy enacted in 1991, when the cardinal visited the United States after he had precipitated a firestorm with comments about Jews supposedly controlling the international media to Poland's disadvantage in public relations, and so on. Jews could not agree on how to react. Some were so mad they wanted nothing to do with Cardinal Glemp, and said they should not even talk to him until he apologized. Seymour Reich, a New York lawyer, resigned as chairman of the International Jewish Committee for Interreligious Consultations (IJCIC) because he could not get agreement on his view that "until Cardinal Glemp repudiates the anti-Semitic accusations he made in his 1989 homily, I do not believe American Jewish leaders should meet with him" (CNS, September 24).

But some did attend a meeting with the cardinal in Washington. Then Cardinal O'Connor displayed heroic virtue in grasping the nettle. Cardinal Glemp was to appear at a Sunday mass with him at St. Patrick's Cathedral October 6, and Cardinal O'Connor set up a meeting in his residence after mass, bringing Cardinal Glemp and some Jewish representatives together for head-to-head (CNS, October 7). At the mass, Cardinal Glemp continued in his non-helpful way. He spoke to the largely Polish-American congregation of many things Polish, but said nothing about relations with Jews, not even offering in general terms a hope they might improve. After mass, a woman approached me and said, "He didn't apologize. I'm glad. What for?"

But Cardinal O'Connor had made a few pertinent comments, saying–with what accuracy I do not know–that Cardinal Glemp had expressed "deep regret" for any misunderstanding, and had reached out "far more frequently than he has been given credit for." The meeting afterward produced an agreement to join together in a program of activities in Poland to improve relations. Some Jews took the pragmatic view that it was best to keep talking and working, and achieve whatever was possible. Rabbi Tanenbaum told me, "You cannot carry out a program if every other week somebody boycotts a meeting or resigns from an office." But Leon Klenicki, a rabbi who was interfaith director of the ADL, said he refused to sign the agreement, though he went to the meeting, because Cardinal Glemp "didn't commit himself to anything."

While the meeting was going on, participants in Cardinal O'Connor's residence could hear Avraham Weiss and associates chanting protests outside. Rabbi Weiss had done his own considerable part to promote disharmony by leading some of his followers to Auschwitz, and carrying his anti-convent protest directly to the nuns. Now, as he led his demonstration outside Cardinal O'Connor's window, New Jersey members of the Catholic League for Religious and Civil Rights counterprotested with signs demanding "Stop Catholic Bashing" and "Stand Up to Our Enemies." The New York police, much accustomed to this style of sidewalk usage, kept the demonstrators separated, and even found space for a third set, abortion advocates who for who knows why had chosen this occasion to resume their chant against Cardinal O'Connor.

I had another opportunity to view Rabbi Weiss's operating style in 1995, when he sent out a press release announcing that he would appear at the Vatican's mission to the United Nations January 23, and give the nuncio a letter for the pope. Such occasions are tricky. You can hardly go without becoming part of the event. If someone is trying to create pressure, getting reporters there becomes part of the strategy. But if something was going to happen, the Catholic News Service needed to check and see what. So there I was. And there was Rabbi Weiss, accompanied by a couple of others. Now that the Auschwitz convent had been moved, the rabbi, identifying himself somewhat vaguely as president of a Coalition for Jewish Concerns, called on the pope to take down a cross still on the former convent, and move a church from another area, Birkenau, that was outside the Auschwitz camp but, according to the rabbi, still offensive for operating in the vicinity. Keeping a church there was part of the "Holocaust revisionism" that would lead people to think the Holocaust was directed only against Catholics, Rabbi Weiss said. "We're not going to tolerate it" (CNS, January 24).

As John Calvin remarked, "It troubles me to burden my readers with a heap of trifles" (*Institutes* IV.xvi.31). But it will be illustrative if I report that in the Polish sphere, bumps on the road to improved Catholic-Jewish relations did not depend on the Glemp or Weiss contributions. Evidence that the demons ruled came in a little incident in 1996, when a committee chose a children's book by a Polish-American author who was Catholic to receive an award from the ADL, and ADL officials decided after the announcement was sent out that they would rather not give honor. The book was *Did the Children Cry?* *Hitler's War Against Jewish and Polish Children,* 1939-45 by Richard Lukas, a history professor living in Florida. After one ADL official notified the publisher, Hippocrene Books in New York, that the award would be presented and set a date, another declared the book was unsuitable for ADL affirmation. "We believe the book underestimates the extent of Polish anti-Semitism before and after World War II," officials of the organization said. When I called Professor Lukas, he told me that he had engaged an attorney who was threatening to sue. So the ADL went ahead and gave the award, but through the mail and with an explanation that it was doing this only to "avoid litigation and further publicity." It was perhaps also partly in response to John T. Pawlikowski, a Servite priest active in Polish affairs, who told the ADL that cancellation of the award could cause "embarrassment and dismay within several Polish-American organizations that have been historically committed to improving Polish-Jewish relations" (CNS, March 6, 1996).

A stranger media event occurred upon a larger stage in 1991. This involved the Dead Sea Scrolls, and some aspects seemed perhaps connected to questions of Jewish-Christian relations, though I could not identify the connections with much precision. On September 4, there was a press conference in New York to announce that some previously unpublished Scrolls material would now go out to the world in defiance of rules that had governed publication to that point.

From the beginning, scholars who took on the task of editing a part of this material were promised that they could be the first to publish it, and gain whatever glory this might bring in the academic Valhalla. However, some of those scholars seemed to delay interminably. They had the excuse that much of the work was quite tedious, and required dealing with fragments, and all the while they must continue teaching their courses and carrying on with other duties. All this considered, some of them were taking an inexcusably long time, and some of the Scrolls–the first ones discovered in 1947 and others in the years immediately following–were still not available in 1991.

Along the way, some scholars working with the Scrolls had produced a preliminary concordance, which means an alphabetical listing of each word with identification of each place it occurs, and the word given with adjacent words to show the context. The break came when Ben-Zion Wacholder of Hebrew Union College in Cincinnati got together with a computer expert, Martin S. Abegg Jr., and found they could reconstruct the full text of documents from the concordance.

I was not told about the press conference, but it made a splash in *The New York Times,* and the next day I wrote a story for the Catholic News Service (sent out September 6). I called Joseph A. Fitzmyer, a Jesuit priest who had worked on the Scrolls, and got from him the basic judgment that some scholars preparing documents for publication had procrastinated unduly, but that the unauthorized use of other people's scholarly work, the concordance, was unethical.

For another view, I called Eugene Ulrich, a Notre Dame professor who was part of a troika overseeing Scrolls publication. He said that he let any interested scholars see photographs of the material he was working on, and thought most of the others involved would do the same. Though in a few cases, he qualified, there had been problems because some of these scholars had been "burned"–he did not say how–in lending photographs.

Later the same September, the Huntington Library in San Marino, California, announced it had microfilm negatives of 3000 Scrolls photographs, and would make them available to other libraries. Then in November, Robert H. Eisenman of California State University in Long Beach and James H. Robinson of the Claremont (California) Graduate School announced they were publishing 1787 Scrolls photographs they had obtained by lawful means they would not disclose.

All this had considerable interest and importance for the academic world, but the Scrolls affair became something remarkable played out for the masses on the public stage. *The New York Times* carried not just one but several major stories. The publication of this material also got the big story treatment in other papers as well as in magazines and all over. Where did editors get the idea it held burning interest for John Doe?

Hershel Shanks, Jewish founder and editor of *Biblical Archaeology Review,* which published the Wacholder-Abegg volume, edited a book of articles about the Scrolls, and it came out the next year. When his publisher, Random House, offered interviews, I took one, and asked him to explain why the publication of these Hebrew, Aramaic and Greek documents that only the tiniest particle of a percentage of Americans would be capable of reading, and few would even care to read in translation, had gotten such a play in the press. He professed to find it surprising himself. But I learned from calling around that elsewhere much credit would be given to his own talent for generating publicity.

On the book's dust jacket, Mr. Shanks was identified as a leader in the movement that succeeded in releasing "the" Scrolls from the scholars who had hoarded "the" texts. That puzzled me since I had on my shelves a couple of volumes containing translated texts from the Dead Sea Scrolls, one collection published as early as the 1950s. In fact, quite a large number of the texts had been published, both in the original languages and in translation, and an immense scholarly literature interpreting them had already come into existence, available in any good theological library. When I asked Mr. Shanks about this, he acknowledged that the reference to his group getting release of "the" Scrolls somewhat exceeded reality.

Perhaps forgetful, Mr. Shanks was, however, sending out a promotional letter for his magazine in 1999, and reasserting the bald claim that "we finally freed the Dead Sea Scrolls." Even the envelope that brought me the letter carried the claim that "we" had liberated "the" Scrolls.

Scrolls were found in eleven caves near the ancient home of the Qumram, perhaps Essene, community that seemed to have lived at the north end of the Dead Sea from about 150 B.C. until wiped out by the Romans in 68 A.D. Publication problems concerned only the Scrolls from what was designated Cave 4. This was the one that held the most, but even some of those, about 20 per cent, had already been published when Mr. Shanks and his associates were crediting themselves with liberation of "the" Scrolls.

"But problems with the Cave 4 texts would eventually discredit the entire publication enterprise," Mr. Shanks wrote in the introduction to the collection of articles, *Understanding the Dead Sea Scrolls.* When I asked him about that sentence, he replied that actually the entire enterprise was not discredited in his own mind, but had been in the minds of the public. If that was so, it was perhaps because somebody was trying to give the public an impression that information of revolutionary importance had been withheld from them. Why some individuals would want to give the uninitiated such an impression was the question that interested me.

For much of the public, the Dead Sea Scrolls seem to exert the same fascination found in the supermarket tabloids and their stories of aliens from outer space or newly-discovered miracle cures for whatever ails you. Mr. Shanks, appealing to this mentality in his letter promoting the magazine, also offered a book that would tell me *Secrets of Jerusalem's Temple Mount,* and not just ordinary secrets, either, but "hidden" secrets. But in all the Qumram texts being published and analyzed, I have never heard of anything emerging that would justify a tabloid headline, or cure your arthritis.

For academic specialists, there is of course much that demands attention. A manuscript containing most of the Hebrew text of Isaiah is dated in the second century B.C., about a thousand years earlier than any Hebrew text of Isaiah previously known. Although there are many variations of spelling and other details, Isaiah's message comes through basically the same, and the discovery of this and other biblical texts at Qumram served mainly to strengthen our grounds for confidence in the copyists who transmitted the texts to us century by laborious century. The Scrolls also help fill in the background for the New Testament period, and enrich the evidence for specialists who write technical articles on the way certain words of the ancient languages were used, or the way certain religious concepts took on different connotations in new contexts. Very professorial.

But I wondered whether some people rushing onto the stage, some Christians, perhaps some Jews, had an idea, perhaps a hope lurking in the shadows, that the Scrolls would reveal secrets, maybe even hidden secrets, to discredit Christianity. Which was something we had seen before. Back in the 1950s, when the Scrolls were really new, Edmund Wilson wrote some articles on them for *The New Yorker* magazine, and later published the articles in a book. Mr. Wilson, of Christian background, was a man who had turned much against the faith of his fathers. In a biography (Houghton Mifflin, 1975), Jeffrey Meyers reported that after the poet Allen Tate converted to Catholicism, Mr. Wilson wrote him, "Christianity seems to me the worst imposture of any of the religions I know of. Even aside from the question of faith, the morality of the Gospel seems to me absurd" (p. 139). The biographer also described Mr. Wilson as "one of the great literary fornicators of all time," and reported that he "seemed to enjoy all forms of sexual activity with all kinds of women" (p. 65), and had "obsessive foot-fetishism" (p. 66). We can easily see how Mr. Wilson, predisposed thusly, might find New Testament morality absurd.

So maybe the Scrolls would prove that Christianity was indeed a fraud. Mr. Wilson lacked scholarly training sufficient to equip him for reading the ancient documents and assessing their value for study of the Bible. But he was the leading literary critic of the day, and for that reason his opinions got a hearing they could not otherwise have received. Many scholars dealing with the Dead Sea Scrolls were also happy to see them get the public attention Mr. Wilson could bring their field, and so welcomed his articles.

Mr. Wilson published his *New Yorker* articles as *The Scrolls from the Dead Sea* in 1955, and republished them with additional material in 1969 as *The Dead Sea Scrolls 1947-1969* (W. H. Allen). Mr. Meyers reported that Mr. Wilson "spent many months acquiring a basic knowledge of Biblical archeology and mastering the complex scholarship in several languages" (p. 358). Mr. Wilson was, to be sure, impressive as a layman in putting together a great deal of information, but even "many months" could make him only an informed layman in a field where scholars spend a lifetime on subdivisions of a field.

Still, the greater problem was bias. Mr. Wilson, his biographer said, was "fascinated by evidence in the Scrolls that disproved the unique origins of the Christian religion" (p. 360). It is hard to see what that statement could mean, or what was understood here by "evidence." The Christian conviction is that Jesus was–is–the Son of God and Savior of the world, and there is not anything in the Scrolls, and in the nature of the case could not be, to prove or disprove that conviction. Mr. Wilson himself wrote that he found "on the Christian side a certain reluctance to recognize that the characteristic doctrines of Christianity must have been developed gradually and naturally, in the course of a couple of hundred years, out of a dissident branch of Judaism" (p. 80). That "branch" was the Qumram community, which he without firm evidence called Essene, and the "must have been," tracing Christian doctrine to it, was a way of trying to undercut the status of the religion he had turned against. The "monastery" of the Qumram community, Mr. Wilson said, was "perhaps, more than Bethlehem or Nazareth, the cradle of Christianity" (p. 97). So, along with gaining public attention for the Scrolls, he spread in cultivated circles the mistaken impression that these documents would serve to explain away the Christian faith. Which was perhaps what many in those circles had joined Mr. Wilson in hoping for.

Mr. Wilson's book on the Scrolls might be considered part of a genre, books on religion that draw acclaim from the culturati but do not stand upon the most solid foundations. *The Gnostic Gospels* by Elaine H. Pagels of Princeton University (1979; Vintage/Random House ed., 1989) might be cited as a later example. Offering Gnosticism as an alternative Christianity, seemingly designed for the Me generation, the Me component of every generation, the "creative" few (p. 150) who see no need of outside help but get all the religion they want from their own innards, she celebrated Gnostics as "restless, inquiring people who worked out a solitary path of self-discovery" (p. 149). Some of us might wonder whether success in that venture would necessarily bring us such a useful discovery, and might consider venturing out to discover other selves more worthwhile. But the self-absorption of the Gnostics enabled them to leave aside the authority of the church and the Bible, and find authority enough in "one's own experience" (p. 151). Professor Pagels got bucketsful of acclaim in prestigious circles, whose occupants apparently found her demonstrating what they wanted to think about Christianity. When the Modern Library, a division of her publisher, Random House, did a publicity event of listing the 100 best non-fiction books written in English over the 100 years of the twentieth century, *The Gnostic Gospels* made the list, ranked 72, just below William H. McNeill's *The Rise of the West* and just ahead of Richard Ellmann's *James Joyce*. (*The Education of Henry Adams* was put in the number one slot.)

But Professor Pagels sometimes got a cooler response from more established scholars in the biblical field. In *The New York Times* Book Review (January 20, 1980), Raymond E. Brown of Union Seminary said scholars found her work, like Edmund Wilson's, made the ancient documents accessible to readers who might otherwise ignore them, but through "underlining the sensational." Actually, orthodox church fathers such as Irenaeus were correct,

Father Brown said, in recognizing the Gnostics as "the crazies of the second century." He also quoted a *Commonweal* (November 9, 1979) review by Pheme Perkins describing the Pagels analysis as "overinterpretation of texts to fit a pre-determined scheme."

For another book to put on the shelf of the same genre, you could add Harold Bloom's *Book of J* (Grove Weidenfeld, 1990), overinterpreting a strand of the Pentateuch from some unknown number of centuries B.C. to make it express the mood of certain self-discoverers in the late twentieth century A.D. From the historical field, you could include works by John Boswell, a Yale professor now deceased, claiming to demonstrate that in a past era the church approved homosexual liaisons. Writing about Job, Karl Barth identified some of the most highly-regarded studies, and then remarked that Carl J. Jung's, titled in the German original, *Antwort Auf Hiob* (1953), was the "most famous of the recent books" but "quite useless" for study of the biblical text, interesting though it was as an expression of Jung's own thought (*Dogmatics IV/3*, 384). I would suppose that something analogous might be said about Sigmund Freud's *Moses and Monotheism* (original German edition 1939).

Actually, so far as anybody has yet heard, the Dead Sea Scrolls say nothing about Jesus or his disciples. And since Jesus and the church are central to Christianity, no proof for Mr. Wilson's thesis could have come from finding some of the phraseology of Christian doctrine in the Scrolls. These materials add depth and detail to the background, but change nothing in the foreground. To go a level deeper, we could recall that Christians believe their faith is in essence what the Old Testament reports as divine revelation, and that the doctrinal development stands in continuity with the theological understanding expressed there. Christians have found the message of their faith expressed from Genesis to Malachi, and in quite specific ways starting with the first chapter of Genesis and its teaching that all begins with the Word of God, or, in a different style, Genesis 3:15 and its promise that the seed of woman will crush Satan with his heel. So in terms of the human concepts involved, the development extended back much further than the couple of centuries Mr. Wilson so boldly asserted to shock us.

The theological continuity can be seen in liturgies that follow the catholic tradition, where it is common to present a reading from one of the four Gospels—Matthew, Mark, Luke and John—after one from some other part of the New Testament, commonly called the epistle reading, and one from the Old Testament. In their separate ways, as Christians see them, the three all present a single message, though the Gospel reading gets the spotlight, coming just before the sermon, with the congregation standing and the reader sometimes chanting the words to accentuate the transcendent meaning.

I saw how instinctive the congregational response to that pattern had become when Pope John Paul II celebrated a mass on the Great Lawn of Central Park in 1995. CNS had an inside reporter who was doing a story directly on the mass itself, and I was assigned to wander around outside and see what was going on peripherally (CNS, October 8). One thing going on was a sort of outdoor theater mass in another area of the park, further up, where people could watch the pope on giant video screens called jumbotrons. When I asked one man why he had come out there when he could get a better view on television and enjoy more comfortable seating at home in Brooklyn, he replied, "I was just thinking about that, after standing here an hour." But people wanted to be there. The atmosphere was casual, and some people were lounging on blankets. When time came for the Gospel reading, nonetheless, many of them stood up, just as they would have done inside a church.

Although this emphasis on the Gospel reading is traditional, it has a misleading aspect. Philip Melanchthon, an associate of Martin Luther, tried to correct the misunderstanding in his *Loci Communes,* which title literally means "commonplaces," but not in the sense of triteness but of themes commonly found in authors. The book has historical importance as the first systematic theology of the Protestant movement, and it includes sections on the gospel and the law and their relationship. For Christians the term "gospel" might be understood generally as what God has given to us, and the law as what he requires from us—both, however, ultimately turning out to be the same thing: the new life in Christ.

Melanchthon warned against thinking "only that is gospel which Matthew, Mark, Luke and John have written, and that the books of Moses are nothing but law" (Melanchthon and Bucer, p. 71; ed. Wilhelm Pauck; Westminster, 1969; Volume XIX of The Library of Christian Classics). On the contrary, Melanchthon said, both gospel and law are found throughout the Bible. The five books traditionally attributed to Moses, the Pentateuch (Genesis, Exodus, Leviticus, Numbers and Deuteronomy), are commonly called the books of the law. But Melanchthon quoted some of God's promises found in those books, and spoke of the "voice of Moses, clearly containing the gospel" (p. 81).

The same point is made in one of the Gospels, John. Though in one context it identifies a distinction, saying "the law was given through Moses; grace and truth came through Jesus Christ" (1:17), in another setting it has Jesus telling the Jews, "If you believed Moses, you would believe me, for he wrote of me" (5:46). The message, of course, was given in a different form in the Old Testament but, as Christians read it, the same God was giving the same good news of his intervention to rescue his people. With all this going for them, Christians will hardly sweat over Mr. Wilson's "couple of hundred years."

But such considerations would mean little to people who longed to see the Dead Sea Scrolls discredit Christianity, and perhaps discredit the Catholic Church in particular. A book published in England in 1991 by two journalists, Michael Baigent and Richard Leigh, directly argued that the overall handling of the Scrolls project was controlled by Catholic clergy engaging in suppression of material contrary to Catholic doctrine. (Since Mr. Wilson had built his theories on material already out in the 1950s, it could seem strange to have others claiming the evidence of fraud was still kept buried in the 1990s, but logic never hinders men with a treasured conspiracy theory to sell.) The English journalists called their book *The Dead Sea Scrolls Deception* (Jonathan Cape). But even the sensation-loving Mr. Shanks had to say "hogwash" to that. And Father Fitzmyer said, "If there is a 'deception' connected with the Dead Sea Scrolls, this book is it" (*America* magazine, February 15, 1992). The editorial team for the Scrolls project did of course include non-Catholics, Jewish as well as Protestant.

The Jewish community was engaged in a campaign at the time to force the Vatican to establish diplomatic relations with Israel, and I also wondered whether some Jews supporting the line about release of "the" Scrolls might feel just a smidgen of anticipation that they would bring to light information embarrassing to Christianity, and maybe put the Catholic Church on the defensive. Why would William Safire feel called to weigh in with a *New York Times* column on such a specialized issue from the world of academic scholarship (September 26, 1991)? In my occasional reading of him, I had not gotten an impression of any deep Jewish piety, but he did seem to display a bit or two of ethnic chauvinism. Some of the Scrolls, he wrote, might "cast light on the psychology of Masada, where Jews committed suicide rather than surrender." Which was raising the decibels rather much. But he also took space to bring in John Strugnell, a Catholic who headed the Scrolls editorial team until he made derogatory statements about Jews in a 1990 interview for the Israeli newspaper, *Ha-Aretz,* and consequently got himself removed. Somehow gaining release of the supposedly secret material became of such importance that Israeli officials who tried to maintain the original agreement about Scrolls publication deserved the term "jerks," in the view of the columnist.

Now these several years later I ask you, Gentle Reader, what have you learned from the Dead Sea Scrolls that has changed your life? They are now all in the public domain, where every Tom, Dick and Harry, or William, who is trained to reconstruct fragmented manuscripts, make informed judgments about what words may have been in missing parts of the manuscripts, read the script of ancient Hebrew, Aramaic and Greek, and translate, can bring the secrets to light. What hidden secrets have they uncovered that changed your view of Christianity or Judaism? "We shall know the truth, and the truth shall make us free," Mr. Safire wrote, making dubious application of Jesus' statement (John 8:32) to the Scrolls material. In what way are you now freer than before? Maybe you are freer of the suspicion that some embarrassing secret has been covered up.

But to go back now to the pope, the attacks on John Paul II for letting Yasser Arafat take some of his time were repeated when a papal audience was given to Kurt Waldheim, in 1987, and the pope called on him during a visit to Austria the next year. Secretary general of the United Nations from 1971 to 1981, Mr. Waldheim had become president of Austria in 1986. He had obscured his World War II record as an officer in the German army, but others belatedly publicized it in the 1980s, and a number of people, with Jews among the foremost, blasted the pope for continuing to treat him as respectable.

The American Jewish Congress devoted the many thousands of dollars required to buy a full page in *The New York Times* (June 26, 1987) for publication of their "open letter" accusing John Paul II of "insensitivity to the meaning of the Holocaust," and asked for contributions to give the letter even more publicity. Signed by Theodore R. Mann, president of the Congress, and Henry Siegman, director, this letter not so delicately raised the question of whether the pope's "forgetfulness" about the Holocaust reflected the church's forgetfulness. "Has Your Holiness dealt with the indifference of the Catholic churches in Europe to the fate of the Jews during World War II?" And because of all that, Mr. Mann and Rabbi Siegman publicly let the pope (and the rest of us) know that they were refusing his invitation to a meeting during his upcoming visit to Miami. "I wish they wouldn't do things like that," Cardinal O'Connor said of the ad (NC, June 29). And he warned that such Jewish actions were creating a backlash in the Catholic community that could have "disastrous" results for Catholic-Jewish relations.

Cardinal O'Connor had been actively engaged in developing ties with Jews, among the most active, but he was one of a very few Christians pursuing that goal who would also talk turkey at times. No doubt every man has fears, but I never discovered what it might be that Cardinal O'Connor was afraid of. In 1990, he took the occasion of an address at a dinner of the American Jewish Committee to state quite directly that he for one was ready for pope-bashing to stop. Receiving the Committee's Isaiah Award for his efforts on behalf of various Jewish causes, he observed that Catholics generally felt rather deeply attached to the pope, and hearing attacks on him from Jews did not make them more disposed to build closer ties. "This is not a threat," Cardinal O'Connor said. "But you have to understand the backlash if the pope is attacked and attacked and attacked" (CNS, May 21).

The cardinal showed some tendency to stay with the practical issues at hand, and keep a distance from the insubstantialities of the theoretical and hypothetical. A Catholic-Lutheran event I covered at St. Patrick's Cathedral had been set up so that he and Lutheran Bishop William H. Lazareth would, so to speak, exchange portfolios. Bishop Lazareth would talk about the papacy and Cardinal O'Connor about the basic doctrine of the Reformation, justification by faith. Bishop Lazareth went according to plan, and presented an ecumenical view of how Protestants might begin to look at the papacy with new eyes. But Cardinal O'Connor maybe worried lest an exposition of theological doctrine fall a little heavily on the ears of his audience, and so talked largely of what a great fellow Bishop Lazarus was (CNS, October 29, 1990).

When I once asked Cardinal O'Connor at a press conference about the issue of converting Jews, he sidestepped the theological question there, too, and addressed the practicalities by observing that the Archdiocese of New York was not sending people out on the streets to seek Jewish converts.

The question of evangelizing Jews has been one of some emotional weight in Jewish-Christian dialogue, and one easier for most Christians to handle in practice than in theory. I suppose the answer lies partly in making a distinction between proselytizing and preaching the Christian gospel to anyone willing to hear. Proselytizing, whether between religions or between sectors of the same religion, carries a repugnant smell. And its religious value is questionable. It may become only a matter of changing the label on a bottle without changing the contents, or sometimes maybe, as I once heard a minister describe shifts of some people from one church to another, changing the label on an empty bottle.

Christians might take some words of Jesus as a caution against a certain kind of convert solicitation: "You traverse sea and land to make a single proselyte, and when he becomes a proselyte, you make him twice as much a child of hell as yourselves" (Matthew 23:15). Those words form part of a polemic against the scribes and Pharisees. But there can be broader lessons in the implication that a zeal to get people into your tent just for the sake of boasting they are now in your tent may do more harm than good.

But to me it seems of the essence of Christian belief to believe that the Christian message is true, and that it brings good news to all people of whatever background or religious culture. When William L. Weiler, an Episcopal priest, was Jewish relations secretary for the National Council of Churches in the 1970s, he once told me of a decision at the Cathedral of St. John the Divine that for a certain period the clergy would accompany the normal reading of the Gospel in English each Sunday with a reading of the same passage in another language, a different one each Sunday, demonstrating concretely its universal character. And he told me that he had signed up to read the Gospel in Hebrew one of those Sundays. That seemed like a logical thing for him to do, but so far as I know, he never followed up on my suggestion that he offer us his reflections on its meaning.

Christians could hardly say the Gospel should be presented in every language in the world except Hebrew. But if you are going to read a Gospel passage in Hebrew at a church service, would you invite Hebrew-speaking people to attend and hear it? There would be little point to reading in Korean if you were not inviting Korean-speaking people to come and hear. And when a minister reads a Scripture passage in a worship service, he presumably is praying that it will be heard with faith. But could a Jewish relations secretary expect to make any progress in Christian-Jewish relations if he were inviting Jews to attend Christian worship services, and to respond to the New Testament message with faith? As a practical matter, Christian ministers by and large do not do much of that. But can they repudiate it in principle?

When I covered a meeting of the United Methodist Board of Global Ministries in 1984 (EPS, April 20), a feature of interest was an address to the World Division by a critic, Gerald H. Anderson, a former United Methodist missionary who was then directing the Overseas Ministries Study Center in Ventnor, New Jersey. He found the mission program of United Methodists deficient on several points, and one was its position on the issue of whether to evangelize people of other religions.

"Any discussion of this issue should begin with the church's witness to the Jewish people, because that is where the Christian mission began," he said. Paul, he noted, would start his missionary work in whatever city he visited by going to the synagogue. And the principle was: "first the Jew and also the Gentile" (Romans 1:16). Leaders of all religious communities will likely object to Christian missionaries trying to convert their people, and Dr. Anderson could logically argue that substituting dialogue for evangelism might be extended from Jews to other groups with a non-Christian outlook, and eventually the Christian Church would cease to preach its message to anybody.

Covering an NCC meeting in 1978, I found board members addressing the issue in relation to Indians (*Christian Science Monitor,* November 6). A policy statement supporting "the sovereignty of Indian nations" also accused the churches of having played "a direct part in the destruction of Indian nations" by the attempt "to civilize and Christianize Indians." The NCC pledged it would "support Indian efforts to maintain the integrity of their spirituality." And it said that "God is revealed to other peoples and cultures in many and diverse ways." Presumably, a similar view could be taken toward people of all non-Christian religions, philosophies and "life styles." But if that had been the view of Christians in past centuries, there would not be any Christians today. Nobody is born Christian; even children of Christians cannot really be put in that category until they have been brought to a conviction that the Christian message is true. So does belief in the Christian gospel and baptism into the church retain any value? We do not really see that worked out clearly in liberal circles.

However, a weakness I saw in Dr. Anderson's presentation was a failure to address the implications of a changed context in Christian relations to the Jews. The nineteen centuries of interreligious conflict have left a climate that makes a direct attempt to convert Jews meaning something different than in the first century—when Paul and other leaders of the first Christian communities were themselves Jews, and did not see their missionary efforts as an appeal to change religions but as an opportunity to get a new understanding of the faith of their fathers.

Paradoxically, it was the very same World Division Dr. Anderson found unwilling to preach the gospel to people of non-Christian religions that later disturbed the Russian Orthodox Church by moving into Russia as soon as religious freedom there allowed, and setting up United Methodism in competition with the Christian churches already established in Russia. Methodists had a little bit of history there from before the communist revolution, so for public relations purposes leaders of the new Russia Initiative spoke of a "renewal" of Methodism in Russia, rather than defend their implicit belief that the religion market in Russia had shelf space for more denominations. Multitudes of Western soul-savers rushed into Russia and tried to get some of the religion business as soon as communism fell. But many of them came from groups that never pretended to have any use for ecumenism, whereas the United Methodist Church had marched in the forward ranks of the ecumenical movement from the beginning. And more paradoxically, it had long been under fire in some quarters for a lessening of zeal for seeking converts in the United States, as its membership fell year by year. And now so zealously off to convert the Russians. It could make a body wonder.

When I did a story on the Russia Initiative for ENI (November 14, 1996), I reported that it began with a 1990 visit to Russia by Bishop J. Woodrow Hearn, president of the Board of Global Ministries, and Randolph W. Nugent, general secretary. By 1996, the board could (and did) boast of 34 United Methodist churches in Russia and other parts of the Commonwealth of Independent States, establishment of a Eurasia Annual Conference and placement in Moscow of a bishop, Ruediger R. Minor from East Germany. A

SIDEBARS

seminary had been opened in Moscow in 1995, nearly a million dollars had been spent in the preceding three years and American congregations such as Highland Park United Methodist Church in Dallas were sending dollars monthly to support United Methodist pastors in Russia.

To show an ecumenical side, United Methodists also gave some help to the Russian Orthodox Church. But the Russian Orthodox naturally felt that if United Methodists were as ecumenical as they had been saying in contacts through the World Council of Churches and other channels, they might have more wholeheartedly oriented their efforts to reinforce the work of fellow Christians already struggling to maintain a historic tradition of church life, rather than setting up competitive shops all over the place. R. Bruce Weaver, a United Methodist minister who coordinated the Russian Initiative from the American side, said Russian Orthodox clergy were assured "that we are not there to proselytize or compete, but to support the work they are already doing." But my impression was that the Russian Orthodox felt no more inclination to swallow that than Jews to think Christian evangelists moving into the Jewish community were only trying to support what the synagogues were already doing. For United Methodists the commitment to ecumenism apparently did not mean working for the unity of the church, but amiable mutual consent to an arrangement where a lot of different denominations would be competing in a friendly way.

Cardinal O'Connor's role in Catholic-Jewish dialogue assumed importance partly because of his prominence in New York life overall. During a controversy over a decision of the Board of Education to remove a schools chancellor, Joseph A. Fernandez, two of his opponents on the board attended mass at St. Patrick's Cathedral one Sunday and received public commendation from Cardinal O'Connor as officials who "voted their conscience." One of them was Ninfa Segarra, later named a deputy mayor by Mayor Rudolph W. Giuliani. Cardinal O'Connor's comment was a matter of only a few seconds, and expressed no opinion explicitly on the chancellor or the issues in dispute, but touched the soul of Ninfa Segarra. An article in *New York* magazine (January 17, 1994) quoted her recollection: "He was really the only one out there."

Andy Logan, a woman who had covered New York City affairs many years for *The New Yorker*, referred to Cardinal O'Connor's comment as "demonstrating to many New Yorkers once again that, no matter who is elected in any November, he is the city's most powerful politician" (June 14, 1993). That judgment in my estimation overflowed, but Cardinal O'Connor was in fact a figure to be reckoned with. If his name appears quite a few times in these pages, it is not because he bribed me, but because he kept himself in the middle of matters far and wide. My own judgment has been that during his tenure as

Catholic Archbishop of New York (1984-2000), he was the only member of the clergy that the mayor had to take seriously. That does not mean the cardinal's views always prevailed of course, but that they—like those of other influentials—had better be taken into account. Political prudence also dictates that the mayor do no disrespecting of the clergy as a group, and that he acknowledge several of them personally as public figures. A few black ministers carry political weight, and some rabbis play a role in New York politics. And various other clergy edge into the picture at times. But no other individual among the New York clergy had impact during the latter years of the twentieth century comparable to that of Cardinal O'Connor.

His role in reviewing the parades that proceed up and down Fifth Avenue past his cathedral both symbolized and enhanced his standing. Not only on St. Patrick's Day, the most publicized, but during parades by other ethnic groups or something such as a Labor Day Parade, the cardinal stood out front to review, and receive parade leaders and dignitaries who interrupted their march to come over and exchange greetings. Presumably, clergy at other churches on Fifth Avenue could come out on their steps and watch parades if they wanted to, but who would notice?

Cardinal O'Connor commanded attention in New York because he had the energy and determination to make himself noticed, and he had the necessary resources and platform. He headed the strongest religious organization in the city, and could involve a sizable array of clergy, nuns, church agency executives and others in any campaign he undertook. He preached most every Sunday morning at the cathedral, except for summer vacations, and was often covered there by reporters and cameras. He expressed his thought most weeks in a column in the archdiocesan weekly, *Catholic New York*. By tradition, the Catholic Archbishop of New York is president of the Catholic Near East Welfare Association, and this means people with special interest in the Middle East seek to make alliances with him. The archbishop also presides over the annual Al Smith dinner, where presidents and other notables speak to help raise money for hospital charities. And for anybody interested in what happens at the Vatican, Cardinal O'Connor became a key operator in that milieu, seated on the boards of several Vatican units and engaged in private conversation every now and then with Pope John Paul II.

My first interview with Cardinal O'Connor came shortly after he was elected president of Catholic Near East, and I wanted to get his views on its work. He had me come to his residence behind the cathedral, and we talked in one of the small sitting rooms. John G. Nolan, later an auxiliary bishop of the Military Ordinariat, was general secretary of Catholic Near East at the time, and Cardinal O'Connor had him sit in with us. As the cardinal outlined his

SIDEBARS

hopes for increasing income from $15 million a year to $50 million, Msgr. Nolan nervously took notes, and I could almost hear him muttering, "How in hell am I supposed to raise fifty million dollars?"

Cardinal O'Connor more than once demonstrated that he fulfilled Robert Browning's ideal of "a man's reach should exceed his grasp" (*Andrea del Sarto*). At one point he spoke of raising a $300 million endowment for archdiocesan schools, but then, after getting reactions of lay leaders asked to help, brought the goal down to $100 million, and eventually let the campaign evaporate when even that much appeared unrealistic. Catholic Near East has never raised anything like $50 million a year, but it does take in enough to serve as a principal support of the Pontifical Mission (originally Pontifical Mission for Palestine, now working in the whole of the Middle East and other areas of Eastern rites). Making trips to check on its work also put the cardinal at times in the international spotlight.

In general, fundraising seemed not one of Cardinal O'Connor's strong points, though he gave time and attention to many efforts. As a chaplain in the Navy, he did not have financial worries, finding his salary and operating costs there all provided automatically from government allocations. So his experience was limited in that respect. And some who had occasion to observe in New York would say that Cardinal O'Connor lacked the finesse of his predecessors for slipping the larger bills out of the fatter wallets and leaving the wallet owners feeling blessed by the experience. I would guess also he may have felt a personal reluctance to cultivate some of the talents sometimes used in cultivating the affluent.

I never had a huge number of interviews with Cardinal O'Connor, but several of my later requests were granted, while the others were allowed to slide along without either yes or no. Like the operating style reported of some governments, certain requests were never denied, but forever delayed with the "not yet." When the birthday of Martin Luther King Jr. was made a national holiday, I was looking for comment and got an interview with Cardinal O'Connor, who had the same birthday, January 15, in an earlier year than Dr. King (1920, to Dr. King's 1929). Before leaving, I asked if we might talk some other time about his view of the ethical principles used in handling archdiocesan investments, a subject that had already received some media attention and was in any case a matter of interest.

He agreed to do that, and to make sure the idea was not forgotten I followed up with a letter to his communications office. Now these many years later, I have never been given the interview, but neither has my request ever been denied–not even after his death could be offered as an excuse. I made the request in January of 1986 (NC King story, January 8), and to this day the only word from the communications office is, "We haven't been given any time for that yet." Presumably, my letter still rests somewhere in a file of pending matters.

On several other topics, I did get interviews, and I found Cardinal O'Connor always handled them in a straightforward way. I never got from him the requests that occasionally came from others for a chance to look at my articles and make corrective suggestions before they went to the editors. He did not give sensitive material and then say, "But you can't print that." He never used the tactic of some people who go off the record in the hope that negative information they are planting in the reporter's mind will somehow come through in the tone of the story, but without their having to take any responsibility for it. No games. He gave his total attention to the questions, discerned their point, acknowledged their legitimacy even when they might take him into choppy waters, and replied in terms pertinent and comprehensible.

The single exception I remember occurred over a report in the *Village Voice* (December 25, 1984) that in 1980, when Ronald Reagan was running for president on an anti-abortion platform, a John O'Connor registered, on October 4, as a Republican. And the registration was in the Pennsylvania town, Chadds Ford, that was the home of the cardinal's sister, Mary Therese O'Connor Ward. With the article was a reproduction of part of the registration showing the date, in a period when Cardinal O'Connor was an auxiliary bishop of the Military Ordinariat and living in New York. People of Irish, working-class background, as Cardinal O'Connor was, usually grew up as enthusiastic members of the Democratic Party. So a Republican registration could signify a significant change of heart. Whether that would mean more conservative politics would depend partly on how you understood "conservative." Military officers tend toward conservatism, and Cardinal O'Connor doubtless absorbed some of that during his long military career. But the conservatism of the military does not exactly match that of the business community. For one thing, there is a different ethos. Military officers have a responsibility to see that every man is accounted for and the wounded are taken care of. In the business world, it is often more like every man for himself, and let the devil take any cripples who lag behind. But when I asked about the *Voice* report, Cardinal O'Connor passed up the opportunity to clarify his history of party affiliation. He gave me a "no," but such an abbreviated and ambiguous "no" that I could not tell for sure. Maybe he meant, "No, that was not me registering as a Republican." But somehow I got a feeling he was telling me, "No way will this interview continue until you get onto another topic." Wayne Barrett, author of the *Voice* article, reported that he, too, found it impossible to get clarification of the affiliation and voting history in his (multiple) interviews.

But generally I got replies, and often quite fully elaborated. They would often run on to considerable length, but not with the irrelevancies I sometimes got from others. No bloviation. That does not mean Cardinal O'Connor told me everything he knew and thought. Nobody with good sense tells all. But even when dealing with explosive matters, he would carefully state a position, and then put no restriction on what I did with it. Publish and be damned, or whatever. Looking down to give intense study to the toe of his shoe, or some piece of design on the rug, he would weave his way through the mine fields, choosing his words with circumspection, and then rest content with the results. No recriminations after stories appeared in print. I wrote a basketful of stories on Cardinal O'Connor, twenty dozen and more, reporting not only on the interviews, but on innumerable homilies, addresses, press conference statements and actions as well. He must have thought at times that this reporting could have been better. I generally did. But he never registered any complaints.

The cardinal's full-elaboration style contrasted with the succinctitude of William F. Schulz, former president of the Unitarian-Universalist Association who became head of the U.S. branch of Amnesty International. When I interviewed him for an article published in the World Council of Churches magazine, *One World* (April 1995), I found he knew what position he wanted to take on most every question I raised, and could state it crisply in a couple of sentences. With a man like that, you can cover a lot of territory in an hour.

With Cardinal O'Connor, better decide on just three or four matters of most interest. Shortly after his arrival in New York, a local television station arranged for him to hold a press conference that the station carried live. But his pattern of thinking through his answers and giving them in rounded fullness did not make for effective television. He was not speaking in sound bites. Under the eye of the camera, too, he studied a spot on the floor as he proceeded carefully and lengthily through his reactions.

The pope got the same elongated answers, it appeared. In 1987, Gabe Pressman of New York's NBC television affiliate, WNBC, filmed an interview with Cardinal O'Connor in Rome right after he had lunched with the pope. The cardinal called it a great experience, but said he always came out hungry from a papal meal. "He begins the lunch–right after prayer–by asking me a question," the cardinal reported of the pope's hosting. "I start to answer and he's eating away, and my plate's lying there with the food on it. Before I know it, the waiter is in to take the plate away, start the next course." And that is repeated, Cardinal O'Connor said. "As soon as the next plate comes, he asks another question" (NC, January 14, 1987). Time for only one O'Connor answer per course.

But a greater problem at the televised press conference was the pack mentality of the reporters. The idea of the Catholic Archbishop of New York going on live television and opening himself up to any and all sorts of inquiries was new, and carried a sort of drama. But most of the reporters came with little but homosexuality and abortion on their minds, and virtually every question returned to one or the other of those topics. At the end of the hour, I finally got in a question about the economics pastoral that was then in process of development by the National Conference of Catholic Bishops, and the cardinal turned to it in the remaining seconds with brief relief. Otherwise, it was nearly all abortion and homosexuality.

Although Cardinal O'Connor was influential and well-liked by many New Yorkers, and adored by some, a good many others came to brand him as something like the Great Satan, and the explanation seemed to lie in the two issues that absorbed the reporters' attention. I think such absorption also led many people to underestimate him in the overall sense. A man who rose to become Chief of Chaplains of the United States Navy and then Cardinal-Archbishop of New York might be presumed to have some competence. But if your mind broods unceasingly on abortion and homosexuality, and you write off anyone whose positions on those two issues differ from yours, you may fail to understand a lot.

To give a random example that the critics would likely ridicule, I understood more after I talked with Samuel M. Taub, a Catholic permanent deacon, when he headed the national Catholic office on the permanent diaconate, and was participating in an ecumenical conference on deacons (NC, March 2, 1987). Comment on particular individuals was not part of the story, but I remember him telling me that Cardinal O'Connor was doing more than any other Catholic bishop to utilize men in this recently-restored office. Critics of the cardinal would likely know little of matters like that, and care a great deal less. But a collection of such points can form a mosaic of effective leadership in the church.

I once heard a Jew define antisemitism as "hating Jews more than necessary." That sardonic definition accepted the reality that we all become objects of hostility at times, and Jews could not expect to escape the ordinary tough and rumble of social conflict. But there is sometimes a depth and intensity of emotion against Jews that cannot be explained by any real or imagined offenses, but comes out of a place they have been arbitrarily assigned in the minds of the attackers. Similarly, I got a feeling sometimes that people with desire for acceptance of abortion and homosexuality weighing heavily and deeply upon them were hating Cardinal O'Connor more than necessary. As time went by, his enemies seemed to tire of attacking him, or perhaps decided they could make more by on-line trading, and moved along. And in 2000, after he had become an octogenarian and the oldest Catholic bishop still in office in the United States, Congress voted him a gold medal. But in his earlier years here particularly, life could get peculiar. People on the other side of issues would naturally be expected to generate some steam at times. But I could see no sufficient provocation for the amount and virulence of the abuse he took—for the *Village Voice* cartoon picturing him in something like Klan collusion, for vulgar and scurrilous signs paraded in front of his cathedral, for the off-Broadway play ridiculing him as "Connor O'John."

Maybe this sort of thing derives partly from the significant degree of alienation of the church from the cultural life of the modern world, for which some responsibility could lie on both sides. When Cardinal O'Connor talked to reporters on his tenth anniversary as Archbishop of New York, he told us that he had not attended any Broadway plays. Since his residence lay within easy walking distance of the theater district, the preeminent theater district of America, that revelation seemed a little startling, though it had not previously occurred to me to wonder about such matters. He was a workaholic, and you heard of him doing little except attending to his job, or getting away from New York for periods of rest in the summer. Shortly after his appointment as archbishop, a Catholic actors group put on a welcoming program for him in one of the Broadway theaters (NC, October 29, 1984). But we did not hear of reciprocal gestures to establish some continuing tie with the theater community.

Looking more generally, it appears Cardinal O'Connor failed to seek out the wealth of artistic expression available in his city—the Metropolitan Opera, Carnegie Hall, the ballet, art exhibits. We seldom if ever heard of him showing interest in these urban resources unless they connected directly with the church.

Perhaps that is not unusual. Another famous clergyman in New York, Harry Emerson Fosdick of Riverside Church, also missed a lot, according to a biography by Robert Moats Miller (Oxford, 1985). Despite Dr. Fosdick's many years in the city, he never got acquainted with the New York of Al Smith, Damon Runyon, Jimmy Walker or Cab Calloway, the biographer said. While Dr. Fosdick did know Carnegie Hall and the Metropolitan Opera House, it "seems likely that Yankee Stadium and Ebbets Field, Small's Paradise and the Cotton Club in Harlem, the jazz spots on 52nd Street and the coffeehouses in the Village, the tiny Chinese restaurants on Spring Street and San Gennaro's festival on Mulberry Street, the West Side tenderloin and 'Texas' Guinan's speakeasy, never knew his presence" (p. 352).

Catholics can say it is the job of the Jesuits to check out such offerings, and it may also be true that the clergy see much that is missed by some who gather the culture bouquets. Still, it must mean something when those preaching to New Yorkers skip over so much of New York life. What it means, I would not try to specify.

The alienation can show up clearly enough. In 1999, as you may remember, the church and culture story was elephant dung. In case anybody wonders, I am here a literalist: dung of the elephant. It seems a British artist of Nigerian background, Chris Ofili, had decided to enhance his paintings by putting on clumps of it. Perhaps for this, perhaps for other reasons, he had become fashionable, and his painting and dunging was represented among various works of the 1990s bought by Charles Saatchi, a London advertising executive. And the Saatchi collection got such a reaction at a London exhibition, the director of the Brooklyn Museum of Art, Arnold L. Lehman, decided to show it and get more notoriety for his somewhat neglected institution.

Now to get into the religion of all this, Mr. Ofili had painted a woman, put a clump of elephantine droppage on for a breast and titled the work *The Holy Virgin Mary.* And he pasted small pornographic cutouts around to add flavor. It was remarked that if he had titled this production "My Aunt Susie," nobody would have given it a second thought, or glance. But presented as Mary, it ceased to exist just as a matter of art. Other works in the exhibit were also of the sort that could make one wonder, and led the museum to title the whole affair *Sensation,* and play up the promise of shock effects. One of the sensation stimulators was, as *The New York Times* described it (October 1), "a device in which maggots feed on a dead cow's head and give birth to flies, which are eventually zapped by an electrical device." Defenders of the exhibit said art was supposed to make you think, and a number of thoughts were produced. Those of the mayor, Rudolph W. Giuliani, ran along the lines of stopping the flow of taxpayer dollars to the museum. While the exhibit had numerous items to appall the masses, the easiest part to get people worked up about, arousing those who enjoy elevating their righteous indignation, was the elephant dung and Mary. Can you now guess which one the mayor would focus on? Mr. Ofili also used elephantage on other works, so putting some on Mary would not necessarily mean sacrilege. But the mayor was contemplating a Senate race, and–some would say "and therefore"–decided to stir up the kind of voters who are readily stirred over such. He stopped the city subsidy to the museum, though a judge later said this violated the right to freedom of expression, and the mayor threatened to put the museum out of its building, which the city owned.

With the mayor carrying on about insults to Mary, unfortunately I was soon having to report that a number of clergy decided they wanted to get themselves into the dung (CNS, September 27). Cardinal O'Connor and

Bishop Thomas V. Daily of Brooklyn gave public denunciations, and other clergy joined in. Another inglorious chapter in the war of clergy against culturati. I get depressed when I see clergy jumping so eagerly onto the stage to play again and again the roles written for them by their critics, the stereotype of the benighted slashing away at any who think new thoughts or try new ways. I pray for a time when the clergy will pause a moment to ask themselves whether God really has called them to take the Simon Legree role in every melodrama of the culture wars. Even the pope now acknowledges that church authorities misspoke in condemning Galileo, a welcome acknowledgement though one might wish it had not taken three hundred years. And one might wish clergy had learned the lesson that it is not necessarily a service to the faith if they react to every new development in their culture with denunciation.

To me, the damage was not to Mary, who probably can look after herself, but to the Christian faith, which was yet again represented by people who made it look like a backwater. I would like to see church leaders working in a positive way to bring about some interaction of church and culture. One could imagine a climate in which bishops and whatnot made a point of getting acquainted with museum directors, and showing appreciation for what they are trying to do for the community. Then, when a politician stirred a flap over something religious, they could call up and ask for an opportunity to see and discuss it. If the first time a church leader shows any interest in a museum is when he decides to deliver a public blast at something he does not understand, he makes a not so especially positive advertisement for his religion.

On strategy grounds, one could lament that church leaders seem never to learn the lesson that "banned in Boston" serves to promote the works they deplore. Keeping quiet, they might let some second-rate material sink more rapidly into the oblivion it deserves. But with the high level flapping, and such as the Catholic League for Religious and Civil Rights demonstrating at the Brooklyn Museum on opening day of the elephant droppings, the report was, as one might have predicted, the museum enjoyed an all-time record attendance (CNS, October 4).

We had similar demonstrations in 1985 when *Hail Mary,* a movie directed by Jean-Luc Godard, supposedly giving Mary an updated treatment with nude scenes, was shown at Lincoln Center as part of the New York Film Festival. I reported that as it opened "at least 2500 protesters thronged outside, reciting the rosary, singing hymns and booing ticket holders who came to see the film" (NC, October 14). Later, I talked with a woman I knew who characteristically interpreted that kind of religious protest as a signal from God that she should see the cause of the to-do. But after she ran the gauntlet of enraged and pious demonstrators, she could not give many stars. "Did I go through all that just to see a second rate movie?" she wondered.

I would not say clergy or lay leaders in the churches should lean the other way, as some do, and acclaim anything that comes into fashion, and pretend to find some deep spiritual meaning in mediocrities produced to exploit the public appetite for sensation. But there could be other options. At least there could be a recognition that the churches will not win over people in the cultural world by charging out into the streets and throwing piety at them.

In 1992, Paul Poupard, president of the Vatican Council for Dialogue with Non-Believers, headed up a conference on religion and the arts at the Lincoln Center campus of Fordham University. When I interviewed him, he said the Council originally focused on dialogue with Marxists, but nobody showed interest in that after the collapse of communism in Eastern Europe (CNS, April 7). So now he was shifting his focus to the West and to areas such as the arts, where if practitioners were not necessarily such hardline "non-believers" as the communists, many of them did operate with religious indifference. But a serious effort led by a cardinal to deal with the relation of religion to the arts could not for sure draw a crowd equal to the thousands that would turn out to pray their rosaries at some film director or playwright they identified as the enemy of righteousness. In a separate article on the conference (CNS, April 7), I could report on attendance of only about a hundred.

To those who did show up, Cardinal Poupard, a Frenchman with doctorates from the Sorbonne, talked about a "general and tragic split between religion and culture in the century now ending." And he found evidence of that in the "trivialization of faith through trivial religious art." I suppose he could have found further evidence in trivial religious protests on the streets of New York, and the demonstrators who show seriousness about attacking people in the arts and not about art itself, or what art can contribute to the human spirit.

In connection with all this, I perhaps should admit that I just do not understand the whole thing about Mary. Karl Barth said the title "mother of God," which was ancient but neglected by Protestants, correctly expressed her significance (*Dogmatics I/2*, 138), but the tradition called Mariology gave us "a luxuriantly unfolding liturgical and ascetic practice with legendary accretions," which "meant a twisting both of the New Testament witness and of the sound christological tradition of the first four centuries" (p. 141). He also called this tradition an "excrescence" that should be "excised" (p. 139). So when I wonder about Christians putting up all those shrines to Mary, and praying to Mary, and holding all those festivals and processions dedicated to Mary, and all those throngs coming out all over the world where somebody claims Mary appeared to him, I am perhaps not alone.

SIDEBARS

As a defense, Christians who venerate Mary say she is honored specifically because she is the mother of Jesus, and not to take the spotlight from him. And I gather that is theologically the most correct thing to say even in the most Mariological circles, though not all feminists seem happy to hear that interpretation. Observing religious practice, however, you can hardly escape the impression that for a good many people venerating Mary, she does compete for glory with her son, and often supersedes him in the fervor she inspires. Then you see people going on to think up as many titles and compliments as they can for her, and then the doctrine is elaborated to say she was perpetually virgin, and conceived immaculately without sin, and taken up body and soul into heaven, and there crowned as queen.

Perhaps this concentration on Mary expresses the same psychological drives that have led people in other cultures to worship mother goddesses. But Karl Barth pointed out that you can always find parallels to Christian ideas and practices in non-Christian religions, and they prove "everything and nothing" (p. 143). The important question for Christians is the connection to the truth of the Christian message. And Professor Barth saw Mariology countering the basic doctrine of Christian grace, seeking to glorify to the creature instead of recognizing that all glory belongs to the Creator (on which, see Romans 1:25). He found a logic in the fact that the same pope, Pius IX, who exalted Mary by declaring the dogma of the Immaculate Conception (1854) was also the pope of the First Vatican Council, which supported those who think they can produce a theology that is "natural" and need not wait for the wisdom from above, and which exalted the papal creature to the level of infallibility. All this fits the mood of those who do not want to acknowledge that, like Lazarus, we are raised from the dead and receive our life solely by the gift of God, and not with the assistance of some power or good will of our own by which we "cooperate," as some like to boast.

In 1997, I reported on an exhibit of art about Mary at the art museum of Newark, New Jersey (CNS, December 11). A new Performing Arts Center was putting on programs related to Portuguese culture, recognizing that Newark had one of the largest concentrations of Portuguese-Americans in the nation, concentrated in a Newark area called the Ironbound Section because of railroads on all sides. The Newark Museum decided it should do something Portuguese, too, and found Mary took a dominant role in Portuguese art. So museum officials put together an exhibit called *Crowning Glory*, with paintings, carvings, textiles and other forms of art related to Mary. There were also items showing the Fatima connection.

Writing for the exhibit catalog, Manuel Clement, a Portuguese-American priest, said Marian devotion developed as "part of the underpinning of

Portuguese national identity," and that the Portuguese had traditionally given Mary credit for their military victories. When they defeated a Napoleonic army in 1808, they sang a "Hymn to the Most Holy Mary for having rid us of the Treacherous and Evil French." So where is the Christianity in all this? The spirit of extolling Mary against the "treacherous and evil" opponent seems not especially unique to the Portuguese. In many places, people who report Mary has appeared to them also report she was taking their side against their opponents. In Medjugorje, a village of Bosnia, Mary even seemed to be taking the side of a Catholic religious order, the Franciscans, in their competition with the bishops. It was not surprising, then, that when I interviewed Ratko Peric, the Catholic Bishop of Mostar-Duvno, the diocese that included Medjugorje, he told me that he agreed with the judgment expressed earlier by other bishops, which was that no supernatural origin of the appearance reports could be affirmed (CNS, August 4, 1994).

To serve as visiting curator for the Newark exhibit, the museum enlisted a professor from the City University of New York, Jerrilynn D. Dodds, a specialist in Iberian art. She told me that she was not a Catholic, but had a strong interest in Mary and the female spirituality presented in her images. Aside from whatever thoughts one might have about spirituality distinguished by gender, the question again arises about how this connects to the message of the New Testament.

Karl Barth suggested in the preface to a volume of the *Dogmatics* taking up the theme of the humanity of Jesus that giving this topic proper attention would make Mariology "superfluous" (*IV/2*, ix-x). And I can see how that might be. If you have been led to think of Jesus only as a stern deity looming over you, a judge ready to send you to hell if you should slip, or at times as a wafer that has undergone some incomprehensible process called transubstantiation on the distant altar, then you might feel a need to approach heaven through someone warmer, more approachable. So you might imagine that in Mary you have someone closer to you than Jesus, someone more compassionate, more willing to forgive you, someone more disposed to assist you than Jesus, readier to respond to your appeals, to plead your case before God, more able to comfort you in your sorrow, ease your pain, than Jesus. Strange imaginings for a Christian. But maybe the feeling of need for such an approach would diminish if Christians saw Jesus was "not a high priest who is unable to sympathize with our weaknesses, but one who in every respect has been tempted as we are," and who "learned obedience through what he suffered" (Hebrews 4:15; 5:8).

But getting back to Cardinal O'Connor, I should not leave the impression that abortion and homosexuality were the only topics that embroiled him in controversy. During a trip he took to Israel and other parts of the Middle East in late 1986 and early 1987, Jews became disturbed because planned meetings with the Israeli president and prime minister in their offices were ruled out of order by the Vatican, which did not want any cardinal acting in any manner to suggest that Jerusalem was recognized as the capital. Cardinal O'Connor took all the blame for the mixup, and worked around the restrictions with ingenuity. The president's office was redefined as his study so that a conversation there would not have to mean anything official.

Some Jews also got upset when the cardinal, visiting the Holocaust Memorial, Yad Vashem, during the same trip, spoke about Holocaust suffering in religious terms as a gift of Jews to the world. The terminology sounded a bit odd and hardly understandable outside a specific theological framework. But the cardinal was obviously trying to show his heart beat with Jewish hearts, as he had on enough previous occasions that they could have known this was the case. And his comments would not likely have drawn fire, absent resentment over the Vatican's non-relations with Israel at the time.

But the Jewish establishment in New York decided it was time to strike a blow for Israel. So Cardinal O'Connor flew home on a Saturday evening, and on Sunday morning *The New York Times* greeted him with a front page story about heads of major Jewish organizations giving him a lambastation. They were "disquieted and distressed," fifty or more of them said, and found his statements in Israel "disturbing and painful." And they spoke of "the failure of the Vatican" to do this and "the failure of the Holy See" to do that.

I later determined that the statement had been distributed around town on Saturday (January 10, 1987), someone apparently having decided that such a good deed as giving the cardinal this demolition job justified a bit of labor on the sabbath. Cardinal O'Connor might have shared the thoughts of the man tarred and feathered and ridden out of town on a rail: "If it were not for the honor of the thing, I would just as soon walk."

The statement was coordinated by Morris B. Abram of the Conference of Presidents of Major American Jewish Organizations, and carried the names of virtually all the presidents. The ADL and Agudath Israel kept their chiefs off the list, but otherwise it was rather comprehensive. Theodore Ellenoff of the American Jewish Committee, Theodore Mann of the American Jewish Congress and Edgar M. Bronfman of the World Jewish Congress, they all lined up to hit the cardinal; ordained and lay they came, Rabbi Herbert Baumgard of the Synagogue Council of America and Rabbi Haskel Lookstein of the New York Board of Rabbis; male and female they punched him, Ruth Popkin of Hadassah and Dolores Wilkenfeld of the National Federation of Temple Sisterhoods; even Marvin Verit of American Professors for Peace in the Middle

East became less peaceful and joined the assault; all–Orthodox. Conservative, Reform–all coming by, each taking his shot at the cardinal's nose. And journalistic coverage with the best possible placement: front page of the Sunday *Times*.

I was among a group of reporters who talked with Cardinal O'Connor after his Sunday morning mass, and found him not greatly amused, in fact hardly amused at all (NC, January 12 and 13). The Middle East journey, he said, was the riskiest he had ever made, personally and professionally, and attacks such as those that had just come from the Jewish leaders would reduce his ability to work for the better Israeli-Vatican relations he was trying to facilitate. If this was what working on problems in Catholic-Jewish relations was going to mean, he could find other ways to spend his time; he was no masochist. He did not understand why they did it, even some of those he had given a great deal of time in trying to address Jewish concerns, or why they released their censure to the press before hearing his explanation of what he had been doing, or even giving him a copy of their attack, and he thought they owed him an apology. But he did not get one.

On many other occasions, however, Cardinal O'Connor was lushly lauded and applauded by Jews, acclaimed and admired, covered with honors, called the greatest, magnified and glorified. Some Jews would have canonized him, could they have gained access to the Vatican machinery. So perhaps Christians just need to understand that Jews have their own way of pursuing their goals, and their descriptions of you should not be overrated, whether they come smooth or come rough. Maybe it is just a matter of different tactics for different stages of the struggle.

When Dr. Fisher, the U.S. Catholic secretary for Jewish relations, gave the John Courtney Murray lecture in 1999, he suggested that some of the conflict over the Vatican's document on the Holocaust the previous year came from a difference in styles, New York Jewish in contrast to Catholic Roman (CNS, May 5). The Vatican thought it had done something creditable in producing the document, something the Jewish community had pushed hard for, and had made many points the Jewish community would like to see emphasized in Catholic teaching. But instead of expressing satisfaction, some Jews only renewed their attacks on the Vatican for not putting as much blame as they wanted on Christianity, the Catholic Church and Pope Pius XII.

Writing of the Middle East, Henry A. Kissinger found it pertinent to explain something about the style of the Israeli ambassador, Yitzhak Rabin: "If he had been handed the entire United States Strategic Air Command as a free gift he would have (a) affected the attitude that at last Israel was getting its due, and (b) found some technical shortcoming in the airplanes that made his accepting them a reluctant concession to us" (*White House Years,* Little Brown, 1979, p. 568). In Dr. Kissinger's second volume, *Years of Upheaval* (1982), he told us, "Israel's domestic political procedures explain its maddening negotiating method, which is to haggle over even the slightest concession, never to make an unexpected compromise, and to settle only when everyone has reached a state of exhaustion that deprives the conclusion of exaltation or even goodwill" (p. 539).

For Christians interested in interfaith relations, a second useful point might be to distinguish between religious Jews, devoted to the God of Jacob and the words of the Scriptures, and those Jews who seemingly care little for any of that but work at promoting the secular interests of their ethnic group. So Christians would just have to recognize that the latter are not necessarily interested in "goodwill," but in using a "negotiating method" that will achieve their goals.

Jews who strive for assimilation, still another category, constitute a problem for the rabbinate, but their blurring of boundaries, their success in directing attention away from the specifics of any religion, may also exert an impact so far not evaluated on the more-or-less Christian society that they become an assimilated part of. Considering the United States a country predominantly Christian by history and outward allegiance of most citizens, I have thought it rather striking that what is perhaps the most popular Christmas song among the American public, *White Christmas,* and perhaps the most popular Easter song, *Easter Parade,* were both written by a Jew, Israel Baline, who was brought to the United States by his parents in 1893 and later changed his name to Irving Berlin. And the songs celebrate their seasons without any allusion to the birth or resurrection of Christ, or anything else that a Christian might recognize as the reason for celebrating. And Christians taken with these songs do not seem to notice the absence. If this is considered a problem, presumably it is a worry primarily for those Christian leaders charged with looking after the religious life of Christians. But I also suppose some Jews, particularly those with religious commitment, might reflect on the twentieth century in Europe and conclude that erosion of the religious substance of a Christian society may not be good for the Jews living there. In a review article on books about Irving Berlin, Brad Leithauser of Mount Holyoke College quoted him as saying music was important because "it changes thinking, it influences everybody, whether they know it or not" (*New York Review of Books,* April 22, 1999). I do not know how Mr. Berlin's songs about Christmas and Easter have changed the thinking of American Christians, but no doubt they have.

Some observers have also seen "domestic political procedures" in the U.S. Jewish community playing a role in its controversies. When Judith Banki did a study issued by the American Jewish Committee in 1979, she reported that "an anti-Israel, pro-Arab attitude has been much in evidence in certain segments of American Christianity" (*Christian Science Monitor,* May 14, 1979). She said the bias came from Christians who developed their sympathies through missionary work in the Arab world, exponents of liberation theology and Arab-American churches, and that all three could be seen operating in the NCC. A similar study by the ADL in 1977 had reached similar conclusions. J Richard Butler, the NCC's Middle East secretary, told me that he did not consider the Banki study a serious effort to influence the churches, and that it was written and publicized without any attempts to speak with the Christian leaders responsible for Middle East work. It was rather, as he assessed, part of a "competition that exists between Jewish organizations, with one wanting to appear to be stronger in defense of Israel than another." And the conclusion: "When these dynamics are at play, sometimes we come out the whipping boy."

But even some of those organizations have not battled as fiercely as the Jewish Defense League (JDL), or as peculiarly. In 1982, surveying some points of Christian-Jewish tension, I included the news that the JDL had taken over offices of the WCC in New York, and had demanded that it reprimand Billy Graham for his remarks on a recent trip to the Soviet Union (EPS, July 31, 1982). The Jewish Press had reported their "demand" that the World Council "censure Graham for giving absolution to the Soviet regime" (May 28).

With many and various such matters on the Jewish agenda, somehow, at some point, for who knows what reason, establishment of Vatican diplomatic ties with Israel became an overriding concern. There seemed to be a rule that no discussion of Catholic-Jewish relations could proceed more than 27 seconds without some Jewish participant bringing it up.

To be precise, diplomatic relations are with the Holy See, not the mini-state of Vatican City. If the acreage in Rome were lost, and the pope took up quarters elsewhere, as popes did at Avignon, France, in the 1300s, the diplomatic relationships would not have to stop. It is likewise the Holy See that has permanent observer status at the United Nations, though in common speech, and in stories of the Catholic News Service, we usually say "Vatican," since that is the current location of the Holy See.

The absorption of so many Jews in getting Israel the prize of diplomatic relations with the Vatican seemed a little curious, because the Jewish community simultaneously stood in the forefront of the battle to keep the Vatican from having diplomatic relations with the United States. After it appeared the U.S.-Vatican tie was probably coming to pass despite the opposition, and as some Jews apparently thought about their desire for the help of U.S. Catholics in getting Vatican ties with Israel, the Jewish front showed some weakening. But even on the day U.S. establishment of relations with the Vatican was announced–January 10, 1984–Rabbi Siegman of the American Jewish Congress condemned it. I and other reporters had gone to his headquarters on the East Side for a press conference announcing formation of an institute on Catholic-Jewish relations, to be led on a part-time basis by Michael Wyschogrod, a philosophy professor at Baruch College. But even while desiring to sell that project, Rabbi Siegman decided he wanted first to charge the Reagan Administration with violating the constitutional principle of church-state separation. The position of American Jews seemed to be, "A diplomatic tie with the Vatican is a very dreadful thing, and Israel deserves to have it."

Thinking more pragmatically, Rabbi Tanenbaum welcomed the Reagan move and commented, "When we have spoken with Vatican officials about the possibility of their establishing diplomatic relations with Israel, they have replied, 'Why should we look favorably on such a move when the American Jewish community has opposed U.S. relations with the Vatican?' Now this impediment has been removed" (*Jewish World*, February 17, 1984). You might wonder whether Vatican officials would speak exactly in such terms, but Jews such as Rabbi Tanenbaum could see the opening for a charge of inconsistency.

I covered Rabbi Tanenbaum a number of times over the course of several years. He did not shrink back from dealing with issues, and when I called him for comment on a story, he usually said something forthright and pertinent–viewing things from the perspective of his community, as you would expect, but in a way that from this perspective made sense. You cannot say as much for everybody you call up.

Back in 1972, I wrote an RNS story (October 16) to report on Rabbi Tanenbaum's acceptance of an Edith Stein Award. That was a delicate affair because the giver, the Edith Stein Guild, named for the Jewish convert to Catholicism, later canonized to the distress of some Jews, was an organization of Jews who had become Catholics, plus some others married to Jewish Catholics or otherwise especially interested. Though attitudes may have been different in the past, and Rabbi Tanenbaum said he had turned down the award in the past, the Guild was not at the time trying to convert Jews, or at least not by any frontal assault. But Rabbi Tanenbaum was frank to take up the issue directly. In a free society, conversions will occur, and will occur in both directions, and should be respected whenever made with integrity, he said. But everyone's goal should be to help all become the best representatives of their religion they can be, he said. "Edith Stein stands for both the glory and the agony of the possibilities. The Edith Stein Guild has not to do with making Jews into

Christians or Christian into Jews, but with the question: Do Christians really take the gospel seriously? Do Jews really take the Torah seriously?"

The institute announced by Rabbi Siegman was one of several attempts made in various parts of the Jewish community to undertake theological dialogue with Catholics and other Christians. But it required bringing water from the rock. Many Jews thought Christian theology or some aspects of it contributed to antisemitism, and they wanted to talk about the connections they saw. But the main bodies of Orthodox Judaism refused to participate in any such enterprise, saying this would imply their convictions were negotiable. If they got to talking about Christian teachings they would like to see modified, theoretically some Christian might some day start talking about reciprocation. Better not start down that road.

So the Synagogue Council of America, which embraced Orthodox as well as Reform and Conservative Jews, could not openly undertake anything called theological dialogue, though on the side people would tell you that theology inevitably did come up whenever Jews and Christians began discussing matters of heartfelt concern. A parallel veto applied to the main Jewish group responsible for dialogue worldwide, the International Jewish Committee for Interreligious Consultations (IJCIC).

The institute established by the American Jewish Congress sponsored a conference in Switzerland, but the biggest news out of that was the flak that came from Jewish critics (NC, January 27, 1984). An Orthodox scholar, David Bleich of Yeshiva University in New York, felt the heat most scorchingly. But the Vatican also got reprimanded for its participation, told by IJCIC that it was supposed to relate to Jews through IJCIC, and only through IJCIC. And Israel Singer, executive director of the World Jewish Congress, was quoted as saying theological dialogue with the Vatican was "undignified" and "demeans us and recalls the Middle Ages when we were forced to talk to the church to stay alive, to see whether they would seek to convert us to their faith or kill us" (*Jewish Press,* January 27). And then I heard no more about the institute.

I later got another perspective from Edgar M. Bronfman, who, when the turn of the World Jewish Congress came to designate the IJCIC chairman, took the post. Along with a couple of other reporters who had asked for interviews, I got a joint session with him and a couple of his associates (CNS, November 26, 1991). Mr. Bronfman was chairman of the Seagram Company, and we were invited to lunch in his dining room at the Seagram Building on Park Avenue. A gracious host, he provided food and drink of quality. Nothing lacking in ambience or service either. You would have liked to have been there.

Mr. Bronfman also turned out to be a man who liked to speak frankly, and was frank to say he considered the Vatican's attitude toward Israel "insulting."

Just look at the crude dictatorships it did exchange ambassadors with while snubbing Israel.

IJCIC's dialogue partner in the Catholic Church was the Vatican's Commission on Religious Relations with the Jews, but officials of this commission wanted to avoid even referring to the question of diplomatic ties. When I got an interview with Pier Francesco Fumagalli, secretary of the commission, in New York, I kept asking questions to clarify this issue, and I sensed him radiating less and less satisfaction. Whether he was focusing his discontent on me for pressing the unwelcomest topic, or on William Martyn, an Atonement brother who was the New York archdiocesan ecumenical officer and set up the interview, or back on himself for letting someone talk him into this abomination, I never knew. But he eventually said enough I could explain the situation somewhat in a CNS story (September 17, 1990).

I clarified further and more authoritatively when I later did an interview with the president of the commission, Edward I. Cassidy (CNS, February 17, 1992). He was not wildly enthusiastic about getting to elaborate on the topic either, if the full truth is to be told. But he said the Commission on Religious Relations with the Jews was in fact authorized to deal only with religious relations and could not move into the area of arranging diplomatic ties with a government. This matter had to be handled between the Vatican Secretary of State and the government of Israel. He did not have authority to negotiate for the Vatican, and he did not see that IJCIC had authority to negotiate for Israel. So the dialogue partners exhibited an awkward fit: the Jewish side unable to take up theology but insistent on pressing the issue of diplomatic relations, the Catholic side unable to negotiate diplomatic relations but ready to talk about religious topics.

To me, it seemed that the way Cardinal Cassidy and Father Fumagalli delayed clearing away the underbrush fell in that category called making things harder than they have to be. It should have been simple enough just to start out from the first and say in the language of the 1960s: we can't relate to that. But times were tense, and people were skittish.

In Mr. Bronfman's frankness, he also characterized himself as a non-religious Jew who did not keep the sabbath or dietary laws, leaving any Christians who read of the interview perhaps to wonder about a religious community that would place in charge of its committee on interreligious consultations a man who frankly said he was not religious. And who said the problems needing to be discussed with the churches were primarily political. With IJCIC directed by a man who was not religious and its dialogue partner at the Vatican authorized to deal only with religious matters, progress could hardly gallop.

Father Fumagalli was in New York for a forum at Fordham University to talk about the Vatican II declaration on the Jews in the document *Nostra Aetate*, which was getting 25th anniversary attention (CNS, September 17, 1990). Elie Wiesel was another of the speakers, and he, too, weighed in on the question of diplomatic relations, and with heavy insinuations. "What is it–what could it be–about the Jewish state that prevents the Vatican from recognizing it as a sovereign state? Doesn't the Vatican understand its absolute importance to the Jewish people everywhere?"

Since the Vatican had said it first needed to see some movement toward resolving the Israeli-Arab dispute, and had identified other points of concern, such as the status of Jerusalem, Mr. Wiesel's way of phrasing the question sounded like an indictment. And since he has an extraordinary skill with words, I suppose he meant it to sound that way. He was implying that he did not believe Vatican explanations really explained its true reasons, and that there must be some underlying, hidden motivation. What could it be?

Then came the Madrid Conference and Israel's agreement to accept a compromise settlement with the Palestine Liberation Organization, and in due order the negotiations for Vatican-Israel relations, by signed agreement December 30, 1993. Now I notice that in a 1996 booklet published by the Anti-Defamation League, *A Challenge Long Delayed,* on the eventual establishment of diplomatic relations (Eugene J. Fisher and Rabbi Leon Klenicki, eds.), Israel's first ambassador to the Vatican, Shmuel Hadas, writes that the reason for the Vatican's agreement was "most of all the shift initiated with the Madrid Conference that set in motion the Arab-Israeli peace process" (p. 31).

Did Vatican agreement on the tie with Israel bring contentment to Jews. Not that you could notice. Cardinal O'Connor and others working on the case sometimes said they hoped to see the diplomatic relations rapidly established so such a major irritant would no longer stand in the way of Catholic-Jewish cooperation on other matters. I do not recall the cardinal itemizing an agenda, but I suppose he was thinking of his interest in social policies to strengthen family life, combat poverty, put more moral content into public education and such. But many Jews just shifted immediately to another grievance: Pius XII and their wish that the Catholic Church anathematize him or something. It began to seem we could never go more than 27 seconds without hearing another Jewish demand for that.

In early 1999, Cardinal Cassidy charged one organization, generally understood to be the World Jewish Congress, with engaging in "a systematic campaign to denigrate the Catholic Church." And when I covered an address he gave later that year, he said Christians and Jews needed to move on, and start working together on issues such as "human rights and questions concerning life itself" (CNS, November 18). But the Jewish community seemed less interested in moving on than in the campaign against Pius XII, and demanded that Catholic officials look around in their archives to see what they could find to serve the cause. Cardinal Cassidy said eleven volumes of documents from the period had been published already, and could they not look at those and find enough information to draw their conclusions? In response, IJCIC joined with the Commission on Religious Relations with the Jews in setting up a Jewish-Catholic team of scholars to study those volumes. But when I covered a press conference the team held after their first meeting, I found them indicating that the look into the eleven volumes would serve only as a launching pad for renewed demands that the Vatican open all its archives to them (CNS, December 8, 1999).

What puzzled me was the way the waging of this battle over Pius XII was delayed for so long after his death. Jews apparently were not attacking him during the Holocaust, but praising him for the assistance he gave to so many Jews. And he lived on for 13 years after the war, and questions about his record could have been put then. But at his death in 1958, he was still held in honor by the Jewish community.

Robert A. Graham, a Jesuit priest working in Rome, became a principal defender of Pius XII. When I covered an address he gave to the United States Catholic Historical Society, I found him tracing the attacks on Pius XII to the 1962 play by Rolf Hochhuth, *The Deputy* (*Der Stellvertreter*). I suppose playwright Hochhuth, a German who also wrote a play accusing Winston Churchill of dastardly deeds, may have had an interest in shifting attention from the people who actually carried out the crimes of the Nazi period, and portraying an Italian pope and a British prime minister as the preeminent culprits of the era. Father Graham told us Vatican records showed Jewish organizations were continually going to Pius XII during the war and asking him to help various people in danger. "They all found out the pope was willing and ready to help," he said. "They were not asking him to make speeches, but to intervene where he had influence" (NC, December 15, 1987).

Another Jesuit, Peter Gumpel, working in Rome on the move to canonize Pius XII, took up the defense against John Cornwell's assault, *Hitler's Pope: The Secret History of Piux XII*. In an article published in *Crisis* magazine (December 1999), he charged that there were many errors of fact and interpretation in the work of Mr. Cornwell, "who has no academic degrees in history, law or theology." But perhaps more significantly, Father Gumpel cited the outlook of Jews during the lifetime of Pius XII. And he reported that on the pope's death, Golda Meier sent the Vatican a telegram stating, "We share in the grief of humanity at the passing away of His Holiness Pope Pius XII. In a generation affected by wars and discords, he upheld the highest ideals of peace and compassion. When fearful martyrdom came to our people in the decade of Nazi terror, the voice of the pope was raised for the victims."

Somehow, Jews have come to be linked with blacks in much discourse about American intergroup relations. Are these two groups to unite in common struggle against white Christians, or to split and struggle a while with each other, Jews finding allies among other whites and blacks among other Christians? I cannot answer that question, but I have had a chance to observe some interesting aspects of the black scene.

BLACKS

CHAPTER SIX

The church burning story was a peculiarity of 1996. Suddenly, the National Council of Churches (NCC) was going all out. The white people down South were so mean that now they had decided to burn down the black churches. "Domestic terrorism," said Mac Charles Jones, a black minister of the National Baptist Convention USA, Inc., who had just come to the NCC as a part-time secretary for racial justice.

We do have a few little Klan groups in this country, and some other white fellows who are not beyond engaging in criminal acts. And occasionally they will set fire to a black church. Sometimes you will read of convictions. No doubt about that.

But if you go on to ask, as I started to do when the NCC campaign heated up, and a congressional committee held hearings in Washington, and President Clinton addressed the subject in a radio talk from the Oval Office, with NCC General Secretary Joan Brown Campbell and a couple of black pastors standing by, and a federal task force being formed, a tougher new federal law being passed and millions of federal dollars being devoted, if you then asked whether more black churches were being burned by white racists than five or ten or twenty years earlier, there seemed to be no way of getting an answer.

When I asked people at the NCC, they said the Justice Department in Washington could give me the data. I was told to call Lisa Winston, assistant to the assistant attorney general for civil rights. But when I did, she said the federal government had no such statistics, and I might find them at an agency of the insurance industry, the National Fire Protection Association in Quincy, Massachusetts. When I called there, I was told that totally reliable figures did not exist, that some states collected data on church arson and some did not, and the association took what figures it could get and extrapolated, and came up with estimates. But there were none yet for 1995 or 1996. And in any case the association never produced separate figures for black churches. And of course no estimates on the number of black churches burned down by mean white people.

But the NCC publicity was beating the drums about not only an increase but a "dramatic increase." The NCC president, Melvin G. Talbert, and the general secretary submitted written congressional testimony (May 21) about an "epidemic of burnings" that was not "random" but "pieces in a pattern," constituting "one of this country's most pressing social and moral crises." Lisa Winston sent me a speech by her boss, Deval Patrick, that had "dramatic increase" ambiguously worked in. And others spoke of a "rash" of burnings.

I eventually got a telephone interview with Mr. Patrick (ENI, November 4), but that did not turn out to be a confidence-building measure. When I asked him how he substantiated the "dramatic increase" language, he grew nervous and moved quickly away. He was just using figures reported to him, he said. He had also spoken of an "epidemic of terrorism," but declined to repeat the phrase when I asked him if he thought terrorism was still abroad in the land. By then, several journalistic critiques of the church burning campaign had appeared, and I asked Mr. Patrick for his response. But he gave no rejoinder to their arguments, and only said he was "disappointed" by them.

A lengthy analysis in *The New Yorker* (July 15) concluded that the truth was "a great deal more complicated" than promoters of the campaign would have us believe, and that there was "no evidence of a master plot by organized hate groups." The *New York Post* published an attack as an editorial with a headline nuanced in the manner you might expect from a paper owned by Rupert Murdoch: "The Great Church Fire Hoax." This assault focused on two agencies allied with the NCC—the Center for Democratic Renewal in Atlanta and the Center for Constitutional Rights in New York—and interpreted the campaign as a continuation of their radical and leftist activity of previous years. The editorial also attacked Don Rojas, lately hired as a spokesman for the NCC's program of response to the burnings, and it said his history included time working with Marxists in Grenada, Havana and Prague.

I reported on the NCC campaign when it got to the Oval Office (ENI, June 11), and on the critical reaction when the August 9 issue of *The Wall Street Journal* presented a skeptical analysis as the lead story on its front page. By then, the NCC had raised several million dollars, including big gifts from foundations such as Ford, and some people were suggesting the campaign was a gimmick. The NCC announced it would use 85 per cent of donated funds for rebuilding churches and the other 15 per cent to address what it saw as the

SIDEBARS

pervasive underlying racism of American society. This, it was contending, had led to what it was presenting as a widespread, growing and coordinated effort of whites to burn down black churches. The *Journal* quoted Rev. Jones projecting a quite ambitious program of seminars in many cities, the hiring of additional staff and the addressing of a lengthy list of issues. The *Journal* had also found a few people who had given the NCC money to help with the rebuilding of churches and who grumbled to learn part of their gifts would be diverted to the NCC's own programs that they did not much care for (ENI, August 12).

The turnaround in the NCC's finances was indeed remarkable. Just the year before, I had done an ENI story about the resignation of Joseph E. Agne, a white United Methodist minister, as the NCC's secretary for racial justice. He felt, he told me, that the NCC's heart was not really in the cause. He had no money to carry out a program, and the last straw came, he said, from being told that there were not even dollars enough for him to buy a plane ticket to go somewhere, anywhere, for a meeting. Later, when I talked with Joan Campbell, she told me a campaign Mr. Agne led to raise funds for his office was $58,000 in deficit when he resigned. He later disputed that, but could not give me alternative numbers.

In any case, the picture had greatly changed. Rev. Jones was doing his work part time and commuting from a pastorate in Kansas City. The NCC was flying multi-person delegations to various places where black churches had burned, and where people would say they thought the mean white people probably did it. Thirty or more pastors of these churches were flown to Washington, where they met with Attorney General Janet Reno and Treasury Secretary Robert E. Rubin, and two of them became the ones standing by President Clinton as he made his radio address. And here was Rev. Jones projecting his expansive program for the coming year.

I figured, however, that the campaign was likely more political than financial in its origins and motivations. Rev. Jones was a board member of the Center for Democratic Renewal, and it had been putting out statistics purporting to show there came a sudden increase in the burning of black churches in January of 1995, which increase it said was gathering more steam in 1996, and which increase it said was to be attributed largely to the mean white people. And Rev. Jones then brought all this with him when he came to the NCC.

What had without question happened in January of 1995 was that the Republicans took over both houses of Congress, and moves were accelerated to cut back on affirmative action, welfare programs and other measures that blacks and the liberal community in general considered vital. One could imagine somebody got the idea that a campaign against the burning of black churches would help liberals regain the initiative and possession of the moral high ground.

Proving arson is not a quick and easy assignment, however. Undoubtedly churches–black as well as white–burned now and then, and I thought the NCC might well have established at the beginning of its existence an office to coordinate response to church burnings year in and year out, and maybe also support Jews dealing with incidents of synagogue desecration. But you could not always immediately determine whether a church burning was by arson or accident, or, if by arson, who or what color of person did it. So, designating one particular year for a campaign, and assuming all the allegations were factual, seemed peculiar. During the presidential campaign of 1996, President Clinton and Vice President Albert Gore provided a photo op by going to one of the burned black churches, Salem Missionary Baptist in Fruitland, Tennessee, and putting in a few hours of work helping rebuild it. And the NCC was there to present a check from its fund. That was in August, but when I talked to Mr. Patrick in October, the federal government still did not have evidence that would enable him to tell me whether or not this example church was burned by whites.

Talk of church burnings proved to be very inflammatory. Burning crosses, burning books, burning churches–there is something psychiatric about burning that excites the imagination and suggests the flames of hell. Soon enflamed black voices in the halls of Congress and elsewhere were demanding action to stop these church burnings. But just as quickly, the wind shifted. When Mr. Patrick resigned in January of 1997, he put out a report indicating that the number of black churches being burned had declined remarkably, and we heard remarkably little from Washington thereafter about it all. And the NCC was soon shutting its program down. So you might say that what was basically a political issue had been resolved politically.

That did not mean, however, that the Center for Democratic Renewal would rest content. On March 10, 1997, it sent a letter to President Clinton, signed by C. T. Vivian, a black minister who was board chairman, and Beni Ivey, executive director, reporting that it found evidence of "a conspiracy to burn black churches," that this was a conspiracy by "white supremacists for the purpose of starting a race war" and that the failure of the Clinton Administration to expose this evidence fully to the public was a matter of concern. Attached to the letter was a report titled *The Fourth Wave,* putting current events in an historical series preceded by the "waves" of the Reconstruction era, the 1920s and the civil rights period of the 1950s and 1960s. And the conspiracy theory was elaborated: "We contend that it is the ideology espoused by the Christian Knights of the Ku Klux Klan, which is based in Christian

Identity and reinforced by *The Turner Diaries,* simplified in a pamphlet written by a known white supremacist in Gwinnett County, Georgia, and sold by the Aryan Nation at its headquarters in Idaho that forms the basis for the conspiracy to start a race war." I never heard whether President Clinton found this theory convincing. Joan Campbell told me the NCC was not endorsing it.

Although the campaign against church burning suffered from a shortage of evidence for its "dramatic increase" rhetoric, I decided the operation was so much to everybody's advantage that, once somebody got it underway, the temptation to carry it on could hardly have been resisted. For the NCC and its allied agencies there was the financial and political return. For a good many black churches, burned somehow, maybe by whites, there was help in rebuilding, and they would wind up with buildings better than what they had before. The campaign brought advantage to President Clinton because it offered another symbolic gesture he could make to show himself a friend of black people while he was signing a welfare bill they found especially damaging. White conservatives gained because delivering a denunciation of church arson was something easily done by all decent people, and members of the religious right, like those in the Christian Coalition, could rush in to get their brownie points. And it was to the advantage of the Ku Klux Klan and whatever comparable groups may have been around because it gave them a national publicity boost, and made them appear much more important than they really were in the total context of American life.

A sad epilogue in 1997 was the sudden death of Rev. Jones. Joan Campbell persuaded him to leave his church, St. Stephen Baptist in Kansas City, and join the NCC full time as head of the National Ministries Unit. He moved into this position March 2, left for an El Paso meeting March 6, suffered an attack during a change of planes at the Dallas-Fort Worth Airport and died of an embolism that evening at a hospital in Irving (ENI, March 11).

Although most black Christians of the United States belong to Protestant churches, covering the black community has at times taken me also to Catholic precincts. Even to the arrest of a bishop. Cardinal O'Connor did not choose to follow the example of those protesters who deliberately violate the law and go to jail to make a point. But he has had a couple of auxiliary bishops who did provoke arrest. One was white: Austin B. Vaughan, who joined the pro-lifers in blocking abortion clinics, spent time with them behind bars and even traveled abroad to get himself arrested in Belgium and the Netherlands, though these countries chose to hold onto him for not many hours (CNS, February 1, 1990). The other was black: Emerson J. Moore, who sought and secured arrest with others blocking the entrance to South Africa's New York consulate as a protest against apartheid. That was back in 1984, and he possibly was the first Catholic bishop to get himself arrested in the United States. He told me afterward it made him feel good to take such a step on behalf of something he believed in (NC, December 6). But he was released immediately after booking, and spent no days in jail.

As a sidebar, I might remark that I have not yet been convinced of the validity of this American tradition of violating a law just to feel good about thinking you have done something to overthrow evil when you haven't really. If someone considers a law unjust, thinks it requires doing something wrong, then refusal to obey can become an act of good conscience. The young men who decided it would be wrong to go to Vietnam and kill people, and who refused to accept the draft, seem worthy of admiration. Many of them endured years of prison rather than act against their convictions.

But in New York, as well as some other cities, we see something different. People almost routinely violate a law about keeping sidewalks or entrances to public buildings open for use by the public. They do not assert that the law is bad, or try to get it changed. They do not contend that the law should allow anyone with a grievance against the government to block the public streets and sidewalks, or entrances to public buildings. But they violate the law just so they will get arrested and, often a motivating hope, get their pictures in the newspapers as propaganda for their cause, while showing disdain for the government and trying to pressure it into change. We of the news media tend to play along, and publicize as significant news what has become choreographed routine. And more than that, the law enforcement establishment of New York acts in collusion, too, seemingly viewing the illegal behavior as all a game. At least when the causes enjoy acceptance among the cultural leadership, violators go through the ritual of getting handcuffed and then shortly turned loose with no disagreeable consequence such as spending a night in jail. Even people who have had responsibility for making and enforcing laws may show this kind of disrespect for law. In 1999, after the killing of a West African immigrant, Amadou Diallo, by white police officers, New York's former mayor, David N. Dinkins, and some congressmen were among more than a thousand protesters who got themselves arrested to show, they said, their objection to police treatment of black people. Then, Manhattan District Attorney Robert M. Morgenthau asked for dismissal of the charges. Since the protests were not violent and the protesters had sacrificed hours of their time to get arrested, they had already paid penalties enough, he said. Proof, if anybody needed it, that the whole affair was a public relations game, with even the district attorney giving it a wink. In New York, the police have been long practiced in this particular choreography, but there must be a degree of demoralization for them in their assignment to serve as actors in charades, required to play the role of the evil oppressor, enduring the hisses of the righteous, while the establishment applauds those the police are obligated to arrest. In the United States, we all have plenty of ways we can protest whatever bothers us. So where is the justification for this display of getting arrested just for the sake of getting arrested?

But such opinions were not pertinent to my reporting, and Bishop Moore became in some measure a friend of mine over the years of his service as auxiliary bishop. He once told me that he ranked Malcolm X as one of his heroes, but he showed nothing of the fiery, denunciatory manner of Malcolm X, and I found him easy to get along with. In 1982, I did a story on his ordination to the episcopacy, which was of more news interest than the usual auxiliary ordination because he was the first black bishop of the New York Archdiocese (NC, September 9). I later did an interview that had some sizzle because he said he supported the presidential candidacy of Jesse Jackson (NC, May 21, 1984). The editor in Washington could hardly believe that a bishop would really make a statement of political choice for publication, a common occurrence among black Protestant clergy but hardly among Catholic bishops, and called me to double check and make sure I could give assurance it really did happen on the record. It may not have been a wise action for the bishop, but that only made it all the more newsy.

The next year, I reported Bishop Moore's account of going with Rev. Jackson for a meeting with Pope John Paul II at the Vatican (NC, January 16). The pope agreed to meet January 3 with Bishop Moore, Rev. Jackson and Herbert Daughtry, a black Pentecostal who also was arrested at the South African consulate. They were particularly interested in asking for the pope's help on the South Africa issue. Then at the end, Bishop Moore told me, Rev. Jackson asked the pope if they could pray. The pope agreed. Then Rev. Jackson asked if they could hold hands. Already in waist deep, the pope apparently felt he might as well try to wade all the way across. So they formed a circle, the pope joining hands with the Baptist and the Pentecostal. Would anybody but Jesse Jackson take charge of a personal meeting with the pope and call for holding hands?

At a press conference afterward, Rev. Jackson said it would be inappropriate for him to report on what the pope said to them in their private meeting. But Bishop Moore told me the pope actually did not get to say much of anything because Rev. Jackson did most of the talking.

I also found Bishop Moore taking an oblique perspective at an occasion in support of illegal aliens (NC, November 11, 1987). I had been struck by hearing people sympathetic to illegal aliens—undocumented immigrants, they preferred to say, as though it were simply a technical matter of incomplete paperwork rather than a violation of law—defend them against the charge they were taking jobs away from American workers. "They only get the jobs Americans won't do." But then people sympathetic to the able-bodies on welfare would defend this group against the charge that they were lazy. "There just aren't any jobs." Bishop Moore did not try to square the circular reasoning for me, but he said that blacks, though harboring no hostility to the illegal aliens, would like to see some of the jobs that were going to them become open to unemployed members of the black community.

Bishop Moore served on the board of Catholic Relief Services (CRS), and that enabled me to get a couple of stories about his overseas travels. And other events put him into the news. But there were puzzles. Twice while he was living at the rectory of his former pastorate, St. Charles Borromeo Church in Harlem, I made appointments—once through his secretary, the other time with him directly—and got stood up. He was not there, and still not there after I waited a good while. And nobody could tell me anything about where he might be, or what he might be doing or when he might be expected to come back. And in the following days I got no explanation from him about being unavoidably detained or whatever. I wondered how the Archdiocese of New York could function with a bishop operating in that fashion. But later I was to hear of more serious glitches than missing an appointment with a reporter. At times, a church full of people waited for him to come for confirmations, and he failed to show.

A perhaps implicit admission that he was responsible for losing contact came after he had spent some months in Rome. Out of the blue, I got a note from him saying he hoped to get back in touch. But he did not follow up right away. Eventually he asked me to come see him at his office in the archdiocesan headquarters. There, he told me that he had been struggling with drug addiction, and wanted a preliminary off-the-record conversation about how I might handle the story if he decided to make it public. I tried to explore with him the possible ramifications—if he told or if he kept carrying the burden of his secret—and left with the understanding he would call me again if he ever came to a decision. So, for an excessively long period I never tried to reach him, and he was assigned to an area of the archdiocese I seldom visited, and our paths did not cross.

One day, when I belatedly woke up, I found he had been a good while away, and the archdiocese would not say where he was, or what he was doing. I assumed the secretive response meant he was somewhere getting further treatment for the addiction. In any case, finding that a bishop had disappeared could have been a story, and the refusal of those in the know to offer any explanation perhaps a bigger story. But CNS editors did not care for aggressive pursuit in a situation such as that, so I let the matter drop, except for asking the

SIDEBARS

archdiocese to transmit a letter I wrote Bishop Moore to say I was still ready to talk with him whenever he might feel ready.

By then, I suppose he was too far gone. Soon, in 1995, came news of his death, followed a little later by a *New York Times* report that he died of AIDS. When I talked about his death with Cardinal O'Connor, a member of the Vatican Congregation for Bishops, he told me that he had never heard any report of any other bishop having AIDS. So Bishop Moore may have been a first for the Catholic hierarchy. Though, I should note, Cardinal O'Connor would not confirm directly that Bishop Moore did have AIDS, pleading the constraints of confidentiality in his dealings with the bishop's family.

Sad as any death from AIDS always is, I was especially saddened by the loss of Bishop Moore because I saw there another in a series of unrealized possibilities for the black community, another of several black men I had observed who were given unusual opportunities, in some considerable measure because they were black, but proved unable to make the contribution hoped for. The U.S. Catholic Church, out of a small pool of black priests, had been much in an affirmative action mode trying to put black faces in the hierarchy. If you were a black priest, your chances of becoming a bishop were many times greater than if you were white. But Bishop Moore's case made me wonder whether the church may have rushed a bit and elevated men to these rather high pressure posts before they were sufficiently seasoned. You could of course see examples of this also in Protestant churches, so it could not be called a specifically Catholic problem.

The issue was pointed up when Bishop Moore was made a bishop at age 44 in the same ceremony with Joseph T. O'Keefe, who was being consecrated at age 63, and after carrying much heavier responsibilities as vicar general of the archdiocese for several years. Cardinal O'Connor reported after Bishop Moore's death that on the basis of personal conversations he considered it certain that the bishop was troubled by pressures he felt in serving as a black bishop in a predominantly white church, a church not accustomed to seeing blacks in positions of authority.

Someone, offering of course no evidence and perhaps speaking only on supposition, told me that Bishop Moore's elevation to the episcopacy originated in a desire by church authorities to put another black priest, Lawrence E. Lucas, a little in the shade. Father Lucas, a native of Harlem and pastor of a Harlem church, was getting a good bit of media attention in the 1970s for his outspoken attacks on various matters he considered manifestations of white racism. To some, he might sound like the primary spokesman of black Catholics in New York. He had put his condemnation of church and society in a book, *White Church-Black Priest* (Random House, 1970), and for a time wrote a column carried in some church papers. But the fierce and repetitive nature of the attacks apparently turned people off after a while, and he seemed to draw less attention as time went on.

The first time I remember covering Father Lucas was in 1971, when he was part of a black delegation that was going to the Vatican (RNS, October 4). On this trip, he joined the director of the National Office for Black Catholics, Joseph Davis; the chairman of that office's board, Charles Hammock; the chairman of the National Conference of Black Sisters, Martin de Porres Grey, and the president of the National Black Lay Caucus who was a member of the Baltimore Black Caucus, Estelle Collins.

Father Lucas, president then of the National Black Catholic Clergy Caucus, hosted a press conference for the group at his church, Resurrection. They said they were going to explore the establishment of a black rite in the Catholic Church and ask for selection of a black as the next archbishop of Washington (neither of which they got). And they were going to talk over the black situation generally.

While discussion of this, that and the other always has potential value, I was struck by the harsh tone of the' rhetoric these black leaders were using about white leaders of their church, and wondered why they were bothering if they considered everything as bad as all that. They released a statement asserting that the white American hierarchy and the apostolic delegate then representing the Vatican in the United States were "dealing with black Catholics as bastard children and with the black community in a dishonest, racist and superficial manner." Father Lucas said his own archbishop, Terence J. Cooke, was "no different" and "superficial at best."

But I should remember that it was not only in the black or Catholic community that you could hear clergy engaging in strikingly harsh attacks against their own churches, or the whole church scene. When I covered the sermon Carlyle Marney gave at the installation of Ernest T. Campbell at Riverside Church, I got another sample (RNS, November 22, 1968). "If a minister is to speak today, his first word must be 'I have sinned,' spoken on behalf of Christendom," said Dr. Marney. I know the feeling. But it might sound better if a preacher's first (and last) word followed more the pattern of Paul's first word to the church in Philippi: "I thank my God in all my remembrance of you, always in every prayer of mine for you all making my prayer with joy, thankful for your partnership in the gospel from the first day until now. And I am sure that he who began a good work in you will bring it to completion at the day of Jesus Christ" (Philippians 1:3-6).

A Southern Baptist, Dr. Marney had fought in Texas and North Carolina pastorates for a more broad-minded outlook in his denomination. But at

SIDEBARS

Riverside Church, he took on the entire Christian world. He accused it of committing three major crimes: "against Judah, against man and against creation." The crime against "Judah," he said, was not only antisemitism but a refusal to accept and use what Christians had received from their Jewish heritage. The crime against man was sanctioning the divisions of race, class and nation. He was not yet into the gender issue. But he sneered at the popular theme of church renewal. "Renew what? Would God want a new version of what we have made out of the church? Renewal may not be the word for the storm that is coming to sweep away our refuge of lies."

I had first heard Dr. Marney in the early 1950s at Baylor University, and immediately recognized him as a unique personality, different in mind and manner from any other preacher I had heard. He had a rich voice and a rich emotional equipment, and a literary mind exploding with unorganized and unclarified ideas. But how could a man who gave his life to working in the church wind up preaching such a negative view of the institution as a totality? And he was far from alone. Attacking the church became something of a fad, in which I myself was led to join at times.

Father Lucas came into the news again in early 1988, and I got to talk with him at the rectory of Resurrection Church. Some of his remarks about the public school leadership of the city had drawn fire from Mayor Edward I. Koch and others, and a statement from Cardinal O'Connor that could, it appeared, be interpreted in various ways.

The city at the time was between school chancellors, as it has seemed to be fairly often, and blacks such as Father Lucas and Al Sharpton were promoting a particular black candidate, Adelaide Sanford, a member of the New York State Board of Regents. Eventually, another black candidate, Richard R. Green of Minneapolis, got the job. But while the selection process was underway, on December 28, 1987, some of the Sanford champions held a rally at the headquarters of the Board of Education in Brooklyn.

Father Lucas was among the speakers, and in a reference to the police, he said, "Those who are killing us in our homes, falsely arresting us in the subways, who are murdering us in the streets, come primarily from the Catholic persuasion." Then he told us about the evil he saw in the schools: "Those who are killing us in the class room, I do not need to tell you from what persuasion they come—you just have to look at the Board of Education and it looks like the Knesset of Israel."

As it happened, the board had only one Jew among its seven members at that point, and it had a black representation of equal size, and a Hispanic. But Father Lucas later said he had in mind not just the board, but the total public school system, with its teachers, administrators and "beneficiaries of contracts meted out in the name of education."

NC wanted to report Father Lucas's response to the controversy, and when I got an interview with him, he did offer explanations of a sort, though it was difficult to tell how seriously he meant them (NC, January 6, 1988). A man talking at home with a reporter may naturally sound calmer than he does stirring up a street crowd, but may also be trying to give different messages to different audiences. Mayor Koch said the rally remarks had "a clear intent to generate antisemitism." Father Lucas said, no, nothing antisemitic at all there, but only a recognition that many Jews were involved in a system that was failing black children. He did qualify by saying that if he had a chance to do it over again, he would leave out the Knesset part.

A sidebar of the incident was the revelation that Father Lucas had a permit to carry a pistol. He said he shot at a club as a hobby, but also carried a pistol at times for self-defense, which I suppose some people might consider out of character for a priest, though it doubtless seemed like a realistic precaution in his circumstances. As I interviewed him, a police car sat outside with an officer keeping watch, the result, Father Lucas said, of his reporting threats that had come to him.

Jews demanded that Cardinal O'Connor disassociate the archdiocese from Father Lucas's comments, and there ensued an exercise in what might be called diplomacy. Cardinal O'Connor did put out a statement, and those who so chose could say he had condemned Father Lucas. He said Patrick J. Sheridan, the vicar general, talked with Father Lucas about his remarks, and "Father Lucas feels that his remarks were taken out of context."

And the cardinal continued: "My personal loyalties to a brother priest cannot justify my condoning rhetoric that, either in or out of context, could be construed by reasonable persons as racist, anti-Semitic, and, ironically, even anti-Catholic, regardless of the intention of the speaker."

Some people called it a sharp reprimand; some said it was mild. Father Lucas told me that he did not see any reprimand at all. "He didn't say whose rhetoric could be characterized that way," said Father Lucas. The meeting with Msgr. Sheridan had been "cordial," and a matter of "putting into context two sentences." But he would concede that the vicar general gave him "a feeling of not being clearly understood."

Whatever the explanation or explaining away, I could sense a man seething with hostility, looking to find any opening that would justify an accusation of racism. The following year, I had a telephone interview with Father Lucas in an effort to get some feature material about a brother of his who had come into the news, and I felt it again (NC, June 5, 1989). For the position of civil rights

SIDEBARS

chief in the Justice Department, the office later held by Deval Patrick, President George H.W. Bush nominated William Lucas, a graduate of the Fordham University Law School who had become an FBI agent and then a county executive and Republican in Detroit. Because of his conservative outlook, put alongside some aspects of his record, the nomination drew a mixed response, dividing blacks and the civil rights community generally, and he eventually failed to win confirmation.

While the nomination was pending, Father Lucas wrote about it in the Harlem weekly, *Amsterdam News* (June 3), and said he did not agree with his brother politically. The goal of overthrowing racism, he said, could not be achieved "in the context of the systems and institutions of white America," because those institutions "like the nation itself are founded in racism." But since someone would get the job now open in the Justice Department, he thought his brother was as good a candidate as could be found.

A by-product of the controversy was letting us learn a little more about the Lucas family. William, we were told, was the oldest of eight children of parents who had immigrated to New York from the Caribbean. There was only one girl in the family—Patricia, who had become a nun of the Daughters of the Heart of Mary, known in the United States as Nardins. But if the family came expecting to find the good life in America, Father Lucas would testify it seemed to him not good enough. Maybe good enough to stay and keep living it, but not good enough for any expressions of gratitude.

Bishop Moore once told me that he generally agreed with the positions Father Lucas took on issues, though their styles differed. If that meant Bishop Moore felt the same angers, but kept them bottled up inside, perhaps the release Father Lucas got through the oratory of rage came to the bishop through drugs. To me, the final result seemed in one way the same, an inability to make the contribution that their unusual talents and opportunities would have allowed.

Whites confront something of a dilemma in trying to assess the language of radical black protesters. Sometimes I have heard white friends of the protesters urging, "Don't get hung up on the rhetoric." The idea is that when a man suffers severe pain, he will likely speak in exaggerated ways, and it is not the time to start checking on how his sentences diagram or coolly critiquing his use of metaphor. Certainly. On the other hand, it can also be a sign of respect if whites pay attention to the exact words blacks are saying, and a little condescending to declare that they could not really have meant what they were telling you. But then, if you start examining the rhetoric closely and suggesting few whites could agree with it, some blacks and their white allies will castigate you for failure to see the bigger picture of justice, freedom and so on.

As part of the ferment of the 1960s, some blacks even began developing what they called a black theology, and I never knew what to make of that. Trying to make a theology out of your ethnic identification seems right peculiar, and in Christianity, where the leaders of this movement operated, it seemed like an impossible undertaking, just on the face of it. Some advocates or defenders of the movement I suppose would tell us we should not get too literal about the language, but often it seemed pretty literal.

James H. Cone, a theologian whose combination of scholarship and out front radicalism got him a teaching post at Union Seminary in 1969 at the very young age of 31, and a full professorship there four years later, became the leading exponent of this kind of theology. When I read his programmatic work, *Black Theology and Black Power* (Seabury, 1969), I found over toward the end a flat assertion, "Being black in America has very little to do with skin color" (p. 151). It meant, rather, identification with "the dispossessed" and so on. But Professor Cone was himself black literally, and elsewhere said his religious inspiration originated in the church of his childhood in Fordyce, Arkansas, which was black literally. And his book was full of illustrations and references connected to matters of literally black *vs.* literally white. His pages were packed with provocative statements keyed to the literal tensions of race relations in the United States, such as that "black power" is "Christ's central message to twentieth-century America" (p. 1). There were also declarations that this message meant "complete emancipation of black people from white oppression by whatever means black people deem necessary" (p. 6); that God revealed "his concern" was "not for whites but for blacks" (p. 64); that it was not possible for white Christians to "evade the hostility of black Americans" (p. 129); that "unless white America responds positively to the theory and activity of black power, then a bloody, protracted civil war is inevitable" (p. 143); that "black people cannot talk about the possibilities of reconciliation until full emancipation has become a reality" (p. 146); that "in America, God's revelation on earth has always been black, red or some other shocking shade, but never white" (p. 150), and that "God's word of reconciliation means that we can only be justified by becoming black" (p. 151).

Sounds literal enough you could infer black theology meant to use Christianity to promote the political interests of blacks as an ethnic group. Later, in a *Christian Century* article (February 18, 1981), Professor Cone said his outlook had been enlarged to take into account the women's movement and problems of Africa, Asia and Latin America. But he still believed "the gospel is identical with the liberation of poor people from sociopolitical oppression," and for the sake of this liberation he had come to "consider socialism as an alternative to monopoly capitalism."

It may be a little bothersome to whites that quite a few blacks have indicated this sort of thing is just the kind of Christianity they like. But I should note that what whites make of it concerns Professor Cone not in the least. Black theology is not talking to white people, but is developed "to prepare the minds of blacks for freedom," he wrote in *Black Theology and Black Power*. "It assumes that the possibilities of creative response among white people to black humiliation are virtually nonexistent" (p. 118).

Not all blacks endorsed black theology, we should recognize. Julius Lester, a Methodist minister's son who served as the fiery spokesman of the Student Nonviolent Coordinating Committee before he looked into Catholic mysticism and became a Jew, signed up with the dissenters. Writing in *Christianity and Crisis* (March 31, 1975), he reviewed a book of essays edited by Eric Lincoln, *The Black Experience in Religion* (Doubleday, 1974), with contributions by Professor Cone and others of similar outlook. He dismissed these as "little more than political polemics in religious language." And while I guess Professor Cone might not have considered this such a negative judgment actually, the reviewer also put him in the category of those who defined blacks as victims, and implied "their primary relationship is not to God but to white American society." Which I suppose Professor Cone would consider right much against the grain. And the review concluded, "This collection makes it apparent that black theologians are uncertain about their identities–as blacks, and particularly as Christians. The result is a cry of despair masked as the bark of militance."

Recognizing full well that Professor Cone, according to the program, does not give a hoot what I or any other white thinks of all this, it nonetheless occurs to me to wonder whether it is good for blacks, especially young blacks mentally alert enough to delve into such books and then to become leaders in the black community. Are they getting the best preparation for life in America when they are encouraged to take a stance of belligerent hostility toward white society? It can get you a job at institutions like Union Seminary, but how will it work out in the business world? And beyond all that, of course, lies the question of whether it helps those young blacks who will take leadership positions in the church speak in ways authentically Christian.

Aside from any particular policy position, the tone of it all makes one wonder: "Black power seeks not understanding but conflict; addresses blacks and not whites; seeks to develop black support, but not white good will" (p. 16). Or for tone consider: "If the riots are the black man's courage to say Yes to himself as a creature of God, and if in affirming self he affirms Yes to the neighbor, then violence may be the black man's expression, sometimes the only possible expression, of Christian love to the white oppressor" (p. 55). But so far as I could see, the riots in Watts, Newark and other cities were mostly irrational outbursts of black communities engaging in self-destruction, frightening some whites maybe but in the end not so damaging to their interests. And the "bloody civil war" that Professor Cone warned us might become "inevitable" sounded like a far-fetched and hopeless adventure most blacks would not want to get themselves killed in.

The tone in which Professor Cone later on would assure us he did not write out of hostility seemed not so much happier. In a 1990 address at Emory University's Candler School of Theology in Atlanta, he explained: "I did not begin to write black theology because I disliked or hated white people, or even enjoyed exposing their hypocrisy or calling them racist. I do not hate anybody, and I receive no delight in pointing out how inhumane and how brutal whites have been in their behavior against blacks. My only concern is to speak and to live the truth of the gospel . . . ." (from a news bulletin of Union Seminary, Winter 1991).

All this has made me recall a service I attended at Abyssinian Baptist Church in New York when Adam Clayton Powell Jr., the Harlem congressman, was pastor. In his "pastoral" prayer, the passions of his heart were enlarged to offer a petition on behalf of "my colleagues in the United States Congress, who this past week have shown themselves to be hypocrites." Many Americans of all colors might join any day of the week in throwing negative terms at members of Congress, but maybe not so many would assume the Reverend Congressman Powell was somehow an exception.

After James Forman took over the 1969 Black Economic Development Conference in Detroit, and issued a *Manifesto* calling for white churches to give blacks $500 million in reparations, he carried his campaign—on May 4—to Riverside Church, taking note of its endowment from Rockefeller money. He disrupted a worship service to make his demands, and a certain number of people said "prophetic," a word such people commonly use in such situations.

Riverside Church had a considerable portfolio, and Mr. Forman said blacks should get 60 per cent of the income from it. And he wanted the church to give him free office space, give use of its classrooms to Harlem residents and let blacks and Puerto Ricans have the use twelve hours a day of a radio station the church was then operating. "We are dead serious about our demands, and we are prepared to die for their implementation," he said.

Radicals of this sort customarily presented "demands," and the word ceased to mean much. In the apartment building where I live, tenants got steamed up about lack of heat and other building deficiencies during that period and once made a list of needed repairs. The complaints of leaky faucets, cracked plaster and stuck windows were all given to the landlord under the one rubric of "demands," though I do not recall anybody promising to die for a repairman.

Riverside Church never made any pretense of giving in to the "demands" that Mr. Forman said he was "prepared to die for." But Dr. Campbell, senior minister at the time, did lead the church in trying to use the occasion for making a new effort on behalf of poor blacks. Shortly after the disruption, I covered a panel discussion at the church where he said the church would not give any money to Mr. Forman's organization, but that the concept of reparations had "great moral force" behind it (RNS, May 23, 1969). Lucius Walker Jr., a black minister who headed the Interreligious Foundation for Community Organization (IFCO), sponsor of the Detroit conference Mr. Forman took over, expressed hope every church would respond to the *Manifesto*. A white member of Riverside Church, Francis Harmon, asked if he agreed with the *Manifesto*'s statement that "only an armed, well-disciplined, black-controlled government can insure the stamping out of racism in this country." Mr. Walker said he agreed but hoped blacks would not have to follow that course—as though he assumed they could. Philip Phenix, a white member of the church who taught at Teachers College, said he was disappointed that other members of the panel so easily dismissed the "seditious" rhetoric of the *Manifesto*. "It is a propaganda piece and sheer demagoguery," he said.

"I agree," said David R. Hunter, a white minister who was deputy general secretary of the National Council of Churches. "But I wouldn't have said it. It is not what we need to hear." Wherein lay a common deficiency among white liberals, as I saw it. They could not exercise much leadership unless they maintained credibility in their white constituency, and that was hardly possible if they went along with rhetoric like that in the *Black Manifesto*. So it was both bad strategy and a deficiency of candor if they were pretending to agree more totally than they really did. Their approach gave an air of play-acting in the black-white dialogue, and led to cynicism among blacks who could see that the follow-up actions of the white liberals by no means matched what their smiling words seemed to promise. I thought the dialogue would have been healthier if whites like Dr. Hunter had been ready to state forthrightly that they rejected many of the assertions black radicals were throwing around, but recognized an obligation to address black needs that were real.

In 1972, I reported for RNS that Riverside Church had finally launched a drive to raise a $450,000 Fund for Social Justice that would be divided among various community service organizations attempting to help blacks (April 7). That was rather far from Mr. Forman's original "demand" of $500 million, said later to have been raised to $3 billion. But it was something. And in a different world than the one that personal problems brought Mr. Forman to in later years. Apparently unable to make a living, he was reported a decade or so after the *Manifesto* to be approaching church executives he knew from earlier confrontations, but now asking for a handout of ten or maybe twenty dollars.

The problem of black poverty was and is a serious matter. But I could never understand why so many people gave so much attention to Mr. Forman and his "demands." I suppose they all knew the white churches were never going to hand over the big millions in reparations. In some cases it could seem liberal whites were using Mr. Forman to help promote an agenda of their own. They wanted the churches to get more into community development, and they could use him as a kind of threat: adopt the program we want or this big black mad guy may get even madder and tear your society down. I doubted he would be capable of doing that, but many people seemed to operate with the assumption that radical blacks could overthrow the government of the United States if they decided it was the thing to do. That was before the military talent of Colin Powell became known, but whether he would contribute his abilities to a project for overthrowing his country's government might also be doubted. Anyway, back then the word of liberal whites instructed us: Better go along with the demands, however outrageous they may sound to your bourgeois ears. When Mr. Forman and members of his group took over some church offices in the Interchurch Center, it became evident he had white sympathizers inside who would aid him against the churches that they were supposedly working for, and were paid to work for. Covering the takeover, I was a little astonished to find one of them suddenly confronting me, demanding to know where I stood and so forth.

One day in 1970, I was sent up to cover a press conference in Harlem called by an interdenominational group of black clergy that had just organized (RNS, May 11). Giving their little group the rather grandiose name of City-Wide Black Clergy Coalition, they explained that they felt a need for a more unified approach to get attention at City Hall. They were much discontented with the mayor, John V. Lindsay, though he had a reputation as a liberal Republican, much too far out for white conservatives. Later that year, I covered the annual Family of Man dinner held by the New York City Council of Churches to raise funds for its program (RNS, October 27). Mayor Lindsay, the principal honoree, used the occasion to blast President Richard M. Nixon, Vice President Spiro Agnew and other Republican leaders. Dan M. Potter, chief executive of the council, told me Mr. Lindsay's unpopularity among businessmen made it hard to sell dinner tickets, and sales fell to half those of the year before, when Mr. Nixon was honored in absentia. But the clergy at the Harlem press conference told me, "We are totally disillusioned with Lindsay. In a way he is dangerous as Nixon because he goes under liberal credentials."

How seriously one should take such rhetoric is difficult to determine. But these clergymen said Mayor Lindsay had failed to give as much attention to a recent bomb explosion at a black church as he did to bombings at synagogues.

I try to stay neutral when I am reporting on issues, and so did a story simply telling what the City-Wide Coalition had said. But I less easily remain neutral when attacks come against me, as when one of the black ministers took the occasion to lecture me on the failings of white people in the media. Actually the truth was the opposite. I was the only reporter who bothered to cover their press conference. Just because they were black, RNS felt some attention should be paid. No black paper or radio station felt that obligation, or gave indication they thought the press conference was worth a reporter's time. And I decided their news judgment was probably accurate. I never heard anything about the group thereafter.

A big international story of the 1970s and 1980s was the Program to Combat Racism launched by the World Council of Churches. It was initiated by Eugene Carson Blake, an American Presbyterian who became WCC general secretary in 1966. In 1969, he arranged a racism consultation in London, with the duties of chairmanship placed in the hands of George S. McGovern, a Methodist minister's son who was then a senator from South Dakota and in 1972 the Democratic nominee for president. The consultation prepared the ground for bringing the World Council into its program of "combat."

While most everybody would condemn racism, particularly in other people, the WCC move did not get the backing of everybody. But the WCC plowed ahead, showing its combative heart by giving money to black guerrilla groups fighting to overthrow the white governments of southern Africa. Grants were announced from year to year, and went to groups in many parts of the world, but southern Africa got the lion's share, and maybe the elephant's as well. And after blacks took over the governments there–Mozambique (1975), Angola (1975), Zimbabwe (1980), Namibia (1990) and finally South Africa (1994)–the oomph departed from the program.

The WCC routinely emphasized a provision that its grants went only for the medical, educational and other humanitarian activities of the recipients, and not for guns. It also would remind critics that the grants came only from a special fund derived from contributions of program supporters, and none of the general gifts made by churches to the WCC went in this direction. But critics were not appeased. Recipients in southern Africa were engaged in violent activities to achieve their goals, sometimes violence against dissidents in their own ranks, and they tended to mouth a Marxist ideology. How much their leaders actually knew about the turgidities of the Marxist canon may be wondered. But that did not matter to the WCC, or to its critics. The WCC was not just doing humanitarian work, as church leaders in the United States some-times attempted to argue against their conservative critics. It had other pro-grams for relief operations in Africa and helping needy blacks, whether they were involved in these struggles or not. The point of the racism grants was to give a public endorsement. Guidelines adopted by the WCC Executive Committee in 1970 specified that money from the "special fund" was to "sup-port organizations that combat racism, rather than welfare organizations that alleviate the effects of racism." Southern Africa was identified as a priority, so the groups there stood at the center of international debate. Grants from this special fund also went to a number of organizations in the United States, and I suspect some of them could have aroused the conservatives right much had more been publicized about what they were saying and doing. But I saw little commotion along that line.

A sidebar consideration for me was the fact that the churches that belonged to the WCC did not seem much engaged in all this. At times, staff of the WCC like to make a public relations pitch that the Council is not the staff in Geneva but the member churches. However, in this case it appeared the Program to Combat Racism, and especially its grant-making, was pretty much a case of staff using the structures of the Council to do something they took a keen interest in but the member churches not so much.

Instead of staff in general, perhaps I should specify Dr. Blake and people he brought in to manage the program. After his death in 1985, a man who had been closely associated with him in the WCC years while working for another Geneva organization, Lewis Wilkins of the World Alliance of Reformed Churches, wrote a tribute that highlighted this program as a major part of the Blake legacy: "He got the Program to Combat Racism through a European-dominated bureaucracy almost single-handedly, against overt and covert oppo-sition from most of the WCC staff and in the Central Committee." Which statement was written in admiration but, viewed from the other side, amount-ed to saying that it was largely a personal project of the general secretary, and that most of the WCC staff and some significant portion of representatives of the churches on the WCC's main governing unit, the Central Committee, did not consider it a wise move. But Dr. Blake had sufficient force of personality to push it through anyway, and after it was in place the WCC could not with-draw without opening itself to accusations of caving in to racist pressures.

Dr. Blake could keep the program going because he found ways of raising the money for it without dependence on the WCC's member churches. A curiosity to me through all the intense debate over the grant recipients was the lack of information on where the money was coming from. The WCC always proceeded openly in telling which organizations were getting grants year by year, and exactly how much they got. But I never saw any reports from the Council on who gave the money. When I was in Geneva in 1980, I once saw a list, but it was too limited in its identifications to provide a useful picture. It might say something like "Trinity Methodist–$147," with no indication of which "Trinity Methodist," or which town or country it might be in. Anyway, such incidental gifts could not provide the bulk of the grants that were sometimes $100,000 or more.

Once, writing an article on the WCC, I was told by someone close to the situation that not one of the U.S. denominations in the WCC was contributing as a denomination to the special fund (*New World Outlook*, November 1988). Another of the U.S. figures related to the WCC said frankly in talking with me that he had voted to tell the WCC staff they could do the program if they wished, but he would not try to raise any money for it. I thought that was an irresponsible position, in the most specific sense of official irresponsibility, and people with votes ought to vote what they actually thought their churches were prepared to do. But I assume he and other U.S. church leaders took that position because they felt more comfortable going along with something described as fighting racism, but calculated that fund raising for their own denominations would be damaged if members thought some of the money would wind up in the hands of Marxist guerrillas. Occasionally a sub-unit of a U.S. denomination might contribute $1000 or something to the special fund, or maybe people at a university chapel would devote a service to the topic of racism and decide to send the offering to the WCC for help with the grants. But such gifts were hardly basic to the budget.

There were indications that the special fund got much of its money from governments that found the program congruent with their policies on southern Africa. Anwar Barkat, who directed the program for a time, told me that Sweden and the Netherlands were particularly important funders. But I never learned how much the churches in those countries were involved. In 1993, I visited Uppsala, Sweden, and got a chance to ask the Swedish (Lutheran) Archbishop, Gunnar Weman, exactly which department of his country's government supplied the kroner for the WCC's special fund. But he said he did not know.

A 1997 book, *The ANC and the Liberation Struggle* by Dale T. McKinley (Pluto Press), said the African National Congress, Nelson Mandela's organization, set up its office in Tanzania with support from the Soviet Union and other Eastern European countries, but also got help from Scandinavia, "particularly Sweden." The author also said the organization's 1991 congress revealed that the Swedish International Development Agency contributed "a substantial percentage of the ANC's budget" (p. 119). So maybe it could have contributed to the WCC fund also.

While I was filling in as temporary editor of the WCC's news service, EPS, in 1993, I was able to get a little information about the contributions to the special fund, and write what possibly was the first EPS story on the subject in its history of more than two decades (September 30). The WCC said some donors wanted their gifts to remain confidential, so it did not release any names. But it did report the totals received in various currencies, and that gave some indication of where the contributors were geographically. In 1992, the largest amount came in Dutch guilders and German marks. After that came Swedish kroner, though in 1992 those were reported to have all started their journey in Norway and come through Sweden because the WCC had a convenient bank account there. The number of U.S. dollars and British pounds seemed hardly worth mentioning, though of course I did mention them anyway for whatever glory or shame the donor countries might deserve.

You might think the black denominations of the United States would rush to rank among the foremost supporters of this WCC program, that they would want to give and announce publicly that they were giving, even if they could offer only symbolic amounts, that they would look on helping finance such a program as a plus in raising money from their members. You would think wrong.

The black denominations may have only a single talent of financial resources to match against the five or ten of the major white denominations, but they do show an ability to raise some money for projects that arouse their interest. And the main black Baptist and Methodist denominations belong to the WCC and the NCC. But so far they have not chosen to put much money in the common pot, even when it is explicitly devoted to serving black interests.

When Philip R. Cousin, a bishop of the African Methodist Episcopal Church, became NCC president in 1983, he said the black denominations had not felt fully a part of NCC life because no one from those denominations had ever been named NCC president before, though blacks from the predominantly-white denominations had been. And Bishop Cousin predicted gifts from the black denominations would increase in consequence of his assumption of leadership. But they did not.

Then, there were other sidebars to the black movement. In 1970, as one of the offshoots of the ferment of the era, New York had riots among the largely black population in the city prisons, and thereafter efforts to improve prison conditions. Mayor Lindsay energized a dormant evaluating body, the Board of Correction, and one part of its effort was giving attention to prison chaplains. William J. vanden Heuvel, board chairman, decided that bringing in more clergy and other people from religious groups would get the broader community involved and concerned about the prisons and their inhabitants. A black pastor, M. L. Wilson of a Baptist church in Harlem, Convent Avenue Baptist, was a board member who chaired a Task Force on Prison Chaplaincy set up in 1972. It held what Mr. vanden Heuvel told me were probably the first hearings on prison chaplaincy of any governmental body in the United States.

My interview with Mr. vanden Heuvel was one of the first times the name of Louis Farrakhan impinged on my consciousness in any memorable way. He was one of those who spoke at the hearings, and the most impressive, Mr. vanden Heuvel said. "He gave a brilliant hour of testimony, describing the role of the Muslim faith in restoring a sense of dignity, self-respect and responsibility to men." And as a result "we are going to do everything possible to give the Muslims access to the prisons and encourage them to play a role" (RNS, April 26, 1972).

In 1981, I got a chance to talk with Desmond Mpila Tutu for an article in the United Methodist magazine, *New World Outlook* (May). I quickly decided he was seeking to follow the New Testament advice on operating as wisely as serpents though harmlessly (to his own cause) as doves (Matthew 10:16). Do you support the moves to get American business out of South Africa and put pressure on the government there? I asked. He responded by reminding me that advocating such a position would make him a violator of the "economic sabotage" act and subject to a sentence of at least five years. So he talked along and expressed hope that the blacks of South Africa had "intelligent friends who know what we are trying to say." He would also point out that he saw no evidence the existing relationship of business to South Africa was making things better. Opponents of change said any withdrawal of investment would hurt poor blacks. But this black priest, later to be bishop and archbishop, said blacks were then suffering without purpose, and would suffer more willingly if they could see a purpose and goal.

It was also from Archbishop Tutu that I got the African insight: "It's difficult to wake up someone who is pretending to be asleep."

When Archbishop Tutu talked to me, he was enhancing the international visibility that gave him a measure of protection. In 1980, he was told to turn in his passport–for criticizing Denmark's purchase of South African coal, he supposed. But he got the passport back the following year, and immediately began using it to visit the United States under sponsorship of the NCC. Despite Archbishop Tutu's calibrated circumlocutions on the trip to the United States, and to Europe at the same time, however, his passport was confiscated again by the government when he got home. Then later he got it back once more, and Americans saw Archbishop Tutu again and again. The South African struggle was waged to a large degree in the United States, and it sometimes seemed that the bishop, like Dom Helder, was spending as much time here cultivating support as he was among his own people.

When Frank Chikane, a black minister of a Pentecostal group established by U.S. missionaries, Apostolic Faith Mission, became general secretary of the South African Council of Churches, much of his work, too, was attending to international alliances. I interviewed him in Jacksonville, Florida, where he was attending a meeting of the NCC, and I wrote a report on the cooperation of the Catholic Church as an "observer member" of his council (NC, November 10, 1987). He had earlier headed an Institute of Contextual Theology that issued a widely-publicized Kairos Document, presenting a theological critique of the racial policy of South Africa's government. When I asked Mr. Chikane whether he was the drafter of this document, he replied, "I facilitated the process." And I wondered whether his lingo indicated he had been spending too much time around church bureaucrats in Europe and North America.

Now as for Jean-Bertrand Aristide, the Catholic priest who became president of Haiti for a time, my interview with him can only be called surreal (CNS, October 1, 1992). He had already been dismissed from his order, the Salesians, for continuing with his politics despite instructions to stay more priestly. And Pope John Paul II was known to oppose the idea of Catholic priests taking political office. How could Father Aristide as a Catholic priest act in such direct opposition to the wishes of the pope? "The pope is a chief of state; I am a chief of state," he explained to me with serene irrelevance.

Father Aristide was in New York to address the General Assembly of the United Nations, where he was still recognized as Haiti's president though the military had taken over the government and sent him into exile. He used the UN platform to attack the Vatican for appointing a nuncio to Haiti, an action he saw as recognition of the military government (CNS, September 30). The Vatican said it was only replacing a former nuncio who had been reassigned, and not making any political statement. But the priest-president-in-exile, addressing the diplomats in French with some use of Creole, charged that the Vatican was "the only state that has chosen to bless the crimes that it was obligated to condemn in the name of the God of justice and of peace."

He also played the race card in what I suppose many people would see as a personal insult to Pope John Paul II. Would the pope, he wondered aloud before the representatives of all the world, have taken the same attitude had the Haitians been white, or perhaps even Polish?

Like a few other politicians in various countries, Father Aristide had gained popularity among his impoverished supporters by leading them to expect more than he could have any hope of ever delivering. But I thought he would have to see that his position in relation to the Catholic Church was impossible.

222 ———————————————————— SIDEBARS

Eventually he did get the inevitable laicization, but at the time I talked with him in his suite at a New York hotel, he was serenely pretending to be asleep.

As a little sidebar, reports had come that he was talking with the Episcopal Bishop of Long Island, a black named Orris G. Walker, about becoming an Episcopal priest. In the Catholic Church, he remained a priest at that time, but was not authorized to function, because the Salesians had expelled him, and he had not affiliated with any other order or any diocese. There had been a good bit of trade in unhappy clergy between the Catholic and Episcopal churches, and for other Catholic priests at odds with their superiors such a move could have seemed almost normal. But I thought it unlikely Father Aristide could have maintained his political standing in Haiti if he renounced the Catholic Church altogether.

In my interview, speaking here in English, he confirmed that he had talked with Bishop Walker, and called him a friend and brother, but refused to say anything about what they had discussed. He did not rule out anything. "I am an ecumenical man; I am not the prisoner of any religious structure," he said serenely and surreally.

The attempt to unite leadership roles of church and state has also been conspicuous in Africa. For a little while in the 1970s, I was writing some articles for *Grit,* a weekly published in Williamsport, Pennsylvania, as a national paper for rural and small town America. One of the articles (June 25, 1978) dealt with United Methodist Bishop Abel Muzorewa, who had received international attention, and criticism from some other United Methodists, for entering into a compromise political alliance with the white leader, Ian Smith of Rhodesia, later to become Zimbabwe. But I could also point out that another black clergyman, Ndabaningi Sithole, in a church related to the U.S. United Church of Christ, also had a leadership role in Rhodesian politics. And looking elsewhere on the continent, I noted that the president of Liberia, William Tolbert, was a Baptist minister, and another United Methodist bishop, Bennie Warner, was Liberia's vice president. I did not try to answer the question of whether this tradition did more to politicize the church or sacralize the particular clergyman's style of politics. I do not favor an absolute separation of church and state, like some of the "wall" people in the United States. But the record suggests both church and state are better off when leaders recognize some demarcation of territory.

From blacks, let us now move to yet another group that has been part of my reporting activity, the Orthodox. I never had any chance to get acquainted with them before I came to New York, but I have had many good opportunities here. So I can now tell you something about Orthodox life.

ORTHODOX

CHAPTER SEVEN

"I was surprised," Theodosius told me. Metropolitan of the Orthodox Church in America (OCA), he should have been as clued in to the Orthodox world as anybody. But Bartholomew flabbergasted him as much as me.

As Ecumenical Patriarch in the city that the Orthodox still call Constantinople, although the Turks have long since changed the name to Istanbul, Bartholomew stood as first among equals in the Orthodox world. And, formally, he did not recognize the status claimed by the OCA and Metropolitan Theodosius. In 1970, the Moscow Patriarchate gave the OCA total independence, called autocephaly. But action in Moscow did not carry weight in Istanbul. Though autocephaly (self-heading) was a Greek word, it did not please the Greeks when applied to the OCA. The Ecumenical Patriarchate said autocephaly could occur only by the common consent of all, especially the consent of itself. And the OCA idea of providing a vehicle for the unity of all American Orthodox in an independent church, unhampered by directives from the mother churches abroad, did not strike Constantinople as a good idea at all. The Ecumenical Patriarchate had under its jurisdiction the Greek Archdiocese based in New York, the strongest Orthodox group in the United States, and felt no inclination to let it go. If there was to be unity among American Orthodox, the way was via connecting to the Greeks under the rule of Constantinople.

Despite all that, when Patriarch Bartholomew visited the United States in the fall of 1997, he accepted an invitation to speak at the OCA seminary, St. Vladimir's in Crestwood, a community in Westchester County. A gesture of significance. What might he say?

The patriarch was doing many things during his U.S. tour, and I was to send a story to ENI (October 28). Since not everything could be or needed to be included, I focused on the St. Vladimir's appearance as the event with broadest interest and most news potential. I was interested to find out what Patriarch Bartholomew, relatively new in his post, would have to tell us about his concept of Orthodox unity in America.

As it turned out, he had nothing to tell us. Absolutely nothing. He did speak at some length—about pollution in the Black Sea, which he seemed not to favor, about the need for careful translation of liturgical texts, about ways the Orthodox had suffered so many times in so many places. But regarding the question foremost in the minds of his audience, zilch. I noticed that even one of the prelates in his own entourage found it not of absorbing interest, and sat on the platform gazing distractedly about.

When the patriarch sat down, Metropolitan Theodosius had a few minutes at the microphone, and launched directly into the topic of the moment. He said that "in all candor" he wanted to let the Ecumenical Patriarch know that Orthodoxy was not meant to be a tribal religion confined to ethnic ghettos. And he requested that Patriarch Bartholomew notice on his American travels the spiritual hungers that might be met by the Orthodox faith, but not by a divided and competitive assortment of Orthodox clans.

When I talked with Metropolian Theodosius afterward, he pointed out that the visit to St. Vladimir's was the "ideal occasion" for addressing the unity issue that had been hanging over American Orthodoxy for decades. So we were all left to wonder yet again at the Orthodox world, which had earned and con-tinued to earn the descriptive term "byzantine," derived from Constantinople's older name, Byzantium. Why would Patriarch Bartholomew bother to put St. Vladimir's on his schedule if he was not willing to say anything pertinent, not even to say in some general manner that he hoped for unity in the sweet by and by? At ENI, the editors decided the gesture of the visit did not amount to much, and demoted it to second place, after some inconsequential material about Bartholomew expressing regrets and all regarding the failure of many Christians to behave well during the Holocaust.

The day before the visit to the seminary, Patriarch Bartholomew met with bishops of the various Orthodox jurisdictions at the Greek cathedral in New York. His printed schedule indicated he would hold a press conference after-ward, so of course I got myself over there to hear his assessment of matters. But we got no patriarch and no explanation. As a fallback, it was said a metropol-itan traveling with him would tell us whatever the patriarch wanted us to know. But then, no metropolitan either. We did finally get some American bish-ops, who discoursed of this and that, but no direct word from the Bosporus. And my request for an interview with Patriarch Bartholomew—promise you will not be shocked by this?—did not meet with approval.

Before Bartholomew was elected patriarch, he made a U.S. visit with his predecessor, Dimitrios. There was not much hope of getting news from Patriarch Dimitrios because he was old and frail, not many years from the time of his final departure, and did not speak English. I was told that Bartholomew, who did speak English well, was the one who could tell me something about the goals of the trip. But he declined that opportunity, too. So I have to conclude that communication is just not his thing.

During the 1997 visit as patriarch, Bartholomew also had on hand the prickly aftermath of his choice of Spyridon, the man he had recently chosen to replace Iakovos as archbishop of the Greek Archdiocese. Spyridon, a native of the United States but for most of his career located elsewhere, most recently in Venice, had shown the delicate footwork of the bull in the China shop, and broken quite a bit of the crockery. Not only were many of his own Greeks disgruntled, but he had measurably worsened relations with other Orthodox groups, creating a not-so-pleasant atmosphere for his patriarch to fly into.

Leonid Kishkovsky, ecumenical officer of the OCA, became upset enough to go public in an editorial in the OCA paper, *The Orthodox Church* (July-August). "Orthodoxy in America is confronted by a crisis," he said. The editors of ENI, who could be a little byzantine themselves, refused for unexplained reasons to carry my reports on that, giving me an impression they had some political motivation for protecting Bartholomew and the Greeks. But Father Kishkovsky's words carried weight enough that the archbishop, presumably at the direction of the patriarch, stepped back a little.

One dispute concerned the Standing Conference of Orthodox Bishops in the Americas (SCOBA), the primary vehicle for cooperative action. Archbishop Iakovos had chaired the group, and Archbishop Spyridon started out insisting he had to be considered chairman automatically, just because he was who he was, representative of the Ecumenical Patriarch. He did in fact appear to be the only candidate. None of the other bishops was campaigning for the job, but they said they had the right to elect. And Archbishop Spyridon eventually conceded, just in time to get this impediment to good Orthodox relations out of the way before his patriarch arrived.

Another complaint involved the Orthodox Christian Mission Center in St. Augustine, Florida. The director, Father Dimitrios (Couchell), was a Greek who was trying to make the center representative of all the Orthodox, until the new archbishop came in and declared that Greeks were carrying so much of the financial load they deserved to exercise full control. But with prospects for foul weather threatening to dampen enthusiasm for the impending patriarchal visit, he found ways to give a little on that point also.

Internally, the Greek Archdiocese got thrown into turmoil by Archbishop Spyridon's heavy-handed intervention into a disciplinary dispute at the archdiocesan seminary, Holy Cross in Brookline, Massachusetts. Just the very next year after his installation, I was reporting for ENI (August 7, 1997) that Archbishop Spyridon had removed the seminary president and three of the long-serving and widely-appreciated professors, to the consternation of Greeks far and wide. Since the four were all priests, the archbishop claimed that he was merely reassigning clergy, a normal activity of bishops. But I do not think many people bought his interpretation. More trouble came with other actions that seemed to arise from an assumption that an archbishop need not care what anybody else might think. So rebellion broke out openly in the ranks, sometimes rather high ranks.

Archbishop Spyridon confronted opposition not only from nationally-connected staff and former staff of the archdiocese, not only lay leaders who could talk about withholding or redirecting gifts of substantial size, but also some of his own bishops, who would join Father Kishkovsky in speaking about a crisis. So the storms continued, and in 1999 Nikki Stephanopoulos, press officer of the archdiocese and wife of the cathedral dean, Robert G. Stephanopoulos, put out a press release announcing cryptically that the authorities at the Istanbul Patriarchate had "transferred His Eminence Archbishop Spyridon of America to the Metropolis of Chaldea in Turkey, pending a new assignment." And Archbishop Demetrios, a 71-year-old native of Greece who had formerly taught at the Holy Cross seminary but had lately been researching something or other in Greece, would become the new Archbishop of America.

Through the years, I have done a number of stories on the Orthodox, and have from time to time been invited to enjoy their hospitality, which can be quite lavish. Somehow I happened to be around Archbishop Iakovos at the right moment and got invited to a lunch he gave for Cardinal Jan Willebrands at the headquarters of the Greek Archdiocese. I sat across from a Greek layman who I surmised took some responsibility for the archbishop's wine cellar. When a waiter came to pour the red for the meat course, starting with the cardinal, this layman gave a sharp look to the label, and did not see what he was looking for. He motioned the waiter over, confirmed his fears with a closer inspection, and sent the waiter immediately to grab the cardinal's glass before he had a chance to take a sip, and whisk it all back to the pantry. Then out with a clean glass and the bottle designated for the occasion.

Cardinal Willebrands himself seemed somewhat knowledgeable about alcoholic refreshments, and told stories about impressive wine cellars he had found among some European prelates. There was also a bit of humor about a

French bishop visiting Eastern Europe and evading any expression of agreement with the presumption that a local version of cognac could be considered cognac as the French understood the term. I do not remember, but the story possibly referred to Georgia. When the Orthodox Patriarch of Georgia, Ilia, came to New York in 1998, he gave me a bottle of Georgian brandy that seemed quite worthy of respect, whether you were French or otherwise.

But getting back to Metropolitan Theodosius, in January of 1978, shortly after the OCA chose him as its new primate, I submitted a request for an interview. Soon I had a letter from Father Kishkovsky, then an assistant to the chancellor, agreeing and saying I would be contacted about arrangements "when the metropolitan returns next week from a pastoral visit upstate." Then, I drummed my fingers a spell.

Finally, about a year later, on January 23, 1979, with not a word in the interval, Father Kishkovsky called and said, "Your appointment is at eleven o'clock in the morning." Fortunately, I had no prior engagements, and got on the train for Syosset, where the OCA operates out of a previously-private mansion, and wrote a story for NANA on the (formerly) new metropolitan (February 16). Time means something different in the Orthodox world.

The OCA had earlier been the Russian Orthodox Greek Catholic Metropolitanate of North America, commonly known as the Metropolia, officially under the Moscow Patriarchate. But in the circumstances of communist dominance over the Patriarchate, the Metropolia pretty much went its own way. As time passed, many of its members became impatient to establish an American Orthodox church that was totally independent and not even formally subject to commands and vetoes from the Old World. And those members pushed the idea of unity for all U.S. Orthodox.

Some observers would suspect the Constantinople/Istanbul Patriarchate insisted on keeping its American archdiocese captive for the financial and political support Americans could provide. "The Ecumenical Patriarchate is a racket," an exasperated John Meyendorff told me at the time it was condemning the OCA's claim to autocephaly. In later years, when he had become dean of St. Vladimir's, and no longer felt such an urgent need to defend what was long since a reality, he took a statesman's stance, and declined to repeat his earlier remarks, conceding only a small smile of remembrance.

Elsewhere in American Orthodoxy, too, the desire for unity was fermenting. But the Ecumenical Patriarchate continued to disapprove, and in 1994 it disapproved most mightily when bishops from all the Orthodox jurisdictions in the United States gathered for the first time at an Antiochian conference center in Ligonier, Pennsylvania, and announced an intention to move toward unity, and to hold an annual assembly (ENI, December 5). Reverberations were thunderous. Archbishop Iakovos had to hustle to pacify Patriarch Bartholomew, and give assurance the American sons and daughters had not the slightest wish to declare independence from their beloved mother.

The OCA has also had trouble on the Russian side. It understood that the two dozen or so parishes still under the Moscow patriarch would be gradually transferred until the OCA would have them all. But in the intervening years the OCA had found movement hardly perceptible.

When I went over to interview Klement, Moscow's bishop in America for a time, he told me that he did not want to approve transfers when they might precipitate a parish split (*One World,* July 1985). "I try to encourage a unanimous decision," he said. The likelihood of getting a unanimous decision from any congregation of any denomination is small. So the transfer expectation has not been fulfilled.

The OCA has been seeking to de-emphasize Russian ethnicity, and make itself indigenously American. Many of its members, including some bishops, came from Protestant backgrounds, and carry no Russian genetic material. But the Patriarchal Parishes play up the Russian connection. Bishop Klement said many members returned to Russia for the Feast of St. Sergius of Radonezh on July 18 at Zagorsk, and came away feeling they did not want to relinquish the spiritual tie with the church there.

In the Cold War climate that still existed, and in consideration of Bishop Klement's relative youth and inexperience in the United States, we can understand that he did not immediately warm to the idea of submitting to back and forth with an American who was planning to put it all in a magazine of international circulation. It took me about eighteen months to pull off the deal. The bishop required first that I submit questions in writing. Those he turned over to one of his priests, who was supposed to get material together for answers. But then the priest was needed in Scranton. And so on.

When the interview finally came, Bishop Klement asked to see a copy of my article before it was printed. In such cases where I am just beginning to establish rapport in situations necessarily difficult, and do not feel I can deliver a total negative, I have sometimes agreed to type up the notes I have taken, and submit them for review, without any indication of how material might be handled in the article subsequently. I did that for Bishop Klement, and the notes came back with only minor changes, and those perhaps not a correction of my note-taking but of himself, stating something in a more qualified way. As a generalization, I can report that most anyone who looks over notes from an interview will decide on reflection to make his statements blander, and diminish the vivacity of live encounter.

For any lacking acquaintance with the Orthodox world, I should explain that there are two families, commonly distinguished as Eastern Orthodox and Oriental Orthodox, though the distinction of terminology has no intrinsic logic because "oriental" means "eastern." This linguistic distinction without a difference provides us with a way of steering clear of the question of who is most truly orthodox, and of showing ecumenical respect for everybody's conception of himself. So we have come to speak of those in communion with the Ecumenical Patriarch, such as the Greeks and the Russians, the Romanians and the Bulgarians, the Serbs and some others, as Eastern Orthodox. And those who are not in communion with him—the Armenians, Copts, Ethiopians and some Syrians and Christians of this Syrian background in India—are grouped as Oriental Orthodox. These Oriental communities were the ones that were not represented at the Council of Chalcedon in 451, and did not ratify its decisions, and so were not recognized as orthodox by the others. Today, people from both families tend to say they really do not have any basic differences on theology, and the separation might be overcome before too long.

I have had one interview with a pope, and that was in the Oriental Orthodox family—Pope Shenouda III of the Coptic Church (*Christian Science Monitor*, May 2, 1977). On a visit to New York, said to be the first of any Coptic pope to North America, he occupied a suite at the Waldorf-Astoria Hotel, and I was allowed a half hour to talk with him there. I found him quite ready to reveal information on how many people were members of his church, in and outside Egypt, and how many parishes and schools it operated. When I asked him to point the path to peace in the Middle East, however, he insisted on leaving that task to political leaders. His title might be august, but he lived in such a tenuous environment he could not feel free even to offer the usual generalities about steps toward overcoming the Arab-Israeli tensions. And even his circumspection did not preserve his freedom. The president of Egypt, Anwar al-Sadat, later exiled him to a desert monastery, perhaps as part of the politics of managing the Muslim fundamentalists.

In an arrangement somewhat unusual, Pope Shenouda had all his delegation of a half dozen or so sit with him for the interview. I dislike having other people sit with the principal, because they can rarely refrain from throwing in their two cents worth, or what in my estimation is often worth less. (Joseph Zwilling, communications chief for Cardinal O'Connor, and now for Cardinal Edward M. Egan, is a sterling exception, always attentive but never interjecting an unsolicited word.) The in-sitting occurs because top officials often like to have an underling or two present so they can corroborate if the principal wants to protest misquotation. Or sometimes the principal may foresee a need to call on an aide for details, or maybe just wants the aide to become better informed through hearing the interview. But a half dozen? The Copts all turned out to be genial guys, however, and we got along well enough. At one stage, one of them let his curiosity rise to the top, and asked if he could reverse the interview and get me to answer a question. I said, "Okay, but it doesn't come out of my time."

Some of the Ethiopian Orthodox I found up in a decrepit part of the Bronx. Their building was the only thing they could immediately afford, but they did not seem to think decrepit suited people of their heritage, and I was told they were looking for something better. The communist takeover of Ethiopia from Emperor Haile Selassie in 1974, combined with drought conditions, especially severe in the next decade, sent a good many Ethiopians to the United States. Abba Haddis, a priest I talked with at the Bronx church, Holy Trinity, told me, however, that this congregation began with blacks who were not Ethiopian Orthodox but wanted a connection with an ancient African church. Abyssinia was a former name for Ethiopia, and some other blacks had shown the same desire for a connection by naming an important New York congregation the Abyssinian Baptist Church.

The communist government of Ethiopia had complicated the church situation. Theophilos, the patriarch in Addis Ababa, was deposed and presumably murdered. No one had any idea where he was. Tekle Haimanot was put in his place, and the new patriarch consecrated some new bishops, including Archbishop Yesehaq, who was sent to look after churches in the Western hemisphere. But Bishop Paulos, who had served under the previous patriarch and then spent several years in prison under the communists, also came to the United States. He operated independently and conducted services, using the ancient Ge'ez liturgy and delivering sermons in contemporary Amharic, for a congregation that met in a chapel at Riverside Church.

In 1992, after the communist government departed, the wheel turned again and Paulos went home to become patriarch. He had at least two specific qualifications. For a church with a clergy mostly suffering from poor education, he stood out for his background of graduate study at Princeton. The other was his origin in the province of Tigre, which might help him get along with the new rulers, who happened to be from Tigre. During the time Bishop Paulos led the New York congregation, the structure of Ethiopian church authority rested in a state of ambiguity. But the Orthodox seem to have a capacity for tolerating ambiguity. So Bishop Paulos did his own thing, but told me that he was not planning to create a schism. His congregation was called the Ethiopian Orthodox Towahedo (Unity) Church of the Savior.

SIDEBARS

The Russians and Ethiopians were not the only ones that had their internal life disturbed by the communists. For most all the Orthodox in areas under Soviet domination, the question of how church members outside should relate aroused conflicting thoughts. Some members in the United States would say that any church leaders in the old country who accepted communist control had betrayed the faith, and deserved no loyalty. Others wanted to remain connected, and argued that the mother churches were justified in accepting external restrictions if they could maintain their internal life and continue to meet the religious needs of their members. So we wound up with two Armenian groups in the United States, one loyal to the chief, called catholicos, in Etchmiadzin, the capital of Soviet Armenia, and the other to the catholicos of Cilicia, based in Antelias, near Beirut, Lebanon.

We also wound up with two groups of Romanian Orthodox. As bishop of the one more obstreperously anti-communist, we got the much-publicized Valerian D. Trifa, who was accused of taking an energetic role in a fascist organization, the Iron Guard, in his native Romania during the Second World War. I did a NANA story about him (July 23, 1974), and found my chief source of information in a Jewish dentist in New York, Charles Kremer. The dentist, a native of Romania, had come to the United States long before the war, but he took up the Trifa case as his own personal cause and pursued it doggedly.

As head of a church body that belonged to the National Council of Churches (NCC), Bishop Trifa held membership on its governing board, though people did not remember him showing up much. Dr. Kremer had taken his case to NCC leaders some years before I talked with him, but they apparently just put it aside without any action at that point. The same basic charges had also been published in 1960 by Ralph Lord Roy in his *Communism and the Churches* (Harcourt Brace, pp. 400-01). But I can imagine NCC leaders felt that trying to sort out issues of decades before, in a distant country that none of them knew much about, lay beyond their capacities and current duties. Quite the contrary, thought Dr. Kremer. He considered it outrageous that such a man as Bishop Trifa could still be regarded with respect in an organization like the NCC, so he kept on and eventually got other Jews to take up the case, and pushed it to the point that the NCC finally did ask the bishop to step aside while investigations went on. The Trifa case was also pursued with authorities of the U.S. government, and he was eventually deported, and went to die in Spain.

Among my reflections was how formidable an opponent Bishop Trifa had in a New York dentist. Maybe in the larger picture of international powers a dentist will not ordinarily stand at the top. But Dr. Kremer was a man of determination, willing to stay with the case year in and year out for as long as it took. Located in Manhattan, he could easily present his material to reporters like me, to members of the Jewish community and to anyone else who might show interest. As a native of Romania, he knew the country and the language, and he had made trips to gather information. He showed me a filing case with drawers full of documentation. And whenever Bishop Trifa got any recognition from anybody, Dr. Kremer was quick to write a letter of protest. With a man like that at work, the pot will always boil.

I had visited St. Vladimir's Seminary a few times before the day I went to cover the patriarchal astonishment. One of the first times was to get some insight into the thinking of Orthodox women. I had often heard or read discussions about Orthodox women, and their situation in churches that were not moving along on gender issues in the manner of liberal Protestants. Since so much was being said about these women, it somehow occurred to me that it might be worthwhile to see if they would like to speak for themselves. When I inquired about individual women to interview, the consensus seemed to light upon Constance Tarasar. She was based at St. Vladimir's, doing some teaching and editorial work, so I took the train up, and used her thoughts as the basis for a report to EPS (March 17, 1984).

Striding across the campus in her slacks, she did not look to me like she was much beaten down by "patriarchy" or oppressions of the tradition. A third-generation American from Minneapolis, she was somewhat removed from the immigrant culture of many U.S. Orthodox. And she had become acquainted with the broader Christian world through ecumenical assignments such as representing her church at assemblies of the World Council of Churches. But she told me that as an Orthodox Christian interacting with people of other churches "you gradually realize you do think differently." Back in 1965, she had become the first woman to get a theological degree from St. Vladimir's, and her example had been followed by thirty or more others at the time I talked with her. For this contingent overall, she could report that they naturally favored equal pay for equal work and a few other such goals of the feminist agenda. But on abortion, she said, they "tend to be on the side of life." And they opposed elimination of the trinitarian terms of Father, Son and Holy Spirit.

"Most if not all Orthodox women agree that ordination to the priesthood is not an option," she said. "The reasons haven't yet been formulated in dogma, but it is based on a theological intuition. I don't think it's just a matter of a time lag by immigrant communities. Younger Orthodox women see things the same way."

But with this outlook, she found work in the ecumenical world sometimes a strain. "You don't want to be the person who's always disagreeing, but the way issues often are framed you have no choice." At the previous year's WCC assembly in Vancouver, she had triumphed to the modest extent of getting into a document an acknowledgment that Orthodox women did have an alternative view. "One small step for Orthodox womankind," she remarked.

To outsiders, the Orthodox seem disposed to bow and scrape before the hierarchy more than many others would consider fitting. But I am not sure they always remain as submissive as we onlookers might imagine. I was at the headquarters of the Antiochian Orthodox Archdiocese in Englewood, New Jersey, one day, sitting in the reception area while I waited for an appointment. There, I had to overhear one side of a conversation between the receptionist and a priest who apparently was ready to tell the hierarchs to shove it. I could not hear what he was saying, and saying, and saying, but the long-listening receptionist finally felt compelled to tell him, "Father, I can't pass along messages like that."

I was myself another troublesome fellow the same receptionist put off for a while. Calling to ask about an interview with the Antiochian Metropolitan, Philip Saliba, I would get her explanation that he was especially busy at this time of year, and she would have to hold my request until a more convenient season. And this evasion I got a number of times. When I eventually realized I was moving into the second or third year of this, and any time in the year I called was described as an especially busy time for the metropolitan, it became pretty evident I was treading a path of futility. But later, I came into contact with a priest of the church who was interested in getting it some public notice, and so was able to arrange an interview for me, and with it a very nice lunch, with Middle East touches.

At the time, I was writing an article for the World Council of Churches magazine, *One World* (October 1990), keyed to the visit of Ecumenical Patriarch Dimitrios to the United States, the first visit of any Ecumenical Patriarch while in office. With a goal of explaining something of the Orthodox situation overall, not that anybody could explain it but doing my little bit, I asked Metropolitan Philip for his assessment. It was not upbeat. He had observed that the Greek publicity always emphasized the role of the Ecumenical Patriarch as spiritual leader of all the world's Orthodox. But somehow the non-Greeks never got consulted on arrangements for the visit. Metropolitan Philip was vice chairman of SCOBA, and wanted to host a gathering where all the Orthodox bishops could talk with Patriarch Dimitrios about Orthodoxy in America. But he was not allowed, though many other events of lesser importance, in his estimation, were loaded onto the schedule. "The most needful thing was not done," the metropolitan told me.

Another of the bemusements from Orthodoxy came when arrangements were made for Cardinal O'Connor to host a lunch for Patriarch Dimitrios, and close to the time was told he could not. The patriarch, it was said, could not accept hospitality from anyone until the prospective host had first been hosted by the patriarch. Perhaps he would be thought to be putting himself under obligation.

A challenge to any stereotypes of Orthodoxy all this might have been planting in my mind came in 1984, when I found some conservative evangelicals at a Greek Orthodox meeting. That is not the kind of place conservative evangelicals normally hang out. But a group of men who had worked for Campus Crusade for Christ, a movement founded and led by Bill Bright, came to feel they had a deficiency in their religion diet. I would guess they were missing the sense of structured community that would position them more securely in the Christian tradition. Conservative evangelicalism has zeal, but its connections across the broader reaches of time and space seem thin. So these former Crusaders looked to the early centuries of Christianity, and decided something like Orthodoxy was the thing. They were influenced partly by OCA Bishop Dmitri of Dallas, himself out of a Southern Baptist background, and explored the possibility of affiliating with the OCA. Then they looked at the Greeks a while before eventually finding a home with the Antiochian Archdiocese and Metropolitan Philip. They wanted to stay together and maintain their group identity within whatever church they joined, so working out a way to handle that presented some impediments elsewhere.

Although the representatives of this group that I met professed to be now fully Orthodox in mind and heart, they still carried a manner that clearly set them apart. Looking at one of them, I had to reflect that he did not look like an Orthodox duck. And when we talked, he did not quack like an Orthodox duck. And when he then went to the other side of the room, he for sure did not walk like an Orthodox duck. These men had quite different social origins and a different cultural formation, and such peripherals have often turned out to be as important as doctrine and hierarchy in dividing the Christian community.

Maybe these formerly Crusader Orthodox have by now changed. I was once told that some Americans converting to Orthodoxy tend to overstress absorption of the secondary characteristics of immigrant culture. "He has been Orthodox for only a year, and already he is speaking broken English."

Lacking a suitable travel budget, I have not often journeyed far from New

York in my reporting. But when Juvenaly, Russian Orthodox Metropolitan of Krutitsy and Kolomna, and an influential figure in the Moscow Patriarchate, came to the United States in 1987, I found it worthwhile to beg a ride from a couple of Orthodox friends and ride out to South Canaan, Pennsylvania, to ask him what was going on in the Soviet Union. What was going on in South Canaan was an annual Memorial Day observance at a monastery, which had graves of many prominent clergy as well as other Orthodox in its cemetery.

So what about this talk of glasnost we hear, Metropolitan Juvenaly? "The spirit of relations between church and state is warmer," he said, speaking through an interpreter. "Of course, it will be very hard to believe that because glasnost has been introduced in our society, all things will change as if by a miracle. But it is a positive thing, and we welcome this sign." One concrete bit of evidence, he said, was a new willingness of newspapers to print stories about local officials who violated the legal rights of the church. "The articles are very important as a warning against the same thing elsewhere," he said. And church officials were allowed to talk publicly about subjects other than peace. "Now we step up onto a new stage" (EPS, June 16).

Now, perhaps we have come far enough I should show that not every single one of my articles has focused directly on religion.

SIDEBARS

OUTSIDE THE RELIGIOUS WORLD

CHAPTER EIGHT

I saw a little item in *The New York Times* one day about one Jack D. Belsky, who had been dismissed from his job as a high paid executive in charge of New York's bus service (February 7, 1976). The Transit Authority also stripped him of his pension rights because, it said, he had used agency personnel to build cabinets and furniture for his Florida home, and had falsified expense records.

The name connected. In 1973, the North American Newspaper Alliance (NANA) had asked me to do a series, one of those they called *Spotlite* on developments in mass transportation (issued November 10). By some happenstance, the city press office I asked for help arranged for me to interview Mr. Belsky, who seemed like a good choice because he was just back from a national meeting of people in mass transportation, but turned out to be not such a good choice because he did not seem to have picked up any ideas at the meeting. One might guess, in fact I did guess, that he spent his time there in the bars with his cronies, but I was not able to establish that as fact. What I did establish was that he operated some place other than on top of his brief.

Preparing for the interview, I had read a few articles and collected some clippings to serve as conversation starters. Alas, they served more as conversation stoppers. Whichever item I asked about, Mr. Belsky seemed not to have heard about it. Several times he jumped up from the table and went over to look through a stuffed briefcase and stack of papers he brought back from his meeting. But locating whatever he might have had in mind seemed beyond him. I was able to report his judgment that battery-operated buses were not yet feasible, and his misinformation that New York would probably soon begin using the double deckers seen in London. These years later, you do see a double decker now and then used for tourist sightseeing on New York avenues, but not for transporting the general public.

Fortunately, the Belsky experience has been rare in my interviewing. But it does give you a sinking feeling when you do your proper preparation to conduct a proper interview, and then realize along the way that the man you are depending on for authoritative information may not grasp the subject as well as you do.

Writing for NANA, a syndicate that had seen its better days but still reached a number of outlets, enabled me to range every now and then into interesting areas beyond my normal religion beat. I could occasionally get a little into New York City politics, and in the three-part *Spotlite* mode investigate broader themes.

In 1978, when U.S. officials were negotiating treaties to turn over the Panama Canal to Panama at the end of the century, I wrote a NANA story (April 12) to point out that the proposed turnover was not an act of sentimental do-goodism, but the judgment of some quite conservative people that this move would best serve the interests of the United States. Ronald Reagan, then courting the conservatives for his upcoming presidential campaign, took the stance of historical romanticism, and called for hugging the canal to the U.S. bosom forever. But William F. Buckley Jr., among the foremost of conservatives, saw that the U.S. position in Panama could be maintained only by brute force, and that holding on in such fashion would damage U.S. relations throughout Latin America. Since the United States gained plenty of pesos from business dealings with Latin America, and Panama helped certain business interests by such measures as providing an economical place to register ships, some settlement seemed advisable. And when I heard the U.S. negotiator, Ellsworth Bunker, explain one day what he was doing, I realized he was in person a very conservative gentleman, looking out for the long range welfare of his country, and not someone disposed to give away the store.

Assignments for church agencies could likewise take me at times out of the church orbit into topics of general interest. In 1981, I covered the annual meeting of the Lutheran Education Conference of North America, a gathering of presidents of Lutheran colleges, when it met in New York, and I wrote a couple of articles for the news service of the Lutheran Council in the USA (February 9).

One of the more interesting speakers was Alexander Austin of the University of California in Los Angeles, who was president of the Higher Education Research Institute. From him, we got a glimpse of where academic standards were heading. Reporting on surveys at 550 colleges across the country over the preceding 15 years, he said entering freshmen came from high school with better grade averages each year, but each year showed by test scores that they had worse academic preparation. We could suppose the former came from a desire of teachers to ingratiate themselves with students and parents, and the latter partly from devoting too many hours to junk and sleaze on the tv.

During this period, seminaries were also trying to attract students by making things easier. In degrees, there was an inflation of nomenclature to cater to student vanity. Previously, students had received a Bachelor of Divinity, or B.D., degree after three years of study. Since they already had bachelor's degrees in arts and sciences from college, they did not derive much ego gratification from another bachelor's. If you assume any degree is worth only whatever you learn, nomenclature does not worry you so much. But seminaries were scrambling for customers who brought other assumptions, so the basic degree was upscaled nomenclature-wise to Master of Divinity, or M.Div. Some of the seminaries–thankfully not my alma mater, Union Seminary–also started offering a class B doctorate, called Doctor of Ministry, or D.Min., for people who were not academically inclined but relished the thought of hearing themselves called doctor. Many seminaries set up these programs to accommodate the full-time pastor or agency executive, who could take a few night courses, do a little research in the breaks between appointments and soon call to instruct his secretary that the telephone should now be answered: "Doctor" Smith's office!

Religious News Service (RNS) also sent me outside the religious world on occasion, one day down to the Lower East Side to interview an Indian woman who had come from the Northwest in hopes of getting public backing for one of the fishing struggles that constantly absorbed Indians in that and some other parts of the country. Treaties commonly let Indians retain the right to hunt and fish in their accustomed manner, and the application of those provisions in modern times became the subject of unending litigation. When state governments passed conservation measures to control hunting and fishing, Indians would often say they did not have to comply because they had their treaty rights from the federal government. Anyway, no conservation measures would be needed if all the white people would go back where they came from.

What struck me about the woman I went to interview was the way she put her cause in personal terms. She had a little boy a year or two old with her, and she told me her hope for his future was that he would be able to fish in the same river in the same manner as his father and grandfathers and earlier ancestors had done for all the centuries past. I had been used to hearing more of parents who wanted their children to go beyond the level they had achieved, and do more and better. No such ambition here.

Many Indians of course follow the more usual pattern of looking for upward mobility in American society. In 1971, I wrote a feature for NANA (May 1) on the American Indian Community House, a program to bring together New York Indians from all tribal backgrounds, and found about 30 tribes represented among the members who had come from elsewhere to get into the New York job market. None claimed a continuous history of tribal life in the area.

The leaders were people such as Mifaunwy Shunatona, who had represented Oklahoma in a Miss America contest and then come to New York to do professional singing and dancing; Louis Mofsie, an art teacher at an elementary school, and Louis D. Bayhylle, a personnel officer for a hospital of the Veterans Administration. Other Indians of the New York area included the Caughnawaga Mohawks, who had a stability that enabled them to work on heights, and who helped build the bridge named for Giovanni da Verrazano, perhaps the first white man to enter New York Bay. They also helped build the World Trade Center, which aptly connected them to the globalizing of economic life that had brought them their white problem to begin with.

Indians and others no doubt have a right to try to maintain their traditional ways, as we all do, but the world turns as bridges and skyscrapers reshape its movements, and the possibilities for any of us living the lives of our ancestors are always receding. The question for friends of the Indians is whether we are doing them a favor when we encourage them to entertain unrealistic hopes.

Later, I was able to look into the Indian treaties a little more in doing a series for NANA (*Spotlite,* October 5, 1975). From this research, I concluded that when critics of American policy regarding Indians complained of broken treaties, the answer was that the allegations were unfortunately untrue.

All Indians are today considered full citizens of the United States, with the same rights and entitlements as other citizens, plus all the services provided by the Bureau of Indian Affairs and Indian programs of other agencies. For the federal government to deal with some of its citizens on a treaty basis, as though they were foreign nations, as independent of the U.S. government as Canada or Mexico, seemed to me a curious anomaly and anachronism, but one I gather many Indians seek to reinforce. For Indians themselves, the anomaly carries the disadvantage of keeping their minds unduly focused on the past, when they need to look ahead and recognize that any worthwhile future will have to be worked out through interaction with the American society that is and is coming to be.

The "Trail of Broken Treaties" routine, sad to say, keeps Indian energies absorbed in fighting over grievances. Doing research for the *Spotlite* series, I read that Indian law had become a specialty, and lawyers could make a lifetime career of it because treaty disputes would forever bring them new business.

This history began with a treaty enacted by the Continental Congress in 1778, and a total of some 370 more were made with Indian tribes before Congress decided in 1871 that it would stop approving them. But those already in force were not annulled, regrettably, and federal courts have continued to recognize them. The problem in particular disputes is that the treaties are, of course, not the only documents with legal authority. The federal constitution, laws and judicial traditions have to be considered, and state laws given whatever weight they merit. Then treaty provisions devised for conditions more than a century ago have to be applied in the quite different circumstances of today. Cause for much head scratching among the judges and much lucrative litigating among the lawyers.

More recently, many tribes have been persuaded to let gamblers operate on their lands, where they are exempt from state controls. If Americans generally come to regard the gambling industry as acceptable, presumably state restrictions will be eased, and the Indian advantage erased. But in any case, living off gambling income does not help Indians build a future in which they will be productive contributors. That, I would suppose, must be the goal of any outsider who really wants to be a friend of the Indians and not merely a historical romantic.

Although it is conventional to say whites stole the land of the Indians, Felix Cohen, a specialist in Indian law, noted even back in 1947 that most of the land in the United States had in fact been purchased. Doubtless the government dominated the negotiating process, and the purchase price may have been low, but purchase in some manner was the old fashioned way, as with the tradition about the Dutch and Manhattan. And since 1947, many additional payments have been made to settle with various tribes claiming they deserved compensation for land they formerly held, or roamed across.

In 1971, Ramsey Clark, who had been U.S. attorney general under President Lyndon B. Johnson, got Alaska natives a cool billion dollars for land there. Which back then still meant serious money, and which if prudently invested in the white man's stock market would have left them today pretty close to sitting on top of the world. When I was doing the *Spotlite* series on Indian treaties, I went down to interview Mr. Clark in his Greenwich Village apartment, where I felt honored to have the former attorney general of the United States hand-grinding the beans for our coffee. He called the proposal of Vine Deloria Jr. to make the United States return to dealing with Indians on the treaty basis that prevailed before 1871 a backward step, which he said would create something like the bantustans of South Africa. "For good or ill, we are now tied up together," he said.

I had been down to interview Mr. Clark once before, when he was (unsuccessfully) seeking the 1974 Democratic nomination for U.S. senator from New York, and expressing a typical politician's blithe certainty he could defeat the Republican incumbent, Jacob Javits (*Monitor,* March 27). But also of interest at that time, his successor as attorney general, John N. Mitchell, was undergoing the legal action that led to his conviction on felony charges. During the presidential campaign of 1968, Mr. Clark came under attack from Richard M. Nixon, who charged that he was soft on crime or something like that. Mr. Nixon promised to appoint a different kind of attorney general.

"That's the one campaign promise he really kept," Mr. Clark told me in one of the comments the editors decided were too pointed to print. "It's not really irony. It is exactly what you would expect. They politicized the Department of Justice, and that is terribly dangerous."

However, Mr. Clark always remained so conscious of failings in American life, and so unable to see virtues or strike a balance, he eventually marginalized himself. "I have some very strong feelings about the failure of democratic institutions," he told me. And he did not seem to feel their strength and resilience, or the relative health of American institutions compared with those of some other countries.

Mr. Cohen wrote, "The purchase of more than two million square miles of land from the Indian tribes represents what is probably the largest real estate transaction in the history of the world . . . . We have driven hard Yankee bargains when we could . . . . But when Congress has been fairly apprised of any deviation from the plighted word of the United States, it has generally been willing to submit to court decision the claim of any injured Indian tribes . . . . There is no nation on the face of the earth which has set for itself so high a standard of dealing with a native aboriginal people as the United States, and no nation on earth that has been more self-critical in seeking to rectify its deviations from those high standards" (Lucy Kramer Cohen, ed., *The Legal Conscience: Selected Papers of Felix S. Cohen,* 1960; pp. 287-88).

Since he wrote, the United States Court of Claims has taken many more actions to rectify past injustices. Other countries–New Zealand offers a notable example–have also taken new action on behalf of aborigines, so the national comparison may need revision. But the more important issue remains what aboriginal people will do themselves to build their future.

One complication in the way of correcting past injustices in the United States arises in considering the considerable amount of ethnic mixing that has occurred. If one of your parents is descended from a group identified as the oppressed, and the other parent from the group called the oppressor, should you be receiving reparations or paying them?

Asked to do an article for *Response* magazine about the Indian Law Resource Center (March 1989), I took Amtrak down to Washington one day, and talked with the director, Richard Timothy Coulter. He was operating as an Indian as he tried to get sovereignty for Indian tribes. But it turned out he was only maybe one-eighth Indian (Potawatomi) himself. If you are by ethnic background one-eighth victim and seven-eighths persecutor, how much standing do you have to demand that the United States government take special action in your favor? Does your one-eighth deserve sovereignty and exemption from U.S. law, and your seven-eighths owe a loyalty to the U.S. Constitution?

Writing for NANA also gave me a chance to interview Howard Fast, and write a news story (October 20, 1972) on his novel, *The Hessian* (Morrow, 1972). It became a news story not only because of the fame of the author but also because it had a newsy theme of implied opposition to the Vietnam War. The actual story concerned a young German mercenary who served with the British trying to put down the American Revolution. But Mr. Fast used it to provide himself with opportunities for writing lines of direct relevance to the current anti-war movement in the United States—the moral dilemma of a soldier trained to follow orders blindly, the weary character who says the war "should be done with and drags on and on and on" (p. 19).

I was also interested in talking about Mr. Fast's political history, but he was not. In 1943, he risked the popularity he had gained with novels such as *Citizen Tom Paine* and *Freedom Road* by joining the Communist Party, an action that he explained as a reaction to Adolph Hitler. But he was one of those who left after Nikita Khruschev's 1956 speech denouncing the crimes of Joseph Stalin. Why it was more acceptable to support communism while Stalin was committing his crimes than after the party leadership had denounced them, I could not see. Could it possibly be that people of Mr. Fast's ilk, of whom there were a good number, at some perhaps subconscious place in their psyche actually liked communism better in its ironfisted Stalinist form than in the more ambiguous defrosting period afterward? But in a 1957 book, *The Naked God,* Mr. Fast gave additional explanations. He was disturbed to find the party accusing him of "bourgeois Jewish nationalism" when he wrote about Jews of the Maccabean period in *My Glorious Brothers,* published the year, 1948, of the establishment of the State of Israel. But he had not turned to the right as ex-communists such as Whittaker Chambers had done. "I'm still at the place where I've always been," he told me. "It was other things that changed." Then he developed a headache, and our interview was cut short.

Later, in 1990, I saw in *The New York Times* book review section (November 4) that Mr. Fast had published another memoir, *Being Red* (Houghton Mifflin), that seemed partly an attempt to justify his time in the American Communist Party. The reviewer, Maurice Isserman of Hamilton College, wrote that Mr. Fast gave "evidence of extreme naivete or crude apologetics," and commented, "Mr. Fast does not seem that naïve." On the basis of my one short interview, I was more inclined to think he fell in that company of men who can contemplate only one idea at a time, and fail to balance it with others to get a comprehensive view.

When Jimmy Carter came into office talking about support for human rights, I developed suspicions that this theme might be largely a feel good therapy for Americans. As he began campaigning, some Americans were not feeling so good about their country and themselves. The disasters of Vietnam and the constant bombardment of depressing news from the Nixon-Agnew administration had been downers. But under a new president, we might hope, the human rights talk could serve as a way of putting all that out of our minds, saying none of it represented the kind of people we were, but that we were still and all actually the good people of the world, the people for human rights, and we were the ones God had commissioned to tell other people how they had to behave in order to be considered good like us.

However about that, in the mood of the Carter era, forming a non-governmental coalition to campaign for human rights seemed to some people like a good idea. So in the fall after his 1977 inauguration, I was covering a National Conference on Human Rights that had been convened in New York with the idea of uniting all the human rights forces of the United States, somewhat as many civil rights organizations had coalesced for a combined effort in earlier years (NC, October 10). Bayard Rustin, a veteran labor and civil rights leader who was then president of the A. Philip Randolph Institute, chaired the meeting. He tried to bridge the divisions, but at the end of the day failed to find enough unity for a continuing coalition.

You might think everybody in the United States automatically supported human rights. Maybe so, but not everybody for sure had the same understanding of what that meant for strategy. Participants in the conference broke down broadly into two main groups. One saw the human rights problem primarily in the Soviet Union and its allies, and wanted campaigns focusing there. The other group said that whatever the Soviet problem, they wanted the coalition to concentrate on human rights abuses more immediately at hand, those in the United States, and then on violators among U.S. allies, such as South Korea.

"If this coalition is to be successful, the Cold War overtones must be diminished," said the representative of the U.S. Catholic Conference, Patricia Rengel. Similar comments came from the National Council of Churches, American Friends Service Committee and others. In the camp for a Soviet focus stood people such as Rita Hauser, who had been U.S. representative to the UN Human Rights Commission, Leo Cherne of the Jewish agency, International Rescue Committee, and Tom Kahn of the AFL-CIO.

George G. Higgins, a Catholic priest who specialized in trying to keep the church connected to the labor movement, stood up to say he had never been to a coalition-forming conference where he heard so much applause. Usually, when people met to form a coalition, they concentrated on technical questions about how they would operate, he said. But applause for speakers of diverse viewpoints, coming from their respective camps, gave him the feeling of attending a rally. "I think there will be a coalition," Msgr. Higgins told me afterward. "But they will have to broaden the group." It turned out that he was overly optimistic, however.

For me, the meeting had one personal aspect that made it memorable. Theodore Jacqueney, managing it as executive secretary, told me someone had come before I arrived and tried to get press credentials under my name. I cannot remember ever hearing of anybody else, before or since, who imagined there was advantage to be gained in pretending to be me.

Floundering about as I began trying to make my way as a freelance journalist, I tried submitting a few unsolicited features from New York to daily newspapers around over the country, and in these I sometimes departed from the religious field. On rare occasions, they did sell, and at that point any sale was encouraging. But the good news was at the same time really something like excitement over fool's gold because it kept me engaged too long in what was professionally a hopeless effort. Daily papers get so much material from the Associated Press and other syndicates that unsolicited submissions from an unknown freelancer stand little chance.

One feature that enjoyed a limited success was a sort of humor piece on put-downs used by the drama critic, Clive Barnes, who was then writing for *The New York Times* and later moved to the *New York Post*. After seeing a musical, *Ari,* based on the book, *Exodus,* by Leon Uris, Mr. Barnes wrote, "There are no genuine show-stoppers to the musical, which is probably just as well for it does seem the kind of show that once stopped would have difficulty in getting started again." Reviewing a production of the Sophocles classic, *Antigone,* he started by damning with faint praise: "The scenery was splendid." But he immediately added: "The production's basic and irremediable fault came when they brought on the actors." Regarding a musical titled *Merriwell,* he commented, "This is the kind of music that if you came out of the theater humming it, you would never notice."

Presumably the humor attracted some interest, and the article was bought not only by the Richmond (Virginia) *Times-Dispatch* (July 18, 1971), which had an editor who knew me, but more encouragingly by the *Portland Oregonian* (July 3), which had nobody who had ever heard my name so far as I knew.

The hopelessness of my efforts became apparent, however, when I tried an article on a rare but serious disease called dysautonomia, which was genetic and seemed to be found only among a specific segment of the Jewish population. I quoted a geneticist at Johns Hopkins University, Victor McKusick, who said the ancestry of all known victims could be traced to the medieval German Rhineland, from which Jews had migrated to Eastern Europe and subsequently to the United States, Israel and elsewhere. He suggested that a mutation occurred about 1000 A.D. in the genes of some Rhineland Jew, who passed it to later generations.

I sent the article out on speculation to a number of papers, including the *Miami Herald*, the latter on the supposition that Miami editors would consider it of interest and importance to the considerable Jewish community there. When the article found no buyer in Miami or elsewhere, I sold it the next year to the North American Newspaper Alliance (NANA). And then the *Miami Herald*, a NANA client, used it (August 17, 1972)–the editors presumably deciding, as I had guessed originally, that it was of interest and importance to the considerable Jewish community there. This experience showed me that even if the writing was up to standard and the subject pertinent, an article still might not sell.

Another topic that brought me a thimbleful of success was an effort led by some people in New York to buy an apartment in Florence where Robert and Elizabeth Barrett Browning had lived, and to preserve it for the visits and use of Browning admirers. I had become acquainted with Philip Kelley, president of the New York Browning Society and executive secretary of a Browning Institute that bought the apartment, and we enjoyed some camaraderie because we were fellow alumni. Our alma mater, Baylor University in Waco, Texas, had become a Browning center of sorts, because an eccentric chairman of the English department, A. J. Armstrong, developed a crush on Robert Browning. He appealed to moneyed Texans who thought culture was something you could buy on a trip to Europe and bring home on the boat with you, or who perhaps just wished to imitate the ancient Romans who enhanced their city with the cultural loot from Greece. With money made by leading these Texans on tours and received from them and other admirers by donation, Dr. Armstrong bought up anything related to the Brownings that the English would sell, and hauled it over to Waco. When I entered Baylor in 1950, the university was just finishing a new building for the English Department, named the Armstrong-Browning Building, and had there not only a special library of books by and about the Brownings, but also a mini-museum of Browning artifacts.

In the clear light of day, you would have to see that the whole thing was more than a little ridiculous, a Southern Baptist institution in the middle of Texas seeking to glorify Robert Browning and, to a lesser extent, his wife. In certain sectors, Browning had a reputation for being spiritual, and those Texas Baptists with a half-baked hankering for culture could imagine that he offered the most inspiring way they could get it without losing their religion. But the spirituality could be a little vague. In *From Dawn to Decadence: 500 Years of Cultural Life: From 1500 to the Present* (HarperCollins, 2000), Jacques Barzun did not find Robert Browning taking any leading role. But he commented that this poet's peculiar way of putting his lines together "generated the Browning societies," composed of "readers determined to help each other find out the obscured meanings" (p. 562). To me, it also seemed a little peculiar that the considerable sums available to Dr. Armstrong were devoted not to stimulating students to become creative themselves, like the Brownings to whatever degree they were, nor even to promoting scholarship about the Brownings, but to splendorizing the Armstrong-Browning Building, and most especially a quasi-sacred space with a copy of the clasped hands of Robert and Elizabeth in a glass case on the quasi-altar, something like bones of the saints in some Catholic churches.

Jaundiced as my view of all this might be, in 1971 it gave me an opportunity to sell a story to the Waco *Times-Herald,* where the editors saw anything Browning-related as of some local interest (November 10). I could report that some of the furniture originally in the Florence apartment, Casa Guidi, was now at Baylor, and that Mr. Kelley was thinking of trying to borrow or copy some of it for use in the repurchased apartment.

The article was also bought by the St. Louis *Post-Dispatch* (December 19), the Roanoke *Times* (November 7) and the Ann Arbor (Michigan) *News* (December 9). Mr. Kelley was from Arkansas City, Kansas, and that enabled me to sell the article there: to the *Daily Traveler* (October 27). But I never enjoyed equivalent success with any other topic, and the sale of Casa Guidi articles was of benefit mostly for experience and ego gratification. There was not enough money in it to justify the time.

When I was writing for the education editor of the *Christian Science Monitor,* Cynthia Parsons, she let me look into the possibilities for moral education of a non-religious type in the public schools. In this quest, I did an interview story (November 6, 1978) with Hugh Scott, dean for programs in education at Hunter College. He gave me two hours, and wrestled with my questions. But to little avail. Yes, he would have to acknowledge the validity of offering moral education. But doing that in the public school was daunting.

He could not use the word "morality" with ease, but tended to slide off into speaking of "values education" or "civic responsibility." Unable to look for a basis to moral education in religion, public schools might turn to documents such as the Declaration of Independence or the Bill of Rights, he suggested. Who is to say what is "good moral character"? Earlier, as schools superintendent in Washington, D.C., he found he could hardly enforce even a dress code. But aside from the church-state issues, Dr. Scott seemed so fixated on viewing children as victims of adult society, he could hardly get around to thinking of them as people in need of some moral education for their daily activity of making decisions about how they would treat each other, how they would behave outside the school and how diligently they would work to turn themselves into worthwhile citizens.

One professor in his department, Lisa Kuhmerker, was offering an elective in moral education. But Dr. Scott was not sure he had a mandate to train teachers in that field, and suggested maybe the topic should be left to the liberal arts.

In 1982, I went back to Hunter for a *Monitor* article on the president, Donna Shalala (September 13). I did not take up the topic of morality with her, but focused on administration. She led with, "The floors are clean, I hope you noticed." She had earlier taught at Columbia University Teachers College, but she was finding she liked her new work. Administrators served the cause partly by creating a good learning environment, as in making sure the floors got cleaned. "It affects how students feel about the institution and how faculty feel, and therefore how students are treated," she said.

Dr. Shalala told me how she divided her time, with fourths of it devoted to this and that. Then, taking into account her efforts at keeping up with paperwork, and engaging in a lot of outside activities, it became clear she was currently using something more than four fourths of her hours. But she could not catch a few winks or even rest her eyes in one of the many meetings she was attending, as she recalled doing on occasion when she was a faculty member. "Now I can't do that, or they'll say the president isn't interested in what they're doing."

She had been assistant secretary of Housing and Urban Development in the Carter Administration, so I took the opportunity to ask what she had learned about administration from President Carter. "Negative," she said. "Personally, I liked him enormously. But he wanted more information than was appropriate for his level. And he didn't conceptualize, didn't put the details into the big picture."

When I interviewed Frank J. Macchiarola, schools superintendent for New York City, I found him able to talk about moral education a little more easily than Dr. Scott. In another story for the *Christian Science Monitor* (March 26, 1979), I could quote his declaration that "the policy of this administration will be to promote moral education."

He was able to see and identify several areas where public schools could deal with the moral dimension: holding up exemplary "heroes" from American history, bringing children into contact with other races and with the handicapped, studying topics such as the Holocaust and so on. And as a practical matter, he thought a good athletics program would drain off energies that otherwise might go into juvenile delinquency and vandalism. He had recently watched some students at an athletic event and reported, "They were so tired and exhausted after that, no way could they get in trouble."

A contrary sidebar to this story, however, was a call later from Mr. Macchiarola's p.r. woman, reprimanding me for asking him questions about moral education. What kind of story was I planning to do anyway? To have the p.r. flack trying to tell me what kind of questions I should ask was not a matter I was going to take seriously. At least not in the flack's terms. But I did find it instructive that whatever the outlook of an individual such as Mr. Macchiarola, there was a prevailing culture in the public school sphere that said concern for the moral was out of place there.

To sidebar the sidebar, this p.r. woman was not unique but one among several who have come along over the years to make me marvel that people whose own relations with the public seem especially poor will choose to go into public relations as a profession, like neurotics becoming psychotherapists.

In 1977, I got into Scottish nationalism, and wrote a NANA story on an interview with the chief economics man of the Scottish National Party (August 22). That was Douglas Crawford, a member of the British parliament who was visiting New York to assure Wall Street that the goals of his party would be good for business. They were not promising a shift to the right, as Margaret Thatcher was to bring later, but he held out the prospects of taxes, personal and corporate, reduced a little from the levels of the United Kingdom. Mr. Crawford was frank to say an independent Scotland would not give business a totally free hand. But he promised some beneficial changes in governmental regulations, and direct flights to the continent, eliminating the existing inconvenience of routing through London.

An important factor behind Mr. Crawford's confidence in the economic future of an independent Scotland was the prospect of the oil revenue from the North Sea. I suspected this factor might just possibly make the English more reluctant to give up Scotland. But the economics man seemed to feel sure they would readily agree and, in a benevolent mood, he said an independent Scotland would give loans to keep England from going bankrupt.

Mr. Crawford had also been to Washington, and reported that he found officials there displaying an attitude of "total pragmatism." They were happy to learn, he said, that Scottish nationalists were not just a bunch of kilted romantics dancing to the bagpipes. So twenty years later, the Scots did get to vote for a regional parliament, but not for independence. And I gather they still lack control of that oil.

But back now to the religious world, where much of my time has been spent with the National Council of Churches.

Tracy with Bishop Anthimos Draconakis at the Greek Orthodox Cathedral, NYC, Sunday 17 April 1977. Photographer unknown.

Went this morning to the Greek cathedral for the consecration of the cathedral dean as bishop –Anthimos Draconakis. The consecration lasted from 10 until about noon and then the regular liturgy went till about 1:15. Terry Kokas had reserved me a place in the very front pew, and I was the first one in that pew to arrive, so I felt rather conspicuous. After the service I walked with another visitor, Carlyle Adams of Albany, and the head of the Greek Orthodox women, Mrs. John Pappas, to the Carlyle Hotel for a luncheon. Adams and I were taken in beforehand for sherry with Archbishop Iakovos and Chancellor Bacopoulos. At the luncheon I sat with Terry, Takis Gonzouleas, Pam Ilott of CBS who taped this morning and her associate Bernie [Seabrooks].

Tracy with Romanian Patriarch's vicar, Bishop Antony, center, and Greek Orthodox Bishop Silas of New Jersey, right, 1979. Photographer unknown.

Thursday 26 April *At noon I went to the Greek archdiocese for an Easter luncheon. The patriarch of Romania, Justin, and a couple of his bishops [Antony and Silas?] were there. It was the first time, I was told, that a Romanian patriarch has visited the U.S. He is going to 50th anniversary celebrations of his U.S. diocese - in Detroit.* ***Friday 11 May*** *Went to a luncheon at Park East Synagogue hosted by the Appeal of Conscience Foundation for the Patriarch of Romania, Justin, and his entourage. The patriarch, with Romania's ambassadors to the U.S. and the present, said all was well in church-state relations and human rights issues in Romania.*

Tracy, standing, with Johannes Cardinal Willebrands, second from the right, Head of the Vatican Council for Christian Unity, and Greek Archbishop Iakovos, right, at the head-quarters of the Greek Orthodox Archdiocese, NYC, Wednesday 17 May 1989. The fourth man is unidentified. Photographer unknown.

SIDEBAR: *Then went to the Greek Archdiocese for a luncheon given by Archbishop Iakovos for Cardinal Willebrands, who will give the commencement address for Hellenic College and Holy Cross School of Theology Saturday. I asked Willebrands if he knew anything about the head of the Orthodox Church of Ethiopia who disappeared at the time of the revolution. But he didn't. I also asked if he saw any way of resolving the conflict over ordaining women. He didn't and expressed hope the Church of England would not approve it.*

Tracy, far right, with Father Kennedy, at lectern, 14 December 1991. Photographer unknown.

SIDEBAR: *This afternoon, I went to Yonkers to cover the installation of Jesuit Father Robert E. Kennedy of St. Peter's College, Jersey City, as a Zen teacher, or Sensei, by Abbot Bernard Glassman, a Brooklyn Jew who founded the New York Zen community in 1980 and moved it to Yonkers in 1982. I rode up on the train and back with Jesuit Faather Matt Roche, who is studying Zen with Glassman. He also brought back another Jesuit, not a Zen student, Father Angelo Paiarro, who is getting a doctorate with Ann Ulanov at Union Seminary and studying psychotherapy at the Blanton-Peak Institute.*

Tracy with Roger Cardinal Mahony, right, and Bishop Thomas V. Daily of Brooklyn, center, Sunday 16 May 1993. Photo by Chris Sheridan/ Catholic New York.

Took the draft [of an article] with me to proofread on the way to St. John's University, where I covered Cardinal Roger Mahony of Los Angeles giving the keynote address of the hospital seminar. He had the topic of 'Dissent Within the Church' but talked mostly of church dissent against society, particularly on abortion and euthanasia. I talked with the St. John's president, Father Donald J. Harrington afterward, and he said they expected to establish a campus in Beijing, the first Christian university to be there. Peter Feuerherd, formerly of Catholic New York and now more happily with the Long Island Catholic, was there and drove me to a subway station.

Tracy at St. Savior Elementary Class Reunion, Montauk Club, Brooklyn, NY, Sunday 14 November 1993. Photographer unknown.

Then I went to Brooklyn for a brunch of 1933 graduates of a parochial elementary school with a Medical Mission Sister, Eileen Niedfield, as speaker. She worked in India till last year and is now in semi-retirement in San Diego but doing interesting work there. I interviewed her after the brunch.

Tracy, Friday, 29 April 1994. Photographer unknown.

SIDEBAR: *This evening I attended a dinner at the Interchurch Center marking the 60th anniversary of RNS. The Religious Newswriters Association is also meeting in New York, and came to the dinner – or some of them. The main speaker was Bill Moyers, who talked at length about the need for more and better coverage of religion on TV. But Elliott Wright also arranged a series of reminiscenses, and asked me to give one. Others participating were Gerald Roumer, Tom Roberts, Charles Austin, Bill Boles and Marge Hyer. The black choir directed by Jim Forbes's wife, Betty, sang – also a little too long. Beverly Brewster coordinated the event, and Charles [Brewster] also attended, and they brought me home.*

Tracy with John J. Cardinal O'Connor, Thursday, 2 June 1994. Photographer unknown.

SIDEBAR: *This evening I went on the fund raising dinner cruise of the Path to Peace Foundation established by Archbishop Renato R. Martino. He gave a posthumous award to King Baudouin of Belgium, which was received by his widow, Queen Fabiola. I sat at a table with the boat owner and his wife and two staff and Archbishop Martino's niece, visiting from Rome.*

Tracy with Archbishop Renato R. Martino, Vatican ambassador to UN, Monday 3 April 1995. Photo by Thien Duangmala.

Ed. note: Martino was ambassador, or nuncio, from 1986 to 2002.

SIDEBAR: *Went back to the UN this morning for a dinner at which Archbishop Martino was given an Italian honor. They used the occasion to do fundraising for the Path to Peace Foundation.*

Tracy with Mario Paredes, Sunday 26 November 1995. Photographer unknown.

Ed. note: Mario J. Paredes was director of the Northeast Hispanic Catholic Center, NY, from its founding in 1974 to 31 July 2001. The Center is located in the Catholic Center where the chancery of the New York archdiocese is located.

SIDEBAR: *Then went to the Douglaston Center for a fundraising dinner to honor the Northeast Hispanic Catholic Center. Cardinal James A. Hickey of Washington was the honoree and spoke. Bishop Thomas V. Daily spoke about him. Cardinal John J. O'Connor, now Center chairman, was scheduled to give the main address, but never made it. He was reported to be delayed in traffic returning from out of town. But I got a report from Mario Paredes that the Center was making a financial turn around, and used it to lead a story I wrote and sent to CNS.*

Tracy, far right, and a gaggle of reporters interviewing Cardinal John J. O'Connor, Sunday 15 April 1996. Photo by Chris Sheridan/ Catholic New York.

SIDEBAR: *I went to St. Patrick's this morning to cover Cardinal O'Connor denouncing President Clinton's veto of a bill banning 'partial birth' abortion and denouncing recent court decisions allowing assisted suicide. Afterward he had a brief meeting with reporters, which as usual was dominated by those with microphones representing broadcast stattions.*

Tracy interviewing Bishop Thomas V. Daily, and Charles W. "Bill" Bell, New York Daily News, interviewing Msgr. Austin P. Bennett, Vicar for Administration, Diocese of Brooklyn, Monday 6 May 1996. Photo by Ed Wilkinson.

SIDEBAR: *I went to Brooklyn, to the building across from St. James Cathedral [the Pavilion], this morning for a press conference held by the Brooklyn Diocese to announce that a woman managing the lay employee pension office had embezzled $1.1 million. Frank DeRosa read a general statement and then Bishop Daily read his own statement assuring retired employees their benefits were not in danger. Jim Lackey told me that he wasn't in a hurry to get the story out, so I waited to write it later in the day, and sent it to CNS tonight.*

Tracy with Carol Marie Herb (left), Editor of Response, a journal of United Methodist Women, and with Beverly Jean Chain, Assistant General Secretary, Mission Education and Cultural Division, United Methodist Board of Global Ministries, Sunday, 4 May 1997. Carol's photo by Beverly; Beverly's photo by Carol.

SIDEBAR: *Today is Carol Herb's birthday, and Beverly Chain's is next month, so I made this a celebration day. I met them at their hotel and gave them the Sistine Chapel prints . . . one of the entire ceiling and one of the creation of Adam. We then went to St. Thomas Episcopal Church for the 11 a.m. service, which turned out to be a confirmation service with Bishop E. Don Taylor officiating. I then bought them a champagne brunch at the Plaza Hotel. We walked home through Central Park.*

Tracy, bored, Grand Ballroom, Waldorf-Astoria, Tuesday, 22 September 1998. Photographer unknown.

SIDEBAR: *I went to the Waldorf to cover the annual luncheon of the Friends of the Cardinal Cooke Guild, working for his canonization. The annual award was given to the priests of the New York archdiocese and received on their behalf by Cardinal John J. O'Connor.*

Tracy, left, with protestors against Iraq sanctions, 5th Avenue, NYC, Monday, 14 February 2000. Photographer unknown.

SIDEBAR: *We then walked to St. Patrick's Cathedral, where some of the group protesting sanctions against Iraq were gathering. Later we followed them to the Hammarskjöld Plaza and listened to speeches by Bishop [Thomas J.] Gumbleton, Father [John] Dear and others. We then watched some of them deliberately getting arrested at the U.S. Mission to the UN. [Tracy's note on the photo: Playing it cool and growing grey in the service of CNS.]*

Tracy, right, with Avery Cardinal Dulles, Friday, 1 June 2001. Photo by Rocco Galatioto

SIDEBAR: *I went to Brooklyn for the annual lunch that Bishop Thomas V. Daily gives for journalists to mark the Catholic communications day. Ralph Penga got an award, and Cardinal Dulles gave a talk on the church and the media. He was supposed to get presentation of the St. Francis de Sales award he was voted by the Catholic Press Association. But the object symbolizing the award did not arrive, so the presentation was postponed.*

Tracy with Joe Zwilling, center, Communications Director, New York Archdiocese and Msgr. Peter Finn, Rector, St. Joseph Seminary, Yonkers, NY, in front of St. Patrick's Cathedral, Thursday 17 March 2005. Photo by Chris Sheridan/Catholic New York.

SIDEBAR: *I tested my stamina this morning by walking to St Patrick's Cathedral, standing there to watch the parade for an hour and then walking over to Second Avenue for my annual Guinness and Irish lunch.*

SIDEBARS

NATIONAL COUNCIL OF CHURCHES

CHAPTER NINE

I have probably spent more time in direct observation of the National Council of Churches (NCC) than any other living journalist. And I'll be danged if I can figure it out.

In 1978, Wayne H. Cowan, editor of *Christianity and Crisis,* asked me to do a general article about the Council (December 11), and as part of that assignment I reported that it had become considerably less than it was a decade or two earlier. I also concluded with the comment that I could not anticipate any future other than still more decline, and I listed several factors contributing to my assessment. I was not happy about writing that conclusion, but I wrote what I saw.

One Council executive protested to me that I was unduly negative, and that he was himself even at that moment engaged in certain initiatives which would serve to put the NCC into the ascendancy once more. I indicated my interest in coming around sometime to learn more about those developments. But before I could get to his office for a corrective conversation, the NCC decided it no longer had enough dollars to keep him on the payroll, and he left town for another job.

At that time, the NCC had a little more than 100 staff at the professional level, called "elected" because they had to be elected by the NCC's executive committee, and this meant a personnel list much shortened from what it had been in previous years. Since the time I wrote, the NCC has been forced by budgetary pressures to cut back still further, several times canceling whole programs, and at the end of 1999 finding itself forced into more drastic pruning, and it now tries to carry on with a professional staff much less than half what it was when I published the analysis in *Christianity and Crisis.*

Some of my reporting on the NCC over the years may have sounded negative, but if so, that was not because I felt disposed to attack the Council, or carried the fundamentally negative attitude some readers may have thought I had. I got a call one day from a man I did not know but who had perhaps seen the *Christianity and Crisis* article, or some of my other reporting on the NCC, and wanted me to give him leads on the Council for something he planned to write. But he was not very forthright about what he was planning, or for whom or why, and it gradually became apparent he was hoping I would tell him where to find some dirt. Since I had engaged in some independent analysis and critique, observing on the one hand this but however on the other, elements of up and down, in and out, ying and yang, he (wrongly) guessed I would be an ally. He seemed to have developed a hostility to the Council because of unhappiness with some policy position, but rather than debate that openly, he contemplated boring in from below to undermine with charges of misappropriating money or something, as a political candidate will try to damage an opponent by dredging up embarrassments from his personal past rather than thresh out issues.

That has not been my line. I have just been struggling to help readers, and myself, understand a little better what the reality of the situation was, and possibly to offer some explanation of why the NCC has fallen so far short of its potential.

The NCC did have true enemies, zealous and faithful, more openly declared than my telephoner. One of the more contentious was Carl McIntire, who seemed to worship the same deity as Ian R. K. Paisley, the off-brand Presbyterian minister who leads the more belligerent Protestants of Northern Ireland. The U.S. soul brother, also off-brand Presbyterian, founded an attempt at a right-wing counterpart to the NCC, the American Council of Christian Churches. He seemed to thrive on attacking the NCC in its earlier years, and showed up at many of its meetings to hurl his accusations jaw to jaw.

I have been a little puzzled to find someone would want to make NCC denunciation his life's work. You can usually find activity vulnerable to critique, whether you are coming from the left side or the right, or some point in between. But it is amazing enough when people take on society as a whole, and live out the totality of their existence as attackers. Even more, to find the meaning of your whole life in fighting one organization seems peculiar.

In the *Christianity and Crisis* article, I noted that some people had enjoyed lucrative careers assailing the NCC. Martin E. Marty, writing one of the responses solicited by the editors, said I was out of date on that, and few people could any longer "make their living knocking the Council" (January 15, 1979). Maybe an exception could be found now in Diane Knippers, who

SIDEBARS

seems to have stepped into the Carl McIntire role in these latter days. She does it with more gentility and less in-your-face vituperation, but shows comparable commitment. The year after Dr. Marty's response, conservatives upset with the liberalism of the NCC and the main denominations in its support group established an Institute on Religion and Democracy (IRD) to serve as an underminer. Edmund W. Robb, a United Methodist evangelist in Texas, chaired the board, which was fairly heavy with disgruntled United Methodists. But there were Protestants of other denominations also, and a few Catholics, including a prominent political philosopher, Michael Novak. A position paper released at a press conference in New York in 1981 was written by Richard J. Neuhaus, a Lutheran minister who later became a Catholic priest (NC, November 11). And eventually, Diane Knippers, a United Methodist turned Episcopalian, became IRD chief.

The United Church Board for Homeland Ministries, an agency of the United Church of Christ and part of the NCC-related sector of church life under conservative attack, got Leon Howell to do a few rounds of investigative reporting and tell something about the funding for the IRD and similar groups. Mr. Howell, a Southern Baptist turned Presbyterian, published his findings in a 1995 booklet called *Funding the War of Ideas*. He reported that IRD income had declined from $705,000 in 1992 to $448,000 in 1994, but in each year most of the money came from conservative foundations, in largest part John M. Olin, Smith Richardson and Bradley.

In earlier years, according to the report, IRD was even more dependent on the conservative grants, and got funding from the Sarah Scaife Foundation, which has Mellon money and is controlled by Richard Mellon Scaife, funder of much of the right wing assault against William Jefferson Clinton. As part of the culture wars, the same foundations and a few like them have also financed other organizations, such as Father Neuhaus's Institute on Religion and Public Life and the Ethics and Public Policy Center, where people such as Elliott Abrams and George Weigle hang out. I doubt that Carl McIntire ever enjoyed such favors.

Attackers often showed most zeal in calling the NCC communist, or communist influenced, or, with more shading, soft on communism, or gullible about communism, or just generally Marxist, leftist, pinko or whatever else. In these accusations they generally overplayed their hand, and so did not get much serious attention from the church leaders who could have made a difference in NCC policy.

If you could get away from the grossness of the debate as it played out in the political atmosphere, and the accusations or insinuations of treason and so on, I might say that in a sense the NCC did exhibit something of a communism problem, as did broad sectors of other components of the liberal political community. It was not, of course, that NCC personnel were communists, as the right wing would allege, but that they were so focused in other directions they would not always find time to take a clear look at the realities of life under communist rule. For reasons sometimes more personal than political, a good many of them tended to make the fight with conservative Christians the primary battle of their lives, and since the conservatives made such a thing about communism, some of the liberals in NCC circles would want to lean the other way, and give the communists the benefit of the doubt. To offer examples that puzzled me, the South Korean government got a great deal of criticism in these circles for human rights abuses, and the North Korean hardly any; the Taiwanese government got a great deal of criticism, and the Beijing communists hardly any. Something had to be at work there besides objective comparison of what those governments were doing for religious freedom and other aspects of human rights. One factor was that the NCC made social welfare benefits a priority, and some people in these circles seemed overimpressed by the communist claim that they had taken care of all such needs in lands they controlled.

In regard to the imbalance in speaking of human rights violations, defenders of the NCC would say it was taking its lead from the churches of the area concerned. Church leaders in Russia, China and so on regularly warned that criticism of their governments by the Western churches would surely cause trouble for them, so please do not.

But in 1977, when I talked to Kim Kwan Suk, general secretary of the (South) Korean Council of Churches, I found the principle of taking your lead from the locals did not apply when U.S. church leaders actually preferred to go in a different direction. Mr. Kim and other South Koreans had been in discussion with executives of the NCC and some of its member denominations when I talked to him. Reporting for the *Christian Science Monitor* (November 17), I wrote, "To the distress of the Koreans, many of these American officials have supported the Carter administration policy of troop withdrawal, and favor reduced U.S. backing of a government they consider a gross violator of human rights." Mr. Kim had himself spent time in the prisons of South Korea, and knew well enough about the violation of rights. But he and his colleagues still worried about "the potential danger of a North Korean invasion," and were dismayed that their U.S. colleagues refused to support the kind of defense measures that people closer to the North Korean border felt they needed. "The United States is a difficult country," Mr. Kim told me with a smile. "It is very hard to change attitudes."

SIDEBARS

In the political climate of the United States, NCC officials of course could not publicly say much of anything but that they did, truly, truly, cross my heart and hope to die, reject communism. But observing day-by-day over the years, one could get an impression they felt no particular anguish about what it was doing to the people who had to live under it. There could even be calls for tolerance to let other peoples operate by whatever systems they preferred, as though the people living under communism had chosen that. I once did talk to an NCC executive unguardedly frank enough to say he considered the apartheid of South Africa worse than Soviet communism, and that the churches therefore should give apartheid precedence among their concerns. One swallow does not make a Capistrano, but I got an impression over time that the Council circles generally rated communism low among their pains. You needed to listen meeting by meeting, watch publication by publication, check which issues got attention and which did not, which parts of the globe were deplored and which were not, who was prayed for and who went unmentioned. When you heard prayers for people who suffered, you would regularly hear mention of blacks suffering under apartheid, along with various groups enduring poverty and oppression in various non-communist countries, but rarely if ever a prayer for those living under communism. Anyone who moved in that direction would have been called a right-winger or something. Looking at all this from the Orthodox perspective, Leonid Kishkovsky once told me (*One World*, January 1992) that an extraordinary number of Orthodox bishops, priests and lay members had suffered martyrdom for their Christian faith in communist countries, but he could sense little regard for these victims in NCC circles.

It was a news event, marking a new departure, when top NCC officials went to Washington in 1987 for a rally on behalf of Soviet Jewry. "We today lift our voices with yours, our Jewish brothers and sisters," said the NCC general secretary, Arie Brouwer. He also reported that he had met with Jewish dissidents during a visit to Moscow, and joined them in calling for "more freedom to emigrate, for more freedom of religious instruction, for freedom of rabbinical education and for more, many more, reopened synagogues."

The rally was held December 6, the day before a Reagan-Gorbachev summit was to open in Washington. And following the rally, Mr. Brouwer went to the (Episcopal) National Cathedral for an NCC-sponsored service with visiting Soviet church leaders to pray for success of the summit. In an article for a New York publication, *Jewish Week* (December 11), I reported that Mr. Brouwer told me that he considered it important to keep the concerns for peace and for human rights together. "We should be free to talk about disarmament and about human rights," he said. But I added that he said he did not know of any NCC leaders previously speaking at an event for Soviet Jewry.

Reporting on the same rally for EPS (December 31), I began, "For the first time that anyone can recall, the (US) National Council of Churches has identified itself with the cause of Soviet Jewry in a dramatic and public way." In doing this, I explained, Mr. Brouwer had to put aside the reservations of those who argued that pushing for emigration of Soviet Jews to Israel would affect the overall Soviet climate in a counterproductive way, and perhaps exacerbate the Israeli-Arab situation. Taking a different view, the NCC general secretary wound up declaring that "American Christians are duty bound to join with American Jews in support of freedom for Jews everywhere, including in the Soviet Union."

But whatever the mix of concern for peace, disarmament and freedom, I still did not see the NCC reaching the point of giving outspoken support to the cause of freedom for all people in the Soviet Union, or joining those many Americans, and those many residents of the Soviet Union, who insisted communism was a bad system that needed to be not just ameliorated but ended, asserting such a position in the way the NCC would unhesitatingly call apartheid a regime of oppression that should be destroyed.

None of this proved that NCC people were secret members of the Communist Party, or enemies of American democracy, or guilty of all those other charges the right wing threw around so carelessly. It was just a matter of the way various tendencies worked themselves out in the minds of some people.

Whatever deficiencies the NCC may have had, I did not march with that considerable company who rejoiced to see it shrivel, and who would have rejoiced exceedingly to see it die. I would have been happy to see it grow stronger, and became depressed watching the continual erosion, and finding myself forced to the conclusion that although the NCC might continue in some form or other indefinitely, the downhill movement probably could not be reversed.

The trend was not just beginning at the point when I analyzed for *Christianity and Crisis*. In a 1970 article for the North American Newspaper Alliance (July 18), I had reported a notable decline just from the previous year. The member denominations had met with financial difficulty, and could not give the NCC support at previous levels. For the first four months of 1970, gifts had been down ten per cent from the year before. The staff had been reduced in early 1969 from 689 to 590, counting here both those "elected" and the secretaries *etc.* who were "appointed," and further cuts were imminent.

People were remarking that you dare not take a vacation because your desk might not be there when you came back.

You might say the NCC peaked at the moment it began, and that shrinkage has characterized its entire history. It was founded November 29, 1950, at a meeting in Cleveland, through a merger of the Federal Council of Churches with several agencies that coordinated interdenominational work in areas such as foreign missions and religious education. Some of those agencies employed larger staffs than the entire NCC has today. The NCC had strength enough in its earlier days to inspire those larger numbers of vociferous enemies, who were showing up at its meetings and accusing it of heresy and collaboration with the communist conspiracy. Programs were more extensive, and the press paid attention. But like the preacher told by a gushing admirer that every one of his sermons seemed better than the next one, the NCC seemed to find every year better than the next.

So a decade after the *Christianity and Crisis* analysis, I was reporting for the World Council of Churches magazine, *One World* (March 1989), that years of slow, steady erosion were yielding to "a period of abrupt retrenchment and realignment." That was a matter of interest to the international community because the NCC had in previous years moved confidently as a major player on the world scene, carrying on extensive programs in many countries and providing budget supplements for a number of national councils. But now I had to tell people on the receiving end of those benefits that they must begin "revising expectations downward" as the NCC curtailed both its own work overseas and the aid it gave to councils in the poorer countries. It had announced "a decision to close some overseas offices," I added.

And the move toward Christian unity did not much progress. In a way, the NCC resembled the nineteenth century movement initiated by the Scottish immigrants, father Thomas and son Alexander Campbell, who had a vision of Christianity beyond the separated denominations but wound up only adding yet more denominations to the religious cafeteria: the Christian Church (Disciples of Christ) on the liberal side and the Churches of Christ on the conservative. The NCC became something like another denomination, finding favor with some Christians, but mostly a segment committed to a particular agenda carried out in a particular way.

Attempts at NCC salvation have come not through renewal of mind but through a series of "restructure" efforts. I suspected each of those proved more detrimental than helpful, but NCC insiders seemed to see restructure as the only way to go ever. In 1999, when difficulties seemed more daunting than usual, and all past restructures had failed to bring success, there came a call for a restructure more far-reaching than usual. Wesley Granberg-Michaelson, general secretary of the Reformed Church in America, said the challenge could best be met by a "process of bringing the NCC as presently constituted to an end so that a new ecumenical vehicle can be born" (*Christian Century,* November 10).

The NCC, lacking power to command, depends on personal ties and intangible connections to its constituency. These are broken when units are eliminated and organizational boxes shifted around. People lose touch. But NCC leaders have tended to interpret their problems as only organizational, and failed to see a need for rethinking to accompany or perhaps replace the restructuring.

After the departure of Arie Brouwer as general secretary, the NCC brought James A. Hamilton, its Washington representative, to New York for an interim period in the office. When I interviewed him for a *One World* article (January 1990), he suggested that the NCC went too far in the 1960s with the idea it should "move out into the streets." Earlier it had put more energy into the approach called study-and-reflection, and drew in many leading figures of American life as participants. But in the 1960s, a lot of church people got overheated and decided they had to rush out and join the crowds marching up and down and shaking fists. If you believed the streets were where it was all happening, who could justify wasting time in study and reflection? I had seen some of that heated hurriness in another context during my college days. Among the more evangelistic types, there were those who decided getting out to win souls for Jesus had such urgency they could not linger for much study and reflection on a college campus. Mr. Hamilton, who had served on the NCC staff since 1958, could remember the days when the NCC had no trouble getting Dwight D. Eisenhower to speak at the dedication of its headquarters. But now, at the time Mr. Hamilton sat in the general secretary's chair, NCC representatives could not even get an appointment to go talk with George H.W. Bush down at his place.

William P. Thompson, who succeeded Eugene Carson Blake as stated clerk of the United Presbyterian Church, took a prominent role in the life of the NCC for a time. A lawyer from Kansas, Mr. Thompson was a man whose ability soon lifted him into prominence in the church world internationally as well as in the United States, and in 1975 he was elected to serve as NCC president for the 1976-78 term. In an address to the NCC board, he observed that "some observers," himself presumably amongst them, had seen a willingness of "some churches" to ask the NCC to undertake "marginal, even bizarre" projects they were not willing to carry out themselves. And he went on to caution that such "must be avoided." Mr. Thompson also asserted that although he favored continuing the NCC tradition of speaking out on social issues, the search for unity was "preeminent" among its reasons for being, and the invitation for addition-al churches to become NCC members should be made "much more explicit." But life in the NCC continued more or less as before. Talking with various NCC leaders individually, you could easily enough get acknowledgment of a need for a change of direction along one line or another. But so many people had a hand in setting the NCC course, and the organization served as the vehi-cle for so many ongoing movements, tendencies and forces, that no one indi-vidual or assortment of individuals could really alter the course of the stream. About the only proposal you could always get agreement on was diving into another round of time-consuming talk about reorganization.

For a while, the NCC was holding an assembly every three years to bring together a large representation of its constituency, an event that could draw attention and build enthusiasm. But in 1969 so many disruptive protesters used the assembly to promote their causes that the wheels were set in motion to eliminate such occasions. The one in 1972, featuring an address by the black radical, Imamu Amiri Baraka (Leroi Jones), became the last (until an abortive effort at something similar much later). People who thought the imamu should not have been invited under any circumstances were especially put out to hear reports that the NCC had paid him $1500 to deliver his rhetoric, a figure more startling then than now. NCC officials refused to comment on those reports, an indication they were probably true, or perhaps understated.

Another restructure was voted at the same time, and among its effects was serving Claire Randall, the new general secretary, as an excuse for dismissing five of the most senior executives, with experience totaling eighty years. One day she had them come into her office one by one, kneel before her and receive a swift beheading.

But she did not announce her action until some time later when reporters started calling up. She apparently thought that she, the first woman elected general secretary, could lop off five of the top males without anybody noticing. When she did get around to issuing a press release (June 21, 1974), it spoke of "deployment" and a commitment to functioning in a "collegial, facilitative, open, flexible style," and only after a couple more pages of such elucidation slipped in the detail that the superfluous five were "given early retirement."

Elliott Wright of Religious News Service reported that Claire Randall told him the changes were necessary if the Council was to "make a real impact on the life of the churches and the nation" (June 20, 1974). But the actual result of firing men with long and well-established ties to many individuals and groups more likely was further evaporation of constituency support. And we have yet to see that "real impact."

Reinforcing the dismissals at the top of general administration, Eugene L. Stockwell of the NCC Division of Overseas Ministries was acting about the same time at the next level to push James MacCracken out of his job as director of Church World Service (CWS), the Council's relief unit. I had no assignment to deal with the MacCracken issue, and went in to see Mr. Stockwell during that period on some other matter. But getting rid of the CWS director had put a number of people on his tail, so he started from the assumption I must be another. I still remember his mixed shock, relief and disorientation as he began to realize that I had come from a different galaxy.

It was reported that under Mr. MacCracken the NCC's relief agency was working in collusion with the United States government, a mortal sin in the eyes of many in Council circles, and showing insufficient dedication to promoting "systemic change" in the countries where it gave assistance. But when I interviewed the next director, Paul F. McCleary, a good while later, it turned out that the relationship with the government, particularly in distribution of Food for Peace commodities, was proceeding much as ever.

Administrative battles are of course commonplace, and those of the NCC, though perhaps unusual in some ways, were more illustrative of an indifference to constituency relations than decisive in themselves. What the NCC needed was something different in perspective. As for Claire Randall herself, I thought she would have been ideally placed if the NCC had made her deputy general secretary for administration. She had a talent for managing affairs, and liked managing affairs, and managed them with energy and dedication. She was not so well suited for the political task of inspiring support out in the provinces, or what President [George H.W.] Bush called "the vision thing." Could she have served as the managerial person while Joan Brown Campbell, who took little interest in the managerial side but excelled in relating to the world outside, was general secretary, they might have made a championship team.

Casting overboard the experience and alliances of the dismissed five failed to reverse the downhill slide, of course. And as Claire Randall approached the end of her tenure, she set the processes in motion for—you perhaps have guessed—a restructure. A presidential panel, chaired by Robert W. Neff of the Church of the Brethren, was asked to come up with something, and much was said about the promise of their enterprise. However, when I once tried to attend one of their meetings, and see what might be developing, Mr. Neff refused to let me in. So I never knew what kind of ideas were presented, but I gradually came to suspect not many of great worth.

The basic concept that emerged—and did not require the panel's lengthy meetings or piles of paperwork—was to make CWS serve not only as the NCC's relief unit, but provide relief for the NCC itself by paying more of the

SIDEBARS

administrative costs of the total organization. CWS had its own fund raising apparatus, known as CROP (Christian Rural Overseas Program) though not by that point still characterized by its name, and enjoyed generally better standing with its constituency than the rest of the NCC. So it received more income than all the other units combined. But it did not feel obligated to bail out the parts of the Council that could not raise their own budgets.

In November of 1983, I got on the PATH train and went to New Brunswick, New Jersey, for a meeting of the NCC board. They took two major actions: one was to approve the reorganization plan of the Neff panel, and the other was to elect a successor to Claire Randall. The successor was Arie Brouwer, who had been general secretary of the (Dutch) Reformed Church in America several years, and then briefly a deputy general secretary of the World Council of Churches in Geneva.

I thought his background, particularly carrying the responsibility of chief executive in a denominational staff and directing its overall program, made him an ideal choice. But it turned out this experience misprepared him, because he brought an expectation that he would be able to exercise the same degree of managerial control at the NCC as he had in his denomination. Actually, the NCC was a considerably different animal, with quite different structures for exercising authority and circumventing authority.

A forceful operator who moved with unrelenting determination, Mr. Brouwer eventually drove the NCC into an internal crisis as he attempted to compel acceptance of the restructure plan, but finally came to concede that he could not. He was directly at loggerheads with the CWS director, J Richard Butler, who had backing from his constituency but after a while decided the hassle was all too much, and resigned. Later, in 1989, Mr. Brouwer made such a polarizing speech to an NCC board meeting that his contract was bought out like he was a coach in the middle of a disastrous season (EPS, June 30 and August 19).

Listening to debate at the New Brunswick meeting where he was elected and the new organizational setup approved, I thought he might have guessed from the beginning that the restructure plan would not fly. Robert J. Marshall, a Lutheran leader, represented CWS in the debate, and gave the message clearly enough: We think this is not a good plan; we think it will not serve our needs; we ask you to do it–not! He spoke for the people who were bringing in two-thirds or more of the NCC's income, and he was ignored. He was–at that meeting–only one person, and the presidential panel were many. So they could easily get their way by numbers. Outside the meeting, however, Mr. Marshall represented most of the people ready and able to put dollars behind their decisions, and the capacity of the NCC board to raise money otherwise was hardly observable.

Sometimes later, when I asked Mr. Brouwer whether the dispute over CWS had ever been settled, he could reply with rue, "Yes, several times."

Feelings inside the NCC went from pretty bad to even worse. William L. Wipfler, an Episcopal priest who had been Latin America secretary and then director of the human rights office, resigned after 21 years on the staff. In a letter to President Patricia A. McClurg and other officers (June 27, 1988), he said he could not credibly work for human rights in the world outside when the NCC was not respecting human rights inside its own house. Within the previous six months "continuous pressure on five staff members has led to the dismissal of one, the resignation of three and the serious consideration of resignation by another," he said. And he was "appalled by the harassment that has taken place" in an attempt to enforce conformity.

Mr. Brouwer contended that his difficulties came from "a small elite of powerful denominational bureaucrats" defying "the whole inclusive people of God" as represented, he said, by the NCC board and, the implicit background thought, by himself as chief agent of the board. The denominational executives he had in view, however, did not agree that the NCC board represented absolutely all the people of God on all issues. These executives were receiving money the donors expected to go for relief. If it was turned over to the NCC board to use for general administration, that could be seen as betraying the trust of at least some of the people of God, those that gave the money. There seemed to be a subconcious assumption: the money just happened to be in NCC accounts, and the only question was what to spend it for. People claiming they deserved equal power in spending did not take equal responsibility for producing. And when the percentage of CWS income taken for NCC administration increased, some denominational executives said CWS was becoming an inefficient instrument. In one of my articles for EPS, I reported that Lloyd VanVactor of the United Church of Christ had gone public about his decision to bypass the CWS-NCC structures and send money directly to an international account set up at the WCC (October 15, 1988).

So what was Mr. Brouwer's alternative strategy after he faced up to the failure of the panel's plan? I found out when I went to Tarrytown, New York, for a board meeting there in November of 1988: restructure. Melvin G. Talbert, United Methodist bishop of San Francisco, was named to head yet another committee assigned to think up something. They emerged with recommendations that called basically for further reduction in staff, though at this point not reduced enough to match the reduced income.

Benjamin F. Chavis Jr., earlier known as a member of the Wilmington 10 and subsequently as the ousted executive of the NAACP, intervened unhelpfully. The Talbert group said income could support only a three-unit Council. But Mr. Chavis, the racial justice executive for the United Church of Christ at the time, rose up to demand that the Council also establish a fourth unit for "prophetic justice." The term as the name of an administrative unit sounded pretentious and incited ridicule, and then became doubly ridiculous because the unit could not raise budget to accomplish much. Mr. Chavis got elected head of the committee overseeing "Prophetic Justice," and let the unit slide into serious deficits, and then more or less abandoned it as he moved to take the NAACP in the same direction, and then go on to his alliance with Louis Farrakhan and conversion to Islam.

Pretentious naming was not new. In 1974, the Council set up a Commission on Justice, Liberation and Human Fulfillment, with a Presbyterian minister from Brazil, Jovelino P. Ramos, assigned as its one-man staff to bring all that to pass. Later on, the "human fulfillment" part was dropped, but I cannot tell you whether that was because the humans connected with it completed their quest for fulfillment, or because they decided the name was too long for the letterhead. Eventually, the Commission itself was dissolved, and its work subsided into an office on "inclusiveness and justice," a sort of "equal employment" office pushing the Council to hire more women and ethnic minorities.

The Commission emerged from the upheavals of the 1960s, when some blacks insisted that blacks be chosen as president and general secretary of the Council and, failing immediate success in that, took the more realistic fallback line of demanding total control of at least one Council unit. Good liberals one and all, Council leaders said they were ready to go along, but then came similar demands from Hispanics, Asians and Indians (there called Native Americans). So when I interviewed Mr. Ramos for an article in *New World Outlook* (September 1974), the minorities were all represented and all calling themselves Third World people, terminology that in some parts of the Third World provoked resisters who did not want third place ranking in anything. Since the NCC regularly came under attack from conservatives for its liberal policies on minority matters, you might think these minority groups would rally around to defend it, uphold its reputation, support its program and do whatever they could think of to strengthen it. You would think wrong. They curiously imagined the NCC leadership was the American Establishment, or at least a significant part of it, and the one part they could really get at. So their goal was to confront the NCC, and hurl their protests and demands at it. And the NCC agreed that this Commission on Justice, Liberation and Human

Fulfillment should devote itself to that mission. Even more than the minorities wanting to do whatever they could to diminish the NCC's strength and reputation, you might wonder about the desire of NCC leaders to pay for that, and get the conflict structured into the organizational charts. But in the atmosphere of those days, a regular observer would eventually become unable to wonder at much of anything.

By the time the Commission got established, it was in a way obsolete, because the NCC had now elected a black president, W. Sterling Cary of the United Church of Christ, and a black Baptist, Lucius Walker Jr., as chief executive of a major Council unit, Church and Society. And the latter position seemed to become a black monopoly, thereafter always given to a black, a suggestion that promoting black goals was the primary agenda of the NCC for American society as a whole. Ethnic minorities were also getting a larger role in other parts of the Council. But the Commission set to work, nonetheless. Mr. Ramos explained that it was meant to be an instrument of confrontation, confronting the people who paid his salary, and demanding that they change to serve Third World struggles for self-determination more in the way Commission members preferred. "That's what we were asked to do, and we're very glad to do it," he said. He had also brought up from Brazil a few radical prescriptions for American society overall, such as that "the people who work the land should control it," ideas I thought might not commend themselves to all the people the NCC depended on for its financing.

Unhelpful as Mr. Chavis had been, the troubles of Prophetic Justice were of course not all his fault. Other units of the NCC also floundered, and the new general secretary, Joan Campbell, launched yet another restructure. Only this time, remembering how many had failed, she called it "transformation." Whatever. She was accommodating to the necessity of further retrenchment. In 1994, I went to an executive committee meeting and heard her report that the NCC would have to rely increasingly on funds from the government, foundations and other sources because financial ills were pushing its member denominations into new rounds of "restructuring and downsizing." The situation was "not becoming stabilized" (EPS, March 10, 1994). And by the time she concluded her tenure at the end of 1999, it had become a great deal more non-stabilized.

To speak of fundamentals, no reversal of the downhill slide was possible because the NCC's supporting denominations were themselves in a state of continuing decline. The largest of them and the one contributing the most to the NCC budget has been the United Methodist Church. It was formed in 1968 by a merger of the Methodist Church with the Evangelical United

Brethren, and the product of this union, too, has had a history of every year better than the next.

Second in importance for the NCC budget has been the Presbyterian Church, which was formed by a reunion of the former Northern and Southern branches. But this denomination has also been losing members and suffering budget problems that brought forced reductions in its own staff and lowered contributions to the NCC. The United Church of Christ, another key supporter of the NCC, has likewise been in retrenchment mode, as have other NCC members such as the Episcopal Church and Evangelical Lutheran Church in America.

From time to time, I asked leaders of these churches about the membership shrinkage, and listened for their references to it in public settings. But I found little disposition to face up. Much of the leadership has persisted in outright denial. Ask them about the national statistics and they start talking about some local congregation in Idaho or somewhere they visited recently and found drawing a full house. Or they would say the membership decline was only a matter of cutting dead wood from the rolls, or something.

When a leader could no longer make himself deny the obvious, his next recourse might be to say something like, well, yes, it was happening for a time, but now it has bottomed out, or is just about to turn around, or is giving promise of turning around at some near date, maybe the umpteenth Sunday after the fourth blue moon. A final fallback position for some was to say, yes, it is happening but it is inevitable–because of birth rates, because of population shifts, because of cultural trends, because of whatever came to mind.

In all these reactions, the same bottom line appeared: There is nothing to be done, and no one should hold the leadership accountable, or expect it to take any remedial action. On with business as usual.

The weakness and decline did not, I would emphasize, change the fact that the NCC was doing a lot of good deeds. And even when it reduced the amount of attention given to "study and reflection," it was still stimulating a lot of thought on issues. You might not like the policy lines it adopted, but you should admire the readiness of the NCC to free church leaders from exclusive absorption with their own localities and organizations, from the customary provincialism and parochialism, and enlist them in addressing a wide range of significant issues, foreign and domestic, facing the American people as a whole. In my years watching the NCC, I have reported on its serious consideration of nuclear weapons and nuclear energy, of public schools and public media, of bioethics, of American relations with Latin America, with Africa, with Korea, North and South, with China, with Cuba, and again and again with Cuba, on farm workers, on affirmative action, on sexual ethics. The NCC has coordinated church response to the needs of poor countries and disaster areas, and it has helped resettle many thousands of refugees escaping dictatorships right and left.

One of the NCC's valuable and non-controversial services was publication of a reference work, the annual *Yearbook of American and Canadian Churches,* giving basic facts about each denomination and ecumenical agency. Another contribution was providing a base of operations for Dean M. Kelley, a specialist in church-state relations who led an unceasing battle for church freedom from government intrusion, and won admiration from many people otherwise far removed from the NCC ethos.

Among the more creative programs in the 1970s was one devoted to helping reduce the tensions of Northern Ireland. David J. Bowman, a Jesuit priest, served as director of this office, and I often went to him for news of the Ulster situation. As a Catholic working for a non-Catholic church body, he was situated to get beyond the usual polemics. On one occasion, after the Irish Republican Army had carried out yet another of its more outrageous acts, I found Father Bowman calling its members "madmen." And he urged Americans to be careful about which Northern Ireland groups they gave money to. "A lot of the money being collected in New York is going to the people who are doing the bombing and killing," he was willing to acknowledge (RNS, July 24, 1972).

Despite the useful work Father Bowman did for a time, NCC relations with the Catholic Church overall have been another puzzle to me. Shortly after the Second Vatican Council, a joint committee studied the possibility of Catholic membership in the NCC, and concluded more or less, "Why not?" (RNS, February 4, 1972). I do not know whether the Catholic bishops ever came to some specific decision, but without giving any formal answer they went on with other things, and did not pursue the matter. They never sent in an application for membership.

Aside from the question of seeking Christian unity, there is the matter of exerting an influence on the outside world. Since the Catholic Church is by far the largest church in the United States, with a membership larger than all the NCC denominations combined, it was evident there needed to be a working relationship if the churches were to maximize their impact on American society. And a certain amount was done. The general secretaries of the NCC and the national Catholic bishops' organization met occasionally. And there were more extensive interactions. During Mr. Brouwer's tenure, he and other NCC representatives made an official visit to the Vatican, and worshiped at the site identified by the Catholic Church as the tomb of Peter, giving prayerful thanks there not only for the apostle but also for Martin Luther, John Calvin and

SIDEBARS

others perhaps not so often recalled with prayerful thanks at that location. When I interviewed Mr. Brouwer on his return, he told me that the delegation met with Pope John Paul II, and the pope "stressed the importance of the ecumenical movement in the United States" (EPS, April 30, 1989).

But there were obstacles, and a lack of comprehensive and persistent striving. The NCC has had a number of Catholics on its staff over the years, but in some cases they have been Catholics out of sympathy with the leadership of their church. So I do not know whether their role has been more of a plus or a minus for Catholic relations overall. NCC opposition to government aid for parochial schools looked to some Catholics like an inexplicable injustice, and opposition to U.S. diplomatic relations with the Vatican like a sign of lingering prejudice. The NCC even joined in a lawsuit sponsored by Americans United attempting to have the diplomatic relations declared unconstitutional. I reported (NC, September 17, 1984) on a meeting of the executive committee where the legal intervention was approved, and only one member voted against the action–William G. Rusch of the Lutheran Church in America. A couple of members abstained, but all the rest took the traditional NCC position that diplomatic relations with the Vatican violated the First Amendment, and the courts should not allow relations to continue.

Doubtless more serious in the back of everybody's mind was abortion. For much of the Catholic community, opposing abortion became the most urgent matter of national policy. But though the NCC had no official position, the liberal Protestants who were dominant in the Council considered abortion a right that must never be given up.

As a national structure, the NCC properly directed its attention primarily to the national Catholic structures in Washington. But since the NCC was based in New York, it presumably might have developed some ties with the Catholic Archbishop of New York, say Cardinal John J. O'Connor in recent years, were the ecumenical flame burning brightly enough to light the way. It could quite properly have sought to undertake some cooperative activity with Cardinal O'Connor as president of the Catholic Near East Welfare Association, or perhaps in connection with some of his other national roles, such as president of the (Catholic) Black and Indian Mission Office. But rapport there seemed lacking. Some people in NCC circles seemed to think they could maintain ecumenical relations with Catholics on a pick and choose basis, or in some vague and general sense without getting down to the specifics of praying and working with particular Catholics they found alien.

Apart from whatever about all that, I was astounded in 1992 when a small group of NCC leaders arranged a two-hour discussion with the head of the Vatican's ecumenical office, Edward I. Cassidy, and mostly wasted the time with inconsequential chit-chat. I was allowed to sit in, and expected the NCC representatives would use the opportunity to get ideas from the top about the best ways of strengthening ties and working collaboratively. Cardinal Cassidy reported that when he was nuncio in South Africa the Catholic Church there cooperated with the South African Council of Churches in some areas, but did not join because it felt the Council was "leading the churches where it did not want to be led" (EPS, March 5). A beautiful opportunity for Council leaders of the United States to engage Cardinal Cassidy in dialogue about ways to pursue their goals without creating a Catholic reaction of that type. But the NCC leaders showed no serious interest in digging into the issues most pertinent to their own situation. Instead, they ran out the clock indulging their curiosity about this and that event abroad they had read about, and asking the ill-informed question, fourteen years into the pontificate of Pope John Paul II, three years after he had met with the visiting NCC delegation, of whether he was downgrading ecumenism. At times around the NCC you could get the feeling of a superficiality that ran quite deep.

Yet, a program the NCC undertook in the 1970s to help Vietnam veterans reenter American society was one of those that served to justify its existence. People associated with the NCC generally held dim views of the war, but they did not take their angers out on the young men sent to fight it, disproportionate numbers of them dragged in from minority and lower class white communities while the Dan Quayles and Bill Clintons found ways to stay out. The veterans were seen more truly as victims, people badly used and then ignored as the nation turned aside from an unpleasant episode and listened to Richard M. Nixon talk about "peace with honor."

One day in the mid-1960s, I was driving along a road in rural Virginia and, seeing a young man who looked like a college student on his way home, violated my rule against picking up hitchhikers. He turned out to be Lewis B. Puller Jr., and I would pass by his home in Saluda, and could let him out at his front door as I proceeded on to my home in Urbanna. He also turned out to be a remarkably open and pleasant young man, frankly telling me that he had flunked out of college, through his very own fault, and was now starting over in a less prestigious institution. Later, he got into William and Mary College, and graduated in 1967. But the next thing I heard, he came back from Vietnam with both legs blown off, and suffering other injuries.

While in the area, I also had a little contact with his father—a retired Marine general, something of a military legend, particularly for his service in the Korean War, and said to be the most decorated Marine ever. General Puller was not a large man, but he had a sort of blood-and-guts, George Patton manner, and carried the nickname of Chesty. Once a woman in Urbanna included him among a number of people invited to her home during the Vietnam War to talk about how people in a small town could work for peace. When General Puller offered his thoughts, it turned out he was not so much interested in working for peace as in beating the tar out of the other side. Almost as much, he wanted to beat up on leaders in Washington for failing to slambang as gung ho a war as he thought was needed. He had even offered to go back into service himself, and show the others how to do it, but his offer was declined. I have wondered how he reacted to seeing his Lewis Jr. come back in mutilated form, neither back safe like himself nor sacrificed in heroic death. Bitter it must have been, and bitter bitter.

Whether physically injured or not, many young men came back from Vietnam hurting from psychological wounds they needed some help in dealing with. So I was glad to be able to report in a *Christian Herald* article (July 1973) that the NCC had a program led by a young Presbyterian minister, Richard Lee Killmer, to offer assistance. Based on my conversations with him, I reported, "Whatever emotional problems the vet already had about his participation in the war, he finds them intensified by the feeling that his country does not appreciate his service, that in fact a lot of people seem to consider him either a brute who went over and killed babies or a fool who let the system take advantage of him."

What the NCC with its limited resources could do to meet this need of such massive dimensions was of course not enough. But Mr. Killmer was making an effort. He was preparing materials to advise local churches on how they could help; he was pulling professionals together to share information on how to deal with emotional disturbances and drug addiction; he was encouraging job and study programs.

I do not know whether any of this touched the young man I saw standing by the road hitchhiking that day, and who would never stand anywhere again. He did get his life together to some extent, and earned a law degree and worked at a job in the Pentagon. In an act of amazing grace, he came to the Vietnam Memorial to support President Clinton when many veterans were turning their backs as this commander-in-chief spoke. But eventually the challenge proved too much. And in 1994 I read in *The New York Times* (May 12) that Lewis B. Puller Jr. had killed himself with a gun. "In public speeches and in conversations with friends, he said the physical and emotional wounds never healed," the obituary told us.

As the NCC declined, erosion also occurred in related parts of the ecumenical world. In 1969, the student leadership of the University Christian Movement (UCM), the U.S. affiliate of the World Student Christian Federation, astonished everyone by voting itself out of existence. Church officials responsible for youth work had irresponsibly abdicated, and taken the supposedly more progressive line that all should be left to the students. Not too long afterward, at a meeting in Washington, one of the students offered a motion to disband, reportedly just to test how thinking went, and was as surprised as anybody else to see it pass.

The movement had moved increasingly into a program of supporting secular causes and away from specifically religious activities. But then the students began to notice that for every cause such as civil rights or anti-war protest they had going, there were secular groups working more effectively. So why should they go to the trouble of keeping a separate organization alive?

For the church in general, keeping the apparatus going takes so much time and effort not many people will do it unless they believe in the church itself. If you see the church only as an instrument for working toward some secular goal, then it will begin to look more and more like a Rube Goldberg design, and you will begin to feel more and more frustrated about how little result you are getting and how absorbed you have to remain with keeping the mechanisms moving.

Some leaders of the University Christian Movement seemingly did not much care for ecumenism, or anything to remind them of the religious background. In an issue of the *Journal of Ecumenical Studies* (Summer 1995) devoted to the movement and later ineffectual attempts over many years to revive it, the analysis of 1960s presidents was cited. Steve Schomberg said it died because there was too much "strain between ecumenicity for its own sake and ecumenicity because there is a political task to be done."

Charlotte Bunch was on the political side: "The world cares little whether Christians are all together; it cries desperately for our insights into and our efforts toward ending racism, imperialism, militarism and other forms of human exploitation." I do not know whether the world knew it was crying desperately for Christian insights, but members of the organization themselves failed to find enough value in that approach to make them want to keep it going. An analyst on the other side, Reuben C. Baerwald, reported that students more closely related to their churches found at the UCM meetings that they were not prepared to deal with "a politically sophisticated movement committed largely to various forms of Marxist/Leninist ideology, class analysis and class struggle as the preferred vehicle of change and redress of the world's injustices." And some of the members were bothered that the others did not want to take any time from their meetings for worship.

One day I was walking past the area where the movement had occupied offices in the Interchurch Center and had recently cleared out of. Someone had left a hand-lettered sign: "Gone out of business–didn't know what our business was." A little later, in December of 1970, I published an article in *Christian Herald* magazine examining some of the issues related to the churches getting more and more involved in the politics of southern Africa. At the end I quoted the sign of the UCM as a caution. I went on to say that we could be confident the church would not go out of business, but that it needed to beware lest its true reason for existence become obscured. The editor, Kenneth L. Wilson, apparently decided my ending lacked punch, and so changed it to leave me asking, "Could it happen to the church?" Later, in another magazine, I noticed a writer had picked up my report on the sign, and changed it still further to end his critique, "It could happen to the church."

These many years later, I remain of the same opinion: The church will not go out of business, however off balance some of its leaders may totter. But I also continue to think the sign offered a useful stimulus to thought. In the years since the UCM did its self-destruct, the entire liberal, mainline Protestant world has been shrinking. One program after another has been given up. Periodicals cease publication, including Mr. Wilson's, and new ones do not replace them. Missionary forces diminish. And one central factor is the reduced sense of the church's distinctive purpose.

Caught up in the mood of the 1960s, some church publications decided they should give less space to churchy matters and more to what was going on in the world. Christians, they would plausibly argue, should show an interest in housing, so let us do an issue on housing. Christians should manifest concern about international trade, so why not an issue on trade? Admirable, surely. Yet, it meant the editors found themselves competing with *Newsweek* and *Time,* and doing it with not a hundredth part of the staff or financial resources. It also meant the subscriber base, more or less traditionally-minded church members who subscribed out of a traditional religious interest, would shrink.

But coming back to the NCC, it may be that the germ of decay was present from the beginning of the council movement. The Federal Council of Churches, which later merged with other organizations to form the NCC, originated in 1908 with the idea of bringing denominations together so they could address American society in a united fashion. But from the beginning of this process, the concept of what the churches should cooperate on was guided largely by the negative idea that America needed to be reformed, and the energies and influence of church leaders should be devoted to accomplishing that.

With such an outlook, the movement for unity was tied to the intrinsically divisive movement for changing society. So the two ideas worked against each other. Many people deplored the pettiness of denominational competition, but when the organization working for unity projected itself into the reform business, the resulting program brought "absolutely not" from some and "don't know about that" from others. The leadership could not get, and I do not suppose ever really tried to get, a constituency consensus on how America should be reformed. Many people might agree the churches should move outside their walls and focus on making a contribution to their society, but would not agree when it turned out some Council leaders believed the way to contribute was to attack the fundamental system by which American society operated. Like the commuter trains leaving Grand Central Station, the conciliar movement would see a few people getting off at every stop, and hardly a minyan would be found on board at the end of the line.

For example, in 1998 the NCC's Racial Justice Working Group announced support for "a national march on the White House in support of amnesty and freedom for all U.S. political prisoners," scheduled for March 27. I doubt that the NCC constituency in any large numbers would agree that there are political prisoners in the United States, which is in fact unusual among nations of the world in its openness to political dissent. The concept is sometimes expanded to include people who say they are violating the law for political reasons, but that seems to diminish the significance of those prisoners in many countries who are incarcerated only for disagreeing with the government.

For another example, in early 1981, the month after President Ronald Reagan took office, I reported that the NCC declared itself in basic opposition to his policy line (*Christian Science Monitor*, February 23). This action could be examined from two perspectives. Some might begin by asking, Was the political line of the NCC better? And its leaders could offer various reasons they thought it clearly was. But one could also wonder, Was it wise for an agency trying to unite American Christians to put itself in a stance of political opposition to a president the voters, many of them belonging to NCC denominations, had just said they wanted to direct the operations of their government?

This tradition fed on itself. People who maintained more balance elsewhere, came to Council meetings with the feeling that here was the place to indulge their impulses for reconstructing society. Measures unacceptable to the denominational membership could be voted at the Council, maybe even some Mr. Thompson would call bizarre, and Council staff would be left to handle the fallout. People who wanted to move the churches further into liberal-left areas naturally gravitated to the Council to take jobs on its staff or serve on its committees. Conservatives who might have provided some counterweight drifted away, or never agreed to spend time with the Council in the first place. People who wanted to stand on the exhilarating frontiers of change could praise the Council as a pioneer. But that was not where most American Christians lived, or wanted to live. So people could view the NCC as an adjunct to the liberal wing of the Democratic Party. And this positioning was reaffirmed and solidified for the beginning of the new millennium when Robert W. Edgar, a liberal Democrat who had represented a Pennsylvania district in the U.S. House of Representatives (1974-86), became the NCC's general secretary in the year 2000.

When I was reporting that Charles Colson, one of the Watergate felons, got the 1993 Templeton Prize for the Prison Fellowship ministry he started in 1976, I noticed how ecumenically he operated, in the general sense of ecumenically (CNS, February 18; EPS, February 28). He took the stance of conservative evangelicals, and belonged to a church of the Southern Baptist Convention, dogmatically averse to ecumenism. But he told us at a press conference that leaders of his organization were drawn from all Christian groups that accepted Christ as savior, the authority of Scripture and the orthodox teaching of the creeds. The work had become international, and in the prisons of Northern Ireland reached Protestants and Catholics, he said. It had grown to employ a paid staff of 280 and operate on an annual budget of $20 million.

It occurred to me to wonder, If such a budget could be raised for such a program, why had this kind of ministry not long before been established by someone in NCC or WCC circles? And the likeliest answer was perhaps that those circles have been too deeply saturated with the feeling that it was society that needed to be changed, not individuals, not even criminal individuals.

But not only people in these circles. I found something similar when I visited a New York prison, the Tombs, one day in 1972 with a Catholic priest, Louis J. Rios, who was going there once a week as a volunteer chaplain (RNS, September 15). Spanish speaking, he had talked with some inmates accused of murder who spoke only Spanish, and took up their case. With his help, they later did get acquitted. But he seemed to take the view that all the inmates were innocent, at least for the most part, rather than offenders against others. He did not manifest a concern to get the inmates generally to develop a different mentality and move toward a new way of life. Instead, he joined them in complaining about the criminal justice system. "The experience of working here radicalizes you," Father Rios told me. "It makes you want to go out and say all this has got to be changed." No doubt there is always room for prison reform, but I would not let that bring a forgetfulness about the need for inmate reform.

From people of this outlook we have come to expect campaigns on behalf of criminals. They will hook onto cases here and there that have been identified as miscarriages of justice–claims that an innocent man was sent to prison or that authorities framed someone they considered a troublemaker to get him off the street. They will campaign for more lenient sentencing of those convicted, more humane conditions for those kept in prison and quicker release on parole. Much of this could be applauded if it were not considered all that needed to be done. Many will say that society, not the criminal, is to blame for crime, and that acts defined as crimes are the predictable result of social injustice. They will not say that the criminals need to renounce the patterns of their past, latch onto a message of change and turn their lives around.

To extrapolate from this, we can see a pattern of dealing with world problems that does not locate responsibility for them in human actions, or the sin that directs human actions, but somewhere in governmental or social "systems." For a characteristic example: In 1973, the general secretary of the World Council of Churches, Philip A. Potter, preached at the Riverside Church one Sunday, and I went up to report on his message (RNS, November 12). He told us that preaching the gospel meant opposing "the systems that oppress people," and that the United States was "the most powerful and wealthy" of those systems. And it has, in fact, been common in much of the rhetoric of these church circles to speak in clichés about "the system," changing "the system" and so on. To me, this seems like a dubious project, because any change will only be from one system to another, and after whatever change we will have something else that becomes "the" system. The New Testament offers a language about "principalities," "powers" and "world rulers of this present darkness" that understands evil as more than the action of certain individuals (Ephesians 6:12). But it does not pretend the evil will be eliminated by changing from one political system to another. Sometimes people who speak of changing "the" system seem to have in the back of their minds a desire to bring about a socialist system, but consider explicit campaigning for that imprudent in the political climate of America. Others seem driven by a vague desire for change in general. A number of years ago, I was struck by hearing a seminarian say that after graduation he wanted to work for "social change," as though that were a profession like medicine or law. However understood, such was taken as the task of the Christian church. So Dr. Potter lamented that too few were engaged in "struggle against the system."

I suppose this concentration on reforming, or in some minds revolutionizing, society has also been a factor in the neglect of evangelism often charged against the NCC and WCC. Billy Graham was among those calling attention to something missing in this area, but people outside his circle have also spoken about it at times. I am perhaps the least evangelistic of all persons in God's universe. But I hardly see how a church can continue to live without giving some attention to drawing in new adherents. Council leaders could never quite come out and say they were against evangelism. But they were averse to what frequently went by that name–practices based on a fundamentalist interpretation of the Bible, often carried out in a way that reinforced the complacency of the powerful and often contributing more to the personality cult of the evangelist than to the spiritual life of those supposedly converted. But NCC-WCC leaders did not really know of a better alternative, so evangelism as a program remained recessive.

Protestant denominations of the NCC have had a few people devoted to evangelism, nonetheless, and at times they have tried to do something through the Council. In 1976, as I reported to *Monitor* readers (April 2), they got the NCC to adopt a statement conceding that its churches had succumbed to a "mistaken polarization" that weakened "the whole life of the church." In the 1960s, the statement said, these churches began emphasizing efforts to rectify social injustices, but "minimized" evangelistic work. They had become "strangely bound" by a reluctance to speak in direct terms about Christ. So the NCC was now calling for renewed emphasis on evangelism, though an evangelism better understood in its bearings on "social and economic justice."

Initiators of that statement said they had made a notable step forward in getting the NCC board to approve their both-and approach. But Rev. Walker, head of the NCC unit on Church and Society, told me that he saw it as getting them to come over to his side, and accept the need for bringing in social justice. So I did not notice any more evangelistic activity coming out of the NCC after the statement than before. Nor did the NCC start writing "both-and" statements to include evangelism when it spoke on social issues. A decade or so later, apparently conscious still of some deficiency and wishing to deflect critics who thought the NCC was too absorbed in secular causes, it talked of upgrading evangelism and linking it with another religious interest to form a Commission on Worship and Evangelism. But nobody ever found enough money to get such a unit going.

To me, this fit in with a broader outlook of people in NCC/WCC circles. I noticed that they often talked about the responsibility of the church to serve human needs. But when they talked about their understanding of what human need was, they sounded little different from the usual social worker. I wondered where the depth was. They did not so often speak of faith in Christ as something that people needed, or of forgiveness of sins, a topic that gets extensive attention in the New Testament.

When Craig B. Anderson, an Episcopal bishop serving as rector of St. Paul's School in Concord, New Hampshire, was installed as 1998-99 president of the NCC (November 12, 1997), he spoke of his efforts to meet "basic needs" when he was bishop in South Dakota and had many Indians in his diocese. What would you expect a bishop to spotlight in his list of our basic needs?

For Bishop Anderson, those needs were being met when he was "feeding the hungry, clothing the cold and combating the structures of oppression and institutional racism," according to an NCC press release. And this has become more or less the conventional rhetoric of respectable church circles.

Partly, I suppose, it is overreaction to the use of piety in some quarters to evade responsibility. To refuse to feed someone who needs food, and cover it over with "God bless you," is of course humbug. In the New Testament, the book of James stands as a corrective to that misuse of religion. "If a brother or sister is ill-clad and in lack of daily food, and one of you say to them, 'Go in peace, be warmed and filled,' without giving them the things needed for the body, what does it profit?" (2:15-16). But an outlook that builds only on this corrective ignores the more basic, more basically human dimension that authentic religion speaks to. For all of us, in or out of prison, on or off the reservation, what we need more than anything else is a new way of thinking and acting. The question left hanging today is whether the church has a message that can help us with that.

Then, a little off the side from the political battle for social change, you could see the NCC engaged with cultural change. When the idea of eliminating "sexist" language came along, people associated with the NCC were much with it. The NCC had sponsored the Bible translation called the *Revised Standard Version* (RSV), which brought it criticism from conservatives, commendation from others and royalties enough from publishers to provide a welcome supplement to the budget (*New Testament*, 1946; *Old Testament*, 1952; minor changes in later editions). In the 1970s, a committee of translators were preparing a revision of the revised, and they came under pressure to use "inclusive" language. In those days, the NCC had a Division of Education and Ministry, which held the RSV copyright and general authority over the project for a new translation. In 1977, I covered a division meeting devoted to the project, and wrote a story for the Women's News Service, an agency operated in conjunction with NANA (September 27).

Bruce W. Metzger, a professor at Princeton Seminary who chaired the translating committee, and another committee member, retired Professor Robert Dentan of the (Episcopal) General Seminary in New York, were put on the hot seats. The session consisted essentially of the NCC representatives telling the translators they were expected to produce a translation without masculine bias, no matter what. The fact that the text being translated had loads of what they called masculine bias was not allowed as an excuse.

Professor Metzger said he and the committee could not eliminate references to God as father, or other male imagery the Bible used in reference to the divine. In passages about humanity, they could agree to adapt in places where

SIDEBARS

the biblical text used "man" in a generic sense, but not where the historical context would indicate male persons were intended.

When Jesus began a parable by saying, "A man planted a vineyard . . . ." (Mark 12:1), the historical situation made "man" proper because it was male persons who planted vineyards in first century Palestine, Professor Metzger argued. That cut no ice with the NCC people. In some developing countries today, women play a big role in agriculture, someone pointed out. Someone else said it was not necessary to indicate gender one way or the other. The translators were also told that keeping masculine language would preserve patriarchal culture, that women would not see themselves in the Bible if the masculine language were kept, that translators were "formers of culture" and should form a different culture, that women were a majority in most congregations, that reference to tradition was a way of justifying oppression. If anyone said anything in favor of fidelity to the text, I missed it.

People who want translators to deviate from the biblical text if necessary to accommodate contemporary feelings can cite one important precedent. That is the handling of the Hebrew name for God, which has the Hebrew consonants YHWH and, scholars say, was perhaps pronounced YAH-weh. In some ancient period, Jews began saying "Lord" when they got to this name, and the vowels for "Lord" in Hebrew were written with the consonants "YHWH" to alert readers that they should say "Lord."

The pious explanation for the shift is that the Jews felt the divine name was too holy to be pronounced. I suppose an analysis in terms of a history of religious ideas might conclude it reflected a change in consciousness that occurred when the idea of tribal gods with different names was given up in favor of a universal deity.

In any case, the development affected translation. When the Hebrew Scriptures were translated into Greek during the Hellenistic period that followed Alexander the Great, "Lord" was used in place of the divine name. In the King James translation into English, that tradition was continued in most places, with the distinction indicated by writing "LORD" all in capitals when it translated "YHWH." In four verses, though, there was use of the name, written "Jehovah" because of the misunderstanding derived from combining the Hebrew vowels for "Lord" with the consonants for "Yahweh" (Exodus 6:3; Psalms 83:18; Isaiah 12:2; 26:4).

Some modern translators have used "Yahweh." That was the case of the Jerusalem Bible, issued by the Catholic Dominican order in French in 1956 and in English in 1966 (Doubleday). Alexander Jones, editor of the English version, wrote in a foreword that "the first duty of the translator is to convey as clearly as he can what the original author wrote," and substituting "LORD" for "Yahweh" would diminish "much of the flavor and meaning of the originals."

However, the RSV translators thought otherwise, and stayed with "LORD," eliminating even the four exceptions of the *King James Version*. Their preface declared, "The use of any proper name for the one and only God, as though there were other gods from whom He had to be distinguished, was discontinued in Judaism before the Christian era and is entirely inappropriate for the universal faith of the Christian Church." Professor Metzger used similar language in his preface to the *New Revised Standard Version*.

Now I wonder, Is it the prerogative of translators to tell us (and the biblical authors) what is or is not "entirely inappropriate for the universal faith of the Christian Church"? I might want to argue that the universal faith of the Christian Church was better understood by an eighteenth century minister in Wales, William Williams, who bridged the distances of space and time to connect with people of a strange language and culture, and give us the hymn, "Guide me, O thou great Jehovah, pilgrim through this barren land."

In the Bible, God is the Lord, to be sure. Never any doubt about that. But the Lord has a name, in the Old Testament and in the New, and he tells us what it is. According to the Torah, God told Moses, "I am Yahweh" (Exodus 6:2). And when that name ceased to be used, another was revealed. According to Acts, when Paul was challenged, by name, from heaven, he asked, "Who are you, Lord?" and received the answer, "I am Jesus . . . ." (9:5). And that was not really a different name, but a new form of the Old Testament name, meaning "Yahweh saves."

Are we to expect that some Re-Re-Revised Version will come along and blot out the name of Jesus, too? Visiting All Souls Unitarian Universalist Church, on New York's East Side, I noticed that their hymnal, *Singing the Living Tradition* (Beacon, 1993), had revised "For All the Saints" as part of the move toward "inclusiveness." The line, "Thy name, O Jesus, be forever blessed," had turned into, "Thy name, most holy . . . ." At All Souls, inclusive language means including Jesus out.

Professor Metzger and colleagues had been promised the freedom to use their best scholarly judgment, and so could not be forced to make the wholesale alterations desired by the Education and Ministry Division. They did respond to some degree, making numerous changes of the type demanded. For Psalms 1, which begins, "Blessed is the man . . . ," they came up with, "Happy are those . . ." Where Jesus began, "If a man has a hundred sheep . . ." (Matthew 18:12), they put, "If a shepherd has . . . ." But in the latter case, they went on to use a masculine pronoun: "does he not leave the ninety-nine . . . ?" And in other ways they failed to do a thorough purging, atop the announced refusal to make God unisex.

So in 1980, foreseeing such a result, the NCC Division of Education and Ministry decided to appoint another committee that would fix the Bible the way they wanted it fixed. In an article for the *Christian Science Monitor* (December 2), I reported that the new committee was to "begin with passages used by churches that follow the lectionary system of designated selections for reading Sunday by Sunday." A move politically astute. The lectionary idea made the project seem a little esoteric, and served to keep it from stirring up as much opposition as it otherwise might. Many of the more conservative people in the NCC constituency would hardly know what a lectionary was, or see any more use for one than for a prayer wheel.

The committee appointed to produce the lectionary did not really translate from fresh, but took the RSV as its base, and only went through to change the "sexist" parts and a few others it found objectionable. It replaced "the people who walked in darkness" (Isaiah 9:2) with "walked in gloom," on a supposition the altered wording might reduce negative attitudes toward black people. And it sought to fight antisemitism by changing "for fear of the Jews" (John 20:19) to "for fear of the Jewish authorities." I have not heard whether that gave joy to the authorities in our contemporary Jewish community, but it fit with the trend to divide humanity into the evil and the innocent, and to evade the biblical truth that we are all guilty.

For this committee, the job overall was not massive, so the NCC was able to publish its first volume of selections, *An Inclusive Language Lectionary: Readings for Year A,* in 1983, and got a jump on the new RSV, which did not appear till 1989. But then it turned out that although an NCC division produced and published the lectionary, the NCC as a totality could not endorse it because the Orthodox churches said, "No way." At a board meeting, Gregory C. Wingenbach, a priest of the Greek Archdiocese, reported that the NCC's Orthodox caucus "absolutely disavows" the lectionary (EPS, November 30, 1983). But like an abortion statement produced earlier under NCC auspices and, because of Orthodox opposition, never formally approved, it nonetheless represented where the NCC leadership stood personally. It happened that the chief of the Education and Ministry Division at the time, Emily Gibbes, was a close personal friend of the NCC general secretary, Claire Randall, and they naturally joined forces to promote the lectionary.

One result of the flight from "masculine bias" was a need to keep repeating the word "God" monotonously. If you go to a resurrection prophecy in Hosea, you find a passage about Yahweh that promises, "After two days, he will revive us; on the third day he will raise us up, that we may live before him" (6:2). But since the lectionary producers could not stand masculine pronouns, they had to make it, "After two days God will revive us; on the third day God will raise us up, that we may live in the presence of God." Or, reworking a favorite verse of the New Testament where we have been accustomed to read, "We know that in everything God works for good with those who love him, who are called according to his purpose" (Romans 8:28), the lectionary substituted, "We know that in everything God works for good with those who love God, who are called according to God's purpose." In John 3:16, the traditional "God so loved the world that he gave his only Son" became "God so loved the world that God gave God's only Child." Which leaves you with little to say but that it is just God-awful.

Another aspect of making this translation non-sexist was referring to God as "Father and Mother." To acknowledge the divergence from the original, the committee wrote "and Mother" in italics, put it in brackets and gave a footnote explanation that it was an "addition to the text." There were also footnotes to acknowledge the addition of Sarah and Hagar when the text had only Abraham, replacing references to the Son of Man with "the Human One" and so on.

These typographical marks reflected honesty of scholarship. But like the all-caps "LORD," they would be lost on people in the churches who were supposed to hear the passages read in worship. In the debates between RSV and new lectionary champions, each side tolerantly conceded that the other's preferred version might well prove useful in private study, but argued that its own should be the choice for public worship. But how would anyone listening to a lectionary reading know that some words were in italics and bracketed and footnoted?

In a warning for those who try to please by rewriting–I do not suppose we need hesitate to say "rewriting" here rather than "translating"–the Bible according to current taste, the lectionary committee also threw out all that "LORD" business the RSV translators were so proud of. For the new generation, it must be condemned as sexist because "lord" was a term used for male rulers. So it was replaced by "the Sovereign One." In an appendix, the committee explained that females, such as Queen Elizabeth II currently, could be "sovereign," the same as males, so this word was better than calling God or Christ "the Lord."

I thought whimsically that the reference to Queen Elizabeth perhaps revealed a subconscious wish for God to become, like her, one who offered a benign presence without attempting to interfere with the governance of the realm. My more serious thought was to wonder how the NCC could have reached the point it would try to get American Christians to stop calling Christ "the Lord," or imagine such an effort would assist it on the journey toward Christian unity. The NCC had originally defined itself as a community of

SIDEBARS

Christian communions that confessed Christ "as Savior and Lord." Now it was telling its constituency they were sexist if they did that, and the NCC would not even let the Bible do it. I'll be danged if I could figure it out.

But the lesson I would draw from all this history is that translators might as well just translate the text, and let each generation deal with it as the Holy Ghost may vouchsafe to lead. I would say rewriting the Bible to conform with the dominant outlook of each new generation actually creates problems. It obscures the distance between the text and the contemporary reader, and contributes to the fundamentalist illusion that the Bible is immediately comprehensible and applicable, and requires no dependence on the Spirit for understanding. People who imagine the Bible provides its own immediate clarity may also decide they do not need the help of other believers for interpretation. That contradicts the reality portrayed in Acts when Philip asked the Ethiopian eunuch if he understood the words of Isaiah he was reading, and the Ethiopian replied, "How can I, unless someone guides me?" (8:31).

Now for another example of the NCC outlook: As 1992 and observance of the 500th anniversary of the discovery of America by Christopher Columbus approached, Council leaders took a totally negative position, and launched a wholesale attack on the totality of American history. I did not fully understand that either.

Some of the same sour spirit had emerged in relation to the 1976 Bicentennial. When R. H. Edwin Espy retired as NCC general secretary at the end of 1973, he set up a small organization to promote Bicentennial observance in the churches. But summing up at the end, he told me that some people had questioned the desirability of even trying to celebrate anything connected with the event (*Christian Science Monitor,* August 19, 1976). He said some church officials expressed fears the observance might turn into a celebration of "civil religion," a term they used to describe "uncritical identification of the will of God with the will of the nation." But the results they feared did not materialize, and the churches that gave recognition to the Bicentennial remained "very self-critical and historically critical," Dr. Espy reported.

As 1992 approached, the sourness had spread, and the church leaders associated with the NCC were "self-critical" and "historically critical" to a fare-thee-well. Partly, they were trying to show sympathy with the Indians, but I found not all Indians were of one mind on the issue. During that period, Carol Marie Herb, editor of *Response* magazine, asked me to write a feature on some church work among the Houma Indians of the Louisiana bayou country (November 1991). So, calling up one Houma for an interview, I naturally took the occasion to ask for his assessment of the Columbus debate. He said he considered receiving the Christian gospel an advantage that outweighed whatever suffering resulted from encounters with whites.

Then in the anniversary year, the Knights of Columbus held their convention in New York, and I covered it for the Catholic News Service. There, the state leader from South Dakota turned out to an Indian, a Sioux-Chippewa named Alfred Jetty, who told me that he was proud to be a Knight of Columbus. And he showed it by wearing a Knights of Columbus medallion executed by an Indian in beadwork (CNS, August 7).

On a down day, an Indian no doubt could get to thinking it has all been downhill since 1491, the last really good year in memory. But there is little likelihood the world will turn back to 1491, so the challenge facing Indians is deciding how to deal with the world as it is turning, and move forward with it.

The NCC attack on the Columbus observance was launched despite the hesitations of some board members. At one meeting, delegates objected to an initial draft of a resolution on the anniversary, and sent it back for reworking. But later, in May of 1990, the board adopted it in a form somewhat revised but still resoundingly negative. "For the church this is not a time of celebration," the NCC said.

Filling the resolution with references to slavery and other evils, and repeatedly throwing in the word "genocide," the NCC portrayed the outcome of the New World's discovery in nothing but dismal colors, and called for making 1992 a year of "reflection and repentance." David B. Reed, Episcopal Bishop of Louisville, proposed that the NCC, while calling attention to the "invasion, genocide, slavery, ecocide and exploitation," broaden the resolution a tad to acknowledge that some people had also found blessings in America. But he was voted down.

I would suppose that in calling on American Christians to make 1992 a year of "reflection and repentance," the NCC did not really mean that American Indians and blacks, or other persons "of color," were expected to repent, but that the resolution was implicitly meant as a condemnation of white America. But how in any case could a church group get to that absoluteness of negativity? To start with, the charges of genocide were of course untrue, as the continuing presence of indigenous peoples from Alaska to Argentina will confirm. Many Indians were killed, and certainly whites could have wiped them all out, but total extermination was never the plan. Today, I have read, 554 Indian tribes have secured recognition by the United States government, several of them still in the territory of the 13 original colonies, and more tribes are presenting claims for recognition. A campaign of genocide would not have left such a presence among us.

It seemed to me, however, that the more serious matter for a Christian body was the lack of any sense of gratitude. "It is very meet, right and our bounden duty, that we should at all times, and in all places, give thanks unto thee, O Lord," Episcopalians say as they follow the *Book of Common Prayer*. But members of the NCC board reviewed 500 years of American history, and could not find anything for which they would call on Christians to give thanks.

This refusal to express gratitude on the occasion of the 500th anniversary of the discovery voyage was especially striking in view of the extraordinary opportunities people from all over the world have found to begin new lives in the New World. "Of color" or otherwise, they have come from all countries, and residents of all countries continue to decide they can find a better life in America. I catch a taxi, and the driver has recently come from Ghana, or perhaps the next day Nigeria, or Ethiopia, or Pakistan or Bangladesh. I could not endure the stress of taxi driving in New York, but many people move into the occupation as a step up from whatever life they had in Afghanistan or India or Haiti. America today, as always, shines as a land of opportunity. Thank God.

Because a good many blacks have been so severe and tiresome in their forever badmouthing of America, I am tempted to say that America has been good especially for black people. Nowhere in Africa or in any other part of the world has black culture been able to flourish and show its strength and vitality to the extent it has in the United States. When I went up to Harlem to visit the Schomberg Center and write an article about it for the *Christian Science Monitor* (November 24, 1980), I found it was not merely an important library for blacks in New York but an institution of international significance. Jean Blackwell Hutson, who had been in charge until recently getting broader responsibilities for black-related materials in the New York Public Library system, told me American collections like the Schomberg Center had also provided a crucial resource for Africans. "Because of the way colonialism worked, often we knew more here about the total African experience than the Africans did," she said. Among those she said had made use of the Schomberg was Kwame Nkrumah, who later became president of Ghana and brought her over for a year to help the University of Ghana develop its library. To look also on the economic side, there is no large black population in any region of the world that has achieved a standard of living as high as is enjoyed by blacks in the United States. Nigeria, the most populous African country and one especially well-endowed with natural resources, has a per capita income moving about somewhere under the $1000 per year level. In the United States, black income per capita is something over $10,000. It is not necessary to ignore slavery and other evils, or current white-black disparities, in order to acknowledge that all Americans have reason to say a prayer of thanksgiving. But for the NCC, the souring of 1992 was another step in distancing itself from the American people.

Negativity absolute about America had for some time been acquiring a fashionable reputation. When I covered an address by William Stringfellow, a prominent lay Episcopalian, in 1972, shortly after President Nixon's reelection, I heard him assert that Christians "discern in the incumbent American regime the same spirit of the Antichrist which Christians in the primitive church exposed and opposed in the Roman state" (RNS, December 18). During that era some people were also deciding it was cute to use the spelling "Amerika" as an indication the United States resembled Hitler's Germany, and they sometimes found toleration within NCC circles.

When Joan Campbell was installed as NCC general secretary in 1991, a call for the NCC to approach its overall task in a different way came from a source that might have been surprising to some observers of the ecumenical movement—her counterpart at the World Council of Churches (WCC). Emilio Castro, a Methodist minister from Uruguay who was then WCC general secretary, addressed the gathering, and said he and other Christians abroad continually felt a temptation to come to the NCC and ask, "Why don't you do something about your government?" But a council of churches, he advised, is "a place of prayer," not a "power or pressure group."

"Joan," he counseled, "keep that in front of the churches, members of this Council, keep that clearly in front of the American public–that what we need to bring to them, what we want to share with them, is that dimension of God in Christ, God in us, that is strength for today and new possibilities for tomorrow."

Mr. Castro also touched on another vulnerable point of the NCC as he urged the new general secretary to stay "close to your people." And he commented, "It is only if you really bring along the prayers of your churches, the support of your congregations, that you will be able to transmit to the consciousness of your country their responsibility in relation to the rest of the world" (*One World*, August 1991).

But how much of that any general secretary could initiate was limited because the member churches control the NCC, and the Protestant denominations that play the biggest role in the Council often have leaders with comparable distance from their constituencies, as well as a continuing desire to operate as "a power or pressure group."

Although their group does not really have enough power to exert much pressure. In the same issue of *One World* in which I reported on the installation of the new general secretary, I also pointed out that the limited effectiveness of the NCC as a political force had became evident yet again during debate over the Gulf War against Iraq. Whether the churches should have taken a stance against the U.S. policy is of course a separate question. But the NCC leadership, including heads of its member denominations, including Presiding Bishop Edmond L. Browning of President George H.W. Bush's Episcopal Church, did speak sharply against U.S. engagement in the war. And to no discernible effect.

At a board meeting in November of 1990, as the U.S. military buildup in the Middle East indicated an imminent unleashing of the move to force Iraq out of Kuwait, the NCC issued a "Call to Action" that spoke of countering President [George H.W.] Bush's policy with "demonstrations at recruitment offices, military bases and other appropriate locations." But little if any of that ever occurred, even by the board members who voted the "Call to Action." But, then, it is not rare that NCC board members assume their part of the action has been completed when they have cast a vote.

Another example of NCC leaders operating at some distance from their constituency had come following the Vietnam War. The NCC relief agency, Church World Service (CWS), wanted to work for reconciliation, and joined with other agencies in an aid effort called Friendshipment. A project they got going in 1977 and completed the next year was sending a shipload of American wheat as a gift to the Vietnamese. Although the wheat would make needed noodles, the gesture was largely symbolic. Earlier, CWS had bought $500,000 worth of rice in Asia and sent it to Vietnam, a project that delivered more calories per dollar. But there was the thought that American farmers giving wheat they had grown themselves to the people Americans had so recently been bombing would provide a more direct way of showing the Vietnamese that the American people did not share the attitude of the American government, but wanted to be friends.

It was a nice idea. It overlooked the reality that not just a few Americans did share the attitude of their government, and that communism remained a problem for the international community, Vietnam War or no Vietnam War. But the proposal also seemed to proceed from not much acquaintance with wheat farmers. Probably somebody moving around in the anti-war circuits had come across a farmer or two offering to give the Vietnamese some of their wheat. But the project called for ten thousand metric tons.

Doing a story for NANA (December 27, 1977), I talked with Cora Weiss, a wealthy Jewish woman who worked with Christians on a number of projects and served as a consultant for Friendshipment. How many wheat farmers of Nebraska she had talked with I cannot tell you, but she assured me they were ready to donate tons of wheat to the Vietnamese, as she said farmers in other

Midwestern states would do. And it was all to go by rail to Houston for loading on a ship scheduled to sail March 1, 1978.

But later we heard farmers were not donating in sufficient tonnage, and interested people who did not grow wheat could maybe give some cash for buying the additional amount needed. My recollection is, so little money came in that CWS had to reallocate funds given for some other purpose to cover the shortfall. The ship finally sailed April 2, and was said to be the first to leave an American port for Vietnam after the war. But no one would ever say how much of the wheat was given by the growers.

A little later, I was engaged to serve as ghostwriter for a book by the CWS chairman, J. Harry Haines of the United Methodist Committee on Relief (UMCOR). Published by CWS in 1980 as *A World Without Hunger,* this book included a section on the wheat shipment (pp. 46-48). But even working inside the CWS operation, doing a project on its behalf, I was never able to get any figures on how much of the ten thousand metric tons had been donated by farmers who grew it. At a party, one staff member sipping on something that perhaps loosened the tongue offered me the estimate of maybe ten per cent.

Ghost writing the book gave me various learnings, and one was the limited appetite of agencies, including CWS, for exposure of frailties. When I began, the word from Mr. Haines and others involved was that we should tell the history straight and unvarnished. At times, CWS had succeeded in its ventures; at times, it had fallen short. So tell the good with the bad, give the bitter with the sweet and all that, and let readers see the full picture. This way of operating, I have learned from a few other experiences, generally appeals to officials more in prospect than in retrospect, when they are actually looking at a manuscript in hand.

I did not make any effort to play up the negatives. But there were a couple of projects that did not work out as CWS leaders had hoped. One was the Friendshipment enterprise and the wheat. Another was a plan to build housing in Guatemala after a 1976 earthquake. On generous impulse, Mr. Haines or somebody had promised to come in with strength and put up just lots and lots of housing for the people made homeless. But CWS officials got in much over their heads, and lacked sufficient financial resources, personnel and expertise for maneuvering through Guatemalan society. The project was delayed, and had to be cut back, and the expectant Guatemalans with hopes raised too high were left with feelings of letdown rather than gratitude for CWS benevolence. It was a mess.

As the manuscript developed stage by stage, I gave it to Mr. Haines for review, but he rarely if ever offered any suggestions. When I turned in the final draft, however, and he settled down to consider putting his name on it as author, he apparently decided it did not read like a great promotional piece. So he reworked it to leave no suggestion that any CWS effort had ever wound up with less than total satisfaction for all concerned.

Mr. Haines thought a preface by some personality of perhaps more note than himself would help the book get noticed, and he accepted my suggestion of Cynthia C. Wedel, a former NCC president who was a World Council of Churches president at the time and widely admired. But then he neglected to put her name on the cover or title page; only his own. And she was sent my version of the manuscript rather than his. So her preface had the observation, "Not every episode is a success story, but we learned from our failures." A reader of the published book would have to wonder what she was talking about. After Mr. Haines did his cleanup, every episode was a pure success story, and no one in this part of the NCC ever had any need of learning from failures.

Regarding the term "ghostwriting," I do not mean this in a deceiving sense. In an introduction, Mr. Haines noted that I had contributed to the project, though part of the credit was for editing, which was the stage I had nothing to do with.

Still and all, CWS remained the most popular part of the NCC, and later came discussion about whether their connection should be emphasized in publicity materials as a way of helping the NCC, or minimized to avoid tarring CWS. Many people did consider the NCC name something of a drag. In 1979, the United Methodist magazine, *New World Outlook,* sent me to San Antonio to do a feature on the city in anticipation of a conference that United Methodists were planning to hold there but never did. I talked with a number of the city's church leaders, and one of my more interesting informants was C. Don Baugh, executive of the local ecumenical agency. Amid stories of Lyndon B. Johnson's girl friends, put out to pasture in San Antonio, pasture lush enough to keep them from making trouble, and other bits of local color, he told me his agency had changed its name from Council of Churches to Community of Churches because of undesirable fallout from a name that suggested a tie with the National Council of Churches. That report carried a little extra punch at the time because San Antonio was the home city of the NCC general secretary, Claire Randall.

On another occasion, Dorothy Berry, executive of the ecumenical body of Kansas, told me that similar considerations led to calling it the Consultation of Cooperating Churches in Kansas. The ecumenical idea was widely approved, but officials of the NCC had taken so many public positions lacking general support from the membership of its churches that the store of sympathy potentially available for this embodiment of the ecumenical impulse had largely evaporated.

So with shrinking resources, the NCC was forced to drop one program after another. The Ireland program closed down in 1979. An office relating to the arts was closed. There came a time when there was no more money for the research office. A Commission on International Affairs could not find enough budget to pay the salary of even one executive, though in the early years the NCC could operate an international affairs department with a half dozen or more executives. An attempt to offer NCC seminars at the Church Center for the United Nations had failed. And in 1983, I was reporting, "Faith and Order, which until lately had two staff executives, can now afford only one. Last summer, the Commission on Regional and Local Ecumenism (CORLE) had to dismiss one of its two executives . . . . Most recently, loss of government grants ended a program assisting black colleges" (EPS, December 11, 1983).

At times, the NCC decided that in the interest of supporting the oppressed it had to hurt itself, as in launching a confrontation with the head of one of its member denominations, Presiding Bishop John M. Allin of the Episcopal Church. If you were trying to encourage member denominations to increase their support, you might think antagonizing a denominational chieftain was not a cool move. But the issue involved revolutionary Puerto Ricans, so the NCC ignored its organizational interests. Anyway, Bishop Allin was known to lean toward the conservative side, so any feelings of his could be disregarded. The FBI was trying to find Carlos Alberto Torres, who was suspected of involvement with a group, Fuerzas Armadas de Liberación Nacional (FALN), that claimed responsibility for dozens of bombings, including one at New York's Fraunces Tavern that left four people dead. The group's name–in English, Armed Forces of National Liberation–presumably was meant to indicate they were soldiers in an anti-colonial war, and as soldiers naturally would have a right to blow up people and things. According to reports, Mr. Torres had also been associated with the Hispanic Commission of the Episcopal Church, so the FBI went there looking for information. Bishop Allin seemed disposed to cooperate. But Maria Cueto, who had been head of the commission, and her secretary, Raisa Nemikin, refused to testify before a grand jury, and Federal Judge Marvin Frankel put them in jail.

I reported for the *Christian Science Monitor* (May 24, 1977) that the NCC board voted at a meeting in Cincinnati to send a delegation to "meet with the presiding bishop of the Episcopal Church to aid him in securing the early release of the two women, to restore their salaries and to pay their legal expenses." I also reported that Bishop Allin had not requested any aid.

That was not reporting on the basis of my own observation in Cincinnati, but I talked with Peter Day, ecumenical officer of the Episcopal Church, who had been there. He told me the NCC statement was originally more offensive, criticizing Bishop Allin by name, a detail Mr. Day doubtless reported to the bishop. Mr. Day said he was able to get the statement toned down in committee, and then did not try to argue against it when it came to the board, but of course cast his own vote in the negative.

The election of Bishop Allin, who began a twelve-year term in 1974, represented a conservative shift in the mood of his denomination. Under his predecessor, John E. Hines, the church moved to the beat of the 1960s, supporting the protesters of various stripes. Critics of Bishop Allin argued that the trust of these people, who were often at odds with government authorities, would be lost if the church cooperated with the FBI. So the NCC took the side of the women who refused to cooperate, and against Bishop Allin and officials working with him. While there could be many thoughts about the issues, the NCC seemed to think only about the issues and not at all about how an organization like itself should deal with its member churches, or whether it could express its concerns in quieter and more diplomatic ways. You could say it was one of the admirable things about the NCC that it regularly took up unpopular causes with no consideration of the possible costs to itself. But if an organization expects to stay alive, sooner or later somebody has to count some costs.

Since the NCC action did not warm the presiding bishop's heart, we could easily imagine he may have passed up opportunities thereafter to channel more Episcopal money to NCC programs, or to align his own programs with theirs. Although he did not attend the board meeting in Cincinnati, I found him at one I covered several years later in Louisville, where he took the opportunity to get a few long-simmering matters off his chest. Attacking each other was not the way for board members to make the NCC what it ought to be, he suggested in an appeal for acting by consensus (EPS, June 11, 1984). The Episcopal Church has, of course, remained a part of the NCC, but I have not sensed any desire of the church's leadership to deepen the ties, or sacrifice in the interest of strengthening the common work.

A couple of decades later, when I interviewed a new presiding bishop, Frank Tracy Griswold III, I found him professing to have little knowledge about the NCC or the World Council of Churches. I figured a bishop as prominent as he who had been working in a diocese as prominent as his, Chicago, must have developed at least some general views about the councils and his denomination's role in them. But he claimed to harbor nary a one, and would say only that he was "eager to explore." He would not even offer a perfunctory statement of general support for the concept and efforts of these organizations his church had belonged to from their beginnings (ENI, February 12, 1998).

Although protest groups and church leaders of the type writing the NCC statement against Bishop Allin valued confrontation, he preferred to puff on his pipe and see how he could avoid anything disruptive. After an interview with him, I reported for the *Monitor,* "Bishop Allin likes to sit back in a relaxed atmosphere and explore at length the ways a problem can be approached, moving from one side to the other, defusing tension points and keeping the perspective of all groups in balance" (July 2, 1974). Not the NCC style.

As for the FALN, in 1998 I was writing about them again. I did a story for ENI reporting that fifteen people identified with the group had been in jail for more than twenty years, and people sympathetic to them, including the general secretary of the WCC, Konrad Raiser, were asking President Clinton to give them clemency (January 26).

Jan Susler, their attorney, said the appeal was made on their behalf, but they were not themselves asking for clemency because they did not think they had done anything wrong. Although the FALN had claimed credit for the Fraunces Tavern bombing, no individuals had been indicted for that, and all those in prison were convicted for offenses that did not involve anyone's death. Calling Puerto Rico, I reached Luis Nieves Falcón of the Puerto Rican Independence Party, whose platform had drawn only four per cent of the vote in a 1993 referendum, and he told me that he favored release of the prisoners. But he acknowledged that the man Puerto Ricans had elected as their governor, Pedro Rosello, did not, nor did the man Puerto Ricans elected as their non-voting representative in the U.S. Congress, Carlos A. Romero-Arcelo. The latter denied claims that those incarcerated were political prisoners, and said they were actually only politicians in prison. Nonetheless, the movement for clemency gained a hearing in Washington, and President Clinton announced he was ready to grant it. The prisoners seemed reluctant to meet the clemency condition of promising to avoid violence in the future, but eventually they brought themselves to take the pledge and came out in September of 1999. However, Mr. Torres, who had been located and imprisoned, was not among those granted clemency.

From time to time, the NCC also suffered blows from behind. In 1983, A. James Armstrong, United Methodist bishop of Indiana and NCC president, made an unexpected departure from Indiana one day, and with comparable abruptness resigned as bishop and as NCC president, to the astonishment of the watching multitudes. We were never told what precipitated those actions, but some got an impression maybe an irate husband gave the bishop a word of encouragement: "You'd better be out of town before sundown, or else." Some

SIDEBARS

months later Mr. Armstrong was invited to preach at Christ Church Methodist on New York's Park Avenue, and was processed in behind a choir singing, "Turn back, O man, foreswear thy foolish ways." But I do not suppose there was any design in that, and mention it only as a curiosity.

At this point, though, the NCC lucked out, because the vice president in line to take over the presidency possessed the personal skills to maneuver through a sticky situation with diplomacy and aplomb. That was Philip R. Cousin of the African Methodist Episcopal Church, bishop of its Birmingham area. He was doubly accidental, or providential, as NCC president, because another black bishop, James L. Cummings of the Christian Methodist Episcopal Church (Los Angeles area), had originally been elected first vice president, but died shortly afterward. So Bishop Cousin was named to fill out his term, an honor he had not anticipated, and then got the presidency laid on him in circumstances that could hardly have been touchier. But he rose to the occasion. He was a natty dresser, presided with dignity and talked easily with reporters about whatever they brought up. And he was never touched by any scandal, so far as I know. Showing how a black bishop might have to come in and clean up a mess left by a white bishop could perhaps offset some preconceptions held by some whites.

I got to examine the ecumenical movement more broadly in 1982, when James Solheim of *A.D.* magazine, a quality affair published jointly by the United Presbyterian Church and the United Church of Christ till the costs of quality put it out of business, asked me to write a general piece on the current state of the movement overall (November).

Who to see? To put one of my choices in context: On a day in 1971, on September 14, a young lawyer who was counsel to the president of the United States sent an "eyes only" memo to another White House staff member, Larry Higby, with an attached list of "persons who have both the desire and capability of harming us" (*Hearings before the Senate Select Committee on Presidential Campaign Activities; Phase I, Watergate Investigation;* Vol. 10, pp. 1697-98). This, with later additions, came to be known as the Nixon enemies list, and included people who might be punished by means available to the Internal Revenue Service or other agencies of the federal government. There was in the White House in those days an ongoing program described, in language of the elegance characteristic of the Nixon team, as an effort to find "how we can use the available federal machinery to screw our political enemies" (ibid., p. 1689).

The White House counsel, whose parents had perhaps hoped for better things in naming him for the founder of Methodism, was John Wesley Dean. He put sixteen names on his first list, with no indication of a hierarchy of importance, and no alphabetizing. But somehow he chose to put in first place a Presbyterian minister who was not currently living in the United States but serving in Geneva as general secretary of the World Council of Churches–Eugene Carson Blake. Beside the name were the words, "per request," an indication, I suppose, that this was not Mr. Dean's idea but that someone else had asked him to include this clergyman–with figures such as composer-conductor Leonard Bernstein, columnist Tom Wicker of *The New York Times* and the eminent power broker, Clark Clifford. But there was no indication of per whose request Dr. Blake was listed.

Knowing the general run of political positioning, I could well imagine that Dr. Blake might have a desire to limit the impact of President Nixon on the world. But how was it decided among the astute and ever so worldly wise operators in the White House that this clergyman had a "capability of harming us"? In terms of the raw, quite raw, power important to Mr. Nixon and his associates, most people would consider the World Council of Churches and its executives toothless, or nearly so.

But a decade later, I did think Dr. Blake would have the desire and capability of helping me with my assignment for *A.D.* magazine. I did not want to rehash the never-explained Nixon affair, but to get his views on the general state of ecumenism. So I went up to see him one day in Stamford, Connecticut, where he was living in honorable retirement while Mr. Nixon agonized over how to crawl back from disgrace.

Dr. Blake, after the death of his first wife, had married a woman named Jean, so friends referred to "he-Gene" and "she-Jean." I found both to be gracious hosts, and ready to talk about events of the day and of the past and future.

I had interviewed "he-Gene" in 1974, when he was president of the citizen action agency, Bread for the World, and I did a story for the *Christian Science Monitor* (August 19). He was a graduate of Princeton, college and seminary, and for the interview invited me to meet him at the Princeton Club in Manhattan for lunch. As one way of alleviating global hunger, Bread for the World was asking Americans to give up beef three days a week, on the theory that the grain or land area or whatever required to produce a pound of beef could provide more nutrition for more people through cereal or something. My interview with Dr. Blake fell on a no-beef day, so we ordered salmon, and I had to reflect that lunching on the salmon plate at the Princeton Club raised me to a level of sacrifice quite easy to endure.

Actually, I had an even earlier encounter with Dr. Blake, but he would not have remembered it. On one occasion, during the time I was assistant to the information officer of the World Council's New York office, I was sent to Dr. Blake for information I would use in a piece of literature the office planned to issue. Along the way, as he outlined the material, he began sounding rather informal, and I supposed he was giving me a little background education. But when he noticed I had paused in my note-taking, he became quite direct: "You'd better get this down."

At his home in Stamford, he was helpful and communicative on many points of relevance to my article, all of which I got down, and a bit indiscreet in commenting on a few church leaders, making observations I thought might well be left unprinted. But I was struck by his recollection of an incident in his earlier years, 1940-51, when he was pastor of a church in California, Pasadena Presbyterian. He and some other Protestant clergy were trying to get local government action on a housing issue, he recalled, and they felt city hall paid less attention to them than to the Catholic clergy. As he recounted the event, an official told them something like, "You Protestants will never get anywhere until you get together." Now, at the end of his career, Dr. Blake was still offering this as a paradigm experience that demonstrated to him the need for church unity.

Reasonable and pragmatic as the point was, it derived from a more worldly than religious approach. And while some may not express the point as directly as Dr. Blake, I have sensed that many people in the ecumenical movement seem to lust a little after worldly power. They would like to march into the offices of government and announce that they represent umpteen million church members, and "you'd better pay attention." And they imagine they could then exhibit political muscle without going through the tedious process of changing minds and hearts, much less winning elections.

Dr. Blake had become known for a proposal, made when he was chief executive, stated clerk, of the United Presbyterian Church, to merge his denomination with three others: the Episcopal Church, the Methodist Church and the United Church of Christ. The effort to arrange their merger was formalized under the name, Consultation on Church Union, whose acronym, COCU, stimulated some comment in Europe because in French it meant cuckold. But representatives of the four churches began to meet, and were joined by representatives of some other churches, and meetings went on interminably, seeming to become an end in themselves, and continue even today, though participants these decades later now say their goal is the more limited relationship of a "covenant" tie rather than merger.

Curiously, when I talked with COCU leaders, they acted as though they were really serious about merger, even years after it seemed evident nothing of the sort would come about. However, Dr. Blake quickly lost interest in the process when he realized it was everlasting courtship without serious intention, and directed his energies into other channels.

I did not lose interest, but I was puzzled. It seemed to me that the kind of discussions COCU held might be valuable, but could have been more valuable under the broader umbrella of the Faith and Order Commission of the NCC. The same denominations that were saying they could not give the commission enough budget to keep more than one staff executive on board were paying for two or three in COCU offices. What COCU was doing, as I viewed it, was draining money, time and interest away from the NCC, and making it even less important to the movement for Christian unity.

Thinking of the original COCU proposal, I had the oblique thought that the timing may have held a significance for Dr. Blake that was not generally noticed. He was in San Francisco for an NCC meeting in December of 1960, and while there made his call for merger at the Episcopal cathedral. It was James A. Pike's cathedral, and Bishop Pike, adept at self-promotion, had many people calling COCU the Blake-Pike proposal for a while.

December of 1960 was the month after the election of the nation's first Catholic president, the Democratic candidate John F. Kennedy, showing significant erosion of the traditional Protestant dominance in the public arena. And the final weeks of the presidential campaign were the weeks of Dr. Blake's preparation for his address. There was still a good deal of Protestant-Catholic tension in those days, and the NCC was at odds with Catholics over such issues as parochial school aid, as it still is. And Dr. Blake came from a Midwestern Republican background, though I guess that influence had weakened by the time of the Nixon presidency.

From the standpoint of theology and church structure, the four denominations Dr. Blake asked to merge were not necessarily the most logical candidates. But they were the ones in the Protestant sphere making the strongest effort to influence national policy. I could imagine Dr. Blake thinking to himself, "You Protestants will never get anywhere in the Kennedy years unless you get together."

I never had an opportunity to report on the famous Bishop Pike. But I did hear him a couple of times. In the 1950s, when he was dean of the Cathedral of St. John the Divine in New York, I caught a sermon of his that I still remember–a description of three valued traditions available in the Episcopal Church: high church, low church and broad church. Then in the 1960s, while I was living in Virginia, I head him speak in Richmond after he had gained a national following as a liberal challenger of church conservatives. Many there were who felt a need for extensive change in the church, so anyone who presented himself as a general in the war against the status quo could expect a following. But I quickly decided Bishop Pike was not the one to lead us into more promising land. For one thing, it was immediately evident the bishop exhibited much too much ego. And his taste for the risqué showed some lack of seriousness. There are those who think it is something of a turn-on to hear a clergyman talking dirty, and Bishop Pike played to that a bit.

My negative impressions solidified when I skimmed through the biography written later by his two friends and supporters, William Stringfellow and Anthony Towne: *The Death and Life of Bishop Pike* (Doubleday, 1974). They reported that his funeral was attended by his wife and two ex-wives (pp. 201-02), that as Bishop of California he also had a mistress who committed suicide with the written complaint that "you are unloving" (pp. 56-66), that he was an alcoholic picked up three times by San Francisco police (p. 332), that he claimed to have talked with various dead people in seances with various mediums (p. 141), that he gave little attention to his four children (p. 332), that his associate, John Cogley, at the Center for the Study of Democratic Institutions, reported the bishop was known for "glibness and raw publicity seeking" (p. 167) and that he practiced "cavalier promiscuity" (p. 164). That was Bishop Pike according to his friends; whether his enemies had worse things to say I do not know.

That matter of talking with mediums could be viewed as a curiosity. But people who pride themselves on broad-mindedness may be susceptible to matters of such sort. To speak again of the Cathedral of St. John the Divine, I was there in 1972 covering a conference on parapsychology, introduced by the conspicuously broad-minded bishop, Paul Moore Jr. In a story for RNS, I reported that William V. Rauscher, rector of Christ Episcopal Church in Woodbury, New Jersey, and president of a psychic group, Spiritual Frontiers, hailed the conference as evidence of the growing acceptability of the field (March 27). He said J. B. Rhine of Durham, North Carolina, had established the truth of mental telepathy, and the church could be "a great interpreter for all this." He brought first hand experience of the "spiritual frontiers" to relate: Arthur Ford, a medium, had enabled him to get a message from a dead child for delivery to the parents. Another conference speaker, Martin Ebon, would not be outdone, and testified to watching another psychic, Eileen Garrett, exorcise a barn in the Pennsylvania Dutch country, where the spirit of a man who committed suicide had been frightening the horses. Bishop Moore indicated a slight hesitation about jumping into all this, but as a good liberal recommended the value of "openness to every kind of human experience." Now, in the era of ecology, I suppose he would add that we should also be open to the experience of the horses.

The life of Bishop Pike ended sadly in 1969, when, at age 56, he took the wrong route during a trip to the Holy Land, a wrong route literally as well as symbolically. He had flamboyantly, as most everything he did was undertaken flamboyantly, announced he was leaving the church, and a reorganization at the Center for the Study of Democratic Institutions cost him his post there. Setting off on a trip then to check out the Middle East and walk where Jesus walked, or perhaps drive where Jesus may have walked, he and his third wife, Diane Kennedy, drove a rented car into the Dead Sea area, went the wrong way at one juncture, got stuck, walked for a while and took shelter in a cave. He stayed there while she went looking for help, then tried going on, but eventually fell onto a ledge, where she and a rescue team found him dead six days later (September 7).

He not only took the wrong route in his car, but was taking the wrong route in the journey of his soul. Despite turning against the church, he was still hooked on religion, and had become enamored of S. G. F. Brandon's (worthless) thesis about Jesus operating as some kind of political zealot (Stringfellow and Towne, pp. 40, 169). Pursuing this interest, he had decided it would help a lot if he could go over and find something called the "historical" Jesus out there somewhere. So he arrived at the idea that he could get to the bottom of things, spiritually-wise, by an on-the-spot investigation in the area where the Dead Sea Scrolls were found, a view quite naïve though presented with some gloss of sophistication.

Georg W. F. Hegel pointed out the reality that Jesus has significance because he is present, and is not merely a figure of the dead past (*History of Philosophy,* tr. E. S. Haldane and Frances H. Simson, I, 73-74). And we could say, not merely a figure of faraway places. In *The Christology of Hegel,* James Yerkes noted that "a merely historical preoccupation" with the Jesus of 2000 years ago could do little for us, but was surpassed by "the worship of the believing community" (State University of New York Press, 1983, p. 218). Contrariwise, Bishop Pike imagined that he had moved scientifically into new areas of intellect beyond such simple believers. Casting aside the convictions of ordinary Christians, he would be the one to get back into the first century and dig up the real Jesus. But his sad ending only confirmed redundantly that a man who cannot find Jesus in the Scriptures or in Christian worship will not find him by wandering off out into the wilderness of Judea.

Now to look at another piece of the NCC record: When John F. Kennedy was running for president, the Bible thumpers in Houston were not the only ones warning about the dangers of his supposed submission to the Bishop of Rome. It seems passing strange that any clergy would demand that a public official promise never to let his church membership influence his actions. But some did. Among those spreading alarms about the danger to American freedoms, a group more respectable than the Houstonites included Norman Vincent Peale of New York's Marble Collegiate Church. When some flak came

SIDEBARS

back, he quickly bailed out, recognizing that his column could lose newspaper outlets and that his book sales and lecture invitations could decline. But he remained a friend of the defeated Republican, Richard M. Nixon, and when Mr. Nixon did get elected, could still be found in his corner.

While President Nixon was making his opening to China, I saw a report that it had the backing of Dr. Peale. I thought there could be a story in his reaction, because at an earlier stage he had joined a couple of other political conservatives in a condemnation of the NCC for advocating such a move. To be precise, the NCC as a body had not taken an official stand on the issue. But in 1958, its Department of International Affairs sponsored a conference in Cleveland that came out for admission of China to the UN and for diplomatic recognition of China by the United States–actual China, leaving aside the pretense that Taiwan equaled China. And this more or less represented the drift of opinion in NCC circles.

But Dr. Peale had joined with Daniel Poling of the *Christian Herald* magazine and others of the sort that had little use for the NCC anyway, and said this call for recognizing the diabolical communist government of Red China should be repudiated by all good Christian folk. He was part of a Clergymen's Committee, auxiliary to a Committee of One Million attacking the NCC, that said the statement on China was inconsistent with "the clear principles of morality and the Christian faith." And now here was Mr. Nixon reversing directions and going over to talk and smile and drink with those very same godless communists, and Dr. Peale was saying, "How nice," or something of the sort.

My idea was not to indict the positive thinker for inconsistent thinking, but to get a "how my mind has changed" story. I thought it would interest readers to hear him explain how he had moved over the years to a new outlook on China, and had come to entertain thoughts that formerly seemed unthinkable, however positively one thought.

I was writing for RNS in those days, and got an appointment with Dr. Peale to do a story for it (March 8, 1972). But when he came into the room where I had been told to wait, nowhere near his office, he showed no interest in reflecting on his changing views. To start with, he really did not care to be interviewed by reporters at all, I surmised. Like most any of us, he would no doubt prefer to deliver his wisdom before the adoring multitudes without interruption, and then let people line up to tell him how wonderful he was. It could not be as much fun to sit with some skeptical reporter asking how does what you are saying now square with your talk of yesteryear, and why were you so worked up over whatever, and which of your positions really come out of your Christianity anyway, and which are just your Republican politics? He had been through it a few times, and felt no enthusiasm in his advancing years for what he seemed to fear now loomed as another episode. He was not doing any positive thinking about me, for sure.

He did acknowledge that his views on China had changed, but he would offer no explanation for the change, except some general comment about changing times. He professed not even to remember his earlier condemnation of the NCC, and when I showed him a copy of the RNS story (January 15, 1959) about his action to refresh his recollection, he declined to read it, and said people had often used his name without his approval.

I came away with the impression he really did not have much insight into how his mind had changed, and was not just holding out on me. Eventually I concluded that his mind had changed mostly because a leader he greatly admired, Richard M. Nixon, had said it was time for change. He proudly showed me a Great Wall postcard sent to him by the Nixons from China, written by Mrs. Nixon and signed "Pat," with the initials "RN," presumably penned by the president, on the side. He also said the churches should leave China relations to Mr. Nixon, and then to the people who might want to go over for business purposes. Billy Graham had said he hoped to preach in China some day, but Dr. Peale said he would only want to visit there, and thought preaching was not "the thing to do now." In a further comment, he warned that American influence would corrupt the morals of the Chinese, which was perhaps not an altogether wrong prediction.

One lesson I took from all this concerned the role of political leadership. Politicians can serve effectively when they act in ways that build and hold confidence. So when it is time to take steps that break with the conventional wisdom, people will go along because of a personal trust that has been established. And it is not just the unwashed and unlearned at the bottom who need to be pulled along in this way, but influentials such as Dr. Peale.

Some people with NCC leanings took rather much pride in the thought that even Richard M. Nixon had finally come around to admitting the validity of a position they had recommended a dozen years earlier. I harbored some reservations about that, however. In the first place, it did not necessarily follow that if reaching out to the communist government of China was a good idea in the 1970s, it would have been a good idea when the NCC conference called for it in 1958. Analysts might plausibly argue that Chairman Mao and party had to learn a few lessons from the failure of their Great Leap Forward, go through the break with the Soviet Union that left them in need of international alliances and then experience the trauma of the Cultural Revolution and its manifold disasters before they would be ready for any constructive talks with the United States. Another reservation about the action of the NCC was that it came before development of any constituency support. Whatever logic might have undergirded the declaration, the people represented by the NCC leadership were in no way ready for such a proposal. So nothing came of it except a further loss of confidence in the NCC.

To go beyond that, I thought President Nixon's change of China policy itself need not be celebrated uncritically. Edwin O. Reischauer, the U.S. ambassador to Japan under Presidents Kennedy and Johnson, spoke at a meeting I covered during this time, and complained about the disregard the Nixon administration showed the Japanese (RNS, May 10, 1972). Although they were loyal allies, and had proved their loyalty by remaining aligned with U.S. policy on China even when they might have considered it not especially favorable to their interests, they were now questioning the reliability of the United States as a partner because of the way President Nixon went about his China moves. "Not only did we fail to consult with them on the change," Ambassador Reischauer said, "we didn't even tell them." So the United States suffered a loss of Japanese trust from the melodramatic secretiveness of President Nixon and his security adviser, Henry A. Kissinger.

Caveating just once more, the way President Nixon handled this shift in foreign policy as a stage drama, with its preparatory work kept hidden behind the curtains, deprived the American public of political education. The nation needed a policy debate to help people understand what was involved in its relationship with China, and why leaders such as President Nixon had come to believe it was time to visit Peking. Instead, the change was put through by theatrics, and the American people remained as incapable as before of giving any reasoned response to that mischievous old question, "Who lost China?" And the way Americans even today squabble over the relationship with China—corporations begging for business, moralists castigating on human rights—does not exhibit much greater maturity.

If you want to understand the weakness of the NCC, I would say one pervasive, underlying factor has been putting itself at odds with the business community. Although there were elements of this from the beginnings of the Federal Council, many leaders of the business world were drawn into partnership with leaders of the ecumenical movement for a time. But that element died out or drifted away.

A partnership of ministers and businessmen had earlier made possible the existence of ecumenical institutions such as Union Seminary, founded in New York in 1836 as part of an effort to move beyond the bitterness and pettiness of conflict between and within denominations. Several substantial businessmen helped get the seminary underway, and one of them, Knowles Taylor, made his home available for the initial planning meeting, and chaired it.

The seminary got a boost in its early days from a bequest by another well-to-do businessman, James Roosevelt. This was money originally intended for his daughter's son, James Roosevelt Bayley, but redirected when the grandson, an Episcopal minister, became a Catholic in 1842. The grandson, who later became the first Catholic Bishop of Newark and then Archbishop of Baltimore, could have been influenced by the example of his aunt, Elizabeth Ann Bayley Seton, who left the Episcopal Church to become a Catholic in 1805, and in 1975 would become the first person born in the United States to be canonized.

In the twentieth century, the partnership of church and business leaders became especially notable in the career of John R. Mott, a Methodist layman and YMCA executive who chaired an important ecumenical gathering in Edinburgh in 1910, and who then played a central role in activities that led to formation of the World Council of Churches in 1948. He made diligent and persistent efforts to build personal ties with many of the top businessmen of the United States, and he could always count on them when he needed financing for his projects. C. Howard Hopkins, author of the biography, *John R. Mott* (Eerdmans, 1979), reported various occasions, such as an extended round-the-world tour in 1912-13, when he went to John D. Rockefeller Jr. and other such friends for the wherewithal (p. 387).

The ecumenical councils have not lately had anyone who could operate at the same level. In the earlier years of the NCC, it drew some laymen of national stature. J. Irwin Miller, chairman of the Cummins Engine Company of Columbus, Indiana, and a member of various national entities such as presidential commissions, served as NCC president for the 1960-63 term. Arthur S. Fleming, Secretary of Health, Education and Welfare under President Eisenhower and holder of various other prestige jobs at other times, took the NCC presidency for the 1966-1969 term. Charles C. Parlin, a Methodist layman who had a successful law career in New York and became board chairman of Citibank, not only served on the NCC board, but got a place on the World Council's six-member presidium, beginning with the New Delhi Assembly of 1961 and continuing through the Uppsala Assembly of 1968. I remember him telling about his experience at the Assembly in Sweden, where he learned from a luncheon seating chart that his wife was to sit beside a man he had never heard of, one H. M. Kung. When the luncheon got underway, she found her companion was His Majesty the King. And the NCC drew in some other laymen of note. But I have not been aware of any U.S. layman of national stature giving the councils much time in recent decades.

In the particular case of Mr. Parlin, I got it through the grapevine that when a campaign against the involvement of U.S. banks in South Africa began gathering steam in the late 1960s, church leaders did not draw on the counsel of this layman with high level knowledge of the banking world, but alienated him with public attacks on his and other banks. This might also be judged a proper procedure if church leaders wanted to operate as a small protest group, but hardly so if their goal was drawing the total Christian community into some kind of common effort.

The NCC may have let Saul D. Alinsky, the radical community organizer and founder of the Industrial Areas Foundation, steer it into more confrontation with the business community than would have happened by natural processes. He was the son of Russian Jewish immigrants, and developed a close working relationship with the Catholic Church in Chicago. In the biography, *Let Them Call Me Rebel* (Knopf, 1989), Sanford D. Horwitt wrote, "Alinsky's own interest in the Catholic Church centered largely on its politics, both internal and in relation to other institutions and forces in American society. The rituals and dogma of religion were of far less interest, and indeed, among friends, he could be openly contemptuous about not only Catholic rituals but religious rituals generally" (p. 196). When he went to a seder one year, he "hammed it up" and "poked fun" at the entire ceremony (p. 197). But like a few other people, he wanted to use the political potential he saw in the parochial and diocesan structures of the Catholic Church, and some of their clergy apparently welcomed an alliance with a man of such contempt for religion because it might enable them to enjoy his kind of power. And then church leaders elsewhere wanted his help in pursuing similar goals.

After a black riot in Rochester, New York, in 1965, a few people there brought Mr. Alinsky in to help them organize a campaign to deal with the issues raised. Kodak was based in Rochester, and a principal objective was to pressure it into hiring more blacks. Out of this campaign came the idea of using the voting rights of sympathetic stockholders to squeeze a company. Biographer Horwitt reported that two workers in the campaign, Herbert White of the Rochester Board of Urban Ministry, and Alinsky organizer Ed Chambers, each claimed credit for the idea. But Mr. Alinsky "took full credit for inventing the bigger and more dramatic scenario of a stock proxy campaign" (p. 495). The Alinsky-related organization in Rochester, FIGHT, bought ten shares of Kodak so it could send representatives to the annual stockholders meeting in 1967. But Mr. Alinsky also got some of the national Protestant denominations to use their Kodak stock in support of his campaign.

The churches had accumulated extensive portfolios through investment of their pension, endowment and reserve funds, but they had not previously been known to use their stockholder rights to fight management. Out of Mr.

Alinsky's campaign in Rochester came a shift that made fighting management of the major corporations a routine part of every year's agenda.

In the years since Mr. Alinsky's death in 1972, his influence has continued. In 1987, I was a little surprised to see Cardinal O'Connor going to the South Bronx and encouraging the confrontation tactics that a coalition of Catholic and Protestant churches called South Bronx Churches were learning from their affiliation with the Industrial Areas Foundation (NC, November 24).

At the NCC, a Corporate Information Center was set up, with Frank White, a United Church of Christ layman, as director. It soon made a publicity splash with a critically-oriented report charging that some of the churches denouncing the Vietnam War were making a lot of money out of it through their investments in war industries. This way of trying to embarrass the churches did not bring the Center much financial support, and in 1973 Mr. White's job ceased to exist. But meanwhile, Timothy H. Smith, a Canadian who attended Union Seminary in New York but did not secure ordination, had become executive secretary of an Interfaith Committee on Social Responsibility that had been formed by some church agencies bothered by a mining project in Puerto Rico.

In 1974, Mr. White and Mr. Smith joined forces to form the Interfaith Center on Corporate Responsibility as an organization related to the NCC, though managed by its own board. Mr. White did not stay long, and Mr. Smith moved into the leadership position, where he remained the key churchman of the corporate responsibility movement until he took another job in 2000. The Center has not been able to employ a large staff, but it has gotten an unusually large amount of free work from its board members and constituency committees. Although it was formed under largely Protestant auspices, and Mr. Smith was Protestant, United Methodist, Catholic nuns have been especially prominent in its activities, finding here a satisfying outlet for energies produced by efforts to find new ways of being nuns in the post-Vatican II era.

The corporate responsibility movement became a continuing by-product of "the sixties," and it retained that style into later decades. In 1988, the editor of *Christianity and Crisis,* Leon Howell, asked me to write a general assessment of the movement and the Center (published March 21), and in an introduction I gave something of the flavor:

"Stepping into the offices of the Interfaith Center on Corporate Responsibility (ICCR), on the fifth floor of the Interchurch Center in New York, you wonder if you have wandered into a residual enclave of the sixties. The makeshift, the unshelved clutter of campaigns past, the work space improvisation, the poster-betaped wall, the annotated clipping about another outrage of the oppressor, the dishevelment, the casual dress and manner of people whose place in the line of authority seems to lack clear definition—all suggest a bivouac for movement people who may soon be called back into the streets to escalate the struggle, and who avoid too much tidiness lest they be coopted into the system.

"Yet, there, central to the operation, what the ICCR is and how it has become, sits director Timothy H. Smith, who could easily pass for white middle class, and seems more the type to devise reasonable compromises with executives in suits and suites than to mount the barricades. You cannot quite tell whether the corporate responsibility movement–now at something like age 15 going on 25–wants to run counter-culture or establish a niche for itself in the established order."

But you are reading it here for the first time. The editors for some reason decided they would not print such words, and made me write a more pedestrian introduction: "This is the season when most corporations . . . ." *etc. etc.* The magazine's own shop had a good deal of the same sixties culture, and the people there perhaps wanted it described in more celebratory terms, if at all.

I had written several articles about the corporate responsibility movement before that one, and have written a great many since. But I still do not know exactly what I think about it. On the one hand, it seems like an obviously commendable program for the churches to give moral examination to the companies they are making money out of. But there could be questions about whether much is really accomplished. The churches file a host of resolutions every year, challenging dozens of corporations on their manufacture of military equipment, on their treatment of employees and customers, on their operations overseas, on their policies regarding the environment and on various other matters. They never win any of the votes on those resolutions, and proclaim victory if they get three per cent, the minimum required under rules of the Securities and Exchange Commission for them to be able to bring up the same issue again the next year. But things sometimes do move, and the churches can feel they have been part of the movement. After Kodak, the next major stockholder action was a resolution filed by the Episcopal Church in 1971 calling on General Motors to get out of South Africa. And South Africa remained a principal focus of the corporate responsibility movement until whites there gave up on apartheid. So the churches could feel they at least contributed to the pressure that got Nelson Mandela out of prison and into the presidency.

Now on the other hand, I reported in my article for *Christianity and Crisis* that the Christian Brothers Investment Services, which advised religious orders and other Catholic bodies, was a new ICCR member, and its president, Brother Raymond Blixt, told me his clients did not want to let confrontation become the dominant tone of their relationship with the corporations they invested in. But I added, "To some people, it appears that the mainline churches have already let the combative posture of the ICCR become their primary mode of relating to the corporate world. This has produced, they believe, a considerable degree of estrangement between the national religious leadership and the national business leadership, to the detriment of both sides and of the nation."

When business leaders found themselves attacked on ethical grounds by the churches, and sometimes accused of multiple evils, and accused every year, they would doubtless feel not particularly close to the religious leadership. And those who were members of these churches might fail to feel any team spirit. According to the Alinsky biography, William Vaughn, board chairman of Kodak, went to New York and tried to explain the position of his company to a top Presbyterian official, but reported that this official "just plain wasn't interested in listening" (p. 497).

It was such church officials who set the tone and direction of the NCC. On one side, the NCC theoretically was meant to be inclusive, ecumenical, drawing in people of diverse views and attempting to forge some kind of broader community. But on the other side, it had people who wanted to take a sectarian stance, or the stance of a fringe political party in opposition, siding against most everybody currently wielding influence. If you adopt the latter approach, positioning yourself to fight anyone who has a leadership role in "the system," who is going to finance your system?

The question became more pointed in the 1990s, when Albert M. Pennybacker, a Disciples of Christ minister who had held pastorates in Cleveland and Fort Worth, set up an Ecumenical Development Initiative to raise endowment funds for the NCC and the World Council. The planning got underway in 1990, but I came into it only in 1992, when I interviewed Mr. Pennybacker and reported that the effort, based in New York, was formally launched August 1 (EPS, October 10).

At that time, he could tell me about drawing up a list of two hundred potential donors, or donor families, he thought might come up with gifts in the range of a million dollars each. And he was setting an initial goal of fifty million dollars. I wondered aloud whether the kind of church members who accumulated that kind of money would be disposed to turn over such amounts to the NCC and WCC. But from Mr. Pennybacker's perspective, the money was as good as in the bank. The next year, he sent out a promotional packet announcing even more ambitious goals: "We seek $150 million by the year 2000 for the six specific initiatives described in this package of materials."

One of those initiatives was a campaign to raise a ten million dollar endowment for the work of Faith and Order, and in 1993 I reported on a separate launching for it (EPS, June 26; CNS, June 29). But there were not many reports of progress on that or other parts of the fund drive, and eventually a great many negative rumblings came from people who would rather not be quoted. And when the whole operation was ingloriously shut down at the end of 1998, we did not get any report on what had been accomplished. I had no assignment to do a story, and I do not know whether, as some knowledgeable people intimated, Mr. Pennybacker spent more money on his operation than he raised. But evidently nobody could see enough success to justify a press release.

In effect, Mr. Pennybacker was trying to reignite the ecumenical fires of the 1950s, but too much water had passed over the dam. He named the Faith and Order fund for Greek Archbishop Iakovos, which had its odd aspect. Archbishop Iakovos had taken a pioneering role representing the Ecumenical Patriarch at the World Council in the 1950s. But lately he had been in the news more for suspending the participation of the Orthodox in the NCC over unhappiness with its liberal Protestant elements, and their moves on matters such as homosexuality (EPS, November 10, 1991). There was some expectation that the Iakovos name would motivate rich Greek-Americans to contribute, but my information indicated that rich Greek-Americans would have liked to see their archbishop go even further than suspension, and break NCC ties permanently.

Giving the project another and still odder twist, Mr. Pennybacker sought the endorsement of Ronald Reagan. This took a certain amount of gall, inasmuch as the NCC had so explicitly declared itself in direct opposition to almost everything the Reagan presidency stood for. And now asking if he would let the NCC use his name to raise money. A staff aide to Mr. Reagan sent the requested permission, but there was not even an endorsing letter with the signature of the former president to show potential donors. Nor do I remember ever hearing of Mr. Reagan himself giving anything. And the result was about the same when Mr. Pennybacker also got permission to use the names of former Presidents Jimmy Carter and Gerald Ford.

All of this looked like an effort to resurrect a spirit of ecumenism that existed before the 1960s. From the beginnings of the NCC in the 1950s, right wing types hated it, but in those days it had the ties to more progressive elements of the business and political communities. However, when the directions taken in its subsequent journey caused even those supporters to grow disaffected and drop out, and no replacements to sign on, the NCC and WCC lost the financial strength of those ties, and also the capacity those talented and resourceful laymen brought for operating in the world of public affairs.

One way you could interpret the NCC might be in relation to George S. McGovern, the Democratic candidate for president who was so soundly defeated in 1972, later lost his seat as U.S. Senator from South Dakota and then became something of a Harold Stassen joke as a perpetually unsuccessful candidate to get another presidential nomination. In an article for the *Christian Science Monitor,* I reported shortly after the 1972 election (November 29) that "virtually all the NCC leadership and staff were McGovern supporters." Recalling that Mr. Nixon was the main alternative, one could consider McGovern support a tribute to the NCC, as well as to Mr. McGovern. But it meant that the NCC leadership was somewhat distant from the American people as a whole, and even today, I venture to guess, most people who cast a vote in 1972 would probably say Mr. Nixon was a more capable president than Mr. McGovern would have been, and pursued policies more in line with what they wanted.

But aside from all that, for the NCC, supposedly seeking to represent the broadest possible range of American Christians, it was significant that the outlook of its leadership was not broadly shared. So we might begin by recalling that NCC leaders have been mostly McGovernitish, for good and for ill. In Senator McGovern, son of a Methodist minister, the Christianity of his father had ceased to hold religious interest, but had become mostly social ethics. While NCC leaders did not go that far, they, too, at times seemed to let issues of public policy dominate, and religious conviction recede.

In these circles, the main idea is that America is mostly something bad, and the goal is to do a job of genetic engineering that will make it into some animal of another species, an idea I cannot imagine will draw the support of many American Christians. When Rev. Walker, a black Baptist minister who had headed the Interreligious Foundation for Community Organization (IFCO), became head of the NCC's Church and Society Division, I interviewed him for the *Christian Science Monitor* (January 3, 1974). Explaining his view of the need for the churches to address problems such as racism, particularly the "built-in racism" of institutions, he charged that America was "one of the most repressive societies in the history of mankind," a judgment the editors did not find space to print. Aside from questions that might be asked about Rev. Walker's qualifications for making comparisons with all the other societies in the history of mankind, I wondered how the NCC could expect to inspire support with leadership of that outlook. Most of the people who gave money to pay the bills of the NCC and its member denominations were themselves pretty much in the mainstream of American society. And I could not imagine they

SIDEBARS

would feel particularly generous toward an organization that was dumping on it so much.

When Claire Randall did later dismiss Rev. Walker, she said her motivation was his failure to operate within his budget, not his approach to issues. But he counter-asserted that the action was evidence of an NCC move to the right. Which makes him distinctive. I do not believe many other people have been able to perceive a move to the right in the vicinity of the NCC.

Writing about the NCC, you could cover most all the controversial issues. But a couple have been so contentious, they deserve separate reports. One is abortion.

ABORTION

CHAPTER TEN

Pierre Rinfret came back to the pressroom during the 1990 Al Smith dinner, looking for someone to give him a little notice. He was a political unknown, but a businessman of some means and some interest in the public sphere, and so had won the honor of going to slaughter that year in the election to decide who would be governor of New York for the next four years. Mario M. Cuomo was running for reelection, and Mr. Rinfret served Republicans as the sacrificial lamb, while politicians like George E. Pataki waited for a more favorable alignment of the planets.

Killing time there at the Waldorf-Astoria Hotel before the program started, we reporters had to cool our heels in a holding pen while the big givers finished their dinner in the grand ballroom. So I took the opportunity for dialogue with Mr. Rinfret.

He was identified as a Catholic and as a supporter of abortion, and some people had commented on a tension there, as they did so often in regard to Mr. Cuomo. I asked Mr. Rinfret whether he considered himself a good and loyal Catholic, and he assured me, oh, certainly, he truly did. Seeking a way to tie him in more directly, I asked him along the way for the name of his parish, assuming this was something a good Catholic would normally know. But my question took Mr. Rinfret beyond his depth. He did know what part of Manhattan's East Side was home, however, so together we could eventually deduce that his parish was St. Jean Baptiste, which had a large church on Lexington Avenue.

I knew St. Jean Baptiste as the parish of Catholics living in East Side affluence. But as a sidebar, it had a place in an article I had written some years earlier poking a little fun at certain expressions of the relics cult. Protestants studying church history learn that there was this cult of relics in medieval times, but then there was the Reformation and Renaissance, and now the modern world. If you wake up one day, however, and become aware that the cult of relics continues even in a time some people groping for more newness call post-modern, you can be a little astonished.

Quite a bit astonished, actually, in my case, to find that the Church of St. Jean Baptiste had a piece of Jesus' grandmother set out for you to see and reverence. (You are not supposed to ask which grandmother, but if you just have to know, the one identified since the apocryphal infancy narrative, Protoevangelium of James, written in perhaps the second century, as St. Ann, wife of St. Joachim.) St. Jean Baptiste parish, as the spelling suggests, was founded by French priests, and a member of their order, the Blessed Sacrament Fathers, brought over a tiny piece of bone that is reverenced as part of the skeleton of the mother of Mary.

My article reporting this and other marvels was accepted by editors of the *Christian Century*, a Protestant weekly I occasionally wrote for in the 1960s and 1970s. Tied to no specific event, the article was regarded as one of those timeless features that could be used whenever, and was held in reserve for some week when material might be in short supply. And held and held too long. A new editor-in-chief, James A. Wall, came on the scene, looked at my article, decided I was anti-Catholic and killed it. He simultaneously delivered the final blow to kill my interest in writing for the *Christian Century*, an interest already weakened by heavy-handed editing and microscopic payments. But the magazine does not appear to have suffered from my withdrawal.

I was also surprised to find that New York had a piece of the True Cross, located in a small room off the basement church of St. Francis of Assisi, near Pennsylvania Station and Madison Square Garden. It has been a scoffer's cliché to say there are enough pieces of the True Cross around to build another Spanish Armada. But seeing the one at St. Francis of Assisi Church made me question that. It is only a tiny sliver that I would judge might weigh no more than a postage stamp. One beam could provide wood enough to put such a sliver in every diocese of the world.

Further awareness of the continuing cult of relics came in the summer of 1993, when I went to Geneva to serve as interim editor of Ecumenical Press Service (EPS). One weekend, I took the train to Reims to see the champagne industry centered there. Dom Perignon, a Benedictine monk, was said to have been the one in charge "the night they invented champagne," and was buried at a church in the nearby village of Hautvillers, where his abbey was located until the French Revolution blew it away. So I got myself out to Hautvillers to do homage at the final resting place of this benefactor of mankind.

His location was marked at the head of the central aisle of the village church. But looking around, I discovered that part of the Emperor Constantine's mother, Helen, seemed to reside there as well, brought in the early Middle Ages, taken into hiding during the Revolution and then returned.

When I went to Santiago de Compostela, Spain, to cover the Fifth World Conference on Faith and Order as part of my EPS job, I was intrigued to find under the cathedral altar there a box said to contain the Apostle James or, in Spanish, St. Iago. After the Muslims gained control of Jerusalem, and pilgrimage to the Holy Land became difficult for Europeans, it was fortuitously discovered that the body of James had been brought for burial on the far upper side of Spain, where he was said to have preached on a missionary journey before returning to be martyred by Herod's grandson, Herod Agrippa (Acts 12:2). So pilgrimage could now be made to the apostle's tomb at the place that came to be named for him, and a kind of contact made with the Jerusalem origins of Christianity. Of the apostolic inner circle of Peter, James and John (Mark 9:2), tradition had already placed the bones of Peter in Rome, and John was tied by the book of Revelation to the island of Patmos, off the coast of Asia Minor. James was the ranking figure not yet taken. So Spain took him, and its scallop shell became his logo, as you can sometimes see on his statues. Another kind of contact can also be made today by gourmets dining on the scallop dish known by its French name, Coquilles St. Jacques.

The Evangelist Mark lies under the altar of the cathedral in Venice, I was told when I visited there. And walking down a street in Rome, I stumbled upon one of the lesser churches with a couple of the lesser known of the twelve apostles in the crypt. And I have since become aware that a good many churches claim to house pieces of people from the time of Jesus.

But to me, the relic at St. Jean Baptiste was just about the ultimate, though I guess there are other parts of St. Ann at other churches. A relic of Jesus or Mary might rank higher, but anyone claiming to exhibit their bones would not likely receive the approval of authorities in Rome. Although: in a biography of Martin Luther, *Here I Stand* (Abingdon-Cokesbury, 1950), Roland H. Bainton reported that Luther's prince, Frederick the Wise, had relics of Christ that included "one piece from his swaddling clothes, thirteen from his crib, one wisp of straw, one piece of the gold brought by the Wise Men and three of the myrrh, one strand of Jesus' beard, one of the nails driven into his hands, one piece of bread eaten at the Last Supper, one piece of the stone on which Jesus stood to ascend into heaven . . . ." (p. 71).

Talk of the St. Jean Baptiste parishioner Pierre Rinfret and abortion, however, was ado over relatively little compared with the debates over Governor Cuomo and his zealous support for abortion rights. Mr. Cuomo was a Catholic who would never have any difficulty telling you the name of his parish or the minutiae of its history. He grew up immersed in the life of the Catholic Church, attending parochial school as a youngster, graduating from St. John's University, run by the Vincentian Fathers, and from its law school, and then taking an active layman's role in church affairs. He is even said to have given pro-life talks at one time, before his entry onto the stage of bigger-time politics.

In *Diaries of Mario M. Cuomo* (Random House, 1984), his reflections on his first winning campaign for governor in 1982, he commented that he would rather be at a breakfast of his parish, Immaculate Conception in Queens, than at the Al Smith dinner in the grand ballroom of the Waldorf-Astoria, where he felt the clergy were cool to him (p. 335).

He had also given attention to religion in its intellectual form. I several times heard or read of him citing Pierre Teilhard de Chardin, a French Jesuit priest who specialized in anthropology but also wrote some theological-philosophical books that gained considerable éclat. Since normal people can hardly even say "Pierre Teilhard de Chardin," Governor Cuomo could give his followers a sense that he was operating on the outer frontiers of religious thought, far beyond where bishops and cardinals and the like got bogged down. His political persona, meanwhile, remained that of the committed layman, in true and humble piety protecting the liberties of the people against the power grabs of the ecclesiastical hierarchy.

To me as a reporter, all this mattered not so exceedingly one way or the other. But my curiosity was aroused by the continual appearance in news accounts of the background statement that Governor Cuomo, however zealously he championed abortion, was "personally opposed." A number of Catholic politicians had latched onto the "personally opposed" gambit as a way of justifying votes for abortion while continuing to claim an identity as loyal members of their church. But I had never been aware of Governor Cuomo using that phrase. And I began to wonder whether reporters and other writers in sympathy with his pro-abortion position were inserting it out of a desire to pacify his anti-abortion critics, and perhaps to give those abortion opponents otherwise supportive of his Democratic politics an easier conscience.

I knew of various formulations Mr. Cuomo had used to suggest that he, as a Catholic, in some fashion or another accepted the bishops' teaching against abortion, though the same he, as a governor, would say he had to support abortion rights. And he supported them with zeal, not sadly and reluctantly as some public officials might say pornography disgusted them personally, but that legal action against it would violate civil liberties. In a much-publicized speech at the University of Notre Dame (September 13, 1984), he said, "I accept the church's teaching on abortion." But a man as skilled in dialectic as Governor

Cuomo has to be scrutinized carefully. He did not go on to explain in what sense he accepted church teaching, and made no declaration in the nature of "I regard abortion as the destruction of innocent human life and consider it wrong." I never heard of him using the language of the Second Vatican Council, which linked abortion and infanticide as "abominable crimes" (*Church in the Modern World*, 51). But the "personally opposed," for who knows why most always in those direct quotes, continued to appear. I found in a 1993 book, Stephen L. Carter's *The Culture of Belief* (Basic Books, p. 62), the same phrase still presented as undebated fact, and still given in the usual quote marks. And, as usual, without any indication of the source of the quote.

One might expect to find something in the *Diaries,* a highly personal set of reflections, so I searched there. Governor Cuomo did bring up the abortion controversy in three or four places, but he only accused his opponents of misrepresenting his position, and never said what his position was. At one point, I wrote to a Catholic member of the clergy acquainted with Mr. Cuomo and to the governor's press office, asking each to tell me whether they knew of any occasion when the governor said he was "personally opposed." But neither answered.

My one opportunity to ask Mr. Cuomo himself about this came when I was invited to a press conference held in 1984 at the World Trade Center, where he had an office to supplement the one at the state capital in Albany. I was not normally notified when he was having press conferences, but for some reason my presence on this occasion was solicited, and I used the occasion to ask how he looked at abortion personally. He, building up a head of steam, refused with some fervor to say anything about what his personal position might be, or what the basis of his opposition to abortion might be if he had any.

After the press conference, he was to meet with a women's group, and they were brought in to watch him deal with the reporters. So as he responded to questions, he was partly playing to his spectator section. And since I identified myself as a reporter for the National Catholic News Service, he could identify me as the enemy, and display for his audience with what dispatch he could demolish this minion of the hierarchy.

But in response to a further question, he did say he rejected the position of those who called abortion murder. That was at least a bit of clarification, so I had a story with the lead:

"New York's Gov. Mario Cuomo, a Catholic who has projected himself into the forefront of debate over the politics of abortion, said at a press conference Aug. 9 that he disagreed with right-to-lifers who call abortion murder" (NC, August 10).

Then on September 9, I was truly surprised to read in *The New York Times* that Governor Cuomo was complaining to Michael Oreskes, an Albany reporter, about my story as an example of the misrepresentation he had to put up with. "I was asked at a press conference by a National Catholic Service (sic) reporter, 'Isn't abortion murder?' I gave a perfectly sound theological answer, 'It's murder if you think it's murder.'" But the story came out, the governor said, reporting that he had rejected the idea that abortion was the taking of human life.

I sent Governor Cuomo another copy of my story to remind him that I had not changed the point, but reported exactly what he had said, that he would not join abortion opponents who called it murder. Next, I got a note from him saying he had tried to reach me by telephone, and would I call back? But when I did, he was not ready to acknowledge that he had made a mistaken allegation. With his operating style of coming at you over the wire and reaching out of your phone receiver to grab you by the throat until you cried "uncle," he began going through his paces on what do the bishops want? We are in agreement theologically, but differ only on the politics. *Et cetera. Et cetera.* A good bit of *et cetera.* As though I were the spokesman for the Catholic bishops of the United States.

Moving with a politician's confidence that he can talk his way out of anything, the governor would admit error only in trying to explain such a complex position as he purported to hold on abortion at a press conference. And shifting slightly, he kept me still in the wrong because people less sophisticated than myself, as he flatteringly put it, would not catch the subtle distinctions. But in none of the *et cetera*s did he ever say whether he was "personally opposed" to abortion, or opposed in any other way. And my presence was not solicited for any more of his press conferences.

Daniel Patrick Moynihan, a Catholic who was a Democratic senator from New York, took the same stance as Governor Cuomo on abortion, and got some flak, but moved less aggressively and kept himself more to the margins of the abortion wars. After a few minutes of the easiest detective work anyone ever did, I got the senator's views a little into the limelight of the Catholic press momentarily, but nothing much came of it (NC, June 2, 1987). Without mentioning him by name, the Catholic archbishop of New York, John J. O'Connor, had critiqued his position on abortion in one of the cardinal's weekly columns in *Catholic New York,* the archdiocesan newspaper, and I naturally tried to figure out who he had in his gunsights.

In 1984, there had been something of a brouhaha when Cardinal O'Connor said the Democratic vice presidential candidate, Geraldine Ferraro, was not expressing a Catholic view on abortion, however Catholic she might be personally. But this column referred to "he," so I assumed we were not after a woman this time. The culprit was said to have one of 535 votes, which put him in Congress. I also assumed a battleship would not be sailing out to attack a motorboat, and thought of persons of prominence. Cardinal O'Connor called this figure an intellectual, one accusation never leveled against New York's other senator at the time, Alfonse D'Amato. There was also a reference to the number of years in office, so then all I had to do was call a Moynihan staffer to confirm that some quoted material in the column did come from the senator's literature. More than elementary, but the cardinal's communications department professed to have no idea who he was talking about. In any event Senator Moynihan made no rebuttal, so the story quickly died.

I had seen Senator Moynihan in action in 1980, when he went to Mineola, Long Island, to accept an honor from the Catholic League for Religious and Civil Rights, which wanted to encourage his efforts for parochial school aid (NC, October 6). The League had decided to answer yes to one of the difficult questions of politics: should you give luster to a politician who is working for one cause important to you but working against another? Some anti-abortion protesters condemned the League and came out to picket, and Senator Moynihan spent several minutes listening respectfully to them. "I am very much opposed to abortion," he said. "But I believe this is a choice that women have to make and that a woman has a right to make."

But I had no opportunity there to explore the grounds of his opposition. This was of some interest to me because I found it hard to imagine what a politician's rationale could be. If he really thought abortion was wrong, why would he not make some effort to stop it, or at the very least try to persuade people not to take that route? I do not suppose anyone would put abortion in the same category as something like skipping mass, where one might say, "I am personally opposed to skipping mass but do not think the government should make it a crime." Do those politicians consider abortion a form of child abuse? Could you hear one saying, "I am very much opposed to child abuse, but I believe this is a choice that parents have to make and that a parent has a right to make"? Would a pro-choice politician say something like, "I am personally opposed to the destruction of innocent human life and believe it is a violation of God's will, but every individual should have freedom of choice about whether he will destroy innocent human life or not, and it would be wrong for me to impose my views about this on others"? Is abortion to them like getting a tattoo, or putting a ring in your belly button, something they perhaps would never do, but think others should have the right to do if they wish? Can it be just a matter of esthetics, like personally shrinking from the sight of blood? What is the rationale?

During the months when the Supreme Court was getting ready to issue its abortion decision, Roe *v.* Wade, a task force appointed by the National Council of Churches (NCC) was writing a statement on the same subject with essentially the same conclusion: the individual woman should be left free to make the decision. The statement was not formally adopted as policy because the NCC's Orthodox members would not stand for it, and the document was issued more neutrally as a study paper. But Claire Randall, who chaired the task force, was then elected NCC general secretary. So it appeared that this pro-abortion position was unofficially that of the NCC as a whole. A few years later, I was reporting for the *Christian Science Monitor* (November 14, 1977) that the NCC had called for public funding of abortion for poor women, an indication the NCC started from an assumption that abortion was not only a good thing but a good thing of such basic importance it should by rights be provided for any who could not afford it.

I do not know how many people ever studied that study paper, but I did for a while, and the more I examined it the more confused and superficial it seemed. And it was almost totally devoid of any Christian grounding. It had a section on "theological perspectives," but treated theology as something any-one might rewrite at will according to predilections of the moment. The NCC told us that "it was believed" in "traditional" theology that God was the sole arbiter of life and death, but "theology today allows to humankind far more control over nature and life." Considering the prominence the ecology move-ment has gained today, and the form much of its theoretical undergirding has taken, we might wonder whether that statement would still be rated political-ly correct in NCC circles. But at the time, the authors presumably considered it cutting edge.

The NCC seemed commendable to me in avoiding the extremes. Like Governor Cuomo, it refused to call abortion murder. It also refused to dismiss it as just another "medical procedure" in the fashion of some pro-abortion rhetoric. "Abortion is never a desirable solution," it said. And at one point it could even speak of "affirming the sanctity of life," though only with a quick balancing off by "quality of life." But inside those limits, the statement left a host of questions, and I asked a good many of them in an article published by *Christianity and Crisis* (October 1, 1973). In the intervening years, an uncountable number of words have been written and spoken about abortion, but I cannot see that the discussion has advanced.

To me, abortion seems like a unique issue, not to be put under some gen-eral category with others. The proposal of Joseph L. Bernardin, Cardinal-Archbishop of Chicago, to group it with war, capital punishment and other topics under a tent called "consistent ethic of life" has some value no doubt,

SIDEBARS

but on the whole seems dubious. Each of those topics raises distinct questions and calls for its own analysis. I would make the linkage primarily in that an absolute position is impossible for any of them. Most people with any sort of moral outlook share a dislike for the destruction or diminishment of human life, and a few individuals may feel called to take a pacifist stand. But the complexities of life in this world bring most of us to avoid an absolute pacifism.

In a book published in 1951 in Zurich, and therefore unrelated to the more recent American debates, Karl Barth raised the question of abortion and declared that "a definite No must be the presupposition of all further discussion" (*Dogmatics, III/4,* 417). Why? "For the unborn child is from the very first a child . . . and not a thing, nor a mere part of the mother's body" (p. 415). But Professor Barth went on to argue that human life, including the life of the unborn, was "not an absolute," and ethical discussion had to allow for "the exceptional case" (p. 420). All efforts should be made to preserve life, however, and "genuine exceptions will thus be rare" (p. 421).

I would go with Professor Barth: when the question of abortion arises, the first response is No, but in some cases an examination of circumstances will show reason to allow an exception.

Asserting abortion views as an absolute—absolute condemnation of abortion or absolute affirmation of any woman's right to choose an abortion—seems to block movement in legal policy. Many Americans, possibly a large majority, could agree to some limits. But opponents who are absolutists cannot tolerate compromise that would legalize any abortion ever. And some fervent advocates of abortion insist on the right of any woman to abort at most any moment for most any reason that satisfies her, though I have found some in the pro-abortion sphere will hesitate about endorsing abortion of a fetus just because it is female.

In an interview with one Catholic obstetrician, I discovered that taking a position with the ring of absolute opposition might not work out so absolutely in practice. When the procedure called "partial birth abortion" by opponents, described clinically as dilation and extraction or dilation and evacuation, became a matter of national debate, I went down to get the opinion of James R. Jones, chief of obstetrics and gynecology at a major Catholic hospital in Greenwich Village, St. Vincent's (CNS, April 22, 1996). A physician committed to Catholic principles, Dr. Jones told me that abortion was never needed to deal with the complications women encountered in pregnancy. But he also said that he did set to and handle whatever problems came up, and that he did this knowing in some cases the fetus would almost certainly not survive.

Catholic ethical theory has a principle called "secondary effect," and Dr. Jones said he took that into account. If you are protecting someone's life and, in doing what you have to do, kill an attacker, you are not intending the death of a person, but only accepting the inevitability of this as a secondary effect. In the practicalities of a hospital operating room, the action of a Catholic physician such as Dr. Jones who opposes abortion may turn out operationally much like that of a doctor who says an abortion is needed. Though the descriptions of what happens may differ, no one need fear a Catholic physician like Dr. Jones will just leave a woman to die.

Cardinal O'Connor, among the foremost in opposing abortion, was among the foremost in supporting the Vietnam War while he was serving Uncle Sam as a Navy chaplain. For that war, which was not necessitated by any attack on the United States, large numbers of young Americans, many of them draftees, were taken to fight in Vietnam and, in the case of more than 50,000 of them, meet their deaths. And, what I would suppose was as big a moral issue for a chaplain, forced to become killers, taking the lives of more than a million Vietnamese, according to U.S. official estimates.

I assume Cardinal O'Connor was pro-life when he was defending all that, and defending it specifically as a clergyman, titling his book on the subject, *A Chaplain Looks at Vietnam* (World, 1968). "I believe that the war in Vietnam is very much the lesser of the many evils that would engulf us if we chose not to fight it," he wrote (p. 243). And he reported that he had been giving that message in talks to Marine officers. In the same 1968 book he also sought to encourage support for the war by giving a military judgment: "I believe we can win and are winning."

A pro-life position is not necessarily inconsistent with support of a war, in my view. I am not now and never have been a pacifist. Deciding what action is most pro-life in the complicated circumstances of the real world cannot be settled by absolute rules. So I would say Cardinal O'Connor was making a judgment on Vietnam that was morally possible for someone who was pro-life, but not pragmatically correct. I prefer the wisdom expressed by Reinhold Niebuhr in 1954, when some people wanted the United States to take over the Vietnam War from the departing French, and it appeared, perhaps deceptively, that top leaders of the United States had decided to keep their country out of that morass. "Would it not have been tragic," Professor Niebuhr wrote in the journal *Christianity and Society* (Vol. 19, Number 4), "to sacrifice American lives to hold the line for forces which are unable to hold their own against communism on the economic, moral and political level?"

In the political debates of the Cold War era, many conservatives assumed that if a group or nation was communist, it should be uncompromisingly fought, whatever other factors might be involved. Many liberals, conversely, tended to think that if other aspects of the situation seemed positive, they could ignore the communist factor, and the interlocking with an aggressive international campaign directed from the Kremlin. Reinhold Niebuhr was anti-communist aplenty in those years, but he was intelligent enough to make more discriminatory judgments. In the 1954 comment on Vietnam, he pointed out the "futility" of "relying on military power alone" in a "decaying feudal and colonial order" where people were "filled with resentments against imperial powers."

That futility today remains a force you can feel when you visit the Vietnam Memorial in Washington, and think of the dead in relation to their sacrifice for a goal that was never achieved. The designer of the memorial, Maya Lin, deserves lots of credit, but how about giving a hand to the people on the Commission of Fine Arts that chose the design? How could they have foreseen the power such a memorial would have? The designer, with the sensitivity of an artist, perhaps would be expected to feel into it. But what about those who had the responsibility of deciding, "We will choose this design and build." Some traditionally-minded veterans and their friends could not foresee the power. The idea of just putting names on a black wall in a sunken area struck them as further humiliation, not honor. So they demanded and got some traditional statues by a conventional sculptor, Frederick Hart, placed nearby as an adjunct. But today, it is the wall that moves a visitor to tears, perhaps seeing a woman stretching up on tiptoes with a yearning to touch one particular name, and the adjunct seems worth hardly more than a glance–demonstrating yet again the biblical truth that there is more power in the name than in graven images.

I got another example of Cardinal O'Connor's adaptability in 1995, when he celebrated a mass in memory of an Irishman, Bobby Sands, who had died 14 years earlier on a hunger strike (CNS, May 8). Cardinal O'Connor acknowledged that the church's teaching against suicide might lead people to expect it would decline to honor a man who deliberately starved himself to death. But the cardinal found in this case that honor in the church was justified, and interpreted the death as a protest against injustice. "If one dies while engaging in the strike, the death itself is not intended," he said. Again, I do not consider the cardinal necessarily inconsistent in honoring this kind of action, or suppose, as some might, that his decision came as much out of Irish chauvinism as Catholic theology. The question of consistency lies, rather, in refusing to consider the possibility that there may be cases where abortion turns out to be the most pro-life choice available, where it is not the death that is "intended" but some goal the mother and those associated with her conclude must take precedence, where she finds abortion to be the lesser of many evils she fears might engulf her. I would not expect us to find many such cases, but I would not rule out the possibility there may be some.

Another difficulty I saw in Cardinal Bernardin's proposal was that it seemed designed partly for strategic purposes. Abortion advocates frequently accuse their opponents of showing concern for life only before birth, and subtly insinuate, or baldly assert, that those fighting abortion are hypocrites, not really pro-life but motivated by a desire to subjugate women. When I covered an ecumenical program on abortion at the Cathedral of St. John the Divine in 1973, just after the Supreme Court decision, I also heard a Jesuit speaker bringing up the consistency issue in another way. Herbert W. Rogers, a priest teaching at Fordham University, said the "selectivity" of protests by Catholics cost them credibility when they condemned abortion but let the nation hear "no great Catholic outcry" against the bombing in Vietnam (RNS, February 1). So it could be imagined that a broader theory covering several other issues along with abortion would undercut that criticism. I doubt that abortion advocates will be mollified, however, and my observation is that so far they have not been. But anyway, the approach will not help in the long run if it is not fundamentally valid.

For a satisfying alternative, you could hardly look to the NCC statement. It was largely a question-begging exercise, speaking repeatedly of the "need" for abortion as though that were a given and the issue only how best to meet an undisputed "need." Indicating some awareness that even those who favored it might not consider abortion a really great adventure, the NCC said that amidst the varying opinions "surely it can be agreed that it is imperative to end the need for abortion." Its idea of how to do that lay along the usual lines of providing more and better contraceptives and supplying more welfare benefits to women. But I did not find that persuasive, since the main ones demanding abortion were middle and upper class women who had ample access to contraceptives and needed no welfare benefits, but just did not want a pregnancy to interfere with their careers or their lives otherwise.

From the doctrinal perspective, it was striking that the NCC proceeded by setting "theology today" in antithesis to "traditional theology," relegating nineteen hundred years of Christian thought to obsolescence. Which has been a perennial source of NCC weakness—the reluctance to root its thinking in its own tradition or to hear the witness of past generations.

In 1970, I had heard that deficiency attributed more broadly as something like an American disease when I did a farewell interview with John Macquarrie, a theologian leaving Union Seminary to become Lady Margaret Professor of Divinity at Oxford University. He told me the strength of American theology was its social involvement, but its weakness was "dilettantism, too much craving for the new, whatever the new may be" (RNS, May 7, 1970).

However about all that, we have been at an impasse on abortion. It bothers the nation, and bothers a good many people very deeply. But the anti-abortionists have not been able to persuade the nation–largely, I would guess, because they speak in absolute terms and equate abortion with murder, which common sense recognizes as an exaggeration. The Supreme Court, with its celebrated talent for making sows' ears out of silk purses, has countered with the opposite exaggeration, absolutizing the pro-abortion position.

Abortion is a constitutional right, says the court. Now, really. Or, abortion is a constitutional right "for the stage prior to approximately the end of the first trimester," according to Roe v. Wade (1973), and sort of a constitutional right "for the stage subsequent to approximately the end of the first trimester," but not necessarily a constitutional right thereafter, except for "the preservation of the life or health of the mother." I do not know how the justices of the Supreme Court expect to be taken seriously when they pretend to define constitutional law in its absoluteness according to some "approximately" that nobody can determine. And that "health" of the mother can of course bring in most any sort of psychological as well as physical situation.

It seems clear from the way Justice Harry A. Blackmun wrote the opinion, as well as from his personal comments about it in later years, and the way women who wanted the right to abortion would express personal appreciation for what they implicitly regarded as a personal gift from him, that he was expressing a personal view about how he would like for the law to be, rather than deciding a case according to existing law. I cannot see that he was able to point to anything in the Constitution that would keep Congress or the state legislatures from restricting abortion if they decided restrictions would serve the common good. But the Supreme Court decreed an absolute right, and opponents countered with a demand for a constitutional amendment ruling out abortion absolutely.

This is one of the issues Richard J. Neuhaus has moved into most provocatively. A former Lutheran Church-Missouri Synod pastor who became a Catholic priest of the Archdiocese of New York, he seems to have received a divine mandate to operate as a provoker. I do not know whether I have enough evidence to prove that conclusively. But he does provoke a few people every now and then. And when he does so, he gives the impression of feeling he is fulfilling his vocation.

In one issue of his monthly journal, *First Things* (January 1997), I found he had provoked even a Jesuit friend of his, Avery Dulles of Fordham

University. Provoking the amiable, gracious, balanced, tolerant, later to become cardinal, Father Dulles is a task not easily accomplished. But by concentrated effort and persistence Father Neuhaus could claim success. After he had given the Jesuits one too many zingers, his Jesuit friend suggested in a letter to the editor that he "lay off the irrational attacks" and the "supercilious abuse." In the same issue of *First Things,* I also found Father Neuhaus had provoked a bishop. Ricardo Ramirez, Catholic Bishop of Las Cruces, New Mexico, and chairman of the committee for a national Catholic program, the Campaign for Human Development, objected to "your dissemination of half-truths and innuendo" in a critique of the program published in an earlier issue (October 1996).

But I was looking at the January 1997 issue for the news interest in reactions it carried to a symposium the previous November with the provocative title, "The End of Democracy? The Judicial Usurpation of Politics." Several writers had accused the federal judiciary in general, but with the Supreme Court most particularly in view, of going beyond its legitimate powers in rulings on matters such as abortion and homosexuality. In an introduction to the symposium, Father Neuhaus had asserted, "The question here explored, in full awareness of its far-reaching consequences, is whether we have reached or are reaching the point where conscientious citizens can no longer give moral assent to the existing regime." And he quoted the statement of the Declaration of Independence about the duty of citizens, oppressed by despotism, to "throw off such government."

Father Neuhaus also wrote that he was prepared for the charge that the symposium was "irresponsibly provocative," which was prudent because the charge did come. Gertrude Himmelfarb, a Jewish writer married to the neoconservative theorist Irving Kristol, was a member of the editorial board of *First Things,* but resigned, calling the symposium "absurd" as well as "irresponsible" for comparing the current situation to the colonial. Another board member, Peter Berger, a Lutheran collaborator with Father Neuhaus over decades, also resigned. The far-reaching judgment about the loss of legitimacy in the American governmental system was reminiscent of rhetoric we heard from some of the leftists Father Neuhaus was marching with in the 1960s, and Midge Decter, a Jewish board member married to the former *Commentary* editor, Norman Podhoretz, found it quite disagreeably reminiscent. She did not resign but deplored echoes of "careless radicalism" of the left she would rather avoid. Even Robert H. Bork, one of the contributors to the symposium and a man who himself had shown some disposition to move provocatively, wrote that he did not want his critique of the judiciary taken as a statement that the whole American "regime" lacked legitimacy.

Still and all, when I interviewed Father Neuhaus for a CNS story on the affair (January 23, 1997), I found him, though not saying he was glad about the resignations, still indicating he was quite satisfied with how matters had turned out. He said "a lot of bishops were pleased" by the symposium, it had become "the hot topic in Washington" and it was "a major plus for the journal." He had a letter from Francis E. George, then Catholic Archbishop of Portland, Oregon, later Cardinal-Archbishop of Chicago, saying that the symposium gave a "careful and responsible analysis of the reasons for the erosion of confidence" in the Supreme Court.

Father Neuhaus's style of provocation on the courts and other topics has rather consistently consisted of identifying points worthy of attention, but then carrying them over the edge, somewhere even beyond the regions many of his potential allies could feel at home. Father Dulles said he did not plan to make a break, but thought Father Neuhaus's enjoyment of debate sometimes took him too far.

Something like that is what I might say about the *First Things* debate on the federal judiciary. I do not have any trouble giving "moral assent to the existing regime" of the United States. In fact, I am rather partial to it, careful as I try to be in avoiding the nationalistic idolatry I seem to sometimes see among conservatives. But there can be serious debate about the role of the Supreme Court, the trend to accept it as a sort of House of Lords, a third and higher part of the Congress, tacitly conceded the power of overruling the other two in settling political issues that are especially difficult. Many elected representatives of the people perhaps prefer letting the judiciary step in when an issue becomes dangerously hot, leaving them free to continue with the more agreeable task of funneling pork to the constituents and free from the democratic duty of threshing out public questions through the legislative process. But the preference of legislators need not prevail at this point.

I do not suppose leaving abortion to legislative decision would please absolutists on either side, because it is unlikely either side could prevail absolutely. But it might be healthier for the nation in the long run, and lead to more realistic results. And while we are talking about this, I would say the same thing about much of the church-state litigation. The founding fathers decided the federal government would not have an established religion, but left it up to each state to work out relations as best suited the views and traditions of its citizenry. Massachusetts kept a form of establishment till 1848, evidence the First Amendment did not prevent such relationships on the state level. The current federal support of rigid separation arose only after the Civil War, after somebody spread the view that state involvement in religion, like slavery, violated our rights, and could not be permitted under the new, fourteenth amendment to the federal constitution (requiring states to uphold equal protection of the laws). I suspect it might be well to return to the vision of the founders, leaving a considerable amount of discretion on these matters to the states and, where some national policy is needed, depending more on Congress for that and less on the Supreme Court. On the face of the matter, it seems rather ridiculous for nine justices in Washington, or some majority of the nine, to decide how religion will be handled in every schoolroom or other public space in America, and by every city council.

For a Fourth of July followup to the *First Things* symposium, Father Neuhaus joined with Charles Colson to produce a statement, *We Hold These Truths,* signed by numerous leading figures of the Catholic, Protestant and Orthodox communities, and again raising alarm about actions of the federal judiciary. When I wrote articles about this for ENI (July 4) and the *National Catholic Register,* an independent weekly published in Hamden, Connecticut (July 27, 1997), I noted that Father Neuhaus had put out a press release saying a recent Supreme Court decision overturning the Religious Freedom Restoration Act "can only intensify our alarm." That act had in view situations such as the Catholic church in Boerne, Texas, that wanted to enlarge its building, but could not get a city permit because the church was considered of historical value, and the city wanted it preserved as it was. The congressional act would have given churches the right to ignore such restrictions, and was applauded by many as a blow for religious freedom, while its overturn by the court was denounced as a damnable blow against. But when I called Mary Ann Glendon at the Harvard Law School, a signer of *We Hold These Truths,* I found she considered the overturn decision "fairly sensible." Her general rule, which I feel inclined to adopt without excluding the national Congress altogether, was, "Let the fifty states work out these problems." Incidentally, she also rejected what I would guess was another of Father Neuhaus's efforts at provocation, the statement's use of the word "crisis." She preferred to speak only of a "grave problem."

But for the matter of abortion itself, if I were asked to advise an NCC task force on that topic, which I actually cannot imagine being asked to do, I might suggest beginning with the biblical story of God giving life to Adam by giving him breath.

At the Paris Health Club, where I sometimes attempt the milder forms of exercise, breathing is a big deal. "Breathe," they keep saying. Breathe deep. Breathe regular. Take in lots of air. Don't forget to breathe. Inhale. Breathing, they explain, goes on simultaneously with your other activity. You should not think of an alternation of now one thing and then another, but breathing must proceed continuously, the essential support for whatever else may be happening. So breathe.

Breathing is also a big deal in the Bible. Life comes with the breath, and "when thou takest away their breath, they die" (Psalm 104:29). According to Genesis, the creation of man did not take place the way Michelangelo pictured it on the ceiling of the Sistine Chapel, God stretching out his finger to transmit the spark of life to the outstretched finger of Adam. Rather, God formed man's body out of the earth, working in a way that might make you think of a sculptor, and gave life by blowing wind into the nostrils (2:7). Breath was the decisive element. And the same Hebrew word is used for the three English words, "breath," "wind" and "spirit," and for "spirit" both human and divine.

When Ezekiel dealt with the valley of dry bones, he reported that he had prophesied as God commanded "and the breath came into them and they lived" (37:10). He also said God promised the people of Israel in Babylonian exile, "I will put my Spirit within you, and you shall live" (37:14). The translation issued by the Jewish Publication Society in 1985 renders that verse, "I will put my breath into you and you shall live again."

In parallel with Old Testament Hebrew, the New Testament uses the same Greek word for "breath," "wind" and "spirit." The new life brought by Christ was conveyed when he "breathed on them, and said to them, 'Receive the Holy Spirit'" (John 20:22).

The people who try to make abortion equivalent to murder emphasize the physiological continuities from the moment of conception through development of the fetus to the fully formed person. Whether there is such a thing as a "moment" of conception, some may question, but the continuities are impressive without doubt. There nonetheless remains a crucial difference between the fetus developing in the mother's womb the day before birth and the baby feeding at the mother's breast the day after. And that difference comes from the breath. The decisive event occurs when the baby begins to breathe and, shifting from potential to actual, announces to the world, "I'm here," or something to that effect.

When the pope asks Catholic bishops to offer their resignations at age 75, he does not calculate from the moment of conception. A sensible man, he recognizes that the life that counts, for bishops as for the rest of us, begins at birth. The very last verse of the Psalms gives a summation: "Let everything that breathes praise the LORD" (150:6). It is only after birth that this praise becomes possible. A basic weakness of the anti-abortion movement has been the refusal to acknowledge that getting born makes such a big difference.

But all this is not to say the fetus is worth nothing and deserves no protection, or that anybody has "freedom of choice" to destroy one at will. In New

York, you do not have freedom of choice about how you will treat a dog. So if members of a community decide that what an abortionist does to a human fetus offends their moral sensibilities, they have a moral right to impose legal restrictions. No one need wait until some agreement is reached on how to describe the status of a fetus philosophically.

To me, the most dubious aspect of the NCC statement on abortion was its individualism in leaving this life and death decision totally to one person, with no requirement of getting even a medical opinion that an abortion was advisable, or the agreement of the father, or the parents of an underage girl. The common formula puts it as a right of a woman to control her own body, which is wrong on both ends. Neither men nor women can claim an absolute right to do just anything with their bodies. But anyway, what we have under discussion is not the woman's body, but some body else.

In the Christian view, the however-you-characterize-it in the womb of Mary does not belong just to Mary, but God is preparing there a gift for the whole world. The divine-human potential is reflected in the Gospel stories about Mary in the days leading up to the birth of Jesus (Matthew 1; Luke 1). So everyone has an interest in what is happening. And for that matter, Mary herself belongs to God and not just to herself. "Behold, I am the handmaid of the Lord," she said, correctly (Luke 1:38).

Along with a biblical approach, an ecumenical approach might help the churches on the abortion issue. I argued that point in an article for *The Lamp* (November 1973), a magazine formerly published by the Atonement Friars, a Catholic order that began in the Episcopal Church and makes a special emphasis on working for Christian unity. I was able to point out that although the mainline Protestant churches generally took a liberal view on abortion, several prominent figures in those churches were opposed, and still others were disturbed by seeing abortion gone wholesale. I quoted C. Eric Lincoln, a leading black Protestant professor, who said his former tolerance had turned to opposition: "My vision was of an occasional individual caught up in circumstances so overwhelming and so devastating in potential as to warrant so drastic a procedure as the interruption of life. I was not prepared for the blood letting which has, in fact, ensued." And I was able to cite John C. Bennett, retired president of Union Seminary and a prominent liberal specializing in social ethics: "I have criticized official Roman Catholic pressures on legislatures when they are governed by a single standard of absolutism, but I have felt for some time that Catholic thinking has been a very desirable corrective for much Protestant and secular thinking on this subject."

So I suggested that abortion was an area where the churches might try to proceed ecumenically. It is pretty clear that the way they have been proceeding has not helped much. Both Catholics and Protestants express a commitment to ecumenism on principle. But they show a tendency to think ecumenically only on certain days, or only during the particular hour a meeting agenda gives ecumenism a slot. If the churches actually were committed to ecumenism, would they not approach everything they did with that in mind? And then instead of abortion sitting ignored on ecumenical occasions, it might become a topic of special attention. Just why is it that serious Christians can see this issue in such fundamentally different ways? The roots of this difference could use further examination.

In this connection, I should pay tribute to Charles Angell, the Atonement friar who edited *The Lamp* and demonstrated he actually was ecumenical by letting a Southern Baptist like me occupy a good many pages in his magazine, starting when I was still a village pastor in Virginia.

But before closing, I will let you know that the abortion wars can move from deep seriousness to high comedy. In early 1989, just before Ronald Reagan left the presidency, Grand Master Bertie of the Knights of Malta came over from Rome and gave him an award at a big dinner in New York. Since the president had divorced his wife and married another woman, had apparently given little attention to the religious formation of his children, or to any other aspect of their lives, and as governor of California had led in liberalizing abortion laws, some people might wonder about this conservative Catholic organization honoring him for "his vigorous defense of Christian family values" (NC, January 16). But thus goes the world of honoring politicians.

J. Peter Grace, chief of the W. R. Grace Company, founded by his grandfather, headed the American Knights and took the master of ceremonies role for the dinner. And some unknown influence prompted him to get going on abortion. He decided to give us a routine he had picked up on the anti-abortion circuits about the illogic of anyone wanting to destroy a fetus, recognizing that we all once existed in the fetus state, and surely would not approve of our own self-destruction.

Except that Mr. Grace's tongue slipped a notch and he was saying "feces" instead of "fetus." You must visualize the scene: there in the grand ballroom of the Waldorf-Astoria Hotel, the Catholic lay establishment by the many hundreds all tuxed and gowned before him; to his left on the dais the president of the United States, Grand Master Bertie of the Sovereign Military Hospital Order of St. John of Jerusalem, of Rhodes and of Malta, and other ultra-worthies; to his right a row of cardinals, papal nuncios and whatnot; and there at the podium the chairman of the W. R. Grace Company doing his riff on "feces." He seemed to sense that maybe some in his audience were not quite with him, and redoubled his efforts. We all began as feces. I began as feces; you began as feces. I have forgotten whether he specifically told us that President Reagan originated in feces, or whether, as some said, the president was seen trying to adjust his hearing aid. But it was a grand ballroom event for sure.

Slips of the tongue can happen to us all, of course. One I remember occurred at a prestige affair attended by King Juan Carlos and Queen Sophia of Spain. The master of ceremonies, who may have lacked familiarity with the arts or perhaps had drunk too many toasts to Their Majesties before dinner, told us that for our entertainment of the evening we were privileged to have "the two principal dancers from the Spanish Royal Buffet." In the matter of Mr. Grace, I thought in his daily conversation he was perhaps unaccustomed to using the word "feces," but when referencing this matter would more likely employ an alternative nomenclature. So his lack of previous opportunities to become used to the word would explain his confusion of the two terms.

Sometime later, I interviewed him for a story on the charitable works of the Knights (CNS, March 28, 1990), and at the end asked whether Cardinal O'Connor, their American chaplain, ever explained to him the difference between "fetus" and "feces." Mr. Grace said that it was not necessary because his wife straightened him out as soon as he got home.

So much for violence (abortion); now for sex (homosexuality).

HOMOSEXUALITY

CHAPTER ELEVEN

On the evening of February 27, 1990, Bruce Ritter, a Franciscan priest, turned ownership of Covenant House, the youth shelter, over to its board, and resigned as president. The next morning, Robert M. Morgenthau, District Attorney of Manhattan, announced that an investigation of charges against Father Ritter had not produced enough evidence to prosecute, and he was closing the case. Neither party said that a deal had been worked out, but the time sequence was suggestive.

I was not among those who could claim advance knowledge of accusations about the behavior of Father Ritter. Some people later would say they had known for years, or at least had heard rumors, but my first awareness came when the *New York Post* alerted the general public with a front page story December 10, 1989.

A young man, then called Timothy Warner, a name we later heard was an alias for Kevin Lee Kite, said Father Ritter brought him to New York from New Orleans, used the tax-free funds of Covenant House to provide him with living and school expenses, and demanded sex in return. He reported that the priest told him, "I decided a long time ago that if God didn't like me the way I am, that's his problem."

Under the ownership of Rupert Murdoch, the *Post* had developed such a reputation as a sleaze sheet, the story was met with suspicion. The Catholic News Service decided initially not even to report the allegations, and ran a story only a day later, after other papers had spread the news. I never had any inside sources or access to special information, but mostly followed developments as they became generally known.

Nationally famous for founding and presiding over the Covenant House shelter serving homeless and runaway youth, Father Ritter had occasionally been the subject of stories I did in earlier years. I had never thought he was telling the full and unbridled truth about how he shifted from his previous work to start the Covenant House program, but I had no specific suspicions. As he would recount the move, he was challenged by a student one day while he was serving as a chaplain and professor at Manhattan College, an institution run by the Christian Brothers and now located no longer in Manhattan but in the Riverdale section of the Bronx. He said he was asked why he was not putting his teaching about service into practice—as though service at a college were not service. Whereupon, he left the college and went to the Lower East Side of Manhattan to start helping young people who had been thrown out by their parents or who had run away from abusive homes. Later, he expanded his program and moved into the Times Square area.

I figured that a grown man does not completely change the direction of his life just because of a chance remark by some student, though possibly a chance remark might bring him to a decision if it crystallized thoughts and impulses already floating around in his mind. So I assumed there must be more to the Father Ritter story than we were hearing, that his account had been constructed for dramatic effect and, collaterally, for effectiveness in fundraising.

Father Ritter liked to talk about sex, I also noticed. He got appointed to a Commission on Pornography by the U.S. Attorney General, and when I interviewed him after a day of its hearings in New York, he was plenty hot about "tens of millions of God-fearing Americans" patronizing the "sex industry" and "putting money in the pockets of organized crime" (NC, January 27, 1986). Telling audiences about the young people he served, he would dwell on the sexual exploitation they endured, and go deadpan explicit with more details than some of us might consider necessary to paint the lurid picture. It was in the vein of those preachers who draw audiences by feeding them prurient material, but putting it in a sanctified context of denunciation so listeners can feel free for the vicarious enjoyment.

This was also the style of the fundraising appeals Father Ritter mailed out across the length and breadth of the land. He liked to tell about a twelve-year-old girl working the New York streets as a prostitute, and about various other girls and boys he said were forced into this life to support themselves after they ran away to New York. It worked: readers got a delicious quiver of outrage, and the money poured in.

Another thing I noticed about Father Ritter was an edge of fanaticism. No ambiguity modulated his world. All was starkly good and evil. Fanaticism in individual psychology is generally understood to derive from the suppression of certain elements within the personality. When those elements disturb us, we drive fanatically in another direction to seek escape from their attraction, or perhaps to keep anyone else from seeing the connections we may have. So one might suspect that Father Ritter was struggling with demons.

If so, and if those demons were driving him in the direction alleged, starting the ministry to runaways was a logical move. Among them were young people in need of help, psychologically vulnerable and often experienced in matters sexual. When a benefactor made his moves, they would know what they were expected to do. The young men who brought the charges against Father Ritter said his style was to move into sex with little if any talk about it, before or after. But with street experience, such young people would not need directions.

Father Ritter's supporters, many of them idolizers, found it difficult to believe the charges, even after they began to pile up. At first, it was just the one man. But then an article in the *Village Voice* added that another young man had told a similar story to the author a couple of years before. Then a third young man went to *The New York Times* with an account of Father Ritter engaging him in sex several years before when he was an underage teen. Then there was another.

Staff and admirers of the priest moved forthwith into a protective mode. They talked of the need to defend the reputation of a saintly servant of God, and to make sure he could continue his ministry to youth in need. Less was said about assuring that young people coming for help were really safe from further abuse.

Aside from the scandal, some people questioned Father Ritter's overall way of conducting his operation. For a professional assessment, I went to Mary Ann Quaranta, head of the school of social work at Fordham University and a former national president of Catholic Charities (CNS, March 30, 1990). She said, positively on the one hand, that Covenant House offered some good programs, and some of her students did field work there, but, negatively on the other side, that Father Ritter operated as a loner, not in cooperation with other agencies. Covenant House was seldom if ever represented at the various meetings held by social welfare professionals, she reported.

I later got another perspective from William B. O'Brien, a Catholic priest who headed a drug treatment program called Daytop. Father Ritter, who talked of the youngsters coming to his shelters as though they were merely victims, and nothing but victims, and had no responsibility for how they were handling their lives, announced a policy of accepting any under-21 who showed up. You want in, we let you in. Nobody is turned away. Probably, the literal truth was always a little more restrictive. An applicant who insisted on bringing in guns would likely have found the tolerance had its limits. But in general the policy was anybody under 21 under any circumstances, and that opened Covenant House to exploitation by youngsters just wanting free room and board while they cruised the city streets a few days.

For Msgr. O'Brien, compassion was more the tough love of a Dutch uncle. His philosophy was "totally different" from Father Ritter's, he told me. If a young drug addict became serious about changing his life, Daytop would take him in and do everything possible to help him. If not, forget it. Just accepting youngsters "makes me feel good," but "it doesn't do anything for that kid," Msgr. O'Brien said. "If they just want a warm bed and food, throw them out or they will con the shirt off your back." And if it happens to be cold and snowing out there, well, that could be very therapeutic, the monsignor said (CNS, August 29, 1990).

On the other hand, he had earlier expressed some tough love for people such as Ronald and Nancy Reagan, who he decided were doing their routine about drugs just to get political credit. Mrs. Reagan visited Daytop centers twice during the 1980 presidential campaign and twice the following year, and got Daytop's Prometheus Award in 1981. But Msgr. O'Brien said they became estranged when he started criticizing her husband for cutting drug treatment funds. He said the Reagan efforts were "doomed to failure" because they consisted almost totally of "Rambo-ing" on the borders, sending helicopters to Bolivia, searching boats in New York harbor and other highly-publicized actions on the enforcement side. Of $2.3 billion then allocated to the drug program, almost $2 billion went to enforcement, he said. More programs to help addicts become drug free were essential, both because people buying drugs would always motivate peddlers to keep them coming in somehow, and because every addict would probably introduce a half dozen acquaintances to the habit. So it did little good for Mrs. Reagan to run around repeating her slogan, "Just say no," Msgr. O'Brien told me (NC, September 24, 1986).

As more Ritter closets were opened, there came discovery of certain oddities in his handling of Covenant House finances, and these, along with the revelation that he had kept important actions secret from the board, seemingly disturbed board members more than the possibility that some troubled young people might have been exploited more than helped when they came to Covenant House.

On the night Father Ritter resigned, after the young accusers had become multiple, a Covenant House release said that "the 17-member board reaffirmed its belief in the innocence of Father Ritter . . . ." The next day, in response to Mr. Morgenthau's announcement, board chairman Ralph A. Pfeiffer Jr. issued a statement saying, "The Manhattan District Attorney has confirmed what we have known all along: the charges against Covenant House and Father Ritter were totally without merit." Actually, Mr. Morgenthau had not done that. He

SIDEBARS

only said he did not have enough evidence to prosecute, a quite different judgment. But later, I found Mr. Pfeiffer unwilling to repeat his positive assessment of Father Ritter, and it appeared the discovery of how much financial data the priest withheld from the board made the difference.

To maintain control, Father Ritter had set up Covenant House as a corporation with himself as the one and only stockholder, capable by his own single vote of electing board members and replacing them. "It was an arrangement with which I had not previously been familiar," the New York cardinal, John J. O'Connor, told reporters. Board members came on with no independent mandate to exercise oversight, but as starry-eyed fans agreeing to help a priest they had put on a high pedestal.

One puzzling aspect of the Father Ritter story was the behavior of his order, the Conventual Franciscans, and specifically his province, Immaculate Conception, then based in Union, New Jersey. The provincial served on the board of Covenant House, and donors might imagine he gave some oversight. But apparently not.

As the story developed, it was reported that officials of the province had been informed in previous years that Father Ritter was using boys sexually, but paid no attention. And after the first *Post* story, a young man named Darryl Bassile reportedly went to them privately to tell of his own similar experience, and took his story to *The Times* only after they again failed to respond.

One might speculate that some of the male religious orders perhaps have a considerable proportion of the homosexually-inclined, many of those otherwise oriented having left in recent times to get married. And one could wonder whether Father Ritter may have been protected by people in his order sympathetic to a brother of reputed homosexual tendencies. But a more natural explanation would be that charges of sex abuse were so very unpleasant, and authorities would naturally avoid dealing with them as long as they could.

Conall McHugh was Father Ritter's provincial at the time. But when I would call for the reaction of the order, he would not come to the telephone, but have a secretary refer me to a deputy, Juniper Alwell, who would say the least possible and explain that confidentiality ruled *etc*. It was only the day that *The New York Times* publicized the third man's charges that the provincial finally acted, telling Father Ritter to take a leave of absence while the order carried out an investigation. After investigating, however, officials still refused to say anything about what they concluded.

"If they could have found any evidence he was innocent, you can be sure they would have released it," one knowledgeable priest outside the order told me.

The provincial directed Father Ritter to return to living with other priests in community, but Father Ritter showed the world what had become of the traditional vow of obedience, and told his superior to stuff it. Eventually, with approval from the order, Father Ritter left the Franciscans, resumed use of his baptismal name, John, and got status as a priest in the Diocese of Alleppey in Kerala, a state on the west side of India's southern tip. He found a place to live, reportedly provided by a supporter, at an undisclosed location in upstate New York, and was next heard from when he sent a thousand or so of his principal backers a letter asking for contributions to an agency that assisted his new diocese. Then he stayed out of the news until his death from cancer October 7, 1999.

Shortly after Father Ritter left the Franciscans, I got an interview with Giles Van Wormer, who had succeeded Father McHugh as provincial, and found he also refused to say anything much (CNS, September 4, 1991). He had talked with Father Ritter, but had not bothered to find out why he was leaving or what he was planning for the future. Or so he said, if you can believe that. Father Van Wormer claimed he still could not say whether the charges against Father Ritter were true, and said that letting Father Ritter remain a member of the order for more than a year despite refusing to return to living with the community was no more than had been done for others. I asked the provincial, "If you believed a priest of your order had been falsely accused and his reputation damaged by slander, would you not feel an obligation to defend him?" He said he had not thought of the matter in those terms, and would have to reflect further before he could give any answer.

To sum up, no official of church or state ever gave the public any official judgment about Father Ritter. So the people who had been sending him their money, and giving him the adoration of their hearts, were left with help from nobody but reporters in deciding whether their gifts had gone to a priest who was using his position to satisfy a homosexual appetite. That allowed more leeway for those defenders of Father Ritter who continued to express belief in his innocence, and claim he was destroyed by the media.

Although much was eventually revealed, there was presumably much more to the case than ever came out. I sent word to Father Ritter through various channels that if he wished to present his side of the story to the Catholic press, the Catholic News Service was ready to give him that opportunity. But I never got any response.

At one point, I began making a list of all the people who refused to talk to me about the case, and found in its considerable length confirmation that there must have been a lot that was kept hidden. In addition to Father Ritter and his provincial, the refuseniks included key people such as Robert Macauley, the businessman-founder of the relief agency, AmeriCares, who had guided Father Ritter in financial matters and chaired the Covenant House board until just the month before the façade collapsed. Some key staff under Father Ritter refused to talk, as did some board members personally close to him. As did others.

Mr. Macauley, a Yale roommate and lifelong friend of President George H.W. Bush, was an object of some wonder, a freewheeling operator who drew suspicions that he had been engaged in projects of different character than the humanitarianism for which he was trying to become known. Charles H. Sennott, the *Post* reporter who broke the Ritter story, later wrote a book about the case, *Broken Covenant* (Simon & Schuster, 1992), and presented a curdled view of Mr. Macauley's role at Covenant House. He also said people generally considered Mr. Macauley a CIA man "although he adamantly denies it" (p. 111).

And other people have raised questions about him and his operations. In 1997, when I was doing a story for the *National Catholic Register* (September 28) on a book by journalist Michael Maren, *The Road to Hell: The Ravaging Effects of Foreign Aid and International Charity* (Free Press, 1997), describing conclusions he had reached observing assistance efforts in parts of Africa, particularly Kenya and Somalia, there came Mr. Macauley again. A leaked document from an official of the United Nations High Commissioner for Refugees recommended "extreme caution" in dealing with Mr. Macauley's AmeriCares. The official said experience had shown it to be "an irresponsible, publicity hungry organization capable of making grandiose generalized offers of assistance" and then providing planeloads of "highly questionable" materials not necessarily useful in meeting relief needs (p. 265). According to the Sennott analysis, it was this Mr. Macauley who took Father Ritter's financial operations into the upper spheres.

Father Ritter also accumulated other characters who might raise eyebrows. He got help, including loans for Covenant House, from Charles H. Keating Jr., who began descending into difficulty about the same time as the priest he aided, particularly over a multi-billion failure of Lincoln Savings and Loan. In 1999, a story in *The New York Times* (April 7) told us that Mr. Keating had pleaded guilty the previous day to four counts of fraud, but would not have to return to prison, where he had been earlier in the decade for racketeering and securities fraud. His conviction on the Lincoln losses in a state court was overturned by a federal judge, but prosecutors were appealing, and Mr. Keating also faced a $3 billion civil judgment against him and his associates.

A sidebar to the Ritter story involved a false baptismal certificate that a priest apparently in cahoots with him was said to have obtained for the young man from New Orleans. According to the cover story, which I suppose reflected mostly Father Ritter's taste for the melodramatic, the young man was in danger of his life because of breaking with people who used him as a prostitute, and he consequently needed a new identity, like those the FBI will sometimes arrange for informers breaking with organized crime. After it all came apart, and we learned the baptismal certificate had drawn in an innocent, unaware family, Covenant House said it regretted the pain it had caused and so forth. But it put out a press release (February 5, 1990) with the justification: "We were trying to save the life of someone we truly believed was in jeopardy. This is the mission of Covenant House, to save and protect children." By "children," we mean in this case a man who was initially said to be 20 but soon was credited with six additional years. The release was signed by one John Kells, a communications officer who was shortly thereafter gone.

Michael P. Duval, a Catholic priest who had formerly worked for Covenant House, had subsequently become an assistant in a parish of the Buffalo Diocese, St. James in Jamestown, and found records of a boy, Timothy Warner, who died of leukemia at the age of ten, about ten years earlier, which would put him at the now-supposed twenty years of the young man from New Orleans. Father Duval apparently arranged for a baptismal certificate and a birth certificate in the boy's name, and gave them to Father Ritter for Kevin Lee Kite.

I assumed reports of an involvement of priests in the deliberate falsification of sacramental records would upset people in the Catholic Church. But I seem to have assumed wrongly. I never saw any indication that any church official was really bothered.

At Covenant House, James J. Harnett, chief operations officer and holder of the same post still today, defended as best he could (CNS, February 13, 1990). Playing the argument both ways, he justified the action as protection for the young man's life, but promised Covenant House would never perform such acts of mercy again; compared it with Pope John XXIII as Vatican nuncio in Turkey giving Jews baptismal certificates to save them from the Nazis, but acknowledged the cases were not really comparable.

I did not want to make life more painful for the family of the deceased boy. Like everybody else, I found my stomach turned by the television reporter who would go with lights and cameras and stick a microphone in some woman's face and inquire: "A psychopath has murdered your husband and baby and raped you and burned your house down—how do you feel about that?" But I did not think I should write the story without giving the family a chance to say whatever they might want to about it. So I got the mother on the phone.

One can well imagine the feelings of a mother who has gone through a child's struggle with leukemia and eventual death, and after burying her child and suffering her grief, a decade later sees his name in the headlines in connection with some sordid mess down in New York. And then she hears that this has happened because of the actions of priests of her church. She did not rage against anybody, but she was not a happy woman.

The news of what had happened was several days old at the time I talked with her. But Father Ritter had not called to say he was sorry for the pain she had been caused. And Father Duval, who was now on leave, had not called. And no one from the Diocese of Buffalo had contacted her. The only person who had apologized was a layman who had nothing to do with the incident. That was Frank J. Macchiarola, who was briefly interim president of Covenant House before he was removed, apparently by Father Ritter in behind-the-barn maneuvering with his remaining friends on the board.

Edward B. Head, the Catholic bishop of Buffalo, was yet another in that long line of people who refused to talk to me. I could only get his press officer, David M. Lee, who would speak only in guarded terms, and generally took the approach some people describe as c.y.a., which I suppose refers to an accounting term, cover your arrears. After I called a couple of times, he finally got out a perfunctory statement saying, in effect, the bishop sure was sorry about what happened to this family in his diocese, and sure wished he knew how it happened. I figured that a bishop who was really interested in what one of his priests had done might get him on the phone and demand some straight answers.

Eventually the press officer was able to report that Bishop Head had told the priest his action was wrong. But the press officer was still playing games. What did the bishop determine that the priest had done that was wrong? Msgr. Lee would rather not say. He thought it had been in the newspapers. Allegations had indeed been in the press, I said, but what had the bishop concluded? I never learned. For Msgr. Lee, it was c.y.a. to the end (CNS, March 22, 1990).

Mary Rose McGeady, a nun of the Daughters of Charity who was chosen to take Father Ritter's place, told me that she had heard nothing from him. Since the needs of the young people continued, and the work of Covenant House continued, one would suppose Father Ritter, whatever his own distress, undoubtedly quite considerable, would write Sister McGeady to say he was praying for her as she took on the responsibility of keeping the work going, and tried to continue what he had begun. How could he not do that? When he later sent his letter to key supporters, and asked them to assist the foreign diocese that gave him shelter from the Franciscans, one would suppose he might also write, "And I hope you will continue to support Covenant House even though I am not there, because the help it gives homeless and runaway youth is still desperately needed and very close to my heart." How could he not do that? Somehow he found strength to not do that either.

And now we need to note that homosexuality was not merely a matter of individual cases, but became a movement of surprising strength. The National Council of Churches (NCC) got hit when the Universal Fellowship of Metropolitan Community Churches (UFMCC), a homosexual denomination started by a former Baptist and then Pentecostal minister, Troy Perry, applied for NCC membership. It seemed obvious that the NCC could not get a consensus of its members to accept this denomination, and that its most prudent response would be to put the whole matter aside. Seemed obvious to me, but not to the NCC leadership.

So the Council entered into a painful, prolonged process of working over the idea, appointed a committee of theologians to confer, and used up much time, energy and good humor without ever making the UFMCC any happier. In the end, the application was not approved, as anyone might have predicted at the beginning. Maybe the idea was to just start getting the legitimacy of the topic as an agenda item accepted, and to begin softening up the opposition in hopes of victory somewhere down the line.

When I went to the NCC board meeting in Hartford, Connecticut, in November of 1983, I found the UFMCC issue at the center of attention. The reality was that liberal Protestants in the Council generally wanted to be liberal, and the Orthodox wanted to be orthodox. Withdrawal by the Orthodox was a live possibility if the UFMCC gained admission, and the Orthodox found allies among some black delegates. The largest black denomination, the National Baptist Convention USA, Inc., which normally sent small delegations, often composed of volunteers who happened to have nothing much else to do, filled all its seats at Hartford with a representation that included denominational heavyweights. But they were not sympathetic to the homosexuals—or to the NCC's new *Inclusive Language Lectionary*, another topic of debate there.

In a compromise that satisfied nobody but kept the NCC together, the board voted to "postpone indefinitely" any action on the UFMCC application. But then there were committees and dialogues with the UFMCC, and it later applied for observer status, a relationship established with such groups as the American Jewish Committee. This question came up for a vote at the November 1992 board meeting, with the alignment somewhat similar to that of 1983, but with liberal Protestants now even more insistent on supporting the homosexuals.

The NCC had received rather specific warnings that giving the UFMCC observer status could mean the loss of not only its Orthodox member churches—all nine of them—but also certain other members such as the (U.S.) Korean Presbyterian Church and maybe some of the black denominations.

Despite the clear potential for a breakup of the Council, the UFMCC lost by only the narrow vote of 91 to 80. Subtracting the Orthodox delegates from the negative side would leave you with a majority of the Protestant delegates voting in favor, ready to see all the Orthodox and some others depart, in effect ready to see a dissolution of the Council. Formal dissent from the negative decision was registered by the United Church of Christ, United Methodist Church and Swedenborgian Church. "If we have unity without integrity, we have no unity at all," said President Paul H. Sherry of the United Church of Christ.

Orthodox members contribute only miniscule amounts to the NCC budget, and their churches generally have weak staff structures, so they play less of a role in Council programs. Many Protestants might welcome their departure, and perhaps say it would allow the NCC to stride forward. But withdrawal by the Orthodox would leave the NCC existing only as an agency of a dwindling band of liberal Protestants, no longer able to present itself as an ecumenical body working for the unity of all Christians. The NCC would then have less interest for Roman Catholics committed to ecumenism, for other denominations outside the NCC or for conservative elements within the NCC's liberal Protestant denominations.

Homosexuals pushed on, nonetheless. In 1994, when many of them had come to New York for the annual Gay Pride Parade, and the 25th anniversary of the Stonewall Rebellion, when homosexuals at the Stonewall bar in Greenwich Village had chosen to fight police raiders rather than run, some of those connected to the homosexual denomination decided to use the preceding Friday, June 24, to put more pressure on the NCC. They gathered enough members and sympathizers they could circle the Interchurch Center, where the NCC has its offices. And they served notice: "We will stand against you, we will stand up to you, in your face, until you hear us and change." That from Nancy Wilson, their ecumenical officer, operating in what had not previously been certified as the style of ecumenical dialogue. But among those standing before the ecumenical officer and giving some kind of support was the NCC general secretary, Joan Brown Campbell. "I couldn't figure it out," Troy Perry said later (EPS, July 10, 1994).

I have been generally surprised by the rapid growth in political strength of the homosexual movement. But in 1977, when I was asked to write an article for *Christianity and Crisis* on the issue of ordaining homosexuals (May 30), I became aware that liberals in the churches had by then reached a consensus that homosexuality was morally acceptable and measures against homosexuality morally unacceptable.

The following year, the United Methodist News Service asked me to cover a meeting of the denomination's New York Annual Conference, where the key issue was the status of Paul Abels (story June 12). He had been pastor of Washington Square United Methodist Church in Greenwich Village for some years, but a homosexual relationship he had entered into had just recently been publicized. Some in the leadership of the Annual Conference thought he could not be allowed to continue as a pastor, but the conference voted after a long closed session that he would. The majority of the rank and file clergy saw no objection to appointing a homosexual as pastor of a congregation. As soon as possible, however, Mr. Abels retired, and a little later he died of AIDS. A plaque honoring his memory can be seen today on a wall in Washington Square Church.

He was of course but one of many young or relatively young homosexual men who have died in these recent years, a development that has cast a shadow over many green fields. And when you have seen these deaths occur among your family and friends, as I have, you will necessarily become deeply saddened. The death of any young person has a special sadness to it, but many of these young men dying of AIDS were people of quite exceptional ability. So you also had to reflect on the immensity of the contribution they could have made but now cannot.

However, I have not been able to see that it is necessary or even logical to move from that sadness to a moral endorsement of the activity that transmitted the fatal disease. The persistence of the liberal stance when it became known that homosexual activity was a principal way of spreading death seemed almost incomprehensible. Sometimes it could even seem that the homosexual community was using the AIDS crisis to promote its agenda, insinuating that anyone who declined to endorse homosexual behavior was coldhearted and lacking in compassion toward these young men prematurely wasting away.

When Cardinal O'Connor observed that following the moral teaching of the church was the best medical advice for avoiding AIDS, it seemed to me his statement was true, obviously true, and a truth much in need of emphasis when AIDS was taking so many lives. But he was fiercely attacked for speaking this truth out loud. Many homosexuals and their allies could only keep chanting their mantra–"condoms, condoms, condoms"–and demanding that everybody repeat on the beat.

Cardinal O'Connor's response to the AIDS epidemic took several forms, extending himself both to deal with a medical tragedy and to blunt the allegation of the homosexual community that the church was cruel in refusing to endorse the homosexual activity that transmitted a large percentage of the HIV infections. He encouraged the work of Catholic hospitals in serving AIDS patients, he turned over an unused convent to Mother Teresa for an AIDS ministry, he served on a commission investigating what could be done about AIDS on a national basis and he spent time in visits to individual AIDS patients. None of that softened the hearts of his critics–such as Tony Kushner, a playwright perhaps best known for *Angels in America: A Gay Fantasia on National Themes* (Part I, 1992, Part II, 1993). *Cathedral News,* publication of the Episcopal Cathedral of St. John the Divine, reported in its winter 1994-95 issue that Mr. Kushner spoke there at an October 9 observance of the National Day of Prayer for AIDS in the Episcopal Church. In what I suppose some might call the spirit of ecumenism, Mr. Kushner included the Catholic Archbishop of New York in his prayers, and called on God to "enlighten the unenlightened: the pope, the cardinals, archbishops and priests, even John O'Connor, teach him how Christ's kindness worked: remind him, he's forgotten . . . ." I cannot recall ever hearing or hearing of anyone offering such prayers for an Episcopal bishop from the pulpit of St. Patrick's Cathedral.

Then in early 1987, Cardinal O'Connor was abruptly confronted with a challenge on a different level, illustrative of the many angles in the life of an archbishop. He returned from an overseas trip to find that a Catholic woman had gone to *The New York Times* with her complaint about the rector of St. Patrick's Cathedral refusing to let her get married there when he found out that the groom had AIDS. The couple, Maria and David Hefner, had been married in a civil ceremony three years earlier. But she said it had been her dream to get a church wedding in St. Patrick's Cathedral, and now with Mr. Hefner, a Protestant, dying of AIDS he agreed to join in making her dream come true. A hairdresser from Brazil, he had reportedly lived a homosexual life at an earlier stage, but then turned his interest to Maria when she became one of his customers.

At St. Patrick's, they talked with a Capuchin priest, John Clermont, who agreed to officiate at the wedding, and it was set for Valentine's Day. But when the cathedral rector, James F. Rigney, learned that the groom had AIDS, he made Father Clermont call the couple and cancel the wedding. When I tried to talk with Msgr. Rigney about the case, he was unwilling to explain his decision, or spend any large number of seconds talking with me at all. But I did get to discuss the case in general terms with William B. Smith, professor of moral theology at the seminary of the New York Archdiocese, St. Joseph's in Yonkers (NC, January 12). A man adept at logic, Msgr. Smith was the kind who could keep concepts in their proper boxes, and proceed thorough interlocking propositions to prove things had to be as they had been ordered, or had to not be as they had not been ordered, whatever he set out to prove. Marital relations could lead to conception of a child with AIDS, and the church does not approve the use of contraceptives. Outsiders might think this couple was perhaps past the stage of sex, but Msgr. Smith pointed out that physical consummation was intrinsic to marriage. Very QED.

Cardinal O'Connor, though, saw himself facing not an exercise in logic but a public relations disaster. A Catholic woman with a dying partner, cherishing a dream to have their union blessed at St. Patrick's Cathedral, and getting a cold shoulder from her church.

The cardinal moved forthwith. He had a secretary call the pastor of the woman's parish, Gerald McGovern, a Carmelite at Our Lady of the Scapular Church, and pass along the word that he should expedite the paperwork and counseling. So on February 14, Father McGovern was at St. Patrick's performing the marriage ceremony for Maria and David Hefner (NC, February 16). And among the guests present to kiss the bride and congratulate the groom was the Cardinal-Archbishop of New York.

When I called Father McGovern, he seemed no more disposed to converse than Msgr. Rigney had been. And Cardinal O'Connor never told us how he had surmounted the insurmountable logic of Msgr. Smith. I suppose maybe an archbishop who would not approve the use of contraceptives to prevent the transmission of life might condone them to prevent the transmission of death. Or other bypasses could have occurred to the cardinal, a man too resourceful to let himself get boxed into places he found confining. But his only explanation of his role in bringing Maria's dream to reality: "I facilitated it."

I should record here that his predecessor, Terence J. Cooke, also showed the compassionate face of the church to people suffering from AIDS at an earlier stage when the general public was even more resistant to any association with the disease. Kevin M. Cahill, personal physician to Cardinal Cooke, and later to Cardinal O'Connor, specialized in tropical diseases, and so got called in when young men losing their immunity through Acquired Immune Deficiency Syndrome began coming down with his kind of infections. So Dr. Cahill put together one of the first conferences on AIDS, and edited a collection of conference addresses, *The AIDS Epidemic* (St. Martin's, 1983).

While he was organizing the conference, Dr. Cahill reported, Cardinal Cooke offered to attend if that would help. So he came and said to participants from various sectors of the healthcare community dealing with AIDS, "I am one with you in your concern, and I rejoice that you are people of hope." The cardinal also offered a prayer that included the words, "Lord, as we face this crisis together, make us instruments of your peace. Heal our divisions and deepen our unity" (p. xiv).

But "activists" of the homosexual community were so sure of the righteousness of their cause that they felt justified in trying to force endorsement of their agenda by outrageous forms of disruptive behavior. When Joseph Ratzinger of the Vatican Congregation for the Doctrine of the Faith came to New York, they decided to show their righteousness by roughing him up a little. As head of the congregation, Cardinal Ratzinger had issued a statement declaring that homosexuality was a "disordered" condition that could not be approved, which seemed like what anybody should have expected him to say, and quite in line with the Christian tradition of moral teaching. But homosexuals and their allies said they were shocked, shocked, shocked.

If anybody doubted just how disordered their condition was, it could be seen when a coalition including ACT-UP, Dignity and others interrupted a lecture the cardinal gave (January 27, 1988; NC stories, January 28) at St. Peter's Lutheran Church, and started yelling "bigot," "fascist," "anti-Christ" and similar tributes. The cardinal had been brought there by Richard J. Neuhaus, then a Lutheran minister but on the journey that took him a little later into the Catholic priesthood, to deliver the Erasmus Lecture. This was a lecture sponsored annually by the Neuhaus think tank–then the Rockford Institute Center on Religion and Society but now, after a break with Rockford, the Institute on Religion and Public Life.

"It is deplorable that homosexual persons have been and are the object of violent malice in speech or in action," said Cardinal Ratzinger's congregation in their statement, issued October 1, 1986. "Such treatment deserves condemnation from the church's pastors wherever it occurs" (paragraph 10). But homosexuals passed over this point and emphasized that the statement went on to say the response to crimes against homosexuals should not be a condoning of homosexual activity, and that no one should be surprised by the occurrence of "irrational and violent reactions" against "behavior to which no one has any conceivable right."

I have observed some of those irrational reactions by people coming out to protest at the Gay Pride Parade that goes down New York's Fifth Avenue on the last Sunday of June each year. When you see guys who can find nothing they would rather do than come out on the street to scream insults and vulgarities at homosexuals by the hour, you know something inside them has gone haywire. On the other hand, it seems to me that anyone with a healthy psyche will feel some natural sense of revulsion at the thought of homosexual activity. So I concluded that Cardinal Ratzinger hit the right notes in the right order: the violence is always to be condemned, but the occurrence of incidents cannot surprise anybody, and our condemnation of them should not lead us to condone behavior that is wrong.

The protesters at St. Peter's, of course, took a quite different view. They handed out a leaflet headed "Expose Cardinal Ratzinger's Lies," and charged him with a "calculated campaign of disinformation and crimes against humanity."

I was there covering for the National Catholic News Service, sitting in a pew with the New York Lutheran bishop, William H. Lazareth. When the objectors jumped up to start yelling and creating their ruckus, Bishop Lazarus went to the platform and stood in solidarity with Cardinal Ratzinger—not necessarily in solidarity with all his opinions but with his right to give an undisrupted address and, for any who might wish, the right to hear it. Police, who had been warned something was afoot and knew the ACT-UP style from too much experience, hovered about, and the disordered were soon removed.

The following year, they were at it again. This time they announced their protest threats in advance, so I was at St. Patrick's Cathedral when they shouted down Cardinal O'Connor during his Sunday morning mass (CNS, December 11, 1989). Prepared for this, archdiocesan officials distributed copies of the homily, so the protesters could not claim they kept the cardinal's message from getting out. And after police arrested dozens of protestors, Cardinal O'Connor was able to proceed with the Eucharist. New York's Jewish mayor, Edward I. Koch, was there to show opposition to the disrupters. But the liberal community of New York overall, I noticed, did not give us many signs of thinking the disruption was a bad thing, as they doubtless would have in the case of conservatives disrupting a liberal event.

For a supplementary, eye-opening example, you should have been with me when former Governor Robert P. Casey of Pennsylvania tried to speak about abortion at the Cooper Union, a private college on the edge of the East Village and historically noted as the site of an important speech by Abraham Lincoln during his campaign for the presidency. People came in chanting, "Racist, sexist, anti-gay, Governor Casey, go away," and carrying signs with messages such as "Gov. Casey—You Are Killing Women." For the Catholic News Service, I reported, "Demonstrators included individual critics of Casey and members of such groups as Women's Health Action and Mobilization, known as WHAM, and AIDS Coalition to Unleash Power, called ACT-UP. A din of chanting, catcalls and yelling continued through an introduction of Casey and when he tried to speak" (October 5, 1992). I also reported that the protesters included people who were taking up the case of Mumia Abu-Jamal, a black journalist facing execution on charges of murdering a Philadelphia police officer in 1982, but that part of the story lost out to editorial trimming.

Governor Casey was unusual as a Democrat who opposed abortion, and the Clinton forces refused to let him speak at the Democratic convention held in New York the previous July. So the Cooper Union event was arranged by the

SIDEBARS

Village Voice under the supposition that everyone had a right to be heard, however much his ideas might offend some people. Nat Hentoff, a *Village Voice* columnist and abortion opponent who called himself a Jewish atheist, introduced the governor and, in an old-fashioned rhetoric that failed to touch the protesters, compared them to Stalinists, fascists and the "goons" that management had sent in to break up labor meetings of a previous generation. The protesters similarly ignored a personal appeal from the president of Cooper Union, Jay Iselin, to give the visitor his right to speak.

Police were on hand, but Governor Casey decided he would rather not speak if he could do so only by having the protesters arrested. So after a few minutes he gave up.

Of special interest to me, again, was the lack of any significant reaction on the part of New York's liberal community, which in other circumstances will talk so long and fervently about the right of all ideas to be heard. You might have thought this element would be offended to know a peaceful visitor to their city had been shouted down by what Mr. Hentoff saw as Stalinists, fascists and goons, and that in subsequent days and years the civil libertarians would have mentioned it now and then as one of the blemishes the city should address. But seemingly not.

At St. Peter's Church, however, the sponsors did let the police do their cleanup job and, despite the temporary disruption, Cardinal Ratzinger enjoyed something of a triumph. He was helped by the contrasting style of the disrupters and perhaps even more by liberal critics in the religious community, who had given him an advance buildup that led some people to expect an ecclesiastical Jesse Helms. Instead, they found a thoughtful, learned, low key man who talked like the former professor he was.

His lecture was in fact so academic as to seem not quite suitable for the general audience that had been gathered. Cardinal Ratzinger titled it, "Biblical Interpretation in Conflict: The Foundations and Directions of Exegesis Today," and he dealt largely with the theories of two German Protestants, Martin Dibelius and Rudolph Bultmann, both deceased, with side glances at the philosophers Martin Heidegger and Immanuel Kant. Not really throwing red meat here.

I spotted Judge Robert H. Bork, a lapsed Presbyterian, in the audience, and went over afterward to ask for his reaction to the lecture. "I'm going to have to read it to fully understand it," he said. He was there, he said, mainly to accompany his wife, Mary Ellen, a former nun with theological education.

Cardinal Ratzinger gave his lecture scholarly weight because it was to serve as the basis of a two-day conference with a small group of Protestant, Orthodox and Catholic scholars. The morning after the lecture, he appeared at a press conference with three of them, including Raymond E. Brown, a Catholic priest of the Sulpician society of seminary teachers and a leading New Testament specialist teaching at Union Seminary. "I would be very happy if we had many exegetes like Father Brown," said the prefect of the Congregation for the Doctrine of the Faith. When I later asked Father Brown about complaints of Cardinal Ratzinger interfering with the work of scholars, he commented, "He is no threat to honest and responsible biblical scholarship." Some conservative Catholics had accused Father Brown of taking positions too liberal, and liberals had painted Cardinal Ratzinger as the enemy. But the two men themselves got along well enough with each other, however eagerly their respective followers might consign the other to perdition.

In the course of the press conference, Cardinal Ratzinger also put fundamentalism aside. "It's naïve," he said. Leaders of the Southern Baptist Convention were even then demanding that their seminary professors hold fast to fundamentalist positions, so I had to reflect that Catholic professors today could keep in good standing with their church authorities, and still enjoy more scholarly freedom than Southern Baptists, who had so often boasted of their escape from the tyranny of hierarchs. Actually, one of the services a hierarchy can offer is protecting the intellectuals of the church, the theologians, from the yahoos. Limits are defined, and anyone working responsibly within that general framework can safely explore.

Father Brown was a prime beneficiary of that protection. Even after his death in 1998, a death that saw him still in good and honorable standing with church authorities, his enemies continued their devotion to blackening his name. When I covered a conference that *Crisis* magazine held in New York on the Jesus Seminar, I found some of the leaders using criticism of the more radical scholars in that project as only a takeoff point for attacks on more mainstream Catholic scholars, and particularly Father Brown and John P. Meier, a New Testament specialist who had recently gone from the Catholic University of America to the University of Notre Dame. However, I could point out in balance that Father Brown had been appointed by Pope Paul VI to the Pontifical Biblical Commission, and later appointed for another term by Pope John Paul II. And the work for which Msgr. Meier was best known, *A Marginal Jew: Rethinking the Historical Jesus* (Doubleday), carried the imprimatur of the vicar general of the Archdiocese of New York, Patrick J. Sheridan. The editors handling my story on the conference presumably decided they would prefer to avoid controversy, and cut out my references to the scholars under attack (CNS, November 15, 1999). That is understandable, but the deletion made it impossible for readers to get a clear picture of what was going on.

SIDEBARS

Dignity, an organization of Catholic homosexuals who rejected church teaching on homosexuality, and one of the groups protesting against Cardinal Ratzinger, held its annual convention in New York in 1985. After reporting on it for the National Catholic News Service, I got a letter of thanks from the convention press officer. He began with the general comment that my stories were "well done," but went on to say he appreciated my "presence with us, as so often the so-called 'institutional' church shuns such alienated groups of Catholics." It struck me as rather poignant that people in this group, who sometimes seemed so belligerent, could actually feel quite grateful for quite modest expressions of respect.

Although NC News Service operated under church sponsorship, and I thought the position of the church on homosexuality was correct, neither the editors nor I ever had any thought but that of course we would report whatever was news. And we in fact did not just a story, but two.

In the first (August 23), I led with the interesting point that the Archbishop of New York held center stage at the Dignity convention without even a drop-by. Carol Bellamy, then New York City Council president and now UNICEF director, addressed the convention and got applause by criticizing Cardinal O'Connor's stand against Executive Order 50, Mayor Edward I. Koch's initiative prohibiting discrimination regarding employment of homosexuals. But she said the cardinal's program to care for AIDS patients was "to his credit." John Hager, president of Dignity, commented that holding the convention in New York showed Cardinal O'Connor that "we're not going away." Conventioneers sang "New York, New York." And in allusion to Cardinal O'Connor, one speaker said they found special meaning in the line, "If I can make it here, I'll make it anywhere."

My second article (August 28) reported the homily of Theresa Kane at the convention's concluding mass. Sister Kane, a member of the Sisters of Mercy, had gained notoriety, acclaim and other responses by publicly confronting Pope John Paul II on the issue of women's ordination. When he visited the United States in 1979, she was president of the Leadership Conference of Women Religious, and in that capacity was invited to address the pope. She used the occasion to tell him to his face that all ministries of the church should be open to women.

A couple of months before the Dignity convention, I had covered the nun, Clare Fitzgerald of the School Sisters of Notre Dame, who followed Sister Kane as president of the Leadership Conference (NC, June 21). Sister Fitzgerald said that throughout her term, everybody continued to talk about what had happened in the confrontation with the pope, and hardly anyone ever realized she had succeeded to the post of president.

With the exception of her mother, who, she told us, belonged to a special breed of Boston Catholic Irish, old school. Making a visit back home, the president of the Leadership Conference let herself in the back door, and even before she could put her suitcase down, heard her mother's voice from the front room: "If His Holiness should visit this country again, I want no fresh mouth out of you."

As famous as Sister Kane had become, her position was of course quite controversial in the church. And when I saw that she was speaking to the Dignity conventioneers, I was surprised that she would want to link her cause with theirs, and so directly and personally. But since then, I have seen the tie of the women's movement with the homosexual movement so much, it seems standard, and now I wonder whether they are separable. Maybe they are only two forms of the same movement, and find their unity in the principle that gender does not matter, that a person of either gender is equally serviceable for any purpose.

I do not know what it means, but it does seem inescapable that a rather high percentage of those leading the women's movement in the churches have been either lesbians or divorcees or both. Has it been a mere coincidence or in some way logical that when the United Methodist Church became the first of the major churches in the United States to give a woman the office of bishop, she turned out to be a divorced woman? Was it strange, or was it predictable, that when the ecumenical group of feminists held their Re-imagining Conference in Minneapolis in 1993, their contribution to the World Council of Churches' Ecumenical Decade of Churches in Solidarity with Women, they gave lesbianism a remarkably prominent place on the program? The planning committee arranged for a group session on "Lesbians and Churches Acting Together" and another on "Prophetic Voices of Lesbians in the Church." But according to a newsletter from the conference organizers afterward, when some women "became aware that there was not an adequately visible lesbian and bisexual presence at the plenary level . . . through the process of open negotiation a ritual moment was added to Saturday's plenary."

Melanie Morrison, a founder of CLOUT (Christians and Lesbians Out Together), spoke to that plenary and asked everyone to wrestle with the question, "What does it mean for us to be in solidarity with lesbian, bisexual and transsexual women in this decade?" She then invited the women in those categories to join her on the stage, and dozens did.

Then, at the final Sunday worship service, the preacher, Christine Marie Smith of United Theological Seminary (United Church of Christ) in New Brighton, Minnesota, felt called to announce, "I share this sermon with you as a United Church of Christ pastor and lesbian clergywoman."

But to say another word about Dignity, in New York we saw its operations on the chapter level as well as the national. Before the Gay Pride Parade in 1995, I went to St. Patrick's Cathedral for Cardinal O'Connor's mass, and going in was handed a Dignity leaflet asking why the cathedral had been "allowed to become a citadel of homophobia." Actually, it had become a center of Dignity's self-promotion efforts. Through the years, Dignity members had repeatedly gone there, with announcements beforehand to reporters, and demonstrated till the routine got old and lost its flavor.

But the charge of "homophobia" was more curious. To tell the actual truth, Cardinal O'Connor had almost gone overboard in repeatedly, and repeatedly, stressing that the church felt no hostility toward homosexuals as persons, and in urging everyone to avoid expressions of hatred or any violence against homosexuals.

Others in the Catholic Church were of course expressing their compassion as well. I got to see a soap opera in the making when a Catholic priest, James J. Gardiner of the Atonement Friars, got together an interreligious group of clergy to talk about their AIDS ministries on ABC's *All My Children* (NC, February 2, 1988). Agnes Nixon, a Catholic who was the creator of the show, introduced an AIDS theme, and wrote the clergy into the story line so they could talk about the pastoral approach they took.

What the Catholic Archbishop of New York could hardly be expected to do, however, was call homosexual activity morally acceptable, or declare church approval for an organization such as Dignity that existed to oppose church teaching.

In 1987, Paul Moore Jr., the Episcopal Bishop of New York, was invited to give the homily at a mass sponsored by Dignity, and I went down to report on that occasion (NC, January 21). The mass was then held each Saturday evening at the Church of St. Francis Xavier, a Jesuit church on the edge of Greenwich Village. But someone in the headquarters of the Catholic Archdiocese of New York heard about the plans and sent word to the pastor, Michael E. Donahue, that he was not to let Bishop Moore give the homily. So things were rearranged to place the bishop's talk at the conclusion of the mass, where whatever might be said need not be considered the homily. But Bishop Moore processed in with other priests, wearing vestments, and had a period of kneeling in silent prayer before the altar with Bernard Lynch, an Irish member of the Society of African Missions, who had somehow wound up working with homosexuals in New York. In the non-homily, Bishop Moore expressed his sympathies for homosexuals, recounted a controversy over his ordination of a lesbian and speculated on the coming acceptance of homosexual marriage. The service was billed as an observance of the Week of Prayer for Christian Unity, which officially began the next day. But it seemed like a less than felicitous expression of the ecumenical spirit for a bishop to go into a church of another denomination to encourage a dissident group. It is not possible to imagine Cardinal O'Connor would have done that, or otherwise given public encouragement to an organization of dissident Episcopalians.

Catholic judgments on homosexuality are not just Catholic or Vatican views, I perhaps should point out for any who might get that impression. Karl Barth, as deeply rooted in Reformed Protestantism as anyone could be, also saw homosexuality as "the physical, psychological and social sickness, the phenomenon of perversion, decadence and decay, which can emerge when man refuses to admit the validity of the divine command." That divine command, he pointed out, tells man to recognize "the togetherness of men and women" as the basis of humanity. "The command of God shows him irrefutably—in clear contradiction to his own theories—that as a man he can only be genuinely human with woman, or as a woman with man. In proportion as he accepts this insight, homosexuality can have no place in his life, whether in its more refined or cruder forms" (*Dogmatics III/4,* 166). In the current climate, probably not many people interested in gaining the good opinion of the cultural establishment would use that word "perversion," but I do not see on what basis anyone could say Professor Barth was wrong.

I have been impressed, though, by the way the term "homophobia" has succeeded in intimidating people and blunting criticism of the homosexual movement. As used in the movement, the term seemed to become a weapon against anybody who declined to express moral approval of homosexual acts.

In 1989, I did a CNS story (July 11) on a book, *Sex and Morality in the U.S.* (Wesleyan University Press), that presented a 462-page analysis of a study conducted under the auspices of the Kinsey Institute at the University of Indiana. The research material, collected in 1970, was dated by the time the book got into print, but retained some interest for the finding that, at least as of that date, reports of a "sexual revolution" in American society had been overstated (pp. 3-15). It would not seem so overstated in the post-Monica era, perhaps. But along the way, the book also reported that "homophobia" was a term apparently introduced by two authors, Kenneth T. Smith in 1971 and George Weinberg in 1972, and that the idea anti-homosexuality was a "phobic" response lacked "convincing support" (p. 204). So we could conclude that although people manifesting the irrational reaction cited by Cardinal Ratzinger might be expressing homophobia in the sense that an irrationally negative reaction to foreigners can be called xenophobia, disapproval of homosexuality could not be labeled a phobia psychiatrically.

Further indication that the word had been made up for the current movement came when I later checked the second, 1989, edition of the *Oxford English Dictionary*, and failed to find it. Use of "homophobia" as a term of attack was, however, a shrewd way for homosexuals to promote the idea that it was not themselves but their critics who suffered from a vile disease. And it was an impressive accomplishment of public relations that the homosexual community could so quickly get so many people to saying the word so often.

In 1999, when I checked for "homophobia" in the subject index of the New York Public Library, I found it, but most of the books with the word in the title were recent. The library had set up a cool three dozen subdivisions of this relatively new subject, in fact, apparently viewing it as a growth stock, though at the time most subdivisions had only a single entry. Starting with "homophobia" *per se,* the subdivisions ran alphabetically from "homophobia–economic aspect," "homophobia–fiction" and "homophobia–France" to "homophobia–United States–religious aspects." Along the way there was also "homophobia–religious aspects–United States," so you could play it either way. And the New York Public Library saw need for a category of "homophobia–religious aspects" in general, as well as "homophobia–religious aspects–Christianity" and "homophobia–religious aspects–meditations." But I suspected that the library could have simplified, and conveniently grouped most of its listed books under a single category, like "homophobia–propaganda theme."

The same Kinsey report disputed claims of homosexuals that they represented ten per cent or more of the population, appearing as a more or less predictable minority by birth, like a certain percentage came out left-handed. This attempt to make homosexuality seem normal on the basis that such a tremendous lot of people practice it may factor, too, into works such as Marcel Proust's *Remembrance of Things Past* (Random House/Vintage edition of 1982; tr. C. K. Scott Moncrieff and Terence Kilmartin). He speaks of the ambassador who presides over a "little Sodom" where every member of the staff except himself was characterized by "inversion," and the staff as a whole constituted a "battalion of transvestites" (II, 699). But the numbers really seem beside the point. Homosexual activity would still be abnormal even if it could be proved that everybody in town was acting that way.

I saw, of course, that many defenders of homosexuality argued that individuals were so inclined by birth, or that an unchangeable disposition in this direction was created by something that happened very early in childhood. However, the argument seemed dubious to me, and I found that Beverly Wildung Harrison of Union Seminary, writing from a stance of pro-homosexual advocacy, spoke of homosexuality in terms of a decision. In *Making the*

Connections (Beacon, 1985), she wrote that it was "time for men to acknowledge" that "many women choose lesbian relations because more and more women have moved beyond male dependency and will not accept intimate relations that lack mutuality" (p. 143).

The United Methodist Church has provided an example of a denomination split on the issue of homosexuality, and has wound up trying to stand on both sides of the river at the same time. Wanting to show itself blessedly liberal, broadminded and tolerant, it declared that homosexuals have "sacred worth" and should get their rights. Wanting also to maintain the traditional stance against homosexuality, it said the practice was "incompatible with Christian teaching," and United Methodists refused ordination to "practicing" homosexuals. This dual approach had the political attraction of seeming to offer something to each faction of a polarized membership. But Jeanne Audrey Powers adroitly exposed the futility of that maneuver in a 1995 address to a pro-homosexual group (ENI, July 4, 1995). A United Methodist minister and until 1996 an executive of the denomination's ecumenical unit, she announced that she was a lesbian, always had been, but as for whether she was practicing—well, that was nobody's business.

Many people in the churches were trying out the compromise tactic of saying a homosexual "orientation" was okay, but homosexual acts were not. That of course did not satisfy homosexuals, but I wondered whether it could really express a Christian view either. If you followed the indication of Jesus in the Sermon on the Mount, going back beyond acts to examine the disposition of the heart (Matthew 5:27-28), you might wind up concluding that the orientation was more wrong than the specific activity a guy might get into from time to time.

It will usually be a bit impractical for churches to prove who is practicing what in the area of sex, or proving whether any deviation discovered is only an occasional incident or a regular practice. They can realistically assume that, sin pervading human life as it does, a good many clergy will from time to time slip into practices they ought not. What the churches reasonably and practicably can do is keep their teaching clear, and ask that those who seek ordination make a commitment to teach in accordance with the standards of the church. Serious nonconformity by clergy could then be dealt with on a case-by-case basis as prudence might direct.

In any case, the attempt to distinguish "practicing" homosexuals from some other kind assumed to exist has a questionable aspect to it. However much a man may yearn to be out playing on the links, we can hardly call him a golfer unless he golfs. From some such perspective, we could say that "practicing" homosexuals are the only kind there are, and we have no good reason for pasting the label on someone who has not been doing it.

From some people in the churches, we also got attempts to explain away the biblical passages condemning homosexuality. These condemnations are direct, explicit and sharp, both in the Old Testament and in the New. The same Old Testament book, Leviticus, that gives us the command to "love your neighbor as yourself" (19:18), and to love "the stranger" (19:34), makes it clear that by "love" it does not mean homosexual activity (20:13). And the same New Testament author, Paul, who wrote about love with the eloquence of I Corinthians 13 also let us know that homosexual activity did not express what he meant by "love" (Romans 1:26-27). But the Bible only condemns bad homosexuality and nowhere says it is against good homosexuality, the argument of some more or less boils down to. Their form of biblical exegesis sounds like a rather pure form of sophistry. But whatever may be said on such points one way or the other, the debates appear secondary, and perhaps diversionary. It has always seemed to me that homosexual activity could be recognized as wrong intrinsically, just because of what it is, without regard to whatever biological or psychological theories might be offered to explain how the inclination originates; and recognized as contrary to the biblical vision of life, regardless of any disputes over how specific passages should be interpreted.

Traditional Christian teaching against homosexuality does not reflect merely the cultural views of a particular era or region, but corresponds to the way we exist from creation. It is the human race that is heterosexual. Jesus set forth his conception of the basic order of things by describing humanity in its original appearance: "God made them male and female" (Mark 10:6, referring to Genesis 1:27). And as Karl Barth or somebody has observed, it is a sign of the goodness of this creation that man and woman delight in each other. Where that does not happen, something has gone badly awry.

From specific issues, we can now look at the broader question of how the church does and should relate to the movement called the social gospel, or what is more or less the same thing in another form, liberation theology.

SOCIAL GOSPEL/
LIBERATON THEOLOGY
CHAPTER TWELVE

Thomas Merton, the Trappist monk, was remarkable in too many ways to count, and his influence keeps coming at you from every direction. I once wrote a story on Dave Brubeck and a mass he was commissioned to compose, *To Hope: A Celebration!* When I interviewed him, I was surprised to find him recalling Father Merton as a stimulus to his thinking. The priest had ignited a reconsideration of his musical ideas by remarking that he found the Gregorian chant at his abbey, Gethsemani in Kentucky, stronger than Bach. "I almost jumped out of my chair because Bach to me is so strong," Mr. Brubeck recalled (NC, August 30, 1982).

One way Father Merton keeps coming at me in New York is through the Merton Lecture that is given every year at Columbia University, where he was a student when he entered the Catholic Church, the experience recounted in *The Seven-Storey Mountain* (Harcourt, Brace, 1948).

In 1987, the lecture turned out to be mostly homiletical and not a news story, but still an educational benefit for me. The lecturer was Joan Chittister, a Benedictine nun who goes about preaching a zealous message of social radicalism. The audience seemed to consist largely of her followers, and at the end they gave her a resounding and prolonged standing ovation. But there was a lot of highly controversial material in her address, and I thought it perhaps not prudent for the representative of the National Catholic News Service to be seen jumping up and applauding it all. So I kept my seat, wanting to avoid any activity that could be interpreted as making a statement of my own. But the standing ovation went on and on, and then on some more. The people who like that sort of thing, boy, they sure do. I seemed to be the only reporter there, and as I remained conspicuously alone sitting down while everybody else stood to clap and clap and clap, I realized I was making more of a statement by not conforming. So I decided on a change of policy: From now on, if everybody else stands to declare appreciation, I will, too, thinking in my own mind that however bad some may judge it to be, the speaker can still deserve thanks for not making it any worse. So if you see me politely applauding somebody's sizzling remarks one day, do not make too much of it. The next day I may be across town politely applauding the speaker who pours cold water.

When Boutros Boutros-Ghali was pursuing his hopeless, inexplicable and embittering attempt to get a second term as secretary general of the United Nations, when he knew the powers then prevailing had predetermined that he could not have it, he reminded us that President Clinton had said some nice things about him at a dinner. But Madeleine Albright, then the U.S. ambassador to the UN and a facilitator of the secretary general's redeployment, observed that one should not make too much of a dinner toast. Nor should one make too much of the applause of politeness.

The year after Sister Chittister, we got something of different character in a Merton Lecture given by John P. Meier, a Catholic priest who was a prominent New Testament scholar at the Catholic University of America in Washington. He would become even better known in 1991, when he published the first part of a three-volume work, *Marginal Jew: Rethinking the Historical Jesus* (Doubleday). His lecture–delivered, like all the Merton Lectures, in St. Paul's Chapel–turned out to be a critique of the way liberation theologians used the Bible.

Now, if you have decided certain people are demonic, you may feel zest in criticizing them. But life gets trickier and your stomach feels queasier when you set out to deal with others you have decided are basically good people, intelligent and well-motivated, working hard to accomplish worthy objectives, but going about it in the wrong way. From this perspective, if you do not want to join with right wingers mad about threats to their economic interests, critiquing liberation theologians becomes a complex affair. So as a preliminary, Father Meier let us know that he admired these theologians personally, and applauded their efforts to improve social conditions for people who were impoverished. But he found them hasty in drawing parallels between the political situation of Latin America in the late twentieth century and what Jesus and the early Christians were doing in the first century.

Although liberation theology as a movement came out of Latin America, some people in the United States have been working along similar lines, and there is a continuity with trends in North America and Europe commonly identified as the social gospel.

Norman K. Gottwald of New York Seminary can serve as our example of U.S. interpreters of the Bible who have tried to make it a political document pointed toward the left. To do this, he more frankly than some others acknowledged that he could not take the Bible as it was, but had to set aside large parts as distorting additions to a supposedly original message centered on class conflict.

While not a dominating figure in the field of biblical study, Professor Gottwald has not been left in the backwaters either, but attained eminence enough to be elected president of the leading professional body, the Society of Biblical Literature. His approach was set forth in his 1992 presidential address, "Social Class as an Analytic and Hermeneutical Category in Biblical Studies," published in the society's *Journal of Biblical Literature* the following year (Vol. I, pp. 3-22). After looking through the Old Testament for evidence, he came to the New, and said:

"An array of repeated themes in the Jesus traditions speaks overwhelmingly for his deliberate participation in social conflict: his focus on the destitute and marginalized elements of the populace, his open table fellowship, his severe strictures on wealth, his cavalier attitude toward the legitimacy of Roman and Temple taxes, his symbolic attack on the Temple economy, his healing of sickness and demon possession as symptoms of social oppression, and his rejection of the ideology that the personal sin of the victim was the cause of all or most of the social misery he encountered" (p. 17).

Others have joined Professor Gottwald in giving the Gospels this political twist, but I have not been able to see the justification. It is not merely that he went overboard with words such as "overwhelmingly," but that the whole body of Gospel material points so unambiguously in the other direction. The quotation I have given seems wrong on every point: Jesus did not involve himself in social conflict as a specific overall strategy, but in the situation of man as such. His focus was on whoever he met, at times maybe a centurion or Nicodemus, a ruler of the Jews, not particularly on the "destitute and marginalized." His apostles were chosen from among ordinary men, not the down and out or the ostracized. His "open table fellowship" was a matter of eating with sinners, not necessarily those low on the power scale. On taxes, Jesus did not show an attitude that could be called "cavalier," an upper class outlook, but supported the right of the state to collect. His "attack on the Temple economy" expressed a concern for the Temple, not the economy. We do not read of him trying to clean up the governor's palace, where we might expect anybody concerned about economic reform to begin. The sickness and demon possession conquered by Jesus were not "symptoms of social oppression" but expressions of the power of Satan, and the two were not equated in "the Jesus traditions."

Professor Gottwald was ready to admit that not all the New Testament supported his position, so he took the biblical material apart and found that passages he believed would have supported him more explicitly got toned down by "redactions," editorial revisions. And then he proposed that by determining—we know not how—the way particular teachings would have been taken by a "Palestinian peasant audience struggling under the burden of multilayered surplus extraction," we could find out "what Jesus had in mind" (p. 18). We might have expected Professor Gottwald to say "Jewish" peasant audience, since Jesus focused his ministry on "the lost sheep of the house of Israel" (Matthew 15:24). But in leftist politics today, a spotlighting of the "Palestinian" oppressed may carry more resonance.

However may be the case about "multilayered surplus extraction" and all that, we do not have here a debate between traditionalists and those who have broken through to freedom, scientific research or whatever. Some people seem to suggest we get only two choices, but actually we can consider alternatives. Rudolph Bultmann (1884-1976), a New Testament professor in Marburg, Germany, and not much of a fundamentalist he, concluded that the message of Jesus was connected with a hope that expects salvation not from a change in social and political conditions but from "a cosmic catastrophe which will do away with all conditions of the present world as it is" (*Theology of the New Testament*, tr. Kendrick Grobel; New York, Scribner's, Vol. I, p. 4). Getting to the comprehensible core of that message requires some digging, of course, but it is digging in a direction away from Professor Gottwald.

In any case, I cannot see why the church should set aside the interpretation of Jesus given by the New Testament authors, and replace it with some professor's speculation on what may have occurred in the thought processes of some first century peasants, which nobody has or ever will have any way of learning anything about.

Liberation theologians did not necessarily go at the Bible the way Professor Gottwald did, but they had similar goals. For a time, their movement was among the most debated subjects in the religious world, and a topic I naturally asked about when I interviewed visitors from Latin America. Gustavo Gutiérrez, a Catholic priest working in Lima, Peru, published what became the basic text, *A Theology of Liberation*, in Spanish in 1971 and in English translation (Orbis Press) two years later. Reading it, I recognized the motivating concern to help people living in poverty, but was left with many questions.

On the political side, the questions centered on the issue of whether movement in a Marxist direction, where Father Gutiérrez and his colleagues seemed to be heading, would really alleviate the problems of poor people, or do it better than other approaches, or would perhaps take away what freedoms and opportunities poor people already had. But liberation theology also raised questions on the religious side. Was its teaching really the message of the New Testament?

Father Meier did not speak of Father Gutiérrez specifically, but described the liberation theologians generally in terms such as "naïve" and "outdated" in reference to their assumption that they could write an objective historical account of New Testament events, separated from the interpretation given to those events by the New Testament authors, and then draw direct lessons in keeping with their goals for changing society.

Jon Sobrino, a Jesuit who, like the founder of his order, Ignatius Loyola, was a Basque, though born in Barcelona because his parents wanted to get away from Franco's armies, was one of those singled out by name for "fraternal correction" by Father Meier. The corrector said liberation theologians such as Father Sobrino and Juan Luis Segundo, a Catholic priest in Uruguay, showed a "fatal attraction" to S. G. F. Brandon, an English scholar who contributed to the portrait of Jesus as a political agitator by connecting him to the first century zealots, a party that actually did not arise until after the time of Jesus.

Father Meier also said the books of Father Sobrino, who had been teaching many years in El Salvador and oriented his work to the situation there, sought to base a liberation program for Latin America on a use of the New Testament that could not be sustained by scholarly methods. And Father Sobrino's references to the poor, understood in the literal sense, were not valid for the New Testament, he said, because there the poor were understood in the manner of Matthew's Beatitudes, "Blessed are the poor in spirit" (5:3). He said Father Sobrino then went further astray in asserting that opposition to Jesus arose because of his concern for the poor. Actually, Father Meier said, the New Testament shows the opposition arising because Jesus accepted tax collectors, who were oppressors. It was a shocking aspect of the behavior of Jesus that he would "eat with tax collectors and sinners" (Mark 2:16).

Talk about the poor is something we are often needing to watch out for. We hear an awful lot of it if we go to the right gatherings, and for the first hundred thousand hours or so it can sound very pious. But later on we may begin to sense a certain amount of cant coming through this rhetoric. At a 1968 meeting in Medellin, Colombia, the Catholic bishops of Latin America declared a "preferential option for the poor." And that has become a central theme of liberation theology, and even something of a cliché to be heard all over the field of Catholic discourse. As a slogan, it sure beats "preferential option for the rich and famous," which seems to be the tacit commitment of some clergy. But taken as a primary expression of church life, "preferential option for the poor" puts the Christian message off-center. God's preferential option is for sinners, fortunately. "Christ Jesus came into the world to save sinners" (I Timothy 1:15), who may be found in all classes.

Anyway, the New Testament could give you different ideas than government statistics about just who are the poor, and who is rich as God evaluates the human scene. In the letters to the seven churches of Revelation, believers at Smyrna are said to be rich despite their poverty (2:9), but those at Laodicea talk about their wealth "not knowing that you are wretched, pitiable, poor, blind and naked" (3:17)

In the rhetoric of politicized theology of the left (not to forget the existence of a politicized theology of the right), we also hear much talk of the oppressed and their oppressors. Reference to a concordance will show, however, that this is mostly Old Testament language, and is found rarely in the New Testament. Which is not to say the language is passé, but only that it must be interpreted from a New Testament perspective if it is to take its place in the interpretation of Christian ethics. References comparable to the concept of oppressors in a literal economic sense can be found in the book of James. But the central New Testament idea is better expressed in the preaching of Peter that Jesus "went about doing good and healing all that were oppressed by the devil" (Acts 10:38).

In Christian thought, we are all oppressed by sin and the devil, and as sinners we all oppress each other. In the structures of this world, to be sure, those who are bigger push around those who are littler. But even in the terms of this world, the question of who is big and who is little cannot be so simply determined. It is common to speak in global terms of the North oppressing the South. But then it also becomes necessary to analyze societies of the South in class terms, and distinguish oppressor and oppressed classes. When feminism is added to this mix, then even peasant men are lumped in the category of oppressors. And so on.

Here we again come across the tendency of many people to get themselves recognized as the oppressed, the yearning sometimes called victimology. History is recounted and past injuries are rubbed raw every morning so they will bleed afresh and justify a hostile, aggressive stance toward the accused. I once (CNS, September 27, 1991) interviewed Clarence Gallagher, a Jesuit priest who was rector of the Pontifical Oriental Institute, when he was visiting New York from his base in Rome. He told me that progress toward Catholic unity with the Eastern churches was often blocked more by history and emotion than by doctrine. The Greeks, he said, keep bringing up the rampage of the Crusaders at Constantinople in 1204. "It was a terrible thing, but they talk about it as if it was just last week," he said.

I had interviewed Father Sobrino when he visited Maryknoll for a commemoration of liberation theology earlier in 1988 (NC, July 21). And I got to talk with him again in 1995, when he came to New York for a meeting of the Catholic Theological Society (CNS, June 16). Despite all the "fraternal correction" he had been offered, he was continuing to advocate liberation theology as a "must," I found. But in 1995 he conceded it was not doing so well. One key factor, he pointed out, was a change in the composition of the hierarchy. In the 1960s, when liberation theology was launched, Dom Helder Camara of Brazil and several other bishops gave their support, and protected the theologians developing it. But as those bishops retired, Pope John Paul II replaced them with more conservative types. In El Salvador the outspoken archbishop, Oscar Arnulfo Romero, was followed by a more moderate Arturo Rivera Damas, whose replacement in 1995 was a member of Opus Dei, Fernando Saenz-Lacalle. Another factor, Father Sobrino said, was a lowered vitality in the parish sub-groups, called base communities, that had sought to implement the goals of liberation theology locally. And he could not point to younger theologians publishing in this tradition who showed stature comparable to the founders. In the pragmatic sphere, he also had to acknowledge that the efforts of Fidel Castro in Cuba and the Sandinistas in Nicaragua failed to produce the results people in the liberation theology camp had hoped for. The following year, I talked with Cardinal Lucas Moreira Neves of Sao Salvador da Bahia, Brazil, and found he had a simpler analysis: Brazilian Catholics who had been relying on Marxism abandoned it after it collapsed in Eastern Europe (CNS, May 13, 1996).

When critics attacked liberation theology for its Marxism, defenders in the United States commonly replied that the Marxism was used only as a tool for analysis, and liberation theologians did not necessarily want to put their societies under the rule of communist parties. In theory, people who adhere to a particular philosophy or theology could adopt diverse positions on how its goals should be pursued in the practical sphere. But when I interviewed César Jerez, a Jesuit who was a university president in Managua during the Sandinista years, he drew a correlation: People who liked the theology of Father Gutiérrez generally liked the politics of the Sandinistas, and those who did not, generally did not.

Theologians who used Marxist analysis tended to take a Marxist view of what the problems were, it seemed to me, and then of what the solutions were, differing mainly perhaps in desiring a revolution with less violence, and in requesting permission to carry on afterward with some sort of religious activities. I figured that if a man was Marxist in diagnosis and in remedial action, it might not matter so much whether he called himself Marxist in the total sense or not.

It was at the headquarters of the Maryknoll Fathers in Ossining that I talked with Father Jerez. This town, located in Westchester County, a few miles above New York, is by coincidence also the location of the prison nicknamed

Sing Sing, but I have not drawn any conclusions from that. Father Jerez, like Father Sobrino, had come to Maryknoll for the conference the society was hosting in the summer of 1988 to commemorate the 15th anniversary of the English edition of Father Gutiérrez's *A Theology of Liberation,* the 20th anniversary of his coining the term, theology of liberation, and his own 60th birthday, celebrated with the traditional tribute volume of essays often called by its German name of festschrift. *A Theology of Liberation* and the *festschrift* were published by Orbis Press, an arm of the Maryknoll Society. The press had been established by Miguel D'Escoto, a Maryknoll priest who became Nicaraguan foreign minister under the Sandinistas, and it served as the main publisher of books in the school of liberation theology.

Father Gutiérrez himself was at Maryknoll lecturing and holding a press conference, and I also interviewed him (NC, July 12, 1988). He turned out to be a likeable fellow. A short pear shape, he lectured with seriousness and humor, and made expressive use of his hands. I got an impression he had the humility to take a servant role, and wanted to operate as a theologian of the church. That was in some contrast with Hans Kung, the Swiss priest who was a Catholic and a theologian but in the Vatican's view not a Catholic theologian. Father Kung gave off a little of the Muhammed Ali aura, and you could imagine him saying, "Bring on the pope! Bring on the pope! I'll show you how to one-two pontifically rope-a-dope a pope!" Though in balance, I must immediately add that Father Kung was totally cordial to me when I interviewed him for a story I was doing on one of his books (CNS, April 16, 1992).

At Maryknoll, Father Gutiérrez went all out to present himself as a theologian of the Catholic Church, seeking to expound his ideas in harmony with the popes and bishops. And he seemingly was ready now to play down the political. At the end of my interview, he protested, "You haven't asked anything about my book on Job."

He acknowledged that the 1984 and 1986 instructions on liberation theology from the Vatican Congregation for the Doctrine of the Faith—the first, particularly, critical of liberation theology but not naming individual theologians—were "relevant observations for myself," and had led to his changing some of the ways he expressed his views. He added, however, that concern for the poor remained his starting point.

Although Father Gutiérrez indicated that the political matters covered in *A Theology of Liberation* were not central to his concern, they were central to mine at that stage, because it was largely the way liberation theology was structured to enlist the church in support of leftist politics that made it an item of news interest. So I led off asking Father Gutiérrez if he were a socialist, and he countered pragmatically that it depended on how the term was understood.

I thought a theologian who had been speaking and writing and quoting other authors as much as Father Gutiérrez might be ready to give first a simple yes or no, and then if necessary explain in what sense yes or no. Were anybody interested enough to ask, I would have no trouble saying straightforwardly that I am not a socialist. But he was presumably answering guardedly to protect himself in the world of North American polemics.

Father Gutiérrez then settled on a formula: "I accept the possibility of the socialist way." I suspected his heart was a little more into it than that, but maybe not. At the time, his own country was troubled by a radical Maoist group called Sendero Luminosa (Shining Path), and he did not equivocate in denouncing them for their campaign of murder, which did not exempt the poor. More significant for the international debate, he also declined to give the nihil obstat to Fidel Castro, a hero to so many left-leaners in and out of the church. Father Gutiérrez said Cuba had done better than some other Latin American countries in providing for food and health. "But Cuba has problems for me and other people in regard to freedom," he said. "The human being needs freedom as well."

Orbis put out a new edition of *A Theology of Liberation* to mark the 15th anniversary, and Father Gutiérrez wrote a new introduction for it. Of special interest to me, this introduction included a retraction of what was called the dependency theory. According to this theory, poor countries such as those in Latin America were poor because dominating capitalist nations so arranged the world economy as to keep them in poverty, and let them only supply raw materials for the manufacturing centers. Poor countries were kept economically dependent by deliberate decision. But in the new introduction, Father Gutiérrez said social science no longer supported that theory, so he was giving it up.

"It is clear," he wrote, "that the theory of dependence, which was so extensively used in the early years of our encounter with the Latin American world, is now an inadequate tool, because it does not take sufficient account of the internal dynamics of each country or of the vast dimensions of the world of the poor" (p. xxiv).

To me, that was a significant shift, but I heard none of his supporters taking note of it. The retraction was not an incidental matter such as finding advances in medical science made some illustrative allusion to heart disease unusable. The dependency theory in one formulation or another gave thrust to all the many theologies developed throughout the world that in one way or another identified themselves as forms of liberation theology. In essence, they all said, "The problems of me and my kind are caused by you and your kind." If we now had to consider our "internal dynamics," we were off on a different path.

Why was there so little reaction? My impression is that many people enthused about liberation theology were not bothering with close reading of what the liberation theologians actually said, but just thought it was a good thing to take the side of the poor, and were happy to see that the liberation theologians talked about doing that. And I suppose many enthusiasts were drawn by the excitement of revolutionary rhetoric.

However excited, though, people of this outlook often tried to deny they were aligning themselves with Marxists, rather than defend their choice explicitly as the best option they saw in the circumstances. Roy L. Bourgeois, a Maryknoll priest who later became leader of the movement to close the School of the Americas, the U.S. government's facility for training Latin American military officers, set off international alarms by disappearing in El Salvador one day in 1981. He showed up eleven days later, reporting he had been out with the armed opposition to the government. On his return to the United States, he appeared at a press conference at Kennedy Airport, and I was sent out to cover it (NC, May 8). The Maryknoll superior, James P. Noonan, had reacted indignantly when the president of El Salvador, Jose Napoleon Duarte, suggested Father Bourgeois might not have been abducted by right wing forces, but maybe joined the guerrillas voluntarily. Father Noonan, refusing to entertain such a thought, insisted that the El Salvador authorities should go to any lengths to rescue Father Bourgeois, and that the U.S. government should make them do it.

So the superior now sat with a bit of egg on his face as Father Bourgeois stood at a lectern, smiled broadly and declared that a chance to learn about the struggle of the people "transcended" his responsibility to the Maryknoll Society, and its requirement about checking decisions with superiors.

One of the comments he got in talking with the people, he reported, was, "We don't need communists or Marxists to tell us we are hungry." When he asked about Marxist influence, "They laughed at me." Since the Farabundo Marti Front for National Liberation (FMLN), the coalition leading the guerrilla struggle, included the Communist Party of El Salvador and a couple of its offshoots, the nature of the laughter may not have been as he seemed to interpret it. But the comment illustrated the tendency of some church representatives to evade issues. Not many of those aligning themselves with Marxist movements were ready to argue directly what appeared to be their real view: we believe the cause of these people is valid and deserves our support, regardless of the ideological terms they use in promoting it and regardless of the international ties they have established.

Father Noonan said the action of Father Bourgeois was "a serious mistake" that Maryknoll "deeply regrets," but that he remained in good standing, and there would be no disciplinary action. Father Bourgeois acknowledged no mistake or regret. But he was only one of many people in the churches who worked against the U.S. policy of resisting global expansion of the Marxist movement. Looking at a particular society, these critics of U.S. policy tended to see the Marxists as the good guys, sweeping away the oppression and despair of the past, but would not linger even to ask whether existing evils might possibly be replaced by greater.

In the 1980s, El Salvador became a focal point for these issues. A coup in October of 1979 created alarm and pessimism about any improvement in conditions there. Then in 1980 came the assassination of Archbishop Romero, on March 24, and on December 2 the killing of four Catholic missionary women from the United States: Maryknoll Sisters Ita Ford and Maura Clark, Ursuline Sister Dorothy Kazel and laywoman Jean Donovan. Ronald Reagan, elected in November that year, threw his support behind the government of El Salvador, and much of the mainstream church community organized to fight his policy. We saw a phenomenon often repeated: the U.S. government declaring it would support an existing regime to prevent a Marxist takeover, church officials denouncing evils of the existing regime but denying, playing down or ignoring any connections to the international communist movement. When the matter of foremost concern to the U.S. government got no serious attention from church critics of government policy, the public was deprived of a clarifying straightforward debate.

In 1981, a high level delegation from the National Council of Churches visited the El Salvador capital, San Salvador, and came back to issue a report that did not even mention the Marxist or international communist aspect. The only allusion came when they reported, "We heard calls for the cessation of all outside support of the warring parties, whether from the U.S. or from socialist nations." But if you thought you were about to get into some even-handed analysis, they exposed your naivete by immediately going on to add: "Nevertheless, the massiveness of U.S. support is singled out over and over again for particular objection, though the U.S. ambassador urges even greater U.S. assistance." The report gave the impression that the only factors worth noting were violence by the government of El Salvador, and the support it got from the United States.

Writing an analysis for EPS (June 26, 1983), I reported that the NCC board unanimously approved a resolution opposing economic or military support for the El Salvador government. The resolution argued that the conflict in El Salvador was the result of past U.S. support for dictatorships, and of missionary work that separated faith from politics. Not Soviet and Cuban intervention, as Reagan officials said. "Although there are some honorable exceptions to these historical patterns, we consider Central America today with a deep sense of repentance for our national and ecclesiastical complicity in current problems," the NCC said. And I could report that the NCC's position reflected what it heard from the Latin American Council of Churches. Those leaders wrote that U.S. churches should act to "change the course of oppressive, militaristic and dishonest policies of your governors."

Oscar Bolioli, a former president of the Uruguay Methodist Church who had become Latin America secretary for the NCC, told me that on a joint visit to Washington leaders of the NCC and the Latin American Council found State Department officials would not agree with their analysis, and the visiting church leaders could not get in to talk with anybody at the White House. So President Reagan showed more ability to stay the course than they did to "change the course." And when the Soviet Union decided it could no longer subsidize Cuba, and Cuba's ability to carry on international activities diminished, the guerrillas of El Salvador decided to end the civil war, an indication Soviet and Cuban intervention may have had more to do with it than the NCC had ever acknowledged.

When I talked with the Catholic auxiliary bishop of San Salvador, Gregorio Rosa Chávez, in 1990, he told me that the change of government in Nicaragua had affected the guerrillas in his country (CNS, April 10). Despite denials, Sandinista support for them had been "obvious," he said. But at that point, the influence of Cuba still remained "muy grande," he added. "I am not a military strategist. But it seems there are many ways they are helping."

In the same interview, Bishop Rosa registered a protest about attempts underway to use Archbishop Romero for political purposes. "That's a big temptation for some groups," he said. They spoke of him only as a prophet against social injustice, when he was also a pastor "in love with Christ and with his church."

Bishop Rosa said the two statements such groups most often attributed to Archbishop Romero were both of doubtful authenticity:

"If they kill me, I will be resurrected in the Salvadoran people."

"A bishop will die, but the church will remain because the church is the people."

Bishop Rosa said both were found only in an interview by an unknown journalist printed in a Mexican newspaper, *Excelsior*. Revolutionaries quoted the statements so often, he suggested, out of a belief they could be used to serve revolutionary goals.

Another consideration regarding the El Salvador situation that occurred to me, however, was the pertinence of a test used in ethical theory regarding the "just war." Among other criteria, the *Catechism of the Catholic Church,* issued by the Vatican in 1994, says that in order to consider recourse to military conflict justified "there must be serious prospects of success" (paragraph 2309). True as it was that the government and paramilitary forces of El Salvador inflicted gross brutalities, a question or two could be asked of those church leaders who encouraged Salvadorans to enter into and continue a civil war: Was there a realistic prospect that their resort to violence would succeed? And these years later, what can be seen as the accomplishments that justify all the killing, all the destruction, all the disruption of life, sending so many thousands into exile from their homeland?

In Nicaragua, some did not merely take the position that the United States should stay out and in neutral fashion leave the Nicaraguans to settle their own affairs. Rather, they gave their hearts to "the Revolution." The Sandinistas, like Fidel Castro earlier, had strong support in the circles called "justice and peace," or "peace with justice," as they sometimes said. The United States was supporting and coordinating "an effort to destroy the hope of the Nicaraguan people," said a "litany of contrition" used at a service I covered in 1983 at the Church Center for the United Nations (NC, July 7). Held July 6, it was coordinated with a visit to Nicaragua at the time by people from the Carolina Interfaith Task Force on Central America. From the Church Center for the UN, worshipers went a block up First Avenue to the U.S. Mission to the UN, and left a letter to Ambassador Jeane Kirkpatrick, telling her that the U.S. government was supporting people who were "killing Christians in the name of Christianity." The letter was signed by representatives of the Maryknoll Sisters, the Justice and Peace Office of the Maryknoll Fathers and Brothers, the Human Rights Office of the NCC, Church Women United, a coalition of women's religious orders in the Intercommunity Center for Justice and Peace, an Interreligious Task Force and other groups. Not just a fringe movement here.

The predisposition to side with revolutionaries could be found in other areas as well. In 1970, one of my RNS assignments was to write about the Young Lords (January 22). That was a radical Hispanic group that had taken over the First Spanish United Methodist Church in East Harlem the previous December 28, and demanded that the church let them use its building for a breakfast program, a day care center and a "liberation school." The Young Lords condemned the church because it was "only" conducting its worship and other church activities, and not, according to their standards, serving the community. Legal action and the intervention of sheriff's deputies were required to get the building back in the hands of the church.

A remarkable aspect of all this was the amount of support the Young Lords got from national church leaders, taking their side against this local church. At the Interchurch Center, many of the most prominent executives in the United Methodist Board of Global Ministries, NCC and other church agencies signed letters to United Methodist Bishop Lloyd C. Wicke of New York and other officials calling for them to join forces with the Young Lords also. Those who seized control of the building, I pointed out in the RNS story, were proclaiming their admiration for Marx, Lenin and Mao, and calling themselves a "revolutionary political party" that believed "armed self defense and armed struggle are the only way to liberation." Recalling the atmosphere of those days, I would not know whether to say the church executives backed the Young Lords in spite of their radical rhetoric, or because of it. While people in the churches have many and varied ideas about what kind of social programs churches should operate, it seemed to me in any case a little strange that so many church leaders would support an armed revolutionary group trying to force a church to set aside its own view of what its ministry should be, and adopt theirs. But it was then the fashion in much of the respectable church world to fall in step with secular revolutionaries any time they came into conflict with the church.

It became a sort of general principle in such quarters that the church itself should be "revolutionary," without too careful discrimination about just what that would mean as push came to shove, or how various revolutionaries might be expected to act if they gained power. In 1971, when I covered a 30th anniversary dinner of the journal *Christianity and Crisis,* I found John C. Bennett, chairman of the editorial board, asserting it was not sufficient to get out of Vietnam, but that the United States should end "our whole counter-revolutionary foreign policy" (RNS, March 17). The United States, he said, was "trying to control as much of the world as we can in the interest of our own ideology." I did not know what the ideology of the United States was, or whether we as a nation even had one. But I thought there was more involved in the international struggle with the Kremlin than anybody's ideology. The struggle sometimes put the United States in bed with people who did not smell very good, and that could always justify some reconsideration, but I never imagined the struggle could just be abandoned.

Dr. Bennet, who was praised at the dinner by General Secretary Eugene Carson Blake of the WCC as one of the foremost contributors to ecumenical social thought, also said the church should change "so that it may cease to stand in the way of its own radical message." In those days, it came to seem that many people would rather say the word "radical" than eat ice cream. Sometimes they would go learned on you and start explaining how the word derived from the Latin for "root," and meant going to the root of an issue, which could mean whatever the person rooting around might wish.

To some extent, all this was just replaying tunes from the 1930s. Reinhold Niebuhr had once edited a little journal called *Radical Religion,* but in 1940, deciding it was time maybe to think about the need for a conservative force against the radical change the Nazis wanted, changed the name to a moderate-sounding *Christianity and Society.*

Curiously enough, the founders of Union Seminary, from which Dr. Bennett had just retired after a long career as professor and then president, included businessmen of substance who did not consider radicalism such a sweet dish. The initial statement of seminary purpose read: "It is the design of the founders to provide a Theological Seminary in the midst of the greatest and most growing community in America, around which all men of moderate views and feelings, who desire to live free from party strife, and to stand aloof from all extremes of doctrinal speculation, practical radicalism, and ecclesiastical domination, may cordially and affectionately rally."

When I entered Union in 1959, that statement was being read publicly from time to time–at opening ceremonies and the like. I heard it oft times. But after I left–not to imply, because I left–that ceased to be the case. The wind shifted, and the mood became pro-radicalism, and the more practical the better. A group of cheeky students once formed a group they called the "practical radicals." And in 1975, Dr. Bennett published a book he titled *The Radical Imperative* (Westminster). So we were not really where God and the Union establishment would want us if we were not radical. In the background lay the rather practical, going to the root fact that a good portion of Dr. Bennett's salary at Union had been coming from earnings on capital the seminary had invested on Wall Street. When a president's ability to pay seminary bills next month depends on the smooth functioning of the capitalist system, just how radical can he really want to be? You could find in there what I suppose the Marxists might call a contradiction.

To all this, I must add that Dr. Bennett in person was among the most moderate of men, and only got into this radicalism routine I would guess because of the extraordinary tensions that swirled around Vietnam, Richard M. Nixon, the civil rights movement and other aspects of what are called "the sixties." Dr. Bennett had a wife, Anne McGrew Bennett, who started life in a sod house in Nebraska and who really was a radical personality type, pushing him along when she could. In an earlier generation, she would have been one of the women with the hatchets going after the booze. But her husband was always telling her, and the rest of us, that you also had to take into account other aspects of the situation.

When I published a profile of Dr. Bennett in the *Christian Science Monitor* just after his retirement at the end of June 1970, I referred to his reputation as a radical, qualifying it in places, and also mentioned that he was a shy man. After *Monitor* editors put the phrase "shy radical" into a headline, Dr. Bennett wrote me, "I suspect that if the truth were told I am shyer than I am radical, but your interpretation is a pleasing one . . . . I hope that your journalistic opportunities abound."

The affair of the Young Lords had the incidental effect of revealing that, however much radicalism may have seeped into the United Methodist Church one way or another, officials of the denomination in New York were not totally in the radical stream. Some of the Union Seminary students had shown their support for the Young Lords by taking over Bishop Wicke's office in the Interchurch Center, which did not win his sympathies. And to the letter signers, one of those addressed, District Superintendent Wesley D. Osborne, shot back, "Not one of the 63 signers, 'staff of church agencies,' made an effort to talk with the addressee before issuing their terms." Writing January 16, they had called for him to withdraw support from a legal injunction against the Young Lords and "do everything in your power to facilitate the participation of the Young Lords with the church in a free breakfast program and other forms of community service." And they gave Mr. Osborne his deadline: he had till January 20 to get it done.

Some three years later, doing a "whatever happened to" article for *New World Outlook* (July 1973), a publication of the United Methodist Board of Global Ministries, I reported that the East Harlem church under a new pastor was getting increasingly involved in the community. As for the Young Lords, who had rather grandiosely set themselves up as a kind of revolutionary government, with one young fellow called "minister of defense" and another "minister of information" and so on, well, "nobody has heard much about them for a while."

The Young Lords got not only the support of with-it church executives, but many others who vibrated to radical rhetoric as the fashion of the hour–Jane Fonda and so on. Then, with the photogenic young revolutionaries in their dashing berets getting so much publicity, politicians decided to score their points, and the church was able to get city funds for a day care center.

One factor in the limited program of the church had been that its small membership of mostly low income members were struggling to pay off the debt incurred by the necessity of rebuilding the church after a fire. But the new pastor, Pedro Pirone, told me that in any case he had reservations about handout operations for adults. "I don't like to see eighty people in a line waiting for a handout like we had last summer," he said. "Any time you give a person something like that, you also take something from him–something of his dignity and self-respect."

There had been a second takeover of the church in October of 1970, after a Young Lord jailed for attempted arson, Julio Roldan, was found hanged in his cell. The authorities said it was suicide, but the Young Lords claimed he was murdered, bought his body to the church and stood guard with guns at the church entrance and on both sides of the casket. Years later, Pablo Guzman, who had been the "minister of information," wrote about this in an article published in the *Village Voice* (March 21, 1995) and reprinted in *The Puerto Rican Movement*, a book of essays edited by Andre Torres and Jose E. Velazquez (Temple University Press, 1998). According to the minister's information, a "hard-liner," Gloria Fontanez, had gained power in their group, and insisted on staying with the "issue" of Mr. Roldan's supposed murder by the police "regardless of its actual truth." And he added that "the majority went along." Which strategy I gather is not particularly unusual among groups of this type.

For my article, "whatever happened to," I talked with Norman Eddy, a minister who, with his wife, Margaret, both Anglos, had lived and worked in East Harlem for decades as leaders of the East Harlem Protestant Parish. For all the talk of the Young Lords about "the community," they were no more a part of it than the church members had been, Mr. Eddy told me. Many of the church members lived elsewhere, and came into the area only to go to their church, which is not a rare phenomenon in New York church life. But Mr. Eddy said the Young Lords also had only a base of operations in the area, and mostly lived in other places.

"Very few people of the neighborhood ever supported the Young Lords," Mr. Eddy said. In his estimation, they had more support among the denominational executives in the Interchurch Center than they ever got in El Barrio.

Questions about the handout operations of churches also arose in my mind when I was reporting on one of the larger feeding operations in New York, the lunch program of Holy Apostles Episcopal Church. In the early 1990s, I was doing some writing for the Episcopal Presiding Bishop's Fund for World Relief. It supported domestic as well as foreign projects, and Katerina Katsarka Whitley, editor of its publication, *Lifeline*, asked me to write about some of the grant recipients in the United States, one of which was Holy Apostles (Spring 1993). From one perspective, the Holy Apostles lunch was of course admirable, giving a hearty free sufficiency of calories each day to 700-1000 people, mostly men. But seeing them lined up waiting for the free lunch, it was striking to see they were not an old broken down crew, but included large numbers of relatively young and energetic men. If they were hungry and had no other way to get food, you could say the church should feed them first and ask questions later. But if sometime later you did get around to asking questions, one of them would have to concern the kind of future they were anticipating, and how they were employing their energies to move toward it. The church fed them every day, and this gave them another opportunity every time to continue another day in whatever style of life they were engaged. But it was not offering them an opportunity to contribute, to give as well as receive.

This issue emerged in a quite different way in 1997, when I covered an address by Rick Santorum, a Republican senator from Pennsylvania, to a fundraising dinner of the Catholic Campaign for America (CNS, February 21; *National Catholic Register,* March 9). This group was generally on the conservative and more or less Republican side, and it was giving Senator Santorum its Catholic American of the Year Award for his leadership in the congressional fight against partial birth abortion.

But the senator had other things bothering him as well. He had been spearheading efforts to change the welfare system, and was unhappy to find his church lobbying against the proposals he was pushing. William S. Skylstad of Spokane, chairman of the Catholic bishops' Committee on Domestic Policy, said the bill that President Bill Clinton eventually signed, a bill that moved in the direction Senator Santorum was pointing, was "deeply flawed" and "fails too many poor children."

So addressing the Catholic Campaign for America, Senator Santorum felt led to criticize his church for that stance in the welfare debate, and to launch an attack on Catholic Charities, the program operated by the bishops in their various dioceses to help people deal with problems of poverty. Catholic Charities should not even be called Catholic, the Catholic senator told this conservative Catholic audience. Most of the funding came from the government, and the government did not allow programs using its funds to include a religious component. The agencies of Catholic Charities "do nothing Catholic," said the senator. It was a somewhat remarkable address, since the use of the name "Catholic" for these programs was done under the authority and direction of the bishops of his church.

Since when, I wondered, did it become the prerogative of laymen to decide what could or could not legitimately be called Catholic? Normally, I have thought, it would be viewed as the right and responsibility of the bishops, led by the Bishop of Rome, to decide what is Catholic. Not too long before, the bishops of the United States had put out the word that Catholics for a Free Choice, an organization promoting the right to abortion, could not legitimately be considered Catholic. But the bishops had not questioned the name of Catholic Charities, which was a part of their own program.

A sidebar to this story concerned the role of Cardinal O'Connor. He was the "ecclesiastical adviser" to the Catholic Campaign for America, and attended the dinner and spoke, but left before Senator Santorum's turn. In the cardinal's absence, Senator Santorum referred to a private conversation with him earlier in the day, and referred to it in a way that could easily have led some listeners to get the idea that the cardinal had endorsed the senator's views.

I rather doubted that Cardinal O'Connor would do that, and thought in any case I should give the him a chance to speak for himself. I sent him a fax, and pretty quick had a secretary phoning and telling me Cardinal O'Connor was ready to talk. As I suspected, he was not disposed to join any campaign against Catholic Charities. It was still Catholic even if "it might be restricted from explicitly talking about Jesus" in government-funded programs. "I have not thought of Catholic social services as a medium for the direct, oral teaching about Jesus," he said. "We are motivated by the reality of Jesus, and try to treat people accordingly."

In my view, however, Senator Santorum had hold of a corner of a real issue, questionable as his way of addressing it doubtless was. He could perhaps have stimulated some serious thinking, rather than just another controversy, if he had maybe raised the subject as a point of concern, asked a few pointed questions and offered a couple of suggestions on the basis of his experience as a legislator–rather than making his slambang attack.

As an outsider, I had gotten the impression that, in theory, conservative Catholic laymen might be expected to support and follow their bishops, and at least try to give some measure of outward respect to their decisions, even if the wisdom thereof was not always immediately apparent. Liberal Catholics may, of course, talk any which way. But I had not anticipated that a conservative Catholic layman would mount a public platform and deliver a broadbrushed assault on a major program the bishops were struggling to carry on. Shows you how little I know.

However, I noticed in the rhetoric of Senator Santorum, deeply conservative Catholic as he presumably was, something of the tone we often hear from conservative evangelicals of the Protestant denominations. In that world, we have sometimes had people using welfare services in an effort to evangelize, which would not comport with government-funded programs that excluded religion. But that practice has also led to debate about the validity of evangelizing with welfare programs, whether government funded or not. If a derelict comes in hungry, should you make him listen to a sermon before he can have a bowl of soup? In foreign missionary work, there was talk of "rice Christians," those who became Christian, or pretended to, in hopes of getting food and other aid. All that sort of thing, I think, is rather universally deplored today, at least by people who reflect on it.

But there is another aspect that Senator Santorum and I wonder about. Is the church doing all it ought to for someone in need if it only answers the questions, "What shall we eat? or, What shall we drink? Or, What shall we wear?" (Matthew 6:31). Church leaders might reply that they are offering different kinds of service at different times, and so on. But it is not clear that they always keep the various dimensions related.

Now, regarding the inclination toward leftist politics in the broader movements called social gospel or liberation theology, we should recall that this is no recent development, but was characteristic of such groups a century ago. And it was tied in with the aspect of the ecumenical movement associated with councils of churches. That can be seen in the Federal Council of Churches, which was founded in 1908 and joined other agencies to form the National Council of Churches in 1950. Charles S. Macfarland told the earlier story in *Christian Unity in the Making: The First Twenty-Five Years of the Federal Council of the Churches of Christ in America 1905-30,* which the Federal Council asked him to write, and which the Council published in New York in 1948. He was secretary of the Council's unit dealing with social issues in 1911, when Council leaders, strapped for cash, asked him to serve also as executive for the whole organization. This was perhaps a symbol of the way wrestling with social issues has tended to set the tone for the total history of councils of churches.

A meeting at Carnegie Hall in New York in 1905 prepared for the launching of the Federal Council, which followed at a December 1908 meeting in Philadelphia. Two of the principal concerns were peace and labor rights. As would be the case for the whole century, the movement drew well-meaning people who wanted to do good but declined to face some of the realities of human sin and weakness, or who imagined these could be overcome by enactment of some changes in Washington. The mentality that produced the Prohibition Amendment. Mr. Macfarland recorded in his book, published three years after the end of the Second World War and in the beginning of the nuclear age and the Cold War, that in 1905 David J. Brewer, the son of missionaries and at the time an associate justice of the U.S. Supreme Court, voiced the belief "that a Federation of all the churches will soon make it plain that as for this nation, there must be no longer war or a getting ready for war" (p. 31). Wishful thinking that would not prepare the country for life in the twentieth century. And it was this thinking, deeply saturating the mind of liberal Protestantism, that Reinhold Niebuhr still had to fight in the 1930s when he was trying to arouse resistance to the Nazis.

In an address at the 1908 meeting, Charles Stelzle of the Presbyterian Church predicted that wars would cease "when the workingmen of the world decide that they will no longer go out to shoot down their fellow workers in order to satisfy the greed and selfishness and the avarice of their rulers" (p. 48). Okay, but how does that help us deal with Hitler and Stalin? It perhaps could not have occurred to Mr. Stelzle that some workingmen might shoot down their fellow workers to satisfy their own greed, or their own sense of entitlement or national pride.

A Brewer-Stelzle tone has pervaded much of the rhetoric heard in the councils of churches through the decades, and has cost them the confidence of many church members generally sympathetic to the goal of Christian unity. At the 1908 gathering, delegates "without dissent or hesitation" approved a resolution: "This Federal Council places upon record its profound belief that the complex problems of modern industry can be interpreted and solved only by the teachings of the New Testament, and that Jesus Christ is final authority in the social as in the individual life" (p. 44). They probably did not pause to ask themselves how that might sound to their fellow citizens of other religions. But in any case they could have used a little instruction from Father Meier to let them know their belief about drawing direct lessons from the New Testament for modern industry was perhaps not as profound as they imagined.

In 1978, I went to Riverside Church one Sunday, September 9, to hear Bishop K. H. Ting, leader of official Protestantism in China. Since he and his associates had survived by going along with the communist authorities, Carl McIntire sent a busload of his followers up to picket and protest. Mr. McIntire, among the most faithful of protesters for a generation, was himself under the weather that day, but the bused in disciples carried his spirit.

Coming out of the church after the service, I went over for a little dialogue with one of the women holding picket signs. But when I began asking for fuller explanations, she exhibited discomfort and passed me along to one of the zealous young preachers in the group. I asked him if he really thought Riverside Church was communist, and he gave evidence by pointing out that just on the other side of the street was Union Seminary. So? And that was where Harry Ward had taught.

Professor Ward had been long since retired from his seminary post and a good while dead, and when I asked at the Union bookstore about his biography, the clerk showed no awareness that such a mortal ever existed. But the enflamed protester in the course of about two minutes could move from Riverside and Bishop Ting of China to Professor Ward and Union Seminary, and tie everything up neatly in the communist bundle.

From the standpoint of American church history in its fullness, Harry Frederick Ward (1873-1961) can be rated a secondary figure. But he had an importance that ought not be disregarded. A Methodist born in England, he came to the United States as a young man and, like some other immigrants over the years, spent his life trying to change the country where he found acceptance, and make it into something different from whatever about it had attracted him. He played a key role in producing the "social creed" that was adopted by the Methodist Church of the North at its 1908 General Convention, and later that year by the Federal Council of Churches at its founding assembly. The "social creed," which was actually not a creed but a statement of church positions on various social and political issues, became a principal expression of the social gospel, shifting emphasis to social reform and away from individual conversion and strengthening of the church.

Professor Ward got a starring role in *Communism and the Churches* (Harcourt, Brace, 1960), a detailed study written by a Methodist minister, Ralph Lord Roy, and published in the *Communism in American Life* series edited by Clinton Rossiter. "No clergyman has played a more important role in the saga of Communism and the American churches," Mr. Roy concluded. He described Professor Ward as "particularly well suited to assist the communists" as chairman of a "united front" organization they were using to draw in non-communist allies, the American League Against War and Fascism. He had a "deep-rooted dedication to the Soviet Union," and "it was through his influence that many churchmen first came into contact with the ideas and apparatus of Communism" (pp. 89-90).

In *Harry Emerson Fosdick: Preacher, Pastor, Prophet* (Oxford, 1985), Robert Moats Miller said Dr. Fosdick, minister of Riverside Church during Harry Ward's heyday, described him as a "personal friend" but "well-known fellow-traveler" who was "lamentably mistaken in his estimate of communism" (p. 468).

After the Russian Revolution of 1917, Professor Ward became the most prominent of the American church leaders who defended the Soviet system. But he was not among the fair number who supported this system in ignorance of what was happening. He spent several months of 1931-32 seeing Russia, and assured himself by direct observation that the new system was working as he thought it should. He reported on that visit in a book, *In Place of Profit: Social Incentives in the Soviet Union* (Scribner's, 1933).

It would seem that in the view of this professor of Christian ethics, the governance of the Soviet Union under Joseph Stalin was ethically superior, far superior, to that of the United States under Franklin D. Roosevelt. A couple of years after President Roosevelt took office, Professor Ward felt moved to publish an article on "The Development of Fascism in the United States" (*The Annals of the American Academy of Political and Social Science,* Vol. 180, July 1935, pp. 55-61). His thesis was: "For the present, the form of American fascism is to be discerned in the course of events under the Roosevelt Administration."

People sometimes comment that the extremes of left and right meet, and such was the case here. This apologist for Soviet communism sounded very much like the similarly-discerning Roosevelt haters of the right, contending that freedom was going down the drain through the president's maneuverings, shifting of power to the executive, the appropriation of more money for the Administration to administer, the growth of all those new bureaus with all their initials–the NRA, the AAA, the PWA–and so on and on.

Professor Ward said the weakness of capitalism had become evident to the whole world following the First World War. That system would have to be replaced, or propped up with special measures. "In Russia a new form of state power has been developed for the purpose of replacing the capitalist economy. In the rest of the world a modified form of the state power is appearing for the purpose of reenforcing the capitalist structure." In the United States, as he saw it, the move toward fascism was shown–in 1935–by the fact that "we are planning war as never before in our history." And his considered conclusion: "It is when war is declared that the full development of the fascist state in this country will be attempted."

Over the course of a very long life, Professor Ward influenced a succession of left-inclined students, and gave his approach institutional continuity by organizing and leading the Methodist Federation for Social Service (from 1947, for Social Action). And he got his thinking into the minds of a broader public through a constant stream of books and articles. Reinhold Niebuhr, also an ethics professor at Union Seminary, had enough leftist connections himself to draw heavy suspicion from conservatives, and in 1932 ran for Congress on a Socialist ticket. But even he found his colleague impossibly far out–a "very naïve Christian Marxist," who was under "Stalinist illusions," as Dr. Fosdick's biographer reported the Niebuhrian view (p. 468).

Professor Ward was a leader in the founding of the American Civil Liberties Union (ACLU), and chaired its board from 1920 to 1940. But the ACLU found its image damaged when some of its leading figures, including the chairman, claiming to champion individual freedom to the uttermost, persisted in defending Stalin's regime. Samuel Walker reported in a history of the ACLU, *In Defense of American Liberties* (Oxford, 1990), that the chairman resigned in 1940 because the board decided no one who supported "totalitarian dictatorship" anywhere, whether in the Soviet Union or in the Nazi and fascist countries, could serve on its governing committees (p. 131).

Eugene P. Link, a student of Professor Ward at Union and later a history professor at the State University of New York in Plattsburgh, wrote the biography, *Labor-Religion Prophet: the Times and Life of Harry F. Ward* (Westview, 1984). He reported that Professor Ward resigned as ACLU chairman because he opposed any "test of consistency in defense of civil liberties" (p. 108). It was "cloudy thinking" that treated the Soviet Union and Nazi Germany "as the same kind of dictatorship, to be equally condemned" (p. 104).

So far as we can see from the biography, however, Professor Ward never condemned the Soviet dictatorship at all. To him, the deepest of all the world's evils was the profit motive, which in his thought seemed to rank as something like the sin against the Holy Ghost. The fact that a man would start a business, and would try to make it profitable, was the root of all misery and oppression. The really great thing about the Soviet Union was that it had eliminated this evil, Mr. Link explained, and created something new that would "change human life forever after" (p. 138).

So Professor Ward naturally made allowances when people said the communists were turning against loyal members of the party in the show trials, or when they raised questions about the Soviet Union entering into a pact with Hitler. "He would say to his students," the biographer and disciple recounted, "that the Soviets made puzzling turns at times in their policies, but if they did not revert to profit making they were to be trusted against all the judgments made by those who lived in national economies dominated by profit motives" (p. 139).

Is it a paradox that this leader of the ACLU, which tended to absolutize individualism, became a chief apologist for Stalinism, an especially cruel form of collectivism? Or should we expect that a mind inclined to absolute solutions will oscillate from one to the other?

Professor Ward was only the most prominent of a good many clergy who let their desire for a better society draw their hearts in one degree or another to the Soviet system. They heard the beautiful ideals expressed, and made themselves believe all those goals had been achieved on the Russian soil, or were well on the way to full realization. But this did not start with Russia. Edmund Burke, in *Reflections on the Revolution in France,* wrote about a Unitarian English minister, Richard Price, who preached a sermon praising the French Revolution without giving attention to the darker consequences for liberty, equality and fraternity that Burke foresaw would follow from its principles, so different from those of England's Glorious Revolution (or the American).

I suppose a question could be asked about Reinhold Niebuhr's judgment that his ethics colleague was naïve, whether such men really were that naïve or only sounded so because they were trying to work out a line of argumentation that would seem plausible in the American context. None of us ever know all that would come from policies we support, but maybe they were astute enough to know what kind of system Lenin and Stalin imposed on Russia, and knew they wanted one like it for the United States. No way for us to be sure about that, but it would perhaps show more respect to give them credit for knowing what they were doing.

Professor Ward was astute enough to see that reaching his goals would require changing the United States Constitution, and that many Americans would likely object to such a move for such purposes. In 1933, he got the idea that "a revolutionary hour had come," according to his disciple-biographer (pp. 178, 183). So he gathered a few like-minded individuals around, and set up a "New America" organization that grew to include twenty local units and, in 1936, drew 65 people for what would be its only national meeting (p. 186). With this cadre, Professor Ward envisioned winning a national election that would enable Congress to "nationalize natural resources," "write a new constitution with courts to resemble people's tribunals" and "liquidate state governments," among other desired actions. But to avoid "unnecessary prejudice," the leaders would not tell outsiders about the means that would be used in achieving the objectives of what was "a revolutionary organization and not another political party" (pp. 180-81).

Pretty soon, it all ended ingloriously, however, because Professor Ward's doctor told him to cut down on his activities, tensions developed among the leaders of "New America" and the one and only national organizer, a Congregational minister named Thomas Wright, came down with a malady called "middle class acculturation" (pp. 186-87). Maybe "naïve" would be a suitable word for Professor Ward's conception of himself and his capacity to change the United States somewhat as Lenin had changed Russia.

But rambling back to the conciliar movement, I get the impression that although people in the Federal Council leadership were speaking of unity, they were not really thinking of the unity of all Christians on a religious basis. Catholics were not involved, nor were Southern Baptists–two groups that increased their role in American life over the course of the century, while the denominations that formed the Federal Council were suffering a relative decline.

Regarding those joining in, George W. Richards, a Council leader, wrote in a foreword to Mr. Macfarland's book, "They began to feel, however vaguely, that they might differ in doctrine, worship and government, and yet cooperate for the moral and social betterment of nations . . . . Nothing but a new inter-denominationalism, recognizing both the unity of the spirit of Christianity and the diversity of its forms, conserving the freedom and personal initiative which go with denominations, and yet engendering cooperation in place of competition and subordinating denominational welfare to the advancement of the kingdom of Christ upon earth–this alone will satisfy the demands of the Christian consciousness today" (p. 13).

If there was to be Christian unity, however, the churches would need to focus more intensely on their differences "in doctrine, worship and government," get to the root of those differences and find a way to move beyond them without losing the central convictions of the Christian faith. The council of churches movement was off on the wrong foot at the start. Later, the

Faith and Order emphasis would come in as a partial corrective, but it never gained equal status with the programs to reform society. And what attention did go to Faith and Order often amounted only to a matter of asking it to write some theological rationale for the "betterment" campaigns.

Although doctrine was not given direct attention at the founding of the Federal Council, it could not be ignored even then. Membership was limited to denominations that believed in the Trinity, though some local federations had taken in Unitarians, and in later times some local councils of churches would accept synagogues. But if the goal was "moral and social betterment," what conclusive reason could there be for making any doctrinal requirements? The criterion then would be only a common understanding of "betterment," and how to produce it.

As an incidental sidebar, it is of interest to see that practical problems which were to persist throughout the century also emerged in the earliest days. At the Federal Council's executive committee meeting in 1909, it got a report that of the $30,000 budget it sought from its membership of about 30 denominations, only $9000 came in. Some individual gifts—the largest being $500 each from John D. Rockefeller and Cleveland Dodge—helped cover the expenditures that had been kept to $14,000. But the councils never became a funding priority for their member denominations. In talking of issues, we should not fail to recognize that any organization has to deal with administrative headaches. And one of the continual challenges is keeping the key players all together and all engaged. At the 1909 executive committee meeting, the chairman was absent because of illness and the vice-chairman because of engagements elsewhere.

In the midst of these institutional matters, however, we should perhaps take time to point out directly that the social gospel preached in the conciliar movement is not the gospel of the New Testament. The social gospel is in fact not gospel at all, but law–as the terms are conventionally distinguished in Christian theology. Advocates of the social gospel place demands on their hearers to support various social causes, and to feel guilt for whatever worldly advantages they may enjoy. The message is "ought." You ought to do and you ought to feel. Always the lash of the "ought." The New Testament, too, leans heavily on moral obligation, but as the second point, the grateful response to the main point, which is the message of what God has done.

Actually, I do not see anything specifically Christian about "betterment" campaigns, about working for peace and labor rights, helping people overcome poverty or doing other good works, which we can often see accomplished by people of any religion or none, and sometimes maybe more notably and effectively by others than by Christians. What makes Christianity distinctive is not ethical performance or a specific brand of ethical teaching but simply a message about Jesus Christ, and a community that is formed as people respond to that message.

Confusion about that leads to trouble. To give you a random example that is not especially important but illustrative of a lot of stuff, I see the University Press of America, based in Lanham, Maryland, published a book in 1999 by a former Catholic priest titled *The Church's History of Injustice and Why This Priest Left*. The catalog said the author, John F. Sheehy, examined "the church's actions, finding prejudice against Jews, marriage, women, homosexuals and others, along with such prominent events as the Inquisition, the Crusades and heresy," and that he became "distraught." For a member of the clergy, getting distraught may be more of a sin than stealing out of the collection plate. But we are told that one did, and became a "business consultant" and adjunct professor of philosophy at Purdue University North Central, after concluding the church was "outmoded and no longer functional in any area of social justice."

Some people who remain committed to the church would try to argue with him and say, look at the church in the civil rights movement, look at the church supporting the farm workers, look at this, look at that. And one no doubt could make various comments for balance. But instead, I would say the critique missed the point. Sad to say, ex-Father Sheehy must have gone to church a while before deciding to become a priest, spent some years in seminary and then functioned a while in the clergy, all without ever being told what the whole thing was about. Sin affecting us all as it does, what people in the churches do to adress the many social needs and issues will always come up troublingly deficient. But the purpose of the church is not to promote whatever causes John F. Sheehy may have latched onto; it is to convey the message of what God has done and wants to do for John F. Sheehy. If he had gotten that message, he might have discovered there were better moves a priest could make than becoming a business consultant (not that I have anything against business consultants). Sad if he preached to his congregations and served communion to his people and never got the Word himself. Sad if a priest never got to stand with Isaac Watts and hear the angels sing:

> Joy to the world! The Lord is come:
> Let earth receive her king;
> Let every heart prepare him room
> And heaven and nature sing.

Although the social gospel is not the gospel of the New Testament, I should note here that the New Testament does contain a dozen or so passages that people in the school we are calling social gospel/liberation theology can and characteristically do use in an effort to claim biblical support. Advocates of this view often start with the inaugural sermon of Jesus at Nazareth (Luke 4:16-21), and some seem to have discovered no other verses. But the generality will sooner or later go on to cite the Last Judgment scene of Matthew 25 and perhaps some other Gospel passages, such as the parable of the Good Samaritan (Luke 10:29-37), then bring in the Acts report of the early Jerusalem community having all things in common (4:32), perhaps for the sake of feminists quote also the assertion of Paul that in Christ there is neither male nor female (Galatians 3:28), turn to James for a passage or two condemning the rich and possibly end with the prophecies of Revelation 13 and 18 regarding the fall of Babylon, taken as a symbol of Rome or perhaps updated as Washington, or winding up with the coming of the new heaven and new earth (Revelation 21:1). Then perhaps back to the Old Testament for a few other passages, chosen as selectively and interpreted as tendentiously.

It is characteristic of a sect to create a system out of a few verses selected from here and there, force other parts of the Bible to fit into the system and pass over in silence those chapters that seem unmanageably contradictory. The social gospel/liberation theology tradition in this sense has been a sectarian movement. And although it showed strength throughout the twentieth century, it has not persuaded the church as a whole.

Any valid interpretation of the New Testament, I suppose, would require an approach that in one way or another took account of all the verses. And it is not possible to read the New Testament as a whole, or even a single New Testament book, say John or Colossians or I Peter, as a whole, and conclude that social justice is what it is about. That is not to say social justice is a bad thing. No doubt all sensible people would welcome movement toward more social justice, though we may feel some reserve when so many people concentrating on this goal seem to operate with unstated assumptions about exactly what social justice means and how you get there. But the New Testament really is talking about something else.

The New Testament orientation is actually so much the other way that modern Christians often seem flustered by it, and squirm and stutter explaining away the more unpalatable parts, when they do not try to pretend those parts out of existence. Well, we are told, Jesus laid down the principles and it took a while to work them out, or the clout of the Roman Empire kept Christianity from showing its true revolutionary colors right at first, and the social radicalism that really constituted the pure original Christian message had

SIDEBARS

to be kept out of the New Testament for the sake of political acceptability. But if Christians were never preaching the true implications of New Testament principles until the Enlightenment started proclaiming "the rights of man," how sure can we be that those really were the implications?

Although Jesus and the apostles lived under the Roman imperial system, they did not practice or teach resistance to imperialism, or talk about a right of national self-determination. Jesus endorsed payment of taxes to Rome–Caesar–the imperialists (Matthew 22:15-22), and in the Sermon on the Mount counseled compliance with enforced servitude–carrying the soldier's pack for two miles rather than the required one (Matthew 5:41).

Jesus as liberator did not present himself as the leader of a slave revolt like Spartacus, but offered liberation to those who could not see that they lacked it (John 8:31-36). The New Testament commands those who are literally enslaved to render good service as part of the Christian ethic, and it rules out any questioning of this obligation in cases where the slave's owner is a fellow Christian: "Those who have believing masters must not be disrespectful on the ground that they are brethren; rather they must serve all the better since those who benefit by their service are believers and beloved" (I Timothy 6:2). Similar teaching about the moral obligation of slaves to be good slaves is also given in other books of the New Testament: Ephesians 6:5-9; Colossians 3:22; Titus 2:9-10; I Peter 2:18-25). This does not mean Bible believers today ought to campaign for a slavery system. But it is pretty clear that the message is not egalitarianism.

Some feminists have tried to find New Testament support for their goals by quoting Paul: "There is neither Jew nor Greek, there is neither slave nor free, there is neither male nor female; for you are all one in Christ Jesus" (Galatians 3:28). But in the New Testament, oneness in Christ means the unity of a body (Romans 12:4-8; I Corinthians 12), where the parts are different and serve in different ways, and are yet all essential and deserve respect for their varied contributions. Paul's statement does not necessarily imply that male and female have or ought to have the same roles in or out of the church. The point made in Galatians could be expressed in a parallel verse of Colossians without any mention of the male-female aspect: "Here there cannot be Greek and Jew, circumcised and uncircumcised, barbarian, Scythian, slave, free man, but Christ is all, and in all" (3:11).

Luke, a book especially valued by advocates of the social gospel, includes the story of Jesus refusing to adjudicate a property dispute between two brothers (12:13-15). "Who made me a judge or divider over you?" Jesus asked. Refusing a request that he intervene to right what one brother claimed was an injustice, he said that his job was warning all parties against attempting to find their security in material goods. The New Testament does not portray a Son of God who came down from heaven and endured crucifixion in order to bring about an equitable distribution of property. Securing an equitable distribution of property is no small matter, and the world needs wise and honest judges to make the decisions. But that is not what the New Testament is about.

All this, of course, is not to suggest that Christians should support social injustice, but only that the New Testament is concerned about something else—the conquest of death, the forgiveness of sins and the uniting of hearts and minds in a fellowship that may be egalitarian in its inward meaning but hardly in the political sense. The New Testament authors do not encourage those of us on the lower levels of society to fight for a more equal status but, aware that every society will be structured in some fashion, to make the best contribution we can from whatever place in the structure we happen to occupy.

If we start out seated at the lower end of the table, possibly we will eventually be called to move up higher (Luke 14:10). Or, if we begin as slaves, wage slaves or however, we naturally will take whatever chance comes along to better our situation (I Corinthians 7:21). But the New Testament does not encourage us to get pushy.

A perspective different from that of the social gospel can also be illustrated in reference to the parable of the Good Samaritan (Luke 10:29-37). When we read a story, we learn about ourselves when we notice some character corresponding to our own place in the world, one we can say we identify with. Reading the story of the Good Samaritan, interpreters conventionally say we all in reality tend to act like the priest and Levite, who pass by on the other side, but ideally should become like the Good Samaritan in giving help to the needy. From a deeper point of view, however, we might see ourselves more as the man lying by the side of the road, overcome by the challenges of life and unable in our own strength to keep going. Taking that view, we would recognize we are first needing the help of a Good Samaritan ourselves before we could start filling that role for others. A close reading will show this interpretation also fits the literary structure of the parable. It begins with the question, "Who is my neighbor" that I am expected to love? And the story ends with Jesus phrasing the exam question, Who "proved neighbor to the man who fell among the robbers"? The poor fellow lying helpless in the ditch is not the neighbor. That man is me. The neighbor I am to love is the Good Samaritan who helps me out. When I am able to carry on with my life, it is because of the help I have received from those passing along who came to me and supported me with their strength. The neighbor I am called to love is the one who has given me this help, a prerequisite if I am ever to be capable of being any use to anybody else. From this perspective, Christianity develops an ethic of gratitude that does not begin by laying obligations on me, subjecting me to rules and regulations, but by creating inside me a desire to show gratitude for what I have received.

If you wanted to find a single verse in the New Testament that would summarize the Christian message, many Christians traditionally would have pointed you to John 3:16, which in the King James Version I learned as a child reads: "For God so loved the world that he gave his only begotten Son, that whosoever believeth in him should not perish but have everlasting life." Preachers have repeatedly taken this verse as the text of their sermons, and Sunday school teachers have regularly asked children to memorize it. Then I find that in *Crossing the Threshold of Hope* (Knopf, 1994), Pope John Paul II cites John 3:16 seven times, more than any other Scripture passage. If the emphasis on this verse I knew growing up among West Texas Baptists corresponded to what he received from his heritage of Polish Catholicism, there must be something about it.

But now in the social gospel/liberation theology approach, that verse seems to have been replaced by a passage from the inaugural sermon of Jesus at the synagogue of Nazareth:

> The Spirit of the Lord is upon me,
> because he has anointed me to preach good news to the poor.
> He has sent me to proclaim release to the captives
> And recovering of sight to the blind,
> to set at liberty those who are oppressed,
> to proclaim the acceptable year of the Lord (Luke 4:18-19).

When Dr. Bennett, a leading representative of the social gospel, became president of Union Seminary, he concluded his inaugural address by quoting those words (April 10, 1964). When Penny Lernoux's book about the Maryknoll Sisters, *Hearts on Fire,* was published by Orbis Books in 1993, an afterword by the president of the order, Claudette LaVerdiere, quoted the same verses, and said they contained the words that "guide us on the way" (p. 286). And these are but a couple of the more noteworthy examples of a practice which has had innumerable practitioners.

The passage is quoted so often, and is so regularly used to promote a certain agenda, you could almost bet as soon as someone starts it that you are hearing from an evangelist for a sect, and must beware of where you are being led. So, concerning this passage a few things need to be said, and among them, firstly,

That it is a statement Jesus is reading from the Old Testament–Isaiah 61:1-2. Here, a question of Christian use of the Old Testament is involved. The church considers the Scriptures of ancient Israel, the Hebrew people, to be the Word of God, and incorporates them with the New Testament as part of its Bible. The church calls the Hebrew Scriptures the Old Testament, not as a negative value judgment, as though they were obsolete, not as though old Scriptures were any less the Word of God than new, but as a statement of the relative place of the Scriptures given before and after Christ. The "New" is not new in the sense of totally different, but in the sense of a renewed or restored covenant, given in a new form as anticipated in the "Old" by Jeremiah (31:31-34).

So the church will understand the Hebrew Scriptures in its own way, from its own perspective. It is not, of course, a matter of pretending to some superior knowledge of the Hebrew language, or some academic distinction in the interpretation of ancient documents, or any such foolishness. It is a different spiritual perception, so the same melody is sung but transposed into another key, or the same fabric is seen in a different light. It is a specific framework in which the Hebrew Scriptures disclose a new meaning for the Christian community. The Old Testament, then, is not for Christians the Bible of another religion, but of their own faith. When they read the Hebrew Scriptures, they hear the same message that they find in the New Testament, though given in a different way.

The church gets its understanding of the Old Testament from the Risen Christ. According to Luke, Jesus met with his disciples after his Resurrection, and spoke to them about the fulfillment of "everything written about me in the law of Moses and the prophets and the Psalms." And he "opened their minds to understand the Scriptures" (22:44-45). It is, incidentally, from the same source, and not from historical research, that the church has learned how to understand the earthly life and teaching of Jesus. It was in the light of the Resurrection that his followers "remembered his words" (Luke 24:8), and saw their truth.

I mention this auxiliary point partly because there has been going on a silly something called the Jesus Seminar, which is mostly a bunch of professors who imagine their historical research qualifies them to act maybe like members of Congress, and decide by majority vote which sayings of Jesus he will get credit for actually saying, decide whether he definitely or probably did or did not actually teach some of the teachings attributed to him. Since not a single one of these professors happened to have his tape recorder turned on at the time Jesus was making his remarks, or even has access to summary minutes of the

SIDEBARS

meeting taken when Jesus was in conference with his apostles, the whole thing is only a pointless matter of guesswork. I do not assert that this professorial voting is the silliest thing going on in the academic world, but it no doubt ranks high. The New Testament gives us the teaching of Jesus in the form that the Holy Spirit, his Spirit, used in conveying it to the mind of the church, so anyone willing to hear the Word of Jesus will pay attention to these words.

All this brings us to the point that the words of Isaiah read by Jesus at Nazareth are accepted by Christians as true, but that they take on a different meaning when viewed in a New Testament light. Social gospellers, with left wing literalism, take them in their surface meaning, and go on to speak of the sermon as though Jesus were a proto-Marxist outlining the objectives of a political movement he was launching.

Alert to the possibility Jesus might be giving the passage new meaning, a reader, secondly, could well spend a few moments reflecting on the proclamation of release to the captives. Neither Luke nor any other New Testament author records any instance of Jesus ever releasing a captive, either a prisoner or a slave, or suggesting that anyone else do so, or even bringing up the subject again after that day in Nazareth. According to Luke, Jesus did heal a slave once at the request of the owner, a centurion, but did not free the slave, or give any indication to the centurion that it might be a nice thing to do (7:1-10). This must be puzzling to anyone who has been led to believe that "deliverance to the captives" in some literal sense was central to the purposes of Jesus.

But, thirdly, we should observe that the point of Luke including the sermon was not to give the Old Testament quotation in itself, as though he were afraid you would not be able to locate it in your Bible, but to give the comment Jesus made on it: "Today this Scripture has been fulfilled in your hearing" (Luke 4:21). The things spoken of are no longer just future hopes or goals or ideals, but have become present reality as well, things present as well as things to come. We continue looking forward to a time of complete fulfillment, but we receive a measure of fulfillment here and now.

The point of the passage is to say something about Jesus, not to speak of desirable goals for society. The one who brings fulfillment is here, and fulfillment consequently has to be understood in some deeper way than before, because the visible reality was not changed so much during the lifetime of Jesus, and has not been in the centuries since, nor do we have any good reason really to expect change of that sort in our time. The world remains a place where people are impoverished and enslaved, where Herods massacre infants and where we must struggle against blindness and other handicaps. But Jesus said the prophecy of Isaiah had been fulfilled. However, this sentence in which Jesus declared the present meaning of the passage from Isaiah is remarkably often omitted when the Nazareth sermon is cited, including both examples I gave above. That is like telling the first part of a story and then forgetting the punch line.

To get a better understanding of the New Testament faith, people focusing on the Nazareth sermon could read further in the same chapter of Luke, and ponder another synagogue story, one about Jesus delivering a man from a demon in Capernaum. Those looking on reported the impression made by Jesus: "With authority and power he commands the unclean spirits, and they come out" (4:36). In the New Testament, a man's basic problem is not external oppression—the Romans or Pharisees or whoever—but the unclean spirits inside, and the contribution of Jesus is to get them out.

Among those I hear speaking from the standpoint of the social gospel or liberation theology, generally much is also made of being prophetic and speaking prophetically. The controlling image behind this outlook seems to be Amos at Bethel, condemning those who "sell the righteous for silver" (2:6) and who engage in religious ceremony when God would prefer that they "let justice roll down like waters and righteousness like an ever-flowing stream" (5:24). Amos is set in opposition to established religion and governmental authority when the priest of the Bethel sanctuary, Amaziah, sends word to King Jeroboam that "Amos has conspired against you" (7:10), and demands that Amos "never again prophesy at Bethel, for it is the king's sanctuary" (7:3).

Pictured thus, prophecy means criticizing the established order, political and religious, and criticizing from the standpoint of concern for improving the condition of the poor and oppressed. Since the emphasis lies on criticizing, Amos fits in with the outlook of clergy who think they are prophets because they suffer from a bilious disposition. And observing some of those "prophets" rushing out so zealously to remake the world, those Lyndon B. Johnson used to call the red hots, we can hardly escape the thought that the world might be better off if they would first pause a moment to let God remake them. Many of the people talking about the prophetic seemingly neglect to consider that the Amos tradition represents only one strand in the many-splendored world of biblical prophecy. The work of prophets is to speak the Word of God, and this means words of comfort as well as judgment, and also hope, guidance, forgiveness and many other words. In Handel's *Messiah,* listeners hear in an especially compelling way the prophetic word from Isaiah, "Comfort ye, comfort ye my people, says your God. Speak ye tenderly to Jerusalem . . . ." (40:1-2).

If one wants to take an Old Testament prophet to serve as a model, the choice of the Old Testament itself was Moses. When God raised up a prophet in the future, it would be one like Moses (Deuteronomy 18:18). And the important point about him was that he was a man "the LORD knew face to face" (Deuteronomy 34:10). In the New Testament, a direct connection was drawn between Jesus and the prophet like Moses that had been promised (Acts 3:17-26).

But the issue of Old Testament prophecy does not have to rest on Moses alone. There is more even in Amos than the "prophetic" camp would want you to know:

> "Behold the days are coming," says the LORD,
> "when the plowman shall overtake the reaper
> and the treader of grapes him who sows the seed;
> the mountain shall drop sweet wine,
> and all the hills shall flow with it.
> I will restore the fortunes of my people Israel,
> And they shall rebuild the ruined cities and inhabit them;
> They shall plant vineyards and drink their wine,
> And they shall make gardens and eat their fruit,
> I will plant them upon their land,
> And they shall never again be plucked up
> Out of the land which I have given them,"
> Says the LORD your God (9:13-15).

A preacher who takes that tack and tone can be called prophetic. But any who proclaim themselves to be prophets, we might add, stand in danger of turning out to be false prophets. "I am no prophet nor a prophet's son," said Amos (7:14).

More important in my view, while the prophecy of the Old Testament has many facets, a Christian presumably would want to start from a New Testament perspective. "He who prophesies speaks to men for their upbuilding and encouragement and consolation," Paul wrote (I Corinthians 14:3). And summing up the overall import, the New Testament tells the Christian community that the prophets of the Old Testament "prophesied of the grace that was to be yours" (I Peter 1:10).

On a visit to Sweden, I picked up a booklet, *Nathan Soderblom as a European,* published in 1993 by the (Lutheran) Church of Sweden in its Tro & Tanke series (ed. Sam Dahlgren). Archbishop Soderblom, who died in 1931, was notable in international church circles for promoting church involvement in social issues. Himself sympathetic to socialism, he led in arranging a gathering in Stockholm in 1925 that launched what was called the Life and Work movement, which emphasized church responsibility for the social order and continued as one of the movements leading to formation of the World Council of Churches in 1948. But in contrast to many church leaders who have worked along this line and emphasized confrontation with their governments, Archbishop Soderblom, I read, was "a good Swede in that he never harmed the foreign policy of Sweden by his appeals and expressions of opinion, but acted loyally within the framework of its general outlines" (p. 50). I do not think clergy should necessarily make that a universal rule, but it does show the availability of options even within the tradition of clergy concerned for the health of the social order.

Some clergy speaking out on issues of the day in more recent times have also shown a capacity for modulated responses. From the stance of "prophetic" confrontation with the government, a number of clergy decide they should go to jail to make a witness. But others find they can express their concern plenty of other ways. I once heard Cardinal O'Connor take up the question when pro-lifers were praising Operation Rescue participants for blocking access to abortion clinics and accepting some jail time. When one of his own auxiliaries, Bishop Austin B. Vaughan, did that, the cardinal expressed full support for him. But Cardinal O'Connor said he did not feel led to take the same route himself. It would put a Catholic policeman in a difficult position if he were forced to arrest his bishop, he said.

Daniel J. Berrigan, a Jesuit priest, has made something of a career of getting arrested and going to jail, following the tradition of Dorothy Day. And he has recommended that bishops adopt the habit. "We really need a few bishops in jail," I heard him remark in a talk about his campaign against nuclear weapons (NC, May 2, 1983). But he added that "this word is not always well received." One who did not well receive it was Leroy T. Matthiesen, Catholic Bishop of Amarillo. I interviewed him in 1983, when he had come into the news for asking workers at an assembly facility for nuclear warheads, Pantex near Amarillo, to reflect on the morality of their work. Because of his call for reflection, a number of protest types coming there to do their thing sought to enlist him. "People come in and invite me to climb fences and get arrested and spend a year in jail," he told me with some bemusement. But he had not felt called to go along.

Nor do so many Jesuits follow Father Berrigan's example. When hundreds of his friends and admirers gathered to celebrate his 75th birthday at St. Francis Xavier Church in Manhattan, his superior in the Jesuit community where he lived on the West Side, Donald J. Moore, said the presence of Father Berrigan had made members of the community better Jesuits. But the superior also told us that he himself had never felt called to get arrested and go to jail (CNS, May 6, 1996). I do not know whether people such as Father Berrigan like the idea of becoming symbols, but it seems to me that is what happens.

Their behavior is not imitated, but praised as a symbol of a more far-reaching commitment the admirers cannot achieve, or do not think they ought to achieve in the same way.

Now, there is a New Testament passage used by the "prophetic" camp, the social gospel/liberation theology circles, so often we better spend extra time on it. If you want to play oneupmanship in righteousness, you need to know this passage, because they will be laying it on you a lot.

I am referring to Matthew 25:31-46, where Christ is heard saying at the Last Judgment the words of commendation to those at his right hand:

"I was hungry and you gave me food, I was thirsty and you gave me drink, I was a stranger and you welcomed me, I was naked and you clothed me, I was sick and you visited me, I was in prison and you came to me . . . . As you did it to one of the least of these my brethren, you did it to me" (vv. 35-40).

Then he warns that those who have not performed those services will hear the judgment, "Depart from me, you cursed, into the eternal fire prepared for the devil and his angels" (v. 41). The sort of people who normally push this line, after they have first gotten you good and scared, will no doubt eventually come around to telling you that there really is no such thing as the eternal fire, and maybe not even any devil. But they would like to keep you a little apprehensive so they can get the full benefit of the way they read this scene.

Since it is truly a commendable act to help people who stand in need, we have to join in praising those who feed and clothe and visit. Who can knock it? But telling Christians they will be consigned to the eternal fire unless they do these good deeds is not really the meaning of this section of Matthew 25. Richard J. Niebanck, the first to get me reexamining it, noticed from his standpoint as a Lutheran that the common interpretation of the scene contradicted what Lutherans were preaching as their (and Martin Luther's) basic view of the Christian faith. "Justification by grace takes a holiday when the gospel for the day depicts the Last Judgment," he wrote in a 1980 study published by the Lutheran Church in America (*Economic Justice: An Evangelical Perspective*, p. 79). The misinterpretation, he said, began as early as the second century, when some Christians no longer understood the original context of the passage (pp. 78-79).

Matthew is generally thought to have been writing for a Christian community composed in his time largely of Jews. They did not think of themselves as renouncing the faith of their fathers, and starting a new religion, but of finding the fulfillment that had been promised, and forming a renewed community of Israel with a new Torah from words delivered on another mountain, the Sermon on the Mount. But at the time that Matthew was writing his gospel, his intended readers formed a community facing persecution. *A priori*, should we not suppose he would try to offer them something helpful? We can hardly imagine Matthew sat down to write with the question in his mind, "How can I massage their guilt feelings, deepen their anxieties about the future and maneuver them toward the leftist politics of the twentieth century?" Rather, he was telling them no need to worry, because they had a protector with the will and capacity to look after them.

The clue to the interpretation of this section of Matthew lies in the introductory verse (32): "Before him will be gathered all the nations." It is not the disciples of Jesus, who in the New Testament are thought to form his body, that are to be judged when the Son of Man comes at the end of the age, but "all the nations." The Christian community is not itself one of the nations, but a separate group that has the job of going to make disciples of "all nations" (Matthew 28:19).

In biblical thought, the concept of "the nations" has a distinctive meaning, and you might well begin your study by reading an article on "nations" such as the one Professor Duane L. Christenson of the American Baptist Seminary of the West in Berkeley, California, wrote for the *Anchor Bible Dictionary* (Doubleday, 1992). The "nations" are what are also known from the Jewish standpoint as the Gentiles or, in Yiddish, the goyim. And the disciples of Jesus are told they should not be like the nations. "In praying do not heap up empty phrases as the Gentiles (nations) do" (Matthew 6:7). According to the Old Testament interpretation, Israel was not one of the nations, not a nation like the others, formed naturally by people with a common blood and soil, but a special people that existed because of God's special act in creating it. Israel was meant to be, as Balaam said, "A people dwelling alone, and not reckoning itself among the nations" (Numbers 23:9). And it was a turning away from God when the people of Israel told Samuel they wanted "a king over us, that we also may be like all the nations" (I Samuel 8:19-20). In the New Testament, you can find the same outlook expressed in Revelation, where John was told "the nations" were not in the temple of God, but were left outside (11:1-2).

Carrying the Old Testament concept forward into a new context, Matthew is aware that under present circumstances, these "nations," the outside forces of the world, are judging members of the community Jesus has formed, and often condemning and acting against them. Jesus warns that "they will deliver you up to councils, and flog you in their synagogues, and you will be dragged before governors and kings for my sake, to bear testimony before them and the Gentiles (nations)" (10:17-18). His disciples cannot expect that to change. "When they persecute you in one town, flee to the next, for truly, I say to you, you will not have gone through all the towns of Israel before the Son of Man comes" (10:23). No end in sight. They will be hated by "all nations" (24:9).

Still, they must carry the Christian message to the whole world "as a testimony to all nations" (24:14). But in the final judgment, it is these "nations" that will be brought before the real Judge, and there find themselves judged according to how they have treated those he adopted as his brothers. The thought here is that "the Gentiles are judged by the standard of their conduct to Jewish Christians," Professor Willoughby C. Allen of Oxford University noted in the *International Critical Commentary* volume on Matthew (T. & T. Clark, 1907, p. 265).

Here, the Christian community, as the new or renewed Israel, is getting the same assurance from its Lord that was given to Old Testament Israel as it lived encircled by hostile nations: "Blessed be everyone who blesses you, and cursed be every one who curses you" (Numbers 24:9). And the Old Testament elsewhere elaborates on how this theme plays out in particular cases. For example, Ezekiel 25 itemizes the way punishment came to the Ammonites, Moabites, Edomites and Philistines for their mistreatment of Israel. The Babylonian Exile and destruction of the Temple may have left some Israelites tempted to despair, but the prophetic vision for them remained: "The nation and the kingdom that will not serve you shall perish" (Isaiah 60:1-2).

In terms of what could ordinarily be perceived, many of those in the Christian community were insignificant, as Paul pointed out quite frankly. He wrote to the church in Corinth: "Consider your call, brethren; not many of you were wise according to worldly standards, not many were powerful, not many were of noble birth" (I Corinthians 1:26). Even the Apostles Peter and John, key leaders, were "uneducated, common men" (Acts 4:13). But the King of all kings took them into his family, adopted them as his brothers, and assured them, "He who receives you receives me" (Matthew 10:40). So those outside will be surprised to find in the end that their standing will be determined according to how they treated even the lowliest members of this community, "the least of these my brethren."

Similarly, Paul assured the church in Thessalonica that "God deems it just to repay with affliction those who afflict you" (II Thessalonians 1:6). They are not to do the repaying themselves, of course, but to take comfort from the fact that God acts for them.

Understanding matters in this way, we can conclude that those who have been adopted into the family of Jesus are not facing judgment. Insofar as they have been incorporated into this community, they have already been judged, found guilty and pardoned. Christians are spared a lot of anxiety because they do not have to wait until the Final Judgment to find out where they stand. Christians know they stand on the left side with the goats, and their only hope is to throw themselves on the mercy of the Court. So the question becomes, is it possible that this Judge will be merciful? And the Christian message says, boy, you better believe it. As a consequence, believers do not fret anxiously about the future, but move into it with confidence that they cannot suffer any ultimate defeat ever, considering who they have on their side. In Matthew 25, the thought is the same as that expressed in the *Heidelberg Catechism* (1563), a principal statement of Reformed Christianity, when it answers the question, "What comfort does the return of Christ 'to judge the living and the dead' give you?" (question 52). Yes, comfort.

And the man of faith is to answer: "That in all affliction and persecution I may await with head held high the very Judge from heaven who has already submitted himself to the judgment of God for me and has removed all the curse from me; that he will cast all his enemies and mine into everlasting condemnation, and he shall take me, together with all his elect, to himself into heavenly joy and glory."

The good news of Matthew is that when we get to the Final Judgment, we will find the Judge is on our side, that he is in fact our brother, not disposed to condemn us but to get us out of the predicament we are in, and to consign to damnation all that has kept us from the life we were meant to live. And it is not the message of Matthew alone, we should notice. John gave the same good news in reporting the words of Jesus that the believer "does not come into judgment" (5:24). And on the basis of the Christian message, Paul could assure his readers that they would find "no condemnation" in their future (Romans 8:1).

Now from the Bible back to the news, and a special case of Christians tying onto politics of the left. In 1977, I went out to cover a meeting of the Christian Peace Conference (CPC) at a black church, St. Alban's United Presbyterian in Queens, for *A.D.* magazine (September). A small assortment of secondary figures from several countries had come to this obscure church to discuss racism. The gathering could not be considered a major news event in itself, but it was of interest just because it was the CPC, and was meeting in the United States.

To that point, I knew only what I had read about the organization, which was widely viewed in the West as a propaganda tool of Soviet communism, an arrangement by which some church leaders in communist countries gained a few drops of freedom in return for defending their governments out on the international stage. I eventually concluded that this judgment was more true than not, but not the total truth. The organization was not a propaganda machine solely, but a group of committed people.

The Queens meeting provided my first chance to meet Karoly Toth, a Hungarian Reformed minister who was then CPC general secretary, and later president after he became a bishop of his church. I talked with him and found him open and in fact eager to explain what he was doing. He was, in the midst of giving information, also imploring me to recognize that he and his colleagues were not betraying the faith, but struggling in uniquely difficult circumstances to keep it alive. He was happy about a statement his group had just adopted against racism, and said at least some of it would be printed in newspapers of the communist countries, and give the CPC more standing. I gathered that he felt Christians were on the defensive not just politically but also morally, and could be legitimately held in suspicion by communists because the churches had not made the witness to social justice they should have.

Mr. Toth denied that positions of the Christian Peace Conference always coincided with those of the Soviet Communist Party. Whereas the party blamed the arms race solely on the West, the CPC held both sides responsible, he said. The CPC had always called for Arab recognition of Israel, regardless of the shifting communist stance, he added.

When he returned to Hungary and took up his bishop's post there, he was followed at the CPC by a Czech Reformed minister, Lubomir Mirejovsky. I got a chance for a long talk with the successor when he came to the United States in 1988 for a meeting in a series called Karlovy Vary, named for the Czech city where the series originated as an effort to keep Eastern European and U.S. church leaders talking across the Cold War divisions (EPS, May 7). I found he, too, was open and ready to speak with some degree of frankness about the political situation he dealt with. On the personal side, he told me that he had four children, and they were all still committed to the church despite the limitations this placed on their future, and despite years of teachers saying, "Your parents are telling you fairy tales." I thought such a response by children had to be considered an indication of strength and integrity of faith inside the personal circles of family life.

But the CPC enterprise overall still seemed questionable. Mr. Mirejovsky at that stage, when Mikhail Gorbachev remained in office, talking of glasnost and perestroika, claimed the new turn in Soviet politics vindicated him against his critics of both left and right. The left had said there was no longer a place in society for religion, but the general secretary of the Soviet Communist Party now conceded there could be. Right wing critics who had dismissed the CPC as nothing but a tool of the communists would now have to recognize it was something more, he said. "Thank God, I could live long enough to see it."

He still had warnings for the church. It had to get more involved in dialogue with the communist parties because they would become stronger if glasnost worked, he said. Maybe a principal source of CPC error, I would guess, derived from a persisting overestimation of communism's status in the context of ultimate reality: This is the future, and we must somehow accommodate.

Despite the sophistication and seriousness with which General Secretaries Toth and Mirejovsky worked, in the end their public statements and the overall stance of their organization always came out something like an echo of the Kremlin line. In my interview, Mr. Mirejovsky tried to offer some plausible and not too self-certain justification for the backing he had given the Soviet invasion of Afghanistan. And, we can recognize, a man did not have to be a communist to agree with a Soviet position on some particular issue. Considering most any point in isolation, there would be independent-minded observers in the West dissenting from the dominant Western view, and moving in some parallel to the Soviet line. But when the CPC was viewed as a whole, looking at all its positions over the years, as a whole it did look like a branch of the communist propaganda machine.

Perhaps underlying it all was a belief not only that communism would prevail, but that something in the nature of things made it right for communism to prevail, and right for the churches to capitulate. The CPC was founded by Josef Hromadka, a Czech Reformed theologian who had spent some years in the United States, and who personified the CPC's strength and weakness. In 1948, he and John Foster Dulles, later to become President Dwight D. Eisenhower's Secretary of State, presented contrasting views to the founding Assembly of the World Council of Churches (WCC) in Amsterdam. Professor Hromadka talked of "spiritual and political decay" in the West, an approaching end to "the era of the Western man" and a "terrific breakdown and failure" in the West after the First World War. He saw Western leaders "paralyzed by the horror and fear of the great social revolutionary process" which had started in Russia in 1917, and which was "irresistibly breaking through the walls of the liberal, bourgeois Western society." In plain words, the Soviet communists were winning, and the West deserved to lose.

In fact, of course, the West was by no means paralyzed at the time Professor Hromadka spoke, but under the confident leadership of President Harry S Truman was implementing the Cold War strategy that prevented a hot war between the two blocs and kept communism to some degree contained until it collapsed from its internal weakness.

Anyone who reflects on the nature of the Stalinism that existed in 1948, and in general outline was known then to be a system of cruelty and oppression, even if many details were disclosed only later, can hardly imagine an intelligent observer talking of "a great revolutionary process." But in the person of Professor Hromadka, an intelligent observer did, and in the same speech went on to extol "the advancing social transformation under the leadership of the Soviet Union."

He conceded a "tendency" toward totalitarianism, a "certain" disregard for the individual life, but argued that communism nonetheless "represents, although under an atheistic form, much of the social impetus of the living church, from the apostolic age down through the days of monastic orders to the Reformation and liberal humanism." So "our great task," said Professor Hromadka, speaking presumably for the churches joining hands in the WCC, was to "understand our own failures, omissions and intangible selfish motives" and "acknowledge the right of the new barbarians" to their share of the good things of the world.

What appeared to the West as Soviet imperialism, said this Czech theologian living in Prague, might be only their defense against "efforts to deprive the Soviet people of the fruits of victory and to bring the great socialistic experiment to its fall."

Overly-optimistic people might have spoken of a "great socialistic experiment" in 1918, or maybe some, in overreaction to the Great Depression of the 1930s, might still have said such words of wishful thinking in 1938. But after seeing the dictatorial system imposed by Lenin work itself out in practice, using terror as a motivating force, and after the evidence of two decades of Stalinism, who in 1948 could rationally speak of a "great socialistic experiment"?

But Professor Hromadka spoke for the mood of a number of people in positions of church leadership, particularly those who linked socialism in some way to the kingdom of God, and saw the Soviet Union therefore as a society on the correct road, even if imperfections understandably remained in the manner of implementation.

At times, church leaders were beguiled because communists used language of the churches in their campaigns to weaken the churches. When I interviewed David M. Stowe, executive vice president of the United Church Board for World Ministries (United Church of Christ), for an article in the publication *Seventh Angel* (November 1984), he told me that his nineteenth century predecessor, Rufus Anderson, had encouraged the churches of China to become "self-governing, self-supporting and self-propagating." But in the twentieth century, the communist Chinese leader Chou En-lai found that formula, somehow, somewhere, and made it a slogan for the communist effort to break the ties of the Chinese churches with the churches outside, and leave them weaker and more easily dominated by the government.

If you were one of those beguiled about communist China, you would rethink if you talked with Zhang Xiao Lin. I interviewed him in 1989, when he was in New York working on a doctorate in library science at Columbia University. He had financial support from the United Board for Christian

Higher Education in Asia, a coalition of church agencies, and I was asked to do an article about Mr. Zhang for the board's publication, *New Horizons* (March).

When I asked him if he got through the Cultural Revolution okay, he said, "Not really." In 1968, when he was about 12, the Red Guards came and took his parents away. His mother was later found floating dead in a river, and his father was held prisoner for six years, he said. An uncle then took care of Mr. Zhang.

His parents were not dissidents. They were, in fact, serving the communist system, his mother a school supervisor and his father an official in the Sichuan Agriculture Bureau, Mr. Zhang said. But Mao Tse-tung had decided to shake things up in a way that led some Western Christians to conclude the kingdom of heaven had finally arrived, and had set up its headquarters in China.

In 1974, still in the era of Mao Tse-tung and the Gang of Four, the Lutheran World Federation and a Catholic research center in Brussels, Pro Mundi Vita, brought together about a hundred church officials interested in China for a consultation in Louvain. One of the workshops there issued a report that said, "Oppressed people and the poor of the world watch carefully what is going on in China, hoping to find there, rather than in the church, a solution to their own problems." Donald E. MacInnis, a consultation participant, told me a common theme of discussion there was that Christianity had failed to achieve social justice where it was predominant, and on that score could learn from China (NANA, November 6). This was all rather remarkable from several angles, one of them the reality that in 1974 people in the West did not really know much about what was going on in China, other than a lot of mindless propaganda from Mao's *Little Red Book* and so on, and virtually nothing about what was going on outside the main centers where officially-guided tour groups were allowed to see a few showcase projects. Ever so much less would the poor and oppressed of the world outside China have had any opportunity to "watch carefully" the developments there. I doubt that any of them had a chance to see Mr. Zhang's mother floating in the river. We would have to suppose consultation participants were mostly projecting their own preconceptions about communism, even if we did not have the later knowledge that Chinese leaders such as Deng Xiaoping concluded China could not advance unless it reversed much of Chairman Mao's economic policy and began learning from the capitalist world.

Another assignment from the United Board got me an invitation to tea with Mrs. Maurice T. (Elizabeth) Moore, a sister to publisher Henry R. Luce and a former president of the board. Their father, Henry Winters Luce, was a missionary to China, and after it became open to Western visitors again, Mrs.

Moore had been able to return and see some of the places she knew from her earlier life. She told me that her group was taken to the campus of a college where her father had worked. She recalled his strenuous efforts to raise money in America to pay for the college buildings, and found the communists who had taken control were not acknowledging that, much less expressing any gratitude for the help their educational system had received from American Christians.

I had also done some reporting on the United Board through an interview with Nathan Pusey, retired president of Harvard University, who had become president of the Board (*Christian Science Monitor,* December 10, 1979). As payment for colleges its sponsoring bodies had operated in China, the agency had been allocated $9.2 million of the funds that the United States got the Chinese government to pay as compensation for confiscated property. The United Board had decided it would use the money to help Chinese universities through such projects as bringing scholars to the United States for advanced study. "We have no interest in proselytizing in the old style," Dr. Pusey said. "But we may be able to help increase the awareness of certain values. We want to see China develop a fuller life in spiritual and intellectual terms, as well as material." He also told me that he had a personal interest in all this because his son, James, teaching at Bucknell University, was a China scholar married to a Chinese woman. "My grandson, who is four, is growing up completely bilingual," said the proud grandfather.

Professor Hromadka, ten years after addressing the founding Assembly of the WCC, two years after Nikita Khruschev launched the deStalinization program, led in the founding of the Christian Peace Conference. With offices in Prague, this agency assumed a degree of importance as a rallying center for church leaders who favored an accommodation with Bolshevism. Except that the Moscow-Beijing split made it difficult to enlist Chinese church leaders.

For church officials in Eastern Europe, aspects of the program had validity, as I saw it. At the time, the communists were firmly in charge, holding every sector of society in an iron grip, and for all anyone could see might rule for the foreseeable future. If the churches agreed to encourage support for government authorities, they would be given a degree more freedom. For individual church leaders, the compromise brought the concrete benefits of permission to travel and join people of other countries in discussing public affairs. I was not myself inclined to glorify the more obstreperous dissidents who were defying laws on church registration and the like, and getting themselves thrown into prison and lionized by conservative circles in the West. They might assert such was the way of witness, but I thought those Christians who went about their business more sedately were also making a witness, and perhaps more effectively. When communist theory held that all religion was destined to wither away, these Christians showed their colors by just not withering.

No one can prove what a different strategy would have brought. As defenders of Pope Pius XII argue that any attempt by him to speak out against Nazi persecution of the Jews would not have helped the Jews but only brought worse persecution to the church, defenders of Professor Hromadka and his confederates can say a strategy of resistance could have left all Eastern Europe in the totally religion-free condition of Albania.

When I talked with Jan C. Korec, Catholic bishop of Nitra, Slovakia, in 1992, after the end of Soviet rule but before Slovakian separation from the Czechs, he told of a triumph over communist opponents who controlled all power–army, police, education and public media (CNS, February 25). "They had everything, and we had nothing–only the faith," he said. "Nevertheless, the system of Marxism collapsed–not from outside but from inside." Cardinal Korec had put himself into the resistance to the extent he was imprisoned from 1960 to 1968, and was watched carefully after his release. So the church won out over communism, but emerged with the necessity of starting "from zero," with all organizational resources destroyed.

Professor Hromadka could have thought pragmatically that a better way would be to offer less political resistance and preserve more of the church structures. But in his heart he apparently really had no inclination to resist, and viewed the Soviet system more as an advance toward the goals his heart embraced.

In 1966, a number of Americans, wanting to maintain contact with the churches of Eastern Europe and show openness to the socialist systems there, formed a U. S. branch of the Christian Peace Conference. But the most important of the Americans bailed out after 1968, when Professor Hromadka was expelled from the CPC leadership for criticizing the Soviet-directed invasion of his country. Metropolitan Nikodim of the Russian Orthodox Church came in and took over the CPC as president, and there was never any question of criticizing Soviet actions after that. The unhappy Americans then formed a new group called Christians Associated for Relations with Eastern Europe (CAREE). A few individuals continued with the Prague organization, however, and in 1987 I could report for EPS that a new North American affiliate of the CPC had been organized (December 31). W. Christoph Schmauch, who had fled East Germany as a young man and directed a conference center in Conway, New Hampshire, led the new group, assisted by the CPC's United Nations representative, Philip Oke. A group of 34 interested individuals met at the CCUN in late October to get the CPC affiliate revived–just in time to go down with the international group as the Soviet era ended.

At the WCC's founding Assembly, Mr. Dulles touched many of the bases that critics of the West generally set forth as essential. Renouncing all thought of a military solution to the East-West tensions, he said that "another world war would engulf all humanity in utter misery and make almost impossible the achievement of the good ends for which, no doubt, the combatants would profess to be fighting." He said there was no such thing as a "holy war." He said violent change would occur where the world made no provision for peaceful change. However, in contrast to Professor Hromadka's talk of "moral, spiritual and political decay" in the West, Mr. Dulles listed accomplishments of the West in building societies of law and in bringing areas such as health and education to higher levels. He simultaneously acknowledged that "all societies are un-Christian in many respects," and quoted Arnold Toynbee's judgment about Western civilization using up its "spiritual capital." Mr. Dulles said attempting to crush communism by force would be "wrong and stupid." The answer, he said, was for those with faith to "translate their faith into works" more vigorously and provide an example others would follow.

What Mr. Dulles was too clear-sighted to do was speak of some promising enterprise in the Soviet Union. He saw that Soviet communism was not a great socialist experiment, but a problem that must be confronted, the preeminent problem of the day in international affairs. "While some good things have been done for the proletariat," he said, "both theory and practice involved coercing, terrorizing and liquidating those whose reason and conscience compel them to reject the order sought to be imposed." And countering what would be the basic assumption of Professor Hromadka in the CPC, Mr. Dulles declared, "The Soviet communist regime is not a regime of peace and, indeed, it does not purport to be . . . . It is inevitable that orthodox communism should reject peaceful ways, except as a matter of temporary expediency, because it rejects the moral premises that alone make possible the permanent organization of peace."

I imagine Professor Hromadka, at least within his own mind, wrote off Mr. Dulles as merely an apologist for a capitalist nation that was exceptionally reactionary. But there were others whose warnings should have seemed worthy of his respect. In a December 1962 letter to "Dear Joseph," Karl Barth said he had been disturbed "for years" by "the arbitrariness with which you not only champion one of the fronts personally but also expect the church and the world to do the same." The letter went on to criticize a recent essay by Professor Hromadka presenting "Nikita, Mao and even Fidel" as the symbols of freedom and peace, and President John F. Kennedy as "an incarnation of the old social and political order that has been outdated since 1917 and is now crumbling away." Professor Barth, who himself was sometimes accused of coming too close to putting Soviet totalitarianism and Western democracy on the same level, protested, "My hair stands on end at this black and white depiction and the demand that we should adopt it" (*Letters* 1961-68, eds. Jurgen Fangmeier and Heinrich Stoevesandt; tr. and ed. Geoffrey W. Bromiley, Eerdmans, 1981, pp. 82-3). This came from a man who would also in the same letter criticize theologians such as Emil Brunner and Reinhold Niebuhr for their way of defending the West. In fact, it was part of the condemnation to assert that Professor Hromadka on his side was about as bad as they were on theirs. The previous year, Professor Barth had also written to Hungarian Bishop Albert Bereczky concerning the CPC, "To this day, it is not clear to me what the movement means by peace" (pp. 10-11).

After the collapse of Soviet communism, there were accounts to be settled. Writing an analysis for the World Council of Churches magazine, *One World* (April 1990), I could report an attempt at self-justification issued in late 1989 by the three top leaders of the CPC: General Secretary Mirejovsky in Prague, President Toth in Budapest and Continuation Committee Chairman Filaret in Kiev. They argued that the CPC had only been trying to keep the Christian faith from being identified with a single political order, Western liberalism, and that Professor Hromadka also viewed socialism with "critical candor." To that we must candidly say, if there was candor, it was little known until after the Soviet invasion of Czechoslovakia.

In 1992, Ernesto Cardenal, a Catholic priest who had been Nicaraguan minister of culture under the Sandinistas, and got his priestly faculties suspended for that, came to New York and read some of his poetry at Union Seminary. He showed up looking the part of the leftist poet-priest: white beard, informal dress and his trademark black beret riding high over piles of snowy white hair. Lydian Lebron-Rivera, president of the student Hispanic caucus, introduced him and quoted his statement, "It was the gospel of Jesus Christ that made a Marxist of me," a quote that might have aroused resistance in some audiences but in the Union context seemed to be a way of giving a visitor a buildup.

I got a chance to talk with Father Cardenal a few minutes afterward, and found he remained firm in his Sandinista commitment. "The Nicaraguan revolution was the first in the world to take place with Christian support," he told me. "It is an example for the future." For CNS (April 14), I could also report his view that the Eastern European system had not been true Marxism but a perversion of it, as societies formally Christian were often perversions of true Christianity, and the collapse of the Eastern European system therefore did not represent a failure of Marxism. I did not hear such judgments coming from Sandinistas when the Soviet system was still going, and they were relying on its support. But it seemed not only Father Cardenal but major portions of the leftist world decided to disengage semantically after 1989.

Earlier, writing an article for *Response* magazine (February 1978) about a delegation from Church Women United visiting Eastern Europe, I had the disconcerting experience of getting a protest from them for beginning with the statement, "Christian faith remains alive in the communist countries of Eastern Europe, representatives of Church Women United (CWU) have found, and many women there continue to live as women of faith." I imagined this would be read as upbeat. But the editor let people from CWU preview my manuscript, and objection was raised. The word "communist" had a harsh sound to them, and to make nice and build friendship they insisted on saying "socialist" countries. I was able to keep a reference to communist governments and Communist Party leadership, but only down in the body of the article. After 1989, however, even former supporters seemed happy enough to call the failed and repudiated system "communist," apparently hoping to save the term "socialist," as well as "Marxist," for continued use.

A different kind of settling of accounts became necessary in China. Bishop Ting visited the United States in 1992, and at a press conference reported that after 1989, authorities in his country began clamping down on the churches, out of a belief that church influence was to blame for the downfall of communism in Eastern Europe. He told Chinese officials, he reported, that the churches in Eastern Europe lacked the strength to bring about such a result, and in any case many church leaders had supported the governments there. So I posed the question: To the extent the churches may have contributed to the changes, would Bishop Ting blame them or credit them? But he said answering this question would not be possible until he had given it more thought. He had not survived more than four decades of communist dictatorship by going out on limbs, I recognized.

Writing the self-justification of 1989, the three top leaders of the Christian Peace Conference tried to disconnect from socialism. "In the current situation of democratization and restructuring of socialism as it exists in practice, and the complete collapse of Stalinism, the CPC wants to stress that the task and implementation of its Christian witness for peace neither were nor will be linked with the socialist order." Along with self-defense, the CPC leaders also offered a concession: "It is true that during the difficult period of the Cold War and in an atmosphere of strong ideological pressure, the CPC accepted some compromises, made mistakes and in some cases gave way to pressure." But no specifics.

That was quite a new tone. When Christoph Schmauch, a deputy general secretary of the CPC, invited people to form the new North American affiliate not so many months before, he could quote a triumphalist rhetoric from the organization's working committee meeting of 1987: "Positions taken by the CPC long ago have not only been vindicated by history, but have come right into the center of the ecumenical agenda, and become the accepted wisdom of the entire ecumenical consensus." That you can say if you keep claiming all you were doing all those years was just going around singing "give peace a chance."

The attempt to distance the movement from the socialist order disturbed some of its members, however. A broader group of leaders, the international secretariat, declared in a February 1990 statement that the sentence about absence of linkage with the socialist order was untrue. This group reaffirmed the belief that socialism was compatible with biblical teachings on social and economic justice, and was "still relevant to all parts of the world." The Mirejovsky-Toth-Filaret troika was thrown out, and the CPC was kept in feeble operation under the leadership of a British clergyman, Kenyon Wright.

But no one seemed much interested anymore. Later that year, when I interviewed Jiri Lukl, Bible secretary for the Czechoslovak Ecumenical Council, he told me all the Czech churches that formerly participated in the CPC had withdrawn, and had in fact joined originally only because the government made them.

Professor Hromadka's life wound up as a tragedy. He gave his post-World War II years to a campaign for building friendship with the Soviet Union and soliciting church support for its program. And he did this despite all the indicators that should have warned him he was sacrificing to Baal. He defended "the great socialistic experiment" of the Soviet Union at the WCC founding Assembly just months after the 1948 coup that brought Czechoslovakia under a communist government and Foreign Minister Jan Masaryk to his death, reportedly by suicide. Professor Hromadka continued on his path despite the Soviet actions against democratic movements in other countries of Eastern Europe and despite the Soviet invasion that crushed the Hungarian uprising of 1956. He defended the Soviet Union despite the building of the Berlin Wall, despite the invasion of South Korea in 1950, despite the Soviet obstructionism that crippled the United Nations and despite the continuing Soviet insistence on rigidly limiting cultural as well as religious freedom. He defended it despite the Soviet suppression of Jewish communal life. He broke free only in August of 1968, when the tanks called by the Soviet Union from five of its satellites rolled into the capital of his own country and crushed the Prague Spring. Finally he saw, and then he wrote a pathetic letter to the Soviet ambassador in Prague:

SIDEBARS

"During my travels abroad I was asked time and again whether I did not fear Soviet intervention. My firm answer, however, was that I regarded that as out of the question, as I had too high an esteem for the wise statesmanship of the Soviet political leaders. For this very reason the occupation on the part of the five allies amongst our socialist neighbors has been all the more painful an experience for me. My deepest feeling is of disillusionment, sorrow and shame." And he was forced out of the leadership of the movement he had founded. And in December of the following year, he died.

The CPC continued to honor Professor Hromadka's memory, but passed over the last episode of his life, and continued to give unquestioning support to the Soviet system until its collapse.

His life was a tragedy, which means a lot of good led to bad results. I never heard anything negative about his personal character. And when I talked with disciples Toth and Mirejovsky, I could not sense anything false in them. I found no reason to doubt that CPC leaders were men of Christian devotion, men of integrity, who believed in what they were doing. But their house was built on the sands of self-deception, and when the storms came it fell.

Church leaders who looked to Soviet communism as the way to the kingdom of God came to their position partly because of their participation in a broader stream of Western intellectual life that proceeded on a similar course. Tony Judt of New York University, in *Past Imperfect French Intellectuals 1944-56* (University of California Press, 1992), gave an illustrative account of another sector, the prominent writers such as Jean-Paul Sartre who expressed sympathy for Soviet communism in its Stalinist form, defended its crimes within its own region as well as its imperialism abroad, and directed all their critical faculties against the West. Even some Catholics, such as Emmanuel Mounier and contributors to his journal, *Espirit,* refused to enlist in the battle against communism, or to acknowledge that the West was defending anything of value. The post-war years were "unique in the near-monopoly exercised by the appeal of Soviet communism within the Left, in the importance of that appeal for a majority of French political thinkers, and in the enthusiasm with which the case for communism was defended" (p. 2).

The most important of these intellectuals did not themselves become members of the Communist Party. But that only confused the situation. "The truly valuable intellectuals"–valuable to the communists–"were not those who joined but those who remained outside the fold, providing the Stalinists with intellectual credibility by their support and their independent status as thinkers, scholars, or journalists" (p. 118).

Efforts of the time to critique this orientation were often undercut by people who careered along by the use of undiscriminating attacks on anyone they decided looked insufficiently fanatical in the anti-communism campaigns, attackers who seemed more interested in using the anti-communist emotion for their own self-advancement than in the issues. A part of that phenomenon, too, was found in the churches. Critics regularly attacked leaders of the mainline churches, and especially the National and World Councils of Churches, from that perspective, and charged that they were allied with communists and doing the work of communists, or perhaps were outright communist traitors themselves. Where a serious debate by responsible people could have been useful, it became virtually impossible because of the atmosphere created by those on the attack.

Church leaders could just say there was no such problem when *60 Minutes* broadcast a segment along those lines, "The Gospel According to Whom?" (January 23, 1983). Claire Randall, general secretary of the NCC, called a press conference to announce that the Council had asked Theodore M. Hesburgh, the Notre Dame president, to represent it in an arbitration of its charges that the program was "unfair and inaccurate," that CBS rejected the idea of arbitration and that the NCC was therefore claiming vindication (NC, June 9, 1983). From time to time, the *Reader's Digest* ran articles of a tone similar to the *60 Minutes* attack, one the same month and another assailing the WCC the previous August. And various of the lesser known media would follow suit, often more crudely.

Such attempts ignored a host of pertinent distinctions–between what the National or World Council did officially and what some related individual or group did or said, between efforts motivated by a desire to avoid war with the Soviet Union and endorsement of Soviet behavior, between admiration for some health and welfare programs of communist countries and support of communist dictatorship itself. The problem was more complex and more pervasive, and deeper, than any particular decision.

A few people in WCC circles tried at times to deal with this issue, and a little something was attempted at the 1975 WCC Assembly in Nairobi. I did not attend but, on the basis of reading reports and talking with people who did go, aired the debate and its aftermath in the *Christian Science Monitor* (October 14, 1976). I reported that William P. Thompson of the United Presbyterian Church believed the WCC had become more open to discussion of human rights in communist countries. At Nairobi, he got into the action by supporting a proposal that the Orthodox representation on the multi-membered presidium be given to someone other than Metropolitan Nikodim of Russia, who, Mr. Thompson argued, was not suspect himself but had to operate under too many constraints. But no competing candidate was found, so Metropolitan Nikodim did get elected. In a 1976 address to the U.S. Conference of the

WCC, Mr. Thompson said Albert van den Heuvel of the Netherlands, who had earlier been communications chief on the WCC staff, and presumably knew a lot about inside workings, initiated the move against Metropolitan Nikodim. In the same address, Mr. Thompson also talked about the broader question of how to deal with issues of human rights in the communist countries. He disclosed that during his previous years of service on the WCC"s Central Committee, he and other Committee members "often discussed this issue privately." But the Central Committee "did not take explicit action in any case in a socialist state."

At the Nairobi Assembly, a Swiss delegate, Jacques Rossel, also proposed an investigation of the Soviet Union's record on the human rights it had promised to respect in the Helsinki Accords. "After urgent protests by Russian delegates, the resolution was modified to call for a study of how all the signers of the agreement were living up to it," I wrote. "But in the course of debate, delegates broke new ground in openly discussing Soviet behavior, and the resolution became the WCC's first human rights action with the Soviet Union among the countries in view." So far as I was ever able to find out, it was actually the first WCC action with any socialist country in view; public critique seems to have been limited to Western democracies and Third World countries that were not socialist. Interviewing Mr. Thompson, I found him somewhat ambiguous in his handling of all this, however. He would acknowledge a problem in some sense, but firmly denied charges the WCC operated on a double standard. "No, sir." So I remained unclear about what exactly was going on behind the scenes. When the World Council had its 1983 Assembly in Vancouver, the Soviet invasion of Afghanistan could at least be discussed, but those delegates who wanted to make a statement against the invasion could not get a majority to support them.

Michael Bourdeaux, an Anglican priest who focused on religion in the Soviet Union from his base at Keston College in England, was more critical of the WCC when I interviewed him (*Christian Science Monitor,* November 1, 1976). He said Jews had shown that publicity in the outside world could affect Soviet leaders, and Christians should try it. Since the Soviet Union was particularly interested in maintaining a good reputation in the Third World, he argued, Third World churches should do more to demand Soviet respect for religious freedom and other human rights. "That's where the World Council of Churches has failed in its duty," he said. "It has great influence in the Third World and hasn't used it."

In 1984, when officials of the Templeton Foundation announced at a press conference in New York that the Keston priest would get that year's Templeton Prize for Progress in Religion, he reiterated his criticism of the WCC, asserting that it had made "serious mistakes" in dealing with Eastern Europe (NC, March 1). But he also criticized Billy Graham, who had come under fire for allegedly showing too affirmative a spirit on a visit to the Soviet Union. Mr. Graham was "not as fully prepared as he might have been." In some circles it was suggested there were only two options: give a smiling blessing to everything or charge into a showdown. But the priest argued that with proper preparation a visitor could make points without becoming so obnoxious the Soviets would throw him out. Donald Coggan, the Archbishop of Canterbury, had shown how it could be done, he said. Here, I suppose, one might have been getting a hint that the archbishop received some of his preparation from Keston.

The churches seemed to have a few other people who were not suffering from poor preparation but from intellectual mushiness. Like Professor Hromadka, some church representatives of the United States and other non-communist countries were so deeply engaged in criticizing Western society that they were disposed to see the alternative offered by the Soviet Union in a glow, and to accept its claims at face value or, in a supposedly broadminded way, suggest that there was good and bad in both societies and we should more or less split the difference, or take the path John L. Lewis found so reprehensible in Franklin D. Roosevelt: to "curse with equal fervor and fine impartiality both labor and its adversaries when they become locked in deadly embrace." Whatever President Roosevelt's justification, it seemed pathological that some church leaders enjoying the religious freedom of the West would put themselves in such an elevated moral position they could curse with equal fervor the governments that protected this freedom and those that crushed it whenever they could.

Because of the fierce climate of anti-communism in the United States, people with a soft spot in their minds for the Soviet system would not find it possible to argue for that system directly. So you could not always tell what they were really thinking in their inner heart of hearts. You had to attempt a judgment by noticing what they ranked as important, and what as unimportant, what bothered them and what did not, who they defended and who they attacked. In some circles, you could sense a compulsion always to interpret actions of the Soviet Union in the best possible light, and actions of the United States and its allies in the worst. There was the will to believe–against whatever contrary evidence might appear–that the perennial blight of poverty and injustice was being overcome: in Russia, and if not there a hundred per cent, surely now in China, or at least finally in Cuba, or in Nicaragua, or wherever true believers were reporting they had seen the fantasy and found it workable. And of course, critics of Western anti-communism were not always wrong.

They could see that a dumb anti-communism might get you into a dumb war, as in Vietnam. But still it was not difficult to get the impression some of them were considerably off-balance.

At the United Methodist Board of Global Ministries, I went in one day for an appointment with L. H. McCoy in the Latin America department to get information for an article one of the board's communications people had asked me to do. But before I could start, Mr. McCoy pulled out a *Christian Science Monitor* article (June 5, 1974) in which I had characterized his assessment of Cuba:

"After a three-week visit last fall, L. H. McCoy, Latin America executive of the United Methodist Church, returned with high praise for the Cuban government, the party and Dr. Castro, criticism of the Cuban churches for not participating in the revolution more actively and condemnation of the U.S. government for its stance toward Cuba."

He had raised a few questions about what was happening in Cuba, and protested that I had given an unbalanced report by omitting them. Maybe so. But for me, the news was the positive comment that I found not only in his report but in reactions of other church leaders when the United States government and most public comment was so strongly negative. That he might express a reservation here or there seemed less significant than the exuberant tone of his report on the Cuban revolution overall, and on the forces that led it. "Both the state and the party are sensitive to and responsible to the people," he had written. In another part of his report that I did not have space enough to cover in my article, some excess of sophistication had enabled him to figure out a way of explaining that Cuban society was "controlled" but not "unfree." I had never visited Cuba or made any special study of conditions there, and of course did not try to argue that Mr. McCoy was wrong. But with so many different opinions around, and so many Cubans risking their lives to get out, I had to conclude it was newsworthy that an executive of a major denomination was viewing the situation in such a different light.

Many of the more liberal Protestants have shown their sympathy for the governing style and substance of Fidel Castro throughout his years of power. And apparently that has been the case inside Cuba as well. When I interviewed Jose Felix Perez-Riera, a deputy general secretary of the Catholic bishops' conference in Cuba (CNS, January 26, 1999), he told me that ecumenical dialogue was impeded there because some Cuban Protestants maintained "close to an official alliance" with the government. While the Catholic Church was struggling to gain more religious freedom and strengthen the role of the church in Cuban society, the president of the Protestant Council of Churches was serving in the parliament and talking like the government. In the world of

Cuban Protestantism, Father Perez said, it becomes "difficult to distinguish political from religious topics."

In the same *Monitor* article quoting Mr. McCoy, I also reported on William F. Wipfler of the NCC saying that many church leaders had become convinced some kind of Marxist revolution was required in Latin America to meet the needs of the masses. And I reported that the NCC board had voted without opposition to call for U.S. diplomatic relations with Cuba and an end to the trade embargo.

This unanimity was in itself a curiosity of the NCC. Time after time, I saw the NCC take positions highly controversial in American church and secular life, far removed from the stance of most officials who won elections, and take those positions without a single board member voicing any alternative thoughts. At other times, only one or two of the more eccentric members might dissent. No doubt large sectors of the membership of NCC churches were voting for Richard M. Nixon, Ronald Reagan and others with a quite different agenda, but often no one at all represented those views in what was supposedly a broad, inclusive ecumenical body. This happened in the atmosphere where the NCC was pushing its member denominations to send board delegates in accordance with various quotas to promote diversity: women, laity, youth, ethnics. But after all that, I could see little diversity of mind.

In the Catholic Church, a related tendency of some intellectuals to live in a separate world appears as a tension between some of the prominent theologians and the bishops, particularly the Bishop of Rome. That became evident at a press conference I covered in June of 1977, when Hans Kung, J. B. Metz and other Catholic theologians reported on a colloquium that had been held at the University of Notre Dame. Although they conceded that another ecumenical council was not likely in the near future, they talked about a Vatican III as a way of indicating they were looking beyond implementation of changes approved at Vatican II, and hoping for more and better revolutions.

They reported that the colloquium, with more than 60 participants, had produced agreement on proposals to ordain women and married men, reexamine the doctrine of papal infallibility, set an age limit for popes, let Catholics elect their bishops and recognize the ordination of Protestant ministers. An impressive list for just one colloquium. But the next year, Karol Wojtyla of Krakow was elected pope, and came to Rome with something else in mind.

There are two views of the Second Vatican Council, I have discovered through reporting debates in the Catholic Church. One group sees the council as an event bringing the church up to date in a process often described with the Italian word "aggiornamento," used by Pope John XXIII, and setting the guidelines for the coming years. A second group sees it as just the beginning of a process of continuing change, and seemingly would like for every decade to produce as much change as the decade of Vatican II. They speak of the spirit of the council, and when they accuse Pope John Paul II, himself one of the bishops actually making the decisions of Vatican II, of abandoning the council, they are not thinking so much of its specific results, but of the spirit of openness to more and more change.

In 1972, a decade after Pope John XXIII opened Vatican II, Lillian Block decided RNS would run a series of assessment articles and then publish them in a booklet. I was assigned to get an Orthodox perspective, and went up to Westchester County to interview John Meyendorff at St. Vladimir's Seminary (RNS, September 18). He had a lot positive to say about the council, but even then thought some Catholics were carrying their updating too far—"far beyond what Pope John expected or wished." Just in those few years, the ultra-updaters had come to "speak of the Council as passé," he lamented.

Much of the disagreement really goes back to the question of authority. Intellectuals who have thought out their theories do not like having to put them aside because some authority figure says so. And as a matter of reality, few people other than the psychologically out-of-kilter really like finding themselves forced to suppress their own judgments at the order of someone else. But it is difficult to see how unity in the church could be maintained without some exercise of authority.

Bishops do exercise a kind of military authority in the Catholic Church, I have observed, and those theologians who think of themselves as independent intellectuals naturally react to that, though the bishops may take it as a matter of course. I was at a dinner of Serra, a lay organization that promotes vocations, one night at the Hilton Hotel when a bishop on the dais saw a priest of his diocese out on the floor dancing. He called another of his priests over, and told him to go bring him the dancer. This priest indicated he would go just as soon as the current dance ended, and the bishop said, "Go right now." So the dancing cleric was brought over and given the word to cool it. Cavorting on the dance floor might be acceptable for the lay folk, but not for priests. It occurred to me that bishops or other leaders in many Protestant churches probably would not try anything similar with their clergy, and if they did would likely get a thumb of the nose or worse.

But getting back to liberation theology and the social gospel, they bring a questionable approach to Christianity because their orientation is to set one sector of humanity against another. In traditional theology, the focus is on the relation of God and man—man as individual, as the human race, as both together—and in Christian ethics, on the relation of man to his neighbor, whatever the type of neighbor. But liberation theology and the social gospel redirect our attention to the conflicts of the poor *vs.* the rich, workers *vs.* owners, whites *vs.* people of color, males *vs.* females, the powerful *vs.* the powerless, the oppressed *vs.* the oppressors.

By contrast, in a commentary on Galatians (Anchor, 1997), J. Louis Martyn of Union Seminary said that in Paul's thought "the human plight consists fundamentally of enslavement to supra-human powers" (p. 97). Karl Barth also spoke of a "plight of humanity" that kept Christians from thinking some other members of the human race were their enemies or the objects of their struggle. "Solidarity in this general and self-incurred human plight binds them to all others and claims them more strongly than the distinction and antithesis which within their plight there may be between themselves and many of the rest" (*Dogmatics IV/4,* 211).

Somewhat as Thomas Aquinas called Aristotle "the" philosopher, I tend to think of Karl Barth as "the" theologian. I have also been helped by the works of Paul Tillich and, in a different way, by Reinhold Niebuhr. In *Communism and the Theologians* (SCM Press, 1958), Charles C. West concluded that Karl Barth gave "the" theological answer to communist charges against religion (p. 349), but that Reinhold Niebuhr showed "greater political realism" in making judgments on how to deal with the communist movement as it actually operated (p. 313). I also found value in Emil Brunner and others. But in theology, I give Karl Barth the gold medal.

He had an erudition that seemed virtually limitless. In tracing the history of a doctrine, he did not merely take the A train of Athanasius, Augustine, Anselm and Aquinas before heading to the Reformers and the moderns. A reader finds him also analyzing the specific formulations of Cyril of Alexandria, Basil of Caesarea, Ignatius of Antioch and innumerable other figures of the second rank, giving extracts in the original Greek and Latin. When he wanted to show the development of a doctrine in Protestantism, he took it generation by generation through the centuries, Lutheran and Reformed. But after working through this intellectual history, and remaining rooted in it, he would move forward to offer his own fresh restatement, taking account of modern developments in science, philosophy and historical criticism, but not surrendering to them. Working out his theology in close relationship to the Bible, he did not merely quote a verse here and there or refer casually to a few biblical themes, but gave space to detailed exegesis of lengthy passages and extensive assortments of passages on the topic at hand.

Readers are shown rather exactly how Professor Barth made it all connect. In one place or another, he offered serious comment on just about every part of the Bible—except that he somehow seemed to have neglected Esther. I find neither the name nor the book in the indexes to the *Dogmatics*. But then Esther never mentions God, which could limit the usefulness of that book for a theologian. All the while, it was recognized that the task of theology is more than "merely to assemble, repeat and define the teaching of the Bible" (*Dogmatics I/1*, 16).

The *Church Dogmatics* of Karl Barth is the most important work in its field, according to Professor Patrick D. Miller of Princeton Seminary. "There is no topic and no text that he does not take up with insight," Professor Miller wrote in a periodical of his trade, *Religious Studies News* (September 1995). "All other works pale beside this one in scope and in depth."

If one wants Christian theology for our time, I would agree, the writings of Karl Barth are the place to find it. He did not skip over any of the rocky stretches, even obscure theological wars of past ages, such as the seventeenth century battle of Dutch theologians over supralapsarianism and infralapsarianism. I doubt that a great many people today take measurable interest in that dispute as originally debated. But Professor Barth scraped away the shell to find what actually aroused the hardheaded Dutchmen on each side, what they felt to be at stake, and he then gave a judgment on the underlying issues and a proposal for expressing the contested points in his own terms (*Dogmatics II/2*, 127-45).

I got a closer look in 1962, when he came to Union Seminary on a side trip from his lecturing at Princeton. He did not have a lecture scheduled for Union, but agreed to make an appearance and respond to questions. One of my fellow Americans showed a perhaps native trait of desiring to keep things simple, or simple minded, and asked why he wrote such big books. But Professor Barth replied genially that he also wrote little books, and wrote the big books to explain what he said in the little books.

It should be added that Professor Barth was a theologian who could also do a detailed analysis of philosophical works such as the *Meditations* of Rene Descartes, as well as the books of more recent figures such as Martin Heidegger. And he knew how to make discriminating judgments when he took up books such as Simone de Beauvoir's 1949 work, *Le Deuxieme Sexe* (*The Second Sex*). He began with the basic appraisal that it was "very pagan in spirit," but despite that he could go on to call much of its content "worthy of attention, especially on the part of men and not least of Christian theologians" (*Dogmatics III/4*, 161-62). As a Baptist, I might also mention that Karl Barth wrote the only intelligent treatment of baptism that I have come across (*Dogmatics IV/4*).

But some will want a more up-to-date judgment on the trends of more recent times than we could get from Karl Barth. So for a finale to such a chapter as this, a tolerant New Yorker might look as far afield as New Haven,

Connecticut, and the creditable corridors of Yale University. There, Brevard S. Childs has meticulously examined the foundational documents of the Christian faith. And in *Biblical Theology of the Old and New Testaments* (Fortress, 1993), he concluded that the message of the church was "sadly muffled" when it was seen as "the political agenda of a 'social gospel' or the realization of the economic goals of a 'liberation theology'" (p. 657).

Yet another way to look at some of the issues troubling the churches in recent times would be in connection with the bandied-about phrase, family values.

FAMILY VALUES

CHAPTER THIRTEEN

I got invited to a press conference held by Eunice Kennedy Shriver one day in 1990. Through the Joseph P. Kennedy Foundation, she had arranged for the production of a book, *Growing Up Caring* (Glencoe/McGraw-Hill), that was to be offered for use in junior high schools as a values textbook. Back of this project, she explained, was a concern about the incidence of mental retardation in premature babies produced by teenagers. She hoped that through the study of this new textbook, schools could lead girls to say no to sex, drugs and other pressures. The material had been tested in 25 schools around the country in a "Community of Caring" program sponsored by the Kennedy Foundation and financed by a federal grant.

When I did a story for the Catholic press (CNS, April 2), I could report that a Jesuit priest, James J. DiGiacomo, had reviewed the text to ensure that it was suitable for Catholic schools. And Mrs. Shriver said that although it had been tested only in public schools, she hoped to see it adopted in parochial schools as well.

But I noticed that the unit on "Caring for Your Family," designed to teach family values, itself had no particular convictions about what was the most valuable kind of family structure. It spoke of different types of families in neutral terms, and avoided expressing any preference for the model of father-mother-child, the arrangement usually set forth in portrayals of the Holy Family but widely rejected as a model by the time this book appeared.

Michael Timpane, a Catholic who was a member of the Kennedy Foundation board and president of Columbia University's Teachers College, spoke at the press conference, and set aside the fiction that public schools stayed neutral on values. "The schools do teach values–all day, every day, whether they call them values or not," he said. One example, he said in critical tones, was their commitment to competition as a value and their lesser emphasis on "cooperative or collaborative activity." However you might think about competition and cooperation, the message from one high vantage point in the educational establishment was that public schools could teach different and maybe better values if they wanted to.

Jack Witmer, president of Glencoe/McGraw-Hill, said *Growing Up Caring* was the first values-based textbook published for American secondary schools. So that was where family values stood.

A sidebar to this story concerned writers. Mr. Timpane had enlisted a professor at his school, Frances Schoonmaker Bolin, to serve as principal author of the text. She was a Southern Baptist and married to William E. Bolin, pastor of the Metro Southern Baptist Church in Manhattan. When I called him up, he told me that he and his wife wrote the text together, but listed only her name as author because of her professional credentials in education. And in a list of contributors he was identified not as a clergyman but only as an "educational writer and consultant." That was to avoid disturbing anybody wary of church influence, he said. And a little later, I heard that the Bolins had divorced. So that is where family values stood.

Was it a paradox that a couple who wrote the book on family values, or wrote the chapter, did not keep their own family together? I do not know about that, but it confirmed my suspicion that maintaining family structures was not a matter of school learning. Past generations did better about keeping their families intact for several reasons, but mainly because they grew up with different assumptions about what families were, and about their permanence, and about the responsibilities of husband and wives. If that is missing, I do not see how anybody can compensate for the deficiency by studying a textbook in junior high school, or by writing one.

Nor by exploiting the "family values" issue politically. The Republican Party has done some of that, but its pretension only opened the way for the unconvinced to point out that a good part of the Republican leadership consisted of men who had violated the teaching of Jesus about putting away wives and marrying other women (Mark 10:11). Ronald Reagan, Robert Dole, Newt Gingrich, Phil Gramm, *etc. etc.* Then in the Monica Lewinsky days, it was disclosed that the House Judiciary Committee chairman, Henry J. Hyde, the epitome of all things proper and a man who paraded himself as a Catholic so much more Catholic than the ordinary Catholic, had in times past conducted his very own adulterous relationship over a number of years. Though that affair extended into his 40s and led to the breakup of his paramour's family, the chairman of the Judiciary Committee dismissed his behavior as merely youthful indiscretion. This was the very same Henry J. Hyde I covered in 1994, when the conservative organization, Catholic Campaign for America, gave him the Catholic American of the Year Award, and he took the occasion to accuse the bishops of his church of dereliction of duty in failing to pressure Catholic politicians enough on abortion (CNS, February 25). So that is where family values stood politically.

When the United Nations designated 1994 as the International Year of the Family, the Catholic Church used the opportunity to emphasize its concern for the family. The National Conference of Catholic Bishops issued a pastoral, *Follow the Way of Love,* and Joseph L. Bernardin, chairman of the drafting committee, came to the UN to offer the document as a contribution to the International Year (CNS, December 8, 1993). He said it was written for Christian families, but offered for the "thoughtful reflection" of all. The International Catholic Child Bureau also arranged a program on the topic with Cardinal Bernardin as speaker. Cardinal Angelo Sodano, Vatican Secretary of State, sent a message conveying the support of Pope John Paul II for the observance. And when the UN General Assembly took up the theme the next fall, Alfonso Lopez Trujillo, cardinal-president of the Pontifical Council for the Family, came to ask for "a decisive, enthusiastic and universal defense of the family on the part of those who govern" (CNS, October 20, 1994).

But a UN information kit on the International Year observed that "nontraditional family types are becoming more and more common, such as cohabitation, same gender relationships, single parent families and reorganized families." And Boutros Boutros-Ghali, secretary general of the UN, spread his benediction broadly: "We celebrate the family in all of its many cultural and social forms." So that's where family values stood internationally.

Also during that year I interviewed the Republican speechwriter, Peggy Noonan, about a new book she had written, *Life, Liberty and the Pursuit of Happiness* (Random House), which had interest for the Catholic press (CNS, July 1). A Catholic who was quite serious-minded about her religious commitment, and/but divorced, she rather refreshingly told me that she did not use the term "family values" very much.

Although a few people have elasticized the word "family" to the breaking point, I suppose we should acknowledge that there have been variations in patterns from one culture to another, and one era to another. Getting Sunday School lessons about the Genesis patriarchs and their multiple wives and concubines, I in childhood was somehow never shocked at learning of such practices in a distant era, and the acceptance of them by the biblical writers. But neither did I ever imagine they could be acceptable now. Joseph Smith and other early Mormons seemed, however, to have read those passages literally as a model for contemporary life, as some other literal-minded Bible believers were also mistakenly grabbing onto other parts of the Old Testament as their models. But I would not think that acknowledging various patterns have been accepted at various times must keep us from maintaining any standards of our own.

In 1975, when I did a story about an Association on American Indian Affairs objecting to the number of Indian children taken from their families by child care authorities, I was told that whites did not evaluate conditions according to Indian standards (*Christian Science Monitor*, October 28). William Byler, director of the association, said welfare departments too often took Indian children from their parents, and put them into foster care, justifying the action on the grounds that the child's development was being affected adversely by conditions in the parental home. He said 25 to 35 per cent of all Indian children of the United States were in foster care, but he thought that parental abuse existed in no more than one per cent of the cases. When a case arises, it should be decided by an Indian review board judging by Indian standards, said the director, himself a non-Indian married to an Indian.

I suppose a decision on this issue might require on-the-spot investigation. If children are being damaged by patterns that some societies take as normal, maybe those societies need to be challenged rather than allowed to continue with a detrimental pattern they can defend on no better basis than just that it is their pattern. Something like that is said increasingly about female genital mutilation. And theoretically it could be said about cultural patterns that are psychologically damaging.

The church and the nation might well give more attention to family values than they do, I would say, provided they can do that honestly and without excessive politicizing or demagoguery. It has been a weakness of liberal churches, as with liberalism generally, that they have not had a clear view of the importance of groups. They are strong on the individual and on humanity as a whole, the masses, the people in their broadest vagueness. But on groups–starting with the family and then extending to the clan, the nation, the race, the economic class, the vocational guild, the religious community–liberals tend to show insufficient regard, or to disparage or condemn. Their hearty applause goes only to me and the masses, not to my family or other concrete forms of community that are the actual location of our lives. In recent polemics, when the concept of the family was given so much political appeal that some liberals felt they had to try for a piece of it, they started redefining the family, making the term mean any- and everything, or nothing. Whoever you happened to lie down beside on any given night, that was your family. And the importance of structured, persisting, particular communities was slighted. It reminds of the statement of Count Stanilas Clermont Tonnerre about how the French Revolution should treat the Jews: "The Jews should be denied everything as a nation but granted everything as individuals." Not every individual Jew has found satisfaction in that principle.

The sharply-increased percentage of unwed girls having babies deplored by Mrs. Shriver and others, is, I suppose, simply a reflection of the permissiveness that has developed regarding most all matters sexual. If it feels good, do it, we have been instructed. And youthful impulses being as they are, in most all times and locales a lot of youthful sexual activity will occur, unless the elders take steps to enforce restraint. And our elders seem not of a mind to impose much restraint, maybe because they are not of a mind to impose much restraint on themselves.

Time was, and not so long ago, when a girl who let some guy get her pregnant without committing himself to care for her and the child was thought to have done something wrong, seriously wrong. Later, with a softening of attitudes came the compassion stage, when many people shifted to speak of such a happening merely as a mistake, or an unfortunate event that had happened to her, and she was to be more pitied than blamed *etc.* Now, in the days of political correctness, she has ascended to the place of honor as "Single Mother." Jesse Jackson compares her to the Virgin Mary.

People will ask, why blame the girl and not the guy? Which is a good question, if the defenders of the girl really carried it through. But it seems more often they only want to mention the guy to get the girl off the hook, and will then quietly let him go, too, so they can proceed to putting responsibility on something called "society," which seems to mean the government's welfare department.

Since the public is so often left with a welfare burden, and the increased dangers from more unsupervised youth, public worriers have begun to ask what can be done about "teen pregnancy." So I could report that President Clinton, a family values man of sorts, had initiated a National Campaign to Prevent Teen Pregnancy, with people such as Sister Mary Rose McGeady of Covenant House enlisted to seek solutions (CNS, December 15, 1998). But talk of "teen pregnancy" misstates the problem, and therefore virtually assures little good can come of all the talk. Teen pregnancy is not in itself necessarily something to deplore. I had a grandmother who became pregnant as a teenager. The difference was, before she got pregnant, she married a reliable fellow, and established a home in which the child could be given the love, care and guidance of both parents.

If we move in on the real problem, irresponsible bearing of children without stable families for their care, criticism would have to extend to many offenders considerably beyond the teen years. Such as the "Murphy Brown" that Vice President J. Danforth Quayle identified as a damaging role model.

As a general rule of thumb, it may be well on various counts to advise that young women avoid pregnancy until they are into their 20s, or until they have finished college or such vocational preparations as they may be undertaking. But older teens can be emotionally mature enough to handle the responsibilities of motherhood. And on the other side, irresponsible behavior does not become okay just because a girl turns 20.

Of course, in a culture where love is not seen as a connection that endures (I Corinthians 13:8), but as a feeling you "fall" into one day and maybe out of the next, divorce often comes along pretty soon, and that brings its own setbacks. Ari Goldman, a former religion reporter for *The New York Times,* wrote a book about a sabbatical he took at the Harvard Divinity School, *The Search for God at Harvard* (Times Books, 1991), and in it told of the pain he had suffered as the child of divorced parents. I never had to undergo that ordeal, but I agree with an idea he put forward, that a child would be justified in suing for damages when the parents divorce and violate their implied contract to provide the child with a united family and home (p. 57). Were I writing the law, I might add a provision for judges to impose triple penalties on those parents who try to justify themselves with the argument that breaking up the family will really be better for the children.

Evidence of a basic shift in American attitudes came with the non-reaction to Hannah Tillich's book. The widow of a theologian of international eminence, Paul Tillich, she published what might once have been considered a scandalous account of her life with him, *From Time to Time* (Stein and Day, 1973). The title, I suppose, can mean whatever you wish, but in the author's mind possibly referred to the varied sexual experiences she and her husband had with varied partners from time to time. Though the book included many expressions of appreciation for Professor Tillich, overall it seemed more like a deeply-angered widow's act of revenge, seeking both to damage the reputation of her famous husband posthumously and to tell the Christian community, which she had repudiated, that this great intellect did not belong to them.

Her account was accepted as generally true by Professor Tillich's biographers, Wilhelm and Marion Pauck, in *Paul Tillich: His Life and Thought,* Vol. I, Life (Harper and Row, 1976). They reported he was "aware that his personal life was unconventional" (p. x). The aggrieved widow wrote more directly: "Our marriage had been broken into small pieces by the relentless assault of the many women–not only his sweetheart who functioned as his secretary and who had lived across the street from us in New York, but the émigré friends, newcomers, students, socialites, wives of friends" (p. 240). And recounting activities with her husband, she reported their common liking for shows such as one in a Harlem basement, where they watched masturbation by "a nude Negress painted gold" and "acts of intimate sex" by a couple–all of which were "filled with the natural vivacity of these beautiful black people" (pp. 176-77). And this theologian might have had his stature reduced a cubit by the account of his childish efforts to hide an "inclination to pornography" (p. 189). Or the report that when his wife confronted him about his relations with another woman he "threw himself on the floor, screaming and kicking" (p. 187).

But in 1973, eight years after the great man's death, all this brought very little reaction. Always men have failed to live up to the principles they professed. Now, some underground erosion had weakened the sense of moral principle so that there was no longer even the outward public show of belief in faithfulness and responsibility.

As a sidebar comment, I would interject here that a man can be immoral in his treatment of his wife or other people, and still be outstanding in his work. In my judgment, Paul Tillich made a worthy contribution in his books, and that remains available, whatever we may learn or think about his personal character. In 1999, the panel advising the Episcopal Cathedral of St. John the Divine on figures it should add to its Poets' Corner recommended Ezra Pound and F. Scott Fitzgerald. But after protests, the cathedral dean, Harry S. Pritchett Jr., decided that Mr. Pound would not get the honor because he had produced antisemitic broadcasts and writings during the Second World War. It was not alleged that the antisemitism got into his poetry, and Donald Hall, a poet on the panel recommending him, said that if the criterion for honor in the Poets' Corner was literary, then "his absence is utterly ludicrous" (*The New York Times,* October 23). If the moral character of F. Scott Fitzgerald and others previously approved for the honor were scrutinized, we might add, very likely reasons could be found for questioning the suitability of honoring them in a church. I once read someone's comment that Robert Frost was a very good poet and a very bad man. I do not know enough to say whether either of those judgments was true. But I would say they both could be simultaneously true. Many people seem to operate on the assumption that if a man did good work, we have to say he was a good man, or that if he acted like a heel we cannot praise his professional contribution. But actually a man, plumber or professor, may be a master of his trade and a disaster in personal relations. For several thousand years now, the world has been seeing bad men sometimes making outstanding contributions and good men sometimes failing to achieve, so we should be getting used to it.

A little later there were the undenied reports that Martin Luther King Jr. had committed adultery on a rather regular basis with a variety of women. Maybe the disjunction of work and personal life was overdone here. Knowledge of his adultery seemingly brought no inhibition about presenting him as a moral leader for the nation, or even for the children who had their schools named for him to keep his memory alive and honored in their minds. Nor was his reputation hurt when it was disclosed that he got his doctorate in part by plagiarism. There seemed to be even a greater determination with him than with others to write his name with the dual titles, "the Reverend Doctor," to emphasize his religious and academic status.

So by the time the nation learned that the president of the United States was calling in a young female intern for oral sex from time to time, there was little reason to expect Americans would be shocked or offended.

And we now had divorce all over the place. Protestant clergy got divorced, and often found it did nothing to diminish their acceptability as religious leaders. Orthodox rabbis got divorced with ditto results. Liberals got divorced; conservatives got divorced. Television evangelists got divorced. That was where family values stood ecclesiastically.

The changing divorce scene became conspicuous in the Catholic Church, which had been known for a rigidly negative position since its widely-publicized disagreement with Henry VIII. But in the 1970s, the Catholic Church quite suddenly became among the more permissive of institutions on divorce. And it was able to change with the simple maneuver of using the acceptable word "annulment" in place of the unacceptable "divorce." I have had Catholic priests give me earnest explanations in earnest tones about some fundamental difference between approving divorce and granting annulments the way they were doing, but so far I have not been able to see it.

When I became aware of the shift, I wrote a *Spotlite* series for NANA (September 7, 1975) reporting on it, and relied on Stephen J. Kelleher as a principal source. A Catholic priest, he had worked in the department of the Archdiocese of New York, the marriage tribunal, that handled requests for annulments, became head of the unit and, after many years of direct experience, decided that the whole system should be scrapped. To explain his views and give some push to moves for change, he published a book laying out the way he saw the system working and misworking. The book was titled *Divorce and Remarriage for Catholics?* And it had the subtitle, *A Proposal for Reform of the Church's Laws on Divorce and Remarriage* (Doubleday, 1973). The tribunal, he reported from years of inside observation and management of the process, was often a "game" of looking for the "loophole" that would justify annulment (p. 143).

In previous years, annulment had been a rare occurrence, given in certain extraordinary situations such as marriage where one party was already married, or was entering into the relationship under some false pretense, or someone was coerced, or wound up married to someone physically incapable of marriage. The annulment said they were never actually married and so, if otherwise eligible, could go ahead and make a union with somebody else.

The great leap forward, or somewhere, came when officials in the church tribunals discovered psychology. With a cooperative psychologist or psychiatrist on hand, it was easy to prove that you, I or most anybody was too immature or mixed up in the head to have entered into a valid marriage. Professionals in psychotherapy have a way of cussing people out in scientific jargon, with terminology about complexes, defense mechanisms, neuroses and so on that can make most any of us seem incapable of most anything normal. But Msgr. Kelleher grew weary of what really amounted to granting divorces "by diagnostic epithet" (p. 163). When a couple have been married for a number of years, perhaps had children and then had their marriage fail, it does nobody any good for the Catholic Church to declare that they were never really married, the monsignor argued.

But Catholic officials had to do something. In the United States, they could hardly have kept the church functioning if they excluded from communion everybody who divorced and remarried. A cynical world might immediately think of the powerful and the rich, and judge that when a Senator Edward M. Kennedy presented himself for communion, a Cardinal Bernard F. Law could hardly turn away a member of a family with so much money to give the church, and carrying so much national influence. But the difficulty was more far-reaching than that. Probably most every bishop by now had some relative or other who had divorced and remarried. Bishops would be troubled to see family members kept forever from communion. And rank and file Catholics who kept dioceses and parishes alive by their gifts and personal service were also divorcing and remarrying in growing numbers. Any attempt to raise a budget or building fund would have to appeal to many divorced and remarried. Lay employees in the diocesan offices might also fall in this category.

The other side of the dilemma was the necessity for the Catholic Church in the United States to act in conformity with Rome, which kept its strict language against divorce. So annulment became the way round.

A couple of decades after the *Spotlite* series, Editor Ed Wilkinson of the *Tablet,* weekly publication of the Diocese of Brooklyn, asked me to do a story on the annulment process there (February 25, 1995). The Brooklyn diocese had been a leader in the move toward using the psychological angle to justify annulments right and left. When I looked into its processes, I found a system where the old juridical forms of a trial were maintained but the inner content had become a pastoral ministry. Mary Josita Walsh, a Mercy sister on the tribunal staff, described her work as a "healing ministry of mercy." Robert J. Young, a priest with the role of "defender of the bond," who in theory was supposed to go into court and argue the side against dissolving the marriage, told me that he had never contested any petition for annulment if the correct procedures had been followed. And when he had served as a judge in times past, he had never refused an annulment to anybody. King Henry, thou shouldst be living at this hour—in Brooklyn!

When conservative Catholics criticized the new policy of handing out annulments in massive numbers, and observed that nearly everybody asking for an annulment got one, tribunal officials would sometimes say that initial screening processes or something kept out the irresponsible who had no good reason for breaking up their marriages. But I found in Brooklyn anyone who would show at least outward respect for the system, and go through the prescribed motions, could be virtually certain of coming out with church approval for his divorce and remarriage.

Edward B. Scharfenberger, a priest who headed the Brooklyn tribunal, told me that he considered the annulment process better than some alternatives. In places such as Italy, he said, the same reality of marriages breaking down was dealt with through such practices as taking mistresses. And I did find Msgr. Scharfenberger and his staff were adopting a pastoral attitude, giving assurance by words, tone of voice and body language that the church was not condemning anything of the past, but stood ready to embrace anyone wanting to make things right.

Which seemed to me quite admirable, though it had to start from the dubious "annulment" premise. This starting point may also be deficient in losing the prior point that breaking a marriage is not the thing to do. Divorce is wrong, and the church needs to remain clear and unequivocal about that. When a man has gone ahead and divorced and remarried anyway, he needs to face up to the fact of what he has done. On the other side, however, telling him to stay away from communion for the rest of his life does not necessarily help. The approach of a church might be to say both that the divorce was wrong, and that you can get forgiveness and make a new start from wherever you stand now. But keeping both points front and center takes effort.

The annulment system also undercuts the basis of repentance. How can a man confess, "I was unfaithful to my wife," or, "I failed to treat her as a man ought to treat his wife," when his church is telling him that he has never been married? The delinquent husband can now say, "I am not a sinner; I have just been suffering from a psychiatric malady." Is that good news or what?

How seriously the annulment theory is taken when people going through the process are not around church officials may be open to question. The issue came into public discussion when the divorced wife of Representative Joseph P. Kennedy II, Sheila Rauch Kennedy, not a Catholic, published a book expressing outrage that the Catholic Church decreed her marriage never to have been. In the book, *Shattered Faith* (Henry Holt, 1997), she reported her former husband had told her the annulment terminology was just "Catholic gobbledygook." That, I expect, might be the view of the average guy.

The climate of opinion on family life has also been reflected in journalism. When I read stories about women and children in poverty, very often I look in vain for some reference to a father. There may be a detailed account of the difficulties faced by a mother, perhaps one who has given birth to several children over a period of a good many years, and the reporter tells nothing about any father playing any role ever. Are the children orphans? Is there a divorced father who is one of the deadbeats refusing to support his children? We might think the reporter or his editor would say there is a hole in the story, something calling for explanation. But apparently today it is not really expected that where there are mothers and children, there will also be husbands and fathers. So that is where family values stand journalistically.

I suppose television should also be treated as one of the forces hostile to family values. I have from time to time reported on the churches making noises about the trash and sleaze on tv, and demanding improvement. But tv has only gotten worse. In 1976, I reported that the Southern Baptist Convention was going to wade into the battle (*Christian Science Monitor,* December 9). The sex and violence routine. So where did that get us? I doubt that even the most boastful Southern Baptists today would claim their huffing and puffing accomplished much.

One might argue that the bigger problem is not the junk on tv but tv itself. When many families seem to make it their highest value, and center family life around the tv set, maybe the primary word should be not to look for the better programs but for the button that shuts the thing off. Churches have often reported that they face increased difficulty drawing their people together because so many members beset by sloth find it easier to sit in the easy chair and watch some tv entertainment. If long hours of tv also keep family members from talking with each other, from sharing in activities, from developing their talents and knowledge, from joining community projects, from acting as good citizens in the neighborhood, then the first reaction should be: turn it off.

Trying to improve the programs could still come in as an immediate second. People opposed to any national action suggest it is enough for those who dislike a particular abomination to switch channels, or turn their own individual sets off. If you have been saving the word "fatuous" for use on some auspicious occasion, the emergence of that argument will give you about as good an opportunity as you can expect to find. Turn off as much as you may, the programs will continue to hurt the total community through the damage done to the millions who continue to absorb them, particularly the young people taking in false values, and conditioned not to concentrate on their algebra books or piano practice. It is not just individuals but the total community that is coarsened if children (or adults) get the impression that it is normal for people to talk to their parents and other members of their family in gross and insulting language. Nor is it sufficient to say we should just encourage parents to exercise more control over what their children watch. We all know well enough the unrealistic nature of that advice, and in any case a great many parents have been showing their values are not necessarily higher than those of the smuttiest producers. TV is a national problem, and dealing with it would require some kind of national effort.

Family values might be considered a sidebar to the story of Dorothy Day, the leader of the Catholic Worker movement who died in 1980. She made a deep impression on many people, became a sort of patron saint to many radicals and won respect among a broad constituency of people who were not so far out but admired her decision to use her talents in serving the needy. On November 8, 1997, the centennial of her birth, earlier calls for her canonization were reiterated by Robert Ellsberg, son of the *Pentagon Papers* discloser, Daniel Ellsberg, and editor of the *Catholic Worker* newspaper before becoming editor of the Maryknoll publishing arm, Orbis Books. The day after Mr. Ellsberg's address, when Dorothy Day was honored at a mass at St. Patrick's Cathedral, Cardinal O'Connor said he would shortly gather some people to discuss whether her canonization should be promoted (CNS, November 10).

I had followed the *Catholic Worker* movement to some limited extent, writing about it in a 1978 article for the United Methodist publication, *New World Outlook* (June), and later in a few other articles. And I had become aware that Dorothy Day had a daughter and some grandchildren. But I heard little about them, and wondered what they might be thinking about the canonization talk. Catherine Hennessy, at 37 the youngest of the grandchildren, was living in Brooklyn at the time of the centennial observance, taking an editorial job she did not much care for to earn money for a return to Guatemala and work with the Indians there. So I made an appointment to go over and see her at her apartment, and talk about family reaction to proposals for the canonization. The word I got was: no interest (CNS, November 18). Or to the extent there might be mixed opinions, she could see the possibility of some value for other people. For herself, however, the granddaughter's message was, "I have no

SIDEBARS

interest." The proposal had been around for some time, but the family never even talked about it when they were together, she said. And Dorothy Day's daughter, Tamar Teresa Hennessy, sent word she had nothing to say about the matter.

When I reported this "no interest," Catherine Hennessy protested. Readers might conclude, she said, that the family had no interest in Dorothy Day herself, which was far from the truth. I had also reported that Catherine had written in the *Catholic Worker* about her "fantastic granny," and I did not think readers of my story could justifiably leap as far as she feared. It seemed to me, rather, that the reason for lack of interest in canonization was lack of involvement in the Catholic Church. There were nine grandchildren, seven still living at the time, and 18 great-grandchildren, and Catherine Hennessy told me nobody in the family was then connected to the Catholic Church, or to the Catholic Worker movement. I found this quite remarkable, since the church was central and fundamental to the life and work of Dorothy Day, and the Catholic Worker movement expressed the meaning of her life.

Dorothy Day's family situation seemed increasingly problematic the more I learned and thought about it. Tamar was born to a common law marriage that Dorothy Day had with Forster (pronounced Foster) Batterham, an anarchist sort from an Ashville, North Carolina, family that was friends with the family of novelist Thomas Wolfe. I have not been able to get any idea of what might have motivated Dorothy to live with Forster. He seems to have done some factory work for income, and some fishing for recreation, but to have pursued no significant goals except to stay free to please himself moment by moment. In Dorothy Day's autobiographical work, *The Long Loneliness* (Harper, 1952), she reported that Forster "lived with me as though he were living alone," that he "hated social life" and that he "refused to do other than live from day to day" (pp. 119-20). She was moved to use not very romantic language in describing this man so significant to her personal life: a "misunderstood cast-off" who was "decentralist and anti-industrialist," and whose outlook "probably approximated that of those who came later to be called the Southern agrarians" (p. 113). Now, is that not something to arouse the passion of a woman?

Miss Day, who had impressed people as religious even in her Bohemian days, wrote that she decided to become a Catholic and have her daughter baptized, but the father was such a zealous atheist he could not stand to live with anyone who was a believer. From childhood, I have been puzzled by seeing cases where exceptionally pious women had decided to bed down with exceptionally non-pious men. I suppose psychiatrists could supply us with theories about that. But in practical terms, I thought it would probably have been better for Dorothy, having produced a child with Forster, to stay with him and keep the tie intact. "Tamar was his delight," she reported (p. 147). The couple did remain friends throughout life, and were never estranged. Though not disposed to such conventional bondings as marriage vows, Miss Day had in reality joined in forming a family, which now had a father, a mother and the child of their union. And she used religion as a justification for breaking it up. For a mother to say, "I am going to break up my family and go serve God," makes you wonder if she has the clearest possible conception of what it means to serve God.

I do not suppose we know for sure that Forster would have left. People writing about Dorothy Day tend to imply that her interpretation of all this gave us the only and final word. I have never seen a report of any biographer or reporter bothering to get Forster's view. If Dorothy had gotten her child baptized and stayed on, maintaining a warm family life, we can imagine he might have decided to hang around. I would have liked an opportunity to ask him, "Would you really have thrown your baby daughter out of your heart and home when you learned of her baptism?"

But Dorothy left Forster, which meant depriving her child of having a normal home life with a father present. And though the public justification was religion, looking at Dorothy Day's life as a whole, we could easily conclude she was such an independent-minded career woman she would never have remained bound to any husband, or considered spending her life taking care of a family, even if Forster had accompanied her to mass every single morning and joined her in saying the rosary every single night.

Deprived of a father's presence, Tamar was also deprived of her mother's presence for much of her young life. Catherine Hennessy told me it made her mother angry—as well it might—to hear Dorothy Day's accomplishments dismissed on the grounds she was a neglectful mother. But the granddaughter also reported that Tamar was hurt by the long and frequent absences of her mother. When Dorothy Day was at home, her commitments to the *Catholic Worker* newspaper and community tended to absorb her from very early to very late. And she was often away, travelling about for her writing and speaking engagements, earning the fees and stirring up the donors that kept her operation afloat financially.

In any event, it appears Tamar might have preferred to have more family life and less religion. She married young, and would have married younger if her mother had let her. She married a man in the Catholic Worker movement, William David Hennessy, but after a while they left it. And after nine children were born, he left her, and failed to send any financial support, leaving the family to depend on welfare. Granddaughter Catherine Hennessy told me that the family's experience of living in real poverty left them with ambiguous feelings about the Catholic Worker talk of voluntary poverty.

So what are we to conclude? I do not have a clear recommendation. But there are matters to consider for those interested in family values. Dorothy Day said her concern to give Tamar a Catholic upbringing made it necessary to split from the father, and neither Tamar nor any of her children remained connected to the Catholic Church. Dorothy Day's son-in-law was part of the Catholic Worker movement, launched to serve the poor, and left his own family to the care of the public welfare system.

Most people interested in Dorothy Day seem to focus on areas other than family values, however. Mr. Ellsberg warned in his centennial address that church officials might dwell on Dorothy Day's service to the poor and her orthodox piety, but filter out her "radical pacifism and resistance to the state." Sure enough, the very next morning Cardinal O'Connor did that very thing. But I rather sympathized with the cardinal as he praised Dorothy Day for the aspects of her life he considered commendable, and passed over in silence those he could not endorse. In a subsequent interview, he acknowledged his disagreement with her pacifism and view of government resistance. But he told me that the question of attention to family responsibilities was the one matter that might keep authorities in Rome from moving forward on her canonization (CNS, October 13, 1998).

Dorothy Day, without question one of the notable personalities of her time, has to be admired for her commitment to serving people in need, as well as for her energy and perseverance in sacrificing for the causes she embraced. But questions can be raised about the content of her ideas. While most all of us yearn for peace, the church does not support an absolute pacifism as she did, does not forbid nations to defend themselves against enemies. In a biography (Harper, 1982), William D. Miller quoted her lament that when the Second World War came along, 80 per cent of the people in the Catholic Worker movement "betrayed" its pacifism (p. 345). Many people unconnected with the Catholic Worker movement had also made statements about their unwillingness to fight in any war, and then went off to fight the Axis powers. For most people who declare themselves pacifist, the statement at bottom seems really to mean no more than, "I sure wish we wouldn't have any more wars." Dorothy Day took an absolute stand. But after refusing to support military action even against Hitler, she had to watch one of her own grandsons, Eric Hennessy, go off to fight in Vietnam.

Quite at odds with her outlook, too, the church has a fundamentally positive view of the state. The church knows well enough from its own experience, in the first century and the twentieth and all in between, that the state can exceed its bounds and become oppressive. But from the time of the New Testament, the church has recognized that government officials, Christian or not, are as officials to be regarded as ministers serving the will of God (Romans 13:1-7), and that the emperor should get not only obedience but honor (I Peter 2:13-17). The church knows that the nature of man, his limited ability as an individual and his propensity for wickedness, makes the state necessary for human life, and justifies it in collecting taxes and enforcing respect for its laws. So we have to ask whether Dorothy Day's fundamentally negative view of the state and lifelong commitment to defying it did not so much express the Christian outlook as the Bohemian individualism she embraced before her conversion.

As for the poor, we could also ask how much the ideas she promoted would really help. Her theories of politics and economics seemed to fall into the category of "Wouldn't it be nice if . . . ?" Nice if we could all share the earth peacefully, and meet our needs by working side by side in little cooperatives, or with our own hands out on the land. When she entered the Catholic Church, she apparently brought with her a lot of the leftist or randomly radical theories she had previously advocated about the causes of poverty and oppression, and about how such evils could be overcome. For those who think, as I do, that those theories were mostly mistaken, admiring Dorothy Day for her attempts to implement them from a Christian standpoint becomes a matter to be carried out only with a few qualifications.

Beyond all that, it occurred to me that questions might be asked about Dorothy Day's Catholicism, especially disqualified as I may be to ask them. She acquired a reputation for strict adherence to orthodox Catholic belief and worship. But to me, her version of the faith looks like a rather individualized concoction. In *The Long Loneliness,* she reported that when her confessor told her to suspend her writing, she did not for a moment consider following his directions, but forthwith got another confessor (p. 152).

Her liking for the Catholic Church had its peculiarities. She seemed to enter the church to get in on a religion system, not to become part of a community of people brought together by common convictions and commitments. In *The Long Loneliness,* she criticized Catholic priests harshly, but added, "And yet the priests were the dispensers of the sacraments . . . ." My impression is that she felt religious power was carried in a sort of electrical system, with Catholic priests controlling access to the outlets. So joining the church was something she did to gain the right to plug in. She did not love the church "for itself," because it was "so often a scandal to me," and she did not even know about its social teachings. She quoted a statement by Romano

Guardini, a Catholic theologian who was born in Italy but grew up in Germany and did his work there, that "the church is the cross on which Christ was crucified" (pp. 149-50).

I am not a Catholic, but I would not call the Catholic Church, or any church I know about, the cross on which Christ was crucified. Actually, I do not even know what that statement means, but it sure sounds unappreciative. I would think that if you are a Christian, you love the church, love the church as it is, not some ideal church that exists only in your own imagination, love the church in spite of the failings of all its members, including yourself, love it as the home in which you live your spiritual life, love it as the body of Christ (Ephesians 1:22-23). According to the New Testament, "Christ loved the church and gave himself up for her" (Ephesians 5:25), so I suppose Christians could try to follow suit. At least, I could not consider the church any more of a scandal to me than I am to it.

But now, if the reference to scandal leads you to expect me to detail my own record of behavior, I have to tell you I am not writing that kind of book. Better to move along to a more objective sphere, such as ecology.

ECOLOGY

CHAPTER FOURTEEN

When the ecology movement began to gather steam, a good many people from the churches joined in. The idea that we ought to clean up the pollution and try to leave things in better shape for future generations seemed obviously worthy, difficult as it might be for us to overcome our greed, sloth and shortsightedness and get down to doing it.

The preparatory committee for the Rio Conference on Environment and Development held its final meeting at the United Nations headquarters in the spring of 1992, and I was able to report for EPS that church representatives were there to show their interest (April 15, 1992). People had come from the U.S. National Council of Churches (NCC) and the World Council of Churches (WCC), as well as other religious groups to follow developments and use whatever opportunities might arise to influence government officials. Jean Sindab, an NCC executive who provided staff services for its Eco-Justice Working Group, told me that 35 or so members showed up at one time or another. This group held a "religious roundtable" one day to talk about environmental issues, and the World Conference on Religion and Peace arranged an interreligious service to pray for the success of the UN's effort.

In general terms, ecology offered a cause that everybody could support. The year after Rio, I was reporting on the launch of a three-year campaign called the National Religious Partnership for the Environment (EPS, October 31, 1993). Funded by some of the major foundations and coordinated by an Episcopal layman, Paul Gorman, based in New York at the Episcopal Cathedral of St. John the Divine, it had four organizational components, working in a federative style: Consultation on the Environment and Jewish Life, National Council of Churches, U.S. Catholic Conference and Evangelical Environmental Network.

One of the first projects of the NCC was a conference for black church leaders that Jean Sindab called a success "beyond our wildest expectation" (EPS, December 31, 1993). A separate conference was held for them because they apparently would not come along with the rest of polluting humanity to talk about environmental damage as such, but only show interest if the focus were shifted to view pollution as something done by others in yet another outrageous offense against them. Called the Black Church Environmental Justice Summit, this event was structured to show that blacks were yet again victims. Vice President Albert A. Gore Jr. addressed the group, and said the communities of blacks and other poor people became the main sites for polluting industries and toxic wastes. And the conference adopted a Black Church Declaration on Environmental and Economic Justice.

Overall, the environmental movement had its obviously valid and necessary aspect, of course. But it appeared to bring forth a dubious element as well. When I covered a conference on "Earth Community" at Riverside Church in 1990, I found Thomas W. Berry, a Catholic priest of the Passionist order, calling on us to see "the universe as revelatory" and learn to read it as another Scripture. I thought it was the other way round, that we read the Scripture to understand our proper place in the universe. But Father Berry told us the traditional emphasis of Christianity on the redemption of the human race needed more balance, and would get that from a concern for creation and saving the planet (CNS, May 7).

In 1998, I was covering him again, and found him talking about the rights of other species. He judged the United States Constitution deficient because it protected only human rights. "Human beings have human rights, but every being has rights according to its mode of being," he told us. "Insects have insect rights" (CNS, October 22). Such statements may carry weight from some perspective, but they sound a little far out.

Father Berry offered these remarks as the concluding speaker at a conference held at the Museum of Natural History in New York to let people working on ecology from a religious perspective talk with others who approached the subject from a scientific or cultural standpoint. The conference brought to culmination a series of ten earlier gatherings that were each set up to get responsibility for the environment addressed from the standpoint of a different world religion: Buddhism, Christianity, Confucianism, Hinduism, indigenous traditions, Islam, Jainism, Judaism, Shintoism and Taoism.

The series was initiated and directed by John Grim, chairman of the religion department at Bucknell University in Lewisburg, Pennsylvania, and his wife, Mary Evelyn Tucker, who taught in the same department. They carried out the project under the sponsorship of the Harvard University Center for the

Study of World Religions, with principal funding from the V. Kann Rasmussen Foundation of Denmark. The series directors had studied under Father Berry and got him to officiate at their wedding, and at the Museum of Natural History, they were presenting him as the more or less patriarch of those who sought to link ecology with spirituality. So he had to be considered an indicator of the tone of the movement. And that tone seemed not to resonate exactly with common sense. Promoting ecology and tying it into the religious dimension of life seemed like further examples of those causes that are obviously admirable in some general sense, but raise questions by the way they are pursued.

I would say we take care of the earth, as we take care of a house, because it is the place where we make our home, and because we want to pass it along in good condition to whoever might be looking for living quarters when we no longer need it. I cannot see that we need to muddle up with a lot of mystique. If you are trying to keep your home in good shape, how much enthusiasm can you generate for promoting constitutional protection of termites?

In 1997, I got into this topic from another direction when I interviewed Larry L. Rasmussen of Union Seminary. He had written a book on ecology, *Earth Community, Earth Ethics,* published jointly by the World Council of Churches and the publishing arm of the Catholic Maryknollers, Orbis. Now, contrary to the experience of the usual professor of matters theological, he was to get a pile of money. H. Charles Grawemeyer, a deceased trustee of the Louisville (Kentucky) Presbyterian Seminary, had set up an annual prize administered by the seminary and the University of Louisville, and in 1997 they gave this honor to Professor Rasmussen for his book. This meant $150,000—well worth a story (ENI, May 15).

The book was loaded with learning and serious exploratory thought and so on. And I of course never mastered it all. But it did seem to have its worrisome side, characteristic of much of ecclesiastical ecology. What exactly did it mean to say that "the integrity of creation forbids division of human from other kind" (p. xii)? I have always rather liked this division myself. And if, as Christians tend to think, the only Son of God appeared in human form, that suggests a division of some kind.

In the interview, I asked whether Professor Rasmussen could not see a difference between persons and pigs. He would of course not say they were exactly the same, but it was not really clear that he saw a clear-cut distinction either. "It has been a serious error of the last few centuries," he told me, "to restrict the circle of moral worth and value to human beings."

Now, is that all so seriously so? According to the usual story of evolutionary history, disputed perhaps by creationists but probably accepted around the

Union Seminary quadrangle, God let quite a few species get wiped out before man arrived on the scene. How much moral worth and value did they have in the divine scheme of things? If God has decided to bestow such value on man as to arrange for him to live eternally, and has told us of no similar arrangements for other creatures, as Christians have believed from the beginning, and not just in the last few centuries, then perhaps the common outlook has not been so much in error. In original form, everything God made was "very good" (Genesis 1:31). But he began taking a different view pretty quick. He soon noticed that "the earth was corrupt" because of the corruption of "all flesh." So he announced, "I have determined to make an end of all flesh; for the earth is filled with violence through them; behold, I will destroy them with the earth" (Genesis 6:11, 13). And I suppose that Christians would want to take account of the word that in the end "the elements will be dissolved with fire, and the earth and the works that are upon it will be burned up." It is because of this temporary character of the natural order that Christians are moved to consider "what sort of persons ought you to be in lives of holiness and godliness," waiting as they are for "new heavens and a new earth in which righteousness dwells" (II Peter 3:10-13). All this calls for a serious sense of responsibility, but offers no occasion for anxiety. Those who trust in God "will not fear though the earth should change . . . though its waters roar and foam, though the mountains tremble" (Psalms 46:2-3).

The situation being what it now is, God seems prepared to sustain nature only just as long as it suits him, and does not necessarily give it high marks as such. "His delight is not in the strength of the horse, nor his pleasure in the legs of a man; but the LORD takes pleasure in those who fear him, in those who hope in his steadfast love" (Psalms 147:10-11). And we are told in the New Testament, "Flesh and blood cannot inherit the kingdom of God" (I Corinthians 15:50). Even when the Scriptures spoke of care for animals, Paul contended, the point was not really to assert some divine concern for the animal kingdom. "Is it for oxen that God is concerned? Does he not speak entirely for our sake?" (I Corinthians 9:9-10). The New Testament teaches that offering the blood of bulls and goats in the Old Testament pattern cannot "take away sins" (Hebrews 10:4). But futile as the attempt may be, it is not condemned as a sin against the bulls and goats. As for eating animals, the New Testament regards the vegetarian as "weak in faith," though he is not to be condemned for that but given a warm welcome into the church along with everybody else (Romans 14:1-4).

As a put-down of the Puritans, some people have joked that they condemned bear-baiting (dogs fighting a captive bear), not because it gave pain to the bears but because it gave pleasure to the spectators. If the Puritans in fact

SIDEBARS

held that view, it seems to me they had it right. Taking pleasure in giving pain degrades the human race, and we ought to stop it for the sake of a more humane humanity.

But to return to my peculiar interest in pigs: stopping one evening at a restaurant on Columbus Avenue, I looked over the menu and decided the only thing in my price range that I might like would be the pork chops. So I asked the waiter how they were, and got a kind of frank judgment seldom heard from his species: "Well, they are not as bad as they used to be." And with that recommendation I placed my order. Maybe the waiter had some sense of moral accountability to a fellow human being, and felt compelled to speak honestly. But I cannot imagine he felt or should have felt any moral accountability to the part of creation that provided the pork chops.

Curious as it may seem, I spent a good bit of time in my early years taking care of pigs, and did it more or less conscientiously. But my conscience never told me that I had some moral obligation to them. We take care of pigs because the ham biscuit would be so much diminished without their contribution. Also, I feel the presentation of the pancakes is deficient unless they are garnished with a little pork sausage. And then there are those recurrent days when my happiness depends on a bacon and egg sandwich. So we must make sure the pigs fulfill their destiny.

Genesis reports that God gave man dominion over the creation (1:26-28). Some people in the ecology movement think God made a blunder there, and they have trashed the account in Genesis more than a few times, particularly that word "dominion." They say it has allowed men to think they could exploit and pollute the earth at will, without regard to consequences, and exterminate other species. But it is a fact that God did give man dominion (Psalms 8:6), and it is a little late to be deciding things should have gone otherwise. He gave man the power of mind, and mind exercises dominion over matter, and ought to increase that dominion, not abdicate.

I would say that our degradation of the environment occurs because of the selfishness that makes us indifferent to how our actions will affect others, and because of the short-sightedness that makes us neglect even our own long term welfare. Why else would people, even some of the ecology-minded, suck nicotine into their lungs?

The moral imperative is not to surrender control but to increase the amount of thought given to extending dominion. It is always more dominion we need, not less. And to select a segment of creation to start reordering, I suppose we might try exercising more and better dominion over our own hands and feet and tongues. Beyond that, anyone who responds to the recommendation of Jeremiah that we "plant gardens and eat their produce" while we live here in exile (29:5, 28) will have to exercise unrelenting dominion. In order to make a piece of ground worth planting in, you will have to assert some authority and disrupt the state of nature. And even if you plant, you will not eat much produce unless you exercise enough dominion to decide between species to be cultivated and those to be excluded. In a manner of speaking, you might say that when man's own nature is renewed, he then by nature seeks to improve on nature.

Some of the murky seemed also to come from Matthew Fox, a Dominican priest whose teaching on ecology and related matters brought him into conflict with church authorities. And whose conflict with church authorities led him to defy his Dominican superiors and eventually leave the Catholic Church and become an Episcopalian. I heard him in 1988, shortly before a one-year suspension of his preaching and teaching was to begin December 15. He accepted an invitation from New York's Community Church (Unitarian Universalist), and from its pulpit made his last address before what he unsubmissively called "my house arrest" (NC, December 6).

He explained that he was trying to promote respect for non-human species and the creation as a whole, and he had to get it done right away, despite whatever directives his superiors might give him, because in twenty years it would be too late. And he said that meeting the ecological demand would require Christianity to become something so different people would not recognize it. "It must change that much," he said. Simultaneously, he was reveling in a broad-minded tolerance of all other religions and philosophies, which I gathered should not be expected to change at all.

Christianity does have its narrow aspect, we should acknowledge somewhere along the way. Jesus recommended, "Enter by the narrow gate" (Matthew 7:13). The Old Testament prophet Elisha also took a narrow view in telling the Syrian Naaman that his leprosy would be cured if he dipped himself seven times in the Jordan. Syria has better rivers, Naaman replied patriotically and perhaps accurately by some standards. Eventually, however, he did agree to take the narrow-minded approach, and found it got him what he needed (II Kings 5). I suppose Father Fox would have told him, "Whatever you like. One river is about the same as another, so far as I'm concerned. They all have water."

It may be unfair to mention, but I also noticed that Father Fox chose to locate his operation, the Institute for Creation-Centered Spirituality, in California, which a number of Americans had come to regard as the epicenter of flakiness.

But now, if we are bound up in moral obligation to all species, I presume it goes all the way around and they are morally obligated to us and to each other. And how will we get the pertinent obligatory behaviors enforced? If we should sail out upon the seven seas, and discover that most everywhere the big fish are eating the little fish, and decide in moral outrage that we should stop it, how do you recommend that we proceed?

Francis of Assisi, who is honored by the ecologists quite a lot, is said to have preached to the birds. Did he convert them to vegetarianism, and persuade them that eating bugs and worms was immoral species-ism? Or did he perhaps commend them for singing so beautifully in thanks to the Creator who provided such an abundance of bugs and worms? Do the ecologists have a strategy for making the lion eat straw like the ox (Isaiah 11:7) sometime before the eschaton? Our first and primary assignment is to get the lion and the lamb within the human heart to live in peace. But we may not find the setting where they harmonize until we put our minds in synch with Revelation, which tells us of the conquering "lion of the tribe of Judah" who is simultaneously "a lamb standing as though it had been slain" and whose "blood didst ransom men for God" (5:5-6, 9). Certainly, ecology is a great cause, sensibly pursued, but some of the ecology talk we have to wonder about.

After the Rio Conference, held June 1-12, 1992, Renato R. Martino, Vatican nuncio to the UN, told me that he had proposed that the conference make the human person central, and that his suggestion was accepted. And then that fall, when the UN General Assembly was reviewing the accomplishments of Rio, Archbishop Martino was able to commend it for putting people first (CNS, November 10). He said that the human person was "the central point of convergence of all the issues," and these issues were therefore ethical. "The centrality of the human person means that the world of nature has its converging point in the human being, and that development can only be understood by taking into account the total dimensions of the human being," he said. The Vatican representative said the focus on the human person meant development could not be blocked for the sake of preserving the environment, nor could environmental measures be blocked in the interest of development. I might go with the nuncio.

Now, before closing, I should note that I have occasionally been called on to deal with the sometimes exciting but actually downbeat topic of crime.

CRIME

CHAPTER FIFTEEN

In the mid-1990s, I was doing a lot of reporting for the Geneva agency, Ecumenical News International (ENI), which had an editor with a tabloid appetite. And there were at the time a number of incidents of church embezzlement. So I got to look a little at the phenomenon of insider crime.

I was called to a press conference one day in 1996 to hear Thomas V. Daily, bishop of the Catholic Diocese of Brooklyn, and other diocesan officials report that they had discovered a $1.1 million embezzlement (CNS, May 7; ENI, May 8). According to the story, Vincenza Bologna, a member of a parish of the diocese, and an employee for 32 years, had been put in charge of the lay pension office in 1990. There, she saw her chances and she took them. She would make out a check to a consultant, endorse it herself and put the money in her own account. When the check came back from the bank, she would destroy it, and replace it with a photocopy of an earlier bank notice that some check had been inadvertently destroyed. The man the checks were made out to, who had at times actually been a consultant and gotten legitimate payments, did not know about all these other checks with his name on them.

Such is the human condition. Embezzlement so commonly shocks because the people found guilty—and Mrs. Bologna did plead guilty in a settlement approved by the bishop that kept her from going to jail—are so often people that church officials know well, who are themselves members of the church they are stealing from, who have served faithfully over so many years they are trusted completely.

The experience of the Diocese of Brooklyn was not so unusual. Just the year before, the Episcopal Church had discovered an even larger, longer embezzlement of some undetermined amount in the range of two million dollars by the chief financial officer in their national headquarters—Ellen F. Cooke (ENI, May 2, 1997).

Hanging out in church circles, you not infrequently hear reports of money going astray, diverted from a designated program to one the executive prefers, money allowed to slip away without records so no one knows exactly where it went, money raised for one purpose but spent for something else, too much of the money used to pay for too generous expense accounts. All this might be relegated to the shelf for class B scandals.

But Mrs. Cooke was scandal class A, taking money and a lot of it for her own personal aggrandizement. Among other staff members, she was not so much admired, and some would tell you that even apart from the stealing she was less than an asset to the organization. But the presiding bishop at the time, Edmond L. Browning, took no notice of the mutterings, and remained firmly supportive, until his stomach was turned by finding that as he moved toward retirement she had greatly soured what might have been a more satisfying conclusion to his ministry. In his last years, he was having to handle the aftermath of dismissing staff and cutting programs (EPS, February 28, 1994), while she lived lavishly and enhanced her estate with stolen church funds.

Should anyone have suspected she was raking off a lot of the church's money for her personal use? She was striding in high style, but she and her husband, an Episcopal priest serving as rector of a New Jersey parish, both had good incomes, so possibly they could have been paying the bills with their own money. And she was someone church officials knew well, a member of their church, someone who had served faithfully so many years she was trusted completely. As the wife of an Episcopal clergyman, she surely would not be one to do anything damaging to the church that was the life not only of herself but of her family.

If you were in the New England Synod of the Evangelical Lutheran Church in America, would you have suspected your treasurer would embezzle $800,000 of synod money? George A. Patrick, who had served 13 years and handled the job from his home in Cheshire, Connecticut, was arrested September 19, 1996, and charged with diverting that amount to his holiday homes, college tuition for his two sons and other personal expenses (ENI, September 23). Mr. Patrick was someone church officials knew well, was himself a Lutheran, affiliated with Bethesda Church in New Haven, Connecticut, and a treasurer who had served faithfully for so many years he was trusted completely. He had helped synod officials save money by explaining to them that review of the books by a certified public accountant (CPA) was sufficient, and they could avoid the unnecessary expense of regular audits, Bishop Robert L. Sakson told me.

Such incidents keep happening, and keep getting the churches lots of the wrong kind of publicity, making potential donors even more wary. You might

SIDEBARS

think that when such a case became known, leaders in other churches would hear a warning bell, and say to themselves, "We'd better double check our procedures and make sure we have the best set of controls we can get." When I talked with John Bailey, the Connecticut state official handling criminal matters, he told me that he announced the arrest of Mr. Patrick at a press conference to make other churches aware of the danger, and he hoped they would profit from the awareness. Other non-profit agencies were required to get audits, and though church-state separation left churches free from that legal requirement, Mr. Bailey wanted to show them it might be a good idea, nonetheless. But my impression is that they say to themselves, "Thank God, we don't have to worry about this sort of thing in our church. The people handling our money are people we know, people who actually belong to our church, people who have served faithfully so many years we know we can trust them completely."

The phenomenon was no respecter of denominations. On March 14, 1996, William R. Jones, the former comptroller of the United Methodist Board of Global Ministries, was sentenced to six months in prison after he admitted misappropriating $400,000. His sentence was reduced to time he had already been incarcerated awaiting trial, provided he would try to make restitution.

Francis J. Butler, a Catholic layman directing an agency that represents supporters of Catholic causes, an agency with the arrestingly prosaic name of Foundations and Donors Interested in Catholic Activities (FADICA), told me that churches often tried to save money by failing to set up adequate financial controls. This "false economy" not only left them vulnerable to fraud but undermined the confidence of donors, he said.

Expanding on the Bologna story, I called up Walter B. Smith, a Jesuit priest with a doctorate in psychology, to ask for his analysis of all those trusted employees stealing from their churches. But he just said they were acting normally—normally in the sense of normal sinners. Crime is not something that needs to be explained, he explained. Crime is just the way we are. Placed before temptation, customarily we yield, absent countervailing pressures. In the words of the priest-psychologist, the superego lacks sufficient strength to control the libido. So we all need to work within structures of accountability.

Even the ancient Greeks were astute enough to recognize that you have to find somebody to guard the guards. Policemen become criminals, we are reminded every now and then. It is not especially rare to see a newspaper headline like "Ex-New Jersey Police Chief Who Ran a Corrupt Force Is Sentenced and Fined" (*New York Times,* January 6, 2000). Lawyers can decide the law is for them to use, not to obey. Attorneys who prosecute criminals in court can become the prosecuted. The chief of the U.S. Justice Department can be convicted of a felony. On occasion, judges who send criminals to jail go and deserve to go there themselves.

It is sometimes said in a semi-joking manner that we can see more scientific evidence for original sin than for any other of the church's doctrines. But people still resist acknowledging its truth. After long years of trying to teach modern men about original sin, Reinhold Niebuhr more or less gave up. In one of his last publications, *Man's Nature and His Communities* (Scribner's, 1965), he said that in using the term, valid as it might be from his perspective, he made a "pedagogical error," because people of modern outlook considered him a "regressive religious authoritarian" caught in "an ancient legend" (pp. 23-24).

I think Professor Niebuhr was wrong about that. Wrong about accusing himself of erroneous pedagogy. The most modern thinkers know well enough how to handle the varied levels of symbolic language, metaphor, legend, myth or whatever, and know how to shift mental gears whenever they need to. I cannot believe the cultured despisers are really hung up on literalism. The reason they reject the doctrine of original sin, I have to think, is not because of its connection to the Genesis story, or Augustine's way of interpreting it, but because they reject the truth it encapsulates.

This tendency to shy away from reality is worldwide, I noticed when I wrote an article for *One World* (December 1990) about the World Summit for Children at the United Nations. I reported that the event was initiated by James P. Grant, director of UNICEF, to generate support for the Convention on the Rights of the Child, adopted by the UN General Assembly in 1989. And I reported that it drew heads of state or of government from 71 countries, and mostly high level representatives of 78 more. They adopted a World Declaration on the Survival, Protection and Development of Children, with an attached Plan of Action.

But since it was all for children, it had a touch of sentimentality about it. Even Margaret Thatcher, the iron lady who disdained the wobbly, would get sentimental, and carry on with it far beyond her time limit, when the subject was children. I reported that the Declaration gave little attention to the child's need for moral and spiritual development. Rather, it asserted, "The children of the world are innocent, vulnerable and dependent." I observed that although children, like all other people, are in fact vulnerable and dependent, they, like all other people, are in fact something other than innocent. Anyone who remembers his own childhood, I might have added, would have to concede that children are not at all innocent. All can think of the childhood escapades when they were doing what they knew they were not supposed to do, but were doing anyway, for no better reason than because they just wanted to. My article got an award from the Associated Church Press, after submission without my knowledge by the *One World* editor, Marlin VanElderen. But I do not know that my disquisitions on innocence had anything to do with that, or affected any sentimentalists who preferred to dream on about childhood innocence.

The doctrine of original sin reminds us that there is something fundamentally wrong with man, so deep-seatedly wrong it will never be cured by any amount of education or any amount of change in the government. The stranger thing is that church leaders often fail to learn from this their own doctrine. If they expect to keep their money safe, they will have to remember that all are born corrupted by original sin–and this "all" of course includes themselves.

Henry J. Lyons was perhaps one who forgot how true the doctrine of original sin is. On February 27, 1999, he was reminded when a jury found him guilty of racketeering and grand theft. Pastor of Bethel Metropolitan Baptist Church in St. Petersburg, Florida, Rev. Lyons became president of what has been generally regarded as the largest black denomination in the United States, the National Baptist Convention USA, Inc., in 1994, and held onto the office despite legal challenges to the validity of his election. Then he seems to have adopted the attitude attributed to one of the popes [Ed. Note: Leo X] of centuries back: "God has given us the papacy; let us enjoy it."

The denominational chief was charged with entering into business deals with various companies in which, for a consideration, they would get access to the denominational mailing lists. But the money that supposedly would be going to the denomination seemed to go instead to finance the luxurious living of Rev. Lyons–two automobiles from Mercedes-Benz, one from Rolls Royce, a pleasure boat. And various accompaniments.

All this was discovered by an accidental assortment of circumstances that doubtless made the pastor-president wonder whether God was really with him. On July 6, 1997, according to law enforcement authorities, his wife, Deborah, found papers indicating her husband had become co-owner with another woman, Bernice V. Edwards, of a house in a plush St. Petersburg suburb, Tierra Verde. The disturbed wife, who later acknowledged a drinking problem, was perhaps partly influenced by alcohol that day, but in any case went to the suburban villa, entered using keys she had discovered, and expressed her opinion of her husband's co-ownership by scattering his clothes about and setting fires. As you were probably expecting, these activities caught the attention of the fire department and, in due course, others. And for Rev. Lyons, they brought a stretch of unflattering publicity, and eventually other unpleasant results.

At the time, Rev. Lyons and the other woman, described by the clergyman as a "close friend of my family" and "business partner," were in Nigeria, reportedly looking into its need for aid. He was subsequently reported to have gotten $350,000 for lobbying in Washington on behalf of the Nigerian dictator at the time, General Sani Abacha, but had not registered as a paid lobbyist. Which could have been the subject of another legal action, but I never read of any followup to that.

When I tried to call Rev. Lyons to get his side of things for an ENI story (July 15), I was told he was not available. And though I left my number and word I wanted to report his answer to the allegations, I never heard from him. But at a press conference where reporters asked about the minister's conspicuous consumption, he reportedly challenged them: "What are you trying to imply? That blacks in this country cannot be successful?" But he refused to answer questions about the specific nature of his success.

Rev. Lyons had been more talkative on a previous occasion when I called him. That was in 1995, when his predecessors in denominational leadership had agreed to host the Central Committee of the World Council of Churches at the headquarters in Nashville, and he was finding it advisable to back out. "The National Baptist Convention is not at this point ready to entertain such a prestigious body," he told me (ENI, January 17). He said the denomination would be ready to serve as host in 1997, which however turned out to be the year his wife got herself and him into trouble by starting the fires.

Alluding I suppose to those challenging his election, he also remarked that "I've been up to my ears in one courtroom after another." With this experience, and some we later heard he had undergone previously, perhaps he had become accustomed to spending his time with lawyers and judges, and would not be apprehensive about spending more if his business affairs led him in that direction.

A sidebar curiosity was some comment from Rev. Lyons on the officials who preceded him in denominational leadership. He said they had left him with an "Amos and Andy" operation at the Nashville headquarters. I thought that was not very nice to say about his fellow clergy, and might sound even unnicer in a news story by a white reporter, so I sacrificed that bit of color.

As things began to unravel for Rev. Lyons, information appeared about the deals with the business corporations—a bank, an insurance company, a corporation that owned and operated cemeteries. Along with this came exposure of the flimsy basis of his denomination's statistics. As reported in annual editions of the *Yearbook of American and Canadian Churches* (published by Abingdon Press, with material prepared by the National Council of Churches), the National Baptist Convention USA, Inc. put out the figure of 5.5 million as its membership from 1958 until 1991, when it raised the number to 7.8 million. That grew the next year to 8 million and the next to 8.2 million, where it was left for a while.

It was pretty evident from the round numbers that officials were just guessing, and had no systematic way of counting. But the business executives who made deals with Rev. Lyons apparently looked at the figures as literalists, and thought they were buying access to lists of eight million or more real people who might become real customers. When they found the denominational headquarters had nothing resembling their expectations, they developed symptoms of discontent. So with Rev. Lyons as facilitator of these deals, which we would not have expected officials of any church body to contemplate, the denomination did not get the money, and the businesses did not get the access.

Somewhere along about this time, the (Jewish) Anti-Defamation League and the (black) National Urban League also developed a few symptoms, after they discovered that money they sent Rev. Lyons for his denomination to use in rebuilding burned churches had gone mostly not to the rebuilding of burned churches.

It is disturbing to find that when a clergyman is caught doing something wrong, he may try to lie his way out of it, just like a president of the United States. But the sidebar revelation that troubled me more was the broad and fervent support that Rev. Lyons continued to receive from other leaders of his denomination even after his crookedness became known.

"I'm with him all the way," E. V. Hill told me in a telephone interview. I was doing another ENI story (February 27, 1998) after Rev. Lyons had been indicted by state authorities. (Later, federal charges were also filed, with accusations that he had stolen $4 million, which he apparently understood to be tax-exempt.) Rev. Hill, a nationally-prominent pastor of Mt. Zion Missionary Baptist Church in Los Angeles, had chaired a committee that investigated the charges, and found that while there might be some administrative disorder, Rev. Lyons still made a great president. Rev. Hill had then led in defending him at the denomination's convention the previous September. There, the president faced down his opponents, and comfortable majorities set at 80 per cent by some observers stood with him in successive votes of the executive board, general board and full convention.

Some prominent figures in the denomination gave their president a critical look. In New York, Calvin O. Butts 3d, pastor of Abyssinian Baptist Church in Harlem, told me the president was "woefully inadequate, corrupt and untrustworthy." I do not know whether Rev. Butts has spoken as forthrightly on the ethics of a former pastor of his church, Adam Clayton Powell Jr. But the stance on Rev. Lyons provided a degree of moral illumination in a darkened corner. Charges that Rev. Lyons was cheating businesses, cheating his denomination and cheating on his wife, and according to other reports coming out, had a record of occasional cheatings in earlier years, as did his female "business partner"–all this failed to disturb the majority of the denominational leaders, the people supposedly giving moral leadership and direction to their members.

"I believe he will come out all right," Rev. Hill told me.

Well, let us see. *The New York Times* reported a year later, on February 28, 1999, that the previous day jurors in Florida's Pinellas County Circuit Court found Rev. Lyons guilty of racketeering and grand theft. On March 17, he resigned as convention president. And the next day, in what was apparently a deal arranged with prosecutors, he pled guilty to charges of bank fraud, tax evasion, making false statements to a bank officer and making false statements to the federal government. Prosecutors then dropped 49 other charges. On March 26, the "business partner" pled guilty to two federal charges of tax evasion, and agreed to pay $200,000 in back taxes. Prosecutors dropped 25 other charges against her, but at the subsequent sentencing she got 21 months (*New York Times,* October 26).

On the state charges, Rev. Lyons was sentenced to five and a half years in prison, and after going to the Lowell Correction Institution near Ocala, Florida, he got a four-year federal sentence that would run concurrently. And both state and federal courts demanded that he turn over millions for restitution and taxes. On April 12, prosecutors clearing up loose ends got a woman with a peripheral role in the Lyons enterprise, Brenda Harris, to plead guilty to one part of a multi-count indictment, forfeit money she was holding in bank accounts and give up a $340,000 home, actions that would enable her to avoid a prison sentence.

Along the way, Rev. Lyons had played the race card a little. If that would produce what looked like getting away with murder in the O. J. Simpson case, why not give it a spin for bank fraud and tax evasion? So Rev. Lyons would suggest he fell into misfortune because the white folks were out to get him. Then he would also suggest that what looked like shady financial shenanigans was just the black way of doing business, which I would think other blacks might regard as an insult.

That was somewhat different from the defense of Allan Boesak that he was so busy fighting apartheid he did not have time to watch where the money went. European agencies sent him grants for aid programs he was administering, and much of it seemed to go elsewhere, to his own personal use. Eventually, a South African court decided Mr. Boesak knew enough about how he was using the money for his own luxurious living that he deserved six years.

The Boesak case was truly sad. He was a gifted man, but was another of those who gained prominence by zealous support of causes and then lost altitude by failing to keep watch, or letting his friends help him keep watch, over his personal behavior.

I had occasion to talk with Mr. Boesak only once–a phone conversation when I was doing a story about his agreement to address the 1997 general conference of the homosexual denomination, Universal Fellowship of Metropolitan Community Churches (ENI, March 5, 1997). Mr. Boesak was in the United States at the time, given shelter as visiting professor at the American Baptist Seminary of the West in Berkeley, California, after a year as visiting theologian at the Stony Point conference center in New York State. He told me that he would gladly address the homosexual convention, which was to be in Australia, if his trial did not interfere, which I gather it did. He expressed sympathy for homosexuals, and regret that he had not spoken up for them in South Africa. "I cannot see any real biblical justification for the condemnation gay people have had to suffer," he told me.

Not homosexually-oriented himself, Mr. Boesak had lost stature not only through loose finances but loose heterosexuality as well. Exposure of an adulterous affair led to his resignation from the presidency of the World Alliance of Reformed Churches. And when he went into politics, he was removed from the clergy rolls of his denomination. And then the financial scandal cost him his political career. Really somber. Many people in Mr. Boesak's constituency in South Africa and friends abroad willingly overlooked aberrations in his personal life because he had effectively championed causes they were committed to. But in the end, he had to face consequences.

Ordinary outsider crime has of course cost the churches also. In 1971, I reported for RNS the news, rather startling at the time, that the Riverside Church in New York would institute a security system costing $100,000 a year (January 22). In those days, $100,000 meant much more than today, and in fact amounted to more than the total budget of many ordinary churches.

But Stephen Feke, the business manager, told me, "We'd had thefts, purse snatchings, robberies, night break-ins, attempted rapes–practically everything." So the church decided security guards would be necessary–eight full time and four part-time. People taking church funds to the bank would have to be escorted, and guards would have to stand by when the church was providing its check-cashing service for employees.

"I hate to spend that kind of money on protection that could go into programs," Mr. Feke said. Just at that time, the church was getting ready to try raising $150,000 per year for a period of three years for new efforts to serve black people—its way of responding to the demand of James Forman for "reparations" without turning over money to James Forman.

Riverside's security problem had a news quality because of the prominence of the church and the scale of its response. But I found crime was hitting many churches of the city and requiring the diversion of church funds for security guards, replacement of stolen items and repair of vandalized buildings. A cost of another kind was the necessity of keeping churches locked up more of the time to prevent crime, and canceling many evening services or other activities because people became afraid to go out in the dark. Particularly older people, often a large part of a church program, became prisoners of crime, afraid to leave home in the evenings. "We are finding people increasingly reluctant to come out for programs at night unless a group is coming from their building," one of the Riverside clergy reported.

New York had undergone a discernible worsening of the crime problem in the previous decade. I finished graduate study and left New York in the spring of 1963, and found when I returned in the latter part of 1968 that the sense of safety in the city had deteriorated in just those few years. I could somehow feel the difference, and I was myself a crime victim a couple of times. The change was attributed largely to the growing drug problem, but saying this just pushed the question back a step and left you with the need for explaining the drug problem. It was not just a matter of the drugs, but also of the increasing permissiveness of the period regarding drugs and drug sales, rather open on my block for a while, and the crime that came next, the general rebellion against rules, the process identified as "defining deviancy down." It made people feel uneasy, and it limited their freedom. And it cost money.

The effects of crime also became visible across the street from Riverside Church at Union Seminary. The seminary buildings completely surround two full blocks, with an open quadrangle inside. When I first began going there in the 1950s, the place was generally open. You or anybody could come and go with considerable freedom. But in the 1960s and 1970s, security tightened up, step by step. Someone was placed on duty at the main entrance to watch comings and goings. Other entrances that previously had unlocked doors came to require keys. A basement snack room, where the studious might come any hour of the night to renew their strength with drinks and munchables from the machines, had to be locked at a certain hour to protect the machines from robbers. Eventually, the main entrance was closed altogether, and everyone was routed through a side portal, with a watcher posted and a sign-in book for visitors, who could now be name-tagged.

The religious establishment of Morningside Heights comprises not only Union Seminary and Riverside Church, but also other institutions. (I figured that in a book of this length I should use "comprises" somewhere, dislike the word though I do, just to prove I know how.) Among the Morningside presences is an office building, the Interchurch Center, whose tenant roster is composed of the National Council of Churches, denominational agencies and miscellaneous other non-profit organizations, church-related and other. At the Interchurch Center, a security system was instituted to make visitors stand in line a while and get permission to enter, and badges they had to wear.

But there, the building manager at the time, Carl Tiller, told me it was not so much the crime threat that had worsened but the legal threat. In that period, Americans were showing an increased eagerness to sue each other, and juries an increased willingness to sympathize and award big bucks. Mr. Tiller said recent court decisions had made trustees of buildings such as the Interchurch Center more vulnerable to damage suits if crime hit a tenant and trustees could not show they had taken all possible precautions.

If you remember the doctrine of original sin, however, you will not be surprised to hear that crime did not cease at the Interchurch Center. Staff of church agencies, maybe even maintenance personnel hired by Mr. Tiller, people who wore the insider badges, could commit crimes. When items big as typewriters kept disappearing, you knew they were not being carried under somebody's arm past the security desk. Some insiders would have to have been slipping them out, maybe through the basement or in shipments misdirected to the purloiner's address. Crime is not something that needs to be explained but, as with magic tricks, sometimes we would like explanations of just how it is done.

Now that you've seen how Tracy worked, some of the stories that he worked on, and his thoughts about those stories, move on to the next chapter for a little something about Tracy himself.

THE AUTHOR

CHAPTER SIXTEEN

BIRTH

William Tracy Early was born 20 February 1934 in Snyder, Scurry County, Texas. He was the eldest of three children born to Willis Worley Early, Jr. and Lillian Marian Walton Early. Boyce Don Early was born 7 September 1935 and died 4 October that same year. Grady Gaston Early was born 8 November 1944.

NAME

In childhood, Tracy was occasionally addressed as 'Bill' and even, curiously, as 'Tracy Bill,' the more correct 'Bill Tracy' not being as euphonious in the Southern tradition as in Bobbie Gentry's "Ode to Billie Joe." He once received mail at Baylor University addressed to Tracy Bill Early. He commented, "I've been trying to lose that 'Bill' ever since the 7th grade but haven't succeeded. Now some [at Baylor] have found out about it." (*Journal,* 29 April 1952) In adulthood, he reserved William T. Early for government documents and became to friends, readers, and employers alike–Tracy Early. At Ft. Bliss, the sign outside his quarters simply said Ch. Tracy Early; no first name or initial, no rank. Some of Tracy's friends were surprised when they learned that his first name was William.

When asked to provide basic data for articles for the *New Catholic Encyclopedia,* he told editor David Eggenberger, "I have no institutional affiliation, so I suppose that is out if we wish to uphold the standards of factual accuracy. And I don't particularly care for any titles. How much is mandatory from your standpoint? Can I just be me?" David agreed. (*Journal,* 23 August 1973).

Once when Tracy changed banks, his bank card listed his full name. He requested a change; the second card again had his full name. The third request worked. (*Journal*, 13 September 1997)

In the army, Tracy had to tolerate 'Chaplain' and 'Lieutenant.' In his pastorate, he also had to tolerate 'Dr.,' 'Rev.,' and even 'Rev. Dr.' But he liked none of them.

HIGH SCHOOL

Tracy graduated from Snyder High School on 26 May 1950, just past his sixteenth birthday. Due to an aptitude for academics, and to the change in Texas from an eleven- to a twelve-year system, Tracy was double-promoted from grade one to grade four, thus explaining his graduation at such a tender age. A lover of music from childhood, Tracy took piano lessons and played alto saxophone in high school. He continued piano and sax lessons at college, but quit after two years to devote more time to academics. He continued to play piano and organ for several years after stopping formal training.

Tracy was fascinated with words. A gifted wordsmith, his first by-lined (with picture) article appeared in *Ambassador Life* in February 1947, the month that he turned 13. Entitled "What alcohol does to you," it expressed a conservative attitude which did not persist in such strong form in Tracy's later life.

BAYLOR AND SOUTHEASTERN

In Tracy's unpublished memoirs, he says, "In the meantime, at age 12, I had made a commitment at a Royal Ambassadors camp to surrender to God's call to me to be a minister. And I continued to feel that vocational decision was valid, even in the time I was thinking my salvation was not secure. So from the age of 12, I had a clear vocational direction in mind, and always assumed that my life would be spent as a pastor."

So Tracy entered Baylor, a Southern Baptist university, at Waco, Texas, in 1950 and graduated with a B.A. degree on 28 May 1954. He was a member of the Columbus Avenue Baptist Church. In Summer 1954, Tracy attended the University of Oslo (Norway) Summer School for American Students. He sailed for Oslo from New York on 23 June on the SS Stavangerfjord and discovered the depth of what was to be a life-long affliction with motion sickness. The pleasure of six weeks in Scandinavia was diluted by anticipation of the return trip.

He entered Southeastern Baptist Theological Seminary, Wake Forest, North Carolina, and graduated with a Bachelor of Divinity (B.Div.) degree on 17 January 1958. He was ordained a Baptist minister on 15 May 1957 upon recommendation of the Wake Forest Baptist Church.

At Southeastern, one of Tracy's professors was Dr. Stewart A. Newman. Checking role on the first day of class, Newman got to Tracy's name and remarked that his second teaching job, in the Hermleigh, Texas, public school, was given him by a man named Early. Newman was attending nearby Hardin-Simmons College in Abilene and needed work. Willis Worley Early, Sr., the chairman of the school board, asked Newman to teach mathematics during the 1927-28 school year. Tracy said, "Yes, sir, that was my grandfather." Tracy and Newman became fast friends. In 1987, Tracy wrote to Newman, "I had not found friends like you before, and have not since. You made a fellow wandering Texan feel at home a long way from home . . . . " Tracy and Newman kept up a lively correspondence until Newman's death at age 94 in 2001. Newman, too, valued the 'Texas connection.' In 1997, he wrote to Tracy, "A lot has occurred to you and me both since we left the confines of West Texas."

THE U.S. ARMY

Having answered the call of God, Tracy then answered the call of country. On 22 May 1957 the Chaplains Commission of the Southern Baptist Commission recommended Tracy for appointment as a Chaplain in the Army Reserve of the United States. On 14 August Tracy was appointed Chaplain (1st Lt) in the U.S. Army Reserve. He entered active duty on 16 August and was assigned to the 59th AAA Battalion at Ft. Bliss, Texas, where he served his entire two-year hitch. The Chief of Staff, Col. J.D. Stevens appointed Tracy as Center Stockade Chaplain effective 8 September 1957. (None of this kept Tracy's Local Selective Service Board No. 21 from wondering whether they should maintain his student status.) From 6 January to 11 March 1958 Tracy attended the Chaplain Officer Basic Course at Fort Slocum, N.Y. Despite a disappointing score in 'warfare,' Tracy graduated second of 31 graduates.

Returning to Ft. Bliss, Tracy fell to work. For outstanding service as chaplain of the 1st Gun Bn (COMP) 59th Arty (16 August 1957 to 8 September 1958) he received a Certificate of Achievement from Headquarters Sixth Artillery Group. He performed his first marriage ceremony on 4 May 1958. Later that year Tracy was assigned to the Red River (guided missile) Range Camp northwest of Carrizozo, N.M. While there he served in a unique chapel that had been constructed, using local materials, by soldiers who volunteered their time.

It was during Army service that Tracy first received payment for writing, an article for *Christianity Today* (July 1959) entitled "Why army churchgoing lags."

Tracy left active duty on 16 August 1959. He resigned his commission on 15 February 1960, receiving an honorable discharge. Tracy was not content just to leave the army; he wanted to take all Southern Baptist chaplains with him. He wrote an essay suggesting that Southern Baptists withdraw from the program of the military chaplaincy, leaving ministry to soldiers to local churches. After distributing the essay to a select group, he received feedback. W. Barry Garrett, director of information services of the Baptist Joint Committee on Public Affairs (BJC), agreed, but urged restraint in publishing the essay. James E. Tull, a Southeastern professor, did not totally agree. Dr. Denton Coker, another Southeastern professor, argued that leaving the military would provide aid and comfort to fundamentalist isolationists within the Southern Baptists. (*Journal*, 6, 15, 21 June) It is of course axiomatic that programs with positions of power to be occupied are not easily disbanded. The Southern Baptists did not abandon the army. Indeed, the current U.S. Army Deputy Chief of Chaplains is a Southern Baptist.

> **Sidebar:** *On 4 August 1972 the* National Catholic Reporter *reported that Tracy's Red River Range had been closed down in 1959 and "only the chapel remained until recently when some unusual thieves carted it away. All that's left is the concrete slab foundation which is shaped like a cross."*

UNION THEOLOGICAL SEMINARY, NEW YORK

As he prepared to return to academia, Tracy considered Yale and Union as equals. The Yale/Union dilemma was probably frustrating, but was certainly funny. In 1957, it was Yale *vs.* Union *vs.* the chaplaincy. On 31 March, Yale accepted Tracy, but offered no financial support; on 3 March, Tracy accepted Yale. On 5 April, Union accepted Tracy, *and* offered a $1,000 scholarship. So on 10 April, Tracy accepted Union and then on 25 April, advised Yale that he'd probably be going into the army anyway. And he did. Then in 1959, as Tracy prepared to leave the army, the drama played out all over again. Yale offered a $200 scholarship which Tracy accepted on 12 April; declining Union. When Union sweetened the deal to $2,000, Tracy wrote on 21 April to Richard Niebuhr at Yale to see if they'd match the pot; they wouldn't, so Tracy reversed course and accepted Union's offer on 26 May. The very next day, he received a telegram from Union indicating that the government money had dried up, but offered a $1,300 scholarship plus a $200 assistantship. That was still better than Yale's offer, so on 8 June, he rejected Yale, and entered Union in September. As it turned out, Congress restored the larger government scholarships.

Union's advantage was that Tracy was at the top of the list to receive one of five National Defense Education Act of 1958 fellowships starting at $2,000 the first year. These fellowships were open to criticism. In the same issue of *The Baptist Standard* (19 August 1959) that announced Tracy's receipt of the fellowship, eyebrows were raised and dire predictions were made. Dr. C.E. Carlson, executive secretary of the BJC, said, "We look upon the church's

SIDEBARS

freedom to train her own leadership as one of the most important freedoms that the church must guard." Government support would "inevitably mean some measure of loss of freedom." And Glenn L. Archer, executive director of Protestants and Other Americans United for Separation of Church and State (POAU), asked, "What has happened to separation of Church and State in a country where the training of clergymen is now to be financed from tax funds?" Tracy even received personal criticism from various sources. Alfred A Carpenter of the Chaplains' Commission wished that Tracy were going to a Southern Baptist seminary rather than Union or Yale. Too liberal. Tracy responded that he was still a loyal Southern Baptist. (*Journal*, 17 June) David E. Kucharsky, news editor at *Christianity Today* expressed surprise that Tracy would accept government money, and requested a statement on how a Southern Baptist minister resolved the church/state problem. After consulting with Newman, Tracy replied that he considered the fellowship analogous to the G.I. Bill. (*Journal*, 13 August) A charge not leveled might have involved the intent of the recipient: these fellowships were for Protestant ministers (Tracy was), seeking the degree Doctor of Theology (Tracy was), and intending to become college teachers (Tracy was not).

There were difficulties. Galling, for one in love with writing, Tracy failed the German language examination. The examining professor said, "Mr. Early, it is evident that you know German, but you don't seem to know English very well." The idea, of course, was that one should absorb the thoughts expressed in German, then convey those thoughts in respectable English. In early 1960, he passed the German examination and, later that year, the French examination.

Another difficulty involved housing. At the gentle prodding of the administration, he investigated the International House, 500 Riverside Drive, but opted for more desirable quarters at 414 West 120th Street, Apt. 609, where he roomed with longtime friend and Southeastern roommate Thomas R. "Tom" Frazier. Rent was $103.50 per month. The landlord supplied gas for cooking purposes only, and electricity for lighting purposes only, using not larger than 75 watt bulbs. Cessation of those utilities was the penalty for their use "in connection with heating, cooling, laundering or dishwashing apparatus." A life-long penny-pincher, rent was a concern. Tracy had been advised earlier that rent at Union averaged about $10 per week for a single men's room. "That shocked me a little. I'd expected it to be a little higher than Wake Forest but not that much." (*Journal*, 4 May 1957).

But New York was liberalizing for a West Texas (conservative) Southern Baptist (very conservative). "I've finally decided that a policy of total abstinence is not important enough to maintain." (*Journal*, 23 February 1962) And, after attending a square dance at Union, "I enjoyed it greatly and feel some resentment at those in my denomination whose influence kept me from enjoying this for the last 14 years." (*Journal*, 24 February 1962)

After considering various dissertation topics, he chose *The Doctrine of Revelation in the Theology of H. Wheeler Robinson* in order to become thoroughly grounded in the Southern Baptist tradition in anticipation of a career as a Southern Baptist pastor. Later he would lament that he should have chosen Paul Tillich who "spoke to my condition." With a new direction in mind, Robinson now seemed "a major waste of time." (*Journal*, 24 June 1967) And "how much better off I would have been if I had gone to the University of Texas and studied journalism." (*Journal*, 6 August 1968)

On 21 May 1963, Tracy received the Doctor of Theology degree. In 1973, Tracy was notified that the New York State Board of Regents would grant the Ph.D. in place of the Th.D. upon relinquishing his Th.D. diploma and $50.00. Tracy did not seize this opportunity. Whether it was his fondness for the diploma or for the $50 is not recorded.

Tracy remained close to Union. He published "Union Seminary, ecumenical pioneer" in the national Catholic weekly *Ave Maria* (27 September 1969), "Seminary's library a treasure trove for Bible scholars" in the *Christian Science Monitor* (9 July 1979), and "John Bennett: Shy radical" also in the *Christian Science Monitor* (16 July 1970). He covered the 27 October 1968 sermon by Dr. John C. Bennett, Union president, regarding Russian attitudes toward the invasion of Czechoslovakia. He wrote a rather acerbic article about Union students' presumption of say-so in the selection of a successor to Dr. Bennett. He reported on a new plan of government giving students an increased voice in all phases of seminary life. He represented Southeastern at the 1976 inauguration of Donald W. Shriver, Jr., as 13th president of Union, made small gifts to various funds, and attended class reunions, especially the 40th in October 2003. More significantly, Tracy accepted Union President John C. Bennett's invitation to lecture in the second semester of the 1968-1969 academic year. Tracy was to lead a Practical Theology course entitled "Ministry in the South." Having recently served as pastor of the Urbanna Baptist Church in Virginia, he was well-prepared for the duty. He "found the experience interesting and profitable in many ways." A minor profit is revealed in a note from Head of Circulation of the library:

> "We notice that you took out, as an alumnus, a year's membership in the library on September 16, 1968. As a member of Union Faculty this Spring semester, you automatically have borrowing privileges in the library during these months. So we'd like to make some adjustment – the amount of $4.00 could be refunded to you out of the $12.00 you paid, or we could extend

your membership for four months to January 16, 1970. Perhaps you'd be kind enough to let us know which of the two arrangements you'd prefer."

THE PASTORATE

Tracy had seized every opportunity to broaden his practical experience in pastoral work. Two years as a Chaplain in the U.S. Army contributed to that experience, but he had other, shorter pastoral experiences.

He spent Summer 1953 working with Vacation Bible Schools in the Austin, Texas area.

Summer 1955 found Tracy working with the young people of Rosemary Baptist Church, Roanoke Rapids, NC, with occasional Sunday stints as Minister.

In Summer 1960, Tracy did one-, two- or three-Sunday stints as supply or guest minister at the Elmhurst (N.Y.) Baptist Church; the Hurleyville (N.Y.) Methodist Church; the Woodenmere (N. Y.) Methodist Church; the Simpson Methodist Church, Paterson, N.J.; the Park Methodist Church, Weehawken, N.J.; and the Monroe (N.Y.) First Presbyterian Church.

June through mid-August 1961, Tracy served as pastor of the Rocky Point Community Church Congregational, Rocky Point, Long Island, N.Y.

In Spring 1962, he was pastor of the Memorial Presbyterian Church in Roosevelt, Long Island, N.Y. In Summer 1962, he preached at the Woodlawn Reformed Church, Brooklyn, N.Y.; the Westbury (N.Y.) Methodist Church; the First Presbyterian Church, Monroe, N.Y.; and the South Presbyterian Church, Yonkers, N.Y.

In 1963, he preached at the Farmingdale (N.Y.) Baptist Church; the Elmhurst (N.Y.) Baptist Church; the East Suffolk Baptist Chapel, Westhampton Beach, N.Y.; and the Presbyterian Church, Cutchogue, N.Y.

And, accepting a challenge, from November 1962 through January 1963, he was interim pastor at the First Presbyterian Church, Nyack, New York, which was then undergoing difficulties. Author Percy H. Epler advised, "While I don't want you sacrificed here where half deserted in a faction, still, if you care to take it as a challenge—you will have our prayers—if it is wise for such a young man of promise as you to come here."

After leaving Union, Tracy spent Summer 1963 in England. Then began five difficult years when Tracy eventually found, and soon resigned, a pastorate. There were two major difficulties with his first and only full-time pastorate: getting in, and getting out.

GETTING IN

On 16 September 1963, Tracy moved to Wake Forest, N.C., and began looking for a pastorate. There followed long, agonizing months when it seemed that he would never succeed. Hints of pastorates here and there, teaching jobs, and other opportunities seemed to arise and then disappear. But Tracy's requirements were stringent. "I do not want to be a Minister of Education anywhere. I do not want to work for any denomination but Southern Baptist. I do not want to work outside the South. I do not want to teach." Also, Tracy was a bachelor; many churches expect two for the price of one.

Finally, he spoke with the Pulpit Committee at the Urbanna (VA) Baptist Church where he preached on 16 February 1964. On the 23rd, the congregation voted 62-4 to invite Tracy to be their minister beginning 15 March. He accepted and preached his first sermon as pastor on that date, and transferred his church membership from the Manhattan Baptist Church, N.Y. Six months of searching had finally paid off.

Tracy fell into the work of the pastorate. There were sermons, baptisms, weddings, and funerals. There were visits with the elderly, the sick, and the well. He was elected Sunday School Superintendent of the Mid-Tidewater Baptist Association in Saluda, VA. He served one term as president of the Urbanna Chamber of Commerce and joined the Ruritan Club. He wrote "Thought of the Week" for the *Southside Sentinel* in Urbanna, "Letter from Urbanna" for *The Baptist Program,* and reported on religious conventions and wrote book reviews for the *Times-Dispatch* in Richmond. He wrote and delivered devotionals on the radio station in Gloucester, VA. And he wrote articles for religious journals: treatments of various chapters of his dissertation, on Paul Tillich, on the Klan, on Easter, on race relations. His articles were sometimes accepted, often rejected. But he wrote.

Ladies of the church brought meals and worried about his marital status. Gentlemen invited him to smoke cigars with them. He made friendships that lasted the rest of his life.

Eventually he saw the realities of the life of a small-town, rural preacher. There was the tension between Tracy's essentially liberal beliefs and the conservative mindset of the rural South. There was the mother who consented to her 16-year-old daughter's marriage because otherwise she would just 'run away.' There was the anonymous letter containing an Ann Landers clipping speaking negatively of preachers who dropped by without phoning first. There was the Richmond newspaper that gave the death of Nehru third billing after a bank robbery and car liability rate increases. There was the male parishioner, divorced, upset over his sermon on divorce. There was the female parishioner, white, upset over his sermon on race relations. And there was the parishioner who was "just a few adjustments away" from getting his perpetual-motion machine working.

GETTING OUT

Barely 20 months into his pastorate, Tracy was having second thoughts. "I came to the decision last nite that the career I would really like to have is that of a freelance writer and lecturer on religious subjects, probably living in New York City." (*Journal,* 25 November 1965) As the months passed, that decision became more and more fixed, but "how to get such a position doesn't seem too clear." (*Journal,* 9 January 1967) Tracy investigated any job that involved writing. He inquired about a job as a reporter or editor with the *Times-Dispatch* and other publications. He took Civil Service exams and interviewed with organizations in Washington, D.C., but he was "a little disenchanted with the idea of being a Washington bureaucrat." (*Journal,* 17 May 1967) Finally he concentrated on possibilities in New York, registering with the Union Placement Office and some New York placement services.

In early 1968, Thomas O'Brien of Corpus Instrumentorum asked him to write some encyclopedia articles. Tracy was to say later that those articles, and the corresponding pay, were what finally allowed him to move from preaching to freelance writing. On 14 June, he definitely decided to move to New York. On 7 August, he told the Board of Deacons who expressed shock, regret, and understanding. On Sunday, 11 August, he told the congregation. One parishioner said that she had wondered how a young man like Tracy could be happy in a little town with nothing going on. (*Journal,* 7 August 1968) Another said, "Your talents are certainly buried here," and another said, "I'm sorry to see you leave, but Urbanna doesn't have much to offer." (*Journal,* 12 August 1968) Tracy's last Sunday in Urbanna was 25 August, with resignation effective 31 August.

In an interview for the Newport News (VA) *Daily Press,* he said, "The Christian ministry should be devoted to the truth. Journalism has the same purpose–to let people know the truth. I feel that with my interest and abilities, I can make a greater contribution through writing than in the pastoral ministry." (*Journal,,* 15 August 1968) Tracy already had some experience with reporting. His first set of press credentials came when he reported on a 1967 Southern Baptist Convention for the *Times-Dispatch.*

Every year thereafter, on the last Sunday in August, Tracy refused to attend any church service as an "annual celebration of independence from the church" (*Journal,* 28 August 1983) and from the "gauche and nauseating elements of Southern Baptist life I couldn't stand." (*Journal,* 24 July 1983) Other Sundays, he went because he "chose to go and not out of a legalistic compulsion." (*Journal,* 30 August 1998)

NEW YORK REDUX

Tracy returned to New York on 31 August 1968 and quickly found a place to live. Beginning on 1 September, he looked at apartments on W. 114th Street, at 125 and at 626 Riverside Drive, on W. 11th Street near the New School, and at the Masaryk Towers on the lower east side. On 5 September he leased Apartment 31 at 102 W. 80th Street, where he was to live for the next 37 years. This rent-controlled apartment commanded the then-princely sum of $160 per month for the first year, rising to $170 thereafter. More than Tracy had intended to pay, it was reasonable enough that he felt he could survive, eventually, as a freelancer. Rent-control had its benefits for a penny-pincher; the last month's rent for January 2006 was only $292.57. Although rent-control allowed annual increases in rent, the owners rarely did so, possibly because the allowed rises were so picayune and the protests from tenants so vehement. Returning the apartment to the owners in 2006 meant that the rent could rise skyward; how high I do not know. Or, since the building went co-op some years ago, the apartment may have been sold; again, for what amount can only be guessed. A floor-through basement apartment directly across the street was, in early 2006, for sale for $1.2 million.

W. 80th Street was not such a good location in 1968. "The neighborhood doesn't look too good, and the super showed me the bandage on a chest knife cut he got from trying to stop 3 men robbing the washing machine coin boxes." (*Journal,* 5 September) Tracy was to jest many times that it was his arrival that started the gentrification of W. 80th Street. It is today a handsome neighborhood.

WORLD COUNCIL OF CHURCHES (WCC)

Tracy began work immediately, writing stories for Religious News Service (RNS) while continuing to write encyclopedia articles for Tom O'Brien. Soon, however, he got a regular job. Tracy had written to Faith Pomponio at the WCC (24 July 1967) to ask for a job, but she had nothing. By 1968, that had changed. On 24 September, Pomponio hired Tracy as a 3-day-per-week assistant, "start tomorrow." On the 27th, Pomponio changed that to 5-days-per-week because her secretary had quit, and she could pay Tracy for the extra days out of those funds. Now Tracy was full-time (assistant editor, *The Ecumenical Courier*) to be reduced to three days per week upon hiring of a secretary.

Tracy joined Riverside Church on 1 December 1968, and remained there for the rest of his life. If he prayed for more reliable employment, then prayers at Riverside are answered quickly; on 2 December 1968, Pomponio requested that Tracy's full-time status be made permanent because of "the fine quality of his work." Dr. Eugene L. Smith, executive secretary, New York office of the WCC, quickly approved.

But Tracy was never at ease working for someone else. On 30 June 1969 he left the somewhat volatile Pomponio and the WCC to pursue his long-dreamed-of freelance career.

RELIGIOUS NEWS SERVICE (RNS)

The realities of earning a living, however, meant that freelancing was not to be Tracy's full-time occupation; not just yet. For a little dependable income, Tracy did additional work for the also-sometimes-volatile Lillian Block at RNS. He covered stories, worked in the office, filled in for staff absences, and wrote the weekly radio script. Even though Block offered permanent employment ($9400, 3 September 1969, $10,600, 18 September; $11,000, 25 September 1970), Tracy insisted on being freelance. Despite an occasionally stormy professional relationship, Tracy and Block remained fast friends until her death on 21 March 1981.

A NEW YORKER

Over the next few years, Tracy gradually became a *bona fide* New Yorker. He got a parking ticket and a phone (18 September 1968). He sold his car (29 December 1969) and relied on public transportation for the rest of his life. He was mugged in Central Park (14 July 1971), losing three or four dollars and change and the watch given him in 1948 by our parents. He filed a taxi driver complaint (17 March 1980) and won (14 April). His apartment was burgled (13 May 1982). His pocket was picked (4 September 1985). For the first time in his life, he made an appointment for a haircut (17 December 1985). His apartment, and actress friend Ann Owens, were filmed for an episode of the Dave Letterman show (26 April 1994). He claimed and received a $7 refund for a taxi overcharge (9 September 1994). He dealt with an infestation of mice, "I have a mouse stealing a lot of cheese without getting caught. It is the first time one has been so successful so long. But I keep setting out my two traps in the kitchen and assume one day he will get careless." (*Journal*, 19 August 1995) "Finally caught a mouse that had eluded me through many bites of cheddar." (*Journal*, 22 August) "There seems to be an unending procession of them into my apartment and into my traps." (*Journal*, 6 September)

Life in New York goes on. The 7 February 1978 snow storm, with 18 or more inches, was said to be the biggest since about 1947. No mail delivery. No

New York Times delivery. Tracy "circled around to see how the blizzard conditions affected Eighth Avenue, and found the prostitutes out working."

WORSHIP AND IDEAS

Tracy searched for ideas for articles in every nook and cranny, very often in the churches of New York City. Attending one or two services each Sunday, he worshipped and looked for ideas from the pulpit. With knowledge and experience to back up strong ideas on what should and should not come from the pulpit, he commented on what he saw and heard. On 21 July 1974, for example, he attended the Madison Avenue Presbyterian Church to hear George Landes. "He preached an expository sermon on the rich young ruler and made not a single 'relevant' remark on social and political events of the day. Very gratifying to find there are still intelligent people who can do it."

On the other hand. On 16 February 1976, flipping through the cable tv channels, he saw Jerry Falwell, pastor of the Thomas Road Baptist Church in Lynchburg, Virginia. "It was my first time to see him and he was about as much of a phony as I expected." On 7 March, he attended the 11 a.m. service at Central Baptist Church on Amsterdam Avenue in New York with a mixture of whites and blacks in the congregation. "The pastor is a young white fellow whose sermon was hardly listenable, though not terribly heavy on dogmatic theology. The music was very bad and the atmosphere in general not inspiring. I wonder why people keep going." More happily, on 28 March, he went to the Cathedral of St. John the Divine to see Dorothy Day installed as a Cathedral colleague. "She also said a few words and showed she still has a clear and common-sense mind." But at the Community Church on 23 May where Don Harrington preached, "But his talk of how great preaching would draw people seemed a little curious since his own church there was no more than one third full."

Tracy was no respecter of rank in his criticisms. One Sunday (28 September 1986), he went to St. Patrick's Cathedral to hear John J. Cardinal O'Connor who, he said, "proceeded in somewhat Machiavellian fashion to start out like he was a liberal, for social justice, *etc.,* quoting the pope's sermon on the parable at the Yankee Stadium mass. But then he noted the pope had also spoken of depriving people of truth, and then moved into a song and dance about the pope as a pursuer of truth and wound up with a defense of institutional thought control."

On 16 November 1980, he heard Hans Kung preach at Riverside Church. "Kung preached a lengthy sermon arguing that a Christian could believe in Jesus as the Son of God without accepting the Virgin Birth as literal history. I thought it was a remarkable sermon to come from the pulpit of Harry

Emerson Fosdick, who had delivered that insight more than a half century before. I also thought Pope John Paul II was probably correct in judging that Kung is not a Catholic theologian. Kung seems to develop his theology as a liberal Protestant would on the basis of individual interpretation of the Bible, handled freely, and without regard to the thinking of the church or positions taken by the Bishop of Rome."

Tracy's critiques could be deadly funny. In 1997, he went to the Malcolm Shabazz Mosque in Harlem to cover Focolare leader Chiara Lubich and Imam W.D. Muhammed, son of Elijah Muhammed, "and his disloyal successor who now has the vague title of Muslim American Spokesman for Human Salvation . . . . And there was much talk of unity and some of Muhammed's peculiar meanderings. A self-educated man who appears to be the product of unskilled labor." (*Journal,* 18 May)

Tracy was equally critical of his own church. "I went to Riverside Church this morning, where as usual I was impressed by the lower attendance, compared with the Coffin era, and was offended by the pep rally atmosphere of continual clapping. At the beginning we had a dance by a group of Indians that seemed to have nothing to do with Christianity but a lot to do with being politically correct. The prayers were also slanted explicitly to the left. And the sermon of Jim Forbes was on forgiveness, with some reference to [President] Clinton, and was I suppose intended to contribute to the argument of Clinton supporters that his actions shouldn't be held against him." (*Journal,* 22 November 1998) A Republican-turned-Democrat, Tracy had become "less sympathetic" with Democrats because they were not facing up to questions about Clinton's behavior, but only making partisan attacks on the prosecutor, Kenneth Starr. (*Journal,* 19 November 1998)

And of his alma mater. "I went to Union Seminary to see about buying the Christmas cards the library made to sell this year. But I decided when I looked at it that it didn't have much class. So I went away disappointed with the card and with Union, which overall now seems to be lacking in class." (*Journal,* 7 December 1998

Tracy was a voracious reader, romping through stacks of books looking for information, background on people he was to interview, book review possibilities. He read the Doris Kearns book on Lyndon Johnson. "Decided it wasn't very great. The style is pedestrian, there isn't a lot of new material about Johnson, the psychologizing is dubious and the big lessons she tries to draw in conclusion are mostly fatuous or meaningless." (*Journal,* 12 June 1976)

Tracy wanted good, succinct, to-the-point scholarship. As he collected books, he discarded others to keep his personal library at a manageable size. But he was mindful of the destination of discarded books. He gave his

12-volume *Interpreter's Bible* to President Joseph C. "Joe" Hough at Union Seminary to give to a deserving student (2 February 2001). He gave his multi-volume set of Washington Irving to the Mid-Manhattan Library. Finally (15 February), "I finished rearranging my books, and selecting books to give and throw away . . . . I have culled out the equivalent of three shelves or more [about 15 feet] . . . . Some of the books I decided were not good, out of date scholarship and perhaps in some cases not so good when they were new, so I am throwing them away to keep any potential readers from being damaged by them." Later (31 January 2004), he donated another stack of books to the St. Agnes branch of the public library. In January 2006, I donated the bulk of Tracy's library to Union's Burke Library.

Tracy disliked religious fads. On 10 July 1977, he went to Christ Church Methodist to hear Bishop James Armstrong of the Dakotas. "He gave a pure social gospel sermon, covering practically every cliché point at home and abroad. I gained an insight into the reason I don't much like the social gospel preachers. They assume that the church includes only people of the upper classes, who ought to go down to the slums and do good deeds for the poor and oppressed. Social gospel preachers apparently never think that some of the poor and oppressed might themselves be part of the church. If I have come to church feeling poor and oppressed myself, the message offers me nothing."

CATHOLIC NEWS SERVICE

Tracy worked for two versions of the Catholic News Service. Created in 1920, and originally called the National Catholic News Service (NC), it is the oldest religious news service in the world. It is authoritative, but not official; it is news, not public relations. It is an editorially independent and financially self-sustaining division of the National Conference of Catholic Bishops. The service changed its name, to reflect a less parochial scope, on 12 June 1989 to Catholic News Service, having changed its logo to CNS on 8 June.

Richard W. Daw was director and editor in chief when Tracy began writing for NC in 1977. Thomas N. Lorsung, who started in 1972 as photo editor, was managing editor. On 17 January 1989, Lorsung replaced Daw to become the seventh director and editor in chief. He named James M. Lackey, NC's national news editor since 1984, as general news editor. On 1 February 2004, Anthony J. "Tony" Spence became director and editor in chief upon Lorsung's retirement.

But the path to the connection between Tracy and NC/CNS was a bit rocky. On 12 October 1972, Fletcher Coates of the National Council of Churches (NCC) asked Tracy to do a series of four articles to be placed with NC to introduce Catholics to NCC because of a possibility that the Roman

Catholic Church would join NCC. Tracy agreed to do the articles, but when he informed Block of the arrangement, she told him that NC could not use his byline.

On 18 April 1973, Jo-ann Price Baehr, NC's New York stringer, asked Tracy if he'd like to do some articles for NC. Alas, no; not and work for RNS at the same time.

On 26 June 1976, after leaving RNS, Tracy wrote to A.E.P. Wall, Daw's predecessor to ask if he could use occasional articles from New York. Now that Block's prohibition against the Tracy Early byline at NC no longer applied, Tracy felt that he might pick up a fair amount of work. But on 6 July, Tracy was "very disappointed to get a letter from National Catholic News Service replying that they had no need for any further coverage in New York."

However, on 22 March 1977, Baehr told Tracy that she might get some NC work for him. On 24 March, she told Tracy that she had talked to Lorsung who had suggested that Tracy write to him; he did. On the 29th, Lorsung gave an assignment to Tracy–coverage of a conference on women's ordination at the Bronx campus of Fordham University. Tracy wrote the story and, on the 31st, dictated it to a Western Union operator for transmission to NC offices in Washington, D.C., by Datagram. Later that day, he talked to Baehr who said that she had already talked to Lorsung who had already seen the story and had liked it. Tracy remarked, "So perhaps we are off to a satisfactory start."

Satisfactory, indeed.

Over the next few years, Tracy wrote more and more pieces for NC; some on his own, some while filling in for Baehr. Not content to await assignments, Tracy "wrote Tom Lorsung to suggest some NC articles . . . ." (*Journal*, 16 May 1977)

Like Block, Lorsung offered to put Tracy on retainer. When Baehr fell ill, Lorsung asked Tracy to fill in and said "they would likely be discussing some arrangement with me to get a retainer like Jo-Ann Price has been getting. I mentioned that I wanted to remain independent with the right to criticize the Catholic bishops, etc." (*Journal*, 19 September 1979). Thus, as with Block, Tracy politely declined the retainer.

This is not to say that Tracy was unconcerned about payment received for work delivered. Tracy often pressed editors for raises.

When Tracy was asked to do additional *New Catholic Encyclopedia* articles beyond his initial assignment, he replied on 17 September 1973, "I assume encyclopedia contributors are normally professors living on salaries, and that the three cents a word is a kind of token of appreciation enabling them to buy a little extra something for the holidays. But I have to depend on my writing just to pay the rent, and of course doing encyclopedia articles at three cents a word doesn't do much for that. Is there any chance of the organization allowing you some extra money for those articles that the professors perhaps haven't had time to finish?" By 23 September, Eggenberger had doubled Tracy's rate.

Pay raise negotiations sometimes took an interesting turn. In 1981, after asking the United Methodist Board of Global Ministries for a raise, he "got a call from Helen Kromer, who had been assigned by Beverly Chain to find out what church periodicals etc are paying writers. This is a process I initiated by talking to Beverly, so it is ironic that I should play some role in determining what they find out, which will influence them in deciding what to pay me." (*Journal,* 3 November)

On 16 July 1982, after Baehr's death, Daw, Lorsung, and Tracy ate at the restaurant in the Citicorp building and "reached the historic agreement that made me the NC agent in New York." Lorsung again suggested that Tracy's arrangement with NC be on a retainer basis. Tracy again said he'd "rather not." Lorsung did take the opportunity to upgrade Tracy's phone to touch-tone. High time. Touch-tone had been in use by phone company operators since 1941, and the home version was previewed at the 1962 Seattle World's Fair. In 1984 (*Journal,* 2 February), Lorsung again upgraded Tracy with a Radio Shack Model 100 computer and printer, later (26 March 1986) upgraded to Model 200, fax added (26 August 1991), and replaced with a laptop (31 March 1994). Tracy began using email (7 September 1995). CNS provided a combination fax/printer (30 January 1996). Late one day (8 February 1996), Tracy wrote a story and sent it to Ecumenical News International (ENI) news service. The next morning, he found ENI had already put out the story on ECUNET. "It is exhilarating to be involved in a form of journalism that operates so quickly–in such contrast to the old EPS [Ecumenical Press Service] style by mail. And with my new printer, I could immediately print out copies and mail them to interested people at Union. Theoretically, I might have sent them by fax." Technology marched on. "[Jim Lackey] told me that I might be asked some time later to start communicating with CNS by E-mail, and to get CNS stories from the Web, rather than having printed copies mailed to me. I said I would adapt." (*Journal,* 4 May 1998) Tracy bought an NEC laptop (6 August 1998), and after the usual pain of adapting to a new computer system, first used it to send a story to CNS (28 August). CNS got an AOL account for Tracy (3 September), and he first retrieved a CNS story from the web and felt confident enough in using the NEC to disconnect the old Radio Shack (15 September). He bought his own printer/fax (16 October 2001). Tracy sent CNS' printers back to Joe Larson at CNS (16 January 2002). He bought a new HP laptop (7 February 2005) which is now used by Tracy's uncle and boyhood playmate Laban Walton.

Tracy was not insensitive to the circumstances of his association with NC. During a depressing writing lull in 1983 (*Journal,* 12 April), he commented , "I am only kept alive by my work for NC, and for that I am indebted to Joann's death, which causes me further depression."

Tracy's earlier association with NC had been blocked by Block who refused to let her reporters work for both RNS and NC. In 1984 (*Journal,* 4 April), Tracy was asked to cover an event for RNS. Remembering Block's rule, Tracy made sure that no one at RNS objected to Tracy's dual role. Lorsung, however, "vetoed the idea." *Quid pro quo.* (*Journal,* 20 March 1984) As a freelancer, of course, Tracy could write for numerous markets. In 1982, for example, he interviewed Dorothy Sölle (German feminist and theologian) and visiting European anti-nuclear leaders and wrote stories for *United Methodist Communications,* the *Christian Science Monitor,* the Worldwide Faith News network, NC, and *Religion Today.* (*Journal,* 22 March 1982)

TELEVISION

Tracy sometimes appeared on television. In 1974, Tracy appeared on Russell Barber's NBC-TV show to discuss snake handlers in various religious sects. In 1985, he was on a four-person panel discussing 'How To Get Into The Media,' Tracy representing print media. In 1993, he was on a six-person panel to discuss 'The Week of Prayer for Christian Unity.' He noted that "None of [the panelists] talked about Unity in Christ." (*Journal,* 20 January)

WRITING

One cannot consider Tracy's life apart from his writing. As soon as he learned to write, he wrote, wrote, wrote. After his death, I began cataloguing 18 file drawers of material ranging from that first publication for *Ambassador Life* in 1947 to his last piece for CNS on 17 July 2005. In that process, I discovered the manuscript for the book that you now hold; ready for publication. Deciding to publish *Sidebars* led to ancillary tasks. Posthumous publication seemed to require this chapter giving some outline of Tracy's life and work. That required creating a bibliography of his work (described below).

The record is incomplete; although Tracy was something of a pack rat and kept numerous tear sheets and original manuscripts, there were gaps indicating that material was missing. Thus, his bibliography, while impressive, could be still longer. Tracy also kept a record of his rejections. The Boston Red Sox' Ted Williams, one of baseball's all-time greats, had 2,654 hits in 7,706 times at bat. He hit 521 home runs, but he also struck out 709 times. Tracy took a lot of swings, sending spec pieces to publications around the nation and around the world. So he got a lot of rejections. One, from an editor at *The*

Washington Post on 11 July 1977, said, "This piece covers pretty much the same ground I tramped over a year ago when the CPC [Christian Peace Conference] people met up at New Windsor, Md., so I guess it's a bit redundant for us. Thanks for thinking of me anyway. I see your name cropping up in all kinds of interesting places—you must be getting rich!" But Tracy didn't take rejections docilely. For example, in 1973, the *Christian Science Monitor* rejected a piece on 26 March; five days later, Tracy placed it with the North American Newspaper Alliance (NANA).

Another piece also illustrates his tenacity. In late 1969, Tracy wrote about the possibility of the Roman Catholic Church joining the NCC, for *Ave Maria*. They held it interminably, went out of business, and sent it back with a $25 check. *The Lamp* was next to reject the story. *The Sign* reacted favorably, so Tracy sent them a rewritten version in August 1970. But they also held it and held it. Finally, Tracy had to do more extensive revisions when *The Sign* got around to scheduling it for publication in May 1971. "But they paid well—$200 when I first did it and $100 for the revisions." (*Journal*, 22 April 1971) Sometimes interviewees made reporting difficult. For example, in 1999 Tracy attended a Catholic Hospital Administrative Personnel (CHAP) program to cover Jesuit Father Richard McCormick for CNS. "Unfortunately, he gave about the same lecture he gave last year, but I picked out different aspects and wrote a different story." (*Journal*, 19 May) Then after covering Bishop Joseph M. Sullivan's remarks to the concluding session of the CHAP conference, he "figured out a way to make a story out of [his] disjointed address . . . ." (*Journal*, 23 May)

Tracy wrote for several news services, so it is not possible to know which publications picked up his pieces. Correspondents often referred to having seen one of Tracy's pieces in such-and-such periodical. For example, his piece on John Lindsay (*Christian Century*, 31 March 1971) was printed by the *St. Louis Post-Dispatch*.

Tracy's name did crop up in surprising ways. For example, he wrote so much that he often appeared multiple times in the same issue of the same outlet. His personal record seems to be six: *Interpretive Services* (10 February 1972) and ENI (November 1996). There were five each in *Seventh Angel* (November 1984); *Religion Today* (11 March 1982); and CNS (26 April 1999 and 23 May 2005). And it was not uncommon for him to have two, three, or four pieces appearing on the same day in one of his news services.

Sometimes his name didn't crop up. In a 1984 story about church trouble in Malta, the interviewees could not be named because of possible retaliation by their government. The city in which the interview took place could not be

SIDEBARS

named. Tracy even suggested that "leaving my name off the story could perhaps give them further protection."

But how to categorize Tracy's work? Most voluminous would have to be the news services. Next would be magazines and newspapers. Then there are books, pamphlets, speeches, sermons, radio spots, and consulting reports. Academically, there were reports, themes, papers, theses, and the dissertation. He wrote (usually) with the familiar 'by Tracy Early' byline, but sometimes without, and sometimes with a pseudonym (*e.g.,* Sophia Watson). Sometimes his byline was simply omitted; sometimes he requested that his name not be used, usually because of editorial changes. Sometimes he was the ghost writer (*e.g.,* for Rev. Robert I. "Bob" Miller, Director of Alumni Affairs at Union Theological Seminary and onetime mayor of Englewood, N.J.).

Finally, there are his letters and diaries. He kept letters received, and copies of letters sent. He wrote our mother almost weekly for over 50 years, and she kept those letters. He recorded daily thoughts and deeds in diaries from 10 October 1948 through 15 July 2005 except for a brief period from 31 August 1959 to 2 January 1962 when he wrote, "Since mama has given me this [journal], I have decided to resume the keeping of a diary. I gave it up when I came to New York because I had come to feel it as something of a burden and thought I should live my life with more spontaneity and less routine. Since then my spirit has not become noticeably more spontaneous."

At various times, Tracy studied German, Norwegian, and French, as well as the usual Latin, Hebrew, and Greek required of divinity students. But he claimed no expertise in writing in any language other than English. However, his pieces were sometimes translated. A 1971 piece for NANA was reprinted in Greek. A 1995 piece was printed in the Danish church magazine *UdSyn.* A 1976 four-part *Spotlite* series on illegal immigration was reprinted in Spanish. A 1980 piece was reprinted in France's *Mensuel* magazine. A 1972 *Christian Science Monitor* piece was reprinted in the *Rome Daily Armenian.*

HUMOR

When Tracy's funny bone got funnied, he could be at once hilarious and thought-provoking. Want proof? Read "Klan Kludd: To Be or Not to Be," *Christian Century,* 22 February 1967; "It Takes Only a Moment," *Saturday Review,* 13 December 1969; "A Tourist's Guide to New York Churches," *Christian Century,* 26 August 1970; "Caustic Clive Barnes Packs Lethal Wallop," *Times-Dispatch,* 18 July 1971. Or this: Tracy was asked to contribute to a Book of Letters to be used in connection with an anniversary at *Response* magazine:

> *"It was not merely the lavish expense account that enabled me–via AT&T–to celebrate Christmas in Jerusalem, to make such visits as those to the Houma Indians of Louisiana's bayou country or the handicapped children in Little Rock's Camp Aldersgate, or even to soar off on the memorable journey to Nome, and see–in my mind's eye–the exciting finish of the Iditarod.*
>
> *"It was not merely the creativity with which you set and from time to time adapted deadlines, and the invigorating challenge of finding a manuscript might fall due a couple of weeks before the assignment was given.*
>
> *"It was not merely the pioneering guidance in political correctness, as you formulated policy on such fundamental questions as whether either an Indian or a Native American could be allowed to say something positive about Columbus or something negative about the Sandinistas.*
>
> *"It was, in basic fact, the privilege you offered of writing for an editor committed to giving readers a magazine actually worth their time and attention. For me, association with such an enterprise has meant both pride and delight." (12 April 1994)*

His humor appeared, even in serious pieces. Consider his lead in a story (*Christianity & Crisis,* 11 December 1978) on the state of the NCC: "Only the most presumptuous of outsiders would take an assignment to assess the National Council of Churches (NCC) entire. So let us begin."

At Urbanna, he had introduced the idea of a "Hymn of the Month" with "O Sacred Head Now Wounded" and pointed out the inferiority of "The Old Rugged Cross." "So far I haven't been hung but I'm expecting it any minute." Or, in the later stages of dissatisfaction with his pastorate, and at a deacon's meeting that was poorly attended, a discussion began of a general lethargy in the church with poor attendance and a membership generally showing no enthusiasm. "We discussed the matter at length but came to no conclusions. It is a difficult matter since I've lost interest myself." (*Journal,* 9 August 1967)

Tracy visited the "corporate responsibility" department of the Nestlé American headquarters in White Plains, N.Y, and interviewed Vincent Wipf about an infant formula controversy which prompted a boycott. "He took a rather hard nosed line, refusing to admit any fault in Nestlé now or in the past and talking about many things they've stopped doing. So apparently they've been perfect from the beginning and improving greatly." (*Journal*, 18 May 1979) Sometimes it's easy to see what's happening behind the scenes.

Other times, it's not so easy. "I got a call this morning that Archbishop [Arturo] Rivera Damas of El Salvador was here and could be interviewed. He came for a UN ceremony where the Truth Commission presented its report on violent acts in El Salvador since 1980. So I went over for that ceremony, and interviewed the archbishop in the delegates' lounge afterward, though he hadn't read the report and I hadn't and he didn't have much specific to say. This afternoon I interviewed Father Joseph A. O'Hare, who also hadn't read the report, by phone. And tonight I wrote a story and sent it to CNS." (*Journal*, 15 March 1993) And reported what? That no one had read the report?

PERSISTENCE

Tracy developed an article about different dates set for Easter by various religious groups. Then he pitched the story to 61 outlets from the *Albany Times Union* to the *Washington Post. The Roanoke (VA) Times* printed it on 2 April 1972. *The Christian Herald* printed it in April 1972. But *The New York Times* declined; twice, as both a general, and a special feature. *The New Yorker* declined. *Reader's Digest* declined. *The Atlantic Monthly* declined. *Horizon* declined. *Etc.*

Tracy had gotten some mileage out of the multiple outlet idea in 1971 when he wrote "Orthodox Easter Sunday Different in Many Ways" for NANA, (15 April 1971). That story was printed by the *Sunday Record* of Bergen, N.J., 18 April 1971. A similar Easter story, "All you ever wanted to know about the date of Easter (and were afraid to ask)" was printed by the *Christian Herald* in April 1971. These few successes conceal the cruel facts of the writing life. In 1971-1972 Tracy decided to test the waters of feature writing for newspapers. He found those waters quite choppy.

Mounting his own *ad hoc* press service, Tracy wrote 14 more-or-less general interest features with subjects ranging from Clive Barnes (*New York Times* theater critic) to dysautonomia (a dysfunction of the autonomic nervous system). He sent one or more of these features to 147 U.S. and eight foreign newspapers for a total of 337 submissions. There were 17 acceptances paying a total of $337.50, an average of almost exactly $1 per submission. Choppy waters, indeed, and a test of anyone's persistence.

That persistence spilled out in some creative ways. For example, he often attended and reported on high-toned events requiring tuxedoes and evening dresses. Reporters, sometimes a rather scruffy lot, were segregated to a press area where they observed from afar. Unsatisfactory. Tracy bought a tuxedo so he could mingle with, and gently interview, the paying guests. In 1990, for example, he went to the Pierre Hotel for the Appeal of Conscience fund-raising dinner honoring Vatican Secretary of State Agostino Cardinal Casaroli and a Chicago Jewish businessman Jay Pritzker of Hyatt Corporation. "Press were not given seats at the dinner, but I was in my tuxedo, and Fred Bona of the W.R. Grace Company recognized me and invited me to use the ticket their company president's wife was not using." (*Journal*, 29 October) A sheep in wolf's clothing.

EDITORS

Tracy's humor and persistence were tested as he doggedly resisted the tender mercies of his editors. After collecting a few articles about religious relics exhibited in churches around the world, Tracy thought that *Christian Century* magazine might like to publish an article about them. What Tracy had in mind was a rather tongue-in-cheek approach to the issue. Then began correspondence between Tracy and Dean Peerman, Editor, *Christian Century* magazine:

> 8 September 1971 Tracy to Dean: "I wonder if Century readers might be interested in a report on this."

> 13 September 1971 Dean to Tracy: "Please go ahead with the piece on relics—sounds like it would be entertaining."

> 24 November 1971 Tracy to Dean: "Thank you for the notification you are accepting my article, 'Bone Divine.' And as usual I would like to see the mutilated version of the article before it goes to press."

> 22 July 1972 Tracy to Dean: "Back in April when I inquired about whatever happened to the grandmother of Jesus, you expressed thanks for being prodded a bit. Now more than three months later, you would no doubt be doubly grateful."

> 9 August 1972 Dean to Tracy: "We haven't even rattled that bone divine yet . . ." because "our staff is too small . . . ."

> 12 October 1972 Dean to Tracy: "Here at last is a copy of the edited version of 'Bone Divine.' We hope you find it satisfactory (even thought we know that you don't like to be 'improved upon'!.) P.S. I'm still chuckling over the article; it's 'divinely' hilarious."

14 October 1972 Tracy to Dean: "My, my, my. You do provoke a fellow. Knowing you oughtn't to do it, you stalk straight ahead, muddy boots and all. And as one of your interpolations has it, But to what purpose? In a piece like 'Bone Divine' particularly the exact wording is crucial in order to maintain the exact tone that is needed. So let us begin."

followed by 4 pages of careful explanations of reasons why Dean's editorial changes should be reversed.

15 November 1972 Dean to Tracy: "Believe me, I do not relish writing this letter; in fact, it is one of the most thankless chores I've had in a long time.

"After we had already gotten 'Bone Divine' set in type–and had included most of the changes and restorations indicated in your long memo–Jim Wall, our new boss, read the galleys and decided against publication of the article. He feels that the article is anti-Catholic and a bit smug–and that relics are too easy a target.

"Martin Marty and I both pleaded your case with Jim, but to no avail. (Marty even made the point that at one time he thought you were Catholic yourself, since he had seen you at a number of Catholic gatherings.)

"I guess that Jim is, as he himself said, 'Feeling his oats.' I'm just sorry that you're the victim of this. I feel especially bad in view of the fact that we had your article for such a long time before processing it, and that you spent so much time on emendations of the edited version.

"Of course, we will be making payment for the piece despite the fact that we won't be publishing it. I do hope that you will be able to place it elsewhere–there might be some consolation in being paid for it twice.! And I also hope–fervently–that you won't decide to boycott us hereafter as a consequence of this distasteful episode." [Tracy didn't; he wrote for *Christian Century* at least through 1984.]

Tracy contributed to the *New Catholic Encyclopedia* (NCE) Volume 16 under executive editor David Eggenberger, to NCE 17 under Tom O'Brien, and to NCE 18 under Berard L. Marthaler.

After reviewing NCE 16, Tracy wrote to Eggenberger:

"But it appears that every article I wrote got into the book, and that every article was printed almost exactly as I wrote it, with only a few trifling editorial changes that even objective observers might call improvements."

"So I give you my heartfelt thanks. My writing for newspapers and magazines often endures a lot of painful editorial butchering, and it is very pleasant to find articles printed as written."

Tracy was quick to note good treatment of his articles. "My AJC [American Jewish Committee] story appeared in the [Christian Science] Monitor today with gratifying promptness, and almost exactly as I wrote it, with no typographical errors or misleading headline." (*Journal*, 14 May 1979)

And bad. "Checked the edited version of my A.D. article and found it generally depressing but containing no actual disasters." (*Journal*, 8 April 1980) Lewistine McCoy once pointed out various typographical errors in Tracy's book *Simply Sharing*. "I can't imagine he would think I needed to have someone tell me about those. If he could tell me how to keep editors and printers from making those errors, I would be more grateful." (*Journal*, 30 April 1981) Tracy wanted his copy unchanged, and his byline intact. On 17 October 1988, Jim Lackey, NC's national news editor, wrote a memo about Tracy to his Rewrite Staff:

"Since Tracy Early's copy usually comes in fairly clean, I usually handle it myself. But on those occasions when others in the newsroom edit his copy, we need to be careful not to change his copy in ways that change its meaning.

"Tracy called me this morning about the handling of his interview with Peruvian Archbishop Durand that ran in the service last Wednesday [NC, 12 October 1988]. (Since I was gone, I don't know who did the editing, and I really don't want to know. I'd rather just point out the following for all without placing blame on anyone.)

"One thing Tracy sometimes does in his stories is throw in generally accepted observations about a particular situation without attributing it to anyone. After I made the mistake a couple of times of assuming that the person being interviewed made the observation, we agreed that he would flag such observations with a parenthetical 'not he said' or similar words to warn us against tacking a 'he said' onto the end of the sentence.

"Unfortunately we fell into the trap on the Durand story even though Tracy in his original had added his customary caution. [Details of the error]

"Tracy was pretty concerned that we had Archbishop Durand characterizing Cardinal Ricketts as a Gutierrez protector when the archbishop said nothing of the sort.

"Tracy is an extremely valuable resource for us, and the news desk does its best to keep him happy. So let's take extra care with his stuff. He doesn't mind it when we chop a lengthy story in half or more. (I once told him that since he's often working late at night and can't ask for guidance he should just pour everything into the story and let us cut it here.) But let's be careful that we don't over edit or wrongly edit the stuff we use."

Tracy did not just file stories and forget them; he read the edited versions and noted where they differed from his originals. If necessary, he contacted the editor to find ways to avoid future editing problems. When Tracy's NC story reporting on his interview with O'Connor about the Middle East appeared (26 September 1984), Tracy found that it had been changed around a lot and "in a way that I thought could leave a wrong impression. It also had a factual error. So I called Tom (Lorsung) to talk about it and suggest it might be well for me to review articles that are rewritten. He will consider it." (*Journal*, 28 September)

Tracy was extremely protective of his reporting image as it was inevitably portrayed by the final versions of pieces that appeared in print with his byline.

Not to say that Tracy never made errors. In comparing his unedited version to the printed 1982 *Christianity & Crisis* article (1 November) about day care centers, he noted that one small change indicated "they may have let Eileen Lindner [director of the Child Advocacy Project of the NCC] read it before publication. It was a correct change of a mistake I made, and I can't imagine anyone else would have known to make the change." (*Journal*, 30 October 1982)

In 1979, Tracy got "the NC with my NCC story, and was greatly dismayed to see that it had been rewritten with great stupidity and came out with several erroneous or misleading statements, plus some things put in a rather gross way." (*Journal*, 15 November). On 16 November, "Jo-ann Price . . . said Tom Lorsung . . . had told her of my story getting mutilated in rewriting and of his regret." But, on 19 November, Tracy got "last Thursday's and Friday's NC and found no correction of my NCC story. Called Tom Lorsung who said they put out something about Bowman but otherwise decided the rewrite hadn't significantly altered my story. I'm a little appalled."

In 1990, Tracy submitted a story about the Christian Children's Fund to EPS editor Tom Dorris, and said, "But if you decide it is so badly written that it requires such extensive rewriting that my byline should be taken off, just discard it." On 2 July, Dorris responded, "You will know that I have never extensively rewritten anything you have written, and that your material is among the best written–probably the best written–I receive . . . If my editorial decision would be to run the story without a byline, I will send my edited version to you for you to indicate whether to run that version with your byline, or to run it with no byline, or not to run it at all."

Another time, EPS' treatment of Tracy was simply incomprehensible. "Got an EPS with a story taken from a Church of England paper on the Greeks suspending dialogue with the Anglicans–annoying because I twice sent that to EPS with the NCC-Greek story, and it was cut out both times." (*Journal*, 18 September 1991) The next day, Tracy asked the editor Ken Mubu about the affront. "He offered no explanation."

Tracy's troubles with EPS continued with its successor ENI. Tracy had been paid more than other ENI reporters. When ENI decided that wasn't fair, they reduced Tracy's rate rather than raising other reporters' rates. (*Journal*, 3 September 1996) Tracy was willing to keep writing for ENI in spite of the pitiful pay, but editorial interference eventually ground away Tracy's tolerance. "Got an annoying fax from [Edmund] Eddie Doogue saying he wasn't putting out the story I worked till 2 a.m. this morning to send him. And he wants me to find an angry feminist who will sound off . . . . I am disposed to tell Eddie he is not paying me enough to spend more time on what anyway seems to me like phony tabloid journalism." (*Journal*, 6 June 1997)

And again. "I was dismayed to get a fax from Eddie Doogue saying my story on [Ecumenical Patriarch of Constantinople] Bartholomew was 'too negative.' He sent a fax of his rewritten version in which he put material about Bartholomew's speech at the Holocaust Museum in the lead, and in the second part of the story used some of my material. But the result is that readers are not really informed about the inter-Orthodox unity situation." (*Journal*, 27 October 1997) On the 29th, "Eddie Doogue faxed back my fax of Monday writing on it my assumptions about his handling of the patriarch story were wrong and not appreciated. So we may be headed for a parting or a showdown or something."

On 20 November, "Got a request from Eddie Doogue for more details on [two stories], and sent me his revised versions he was putting out on email. Most of the information he wanted I couldn't get, and felt wasn't particularly important. And he dropped out some information I had that was pertinent. But tonight I faxed back what I could, along with suggestions for repairing some of the damage he had done." And on the 26th, "I am thinking a good bit about the possibility of quitting ENI. Since Eddie Doogue cut my rate of pay by 40 per cent, it means a great deal of work for not so much money. And I don't get a lot of satisfaction out of the reporting itself because he rewrites my articles very extensively, changing leads regularly and changing the thrust of articles and often introducing errors and sometimes discarding articles altogether. Today he sent word that he was not using the article he asked me to do on the report of the Greek Archdiocese's legal committee about the seminary events. I spent a good bit of time and effort on it and called up people to talk and got first hand reactions. And he now says he didn't use it because it was too complicated."

The ENI attitude contrasted sharply with that of CNS. "[Lorsung] again expressed great appreciation for my work–an attitude quite different from what I feel coming from the ENI editors." (*Journal,* 6 January 1998) Then, again, Doogue rejected a story as being "too complicated." "I . . . reminded him that he had done that before, and I very much disliked having to write letters and tell people I took up their time for no purpose." (*Journal,* 4 March 1998) "It is becoming clear I will have to bring things to a head one of these days." (*Journal,* 5 March) The next day, ENI put out a story that was a composite of reporting by Tracy and other reporters. The story concerned a delegation to China led by Archbishop Theodore E. McCarrick. But "the lead of today's story was that McCarrick reported Christianity was growing in China, which was dumb because everybody has known that for a decade or more and dumber still because it did not connect to the point of this delegation." Tracy faxed Doogue saying that "we should talk." (*Journal,* 26 March) The next day, Doogue faxed back that "he saw no need for any adjustments by ENI. So he will not even respond to my request for discussion. I consider his fax an act of personal contempt. And I am not willing to do any more stories for ENI until some attention has been paid to my complaints." Finally, a story that Tracy had written on 19 March was put out by ENI on 6 April–Tracy's last piece for ENI. And Tracy received his last check from ENI on 9 May. Tracy started reported for EPS in 1982, continued when EPS became ENI, and stopped in 1998 only after extreme provocation. Seventeen years of reporting ended by one crummy editor.

Tracy had served as interim editor of EPS in Geneva from 28 June to 24 September 1993. That's one way to ensure that his stories were printed as he wrote them; perhaps he should have stayed on.

Other editors, too, could lapse into heavy-handed editing. "My story yesterday on Archbishop [Rembert G.] Weakland came out considerably messed up by the editing. I assume whoever edited it decided it needed to be simpler and so made it simply wrong." (*Journal*, 17 May 2000)

SENSITIVITY

Tracy's sensitivity in handling controversial issues was well-known and appreciated. In 1997, Sister Annelle Fitzpatrick, director of the Catholic Healthcare Administrative Personnel program for St. Vincent Catholic Medical Centers in New York, called Tracy about a conference to be held at St. John's University. "She is increasingly nervous about publicity because she has speakers who deal with controversial issues, and sensational publicity in right-wing newspapers might cause difficulties in getting along with the bishop. She wanted assurance I would be careful about reporting such things, and I said I would be as I had been in the past. So she will let me cover again. She said she was now denying access to The Tablet and The Long Island Catholic and all others but me." (*Journal*, 24 April)

Not sensitive enough for some editors, perhaps. "My CNS story on Cardinal O'Connor and black bishops finally came out today, cleansed of his reference to 'real tragedies' in reference to black bishops, and my unpolitic reference to Bishop [Emerson J.] Moore [first black bishop in the Roman Catholic Archdiocese of New York] dying of AIDS and the Atlanta bishop [Eugene Marino, the nation's first black archbishop] having to resign for involvement with a woman." (*Journal*, 1 June 1999)

Sensitive or not, some reporting presented extraordinary hurdles. When John F. Kennedy, Jr., his wife Carolyn Bessette, and her sister Lauren Bessette were killed in an airplane accident, CNS wanted Tracy to interview priests involved in the funeral. Few priests were willing to talk about the Kennedys, but Father Richard Fragomeni who served as family consultant and as master of ceremonies at the memorial mass, was willing to be interviewed if the Kennedy family had no objection. Caroline Kennedy approved the interview, so Tracy finally got a story for CNS (2 August 1999). "He had nothing startling to tell, but gave the first authoritative background report made available to the public." (*Journal*, 23 July-1 August 1999)

In some cases, nothing could be done. "Father [Aldo] Tos of St. Joseph's Church in Greenwich Village called this morning and thanked me for coming to the lecture [on interreligious dialogue] last night and apologized for not having time to talk with me and, then, perhaps contrived, he said Father [Jacques] Dupuis [a Jesuit theologian] had just walked in and wanted to talk to me. Father Dupuis asked me not to report a new book he published in Italy last year is to be published in English by Orbis. He said Cardinal Ratzinger would try to stop the publication if he heard about it. I told him the story was already gone, but I would relay his request to the editors for their decision. Since it seemed to involve high politics, I called Tom Lorsung. He called back later to say Nancy O'Brien had dropped that part to shorten the story, so he did not have to decide. Meanwhile, Father Dupuis had got the Orbis editor, Robert Ellsberg, to call me with the same request. I relayed that to Jim Lackey, and he said the story in any case wouldn't go out until Monday." (*Journal,* Friday, 19 April 2002)

Father Dupuis was a bit duplicitous in apologizing for not having had time to talk. After the lecture, "I asked him for the text of his lecture, but he refused to give it, and said that since he was under scrutiny by the Congregation for the Doctrine of the Faith he would rather not have a news story. I told him I could not agree to that, and could do a better and more careful story if I had the text. But he refused." (*Journal,* 18 April 2002)

Sidebar: *From 1981–2005, Joseph Cardinal Ratzinger was prefect of the Catholic Church's Congregation for the Doctrine of the Faith, usually known among Catholics as the Holy Office and among non-Catholics as The Inquisition, from its original name, Sacred Congregation of the Universal Inquisition, whose mission, according to Pope John Paul II, is "to promote and safeguard the doctrine on the faith and morals throughout the Catholic world" On 19 April 2005 Cardinal Ratzinger became Pope Bendict XVI. Because of Ratzinger's reputation, however, Tracy was "surprised" at the elevation.* (Journal, *19 April 2005)*

For more information about the Congregation for the Doctrine of the Faith, about Ratzinger, and about the Dupuis/Ratzinger difficulties, respectively, see:

- http://www.vatican.va/roman_curia/congregations/cfaith/documents/rc_con_cfaith_pro_14071997_en.html
- http://www.ratzingerfanclub.com
- http://www.cwnews.com/news/viewstory.cfm?recnum=34318

People were usually willing to talk freely with Tracy and to have him report on those talks. Not always. When the new cardinal of Hungary, Peter Erdo, was at St. Stephen of Hungary Church, Tracy went to see if there was anything newsworthy. After the mass, Erdo had a "sort of press conference" and "I got in a question or two and at the end had a long interview. But when we finished, Erdo said I had to submit what I wrote to him before I sent it out. I said we did not do that. He said I did not have his permission to use anything from the interview. Actually, he did not say much of significance, but evaded questions on Iraq, [Cardinal J.] Mindszenty etc. I think I have the right to do the article without his permission, but I thought it might not be good for CNS to have an explosion from a cardinal. So I said I would write nothing. Later I called and told Jim Lackey about it." (*Journal*, 26 July 2004) Two days later, Tracy attended a luncheon given by the Appeal of Conscience Foundation for Erdo. Tracy was invited and went, but avoided Erdo who made a few remarks about Sudan that Tracy used for a lead in a CNS story (29 July 2004). The next day, Msgr. Francis Chullikatt of the Vatican mission to the UN called to press Erdo's case for seeing Tracy's story before it went out. Apparently, Erdo visited Chullikatt who mentioned seeing Tracy at the luncheon and thought he would probably do a story. So Erdo asked Chullikatt to try to influence Tracy. "I said I didn't let people check over my stories in advance, and in any case had already sent it." Quite a difference from O'Connor.

And from Archbishop Renato R. Martino, Vatican ambassador to the UN In an interview at the UN, Archbishop Celestino Migliore, Martino's successor, seemed to be a little nervous about being quoted by Tracy and said, without specifics, that on a couple of stories, Tracy got Migliore's positions wrong. "But in general it seemed he didn't like to be quoted at all. He wanted me to write as though I knew all the things he was telling me through my general observation. I wrote a story tonight trying to take account of his concerns, but doubt I can satisfy him and do valid stories. I suspect he is temperamentally uncomfortable being in the spotlight–quite unlike Cardinal Martino [promoted after leaving the UN Mission] who loved to be in the spotlight." (*Journal*, 7 February 2005) In September 2005 when Tracy was in Concourse Rehabilitation and Nursing Center in the Bronx, I was present when Migliore visited Tracy. The attribution issue arose during their conversation; Migliore repeated his desire not to be quoted and Tracy insisted that stories had no "punch" without "Archbishop Migliore said" or "the nuncio said."

Editors can handle a sensitive issue by ignoring it. One was the Father Ritter/Covenant House story that you read about in Chapter 11. "My story for CNS on Father Ritter and the false baptismal certificate came in the mail, and I saw that the editors cut all my sentences that pointed up the stonewalling by Covenant House officials on this, including the statement that [James] Harnett [a spokesman for Covenant House] refused to explain what role Ritter or other individuals had. But anyway the story ran extraordinarily long–840 words–and *Catholic New York* did not let its readers know there was a baptismal certificate story." (*Journal*, 15 February 1990) So CNS omitted the stonewalling; *Catholic New York* omitted the story altogether.

Later, Ritter resigned (27 February) and the district attorney dropped the investigation (28 February) but Ritter's Franciscan superior announced that their investigation was continuing. So Tracy's coverage of the story also continued, but it was hard to get cooperation. After an interview with another Covenant House spokesman, George Wirt, Tracy noted that "he has a gift for talking a lot and not giving much basic information." (*Journal*, 16 March) Stonewalling by Covenant House didn't apply just to the press. In an interview with O'Connor who had been asked to help find a new president for Covenant House, O'Connor said that he had not yet received all of the documents, such as Ritter's letter of resignation, that he needed. Tracy noted that "it is exceedingly curious he felt he needed to put public pressure [via the press] on the Covenant House board to get [the documents]." (*Journal*, 18 March)

THE WORKMAN'S PAY

Tracy's value to NC/CNS was reflected in his pay rates. Tracy noted (*Journal*, 15 July 1978) that his NC word rate was a little bit above NC's standard 5 cent rate, "Which is a bit encouraging." Raises came steadily: 10 cents (29 January 1980), 15 cents (2 August 1982), 18 cents (1 August 1985), 20 cents (1 January 1986), 22 cents (15 August 1989), 25 cents (1 January 1990). Tom Lorsung said, "That's the highest word rate for a correspondent in NC history, but we value your work very highly. Maybe you'll think it's enough so you can invest in an air conditioner. [He didn't.] Even though you're a heat-toughened Texan, I still worry about your well-being in this unrelentingly steamy summer." Up and up: 28 cents (1 January 1992), 30 cents (1 July 1992), 35 cents (1 January 1995), 37 cents (1 January 1998), 40 cents (1 July 1998), 45 cents (1 February 2001). At this point, Lorsung again tried to tempt Tracy onto the CNS staff: "Also, please keep in mind that we are open to establishing a more predictable monthly rate for you if you ever change your mind about wanting to keep working for a word rate." It was not, of course, the idea of working for a word rate that kept Tracy among the freelancers; it was the idea of *not* working for someone else. As 2004 approached, Tracy again thought of asking for an increase. "I called Tom Lorsung to ask about his replacement. He said the choice was being announced today–Anthony Spence . . . . I don't know if it will be good if I hit the new editor with a request for an increase as soon as he is on the job. I will consult with Jim Lackey and see what he recommends." (*Journal*, 8 December 2003)

That consultation soon occurred. "I called Jim Lackey [and] . . . asked for his thoughts on the review of my rates of payment . . . . But with the retirement of Tom Lorsung and impending arrival of a new chief . . . . I have thought it might be wise to wait a while before raising the issue. Jim agreed, and I asked him to mention it whenever he thought the time was right." (*Journal*, 30 January 2004) Forty-five cents turned out to be Tracy's final rate. That's quite a lot. At that rate, this book would fetch over $100,000; you got a bargain.

Of course, there are various ways to get a raise. "Tonight I went to Columbia University to cover the Merton Lecture given by Archbishop Migliore. He talked generally of Holy See diplomacy, and said nothing of special news interest. But I made an 800 word story out of it and sent it to CNS." (*Journal*, 22 November 2004)

Lorsung once expressed some concern about how much of his budget for correspondents was going to Tracy, and that he would like to get it stabilized, but made no specific suggestions. (*Journal*, 27 November 1998) No doubt Lorsung and Lackey could have reduced Tracy's budget bite by reducing the number of stories they asked him to do; perhaps Lorsung was simply hinting that Tracy might reconsider becoming a CNS reporter rather than a freelancer. Maybe the former. "I wonder if CNS is in a financial squeeze. Jim Lackey has been rather reluctant, it seems, to give me assignments this year." (*Journal*, 1 March 1999) And he wondered if "there is a policy of giving me fewer assignments to keep my payments lower. Tom Lorsung had indicated last fall that he thought they had become too high—40% of the total budget for stringers, he said." (*Journal*, 13 April 1999)

Or maybe CNS was just trying to spread the load. "The CNS service today had another example of something that seems to have become fairly common recently—a story that Jim Lackey had told me the service did not need when I asked him about it. This was the formal establishment of the Franciscan Friars of the Renewal. I had done a story reporting they were approved. But today they carried a John Burger story on the establishment—after Jim had told me another story wasn't called for." (*Journal*, 7 June 1999)

Still, even a blind hog finds an acorn once in a while. "I had the upbeat experience of finding that CNS used the [Archbishop Theodore E.] McCarrick story I sent last night just as I wrote it, and all of it—making 800 words. That does not happen often enough." (*Journal*, 12 July 1999)

On the other hand, Tracy proposed an article to Lackey who liked the idea but assigned it to another reporter, Jerry Filteau, "which was discouraging and again made me wonder whether it was worthwhile to stay on the lookout for stories and alert Jim when I find something." (*Journal*, 23 February 2000) Pish, tush. Tracy was 66 and likely to think of retirement at some point; Lackey was probably thinking of potential replacements for New York stringer duties.

Pay rates could be reduced to zero. It is sometimes difficult for a religion-oriented publication to stay solvent. *The Lamp* folded in 1974, *Seventh Angel* in 1985, *Christianity and Crisis* in 1993, *One World* in 1995. In 1982 Tracy was Custombook's "main and most trusted" writer; in 1983 they parted ways over a pay dispute. The *Christian Science Monitor* began relying on staff reporting rather than paying freelancers in 1985. In 1990 EPS temporarily stopped accepting submissions because of financial problems.

CONTROVERSY

Tracy sometimes became involved in controversies such as the Gov. Cuomo affair that you read about in Chapter 10. There, the problem was what was in the story. Often, though, it is what is not in the story. In 1986, Lorsung sent Tracy copies of a letter Bishop Joseph T. O'Keefe, vicar general of the archdiocese of New York, had written to NC protesting Tracy's story on a pro-homosexual rights press conference, and of Lorsung's reply, "a stout defense of me and my reporting." O'Keefe didn't really allege any errors, but seemed to think NC had given the event too much attention, but paradoxically wanted more negative background given on some of the people involved. "It didn't really make any sense, and it is a little dismaying to think such a high post is held by a man of such limited outlook." (*Journal,* 19 March)

Occasionally, sensitive issues caused a parting of the ways. "The Jewish Week that appeared on the newsstands yesterday had an article by a staff member who had used a little of the article I submitted on Rabbi [Leon] Klenicki and the Auschwitz new convent and center. But the reporter had apparently called Klenicki to get more comment—mainly pious hopes of all now being well—and wrote a different story. So I called editor Charles Baumohl today. He didn't have much to say except that I hadn't included the background of controversy over the convent, which I assumed every reader of Jewish Week would be aware of, and my computer transmission didn't come out clearly. But I had not been notified of these problems, so I assume they are not interested in having me write for them any more." (*Journal,* 7 May 1991) And he didn't.

A VALUABLE ASSET

Part of Tracy's value to his clients was that he was a workaholic. "This morning I covered a mass at St. Patrick's [Cathedral] honoring Lech Walesa. Came home and wrote the story and sent it to CNS. But since I have to get up early tomorrow, I went to bed without doing the [Father James] Keenan story—a very rare if not unprecedented case of going to bed without having done any CNS story I had the material to do. But I had told Jim Lackey I might not be able to keep up with the writing when I was out covering things day and night."

(*Journal,* 21 May 1996) After sending two pieces to CNS, he "left for tomorrow the [Our Lady of Mercy] hospital story, perhaps my first time to go to bed without finishing all of my CNS work. But it was after 2 a.m. and I was sleepy." (*Journal,* 18 May 2000) Well, not the first time, but rare. Tracy worried about such things, so he seemed relieved the next day when "CNS only got out my Brooklyn story [about vandalizing religious statues in Brooklyn] and not the [Archbishop Giovanni Battista] Re story. So I assume they would not have put out the hospital story if I had stayed up all night to get it done." Relieved or not, three days later he got two CNS pieces done and sent, finishing about 3:30 a.m., and left another piece to do later.

Tracy was also valuable to those he wrote about. "This evening I covered the annual Path to Peace fund raising cruise, . . . Archbishop Martino had told me that he had sold more tickets than there were spaces on the boat and did not know whether I could be included . . . . But when I got there, he told me that I was on the seating list." (*Journal,* 22 May 1996) Archbishops know to take care of the press. On another occasion, Martino told Tracy that his story on Martino's response to an Amnesty International charge was "the best I had done." (*Journal,* 9 May 2000)

Bishops, too, take care of the press. "I went to Brooklyn for the annual luncheon given by Bishop [Thomas V.] Daily for friendly media people." (*Journal,* 28 June 1996) Apparently the unfriendly must forage for their own grub.

On the 20th anniversary of Tracy's arrival in New York, he reflected that "I have as good a grasp as anyone of the field of religious journalism." (*Journal,* 28 August 1988) True. Tracy knew the institutions, the people, where the bodies were buried. And he kept up with events in the field of religion. NC knew that, as they had demonstrated by making Tracy their permanent correspondent covering the United Nations, in addition to covering religion in general. (*Journal,* 17 August 1988) And Tracy had high regard for NC. In 1989, he remarked that he had written an extremely long story, 1295 words, and sent it to NC "without any idea of what they might do with it" (*Journal,* 3 May) but trusting NC to treat the story appropriately. On another occasion, "Jim Lackey decided CNS should have a story on Cardinal O'Connor meeting yesterday with leaders of the unions striking against the Daily News. So I wrote one and sent it." (*Journal,* 31 October 1990)

HONORS AND AWARDS

I suppose that honors and awards in the field of journalism in religion are few and far between. Tracy was not overly impressed by them anyway, but he did get a few.

In 1956 at Southeastern's graduation exercises, Tracy received a silver cup for an outstanding paper in Church history. It is a handsome chalice, still in its original box as Tracy was loath to display such awards.

In 1974 Tracy received an Award of Merit, in the category of mission magazines, from the Associated Church Press, second place, for his article "God and Man in the 'Big Apple'" in *New World Outlook* (September 1973).

In 1991 Tracy received an Award of Merit, again from the Associated Church Press, for his article "A Summit for Children" in the December 1990 issue of *One World*, a magazine of the WCC. Tracy "didn't know it had been entered, but was of course delighted to hear I'd won what I suppose is my first ever writing award." (*Journal*, 9 May 1991) Well, first since 1974. Marlin VanElderen, editor of *One World*, congratulated Tracy, but told him "it wouldn't mean any increase in rates." (*Journal*, 22 May)

In 2000, Tracy's biography appeared, partly thanks to Martin Marty, in the Marquis *Who's Who in America*. His biography was also included in the 2001 and 2002 editions.

Finally, and disappointingly, "This afternoon I went to the UN to cover a statement by Archbishop Martino. He asked me for my curriculum vitae, and I supposed he was thinking of some honor as he was leaving his UN post. But I wondered whether he was doing it in awareness of my non-Catholic status. After we left the room where he gave the statement, he asked me—with apologies—if I was Catholic. When I told him I was Protestant, he asked for the denomination, and I told him Baptist, but that I belonged to an ecumenical congregation in New York—Riverside. He said he planned to nominate me for a knighthood of the type the Vatican gives to non-Catholics. So tonight I wrote out some facts for a basic biography and gave it to him." (*Journal*, 7 October 2002) Later, Martino "told me that his request for an honor for me had to be approved by the local bishop and the country nuncio before going to Rome for approval, and he had gotten [O'Connor's successor Edward] Cardinal Egan's ok. So I am glad I never got around to telling Egan all my negative thoughts about him." (*Journal*, 14 October) Then, "Martino told me at the UN that people at the Archdiocese of New York—he wouldn't say whether Cardinal Egan or someone else specifically—had vetoed his idea of getting me a medal. They knew I was a Protestant minister and objected on that basis, he said. I am rather disappointed but would rather not get the award than get it without full openness. So I am glad Egan and company were aware—if it bothers them that much. I would not want to get an honor and have them find out later I am a minister and say they wouldn't have approved if they had known what I was." (*Journal*, 30 October)

Curious. As Jim Lackey said in Tracy's obituary, "His byline, Tracy Early, was familiar to millions of readers of the Catholic press in the United States, Canada, and more than 40 other countries around the world where Catholic publications rely on CNS for national and international news. Tracy Early was, both literally and figuratively, the face of Catholic News Service in New York. People he covered for us–from members of the Catholic Worker movement to the last three cardinal-archbishops of New York to the Vatican's nuncio at the United Nations–might not have known his editors back in Washington, but they certainly knew Tracy." Thirty-three years of presenting, via NC/CNS and a host of other Catholic publications, a sympathetic view of Catholicism to the world, but being a Protestant minister made him unworthy of thanks.

OUTPUT

I used Tracy's files and the good offices of people at some of the publications for which Tracy wrote in order to construct a bibliography of his work. I included every piece that I could find. Each piece is listed, one per line, with date of publication [or date written, if not published] and headline or title. The output is extraordinary. Tracy's bibliography, only modestly annotated, contains 58,480 words on 8,047 lines. Printing it here would increase the size of this book by about 25%.

ACADEMIA

It is impossible to tell how many papers up to and including his doctoral dissertation were written. Tracy kept 38 of them written from high school days in 1949 to Union seminary in 1963. School and publications don't often mix, but he had one article in *The Baptist Student;* it was the second article for which he was paid. (*Journal,* 8 February 1962)

CHAPLAINCY

Tracy remained active in writing during his chaplaincy. He contributed to *The Baptist Program, The Border Baptist, The Baptist Standard, The Baylor Line,* a *Chaplain's Desk Reference, Christianity Today,* the *Fort Bliss (Texas) News, The Military Chaplain,* and *Southern Baptist Family Life.*

MINISTRY

He continued writing in the ministry. He wrote two adult Bible teaching guides for the Southern Baptist Sunday School series, and articles for *The Baptist Program, Christian Century, Christian Herald, Christianity & Crisis, Church Administration, Religion in Life, Religious Herald,* Richmond (Virginia)

Times-Dispatch, Society of Biblical Literature, the Urbanna, Virginia *Southside Sentinel,* the *Sunday School Board,* and *Upward.*

Lest you think that the beginnings of Tracy's writing career was a bed of roses, his pieces were also rejected by the *Atlantic Monthly, Harper's, Interpretation, The Journal of Bible and Religion, The Journal of Biblical Literature, The Journal of Religion,* the *National Observer,* the *New York Times* magazine, and *Theology Today.*

BOOKS

Tracy wrote one book, *Simply Sharing* (1980, World Council of Churches), and contributed to several others. His 1984 report on a conference at the Rockford Institute Center on Religion and Society was reprinted in *Democracy and the Renewal of Public Education* edited by Rev. Richard John Neuhaus, Grand Rapids, Michigan: Wm. B. Eerdman's, 1987. In 2001, he condensed Martin Conway's revision of Marlin VanElderen's *Introducing the World Council of Churches.* He contributed to Evelyn Ryland's 2004 history of the *Urbanna Baptist Church 1888-2003: A Little Church with A Large Ministry.* He wrote 35 church histories for Custombook (1979-1983). He contributed a biography of Michael Servetus to *Collier's Encyclopedia* (1975). He contributed 604 articles (from Adler to Zilboorg) to the *Encyclopedic Dictionary of Religion* produced by Corpus Instrumentorum (1968-1970). He wrote 33 articles (from Adenauer to World Council of Churches) for supplementary volume NCE 16, edited by David Eggenberger, of the *New Catholic Encyclopedia;* as one of 500+ contributors writing 810 articles, Tracy seems to have gotten the lion's share.

One article was reprinted in *The Human Encounter: Readings in Education,* second edition, by Sheldon Stoff and Herbert Schwartzbergm, 1973, Harper & Row, New York.

An NCC article was referenced in *Building a Protestant Left: Christianity and Crisis Magazine, 1941-1993,* by Mark Hulsether, 1999, University of Tennessee Press, Knoxville.

And a quote from one of his pieces in *The Tablet* was used in *JOHN CAR-DINAL O'CONNOR At the Storm Center of a Changing American Catholic Church* by Nat Hentoff, 1988, Scribner's Sons, New York. *The Tablet,* but not Tracy, was credited.

NEWS SERVICES

Most of Tracy's post-ministry writing was for news services. He wrote for the Episcopal News Service (8 pieces during 1991-1994), the Independent News Alliance (3, 1980), Interpretive Services (63, 1970-1981), Radio Free Europe

(34, 1984-1985), Religion Today (107, 1980-1982), RNS (245 news stories, 244 radio scripts, 1 Religious News Reporter, 1968-1975), United Methodist Communications News (10, 1971-1984), United Church News (11, 1988), Women's News Service (18, 1970-1980), NANA (252, 1970-1980), EPS (192, 1969-1994), and ENI (180 , 1994-1998). Well, Tracy's 1969 piece in EPS is a little iffy. Tracy said, "This article was just a slight revision of an article written by one of the newspaper reporters in Tulsa, Okla. when the WCC Exec Com met there. I typed it up for possible anonymous inclusion in The Ecumenical Courier, and Faith Pomponio sent it to EPS with my by-line, which I didn't actually deserve."

Then there are NC (1,101, 1972-1989) and CNS (2,149, 1989-2005) for a total of 3,250 pieces over 33 years. He peaked at 193 pieces in 1990, a bit less than two days per piece, and averaged almost 100 pieces per year, or nearly two pieces per week. A remarkable record; perhaps it should've been the Tracy Early News Service.

OTHER PIECES

Tracy's stories also appeared in many magazines and newspapers. You don't want to see the entire list of 682 stories in 102 publications from the *American Baptist* magazine, through *Grit,* to *Worldwide Faith News.* Nor the rejections. *Family Circle, Redbook,* and *Texas Parade. The Review and Expositor* managed to reject Tracy's pieces in three stages of his life: at Southeastern Seminary (1956), in the Army (1959), and at Urbanna (1966).

OTHER PEOPLE

When Tracy was not writing his own pieces, he was ghost-writing. In 1979, he wrote *A World Without Hunger* for J. Harry Haines, published by Church World Service USA in 1980. Tracy got research and editing credit, but with his name misspelled Tracey. In 1969 he wrote an article that appeared in *Tempo,* an NCC publication, "by" Robert I. Miller. Bob liked it so much (Tracy was his "favorite ghost writer") that in 1970 he wrote another Miller "by" article, that appeared in *Presbyterian Life.* In 1972, Tracy wrote a speech for David Yurrich, vice-chairman of Macy's department store.

CITATIONS

Tracy's first citation was probably for an article for *Christianity Today* (July 1959) entitled "Why army churchgoing lags." This article brought many comments from readers, and was cited in David O. Moberg's *The Church as a Social Institution: The Sociology of American Religion,* Prentice-Hall, 1962.

In 1979 *Foreign Affairs* magazine published an Arthur Schlesinger article which cited Tracy's 1978 *Worldview* article that criticized President Carter's human rights policy.

CONSULTING

Tracy also did contract work, press releases, pamphlets, *etc.* for a number of organizations: The Board of Global Ministries of the United Methodist Church; the Migration Office of the Brooklyn Diocese; the Catholic Church Extension Society; the United Methodist Coordinating Committee on Hunger (CCOH); the Lutheran Council in the U.S.A. (LCUSA); the National Council of Churches News; the Planning and Development Unit, Domestic and Foreign Missionary Society, of the Protestant Episcopal Church; the WCC; the United Presbyterian Church in the U.S.A. (UPCUSA); the Christian Life Commission of the Southern Baptist Convention; the Sunday School Board of the Southern Baptist Convention; the United Presbyterian Health, Education and Welfare Association (UPHEWA); and the Jewish Appeal of Conscience Foundation. Look up the word 'ecumenical' in the dictionary and you'll see Tracy's picture.

Over fifty-eight years of published writing from February 1947 through July 2005. Only God knows the word count.

-30-

Tracy's last journal entry was 15 July 2005. He was feeling lethargic and slept most of the time. On 20 July, he was having such trouble breathing that he checked himself into St. Luke's Hospital in Manhattan where he spent three weeks in a drug-induced coma while being treated for necrotizing pneumonia. That treatment, compounded by treatment for relapsing polychondritis, resulted in Tracy's death on 16 December. He was buried next to our father on 22 December in the cemetery in our boyhood hometown of Snyder, Texas. A memorial service was held on 7 January 2006 at Riverside Church in Manhattan. Reaction to his death was fast and extensive.

2005-12-16, Lackey, Jim, "Tracy Early, longtime CNS correspondent, dies," Catholic News Service, U.S. Conference of Catholic Bishops, Washington, D.C., http://www.americancatholic.org/Features/DailyNews/todays.asp?date=12/16/2005

reprinted in the Georgia Bulletin
http://www.georgiabulletin.org/world/2005/12/16/PEOPLE-5/

and in Catholic News
http://www.americancatholic.org/features/DailyNews/todays.asp?date=12/16/2005

http://davidwilliamson.blogspot.com/2006/01/journey-from-tillich-to-barth-and.html
and reposted in
http://danphillips.blogspot.com/2006_01_01_danphillips_archive.html

2005-12-19, staff writer, "Early -- Tracy," The New York Times, New York, p. B8 and
http://query.nytimes.com/gst/fullpage.html?res=9503EEDC1730F93AA25751C1A963
9C8B63

2005-12-21, "Tracy Early 1934-2005," The Snyder Daily News, Snyder, Texas, p. 9

2005-12-24, staff writer, "CNS' N. Y. Correspondent is Dead," The Tablet, Brooklyn,
p. 6

2006-01-07, Bell, Charles W., "Farewell to friend, scribe," Daily News, New York, p. 16

2006-01-05, staff writer, "Tracy Early, 71, News Reporter," Catholic New York, New
York, p. 46 and http://cny.org/archive/ob/obnames010506.htm

2006-01-09, staff writer, "Tracy Early, 1934-2005," Riverside News, Riverside Church,
New York, http://www.theriversidechurchny.org/news/article.php?id=57

2006-01-10, staff writer, "William Tracy Early," The Christian Century, Chicago, p. 19

2006-01-11, staff writer, "Tributes flow for New York freelance religion writer,"
Ecumenical News International (ENI), New York,
http://www.eni.ch/highlights/news.shtml?2006/01

2006-01-19, Woods, John, "A Reporter to Remember," Catholic New York, New York,
p. 9 and http://cny.org/archive/er/er011906.htm

2006-01-20, Lefevere, Patricia, "Noted religion journalist dies at 71," National Catholic
Reporter, Kansas City, Missouri, p. 12 and
http://www.highbeam.com/library/docfree.asp?DOCID=1G1:141493248&ctrlInfo=Ro
und19%3AMode19a%3ADocG%3AResult&ao=

2006-01-20, Winter, Art, "Noted religion journalist dies at 71," National Catholic
Reporter, NCRonline.org, http://ncronline.org/index0120.htm

2006-03-07, Costello, Jerry, "CPA Spotlight. . . . Around The Catholic Press," Catholic
Press Association, http://72.14.203.104/search?q=cache:e1uypPr5QqwJ:www.catholic-
press.org/story6.htm+%22catholic+news+service%22+%22tracy+early%22&hl=en&gl=
us&ct=clnk&cd=14

The New York Times online obituary is perpetually available at
http://www.legacy.com/NYTimes/DeathNotices.asp?Page=LifeStory&PersonID=16061856

ACKNOWLEDGMENTS

Authors often say that it's not possible to thank everyone who helped, but I'm going to try. Errors, of course, are mine; not theirs. If I've omitted your name, mea culpa.

Rev. Charles E. Brewster, Pastor, The First Presbyterian Church, Forest Hills, N.Y.

Stephen Brown, ENI News Service, Geneva

Beverly Chain, Assistant General Secretary [retired], Mission Education and Cultivation Division, United Methodist Board of Global Ministries

Paulette DePaul, Christianity Today International, Carol Stream, IL

Frank DeRosa, Public Information Office, Roman Catholic Diocese of Brooklyn

Avery Cardinal Dulles, McGinley Professor, Fordham University

Dr. Doris Jean Dyke, Professor Emerita, Emmanuel College, University of Toronto

Archbishop John P. Foley, President, Pontifical Council for Social Communications

Rev. Vittorio Guerrera, Attaché, Permanent Observer Mission of the Holy See to the United Nations

Carol Marie Herb, Editor [retired], *Response,* journal of United Methodist Women

Beverly Judge, Executive Vice President, Faith and Values Media

Marv Knox, Editor, *The Baptist Standard*

James M. "Jim" Lackey, General News Editor, Catholic News Service (CNS)

Denyse Leger, Librarian, The World Council of Churches Library

Thomas N. "Tom" Lorsung, Director, Editor in Chief (retired), Catholic News Service

Leigh Montgomery, Library, *Christian Science Monitor*

New World Outlook, General Board of Global Ministries, The United Methodist Church

Katherine Nuss, Information Services Manager, Catholic News Service

Owen Phelps, PhD, CEO, Midwest Leadership Institute

Chris Sheridan, *Catholic New York*

Tod M. Tamberg, Director of Media Relations, Archdiocese of Los Angeles

Cora Vander Broek, Editorial Assistant, *The Christian Century*

John Woods, *Catholic New York*

Joseph Zwilling, Director of Communications, Archdiocese of New York

Grady Early
San Marcos, Texas

Now that you know the "Bone Divine" backstory, I know you want it to be our last chapter. It is; read on.

BONE DIVINE

CHAPTER SEVENTEEN

Visitors to New York generally show more interest in our entertainment, shopping and sight-seeing opportunities than in our spiritual resources. But the spiritual is here for those who want it.

One opportunity you have here that is not available in the average town is the chance to venerate a piece of the skeleton of Jesus' grandmother.

Somehow this attraction has not been as widely publicized as the Rockettes, though in some ways it seems to me even more inspirational. I became aware of it only recently myself and was, I confess, surprised to find we had a treasure of that vintage on display in twentieth century America.

I had of course heard that the churches of Europe possessed such treasures. In the course of reading [Roland] Bainton's biography of Luther, one is told that Frederick the Wise had collected 19,013 holy bones plus four hairs from the Virgin Mary, some of the myrrh brought to Jesus by the Wise Men, a strand of Jesus' beard, one of the nails driven into his hands, and a piece of the bread eaten (possibly on the table but not eaten?) at the Last Supper and other objects, which, if one viewed them on All Saints Day and made the prescribed contributions, would reduce one's time in purgatory by 1,902,202 years and 270 days.

And I was vaguely aware that despite the Reformation, the French Revolution and other storms of history, a number of relics survived into our own day. Rome, as a spiritual center, naturally has them in quantity. Sancta Sanctorum Chapel in Rome has Jesus' sandals, a portrait of him said not to have been painted with mortal hands, and the 28 steps leading to Pilate's praetorium—climbing which, Luther regretted his parents were not yet dead so he could get them out of purgatory. Also in Rome, the Church of Santa Croce in Gerusalemme has three pieces of the true cross, a nail used in the crucifixion, the title Pilate had put on Jesus' cross and two thorns from Jesus' crown of same.

But Rome has no monopoly. In the case of the thorns there seems to have been a rather widespread scattering—one at the cathedral in Barcelona, another at Stanbrook Abbey in England, others here and there, with the main part of the crown at Notre Dame in Paris.

The cathedral at Turin has Jesus' shroud, with his imprint on it. Aachen, Germany, has his swaddling clothes and Mary's cloak. And in Loreto, Italy, there is the house, transported from Nazareth by means unknown, in which Mary was living when Gabriel appeared to her for the Annunciation. Chartres cathedral has a relic that was passed off on the gullible for a long time as Mary's tunic. But more scientific methods of historical research have now shown that it is but her veil.

Knowing all that, for some reason I had nonetheless been led to think of relics as themselves a kind of relic of the medieval age when they served to impress the peasants, not a tradition compatible with the technological spirituality of modern America, particularly our secular city of New York. But the piece of the skeleton of Jesus' grandmother, St. Ann, is displayed here at the Church of St. Jean Baptiste, which serves not peasants but our radically chic East Side. It is a church where you might find a Kennedy or a Buckley if one happened to be in town on a Sunday.

The relic of St. Ann was brought here from France in 1892 by a French priest, who delivered larger pieces of the skeleton to the Shrine of St. Anne de Beaupré, near Quebec. Calvin reports that he knew of two of St. Ann's skeletons existing in his time, plus three additional heads and miscellaneous bones, so Europe presumably had enough, even apart from the natural processes of bone growth, to share some with the new world.

The pastor of St. Jean Baptiste requested a bit of St. Ann for his church after exhibition of the bones on the way to Canada brought the immediate cure of an epileptic and restored sight to a blind woman the following day. Information distributed by a St. Ann Society at the church reports nothing of that sort recently, but the tiny piece of bone does apparently have healing power. At least, a priest blesses oil in its presence and will send you a little bottle full if you send him a little donation.

The exact nature of this power is undefined in the literature, perhaps to avoid questions from the Food and Drug Administration, which might lead to an un-American mixing of church with state. But visiting the shrine one day, I noticed that a handkerchief was lying beside the reliquary. The women coming by, showing their American regard for hygiene, would each take the handkerchief and wipe the glass shielding the bone before kissing it. So I gather the

SIDEBARS

power of the relic reaches as far as curing epilepsy but not to the point of sterilizing glass.

Should there be readers, affected by the skepticism of a skeptical age, who are tempted to doubt what I am reporting, to them I can only say, Come and see. There is a sign by the relic identifying it and they can read for themselves. (And if they are so hung up on proving things, let them prove that it is not from Jesus' grandmother.)

Every Catholic church of course has at least one relic of a martyr in its altar, as, I believe, every Orthodox church. For example, a recently-consecrated Greek Orthodox church on Long Island had a relic of St. George the dragon killer, whom some people might consider almost as legendary as his dragon, placed in its altar.

Relics dating from New Testament times, however, I consider to be in a different category than even extraordinary relics of later saints–spiritually, being more biblical, and historically, being more ancient.

In Jesus' grandmother we have the closest thing possible to what we might call bone of his bone, or bone divine. Ecclesiastical authorities would likely exhibit a critical attitude toward any pastor who claimed to have the bones of Jesus himself on view. Calvin does note that in his time a couple of churches, doing what they could to surmount the unfortunate limitations imposed by the Ascension, were exhibiting foreskins of Jesus, removed at his circumcision. But the possibilities here are obviously limited. The doctrine of the Assumption, likewise, has an inhibiting effect on those who would display the Virgin Mary's bones. As Jesus had no descendants, therefore, and according to one influential school of theology no brothers or sisters, it is to his grandmother that we must go.

And our possession of her bones is very providential on another score, for without them our knowledge of her might not carry a high degree of historical certainty, neither she nor Jesus' grandfather, St. Joachim, being mentioned in the New Testament or any other document of their period. They first appear actually in the late second century Protoevangelium of James–though that point cannot be pressed to the point of justifying radical skepticism. As the *New Catholic Encyclopedia* puts it with scholarly balance, "The Blessed Virgin surely had parents, no matter what their names may have been."

While New Testament relics rate highest spiritually for Christians, from the historical point of view Old Testament relics would be even more impressive, could we but be sure of them. We do read that Frederick the Wise had a nonconsumed twig from Moses' burning bush, and that the bishop of Mainz had one of the nonconsuming flames. Probably some of those relics of Old Testament times are around somewhere today. I have neither seen them myself nor found reliable accounts of them, however, so I cannot vouch for their authenticity.

But I have seen one other New Testament relic of crucial significance here in New York—a piece of the true cross, which any visitor can see in the Franciscan church near Pennsylvania Station.

Scoffers love to say that if all the relics of the true cross were gathered together there would be enough wood to build the Spanish Armada, or some other absurdity. But the relic here is such a tiny speck, if the others are comparable, I think the scoffers may have again overstepped themselves. It would take a great many such particles to weigh an ounce. So a single man-sized cross could yield enough relics to provide one for virtually every church in Christendom, or, at the least, one for every church that knows what religious value lies in putting such objects on display.

Whether the splitting up of relics into tiny bits is the most reverent procedure, however, may be in doubt. In the case of a revered person like Jesus' grandmother, I cannot help but feel there is something unseemly about priests' hacking her up into little pieces for general distribution. I have trouble even visualizing the scene in my mind.

Another question, whether a fragment retains the same power as the original whole relic, poses metaphysical issues on which I am not qualified to pass judgment. What we can be sure of in regard to the cross is that it was intact when St. Helena found it during her visit to Jerusalem around 326, and that it had life-giving power then. In fact, that is how we can be certain that she did find the true cross, from which the bits and pieces scattered about today have come. It was the only one of three she tested that brought a dead man to life. Can just a tiny speck do that? We cannot rule it out as a theoretical possibility, but if the one in the church here has brought any dead people to life, I have not heard of it. And I think it probably would have been in the *Times*.

Unlike the bone of St. Ann, the splinterette does not appear to even be doing the more mundane work—possibly more relevant to a harassed pastor struggling to make ends meet—of bringing in money. It is set in a little alcove in the lower church (basement) and does not seem to be hooked up to any fund-raising apparatus.

As remarkable as it is to think you have your hands on a piece of the actual cross on which Jesus died, or on some comparable relic, it is difficult to decide just what would be the most appropriate thing to do with it. Stewart Newman, a professor of mine at Southeastern Baptist Seminary, used to goad the more literalistic students, who talked so much about the power of the blood, by asking, "Suppose someone had caught some of Jesus' blood and you have a jugful of it—what would you do with it?" I do not know if anyone ever came up with a satisfying answer. Certainly I never did, though I found the question thought-provoking.

As Protestants we were handicapped since our tradition had not prepared us to handle questions of that depth. This is one of the places where Catholics have a clear historical advantage, with their long tradition of meeting the issue in concrete form. At least in times past Catholic churches and monasteries possessing some of Jesus' blood were said to be about as common as those possessing some of the Virgin Mary's milk.

But in talking with some of my Catholic friends about how impressed I am to find the richness of Catholic tradition preserving bones from Jesus' grandmother and other similar treasures, I seem to hear a certain amount of equivocation, with references to symbolic values and the like. No doubt finding the best way to appropriate our traditions is a problem for us all. [Original manuscript dated 16 November 1971.]

INDEX

Note: page numbers followed by "f" denote an additional entry on the following page.

Angell, Charles, 337
Angels in America, 351
annulment, 432-435
Annunciation, 506
Anselm, 422
anti-Catholicism, 151
anti-clericalism, 151
Anti-Defamation League, 145f, 150, 164f,
 189, 192, 196, 457
Antichrist, 294
Antigone, 247
Antioch, 132
Antiochian Archdiocese, 235f
Antony, 253
Antwort Auf Hiob, 170
apartheid, 265f, 313, 458
Apollo Belvedere, 32
Apostolic Faith Mission, 222
Appeal of Conscience Foundation, 77, 253,
 484, 492
Applied Christianity, 95
Aquinas, Thomas, 422
Arab-Israeli peace process, 196
Arafat, Yasser, 147f, 173
Archbishop of Canterbury, 76, 418
Archdiocese of Olinda and Recife, 76
Archdiocese of Washington, 68
Archer, Glenn L., 467
Ari, 247
Aristide, Jean-Bertrand, 222f
Aristotle, 422
Armed Forces of National Liberation, 298
Armenian massacres, 149f
Armies of the Night, 57
Arminianism, 116
Armstrong-Browning Building, 248f
Armstrong, A. James, 248f, 300f, 476
Army chaplains' school, 43, 121
Army Reserve, 465
Arrupe, Pedro, 71
Art Institute of Chicago, 31
art, Iberian, 188
Aryan Nation, 203
Ascension, 143, 507
Associated Church Press, 455, 497
Associated Press, 14, 247
Association on American Indian Affairs, 428
Assumption, 507
astrology, 124
Athanasius, 422
Atonement Friars, 22, 336, 359

Augustine, 62, 138, 422, 454
Auschwitz, 148, 163f, 495
Austin, Alexander, 240
Austin, Charles, 256
Austin, Gerard, 116
autocephaly, 225, 229
autographs, 158
Avery Fisher Hall, 63
Avignon, 192
AWACs, 146
Axis powers, 439

Baal, 414
Babylon, 392
Babylonian Exile, 403
Bach, Johann Sebastian, 365
Bachelor of Divinity, 241
Bacon, Gershon, 149
Bacopoulos, 253
Baehr, Harry, 26
Baehr, Jo-ann Price, 25f, 477-479, 488
Baerwald, Reuben C., 280
Baigent, Michael, 172
Bailey, John, 453
Bainton, Roland H., 321, 505
Bakker, Jim, 123
Balaam, 402
Baline, Israel, 191
Baltimore Black Caucus, 208
Bangor Seminary, 93
Banki, Judith, 192
banned in Boston, 185
bantustans, 243
baptism, 115, 133, 423
baptismal certificate, 345f
Baptist Joint Committee on Public Affairs,
 466
Baraka, Amiri, 269
Barber, Russell, 479
Barkat, Anwar, 219
Barnard College, 143
Barnes, Clive, 247, 483
Barrett, Wayne, 180
Barth, Karl, 41, 58, 120, 138, 156, 170,
 186-188, 327, 360, 363, 411f, 422f
Bartholomew, 225-227, 230, 488
Baruch College, 193
Barzun, Jacques, 249
Basil of Caesarea, 422
Basques, 13
Bassile, Darryl, 343

Batterham, Forster, 437f
Baudouin, 256
Baugh, C. Don, 297
Baum, Gregory, 141
Baumgard, Herbert, 189
Baumohl, Charles, 495
Bayhylle, Louis D., 242
Bayley, James Roosevelt, 310
Baylor University, 209, 248f, 463f
bear-baiting, 446
Beatitudes, 130, 369
Beijing, 264
Being Red, 245
Belickas, Ausvydas, 78
Bell, Charles W., 258
Bellamy, Carol, 357
Belsky, Jack D., 239f
Benedict XVI, 491
Benedictines, 63, 320
Bennett, Anne McGrew, 379
Bennett, Austin P., 258
Bennett, John C., 20, 152, 336, 378-380, 395, 468
Bereczky, Albert, 412
Berger, Peter, 332
Berlin Wall, 78, 414
Berlin, Irving, 191
Bernardin, Joseph L., 17, 39, 326, 330, 427
Bernstein, Carl, 36
Bernstein, Dan, 22
Bernstein, Leonard, 302
Berrigan, Daniel J., 400
Berry, Dorothy, 297
Berry, Thomas W., 444f
Bertie, 337
Bessette, Carolyn, 490
Bessette, Lauren, 490
Best of Friends, The, 139
Bethel Metropolitan Baptist Church, 455
Bethesda Church, 452
Bethge, Eberhard, 41f
Bethlehem, 155, 157, 169
Bevilacqua, Anthony J., 95
Bible, 144, 158f
Biblical Theology of the Old and New Testaments, 424
biblicism, 120
Bicentennial, 291
Big Apple, 74
Bill of Rights, 250
Bird, Thomas E., 149

Birkenau, 164
Bishop of Rome, 75, 306, 382, 420
Black and Indian Mission Office, 277
Black Church Declaration on Environmental and Economic Justice, 444
Black Church Environmental Justice Summit, 444
Black Economic Development Conference, 35, 214
Black Experience in Religion, The, 213
black gospel, 62
black power, 212
black rite, 208
Black Sea, 226
Black Theology and Black Power, 212
Blackmun, Harry A., 331
Blake, Eugene Carson, 217f, 268, 302-304, 378
Blake, Jean, 302
Blanshard, Paul, 153
blasphemers, 134
Bleich, David, 194
Blessed Sacrament Fathers, 320
Blessit, Arthur, 121
Blixt, Raymond, 313
Block, Lillian, 19-25, 31, 421, 473, 477, 479
Bloom, Harold, 170
Bluck, John, 16
Board of Correction, 220
Bob Jones University, 114
Boerne, Texas, 334
Boesak, Allan, 458f
Boles, Bill, 256
Bolin, Frances Schoonmaker, 426
Bolin, William E., 426
Bolioli, Oscar, 376
Bologna, Vincenza, 451, 453
Bona, Fred, 484
Bone Divine, 484f
Bonhoeffer, Dietrich, 41f
Book of Common Prayer, 293
Book of J, 170
booze, 379
Bork, Mary Ellen, 355
Bork, Robert H., 332, 355
born again, 120
Bosnian conflict, 149
Boston Red Sox, 479
Boswell, John, 170
Bourdeaux, Michael, 417
Bourgeois, Roy L., 374f

Communist Party, 245, 266, 413, 415
Community Church, 474
Community of Churches, 297
complicated, too, 489
Concord Baptist Church of Christ, 59
Cone, James H., 212-214
Conference of Presidents of Major American
  Jewish Organizations, 189
Confucianism, 444
Congregation for Bishops, 207
Congregation for Religious and Secular
  Institutes, 95
Congregation for the Doctrine of the Faith,
  101, 353, 356, 372, 491
Congress, 334
Conservative Mind, 127
Constantine, 54, 321
Constantinople, 157, 225
Constitution, 331, 388, 444
Consultation of Cooperating Churches in
  Kansas, 297
Consultation on Church Union, 303f
Consultation on the Environment and Jewish
  Life, 443
Context newsletter, 7
Continental Congress, 73, 242
Continuation Committee, 412
Convent Avenue Baptist Church, 221
Convention on the Rights of the Child, 454
Conventual Franciscans, 343
Cooke, Ellen F., 451f
Cooke, Suzanne Johnson, 50
Cooke, Terence J., 31, 38f, 54, 123, 159,
  208, 352
Cooper Union, 354
Coptic Church, 231
Coquilles St. Jacques, 321
Corinth, 403
Cornell, George, 14f
Cornwell, John, 197
Corporate Information Center, 312
corporate responsibility, 482
Corpus Christi, 150
Corpus Instrumentorum, 471
Corpus Publications, 15
Cost of Discipleship, 41
Cotton Club, 183
Coulter, Richard Timothy, 244
Council for the Family, 95
Council of Chalcedon, 231
Council of Churches, 297

Council of Trent, 11
Courage to Be, The, 118
Cousin, Philip R., 220, 301
Covenant House, 122, 339-344, 346f, 429,
  492f
Cowan, Wayne H., 261
Cox, Harvey, 124
Cox, Nan, 104
Crawford, Douglas, 251f
creationists, 445
Criswell, W.A., 125, 130
Cronkite, Walter, 68
Crossing the Threshold of Hope, 117, 395
Crowley, Donald L., 43
Crowning Glory, 187
Crucifixion, 143
Crusader Orthodox, 236
Crusaders, 370
Cuba, 376, 418, 420
Cueto, Maria, 298
Cultural Revolution, 308, 408
Culture of Belief, The, 323
Cummings, James L., 301
Cummins Engine Company, 310
Cuomo, Mario M., 319, 321-324, 326, 495
Custombook, 498
Cyril of Alexandria, 422
Czechoslovak Ecumenical Council, 414
Czechoslovakia, 412, 414, 468

D'Amato, Alfonse, 325
D'Escoto, Miguel F., 97-99, 372
da Verrazano, Giovanni, 242
Dachau, 155
Daily Traveler, 249
Daily, Thomas V., 185, 255, 257f, 260, 451,
  496
Dallas Cowboys, 130
Daly, Cahal Brendan, 95
Danneels, Godfried, 95
Daughters of Charity, 347
Daughters of the Heart of Mary, 211
Daughtry, Herbert, 205
Dave Letterman Show, The, 473
David, 155
Davis, Joseph, 208
Davis, Stephen T., 143
Davis, Thurston, 68
Daw, Richard W., 26, 476, 478
Day, Dorothy, 400, 436, 437-440, 474
Day, Peter, 299

Ecumenical News International, 16, 58, 67, 89, 106, 226f, 451, 478, 488f
Ecumenical Patriarch, 225-227, 229, 235, 315
Ecumenical Press Service, 16, 24, 220, 320, 478, 488
ECUNET, 478
Eddy, Margaret, 381
Eddy, Mary Baker, 55, 87f
Eddy, Norman, 381
Edgar, Robert W., 283
Edict of Milan, 54
editor, assistant, 472
editor, interim, 490
Edomites, 403
Education and Cultivation Division, 109
Education and Ministry Division, 288f
Education of Henry Adams, The, 169
Edwards, Bernice V., 455
Edwards, Jonathan, 128
Egan, Edward M., 231, 497
Eggenberger, David, 463, 478, 485f, 498
Egypt, 117, 155
Ehrlichman, John D., 113
Einstein, Albert, 47
Eisenhower, Dwight D., 112, 268, 310, 406
Eisenman, Robert H., 166
El Barrio, 381
El Greco, 87
El Salvador, 44, 375-377, 483
elephant dung, 184
Elisha, 448
Elizabeth II, 290
Ellenoff, Theodore, 189
Ellmann, Richard, 169
Ellsberg, Daniel, 436
Ellsberg, Robert, 436, 439, 491
Emerman, Anne, 81
Emmanuel, 162
Encyclopedia of Southern Baptists, 133
Encyclopedic Dictionary of Religion, 15, 498
enemies list, 301
Enlightenment, 393
Episcopal Church, 275, 452
Epler, Percy H., 469
Erasmus Lecture, 353
Erdo, Peter, 491f
eschaton, 449
Espy, R.H. Edwin, 291
Essene, 167, 169
ethic of life, consistent, 17, 326

Ethics and Public Policy Center, 263
Ethiopia, 79f, 232
Ethiopian eunuch, 291
Ethiopian Orthodox, 232
Eucharist, 118
Evangelical Environmental Network, 443
Evangelical Lutheran Church in America, 275, 452
Evangelical Theological Society, 158
Evangelical United Brethren, 274
evangelicals, conservative, 236
Excelsior, 376
Executive Order 50, 357
Exodus, 247
Exodus, 117
Ezekiel, 335

Fabiola, 256
Faith and Order Commission, 56, 298, 304, 315, 390
Falcon, Luis Nieves, 300
Falwell, Jerry, 125, 136, 146, 474
families, reorganized, 427
Family of Man, 216
Family Yesterday and Today, The, 28
Fanning, Katherine W., 89
Farabundo Marti Front for National Liberation, 374
Farrakhan, Louis, 221, 273
Fast, Howard, 245
Fatima, 187
FBI, 9, 298f, 346
Feast of St. Sergius of Radonezh, 230
Federal Council of Churches, 267, 281, 309, 384, 386, 389, 390
Fedor, Jan, 9
Feke, Stephen, 459
Fernandez, Joseph A., 177
Ferraro, Geraldine, 324
festschrift, 372
Feuerherd, Peter, 255
Fifth Avenue Presbyterian Church, 60f
Fifth World Conference on Faith and Order, 321
FIGHT, 311
Filaret, 412, 414
Filteau, Jerry, 494
Finn, Peter, 260
First Amendment, 151, 333
First Baptist Church, 49, 130
first by-lined article, 464

Gifford Lectures, 94
Gingrich, Newt, 426
Gittings, James A., 151f
Giuliani, Rudolph W., 177, 184
glasnost, 237, 405
Glassman, Bernard, 254
Glemp, Josef, 163f
Glendon, Mary Ann, 334
Glick, G. Wayne, 93
Gnanadason, Aruna, 54
Gnostic Gospels, The, 169
Gnostics, 170
God and the Rhetoric of Sexuality, 16
Godard, Jean-Luc, 185
Goicoechea, Angel Suquia, 13
Goldberg, Rube, 280
golden calf, 144
Golden Rule, 127
Goldman, Ari, 430
Goldwater, Barry, 126f
golfer, 362
Gonzouleas, Takis, 253
Good Samaritan, 392, 394
Gorbachev, Mikhail, 58, 77f, 405
Gore, Albert A. Jr., 202, 444
Gorman, Paul, 443
Gospels, Synoptic, 127
Gotham, 72
Gothic architecture, 75
Gottwald, Norman K., 366-368
goyim, 402
Grace, J. Peter, 337
Graham, Billy, 49, 111-116, 118-121, 125,
    192, 284, 308, 418
Graham, Robert A., 197
Gramercy Park, 44
Gramick, Jeannine, 100f
Gramm, Phil, 426
Granberg-Michaelson, Wesley, 267
Grand Central Station, 282
Grand Inquisitor, 28
Grant, James P., 454
Grawemeyer, H. Charles, 445
Great Church Fire Hoax, The, 200
Great Depression, 407
Great Leap Forward, 308
Great Satan, 182
Great Society, 103
Great Wall of China, 308
Greek Archdiocese, 74, 122, 225, 227f
Green, Richard R., 209

Greenwich Village, 51, 327, 349f, 359, 490
Gregorian chant, 62f, 365
Grey, Martin de Porres, 208
Griffin, Barry, 100
Grim, John, 444
Griswold, Frank Tracy III, 299
Groeschel, Benedict J., 38, 40
Growing Up Caring, 425f
Guardini, Romano, 440f
Guatemala, 296
Guerrera, Vittorio, 503
Guest, Edgar A., 98
Gulf War, 295
Gumbleton, Thomas J., 260
Gumpel, Peter, 197
Guthrie, Woodie, 64
Gutierrez, Gustavo, 368f, 371-373
Guzman, Pablo, 381

Ha-Avetz, 172
Habitat for Humanity, 123
Hadas, Schmuel, 196
Hadassah, 189
Haddis, Abba, 232
Haering, Bernard, 28
Hagar, 290
Hager, John, 357
Hail Mary, 185
Haimanot, Tekle, 232
Haines, J. Harry, 296f, 500
Haiti, 222
Haldeman, H.R., 113
Hall, Donald, 431
Ham, Mordecai F., 114
Hamer, Jean Jerome, 95
Hamilton, James A., 268
Hammock, Charles, 208
Hancock, Gerry, 61
Handel, George Frideric, 398
Harlem, 49f, 73, 183, 206f, 211, 214, 216,
    221, 293, 431, 457, 475
Harmon, Francis, 215
Harnett, James J., 346, 492
Harrington, Donald J., 18f, 255
Harrington, Donald S., 152, 474
Harris, Brenda, 458
Harrison, Beverly Wildung, 54, 361
Harry Emerson Fosdick, 386
Hart, Frederick, 329
Harvard Divinity School, 430
Harvard Law School, 334

Newark Museum, 187
Newman, Stewart A., 465, 508
Newport Jazz Festival, 63
Nicaragua, 376f, 412, 418
Nicodemus, 367
Niebanck, Richard J., 401
Niebuhr, Reinhold, 74, 91f, 94, 125, 161,
    328f, 379, 384, 387f, 412, 422, 454
Niebuhr, Richard, 466
Niedfield, Eileen, 255
Nightingale, Florence, 106f
Niilus, Leopoldo, 145, 147
Nikodim, 410, 416f
Niwano Peace Foundation, 76
Nixon-Agnew administration, 246
Nixon, Agnes, 359
Nixon, Pat, 308
Nixon, Richard M., 100, 112f, 216, 244,
    278, 294, 302, 304, 307-309, 316, 379,
    420
Nkrumah, Kwame, 293
Nolan, John G., 178f
Non-Proliferation Treaty, 58
Noonan, James P., 374
Noonan, Peggy, 427
North American Academy of Ecumenists, 33
North American Newspaper Alliance, 99
North Korea, 264
North Sea, 251
Northeast Hispanic Catholic Center, 95, 257
Nostra Aetate, 196
Notre Dame, 30f
Novak, Michael, 101, 263
NRA, 387
Nugent, C. Robert, 100f
Nugent, Randolph W., 176
Nuss, Katherine, 504

O'Brien, Nancy, 491
O'Brien, Thomas C., 15, 471f, 485
O'Brien, William B., 341f
O'Collins, Gerald G., 143
O'Connor, John Jay III, 108
O'Connor, John Joseph, 10, 12, 30, 38-40,
    59f, 77, 98-100, 107f, 151, 155, 163f,
    173f, 177-184, 188-190, 196, 203, 207,
    209f, 231, 236, 256-259, 277, 312, 324f,
    328f, 337, 343, 350-352, 354, 357, 359f,
    382f, 400, 436, 439, 474, 487, 490, 492,
    496, 498

O'Connor, Sandra Day, 108, 126
O'Hare, Joseph A., 97, 107f, 483
O'Keefe, Joseph T., 99f, 207, 495
Ode to Billie Joe, 463
Oestreich, James R., 62
Office for People with Disabilities, 81
Offner, Elliot, 149
Ofili, Chris, 184
Oke, Philip, 410
Okullu, Henry, 44
Olson, Evert, 85
Onassis, Jacqueline Kennedy, 14
One World magazine, 16, 51
open table fellowship, 367
Operation Rescue, 400
Opus Dei, 371
ordination of married men, 420
ordination of Protestant ministers, 420
ordination of women, 160, 420
ordination, 119
Oreskes, Michael, 324
Oriental Orthodox, 231
original sin, 454, 455, 461
Orthodox Christian Mission Center, 227
Orthodox Church in America, 66, 225, 230,
    236
Orthodox Church, The, 227
Osborne, Wesley D., 380
Osbourne, Ozzy, 15
Osiris, 64
Ottomans, 150
Ouagadougou, 117
Our Lady of Mercy Hospital, 496
Our Lady of the Scapular Church, 352
Our Savior Lutheran church, 51
Oval Office, 199, 200
Overseas Ministries Study Center, 175
Owens, Ann, 473
Oxford Dictionary of Quotations, 61

Pacelli, Eugenio, 94
Pagels, Elaine H., 169f
Paiarno, Angelo, 254
Paisley, Ian R.K., 262
Palatine restaurant, 68
Palestine Liberation Organization, 145-147,
    196
Panama Canal, 240
Pantex, 400
Pappas, Mrs. John, 253

Powers, Jeanne Audrey, 362
Prague Spring, 414
prayer wheel, 289
Presbyterian Church, 51, 275
Presbyterian Seminary, 445
Presiding Bishop's Fund for World Relief, 381
Pressman, Gabe, 181
Price, Richard, 388
Princeton, 169, 286, 302, 423
Prison Fellowship ministry, 283
Prisoner of Chillon, 24
Pritchett, Harry S. Jr., 431
Pritzker, Jay, 484
Pro Mundi Vita, 408
Prodigal Son, 161
Program to Combat Racism, 217f
prohibition, 135, 384
Prometheus Award, 342
Proof of the Apostolic Preaching, 134
Propagation of the Faith, 95f
Prophet with Honor, A, 118, 121
prophetic justice, 273f
Protestant Council of Churches, 419
Protestantism, evangelical, 114
Protestantism, Reformed, 360
Protestants and Other Americans United for Separation of Church and State, 153, 467
Protestants of Northern Ireland, 262
Protestants, 33
proto-Marxist, 397
Protoevangelium, 320, 507
Proust, Marcel, 361
Pruitt, Jean, 105
Psalms, 159
PTL Club, 123
Puerto Rico, 300, 381
Pugevicius, Casimir, 78
Puller, Lewis B. "Chesty", 278f
Puller, Lewis B. Jr., 278f
purgatory, 505
Puritans, 72, 132f, 446
purses, silk, 331
Pusey, James, 409
Pusey, Nathan, 93, 409
PWA, 387

Quaranta, Mary Ann, 341
Quayle, J. Danforth, 278, 430
Queens College, 149
Queens, 74

Qumram, 167, 169
Qur'an, 158

Rabin, Yitzhak, 190
race relations, sermon on, 470
Racial Justice Working Group, 282
Radical Imperative, The, 379
radical, shy, 380
radicals, practical, 379
radio devotionals, 470
radio script, 473
Radio Shack, 478
Rainier III, 70
Raiser, Konrad, 300
Ramirez, Anthony, 71
Ramirez, Ricardo, 332
Ramos, Jovelino P., 273f
Randall, Claire, 269-271, 289, 297, 317, 326, 416
Rasmussen, Larry L., 445
rationalism, 120
Ratzinger, Joseph, 160, 353-357, 360, 491
Rauschenbusch, Walter, 139
Rauscher, William V., 305
Re-imagining Conference, 51f, 55, 358
Re, Giovanni Battista, 496
Reagan-Gorbachev Summit, 265
Reagan, Nancy, 124, 342
Reagan, Ronald, 58, 122f, 125f, 128, 146, 152, 180, 193, 240, 282, 315, 337, 342, 375f, 420, 426
Real Anti-Semitism in America, The, 146
reasoning, circular, *see* circular reasoning
Reconstruction, 202
Red Apple, 40f
red hots, 398
Red River Range, 465
Redemptorist order, 28
Reed, David B., 292
Reflections on the Revolution in France, 388
Reform Judaism, 128
Reformation, 55, 139, 174, 320, 505
Reformed Christianity, 60, 404
Reformed Church in America, 268, 271
refusenik, 471
Regan, Donald, 124
Reich, Seymour, 163
Reims, 320
Reischauer, Edwin O., 309
relics, 319, 320, 484
Religion News Service, 19

Sensation, 184
Sephardic Jews, 72
Sepphoris, 161
Sermon on the Mount, 124, 362, 393, 401
Serra, 421
Servetus, Michael, 498
Seton, Elizabeth Ann Bayley, 310
Seven-Storey Mountain, The, 365
Seventh-day Adventists, 55, 131
Seventh-day Baptists, 131
Seventh Angel magazine, 151
Sex and Morality in the U.S., 360
Sh'ma, 75
Shakers, 55
Shalala, Donna, 250
Shanks, Hershel, 166f, 172
Sharpton, Al, 209
Shatila camp, 148
Shattered Faith, 435
Shaw, George Bernard, 139
Shea Stadium, 111-113
Sheehy, John F., 391
Sheen, Fulton J., 12
Shenouda III, 231
Sheridan, Chris, 255, 258, 260, 504
Sheridan, Patrick J., 210, 356
Sherry, Paul H., 349
Shining Path, 373
Shintoism, 444
Shoah, 149
Shriver, Donald W. Jr., 468
Shriver, Eunice Kennedy, 425, 429
Shroud of Turin, 506
Shunatona, Mifaunwy, 242
Sidebars, 479
Siegel, Eli, 34
Siegman, Henry, 173, 193f
Sienes, Ramon Taibo, 44
Silas, 253
Silvi, Sharry, 8
Simon, William E., 101f
Simply Sharing, 16, 486, 498
Simpson, O.J., 458
Sin, Jaime L., 95
Sindab, Jean, 443f
Sing Sing, 372
Singer, Howard, 147
Singer, Israel, 194
Single Mother, 429
Sioux-Chippewa, 292
Sisters in Crisis, 105

Sisters of Mercy, 357
Sisters of St. Joseph, 15
Sistine Chapel, 335
Sithole, Ndabaningi, 223
60 Minutes, 416
Skylstad, William S., 382
Small's Paradise, 183
Smith Richardson Foundation, 263
Smith, Alfred E., 150, 183
Smith, Bailey, 146
Smith, Christine Marie, 358
Smith, Eugene L., 473
Smith, Iam, 223
Smith, Joseph, 55, 163, 427
Smith, Kenneth T., 360
Smith, Timothy H., 312f
Smith, Walter B., 453
Smith, William B., 351f
Smith, Willie Mae Ford, 63
Smyrna, 370
Snyder, Texas, 463f, 501
Sobrino, Jon, 369f, 372
social creed, 386
social gospel, 476
Society of African Missions, 45, 359
Society of Biblical Literature, 367
Society of St. Pius X, 11
Sodano, Angelo, 427
Soderblom, Nathan, 399f
Solheim, James, 301
Sölle, Dorothy, 479
Son of Man, 290
Sophia, 52f, 337
Sophocles, 247
Sorbonne, 186
South Africa, 222, 278, 313
South Bronx Churches, 312
South Korea, 264
Southeastern Baptist Theological Seminary, 464, 508
Southern Baptist Convention, 115, 129, 146, 356, 435, 465
Southern Baptist, 27, 116, 464
Sovereign Military Hospital Order of St. John of Jerusalem, of Rhodes and of Malta, 337
Sovereign One, 290
Soviet Communist Party, 405
Soviet Union, 308, 387f, 407, 414, 416-418
Spanish Armada, 320, 508
Spanish civil war, 45
Spanish Royal Buffet, 337

SIDEBARS

SIDEBARS